C000061000

BANKING LAW IN AUSTRALIA

THIRD EDITION

BANKING LAW

IN

AUSTRALIA

THIRD EDITION

ALAN L TYREE
BSc, MSc, PhD, LLB (Hons)

BUTTERWORTHS
SYDNEY — ADELAIDE — BRISBANE — CANBERRA
MELBOURNE — PERTH
1998

AUSTRALIA   BUTTERWORTHS   Tower 2, 475-495 Victoria Avenue, Chatswood, NSW 2067
111 Gawler Place, Adelaide, SA 5000
Oxley House, 25 Donkin Street, West End, Qld 4101
53-55 Northbourne Avenue, Canberra, ACT 2601
461 Bourke Street, Melbourne, Vic 3000
Suite 32, Hyatt Centre, 23 Plain Street, East Perth, WA 6004

On the Internet at: www.butterworths.com.au

CANADA   BUTTERWORTHS CANADA LTD   Toronto and Vancouver

FRANCE   EDITIONS DU JURIS-CLASSEUR   Paris

HONG KONG   BUTTERWORTHS ASIA   Hong Kong

INDIA   BUTTERWORTHS INDIA LTD   New Delhi

IRELAND   BUTTERWORTH (IRELAND) LTD   Dublin

ITALY   GIUFFRÈ EDITORE SPA   Milan

MALAYSIA   MALAYAN LAW JOURNAL SDN BHD   Kuala Lumpur

NEW ZEALAND   BUTTERWORTHS OF NEW ZEALAND LTD   Wellington and Auckland

POLAND   WYDAWNICTWA PRAWNICZE PWN   Warsaw
WYDAWNICTWO PRAWNICZE   Warsaw

SINGAPORE   BUTTERWORTHS ASIA & MALAYAN LAW JOURNAL   Singapore

SOUTH AFRICA   BUTTERWORTH PUBLISHERS (PTY) LTD   Durban

SWITZERLAND   STAEMPFLI VERLAG AG   Berne

UNITED KINGDOM   BUTTERWORTH & CO (PUBLISHERS) LTD   London and Edinburgh

USA   LEXIS-NEXIS   Miamisburg, Ohio
LEXIS LAW PUBLISHING   Charlottesville, Virginia

National Library of Australia Cataloguing-in-Publication entry

Tyree, Alan L., 1939-   .
Banking law in Australia.

3rd ed.
Includes index.
ISBN 0 409 31318 1.

1. Banking law — Australia. I. Title.

346.94082

©1998 Reed International Books Australia Pty Limited trading as Butterworths
First edition 1990
Second edition 1995

This book is copyright. Except as permitted under the Copyright Act 1968 (Cth), no part of this
publication may be reproduced by any process, electronic or otherwise, without the
specific written permission of the copyright owner. Neither may information be stored
electronically in any form whatsoever without such permission.

Inquiries should be addressed to the publishers.

Printed in Australia by Sands Print Group (WA).

CONTENTS

PREFACE

The most significant development in banking law since the publication of the second edition of this book is the release of the Financial System Inquiry Final Report, the Wallis Report. The Report recommends substantial changes to the regulatory structure. These recommended changes are outlined in Chapter 1.

The Wallis Report also recognises the development of electronic commerce, a development which has the potential to change the face of banking and banking law. The most immediate and obvious impact is the formation of 'Internet banks' and the development of new payment systems known as 'digital cash'. The Report recommended legal and structural changes to facilitate the development of electronic commerce.

There are other less dramatic but no less important developments. The Privy Council has clarified the circumstances under which a banker can be held liable as constructive trustee in the so-called 'knowing assistance' type of case. The result is a substantial retreat from the high points of the *Selangor* and *Karak* cases.

The New South Wales Court of Appeal has reaffirmed the trend of holding bankers responsible for forgeries even when the customer has been 'negligent' in some way. This reinforces the dictum of Lord Scarman in *Tai Hing* that '[t]he business of banking is the business not of the customer but of the bank'. Financial institutions are using the introduction of new payment methods to impose substantially higher obligations on customers.

I repeat the observation of both the first and second edition that no book is written in a vacuum. My debt to writers who have gone before me is substantial. I also acknowledge the assistance of those who have helped me to turn a rough manuscript into one that is not so rough. Special thanks to Alex Craig at Indigo Ink for her invaluable editorial assistance. Thanks also to the staff at Butterworths who have provided the support and encouragement to get the third edition to press.

Finally, thanks to my wife Allison for her support during the difficult times that accompany long writing efforts.

Alan L Tyree
February 1998

Acknowledgments

The author and publishers are grateful to the holders of copyright in material from which extracts appear in this work, particularly to the following:

Canada Law Book Inc
Incorporated Council of Law Reporting for England and Wales
LBC Information Services Ltd
Lloyds of London Press
Sweet & Maxwell Ltd

While every care has been taken to establish and acknowledge copyright, the publishers tender their apologies for any accidental infringement. They would be pleased to come to a suitable arrangement with the rightful owners in each case.

TABLE OF CASES

REFERENCES ARE TO PARAGRAPHS

Streicher v ES&A Bank Ltd [1945] SASR 207 .... 2.42

Sunderland v Barclays Bank (1938) 5 LDAB 163 .... 4.19

Suse, Re (No 2) (1885) 14 QBD 611 .... 11.19

Sztejn v J Henry Schroder Banking Corporation 31 NYS 2d 631 (1941) 12.55, 12.57

TSB Bank of Scotland plc v Welwyn Hatfield District Council and Council of the London Borough of Brent [1993] 2 Bank LR 267 .... 8.85

Tai Hing Cotton Mill Ltd v Liu Chong Hing Bank Ltd [1986] AC 80; [1985] 2 All ER 947 .... 2.34, 2.35, 3.44, 3.48, 5.24, 5.35, 5.41, 7.40, 9.60, 9.88

Tailby v Official Receiver (1888) 13 App Cas 523 .... 11.102, 11.109

Tancred v Delagoa Bay and East Africa Railway Co (1889) 23 QBD 239 .... 11.101

Tarn v Commercial Banking Co of Sydney (1884) 12 QBD 294 .... 3.50

Taylor v National Bank of New Zealand [1985] BCL 895 .... 2.79

— v Russell [1892] AC 244 .... 11.57

Tenax Steamship Co Ltd v The Brimnes (Owners) [1975] QB 929 .... 8.48, 8.72, 8.83, 8.85

Tenore Pty Ltd v Roleystone Pty Ltd (SC NSW, 14 September 1990) 12.53

Thackwell v Barclays Bank plc [1986] 1 All ER 676 .... 7.133

Thomas v Hollier (1984) 53 ALR 39 .... 10.14

Thomson v Clydesdale Bank Ltd [1893] AC 282 .... 3.13, 3.16

Thorpe v Jackson (1837) 2 Y & C Ex 553; 160 ER 515 .... 2.77

Tilley v Official Receiver (1960) 103 CLR 529 .... 5.93

Tina Motors Pty Ltd v Australian and New Zealand Banking Group Ltd [1977] VR 205 .... 5.29, 7.40, 7.130

Tolhurst v Associated Portland Cement Manufacturers (1900) Ltd [1902] 2 KB 660 (CA); [1903] AC 414 (HL) 12.119

Total Oil Products (Aust) Pty Ltd v Robinson [1970] 1 NSWR 701 .... 11.164

Tournier v National Provincial and Union Bank of England [1924] 1 KB 461 .... 4.2, 5.54, 8.85, 12.13

Tubby Trout Pty Ltd v Sailbay Pty Ltd (1992) 113 ALR 748 .... 4.12

Tunstall Brick and Pottery Co v Mercantile Bank of Australia Ltd (1892) 18 VLR 59 .... 2.12

Turner Manufacturing Co Pty Ltd v Senes [1964] NSWR 692 .... 11.137

Turner v Sylvester [1981] 2 NSWLR 295 .... 12.5

Turvey v Dentons (1923) Ltd [1953] 1 QB 218 .... 6.16

Twibell v London Suburban Bank [1869] WN 127 .... 5.58

Underwood (A L) Ltd v Bank of Liverpool Ltd [1924] 1 KB 775 .... 7.60, 7.79, 7.87, 7.111, 7.132 8.73

Union Bank of Australia Ltd v McClintock [1922] 1 AC 240 .... 7.17

— v Murray-Aynsley [1898] AC 693 .... 3.38

United Australia Ltd v Barclays Bank Ltd [1941] AC 1 .... 7.21, 7.22

United City Merchants (Investments) Ltd and Glass Fibres and Equipment Ltd v Royal Bank of Canada [1979] 2 Lloyd's Rep 498 .... 12.50, 12.57

United Dominions Trust Ltd v Kirkwood [1966] 2 QB 431 .... 2.98

United Service Co, Re; Johnston's Claim (1870) LR 6 Ch App 212 .... 4.58, 11.129

Universal Guarantee Pty Ltd v Derefink [1958] VR 51 .... 3.86

— v National Bank of Australasia Ltd (1965) 65 SR (NSW) 102 .... 6.81

Urquhart Lindsay & Co Ltd v Eastern Bank Ltd [1922] 1 KB 318 .... 12.45, 12.49

TABLE OF STATUTES

REFERENCES ARE TO PARAGRAPHS

OUTLINE

STRUCTURE OF AUSTRALIAN BANKING

[1.1] The Reserve Bank of Australia is the country's central bank. It was created by statute in 1959 and took over the central banking function from the Commonwealth Bank which had exercised that function since the mid-1920s.

Four major trading banks account for more than 70 per cent of total banking deposits. The remaining banks include seven regionally operating banks, 17 foreign banks, many licensed as part of the government's policy of deregulation in the mid-1980s, three state trading banks (NSW, SA and WA) and a trustee bank (Tasmania). With the exception of the state banking, the Commonwealth Parliament has the power and the responsibility to make laws relating to banking: s 51(xii) of the Constitution.

For all practical purposes the distinction between trading banks and savings banks has been eradicated. Historically, savings banks provided finance primarily for private housing. This was not entirely a commercial decision, for regulations required that a very substantial portion of savings bank assets must consist of loans secured by property within Australia, or of government loans. Savings banks were, prior to 1989, identified separately in a schedule of the Banking Act 1989, but the definition of 'trading bank' and 'savings bank' was removed from the Banking Act 1959 (Cth) by the Banking Legislation Amendment Act 1989 (Cth). Curiously, the Banking (Savings Banks) Regulations 1960 appear to remain in force. These regulations require a savings bank to hold a certain percentage of all deposits in prescribed investments and limit the types of deposits that the bank may accept.

Perhaps the most important activity of the Reserve Bank is the prudential supervision of banks. This supervision is exercised both by means of statutory powers and by agreements with the banking community which have no direct statutory authority.

THE BACKGROUND TO MODERN REGULATION

[1.2]   Although it is commonplace in modern economic discussions to speak of 'deregulation', there is little likelihood that governments will ever completely 'deregulate' the banking industry. It is worth exploring the reasons for this.

WHY REGULATE?

[1.3]   Although there are significant pressures for 'deregulation' of the financial industries, the demonstrable past failures of pure market forces ensure that governments everywhere will continue to take a close interest in the business of banking.

The characteristic feature of modern banking is that it is 'fractional reserve' banking. In simple terms, the bank 'lends' its credit, not its money. The banking system as a whole is capable of creating 'money', a point recognised by the Campbell Committee as a feature common to banking in most countries: see The Committee of Inquiry into the Australian Financial System, 1981.

This ability to create money is most easily understood by a consideration of earlier practice. Prior to 1900, it was common for banks to issue 'banknotes'. Banknotes were essentially promissory notes issued by a bank: see Chapter 9. Banknotes circulated as cash and loans were made by the bank by giving the borrower notes issued by the institution.

It is clearly possible for a bank in such a position to create 'money'. One of the most extreme examples of the excess which might occur is mentioned in J K Galbraith, *Money: Whence it Came, Where it Went*, Deutsch, London, 1975. He describes a Massachusetts bank which failed in the 1830s which had a note circulation of more than $500,000 supported by reserves in specie of $86.48. It was, as Galbraith observes, 'a modest backing'.

In a system where bank liabilities are used as 'money', it is clear that the financial stability of the entire community is closely related to the stability of the banking system. It is also all too clear from the history of western economies that pure 'market forces' do not provide the necessary stabilising forces. The most devastating example of disruptive forces in Australian banking history is the collapse of the banking system during the period between 1891 and 1893 when 54 of a total of 64 banks closed their doors, 34 of them never to open again. Many of these 'banks' were structures formed solely for the purposes of financing shoddy high-risk real estate deals which were left insolvent by the collapse of the Melbourne property market, but even restricting attention to institutions which could properly be called 'banks' only nine out of 28 were able to remain trading throughout the panic: see T Sykes, *Two Centuries of Panic: a history of corporate collapses in Australia*, Allen & Unwin, Sydney, 1988.

The immediate response to the crash in New South Wales was the Bank Issue Act of 1893 and the Current Account Depositors' Act of 1893. The first

of these Acts proclaimed that certain banknotes were to be legal tender: see F
A Mann, *Legal Aspects of Money*, 4th ed, Oxford University Press, United Kingdom, 1982. The second permitted the issue of treasury notes to depositors on
the security of their questionable bank deposits.

The first Commonwealth note issue was in 1910. There was substantial
opposition from the banks, particularly since the issue of the notes coincided
with a tax on all banknotes issued after that time: Australian Notes Act 1910;
Bank Notes Tax Act 1910. The replacement of private notes by the new Commonwealth notes was completed in a few years, although banknotes were still
issued in Tasmania in the 1930s; see G W Tomlinson, *Australian Banknotes
1817–1963*, Hawthorn Press, Melbourne, 1963 and M P Vort-Ronald,
Australian Banknotes, Adelaide, 1979.

The Great Depression led to international interest in the regulation of
banks. In Australia, a Royal Commission was appointed in 1935 to inquire
into the financial system and to make recommendations. The Banking Commission Report of 1937 recommended substantial increases in the powers of
the Commonwealth Bank to act as central banker, as well as the maintenance
of reserve accounts by each bank which would be a proportion of their total
deposits. The recommendations were opposed by the banks.

NATIONAL SECURITY (WARTIME BANKING CONTROL) REGULATIONS 1941

[1.4]   Debate on the recommendations of the Commission continued until
the outbreak of the Second World War. Exchange control was introduced
almost immediately and by 1941 the trading banks agreed to maintain a
certain percentage of deposits with the Commonwealth Bank that had
assumed the role and powers of a central bank. Further advances were only to
be made in accordance with policies outlined by the Commonwealth.

These arrangements were formalised and extended by the Labor Government in the National Security (Wartime Banking Control) Regulations 1941
which gave the Treasurer, the Commonwealth and the Commonwealth Bank
(acting in its role as a central banker) substantial powers over the lending and
investment policies of the trading banks.

These regulations were substantially re-enacted as the Banking Act 1945
and the Commonwealth Bank Act 1945, but the Banking Act went further in
an attempt to control banking operations. Section 48 of the Act purported to
give the Commonwealth the right to prohibit a bank from conducting any
banking business for a state or for any authority of a state, including a local
government authority. In 1947, s 48 was invoked to order the Melbourne
City Council to cease its banking arrangements with a private bank.

The Corporation responded with a court challenge which ultimately
resulted in a majority of the High Court declaring s 48 to be invalid, holding
that 'state banking' means the business of banking engaged in by a state as
banker, and does not include transactions between a state as customer and a

bank: *Melbourne Corporation v Commonwealth* (1947) 74 CLR 31. The Commonwealth Government countered with the Banking Act 1947 which was an attempt to nationalise the private trading banks. Again the High Court ruled the legislation to be beyond the constitutional powers of the government and therefore invalid: *Bank of NSW v Commonwealth* (1948) 76 CLR 1; *Commonwealth v Bank of NSW* [1950] AC 235.

THE 1959 ACTS

[1.5]   Although the more aggressive initiatives of the Labor Government were thus defeated, the structure of banking regulation would never again revert to the unstructured days which preceded the war. The Commonwealth Bank continued to function as the central bank through the 1950s until the restructuring of the banking legislation in 1959.

The Banking Act 1959, the Reserve Bank Act 1959 and the Commonwealth Banks Act 1959 had the cumulative effect of splitting the old Commonwealth Bank into several separate entities along functional lines. The central banking function of the Bank was transferred to the newly created Reserve Bank of Australia and the trading bank functions to the Commonwealth Trading Bank. The Commonwealth Savings Bank, created by the Commonwealth Bank (Savings Bank) Act 1927, was continued as a separate entity. The 1959 Act also created the Commonwealth Development Bank of Australia which was intended to provide finance for primary production and for the establishment or development of industrial undertakings.

The structure of the Commonwealth Bank was further altered by the Commonwealth Banks Amendment Act 1985. The capital structure of the bank was altered, its name changed to the Commonwealth Bank of Australia and the Commonwealth Savings Bank was made a wholly owned subsidiary. In 1987, the Commonwealth Development Bank was given power to provide finance for all general business purposes: Commonwealth Banks Amendment Act 1987 s 23.

FUTURE REGULATION: THE WALLIS REPORT

[1.6]   The final report of the Financial System Inquiry (the Wallis Report) was made public in early April, 1997. The report contained 115 recommendations on a wide variety of financial system issues, all driven by the observation that there is a 'convergence' of financial markets. This leads to the conclusion that regulation should be based on 'sectors' rather than on institutions.

The Inquiry recommended a single licensing regime for all deposit taking institutions (DTIs). There would remain, however, classes of DTIs such as banks, credit unions and building societies.

For present purposes, the most important recommendations are the establishment of three new regulatory bodies. These are:

- the Corporations and Financial Services Commission will be responsible for establishing and enforcing rules of conduct and disclosure;

- the Australian Prudential Regulation Commission will have primary responsibility for prudential regulation of the financial sector, a role currently performed by the Reserve Bank (see below); and

- the Payments System Board (the PSB) will have responsibility for the payments system, ensuring system stability, access to and control of the payments system.

The Reserve Bank would continue to have responsibility for 'systemic stability'. Since this role seems to overlap with that prescribed for the PSB, the Report recommends that the PSB be chaired by the Governor of the Reserve Bank and should also include one deputy governor.

[1.7] A more uniform treatment of deposit taking institutions is probably desirable. In spite of protests from some of the major banks, there seems little reason why building societies and credit unions should necessarily be barred from the cheque system. Prudential regulation of these organisations should be based upon stability requirements, not upon the particular name or class of institution.

It is less obvious that prudential supervision should be removed from the RBA. The Inquiry identified three main reasons for moving responsibility from the RBA:

- the RBA could not be expected to fulfil the function since its primary relationships are with banks;

- removing prudential supervision from the RBA will emphasise that there is no guarantee of deposits; and

- separation permits the RBA and the APRC to focus clearly on their primary objectives.

The first two of these are hardly convincing, and the third could really be an argument for having all of the functions in one body. After all, the functions are not separate, and if the separate institutions are to fulfil their function there must be a great deal of cooperation. The history of inter-agency cooperation is not overly encouraging.

[1.8] The establishment of a new body responsible for prudential regulation will not change the fundamental principles of regulation. This is recognised by the Report in several places, most notably in Recommendation 35: 'Prudential regulation of DTIs needs to be consistent with international requirements.'

In particular, the Recommendation notes that regulations should be consistent with the standards approved by the Basle Committee on Banking Supervision and should aim to ensure that the risk of loss of depositors' funds is remote.

For these reasons, it seems that prudential regulation is unlikely to change dramatically. Although the federal government has indicated that it will adopt most of the Wallis Report's recommendations, the general approach to prudential regulation described below is unlikely to change.

CURRENT REGULATION: THE BANKING ACT 1959

[1.9]   According to the preamble, the purpose of the Banking Act is '... to regulate Banking, to make provision for the Protection of the Currency and of the Public Credit of the Commonwealth ...'. The scheme of the Act accomplishes these goals in several ways. First, there are restrictions on entry into the business of banking. Second, the Act provides for the prudential supervision and monitoring of banks by the Reserve Bank. Third, there are powers given to the Reserve Bank which may be exercised for the protection of depositors. Fourth, there is a scheme of 'non-callable deposits' which requires that banks maintain deposits of a certain level with the Reserve Bank. Finally, the Act authorises the Reserve Bank, with the approval of the Treasurer, to make regulations for the control of interest rates.

ENTRY LIMITATIONS

[1.10]   Only a body corporate which has the appropriate authority may carry on banking business in Australia: ss 7 and 8. Section 9(1) of the Act confers the necessary authority on the banks which are listed in Schedule 1 of the Act.

The Act provides that any corporation which wishes to carry on the business of banking may apply to the Treasurer for the authority to do so. This continues earlier legislation which restricted the right of entry into the banking business. In fact, there were no new banking 'licences' granted between 1945 and 1985. By 1985, four of the major trading banks held between them approximately 80 per cent of the total trading bank deposits in Australia.

[1.11]   Motivated by business and economic pressures, the government appointed a committee of inquiry, the Campbell Committee, to conduct an inquiry into the Australian financial system. The report of the Committee recommended a substantial reduction in regulation of the financial system and a more competitive environment. This led to certain steps being taken towards deregulation, most of which concerned the relaxation of direct interest rate controls and the announcement that the Treasurer would allow the entry of 10 more banks.

Before the new licences were issued, the Labor Party was elected to office. A commission, the Martin Commission, was appointed to conduct a further inquiry into the financial system. The report of the Martin Commission recommended further deregulation of the industry.

In 1985, the government announced the granting of a further 16 banking licences. The 'new' banks have not had a major impact in terms of market share, but the liberalisation of the financial system has had a dramatic effect on the way in which banks have conducted business. It was '[t]he threat of competition from new banks, rather than the reality of their arrival, [that] stimulated the domestic Australian banks': E Carew, *Fast Money 3*, Allen & Unwin, Sydney, 1991. At the end of 1997 there were 22 licensed banks.

Aside from entry limitations, there are also limitations on the amount of shares which may be held by any one individual or organisation: see [1.12].

LIMITATIONS ON SHAREHOLDINGS

[1.12]   Because of the economic and political sensitivity of the banking sector of the economy, it is common for governments to place some limitations on the size of individual banks or some limitation on the size of an individual's holdings in a single bank. The traditional form of regulation in the United States took the first course, limiting size of the individual institution by placing a blanket prohibition on branch banking.

Australia, when it finally determined to make regulations of this type, took the second approach. The Banks (Shareholding) Act 1972 limits the amount of an individual (or an association of individuals) shareholding to 10 per cent of the aggregate voting shares of any bank: s 10. There is provision for this percentage to rise to 15 per cent upon application to the Treasurer who may refuse the application on the grounds that it is not in the national interest.

[1.13]   The results of the two extreme forms of this type of regulation are not wholly in keeping with the philosophy of the regulators. There are now more than 14,000 banks in the United States and, in recent years, there have been over 300 bank failures each year. This is scarcely a desirable situation and has resulted in moves which will permit branching and, as a consequence, the development of larger and economically more stable financial entities.

The consequences of the Australian approach have indeed prevented any individual from gaining undue influence through control by shareholding, but has resulted in the establishment of a powerful 'management class' which, by virtue of the widely dispersed shareholdings, is virtually autonomous. As a consequence of this autonomy, the banks, or rather the management of the banks, wield precisely the kinds of political and economic power which the limitations on shareholdings were designed to prevent.

[1.14]   The Banks (Shareholding) Act 1972 has been supplemented by Reserve Bank intervention which places limits on the rights of shareholders to appoint representatives to the board of directors of a bank. As a general rule, a shareholder (or a group of associated shareholders) which has an interest of 15 per cent or less is to be represented by no more than one person associated with the shareholder if the board has six or fewer directors and by no more than two on a board consisting of seven or more directors. If there is a shareholding which represents more than 15 per cent, the representation on the board is expected to be no more than the proportionate share.

Again, the effect of the rule is to weaken the power, or potential power, of individual shareholders and, as an inevitable consequence, strengthen the power of the corporate management.

There is no obvious solution to this part of the regulatory conundrum. Economic pressures are clearly favouring the creation of larger banking entities. Once the entity becomes large, it becomes economically and politically powerful and the only choice which is obviously open to the regulators is to change the balance of power between the shareholders and the management. The current Australian position clearly favours the management and seems unlikely to change in the near future.

PROTECTION OF DEPOSITORS

[1.15] One of the characteristics of banking business is that the ratio of debt to equity is extremely high. Since most of the debt is owed to relatively small depositors, it is essential that these depositors be protected from mismanagement and that there is a general level of confidence in the bank. This confidence is for the benefit of the bank and the banking system as much as for the depositors.

The Act gives the Reserve Bank certain powers which are intended to provide this protection and so to maintain the confidence: Pt II, Div 2. The Bank has the duty to exercise these powers for the protection of depositors: s 12. It is important to note that the duty to protect depositors and the powers of the Reserve Bank granted by Div 2 do not extend to 'foreign banks', that is, one which is a foreign corporation which is authorised to carry on banking business in a foreign country and which has also been granted an authority under s 9: see s 11E(1). A foreign bank which accepts a deposit from a person in Australia must inform the depositor that the protective provisions of the Act do not apply: s 11E(2). The Bank of China and the Bank of New Zealand are not foreign banks for this purpose: ss 11D(a), 11D(b).

A bank which considers that it may become unable to meet its obligations or which is about to suspend payments must inform the Reserve Bank: s 14(1). Upon being so informed or, if the bank fails to inform, when the event actually occurs or when the Reserve Bank forms the opinion that such events might occur, the Reserve Bank has the power to appoint one of its own officers to investigate or to assume control of the bank and carry on the bank's business: s 14(2). In the event that the Reserve Bank does assume control it is obliged, subject to an order of the Full Court of the Federal Court to the contrary, to remain in control of the bank until such time as the deposits have been repaid and that it is no longer necessary for the Reserve Bank to remain in control: s 14(5).

Australian assets must be used to meet Australian deposit liabilities in priority to other liabilities: s 16(1). Further, unless otherwise authorised by the Reserve Bank, every bank (except a 'foreign bank' to which Div 2 does not apply) must hold assets other than goodwill in Australia which are adequate to meet its total Australian deposit liabilities: s 16(2). A foreign bank which suspends payment or which becomes unable to meet its obligations has its Australian assets applied to meet its Australian liabilities in priority to all other liabilities of the bank: s 11F.

These requirements are minimal and probably have little real effect either on the actual protection of depositors or upon the confidence of depositors. In the event of a bank failure it seems very unlikely that depositors could claim against the Reserve Bank for any perceived failure of the Bank to carry out its statutory obligations. An attempt by depositors to claim against members of the Isle of Man Finance Board and the Treasurer, both charged with duties toward depositors similar to those imposed on the Reserve Bank, was dismissed as unreasonable: *Davis v Radcliffe* [1990] 2 All ER 536; see also *Minories Finance v Arthur Young* [1989] 2 All ER 105.

PRUDENTIAL SUPERVISION

[1.16] One of the functions of the Reserve Bank is to encourage and promote sound banking practice in relation to prudential matters. The Banking Act instructs the Bank to collect and analyse information in respect of prudential matters and to evaluate the effectiveness of banking practice: s 11B. Although the Act contains a power for making regulations for prudential practice there have, in fact, been no regulations made. The preferred practice of the Bank is to consult with the banks and to establish guidelines which are then published and followed 'voluntarily' by the banks. The aim of the standards developed is to serve as a 'trigger' for discussions on particular aspects of operations. Although the Reserve Bank prefers the consultative approach, it recognises that if agreement cannot be found it may need to serve as the final arbiter. Current practices are available from the Reserve Bank: see 'Prudential Supervision of Banks' — *Prudential Statements*, published by the Reserve Bank of Australia.

'Prudential matters' are those relating to the conduct by a bank of its business affairs in such a way as to keep itself in a sound financial position and not to cause or promote instability in the financial system. 'Business affairs' in this context relates to business carried on by the bank which is not necessarily 'banking business'. 'Prudential matters' also relate to the need to conduct the bank's affairs 'with integrity, prudence and professional skill': see the definition of 'prudential matters', Banking Act s 5(1).

Current practice in relation to prudential supervision is concerned with five main areas. These are: capital adequacy, liquidity adequacy, risk exposure, associations with non-banks and foreign currency exposure. Each of these will be discussed briefly.

However, it should first be noted that although the Reserve Bank is charged with the task of prudential supervision it is unlikely that the Bank owes a duty of care to other financial interests in the exercise of that supervision. In *Minories Finance v Arthur Young* [1989] 2 All ER 105 the plaintiffs suffered substantial losses when a financial institution failed. In an attempt to recover these losses, the plaintiffs claimed against the Bank of England, claiming that the Bank had been negligent in carrying out its duty of supervision. The action was dismissed. It would be 'contrary to commonsense' to allow a commercial plaintiff to recover its losses from a statutory supervisory body: see also *Davis v Radcliffe* [1990] 2 All ER 536.

CAPITAL ADEQUACY

[1.17]   The Reserve Bank considers that it is of the greatest importance that the individual capital resources of a bank are adequate having regard to the size, quality and spread of the bank's business.

One of the shortcomings of the older prudential and monetary control instruments was that they were too closely related to accounting standards. Certain 'off balance sheet' business activities which had the effect of providing financial accommodation, and hence risk exposure for the accommodating institution, were not part of the calculations. These items, which include guarantees, standby letters of credit and bill acceptances, could account for very significant risks.

The problem is worldwide and was addressed by the Basle Supervisors' Group of the Bank for International Settlements, which issued guidelines for a system of calculating 'risk rated assets'. The basic plan of the scheme is that a bank's capital base should be at least a certain minimum percentage of the total of its risk rated assets. Risks are weighted according to their potential for default, and the scheme calls for a bank to maintain a ratio of capital to risk-weighted assets of not less than 8 per cent, with at least 4 per cent in 'core capital': see 'Capital Adequacy of Banks, Prudential Statement No C1', Reserve Bank of Australia, 1985.

[1.18]   For supervision purposes, 'capital' is divided into 'core', also called 'Tier 1', capital and 'supplementary', or 'Tier 2', capital.

Core capital consists of shareholders' funds as these represent the permanent commitment of funds which are available to meet losses. Shareholders funds include paid up ordinary shares, non-repayable share premium accounts, general reserves, retained earnings, non-cumulative irredeemable preference shares and minority interests in subsidiaries.

Supplementary (Tier 2) capital consists of other capital elements which, although important in assessing the overall strength of a bank, fall short of the certainty of core capital. The inclusion of supplementary capital as part of the capital base is subject to a number of restrictions and discounts. The most important restriction is that the total supplementary capital cannot be counted for more than 50 per cent of the total capital base of the bank.

Risks are placed into five categories and are given individual weights of 0, 10, 20, 50 or 100 per cent. Cash, gold bullion, Commonwealth Government money market securities (not exceeding 12 months to maturity) and claims on the Reserve Bank have a zero weight. Other claims are weighted according to the nature of the party. So, for example, most claims on federal and state governments have a weight of 10 per cent, most claims on Australian banks have a weight of 20 per cent, loans for secured residential housing have a weight of 50 per cent and most other corporate and private lending attracts the full 100 per cent rate.

[1.19] 'Off balance sheet' business is first converted to its 'credit equivalent amount' and then weighted according to the category of the counterparty or, where relevant, the guarantor or the collateral security.

The conversion to credit equivalent is done by means of conversion factors. So, for example, guarantees and standby letters of credit acting as guarantees are seen as acting as direct credit substitutes and are converted to a 'credit equivalent' of the face value of the guarantee or credit. On the other hand, certain trade-related items are converted at a fraction of their face value. An example of this conversion is a documentary letter of credit, which is assigned a 'credit equivalent' of 20 per cent of its face value. The differences in the two reflect the different risks associated with the different instruments: see Chapter 11.

Once the off balance sheet item is converted to its credit equivalent, the risk weighting is then assigned according to the identity of the other party.

Each risk is then multiplied by its associated weighting factor and all weighted risks are summed. The current requirement is that the total capital of the bank should be at least 8 per cent of the total risk weighted assets with at least 4 per cent Tier 1 capital.

LIQUIDITY

[1.20] It is clear that fractional reserve banking requires that a bank maintain substantial liquid or near liquid assets. A bank must also manage its day-to-day liquidity in order to meet demands for loans or withdrawals and other expenditures. The older forms of direct monetary control not only facilitated the implementation of monetary policy, but also served to assure a minimal level of liquidity. These monetary controls have now been replaced by the Prime Asset Requirements: see 'Supervision of the Adequacy of Liquidity of Banks, Prudential Statement No D1', Reserve Bank of Australia, February 1990.

The structure of the scheme is that each bank must maintain a minimum proportion of its balance sheet in specified 'prime' assets. Prime assets are those which may be quickly converted into cash in extreme circumstances. Prime assets are additional to the liquid assets which a bank must maintain for management of its day-to-day activities.

Prime assets are cash, claims (other than non-callable deposits; see [1.21], treasury notes, Commonwealth Government securities and loans to authorised money market dealers which are secured by Commonwealth

Government securities. Prime assets must be held in the name of the bank and may not be the subject of any security interest.

Any bank which is in danger of breaching the Prime Assets Requirement is required to notify the Reserve Bank immediately. It is contemplated that the Reserve Bank and the bank in question would then consult in order to identify actions to correct the deficiency promptly.

NON-CALLABLE DEPOSITS

[1.21] Banks are required to maintain an account with the Reserve Bank which is known as the 'non-callable deposit account'. Although the Reserve Bank is required to pay interest on these accounts, the interest rate is lower than the depositing bank could expect to receive from other sources. In effect, the non-callable deposit represents a tax on banks.

The required amount to be deposited may be based either on 'eligible' assets or on 'eligible' liabilities, the choice being made by the Reserve Bank with the approval of the Treasurer: Banking Act 1959, s 18. The required amount may not exceed 1 per cent of the eligible assets or the eligible liabilities as the case may be: ss 20, 22. In determining both the method and the amount, the Reserve Bank must apply the same rules to all banks: s 20(3). Similarly, the rate of interest paid on the non-callable account must be the same for all banks: s 24(2).

RISK EXPOSURE

[1.22] Risk is managed by ensuring a diversified loan and deposit structure. The diversification should consider both geographical and industrial factors. The Reserve Bank has requested banks to be particularly careful in the development of offshore operations and to ensure that these do not outrun their managerial and capital resources.

Australian corporate activity during the 1980s was characterised by the rise of large corporations which were primarily concerned with acquiring other companies. There are economic arguments to the effect that such 'takeovers' serve a very useful purpose in encouraging the target companies to improve their efficiency in order to eliminate the conditions which make takeovers profitable. Others believe that the threat of takeover leads the management of a company to spend so much time on 'defensive' manoeuvres that the efficiency of the company inevitably deteriorates.

Whatever the correct economic analysis, the takeover operation usually requires large amounts of credit. Experience of the last few years has shown that banks are willing to provide that credit and this has led to concerns that individual banks may find that too much credit risk has been concentrated with a single borrower or a single class of borrowers. The events of the 1980s and early 1990s have shown that these concerns are well founded.

A similar situation can arise when particular industries experience periods of unusual growth. The natural, indeed the sensible, method of financing such growth under current taxation law is through borrowings. Since the industry is, *ex hypothesi*, in a period of expansion, the individual will appear to be, and most likely will in fact be, a good credit risk. From the regulatory point of view, however, the overall consequence is that the banking system as a whole becomes undesirably dependent on a single sector of industry. The fear is that such over-exposure will cause undue economic effects in the event that the fortunes of the industry reverse. A collapse in the gold price, the wool price or the sugar price cannot be permitted to lead to a general collapse of the financial system.

[1.23] These considerations have led the Reserve Bank to place 'exposure limits' with regard to individual borrowers or groups of related borrowers. Although the exposure limits were originally applied to each bank individually, the Reserve Bank revised the guidelines to apply the limits to the 'consolidated group', that is, the bank and all its subsidiaries. Banks are required to report any such exposure which is more than 10 per cent of the capital base (Tier 1 and Tier 2 capital: see [1.18]) of the consolidated group. The risk exposure may be to an individual client or to a group of related clients. Banks are also required to give prior notice of any intention to enter into an exceptionally large exposure to an individual or related group of clients.

The Reserve Bank has indicated that it expects such large exposures to be kept under close review and that if the bank has any such large exposure it must be prepared to show that excessive risks are not being undertaken. The Reserve Bank has suggested that any bank which wishes to maintain such large exposures might be required to maintain a higher capital ratio: see 'Supervision of Banks' Large Credit Exposure', Prudential Statement No E1, Reserve Bank of Australia, August 1989.

ASSOCIATION WITH NON-BANKS

[1.24] As banking business has expanded beyond the range of traditional banking functions the main trading banks have formed subsidiary organisations to perform these functions. The Reserve Bank has established guidelines concerning the relationship of banks to these other organisations. In particular, the overriding principle is that the interest of the depositors of the bank is primary.

In order to 'insulate' a bank from the fortunes of a non-bank associate, the Reserve Bank has indicated that there should be prior notification of any proposed equity association of a bank with another institution. If the proposed interest exceeds 12.5 per cent then the bank must notify the Reserve Bank. The notification must be timely so that the Reserve Bank may comment to the bank if there is anything of relevance which it felt should be taken into account before the bank is committed to the other institution.

[1.25] In addition to this specific requirement, the Reserve Bank has established some more general guidelines. The most important of these are:

- a bank's equity association with another institution should normally be related to financial intermediation, and any involvement in non-financial areas should be of substantial relevance to banking business;

- finance for new or additional equity associations should come from share-holders' funds;

- a bank should not give a general guarantee of its associate's liabilities, and should seek to ensure that the associate does not give the impression that the bank's resources are available to meet the liabilities of the associate;

- a bank's financial dealings with an associate should be based on normal banking principles and, in particular, there should be no open-ended commitment by the bank to an associate;

- in those circumstances where a bank does assume direct responsibility for the affairs of an associate, it must ensure that the associate has sound and prudent management;

- a bank should ensure that the size of a subsidiary does not become large relative to the bank itself.

For more detail, see 'Banks' associations with Non-Banks', Prudential Statement No G1, 1985.

FOREIGN CURRENCY EXPOSURE

[1.26] With the collapse of an orderly regulation of the relative values of world currencies, foreign currency has become a commodity to be traded like any other. For a bank involved in international operations, the risk of currency fluctuations must be managed carefully by holding appropriate levels of the currency of those countries where the bank carries on business. Because of the volatile nature of foreign currency markets, the Reserve Bank has an interest in the foreign currency holdings of a bank. The Reserve Bank supervises the domestic foreign exchange operations of individual banks. It has established limits for each bank in respect of the bank's net open over-night foreign exchange positions which can expose the bank to foreign exchange risk.

In addition, the Reserve Bank receives information on a bank's global foreign exchange exposure. These exposures are reviewed with the banks with a view to determining the adequacy of their internal monitoring and control systems: see 'Prudential Supervision of Banks', Prudential Statement No A1, 1985.

LENDING POLICIES

[1.27] Section 50 of the Banking Act gives the Reserve Bank the power to make certain regulations which effectively set interest rates. This power can only be exercised with the approval of the Treasurer.

In fact, it seems that the power has never been used. This is not to say that there has been no control of the type authorised in s 50. The control has been implemented by 'agreement' between the Reserve Bank and the trading banks. Section 50 provides a powerful bargaining chip in any negotiations leading to such an agreement.

Direct controls over interest rates have fallen from favour during the last decade. It seems unlikely that s 50 will be used either directly or indirectly in the near future.

The Bank also has the power to determine policies in relation to advances: Banking Act 1959 s 36. This power specifically includes the power to give directions as to the classes of purposes for which loans may or may not be given by banks: s 36(2). The Reserve Bank might, for example, direct certain policies with respect to housing loans. However, the power of the Bank does not extend to directing that loans be made, or not made, to any particular person: s 36(3).

CONTROL OVER NON-BANK INSTITUTIONS

[1.28]   One of the effects of the moves to 'deregulate' the financial system has been that the distinction between banks and other financial institutions has been blurred. One response to this has been the change in regulatory methods which has already been discussed. Another response is to consider the inclusion of other financial institutions within the regulatory powers of the Reserve Bank.

Part IV of the Financial Corporations Act 1974 provides the formal statutory framework for this extension of the Bank's powers. This part of the Act has not been proclaimed, but its existence has provided the framework for a considerable amount of less formal discussion between the Reserve Bank and various sectors of the financial industry.

FINANCIAL TRANSACTIONS REPORTS ACT 1988

[1.29]   It is widely believed that cash transactions are used to facilitate the evasion of tax and to finance the importation of drugs into Australia. One response of the government to this problem is the Financial Transactions Reports Act of 1988 (the FTRA) which requires certain 'cash dealers' to report certain information to the Australian Transaction Reports and Analysis Centre (AUSTRAC). The stated object of the Act is to facilitate the administration and enforcement of taxation laws, to facilitate the administration and enforcement of laws (other than taxation laws) of the Commonwealth and the territories, and to make information collected for the above purposes available to state authorities to facilitate the administration and enforcement of the laws of the states: FTRA s 4.

In addition to requiring certain financial transactions to be reported, the FTRA also imposes obligations on all financial institutions to verify the identity of persons who are opening accounts with the institution or who are seeking to become signatories on existing accounts. Accounts for which the signatories are not verified in a manner specified by the Act become 'blocked' and liable to forfeiture.

The FTRA further makes it an offence to open or to operate an account under a false name and, since 1991, has imposed a statutory identification scheme for the opening of new accounts or for changing signatories on existing accounts.

Each of these matters will be discussed in the following sections.

AUSTRAC

[1.30]   The FTRA establishes The Australian Transaction Reports and Analysis Centre (AUSTRAC) which is intended to administer the FTRA and to keep records of certain transactions. The Cash Transaction Reports Agency, the forerunner of AUSTRAC, commenced operations in Sydney from January 1989. Its first task was consultation with various industry representatives with a view to defining procedures which would implement the requirements and the objectives of the FTRA with a minimum of expense and disruption.

WHO MUST REPORT?

[1.31]   The FTRA imposes reporting obligations on all 'cash dealers' and solicitors. The term 'cash dealer' is very widely defined and, in spite of representations to the government that it should be otherwise, banks and other financial institutions are specifically included in the definition. A 'cash dealer' is one of the following:

a) a financial institution;

b) a body corporate that is, or, if it had been incorporated in Australia, would be, a financial corporation within the meaning of paragraph 51(xx) of the Constitution;

c) an insurer or an insurance intermediary;

d) a securities dealer;

e) a futures broker;

f) a Registrar or Deputy Registrar of a Registry established under s 14 of the Commonwealth Inscribed Stock Act 1911;

g) a trustee or manager of a unit trust;

h) a person who carries on a business of issuing, selling or redeeming travellers' cheques, money orders or similar instruments;

i) a person who is a bullion seller;

j) a person (other than a financial institution) who carries on a business of:

    (i) collecting, holding, exchanging or remitting currency, or otherwise negotiating currency transfers, on behalf of other persons; or

    (ii) preparing payrolls on behalf of other persons in whole or in part from currency collected; or

(iii) delivering currency (including payrolls);

k) a person who carries on a business of operating a gambling house or casino; and

l) a bookmaker, including a totalisator agency board and any other person who operates a totalisator betting service.

'Financial institution' means a bank, a building society or a credit union. A 'unit trust' includes a cash management trust and a property trust.

[1.32] The Director of AUSTRAC may declare a cash dealer to be an 'approved cash carrier'. These are non-financial institutions which carry on the business of:

1. collecting currency, and holding currency collected on behalf of other persons;

2. preparing payrolls on behalf of other persons in whole or in part from the currency collected; and

3. delivering currency (including payrolls). Since these kind of organisations routinely serve merely as a mechanism for transporting cash from one cash dealer to another, approved cash carriers are relieved of the need to report significant cash transactions.

WHAT TRANSACTIONS MUST BE REPORTED?

[1.33] Unless the transaction is exempt, or unless the cash dealer is an approved cash carrier, a cash dealer who is a party to a reportable transaction must, before the end of the reporting period, prepare a report of the transaction and communicate the information contained in the report to the Director of AUSTRAC. The FTRA imposes an obligation to report 'significant' cash transactions, 'suspect' transactions and, since 1992, certain 'international fund transfer instructions'.

Significant cash transactions entered into by or on behalf of a solicitor in the course of practising as a solicitor must be reported. The reporting obligation is placed on the solicitor: s 15A(1).

'SIGNIFICANT CASH TRANSACTION'

[1.34] A 'cash transaction' is any transaction which involves the physical transfer of currency from one person to another: s 3(1). 'Currency' is the coin and paper legal tender of Australia or of any foreign country: s 3(1). 'Paper money' means money comprising a note written, printed or otherwise made on paper or any other material: s 3(1). In particular, various forms of 'computer money' are not currency: see [8.86]ff.

[1.35] It would clearly be counterproductive to require the reporting of all cash transactions. A 'significant' transaction is one which involves the transfer of not less than $10,000 in value: s 3(1). Where the cash transaction involves the international transfer of currency, the reporting limit was $5000, but this was raised to $10,000 in the 1997 Amendment.

17

'SUSPECT' TRANSACTIONS

[1.36] Although there is no onus on the banker to make inquiries into the business activities of a customer, if some information comes to the attention of the banker which raises a reasonable ground of suspicion that the transaction may be relevant to an investigation of evasion of a tax law, an offence against any Commonwealth or territory law or of assistance in the enforcement of the Proceeds of Crime Act 1987 then the transaction must be reported to the Agency as soon as practicable after forming the suspicion: s 16(1).

Note that the test is 'reasonable grounds to suspect', not 'reasonable grounds to believe'. No action may be taken against the institution or any agent or employee for making a report under this section: s 16(5). It is thought that this protection would only apply if the action is not taken negligently or recklessly, that is, it only applies when the suspicion is, in fact, based on reasonable grounds. Section 16(5) protects against actions for defamation and for breach of the banker's duty of confidentiality: see [4.2]ff.

A person who forms such a suspicion is also under threat from the Proceeds of Crime Act 1987 (Cth) as a person who has received proceeds having reasonable grounds to suspect that the funds represent the proceeds of a crime: see below [1.52] ff. Section 17 provides them protection if the information is passed on to the Agency by deeming them not to have been in possession at any time of the information communicated by them under their s 16 duty. This prevents any prosecution for the offence of money laundering. Of course, if the person is in possession of any further damaging information which is not communicated to the Agency, then that information may be used as evidence against them in a prosecution.

INTERNATIONAL FUND TRANSFER INSTRUCTIONS

[1.37] An international funds transfer instruction is an instruction for the transfer of funds that is transmitted either into or out of Australia by electronic or telegraphic means: s 3(1). Any cash dealer who sends or receives such an instruction must prepare a report unless the dealer is, or is acting on behalf of, a bank: s 17B. Because of the large number of routine international funds transfers, the Director of AUSTRAC may exempt particular transfers or classes of transfers from the reporting requirement: ss 17B(3), 17B(4).

The FTRA attempts to clarify who is the party 'sending' the message when one person sends an instruction on behalf of another. If a cash dealer transmits an instruction on behalf of another person, it is the cash dealer who is taken to send the message: s 17B(6). If a person who is not a cash dealer sends a message on behalf of a cash dealer, it is the cash dealer who is taken to be the sender: s 17B(7). But where a bank is acting on the instructions of a second bank which is in turn acting on the instructions of a non-bank customer, it is the first mentioned bank which is taken to be acting on behalf of the customer: s 17C.

The implementation of various forms of 'computer banking' has caused some problems. Computer banking permits the customer to order the transfer of funds from a computer terminal. The major financial institutions have taken the view that these 'client initiated' transfers are not reportable by them since they are not transfers made by a 'cash dealer'. The argument is doubtful since the way in which a client orders a transfer should not be relevant to the question of reportability. However, it is clear that the spread of this form of account access will require an amendment to the FTRA if its purpose is not to be frustrated.

STRUCTURING TRANSACTIONS

[1.38] Since reporting is not necessary if the transaction is less than $10,000, why not merely make several smaller transactions? The procedure is known as 'smurfing', although the FTRA does not use such colourful language.

In an attempt to deal with smurfing, the FTRA makes it an offence in certain circumstances to structure two or more transactions in a manner which would have the effect of avoiding the reporting requirements. In partic-ular, a person is guilty of an offence where he or she is a party to two or more non-reportable cash transactions and it would be reasonable to conclude that the person conducted the transactions in the manner or form for the sole or dominant purpose of ensuring that the currency involved in the transactions was transferred in a manner and form that would not give rise to a significant transaction or would be an exempt transaction. Regard should be had to the manner and form in which the transactions were conducted, including the value of the currency involved in each transaction, the aggregated value of the transactions, the period of time over which the transactions took place and the interval of time between any of the transactions. Regard should also be had to any explanation made by the person as to the manner or form in which the transactions were conducted: see FTRA s 31(1).

If a would-be money-launderer has his or her ill-gotten gains in the form of 'digital cash' then the problem of detecting smurfing may be nearly imposs-ible. The launderer may simply program a computer to make continuous small transactions through many off-shore accounts: see [8.86]ff and Brent Fisse and Peter Leonard, 'Net-smurfing and other emerging regulatory challenges from electronic payment technologies', *ASC Electronic Commerce Conference*, Sydney, 4 February 1997.

EXEMPT TRANSACTIONS

[1.39] The Act recognises that certain 'significant' transactions are not in fact significant for the purposes of the Act. A transaction need not be reported if it is 'exempt' at the time when it occurs or if it is eligible for exemption at that time and becomes an exempt transaction prior to the time when report-ing is required.

[1.40]   The concept of the exempt transaction depends upon the maintenance of an 'exemption register'. Part II of the Act requires each financial institution to create and maintain a register: s 12. Section 11 of the Act authorises certain entries in the register. The entry may relate to a single transaction or to a class of transactions. When the entry is in relation to a class of transactions, the entry must be associated with a particular person.

If the entry is properly made, then the transaction, or class of transactions, becomes exempt and need not be reported to AUSTRAC. The Director of AUSTRAC is given the power to order a financial institution to delete the entry of a class of transaction or to amend it so that it ceases to apply to transactions of the kind specified.

ELIGIBILITY FOR EXEMPTION

[1.41]   Financial institutions and others clearly make many routine dealings with cash which would be of no interest whatsoever to AUSTRAC. The exemptions listed in s 10 are intended to reflect this obvious fact.

A transaction is eligible for exemption if it is between a financial institution and another financial institution or a cash dealer: s 10(1). Note that a transaction is not eligible if it is between two cash dealers neither of which is a financial institution.

The Act also recognises that certain customers of financial institutions will regularly engage in large cash transactions. Indeed, that is one of the main reasons why they are customers! The FTRA permits exemption of transactions where the customer carries on a retail business, an entertainment or hospitality business (as defined by notice in the Gazette) or a vending machine business. The transaction is only eligible for exemption if it is into or out of an account which is maintained for the purpose of the business and the amount does not exceed an amount that is reasonably commensurate with the customer's lawful business activities: s 10(2).

Withdrawals by an established customer for the purpose of meeting a payroll are eligible for exemption provided the customer regularly withdraws sums for that purpose and provided the sum withdrawn does not exceed the amount that is reasonably commensurate with the customer's lawful business activities: s 10(3).

In both of the above classes of transaction, eligibility for exemption is restricted to 'established customers', that is, a person who has been a customer of the institution for not less than 12 months immediately preceding the relevant time. If a customer transfers an account from one institution to another, then transactions with the new institution will remain eligible for exemption provided they would have been eligible if conducted with the original institution: s 10(6).

Transactions between financial institutions and public authorities are eligible for exemption, again provided that the sums involved do not exceed amounts which are reasonably commensurate with the authorised activities of the authority: s 10(4).

Section 10(5) provides a catch-all category by allowing a transaction to be eligible for exemption if it is so declared by the Minister by notice in the Gazette.

PROCEDURE

[1.42]   If the transaction is eligible for exemption under s 10, then a financial institution may enter it on its exemption register provided the other party signs a written statement to the effect that the party believes that the transaction is eligible and the information provided to the financial institution is, to the best of the party's knowledge and belief, true and correct in all material particulars: s 11(1).

OBLIGATIONS WHEN OPENING ACCOUNTS

ACCOUNTS IN FALSE NAMES

[1.43]   The purpose and efficacy of the FTRA would be frustrated if accounts could be opened in false names. Section 24 of the FTRA makes it an offence to open an account in a false name. If the person opening the account is commonly known by two or more different names, these other names must be made known to the banker: s 24(3). A person is deemed to have opened an account in a false name if the person uses any name other than that by which he or she is commonly known. It is also an offence to operate an account using a false name. This includes any action in relation to an account or any communication with the banker using a name other than that by which he or she is commonly known: s 24(7).

There are a number of reasons why a person may wish to use a name other than the one by which they have been known. The FTRA recognises certain classes of name changes and provides procedures for opening accounts in the new name. A person who wishes to open, or become a signatory to, an account in a new name may do so provided the new name falls into one of the approved categories. These categories are: (a) a name which the person has adopted by marriage; (b) a name by which the person, being a woman who has previously changed the surname by which she is known to that of her spouse or de facto spouse, was formerly known; (c) a name which the person, being a person who has been the victim of violence or threats of violence, or the dependent child of such a person, has adopted or intends to adopt to ensure his or her personal safety; or (d) if the person is an Aborigine or Torres Strait Islander, a name which is a traditional name of the person: see FTRA s 21A.

The FTRA requires that the person give the banker a change of name statement signed by the customer and by a 'prescribed person': see below [1.47]ff. A change of name statement sets out the name or names by which the person has been commonly known, states the name category into which the new name falls, sets out the reasons why the person is entitled to change his or her name, sets out the new name, and states that the new name is one by which the person will be commonly known: see FTRA s 21A.

Such statements are then taken to constitute an identification reference for the person in the new name. It is an offence for a person to knowingly or recklessly make a statement in a change of name statement that is false or misleading in a material particular or to omit from the statement any matter or thing without which the statement is misleading in a material particular.

Account opening procedures

[1.44]   It is not enough to make it an offence to open an account in a false name. What is desired is a procedure that makes it difficult or impossible to do so. The FTRA deals with the problem by imposing stringent requirements on bankers and other cash dealers opening accounts or adding signatories to existing accounts.

The procedure is simple in principle. When a new account is opened, or a new signatory added to an existing account, the cash dealer must obtain 'account information' and 'signatory information'. This information must be obtained before the 'infringement day'. Failure to obtain timely information results in the account being 'blocked' with respect to each signatory until such time as the information is obtained or until released by the Director of AUS-TRAC. The information may come from the person opening the account or may already be in the possession of the cash dealer by virtue of the person being a signatory to another account.

[1.45]   'Account information' is information which uniquely identifies the account in question including any identifying numbers and the name in which the account is held. It must include information and documents which identify the postal address, other than a post office box, of the account holder. 'Account information' also includes particulars concerning the legal personality of the account holder and must include a certificate of incorporation where the account holder is a body corporate. Details of trust arrangements and of business names must be included with supporting documentation where relevant: for more detail, see FTRA s 3(1).

[1.46]   'Signatory information' is information and documents which include the name used by the signatory in operating the account, any other name disclosed to the cash dealer by which the signatory is commonly known and, most importantly, an 'identification record'. If the account is in the name of an unincorporated association, the signatory information must also include a copy of the instrument which authorises the signatory to sign: for more detail, see FTRA s 3(1).

[1.47]   The FTRA provides for two distinct mechanisms for ensuring that accounts cannot easily be opened under an assumed name. The first is the 'identification reference'. The second is a 'verification procedure' carried out by an 'identifying cash dealer'. A cash dealer has the required 'identification record' if in possession of an identification reference or, if an identifying cash dealer, he or she has performed the necessary 'verification procedure'. Any cash dealer may apply to the Director of AUSTRAC to become an 'identifying' cash dealer.

[1.48] An 'identification reference' is a written reference by another person which conforms to the standards established by the FTRA. The referee must be one of a class of 'acceptable referees' as determined from time to time by notice in the Gazette. The reference must contain certain information which is intended to guarantee that the person has been properly identified. The most important requirement is that the referee must state that he or she has examined a 'primary identification document', such as a passport or a citizenship certificate, in the name of the person or, if that is not possible, certain 'secondary identification documents' together with an explanation for the failure to sight a primary identification document: for more detail, see FTRA ss 3(1), 3(5) and 21.

[1.49] 'Verification procedures' may be carried out by 'identifying cash dealers'. The verification procedure consists of certain checks on the identity of the signatory which are intended to establish the person's identity. Documents produced by the intending signatory are assigned scores. The total score must total at least 100 points in order that the proposed signatory is taken to be properly identified. Some classes of signatories are treated as special cases and different procedures are applied. For more detail, see Financial Transactions Reports Regulations 1990.

[1.50] The effect of an account becoming a blocked account is rather draconian. Where an account has been blocked for at least 12 months and the Director of AUSTRAC has been notified of this fact, the Director must take certain steps to notify the signatory concerned. Unless the Director is satisfied of certain matters within three months, all rights and interest in relation to the account are forfeited to the Commonwealth: s 19. The account holder has a right to appeal to a court which may set aside the Director's decision and may make orders which result in the account holder receiving restitution.

RECORD KEEPING

[1.51] 'Account information' and 'signatory information' obtained by a cash dealer must be kept in a form which can be audited: s 20(1). Any record made or obtained in the course of acquiring either 'account information' or 'signatory information' must be retained by the cash dealer for a period of seven years after the closing of the account, although it is sufficient if the cash dealer retains a copy: s 23(1).

PROCEEDS OF CRIME ACT 1987

[1.52] There is a widely held belief that organised criminal activity may best be fought by following the 'money trail'. One legislative response to this belief is the Financial Transactions Reports Act 1988: see [1.29]ff. Another response is the Proceeds of Crime Act 1987 and various state Acts which attempt to confiscate the proceeds of illegal activity.

[1.53] The Act itself states its principal objects in s 3(1):

(a) to deprive persons of the proceeds of, and benefits derived from the commission of offences ...

(b) to provide for the forfeiture of property used in or in connection with the commission of such offences; and

(c) to enable law enforcement authorities to effectively trace such proceeds, benefits and property.

In pursuit of these objectives, the Commonwealth Act imposes significant criminal penalties on those who participate in 'laundering' the money obtained from illicit activities. Since it is obvious that many 'laundering' operations will involve the use of bank accounts, it is important for bankers to be aware of their responsibilities under the Act. The Act also imposes significant record keeping burdens on financial institutions.

The essence of the Commonwealth Act is to create three new offences: money laundering under s 81, receiving or possessing money or property reasonably suspected to be the proceeds of crime as prescribed by s 82, and organised fraud under s 83. The first two of these offences are of direct concern to bankers, since it is possible for the banker to become 'innocently' involved.

In addition, all of these offences impose vicarious liability on individual and corporate entities for the conduct of their agents and employees: s 85. This imposition of vicarious liability for criminal offences violates common law principles and is one of the most offensive aspects of the Act. It also has the effect of making the Act of the utmost importance to bankers. See the discussion at [1.57].

MONEY LAUNDERING

[1.54] A person shall be taken to engage in money laundering if, and only if:

(a) the person engages, directly or indirectly, in a transaction that involves money ... that is proceeds of crime; or

(b) the person receives, possesses, conceals, disposes of or brings into Australia any money ... that is proceeds of crime; and the person knows, or ought reasonably to know, that the money is derived or realised, directly or indirectly, from some form of unlawful activity: s 81(3).

The penalties for breach are severe: a fine of $200,000 and/or jail for up to 20 years if the offender is an individual and a fine of up to $600,000 if the offender is a corporation.

[1.55] Note that the mental element of the offence is an objective one, that the person 'ought reasonably to know'. This imposes a statutory duty on bankers when opening accounts and receiving deposits to take precautions which will reveal the source of tainted funds. The standard of inquiry demanded may be high since the funds need not be directly the 'proceeds of crime' but may be derived 'indirectly'.

There do not seem to be any of the reasonable defences that one might expect. So, for example, it seems that if the banker accepts money when he or she should have a suspicion that it is derived from the proceeds of crime, it will be no defence to establish that it was received with an intention that it would be held for the purposes of returning it to the police or to the rightful owner.

However, where a 'cash dealer' or any person who is an officer, employee or agent of a cash dealer, provides information as required by the Financial Transaction Reports Act, that person is deemed not to have been in possession of the information for the purposes of the offence of money laundering: Financial Transactions Reports Act 1988 s 17. Since the person in question is not 'in possession of the information' then he or she would not be in a position where they 'ought reasonably to know' that the funds are tainted. This is a very oblique method of establishing a defence to a serious crime.

POSSESSION OF PROCEEDS OF CRIME

[1.56] Section 82 creates the offence of receiving or possessing certain money:

(1) A person who ... receives, possesses, conceals, disposes of or brings into Australia any money, or other property, that may reasonably be suspected of being proceeds of crime is guilty of an offence against this section.

Subsection 2 provides a defence, but it is clear that the onus is on the defendant to establish the defence once the fact of possession, etc, is established. It is a defence to the charge if the person satisfies the court that he or she had no reasonable grounds for suspecting that the property referred to directly or indirectly resulted from some form of unlawful activity.

For 'cash dealers', their officers, employees and agents, there is also the 'information defence' discussed above: see [1.55] and s 17 Financial Transactions Reports Act 1988.

Penalties are fines of up to $5000 and imprisonment for up to two years if the person charged is a natural person and a fine of up to $15,000 if the offender is a body corporate. Needless to say, the reputation of a banker charged with such an offence would be severely damaged.

CORPORATE LIABILITY

[1.57] For the purposes of both the offence of money laundering and possession of suspect property, a body corporate may be held liable for the actions of its directors, employees and agents. Any act of these parties will be attributed to the body corporate if it is within the scope of the person's actual or apparent authority: s 85(2)(a).

Further, if any director, employee or agent of the body corporate consents or agrees to another person engaging in certain conduct, then the acts of that person will be attributed to the body corporate provided only that the person giving the consent or agreement has the actual or apparent authority to do so: s 85(2)(b).

If is it necessary to establish the state of mind of a body corporate when engaging in certain conduct, then it is sufficient to show that the person acting had that state of mind provided that the conduct is within the actual or apparent authority of that person: s 85(1).

RETENTION OF DOCUMENTS

[1.58]   A financial institution must retain certain documents for a period of seven years. If the document is an 'essential customer generated financial transaction document' then the original must be retained, but in the case of other, non-essential, 'customer generated financial transaction documents' it is generally sufficient if a copy is retained: s 77(1), 77(2).

A 'customer generated financial transaction document' is any document, signed or not, which is given to the institution by the customer concerned and which relates to the opening, closing or operation of an account, an electronic funds transfer, an international transfer or an application for a loan: s 76(a), 76(b). The document is 'essential' if it relates to any of the above categories except the operation of an account.

The Act provides an exception for documents relating to a single account transaction where the amount does not exceed $200: s 77(4).

CHAPTER 2

THE BANKER–CUSTOMER RELATIONSHIP

[2.1] If one reflects on the many services provided by the modern bank to its customer, it will be apparent that the legal relationship between the banker and the customer must be a complex one. Indeed, it would seem almost impossible to fit even the primary relationship into a single legal category. Yet a classification is necessary if the variety of legal disputes which arise are to be analysed and solved in a satisfactory fashion. It may surprise the reader to learn that the relationship is not defined by statute but rather by a series of common law judgments.

POSSIBLE RELATIONSHIPS

[2.2] The common law analysis of the banker-customer relationship was a surprisingly late development. Perhaps because modern banking had its origins with the goldsmiths of London, there was for many years the possibility that the legal relationship might be one of bailment. On the other hand, it was clear that in many transactions the banker acted in a position of trust and, in still other situations, the relationship could be considered one of agent and principal.

Since it was possible right up to the mid-nineteenth century that the courts might have found the basic relationship to be any one of these, it is worth considering each in turn, for had any of the three been selected as the basic legal relationship which defines the rights and obligations of the parties, banking could not exist in the form in which we now know it.

BAILOR-BAILEE

[2.3] A bailment is the transfer of the possession of a chattel without the transfer of title: see, for example, R M Goode, *Commercial Law*, 2nd ed, Penguin, London, 1995. The transfer may be very informal, as when a person leaves a lawnmower with a neighbour while on vacation, or it may be a formal contractual arrangement such as when a chattel belonging to the debtor is left with the lender as a security for a loan. The owner of the chattel who parts with possession is known as the bailor, the person who receives the chattel is the bailee.

It is clear that there are occasions when the banker acts as the bailee of goods which are deposited by the customer for safe-keeping: see Chapter 4 for a discussion of the duties of a banker who is acting as a bailee. When the goldsmiths of London first began receiving goods for safe-keeping, there is little doubt that they were doing so as bailees of those goods. However, at a later time when receipts were issued and when it was not expected that the goods (that is, gold) returned would be exactly the same as those deposited, it was no longer possible to consider the relationship to be one of bailment.

The business of banking based on receiving deposits and lending money could scarcely exist if the fundamental relationship between banker and customer were one of bailment. It would mean, for example, that when the customer deposited notes and coins into an account, that the banker would be obliged to return precisely those same notes and coins rather than a sum of money equivalent to the deposit. Furthermore, the duties of a bailee are simply not directly applicable to the business of banking, save where the banker is acting in the special capacity of custodian of property which has been deposited for safe-keeping.

[2.4]   It might be thought that money is special and that there might still be a bailee-bailor relationship even though the banker is clearly not expected to return the same identical notes and coins. In legal terms, it is said that money is a 'fungible'. However, it seems that the concept of bailment is incompatible with that of a fungible. In *Chapman Bros v Vercos* (1933) 49 CLR 306 the High Court of Australia held that an arrangement whereby wheat was deposited with a company which would then sell it or, at the request of the 'bailor', return an equivalent amount of wheat if the terms of sale were unacceptable could not be a bailment precisely because the same identical grains of wheat were not to be returned.

There is one very practical consequence of the *Vercos* decision. If the relationship is one of bailment, then the property in the goods or money remains with the depositor. In the event of the insolvency of the banker, the customer would be entitled to receive the full value of the deposit in preference to other creditors of the banker. However, if the relationship is one in which the depositor loses property in the goods or money deposited, then the other creditors of the banker will rank equally and the depositor can expect only a small fraction of the original deposit to be returned. As a result of *Vercos*, a depositor ranks only as an unsecured ordinary debtor who must prove in bankruptcy when a bank fails.

TRUSTEE-CESTUI QUE TRUST

[2.5]   There are clearly occasions when a banker acts in a fiduciary capacity similar to that which exists between trustee and beneficiary. Had the courts held that the opening of an account and the deposit of money established the legal relationship of trust, then once again, modern banking simply could not exist. A trustee is severely restricted in the use to which trust funds may be put and will ordinarily be restricted in the class of investment. The freedom of investment enjoyed by bankers would be restricted, with the economic consequence that financing for all but the safest of projects would of necessity come from non-banking sources. Banks would cease to be the major economic and financial force that they are now.

Had the primary banker-customer relationship been found to be one of trust, then once again, the position of the depositor would have been improved in the event of the banker's insolvency. Since the beneficial (that is, equitable) ownership of the money would remain with the customer, other creditors would be deferred until depositors were fully repaid: see A N Lewis, *Australian Bankruptcy Law*, 10th ed, Law Book Co, Sydney, 1994.

Although there may be occasions where the banker acts as trustee for the customer, it does not do so in the ordinary course of banking business. So, for example, where a bank received rent on behalf of a customer, crediting the customer's account and paying rates on behalf of the customer, it was found that the bank was not receiving the sums as 'agent or trustee': *Midland Bank Ltd v Conway Corp* [1965] 1 WLR 1165.

AGENT-PRINCIPAL

[2.6]   Again, it is clear that there are certain circumstances in which the banker acts as the agent of the customer. Perhaps the most common situation is the collection of cheques, a matter which is discussed at some length in Chapters 5 and 6. There is no legal obstacle to the creation of an agency in which the banker would have the authority to use the customer's money at the banker's discretion. However, the law relating to the remuneration of an agent and the duty of an agent to account would severely hamper the development of modern banking practice.

DEBTOR-CREDITOR

[2.7]   In spite of the difficulties attached to the above possibilities for defining the primary legal relationship between the banker and customer, it was not until 1848 that the primary legal relationship was firmly established as being a debtor-creditor relationship which arises from contract.

In the landmark case of *Foley v Hill* (1848) 2 HL Cas 28; 9 ER 1002, the plaintiff had deposited a sum of money with the defendant banker many years before bringing the suit. The banker had agreed to pay 3 per cent interest but there had not been any interest paid or credited to the account for well over six years. The problem for the plaintiff was to overcome the Statute of Limitations, for if the money owed by the banker was a mere debt, then an action for its recovery was within the scope of the statute: see [2.40]. However, if the relationship between the parties was one in which the banker owed the plaintiff a fiduciary duty, then the statute did not apply.

Lord Cottenham said (at 2 HL Cas 28 at 36; 9 ER 1002 at 1005):

> Money, when paid into a bank, ceases altogether to be the money of the prin-
> cipal ...; it is then the money of the banker, who is bound to return an
> equivalent by paying a similar sum to that deposited with him when he is
> asked for it. Money paid into a bankers' is money known by the principal to be
> placed there for the purpose of being under the control of the banker; it is then
> the banker's money; he is known to deal with it as his own; he makes what
> profit he can, which profit he retains to himself ... He has contracted, having
> received that money, to repay to the principal when demanded a sum equiva-
> lent to that paid into his hands. [Note that there is still the trace of the agent-
> principal relationship in the language used by Lord Cottenham.]

[2.8] Thus, when a banker receives money from a customer, or receives
money from some third party for the account of a customer, the banker does
so as a borrower. The ownership of the money is transferred to the banker
who is then free to use the money in any way that he or she chooses. The
banker is also free to retain the income from or any other benefit of the
money. There is no duty to hold the actual notes or coins or to keep the
money segregated in any way from any other of the banker's money, nor is
there any duty to invest it carefully or prudently. He or she is simply a borrower with a contractual obligation to repay the money to the customer when
certain conditions are met.

[2.9] Approval of the debtor-creditor basis of the banker-customer relationship was given explicitly by the High Court of Australia in *Croton v R*
(1967) 41 ALJR 289. A man and woman who were living together opened a
joint bank account where each had the authority to draw cheques. Both
parties deposited money into the account from time to time. Without the
woman's authority or knowledge, the man withdrew the money from the
account and deposited it in a bank account in his own name. When the
woman discovered this, she complained to the police who charged the man
with larceny. A majority of the High Court upheld his appeal on the basis that
the correct charge should have been fraudulent misappropriation. Barwick CJ
said (at 291):

> Though in a popular sense it may be said that a depositor with a bank has
> 'money in the bank', in law he has but a chose in action, a right to recover
> from the bank the balance standing to his credit in the account with the bank
> at the date of his demand or the commencement of action ... But the money
> deposited becomes an asset of the bank which it may use as it pleases. Neither
> the balance standing to the credit of the joint account in this case nor any part
> of it, as it constituted no more than a chose in action in contradistinction to a
> chose in possession, was susceptible of larceny, though it might be the subject
> of misappropriation.

ADDITIONAL CONTRACTUAL INCIDENTS

[2.10] Although the primary legal relationship is one of debtor and creditor, there are additional contractual terms which must be implied into the
contract in order to facilitate the fulfilment of the parties' expectations. The

first comprehensive judicial acknowledgment of the complexity of the banker-customer contract was in *Joachimson v Swiss Bank Corporation* [1921] 3 KB 110. Although the case concerned the question of when the debt owed by the banker is repayable and, in particular, the need for a demand by the customer, the court went beyond the facts in an attempt to define the nature of the banker-customer relationship.

In *Foley v Hill*, Lord Cottenham LC made it quite clear in his speech that the contractual duty to repay is slightly different from the normal debtor-creditor relationship. Ordinarily, it is for the debtor to seek out the creditor and to make repayment when due: *Wafton v Mascall* (1844) 13 M & W 452 at 458. It is obviously not contemplated that the banker will seek out the customer and repay the debt since that would have the effect of closing the customer's account, a result which is not desired by either party.

[2.11] The confusion regarding the need for the customer to make a demand before the debt became due was possibly a result of the fact that the headnote of *Foley v Hill* neglected to mention Lord Cottenham's qualification to the debtor-creditor relationship. In 1921, Lord Atkin in *Joachimson v Swiss Bank Corporation* [1921] 3 KB 110 undertook a more complete analysis of the banker-customer relationship. In one of the most famous and oft-quoted passages of the law of banking he said (at 127):

> I think that there is only one contract made between the bank and its customer. The terms of that contract involve obligations on both sides and require careful statement. They appear upon consideration to include the following provisions. The bank undertakes to receive money and to collect bills for its customer's account. The proceeds so received are not to be held in trust for the customer, but the bank borrows the proceeds and undertakes to repay them. The promise to repay is to repay at the branch of the bank where the account is kept, and during banking hours. It includes a promise to repay any part of the amount due against the written order of the customer addressed to the bank at the branch, and as such written orders may be outstanding in the ordinary course of business for two or three days, it is a term of the contract that the bank will not cease to do business with the customer except upon reasonable notice. The customer on his part undertakes to exercise reasonable care in executing his written orders so as not to mislead the bank or to facilitate forgery. I think it is necessarily a term of such contract that the bank is not liable to pay the customer the full amount of his balance until he demands payment from the bank at the branch at which the current account is kept.

[2.12] Recall that a term will not be implied into a contract unless it is necessary to do so and that in the absence of the implied term the whole transaction would become 'inefficacious, futile and absurd' (per Lord Salmon in *Liverpool City Council v Irwin* [1977] AC 239 at 262).

It seems likely that bankers would certainly agree that the implied term as to demand at the branch where the account is kept is necessary, for otherwise the customer would be entitled to demand the money at any branch of the bank, irrespective of where the account was kept. Customers, in like manner, would certainly agree that the consequential need for giving notice before ceasing to do business is also necessary, for otherwise the banker would be entitled to repay the account balance at any time and to then dishonour any outstanding cheques. The contractual terms concerning the collection of bills and the payment against 'written orders' are the subject matter of Chapters 5 –7.

The actual decision in *Joachimson's* case can be somewhat confusing, for in addition to holding that a demand is necessary for the debt to become due, the Court of Appeal held that the issue of a writ or the service of a garnishee order nisi by the customer for the amount due would be sufficient demand. It seems strange that the service of the writ can form part of the cause of action, but this is undoubtedly the case.

The *Joachimson* principle that the debt is not due until demand has been made has been approved in Australia: *Re ANZ Savings Bank Ltd* [1972] VR 690; *Bank of NSW v Laing* [1954] AC 135. The service of a garnishee order nisi also has been held to be sufficient demand in Australia: *Tunstall Brick and Pottery Co v Mercantile Bank of Australia Ltd* (1892) 18 VLR 59. Because of some doubts about the matter in garnishee proceedings, there is now statutory confirmation in all jurisdictions: see [3.79]ff. The service of a garnishee order nisi is not a substitute for other conditions such as the requirement to present a passbook: *Bank of NSW Savings Bank Ltd v Fremantle Auto Centre Pty Ltd* [1973] WAR 161.

[2.13]   It is often said that the basic relationship is one of debtor and creditor with 'superadded obligations'. This expression of the relationship does no harm so long as it is understood that all it means is that there is a single contract between the banker and the customer and that the contract has many terms: *Joachimson v Swiss Bank Corporation* [1921] 3 KB 110 at 127. Indeed, much of the subject matter of the law of banking is nothing more than the explanation and the elaboration of the terms of the contract between the banker and customer.

The Privy Council referred to some of the ways in which the banker-customer relationship differs from the normal debtor-creditor relationship in *Bank of NSW v Laing* [1954] AC 135. The plaintiff alleged that a series of cheques were forged. He drew cheques totalling the amount of the cheques which he claimed were forged and presented them to the defendant bank for payment. They were dishonoured and the plaintiff sued. Unfortunately, New South Wales at the time still retained the forms of pleading and the decision in favour of the bank turns entirely on a technicality. However, during the course of the judgment, Lord Asquith of Bishopstone commented upon the ways in which the banker-customer relationship differs from that of the ordinary debtor-creditor relationship. First, the debt does not become due until the customer makes a demand. Second (at 154):

> a further 'peculiar incident' is that the bank is only indebted to the customer for the amount ... standing to his credit as at the time of the demand ... If the 'balance' falls short of [meeting the demand], even by a penny, he [the customer] fails altogether, another distinction which rails off the creditor-debtor

relationship in the case of a customer and banker from that relationship in other cases.

Although directed to the forms of pleading, this statement of the relationship is still relevant when the 'demand' is in the form of a cheque drawn on the customer's account: see [5.51].

[2.14]   The fact that the fundamental relationship between banker and customer is one of debtor and creditor created by contract should not obscure the fact that there are other relationships created by the contract. The banker acts as the customer's agent for the purposes of paying and collecting cheques, a relationship which imposes certain obligations on both parties: see [5.105]. In addition, the banker will perform services from time to time which may be considered as outside the basic banker-customer contract. Such services include the keeping of valuables and giving investment advice: see [4.52]. Whether the rights and the obligations of the parties are considered as separate terms of the basic banker-customer contract, or are considered as governed by separate contracts created from time to time, will not usually be a matter of great practical significance.

FORMING THE RELATIONSHIP: WHO IS A CUSTOMER?

[2.15]   There are a number of circumstances in which it may be important to know if the banker-customer relationship exists between two parties. A banker is only required to honour the cheques of a customer, the banker is entitled to certain privileged statutory defences if collecting a cheque for a customer and a bank owes certain other duties to a customer but not to non-customers: see Chapter 5. In this section, the problem of the time of formation is considered. Termination of the relationship will be considered at [2.23].

There is no statutory definition of the term 'customer'. For many years, there was a body of opinion which thought that a continuing relationship of some duration was required, that it was indeed necessary to show some 'custom': see, for example, *Matthews v Williams, Brown & Co* (1894) 10 TLR 386. At the other end of the spectrum, some thought that, by analogy with the use of the word in other businesses, if the banker had any dealings at all with a person, then that person was a 'customer': see the arguments in *Great Western Railway Co v London and County Banking Co Ltd* [1901] AC 414.

Neither of these views is correct. The cases are primarily concerned with the meaning of 'customer' for the purposes of the bank claiming statutory protection under the Cheques and Payment Orders Act 1986 (CPOA) or its equivalent: see Chapters 5 and 6. In this context, the cases show that a contractual relationship must exist prior to the act which gives rise to the dispute.

However, it may be that a person is a 'customer' for one purpose but not for another. For example, a bank collecting cheques for a 'customer' is given certain statutory defences against charges of conversion when the person for whom the collection is being performed has no title, or a defective title to the cheque: Cheques and Payment Orders Act 1986 s 95. In *E B Savory & Co v Lloyds Bank Ltd* [1932] 2 KB 122, affirmed in *Lloyds Bank v E B Savory & Co* [1933] AC 201, cheques were collected for a person who had an account with the bank, but not at the branch which performed the collection. Lawrence LJ expressed doubt that the person was a 'customer' of the bank for the purposes of the then English equivalent of s 95 of the Cheques and Payment Orders Act 1986. There is, of course, no doubt that the person was a 'customer' of the bank for most other purposes, for it is generally considered that the contract is with the bank, not with the branch: *Garnett v M'Kewan* (1872) LR 8 Ex 10.

[2.16]   It is clear that even a regular pattern of transactions does not suffice to make a person a 'customer' if the transactions are not sufficient to establish a continuing duty on the part of the banker under the usual rules of contract formation. In *Great Western Railway Co v London and County Banking Co* [1901] AC 414 a man, H, had for some years been in the habit of cashing cheques over the counter at the defendant bank. The cheques were crossed and marked 'not negotiable' which meant, inter alia, that it was necessary for them to be presented for payment by a bank: see [6.71] for the meanings of crossings on cheques. H never opened an account at the defendant bank. He obtained a cheque from the plaintiffs by fraud which he cashed at the defendant bank. The plaintiffs claimed to be entitled to recover the amount of the cheque from the defendant bank; one of the issues was whether H was a customer of the defendant bank. It was held that he was not since there was no account and no intention to open an account.

DURATION NOT IMPORTANT

[2.17]   On the other hand, it is now abundantly clear that the duration of the relationship is of no significance. In *Ladbroke v Todd* (1914) 30 TLR 433 a thief stole a cheque and took it to the defendant banker where it was used for the purpose of opening an account. The court held that the account was opened when the cheque was collected and that the thief was a 'customer' even though there was only one transaction during the entire life of the relationship.

This was followed and endorsed by the Privy Council in *Commissioners of Taxation v English Scottish and Australian Bank* [1920] AC 683. Again, the case concerned an account which had been opened with the deposit of a single cheque which had been misappropriated. The decision of the Judicial Committee was delivered by Lord Dunedin who said:

> Their Lordships are of opinion that the word 'customer' signifies a relationship in which duration is not of the essence. A person whose money has been accepted by the bank on the footing that they undertake to honour cheques up to the amount standing to his credit is, in the view of their Lordships, a customer of the bank in the sense of the statute, irrespective of whether his connection is one of short or long standing. The contrast is not between a habitue and a newcomer, but between a person for whom the bank performs a casual service, such as, for instance, cashing a cheque for a person introduced

by one of their customers, and a person who has an account of his own at the bank.

POSSIBLY BEGINS PRIOR TO THE OPENING OF THE ACCOUNT

[2.18]   The *ES&A* case shows that the existence of an account is ordinarily sufficient to establish the banker-customer relationship, but it is not necessary. There may be circumstances where the relationship is established prior to the opening of an account.

In *Woods v Martins Bank Ltd* [1958] 3 All ER 166 the plaintiff was a director of a company but he had no real business experience. In May 1950, he asked the manager of the Quayside branch of the defendant bank to act as his financial adviser. Subsequently the manager told the plaintiff that he might be able to obtain some preference shares on the plaintiff's behalf in a private company called Brocks Refrigeration Ltd. This company was a customer of the defendant bank, a fact known to both the plaintiff and the defendant. At all material times, Brocks Refrigeration Ltd had a large overdraft with the defendant bank and was in need of funds. On 9 May, the plaintiff authorised the defendant bank to acquire the shares on his behalf. There was no account opened until 1 June. The court found that the advice given had been negligently given.

The defendant argued, inter alia, that the plaintiff was not a customer of the bank at the date of the first transaction in May, the time when the advice was given, and that as a consequence they owed the plaintiff no duty of care. Note that this argument would have no chance of success now since the duty of care may exist independently of contract: see [4.27].

[2.19]   Salmon J held that the plaintiff had become a customer by 9 May and that the advice given earlier in the month must be considered as being impliedly repeated at that time. But even if the plaintiff had not become a customer until later, the defendant would still have been under a duty for giving advice of the type that is part of the business of the bank. As Salmon J phrased it (at 174):

> In May, 1950, the plaintiff paid business, not social, calls on [the manager] in his office. The plaintiff made it plain that he was consulting [the manager] as manager of the defendant bank's Quayside branch. The plaintiff was a potential customer and one whose custom [the manager] was anxious to acquire and soon did acquire ... No doubt [the manager] could have refused to advise the plaintiff, but, as he chose to advise him, the law in those circumstances imposes an obligation on him to advise with reasonable care.

We should note that the case was decided at a time when it was thought impossible for the defendant bank to be held liable in tort for negligent advice. Since the decision in *Hedley Byrne & Co Ltd v Heller & Partners* [1964] AC 465 it is not necessary to find a contractual relationship in order to find liability: see [4.28]ff for a discussion of the *Hedley Byrne* liability.

WHO MAY BE A CUSTOMER

[2.20] It is possible for another bank to be a customer, even when the 'customer' bank does not keep an account with the other bank. In *Importers Co Ltd v Westminster Bank Ltd* [1927] 2 KB 297 a cheque which was crossed 'account payee only' was stolen and paid into a foreign bank for collection. The court held that the foreign bank was a 'customer' of the defendant bank for the purposes of the special protective provisions of the Bills of Exchange Act 1882, but the case should not be taken to imply that a collecting bank is always a customer of a paying or further collecting bank. There were special arrangements between the banks for the collection of foreign cheques.

The importance of this decision is now diminished. When a bank is collecting a cheque for another 'financial institution' within the meaning of the Cheques and Payment Orders Act 1986, then it is no longer important to establish that the other institution is a customer since s 95(3) provides special defences for the collecting bank: see [6.92] for a discussion of 'financial institution' and [7.63] for the statutory defences of a collecting bank.

FRAUD AND FALSE IDENTITY

[2.21] In certain circumstances it may be difficult to say precisely who the customer is. So, for example, in *Stoney Stanton Supplies Ltd v Midland Bank Ltd* [1966] 2 Lloyd's Rep 373 an account was opened with a bank by a person who represented himself as having the authority of the plaintiff company. The documents presented were forgeries from beginning to end. The Court of Appeal held that there had never been a relationship of banker and customer between the company and the bank.

Similarly, where a rogue opens an account in a false name, it is the rogue rather than the person whose name has been appropriated who is the customer: see *Marfani & Co Ltd v Midland Bank Ltd* [1967] 3 All ER 967; [1968] 2 All ER 513.

GENERAL PRINCIPLE

[2.22] If there is a general principle to be drawn from the cases concerning the definition of 'customer' then it appears to be that the relationship does not exist unless the banker is contractually bound to provide at least some of the services normally provided by a banker. In determining the existence of the contract, normal principles of contract formation are used. In the *Great Western* case, it is clear that the bank could have refused at any time to collect the cheque for H. It would seem foolish to attach magical powers to the actual opening of the account, so that if a banker had agreed to accept the customer there is no reason why the relationship should not come into existence at that time even if the account is not formally opened until later or never at all.

On the other hand, it would seem impossible to imagine a situation where the banker is contractually bound to provide a full range of banking services to someone who is not a 'customer'. There are many situations where a bank may provide some casual service such as changing notes or providing information. In such a situation, although the bank is probably obliged to perform the particular service with care, the relationship of banker and customer does not arise.

DURATION OF THE RELATIONSHIP

[2.23]   In *Joachimson*, Lord Atkin indicated that the banker could not terminate the relationship without notice. This is because the customer has every right to expect that, in the ordinary course of events, cheques will be met which are outstanding and provided that the other preconditions for payment are satisfied. Lord Atkin referred to 'reasonable notice' being required before the banker ceases to do business with the customer.

[2.24]   What is 'reasonable notice'? In *Prosperity Ltd v Lloyds Bank Ltd* (1923) 39 TLR 372 a suit was commenced by the customer for declarations and an injunction against the banker on the ground that the banker had given insufficient notice of the intention to close the customer's account. The account was, at all material times, in credit. A month's notice was held to be insufficient, but there were very special circumstances and it was expressly held that the period of notice required must depend upon the particular facts of the case.

The special circumstances were that the plaintiffs ran what they called a 'snowball' scheme of insurance whereby a subscriber on payment of £1 15s would receive a book containing 10 application forms valid for a year. Each new subscriber obtained by the first subscriber would fill up one of the forms and go through the same process. The first subscriber would receive a two shillings credit in respect of each of his 'descendants'. When sufficient sums had been credited, an insurance policy would be taken out with an associated company in favour of the subscriber. The scheme is, of course, what is now known as a 'pyramid' scheme and is now illegal in most jurisdictions: see, for example, s 61 of the Trade Practices Act 1974 (Cth). The nature and purpose of the scheme was discussed with the bank before the account was opened. Many circulars had been sent out and many were outstanding at the time when the bank wished to close the account. Since the rules of subscription called for the subscriber to make the sum payable to Lloyds Bank the promoters of the scheme required more than a month to reorganise their business. Although the bank was in breach of its obligations to continue operation of the account, an injunction was an inappropriate remedy since it would be functionally equivalent to making an order for specific performance of a contract for the provision of personal services and the borrowing of money by the banker. The appropriate remedy is in damages for the dishonour of any cheques which the customer might rightfully expect to be honoured but which are in fact dishonoured due to the wrongful closure of the account. As will be seen later, these damages can be substantial so it behoves the banker to exercise some care in closing an account: see [5.70] and [5.74].

[2.25]   The *Prosperity* case concerned an account which was in credit. McCardie J noted that 'The right of a bank to close a banking account which was in credit might be quite distinct from the right to close one which was in debit…' but considered that it was unnecessary for him to discuss the matter further. The problem arises because most overdrafts are given on the condition that they are repayable 'on demand' so that it may be argued that no notice is necessary. Although there seems to be no authority on the question, principle would indicate that reasonable notice must be given before the account is terminated, since the damage to the customer is at least as great as the closure of a credit account: see further [3.10]ff.

[2.26]   The contract of banker and customer is a personal one. It therefore terminates when the customer dies or becomes bankrupt. Where the customer is a legal entity other than a natural person, it would seem that the relationship terminates when the entity ceases to exist as, for example, where a partnership or a company is dissolved. The relationship is also terminated at the time when the bank is dissolved: *Re Russian Commercial and Industrial Bank* [1955] 1 Ch 148.

[2.27]   There may be occasions when the bank must 'stop' the account, that is, refuse to allow further deposits or withdrawals. This is not the same as terminating the banker-customer relationship. Circumstances under which the bank should stop the account are discussed at [3.49]ff.

[2.28]   Certain contractual obligations of the banker-customer relationship may endure beyond the closure of the account and the termination of the relationship. Most important of these is the banker's duty to treat as confidential certain financial affairs of the customer: see [4.27].

CONSEQUENCES OF THE CONTRACTUAL RELATIONSHIP

[2.29]   This section explores some of the further consequences of the fact that the banker-customer relationship is founded in contract.

FAILURE OF THE BANK

[2.30]   The most immediate consequence of the legal nature of the relationship is that the customer receives no preferential treatment in the event of bank failure. The customer whose account is in credit must prove for the amount of the debt and will rank behind secured creditors of the bank and any debts, such as wages, which receive preferential statutory treatment: see [3.51].

ALTERING THE RELATIONSHIP

UNILATERAL ALTERATION

[2.31] A further consequence of the relationship being a contractual one is that it may not be altered unilaterally by either of the parties. This can cause great inconvenience to bankers who wish to change the manner in which business is conducted. For example, in *Burnett v Westminster Bank* [1965] 3 All ER 81, the customer kept accounts at two branches of the defendant bank. After Burnett opened his account, one of the branches adopted computerised accounting methods and issued chequebooks with magnetic ink character recognition (MICR) figures preprinted on the cheques: the use of MICR cheques is discussed at [8.11]. The inside cover of the chequebooks of the computerised branch contained a notice to the effect that the cheques could only be used to draw upon the account for which they had been prepared.

Burnett used one of the MICR cheque forms to draw a cheque in which he struck out the name of the computerised branch and wrote in the name of the non-computerised branch at which he kept his other account. He subsequently wished to stop payment on the cheque and gave notice to the non-computerised branch, the branch upon which he believed that he had drawn the cheque.

Of course, the cheque was paid in the ordinary course of the computer processing and the bank claimed the right to debit the (computerised) account. The court held that the customer was entitled to succeed on the basis that the purported change in contractual conditions by the bank was not effective to bind the customer and consequently he was able to change the form and use it to give instructions to the non-computerised branch. It followed that the stop order was directed to the correct branch and that Burnett was entitled to succeed. Part of the basis of the decision was that the bank was unable to show that the notices in the chequebook had been brought to Burnett's attention. Consequently, the use of the chequebook could not be construed as an agreement by Burnett to abide by the new terms which the bank wished to insert into the contract.

[2.32] Even though the relationship is contractual, it is a contract of a very unusual kind in that ordinarily all, or nearly all, of the terms are implied terms. This is just another way of saying that the terms of the banker-customer contract state rights and obligations which have been defined by the courts over many years. However, *Burnett's* case shows that it is possible that the terms may be changed or overridden by express agreement between the parties even though the same case shows that the change may not be uni-laterally made.

WRITTEN AGREEMENTS

[2.33] Long and complex written agreements are common in North America and it is no doubt tempting for bankers in other parts of the common law world to introduce terms into the banker-customer contract which would throw more of the risks on the customer. For example, it will be seen in later chapters that the general rule is that the customer has no duty to examine the periodic statement and that the risk of forgery is prima facie on the banker: see [5.21]. A common term in overseas contracts is one which requires the customer to read the periodic statement and to report any irregularities within a fixed period of time. In default of so doing, the customer is to be bound by the terms of the periodic statement. Another common term is one which purports to throw the risk of forgeries onto the customer.

[2.34]   A recent decision by the Privy Council indicates that clauses such as these cannot be introduced without making the customer aware of the changed responsibilities. In *Tai Hing Cotton Mill Ltd v Liu Chong Hing Bank Ltd* [1986] AC 80; [1985] 2 All ER 947 a number of clauses were inserted in written agreements or were incorporated by reference.

In one instance, the customer agreed to be bound by the bank's 'rules and procedures in force from time to time governing the conduct of the account'. One of the rules was rule 7: 'A monthly statement for each account will be sent by the bank to the depositor by post or messenger and the balance shown therein may be deemed to be correct by the bank if the depositor does not notify the bank in writing of any error therein within ten days after the sending of such statement ...'.

The customer in fact returned a confirmation slip upon receipt of the statements, but failed to notice a number of forgeries.

In another account operated by the same customer, the terms appeared on the back of a pro forma letter which was signed by the customer. One of the terms read: 'The bank's statement of my/our account will be confirmed by me/us without delay. In case of absence of such confirmation within a fortnight, the bank may take the said statement as approved by me/us.' The customer never confirmed any of the accounts sent.

A third account was opened by request of the customer in which the customer agreed to open the account subject to the bank's rules and regulations. Rule 13 provided: 'A statement of the customer's account will be rendered once a month. Customers are desired: to examine all entries in the statement of account and to report at once to the bank any error found therein; to return the confirmation slip duly signed. In the absence of any objection to the statement within seven days after its receipt by the customer, the account shall be deemed to have been confirmed.'

In this case, the bank never sent any confirmation slips to the company and the company never sent the bank any confirmation of the accounts.

[2.35]   The Privy Council held that although the terms had contractual effect they did not prevent the customer from challenging the validity of the statements since their terms did not bring home to the customer either the intended importance of the inspection of the accounts or the fact that they were intended to have conclusive effect against the customer in the event that no timely query should be raised. In the words of the Privy Council (per Lord

Scarman, *Tai Hing Cotton Mill v Liu Chong Hing Bank* [1985] 2 All ER 947 at 959):

> If banks wish to impose upon their customers an express obligation to examine their monthly statements and to make those statements, in the absence of query, unchallengeable by the customer after expiry of a time limit, the burden of the obligation and of the sanction imposed must be brought home to the customer ... The test is rigorous because the bankers would have their terms of business so construed as to exclude the rights which the customer would enjoy if they were not excluded by express agreement.

It is clear that the Privy Council considered the implied contractual terms of the ordinary banker-customer relationship to be in the nature of common law rights and that express terms which purport to alter those rights will be construed strictly against the party attempting to take advantage of them. In such circumstances, the imposition of express terms becomes difficult and the banker must weigh the advantages to be gained from the terms against the possibility of frightening off customers by 'bringing home' the burdens sought to be imposed. The *Tai Hing* case is discussed further at [5.41].

VARIATION: EFT ACCOUNTS

[2.36] Where an account can be operated by a debit card it will probably be governed by the Electronic Funds Transfer Code of Conduct: see Chapter 9 for a general discussion of the Code. The Code makes special provision for variations in the Terms and Conditions of Use. The scheme is to require written notification for the most serious changes but to allow 'mass notification' for others.

There is one important exception to this scheme: a card-issuer may unilaterally and without notice vary the EFT Terms and Conditions of Use when such changes are necessary to restore or maintain the security of the system or of individual accounts: cl 3.3. This is an important exception to the usual principle of unilateral variation of a contract, but it is a justifiable response to a risk which was never presented by the older technologies.

[2.37] 'Important' changes can only be made after giving the cardholder written notice of at least 30 days prior to the change: cl 3.1. These changes include those which impose or increase charges relating solely to the use of EFT facilities, increase cardholder liability for losses, or vary periodic transaction limits: cl 3.1(i)–(iv).

Other variations in the Terms and Conditions of use must be notified in advance through notices accompanying the periodic account statement, notices on terminals and in branches or through press advertisements: cl 3.2. Where the last two methods are used, subsequent written advice must be provided at the time of the next account statement: cl 3.2.

VARIATION: CONSUMER ACCOUNTS

[2.38] Where the Code of Banking Practice applies (see [9.2]ff) there are special rules governing the unilateral variation of terms and conditions. The structure of the scheme is similar to that of the EFT Code, namely, that some variations are considered to be of such importance that written notice to the customer is required but that others may be notified by advertisement.

If a bank intends to introduce a new fee or charge (other than a government charge) or to vary the way in which interest is calculated or the frequency with which it is credited or debited then the bank must provide written notice to each affected customer at least 30 days before the proposed change takes effect: s 9.1. This does not apply to so-called 'Standard Fees and Charges' or an interest rate change: see [9.2]ff.

In relation to all other changes in the terms and conditions governing the account the bank may notify affected customers by advertisement in national or local media. This 'notification' is to be made no later than the day on which the variation is to be implemented: s 9.3. Such 'notification' is, of course, no notification at all but it is not the only example of the Code depriving consumer customers of common law rights: see [9.2]ff for further comments and criticisms of the Code.

Where actual written notice is required, the bank may fulfil its obligation by sending a notice to the mailing address of the customer which was the last recorded with the bank: s 9.3.

The Building Society Code of Practice and the Credit Union Code of Practice have similar provisions.

CONTRACTS REVIEW ACT 1980 (NSW)

[2.39]   The fact that the relationship is contractual means that it may come within the scope of the Contracts Review Act 1980 (NSW). Since factual situations which give rise to challenges under the Act usually arise in the context of loans, the application of the Act is discussed at [10.145].

LIMITATIONS ACTS

[2.40]   Since the banker-customer relationship is, inter alia, a debtor-creditor relationship which is founded on contract, the rights of recovery are limited by the time restrictions imposed by the Limitations Acts of the various states. An important feature of the Acts is that they are merely a procedural bar, that is, the debt remains in existence after the expiry of the limitations period, but the help of the courts to recover it is no longer available. If there are other procedures for recovery available, they are not affected. The NSW Act is an exception to this general rule: see the discussion at [2.61].

So, for example, if the creditor is in a position to exercise some rights over the property of the debtor, the debt may be recovered from the security even though the right of action for the debt might be barred by the appropriate Limitation Act. This is of particular importance to the banker and customer, for the banker may exercise the banker's lien over a wide range of documents: see [10.93].

[2.41] Time begins to run for the purposes of the Acts from the time at which the debt falls due. However, if at any time prior to the expiration of the limitation period there is a part payment of the debt or an acknowledgment of the debt then the time period begins to run afresh. The clock is also restarted when there is some new promise by the debtor to pay the debt. This may be an express promise or one which may be inferred from some act of acknowledgment of the debt: see *Re River Steamship Co*; *Mitchell's claim* (1871) LR 6 Ch App 822 at 828.

As might be imagined, there is a large body of case law which considers the adequacy of various acts of acknowledgment for the purposes of revival of the procedural remedies. It should be noted that it is not necessary to show any fresh consideration for the new promise to pay, for it is not a new contract which is being formed, but a procedural remedy which is being revived: see J G Starke et al, *Cheshire & Fifoot's Law of Contract*, 6th Aust ed, Butterworths, Sydney, 1992.

Although an effective acknowledgment must be in writing and signed by the debtor, it is not necessary that the acknowledgment be an express promise or that it be prepared for the special purpose of acknowledgment. So, for example, it may be possible to find an acknowledgment in correspondence between the creditor and debtor: see *Bucknell v Commercial Banking Co of Sydney Ltd* (1937) 58 CLR 155; *National Bank of Tasmania Ltd v McKenzie* [1920] VLR 411.

Time begins to run for the purposes of a debt when the debt is due. The particular time may depend upon the type of the account and whether the account is in credit or overdraft.

ACCOUNT IN CREDIT

[2.42] One of the consequences of *Joachimson's* case is that the debt owed by the banker to the customer does not become due until such time as a demand is made by the customer. It follows that when the current account is in credit, time does not begin to run against the customer for the purposes of the Limitations Acts until such time as that demand is made. In the case of a savings or other interest-bearing accounts, there will generally be other conditions precedent to the repayment of the money so that, *a fortiori*, the time period does not commence until these formal requirements have been met.

In *Atkinson v Bradford Third Equitable Benefit Building Society* (1890) 25 QBD 377 an unidentified person presented a passbook and obtained the balance of an account kept with the defendant. This happened two days after the customer died in 1879. The plaintiffs were administrators who were appointed in 1889. The bank pleaded, inter alia, that the action was time-barred. The court held that the action could proceed, but apparently on the basis that the administrators' right of action arose with their appointment in 1889.

It appears that the court treated the action as one for breach of contract. With respect, this is clearly wrong. When paying the rogue, the bank paid away its own money. It is not entitled to debit the customer's account, and it is submitted that the debt became due when a proper demand was made for it.

It has been said that it would be unusual for a bank to plead the statute as a means of resisting repayment of a credit account. Although this may be true, there are several cases where the defendant bank has pleaded the statute: see, for example, *Streicher v ES&A Bank Ltd* [1945] SASR 207; *O'Ferrall v Bank of Australasia* (1883) 9 VLR (L) 119; *Municipal Council of Sydney v Bank of Australasia* (1914) 14 SR(NSW) 363; *National Bank of Commerce v National Westminster Bank* [1990] 2 Lloyd's Rep 514.

However, 'dormant' accounts can cause considerable inconvenience for the banker and represent a generally unproductive relationship. In order to relieve the banker from this burden and to clarify the position with regard to such accounts many jurisdictions have legislation which provides that dormant accounts are transferred to the Crown, but such legislation usually provides a method for the customer, or someone legitimately claiming through the customer, to reclaim the money.

[2.43]   In Australia, this legislation is found in s 69 of the Banking Act 1959 (Cth). The legislation applies to all banks licensed under the Act. Dormant accounts in state banks are governed by various state legislation.

Under BA s 69, 'unclaimed moneys' in a trading bank account shall be reported to the Federal Treasurer: s 69(3). 'Unclaimed moneys' means all principal, interest, dividends, bonuses, profits and sums of money legally payable by a trading bank but in respect of which the time within which proceedings may be taken for the recovery thereof has expired: s 69(1). The term also includes any money in an account which has not been operated on by deposit or withdrawal for a period of not less than seven years: s 69(1). Under the terms of the section, the customer must make a deposit or withdrawal in order to 'operate' the account. This definition allows the bank to debit fees or to credit interest to the account without the account being 'operated': s 69(2).

The report to the Treasurer must contain information concerning the customer which will allow the customer or the representative of the customer to claim the money: s 69(4). The money itself is paid to the Commonwealth at the time when the report is made: s 69(5). This payment discharges the bank's liability to the customer, subject to a claim being made under ss (7). A person who would have been entitled to the money may claim it from the Treasurer and, upon the Treasurer being satisfied that the person claiming is entitled, the funds are paid to the bank for the credit of the claimant: s 69(7). Details of unclaimed money are to be published in the Gazette or made available to the public in some other manner: s 69(9).

There is also state legislation governing the disposition of unclaimed money, but it is provided that these Acts have no effect in so far as banks are concerned: s 69(11A).

Unfortunately, there is no requirement that a bank make an effort to contact account owners.

[2.44]   This legislation solves the 'dormant account' problem if the banker follows the appropriate procedure. If there is a failure to do so, the Acts do not provide any guidance as to the disposition of the money. In at least one extreme case, the court has been willing to consider general evidence to find that an account had been properly repaid and closed by the banker. In *Douglass v Lloyds Bank* (1929) 34 Com Cas 263 the account had not been operated for over 20 years. One Fenwicke had deposited some £6000 with a branch of the defendant in 1868. The account was never operated after 1868. In 1927, some of Fenwicke's survivors found a deposit receipt which showed a balance of £3500. They claimed that amount from the bank with interest. Evidence was given to show that Fenwicke was a man who was careful with his financial matters and that there was reason to believe that the £6000 represented the proceeds from some shares which he sold during the financial crash of the 1860s. The plaintiff had no evidence of the debt other than the deposit book, but claimed that to be conclusive in the absence of any better evidence.

The bank produced evidence to the effect that the books of the particular year in question had been destroyed, but that there was no evidence of any accounts which were still in credit from the period.

In the course of the judgment, Roche J said (at 273):

> I recognise to the full the strength of the fact that the plaintiff produces this deposit receipt, but I cannot ignore what experience tells me, and the evidence in this case shows, that people lose or mislay their deposit receipts at the time when they want to get their money back, and that money is paid over, if they are respectable persons and are willing to give the necessary indemnity.

Roche J was unable to accept that Fenwicke either intentionally left the money there or forgot about it. There was some evidence that the defendant bank had treated the deposit as repaid at least from about 1873.

The bank also argued that the action was time-barred. However, Roche J held that time did not begin to run for the purposes of the Statute of Limitations until such time as an appropriate demand was made.

The case is sometimes said to rest on a presumption that a debt has been repaid after a long period of time, but there is certainly no need to invent a presumption to understand the case. The plaintiffs had a strong case on the basis of the passbook, but there was other evidence to support the bank's defence. It certainly should not be thought that the bank could have won the case without the production of any evidence whatsoever.

[2.45]   The period of limitations is also relevant when a customer claims that there has been a wrongful debit to the account. In *National Bank of Commerce v National Westminster Bank* [1990] 2 Lloyd's Rep 514 the court held that time begins to run from the demand by the customer. The reason being a claim of wrongful debit is, in essence, a claim for a payment of a debt that becomes due at the time of the demand.

TERM LOANS

[2.46]   When the banker is the creditor who wishes to recover, the problems can be more complex. The question in all cases is to determine the time at which the debt falls due for that is the time at which 'the clock begins to run' for the purposes of the Limitations Acts. In the case of a term loan which is stated to be repayable at a specified date, it is that date at which time begins to run. If the repayments are to be made in instalments, then, in the absence of agreement to the contrary, each instalment represents a separate debt for the purposes of the Acts. However, there is frequently an agreement to the contrary since standard form contracts often provide that a default in a single instalment has the effect of making all subsequent instalments due and payable. In such a case, time begins to run for the entire amount from the time of the default. The making of further instalment payments by the debtor is, of course, an acknowledgment which has the effect of restarting the clock: *Falzon v Adelaide Development Co Ltd* [1936] SASR 93.

UNSECURED OVERDRAFT ACCOUNT: THE DEBTOR

[2.47]   Since it would be unusual in the ordinary course of events that a banker would attempt to rely upon the Limitations Acts in order to avoid repayment of the sum standing due in a credit account, the effect of the limitations period when the account is in overdraft or where it is sought to recover from a guarantor is of far more importance.

The problem is complicated by the view of bankers that an overdraft does not become due and payable until such time as a demand is made. As a consequence, it is argued, time does not begin to run against the bank until such time as the demand is made for the overdraft to be paid. Unfortunately there is no recent authority, and the older authorities suggest that time begins to run no later than at the time of the last advance, although it must be admitted that the text writers are divided on the question and none of the authority is highly persuasive.

[2.48]   The opinion of the court in *Parr's Banking Co Ltd v Yates* [1898] 2 QB 460 was that time begins to run from the date of each advance. As a consequence, it might be that some parts of the overall debt are time-barred while others are not: see also the discussion of the rule in *Clayton's case* (*Devaynes v Noble* (1816) 1 Mer 529; 35 ER 767) at [3.7].

Parr's case was an action on a guarantee. The defendant had guaranteed to the plaintiff payment of all moneys which might be owing to it in an account with a third party customer, including all interest and other charges. The guarantee was a continuing one and not to be withdrawn with less than six months' notice. The bank made advances to the customer down to a period more than six years before the action, but not after that period. The customer paid sums to the plaintiff from time to time against the liability, including some payments within the six-year limitation period. The court held that the right of action for the principal sum was barred by the Statute of Limitations.

Although the principal was not recoverable, the interest which had accrued due from the customer within the preceding six years could be the subject of an action. This was in spite of the normal rule with regard to the appropriation of payments by which interest is presumed to be paid before principal. The court ruled that the rule is not applicable in the case of interest on an overdrawn account which according to usual banking practice has been from time to time converted into principal. This forms an exception to the rule in *Clayton's case*: see [3.7].

During the course of his judgment, Vaughan Williams LJ said (at 467):

> My view is that the cause of action on the guarantee arose as to each item of the account, whether principal, interest, commission, or other banking charge, as soon as that item became due and was not paid …

None of the other members of the court were quite so explicit. The importance of the point is that if the view is correct, the banker's right of recovery might be time-barred as to some parts of the debt, but not others.

Bankers do not like the implications of the view expressed by Vaughan Williams LJ, for if the same logic applies to overdraft accounts then it means a very substantial increase in the bookkeeping required for such accounts if rights against the customer are not to be accidentally lost.

[2.49]   The 'demand' theory also received a setback in *Bradford Old Bank v Sutcliffe* [1918] 2 KB 833 where it was said (per Scrutton LJ at 840):

> Generally, a request for the payment of a debt is quite immaterial, unless the parties to the contract have stipulated it should be made. Even if the word 'demand' is used in the case of a present debt, it is meaningless, and express demand is not necessary, as in the case of a promissory note payable on demand.

Similarly, Pickford LJ said:

> It was argued on behalf of the defendant that the words 'on demand' should be neglected because the money was due, and therefore a demand was unnecessary and added nothing to the liability. This proposition is true in the case of what has been called a direct liability, for example, for money lent. There the liability exists as soon as the loan is made, and a promise to pay on demand adds nothing to it, as in the case of a promissory note for the amount payable on demand, and the words 'on demand' may be neglected.

Modern authors suggest that the position may have changed over the years so that the 'on demand' aspects of an overdraft have increased their importance, yet conclude that it would be most unwise for a banker to ignore these old cases: see G A Weaver and R C Craigie, *The Law Relating to Banker and Customer in Australia*, 2nd ed, Law Book Co, Sydney, 1990 para [6.330]; W S Weerasooria, *Banking Law and Practice in Australia*, Butterworths, Sydney, 4th ed, 1996 p 642. The only safe course is to presume that time begins to run at the date of each advance.

Overdraft account: the guarantor

[2.50]   The comments made so far relate to an action by the bank against the primary debtor, that is, the account holder. When the banker is attempting to recover against a guarantor, the situation is somewhat different, for generally the guarantee will be a 'continuing guarantee', that is, one which is expressed to guarantee the balance of the account which is struck from time to time. In *Bradford Old Bank* itself, the action was of this kind and the court held that the contract of surety was a collateral one so that the words 'on demand' should be given their full meaning. Thus, after making the comments above concerning the lack of meaning of the words 'on demand' when used in conjunction with an ordinary debt, Pickford LJ went on to say (at 840):

> It ... has been held ... that this doctrine does not apply to what has been called a collateral promise or collateral debt, and I think a promise by a surety to pay the original debt is such a collateral promise, or creates such a collateral debt ... The only question, therefore is whether, on the construction of the guarantee, the parties meant the words 'on demand' to mean what they say. I cannot doubt that they did. Interest is to run from demand.

Consequently, time did not begin to run against the bank, vis-a-vis the guarantor, until such time as a demand was made against the guarantor. The wording of the guarantee is important, for if the guarantee calls for the surety to pay on the default of the principal debtor, the time when the surety's liability arises might be different: see the discussion of *Commercial Bank of Australia Ltd v Colonial Finance, Mortgage, Investment and Guarantee Corporation Ltd* (1906) 4 CLR 57 at [2.53].

[2.51]   The matter has been considered by the New Zealand court in *Wright v NZ Farmers Co-operative* [1936] NZLR 157; [1939] NZLR 388. This was an action against a guarantor where it was claimed that the rights of the bank were barred by virtue of the dictum in *Parr's Banking Co Ltd v Yates*.

Wright agreed to guarantee to the plaintiff the payment by a husband and wife 'of all goods already supplied or hereafter supplied by you to them and of all advances already made or hereafter made by you to them together with interest thereon at the current rate charged by you and together with such charges as are usually made by you'. The guarantee was expressed to be a continuing guarantee and the amount claimed on the guarantee was some £12,000; the amount of £3255 which represented advances made by the respondent prior to 31 July, 1928, being six years prior to the commencement of the action, was disputed as being outside the Statute of Limitations.

In the New Zealand Court of Appeal, the statement of Vaughan Williams LJ in *Parr's Banking Co Ltd v Yates* was doubted and it was suggested that the real ground of decision in *Parr's* case may have been that there had been no advances made to the principal debtor within six years prior to the commencement of the action. An action for the balance arising upon a series of debits and credits extending beyond a period of six years is, it was suggested, not barred by the statute if it is brought within six years from the date of the last advance. Since that was the case here, the court distinguished *Parr's* case on that ground.

This approach treats the entire debt owed to the bank as a single debt which becomes due for the purposes of the statute at the time of the last advance. The reader should note that it does not confirm the banker's view that the debt becomes due only upon demand. The approach used by the Court of Appeal is out of step with other parts of the law which concern the repayment of overdrawn accounts (for example, the rule in *Clayton's case*) and should be viewed as an attempt to circumvent the invidious effects of the Statute of Limitations.

The case went on appeal to the Privy Council, which chose to distinguish *Parr's* case on the basis of the wording in the guarantee which was signed by Wright. Lord Russell of Killowan gave the opinion of the Judicial Board during which he said:

> It is difficult to see how effect can be given to [the terms of the guarantee] except by holding that the repayment of every debit balance is guaranteed as it is constituted from time to time, during the continuance of the guarantee, by the excess of the total debits over the total credits ... The question of limitation could only arise in regard to the time which had elapsed since the balance guaranteed and sued for had been constituted.

It is important to note that the Privy Council made it quite clear that they were expressing no opinion on the correctness of the decision in *Parr's* case.

[2.52]   The matter was further considered in New Zealand by Perry J in *Commercial Union Assurance v Revell* [1969] NZLR 106. There was an express written contract which contained the words 'I hereby undertake ... to repay ... on demand ...'. The document was signed by the plaintiff in 1957. There was no demand made until mid-1967 and the sole issue was whether the action was time-barred. Perry J followed *Re Brown's Estate* [1893] 2 Ch 300 and *Bradford Old Bank Ltd v Sutcliffe* [1918] 2 KB 833 in holding that the words 'on demand' when used in an express contract which does not relate to a present debt will be given their full effect so that time does not begin to run unless and until a demand is made.

[2.53]   So far as the banker is concerned, the matter is still open, for it is still not clear whether an overdraft account is a 'present debt'.

When a demand is made by the bank on the principal debtor, then time may begin to run against the bank in respect of the amounts of the demand made if the principal debtor defaults. Thus, in *Commercial Bank of Australia Ltd v Colonial Finance Mortgage Investment and Guarantee Corporation Ltd* (1906) 4 CLR 57 a continuing guarantee called for the guarantor to pay all advances owing or to become owing by a customer of the bank 'to the extent of £12,500 in case the customer should make default ...'. The bank demanded payment from the customer on two occasions, one for payment of a portion of an overdraft and one for interest. The court held that the failure to pay on demand gave the bank a cause of action against the guarantor, but only to the extent of the demand and default. Consequently, the Statute of Limitations began to run against the bank as to that portion of the indebtedness only, and the guarantee continued as security to the bank for the balance.

In Australia the matter came before the High Court in *Bank of Adelaide v Lorden* (1970) 45 ALJR 49. The guarantee in question was 'to pay the bank on demand all such advances including all debts now owing …'. Although the issue was not discussed in detail, the court clearly considered that a demand was necessary before the debt became due. Note that there is no inconsistency with *Commercial Bank of Australia Ltd v Colonial Finance, Mortgage, Investment and Guarantee Corporation Ltd* (1906) 4 CLR 57 since in that case the guarantee was payable on default of the principal debtor.

SECURED OVERDRAFT ACCOUNT

[2.54]   Even if time begins to run from the time of each advance when the loan is by way of simple overdraft, it may be that a secured overdraft is in a different position. In *Re Brown's Estate; Brown v Brown* [1893] 2 Ch 300 a mortgage was classified as a 'collateral' debt or promise. Consequently, the mortgage fell within the class of debts mentioned by Pickford LJ in the *Bradford Old Bank* case which do not fall due until a demand is made by the creditor.

[2.55]   The rule in *Brown's* case was expressly approved in *Lloyds Bank v Margolis* [1954] 1 All ER 734 at 738. The case concerned a legal charge which was given over a farm; the defendant objected that the claim was statute-barred because there had been no advances made within the limitation period. Chitty J held that on the true construction of the charge a demand was necessary, but that in any case the charge was collateral security and, therefore, even if no demand was necessary to the bringing of an action of a direct present debt payable on demand, in the present case a demand would be necessary.

[2.56]   Since most large overdrafts will be secured by some kind of a charge or mortgage, this line of cases would seem to be adequate to protect the banker from the worst effects of the decision in *Parr's Bank v Yates*.

In summary, the only safe course of action for the banker is to presume that the debt of the customer becomes due at the date of each advance so that advances made more than six years previously may be statute-barred. However, properly worded guarantees may be enforced against guarantors and 'collateral' debts owed by the primary debtor do not become due until a demand is made.

SAVINGS ACCOUNTS

[2.57]   Savings accounts differ from current accounts in that they ordinarily earn interest and they cannot usually be drawn upon by cheque. There is often a requirement that notice be given before withdrawal. In the past, it was customary to require presentation of a passbook for withdrawals. While this may still be the case for some accounts, it is common practice today to permit withdrawal through ATMs and in EFTPOS transactions.

Savings accounts also differ from current accounts in that they are ordinarily more likely to be governed by a written contract. This document does not contain all of the terms which govern the banker-customer relationship, but will usually describe conditions under which money may be deposited and withdrawn from the account, interest rates to be paid and any other special account conditions. These differences reflect the differences in function which are served by the two types of account. The primary function of the current account is to provide the customer with access to third party payment mechanisms, whereas the primary function of the savings account is to provide investment facilities for funds of the customer and to provide the bank with funds which it may safely invest over longer periods of time.

In spite of these differences in function, a savings or deposit account is in law a loan to the banker: *Pearce v Creswick* (1843) 2 Hare 286; 12 LJ Ch 251; *Dixon v Bank of NSW* (1896) 12 WN (NSW) 101; *Akbar Khan v Attar Singh* [1936] 2 All ER 545. There is probably no right to draw cheques against a savings account, even when the account is expressed to be repayable without notice. The matter is unlikely to ever be raised in Australia, where it is common practice for the contract to spell out explicitly the preconditions for withdrawal of money from the account. In modern practice, the contract will call for the production of a passbook or, where the account permits electronic withdrawals, an EFT card and PIN at an authorised terminal.

Some savings accounts require a specified period of notice before general withdrawals may be made and some are for a fixed period of time. In the latter type, the customer has no right to call for the repayment before the expiry of that period, even though it is not uncommon for a banker to permit such a withdrawal, perhaps with some loss of interest.

[2.58]   The savings account is also similar to a current account in that a savings account is one continuing contract and not a fresh contract made with each deposit by the customer: *Hart v Sangster* [1957] 1 Ch 329. Mocatta J has expressed the opinion that there is no such thing in law as an overdrawn deposit account: *Barclays Bank Ltd v Okenarhe* [1966] 2 Lloyd's Rep 87. Savings accounts are usually accompanied by a passbook in which deposits and withdrawals are recorded. This passbook is, or should be, essentially a copy of the customer's account in the bank's ledger. It is also usual for the passbook to contain the basic terms of the agreement between the banker and customer. These terms are a part of the terms of the contract between the bank and its customer: *Re Australia and New Zealand Savings Bank Ltd; Mellas v Evriniadis* [1972] VR 690. It is usually a condition precedent to any withdrawal that the book must be presented together with a signed withdrawal slip. In many cases, the passbook contains a specimen of the customer's signature which is normally invisible but may be read under an ultraviolet lamp.

[2.59]   The English Court of Appeal has held that the passbook is indicia of title to the account: *Birch v Treasury Solicitor* [1951] Ch 298. The result was that delivery of the passbook in the circumstances of the case was held to be a valid *donatio mortis causa*. The court placed considerable weight on the fact that presentation of the book was a condition precedent to any withdrawal from the account.

It might be thought that the position could be different when the passbook itself contains a statement that it remains the property of the bank or when there is legislation to the same effect. However, the same result was reached by an Australian court even before the *Birch* decision. In *Watts v Public Trustee* (1950) 50 SR (NSW) 130 it was held that a gift of a Commonwealth Savings Bank passbook was good evidence of a valid *donatio mortis causa* of the balance of the account despite legislation which provided that the passbook remained at all times the property of the Savings Bank. The court did not find it necessary to go so far as to say that the passbook was indicia of title: see also *Public Trustee v Young* (1940) 40 SR (NSW) 233; *Harneiss v Public Trustee* (1944) 40 SR (NSW) 414.

[2.60]   Needless to say, a banker who paid some third party merely on the basis of the party's possession of the passbook would be taking great risks, since the possession itself is certainly no indication that there has been an intended assignment. The bank may be exposed to danger even when the customer has 'indorsed' deposit receipts to a third party.

In *Evans v National Provincial Bank of England* (1897) 13 TLR 298 the plaintiff had deposited money with the defendant on terms that the money should be repaid with interest on production and delivery up of a deposit receipt. While in London, the plaintiff wished to pay a small debt and attempted to withdraw the interest from the account. The bank refused. According to the defendant, she then borrowed the money from one Lloyd, signing the receipt over to him as security. The receipt was produced at the bank bearing an apparent indorsement by the plaintiff and witnessed by a third party. This witness was unable to testify due to insanity. When presented with the receipt, the bank 'did not rely upon the signature' but indicated that the payment should be made if suitable identity was produced. Therefore, there could be no estoppel, since the bank did not rely upon the signature. Estoppel also failed since if the plaintiff signed only for a restricted purpose, she would not be estopped since the document was a receipt only and did not purport to be an authority.

THE NSW ACT

[2.61]   The effect of the NSW Limitation Act 1969 s 54(1) and s 63(1) is to not merely bar the remedy but extinguish the right: see *Stage Club Ltd v Millers Hotels Pty Ltd* (1981) 56 ALJR 113; *Maguire v Simpson* (1977) 52 ALJR 125; *Proctor v Jetway Aviation* [1982] 2 NSWLR 264.

If the right is extinguished, then the defendant has the benefit of that extinction even if he or she does not want it, that is, even if the defence is not pleaded. Since banks customarily have declined to plead the Statute of Limitations, the result would be a change in practice. Section 68A of the Act provides that the benefit is available only if pleaded.

SPECIAL CUSTOMERS

[2.62]   There are certain classes of customer which call for special attention. While customers in these categories assume the obligations imposed by the banker-customer contract upon all customers, there are various features which call for more than normal care on the part of the banker.

UNINCORPORATED ASSOCIATIONS

[2.63]   Unincorporated associations are not, strictly speaking, independent legal entities at all. They are groups of people who are formed for some purpose other than gain. Since there is usually no contemplation of profit, they are not partnerships. If the association is with a view towards making profits, then the organisation may be a partnership: see [2.67]. The membership will usually be fluctuating and the members are not normally liable to the organisation in any way save to pay membership subscriptions required by the rules of the association. Such organisations are normally formed for social or sporting purposes and it is not uncommon for them to keep a current account with certain of their members authorised to sign cheques.

ACCOUNT IN CREDIT

[2.64]   There is little problem with such an arrangement so long as the account is kept in credit. When opening the account, the bank should obtain very clear instructions as to who is entitled to operate the account. It is probably prudent to obtain a copy of the constitution of the association or some other documentation which purports to grant authority to the members who wish to open the account.

The lack of a legal entity means that the association may not sue or be sued in its own name. The banker should therefore normally resist any pressure for the account to go into overdraft. Weaver and Craigie suggest that the authorised signatories might be answerable for the amount, but advise that as the matter is by no means clear such arrangements should be avoided: see Weaver and Craigie, op cit, para [5.85]. Ellinger argues that the committee members are personally liable for any overdrafts, but in the cases which he cites it seems that the bank expressly called for the personal liability of the committee members at the time when the overdraft was granted: see E P Ellinger and E Lomnicka, *Modern Banking Law*, 2nd ed, Clarendon Press, Oxford, 1994, p 257 and the cases cited there.

OVERDRAFT ACCOUNT

[2.65]   The problem of the overdraft is compounded by the fact that any property of the club which is used as security for advances may have an uncertain ownership. Property is usually held on behalf of the organisation by trustees which will frequently be the members of the governing body. Even if these parties have the full authority of each member of the club to enter into security arrangements, it has been held that they have no power to contract on behalf of those who become members after the date of the contract. These new members will not be bound unless the conditions are such that the mere fact of becoming a member may be taken to signify consent.

The problem can be illustrated by *Abbatt v Treasury Solicitor* [1969] 1 WLR 561. The club ceased to operate and the question arose concerning ownership of former club property. It was held that once the club had ceased to function the interests of the existing members became fixed so that club property belonged to those individuals who were members of the club at that time. The case does not necessarily mean that a banker could not hold a security interest in the property so that the members of the club own the property subject to the security interest, but it does serve to illustrate that caution is necessary when the ownership is shifting and uncertain.

Similarly, in *Amey v Fifer* [1971] 1 NSWLR 685 (NSW CA) three trustees of a sporting club, claiming to be authorised by the other club members, sued a firm of accountants claiming damages for breach of contract. It was held that an alleged contract with the members for the time being of an unincorporated voluntary association having a fluctuating membership is no contract at all, and the action was dismissed.

INCORPORATED ASSOCIATIONS

[2.66]   In most jurisdictions an association may become an 'incorporated association': see Associations Incorporation Act 1991 (ACT); Associations Incorporation Act 1984 (NSW); Associations Incorporation Act 1963 (NT); Associations Incorporation Act 1981 (Qld); Associations Incorporations Act 1985 (SA); Associations Incorporation Act 1964 (Tas); Associations Incorporation Act 1981 (Vic); Associations Incorporation Act 1987 (WA).

In most cases an incorporated association is treated as a company, but banks may need to be more careful since it seems that the doctrine of *ultra vires* has not been abolished in the same way as in the Corporations Law: see [2.84].

PARTNERSHIPS

[2.67]   A partnership is not a legal personality. It is a relation which exists between persons engaged in certain activities, but the situation is very much different from that of an unincorporated association due to the fact that the rights and obligations of the partners inter se and their relationship with third parties are specified in considerable detail in the Partnership Acts.

Each state has a Partnership Act based on the Partnership Act 1890 (UK). In this discussion, the section numbers will refer to the Partnership Act 1892 (NSW). A partnership is defined by s 1: '(1) Partnership is the relation which subsists between persons carrying on a business in common with a view to profit.'

But the relation between members of any company or association registered as a company under companies legislation is not a partnership within the meaning of the Act: s 2(1).

[2.68]   There are no formal requirements for the creation of a partnership. If the parties are in fact carrying on a business in common with a view to profit, then the partnership relationship may exist even if the parties never give any conscious thought to the formation of the partnership. The partnership may be formed without any public notice of its existence and there is generally no need for any public registration although certain types of partnerships, so-called special partnerships, are treated separately by the Act and require registration.

It may be difficult to know if a partnership has been formed. Section 2 of the Act specifies a number of instances where it is not to be presumed that a partnership exists, but there is only one positive rule, namely, that the receipt by a person of a share of the profits of a business is prima facie evidence that he or she is a partner in the business: s 2(3). But the rule is only prima facie evidence and the section itself goes on to provide exceptions.

The essential feature from the banker's point of view is that each of the partners is an agent of the firm for the purpose of conducting transactions which are within the scope of the business of the firm: s 5. At least when the partnership is a trading firm, each partner has the right to open an account in the name of the firm and to operate it by means of his or her own signature: *Backhouse v Charleton* (1878) 8 Ch D 444. The authority of the individual partner does not extend to maintaining a firm account in his or her own name: *Alliance Bank v Kearsley* (1871) LR 6 CP 433.

A partner in a trading firm has authority to borrow on behalf of the firm, but only for purposes that are within the ordinary course of the partnership business. There is, however, no such authority for partners in a non-trading partnership: *Higgins v Beauchamp* [1914] 3 KB 1192.

[2.69]   Since there is no new legal personality, the Act spells out the liabilities of the partners. The partners are jointly liable for all of the liabilities of the firm and, following the death of a partner, the estate is also severally liable: ss 5 and 9. This liability is not limited to the personal contribution that the partner may have made, nor is it limited to his or her share in the firm's assets. A partner who is forced to pay the firm's debts from private assets is entitled to be indemnified by the firm and by the other partners, but that is a matter which is of no interest or concern to outsiders.

The rights of the partners to act on behalf of the firm may be limited by the articles of partnership. Because of the wide powers which are prima facie granted to each of the partners, this power of limitation is very common, but such limitations do not bind third parties who are not aware of them. However, the practice of requiring multiple signatures to operate a bank account might be so widespread that it could be that a banker who opens a partnership account to be operated by a single signature might be held to have had constructive notice. It is common and highly recommended practice to take an express mandate as to the terms of the account operation.

Similar comments apply to any application for overdraft facilities. An individual partner has the authority which is customary in the type of partnership in question. Thus, a partner of a trading partnership would have the authority to raise credit for the firm's purposes. A partner of, say, a legal firm would probably not have such authority. For obvious reasons it is customary for the partnership agreement to restrict these powers of individual partners. Overdraft or other credit facilities should only be provided on the express authority of all partners.

[2.70]   The dissolution of a partnership revokes the authority of each of the partners to act on behalf of the firm. Dissolution may occur by any one of the partners giving notice to the other partners of his or her intention to dissolve the firm, by the completion of the single adventure or undertaking for which it was formed, by the death of any one of them or by the bankruptcy of any one of them, although the partnership agreement may provide for the continuance of the firm by the survivors or by means of other occurrences which are mentioned in ss 32–5.

In the event of a dissolution, it is important for the banker to note that the only authority which remains is to operate the account for the purpose of winding up the business affairs of the firm. The banker should not knowingly permit the operation of the account for any other purpose. However, the banker is entitled to assume, in the absence of knowledge to the contrary, that the surviving partners are acting within their statutory authority: see *Re Bourne* [1906] 2 Ch 427.

EXECUTORS/TRUSTEES

[2.71]   When a person dies, it is necessary that burial be arranged, that outstanding debts be paid and collected and that the property of the deceased be distributed either as dictated by his or her will or by the law of intestacy where there is no will.

Where the deceased has left a will, it will ordinarily name a person who is to undertake the duties mentioned above. Such a person is known as an executor. The executor has power to deal with the deceased's estate for the purposes mentioned above and, when those duties are complete, holds the remaining property in trust for the survivors. The executor must apply to the appropriate court and, after complying with certain legal obligations and formalities, 'probate' will issue. Probate is official evidence of the person's title to act as executor.

If the person has not left a will, or if the named executor has predeceased the testator or refuses to carry out the duties of an executor, a person will be appointed by the court to carry out those duties. The appointment is by means of letters of administration which are issued by the court and the person so appointed is known as an administrator.

From the banker's point of view, there is little difference between the executor and the administrator, save that the executor derives his or her title and power from the will itself; probate is merely the evidence of these powers. The administrator, on the other hand, derives his or her power from the letters of administration and has no rights until the issue of such.

Executors and administrators constitute a single legal entity so that the basic rule is that any one of them is entitled to operate on the executors' account; this basic rule is modified for some transactions involving real property: see, for example, Conveyancing Act 1919 (NSW) s 153(4). The death or other departure of one of them is irrelevant to the course of the administration and to the operation of the account, unless the person's signature is expressly required for the operation of the account.

POWER TO CARRY ON BUSINESS OF THE DECEASED

[2.72]   Executors have the power to carry on the business of the deceased for the purposes of administration, that is, for the purpose of winding up the estate or of selling the business as a going concern. This would not be expected to continue for any length of time. The executor has no power to continue the business for the benefit of the beneficiaries unless authorised by the will or by the court: see *Re Kerrigan* [1916] VLR 516.

However, when the business of the administration is complete, the executors or the administrators are thereupon transformed, perhaps unknowingly, into trustees who hold any remaining property in trust for the beneficiaries of the estate. In such a capacity, there would be no objection to the trustees continuing to operate the business on behalf of the beneficiaries.

The distinction between executor and trustee is very important to the banker, for once the executors become the trustees, they are no longer a single legal entity and the operation of the account must be on quite different terms: see [2.71].

OVERDRAFTS

[2.73]   Since the executor or the administrator always has the power to conduct the estate business for the purposes of administration, there are bound to be circumstances where the executor wishes to borrow in order to facilitate the winding up process. The lending banker must recognise that he or she does not automatically become the creditor of the estate ranking *pari passu* with other creditors: *Berry v Gibbons* (1873) LR 8 Ch App 747. The true position is that the executor is personally liable to the lender but if the debt was properly contracted, that is, for the purpose of the administration of the estate, the lender may be entitled to the executor's right to indemnity from the estate.

MINORS

[2.74]   At common law, a person under the age of 21 was considered to be an 'infant' and in need of special protection. The protection given by the law was to make most contracts with infants voidable at the option of the infant with the result that the contract was unenforceable against the infant. Although the age of majority is now 18 in all Australian jurisdictions, the consequences of contracting with an infant must still be of concern to the banker.

The banker may safely accept a minor as a customer provided that the account is not allowed to go into overdraft. Cheques drawn by a minor are valid cheques even though it may not be possible for the holder of such a cheque to enforce it against the minor: Cheques and Payment Orders Act 1986 s 30. However, when the banker pays a cheque drawn by a minor there is no attempt by the banker to enforce a contract. On the contrary, the banker is fulfilling a contractual obligation owed to the customer. Debiting the account is merely a part of fulfilling that contractual obligation.

The problem is different if the account is allowed to go into overdraft. The problem of lending to a minor is considered at [10.12].

JOINT ACCOUNTS

[2.75]   A joint account is one which is opened in the name of two or more customers. There are several problems which may arise from the operation of a joint account. First, it is necessary to establish which signatures will be required to operate the account. Second, joint accounts are subject to special rules when one of the owners dies. Third, special problems may arise if the bank pays a cheque on which one or more of the required signatures is forged or missing.

SIGNATURES REQUIRED

[2.76]   In the absence of any agreement, the debt owed by the banker to the customers is owed to them jointly and severally, with the consequence that cheques should bear the signatures of all the account holders: see *Jackson v White and Midland Bank Ltd* [1977] 2 Lloyd's Rep 68. It is common, and highly desirable, for the banker to take an express mandate from the account owners which expresses, inter alia, which signatures are required on cheques. It is not uncommon for a joint account to be operable by a single signature, particularly when the owners are husband and wife.

It is now common for Australian banks to take a mandate which authorises the operation of the account on a single signature: see *DCT (NSW) Westpac Savings Bank* (1987) 72 ALR 634.

[2.77] Ordinarily, when a customer dies, the account vests immediately in his or her personal representative, that is, the administrator or the executor. However, when the account is a joint account and one of the parties dies, the general rule is that the surviving account holders are entitled to the balance of the account. It is not entirely clear whether this rule is part of the general law of devolution between joint owners or is due to an implied term in the banker-customer contract, but in either case, it is based on an implied intention of the parties which may be rebutted by evidence of a contrary intention. However, equitable doctrines may override the general rule: see M Hapgood, *Paget's Law of Banking*, 11th ed, Butterworths, London, 1996, p 171; *Thorpe v Jackson* (1837) 2 Y & C Ex 553; 160 ER 515.

The question of survivorship is separate from the question of the operation of the account, so that it is not relevant to the question that the mandate taken calls for all signatures on cheques or that it allows the account to be operated on the signature of any one of the account holders.

Although the question of contrary intention has arisen most often in cases where the joint account is held by husband and wife and the husband dies, it arises in all cases where the funds for the account have been supplied solely or primarily by one of the account holders, for in such a case, there is a presumption that the other party or parties holds the sum in trust for the party who provided the funds. The resulting conflict between the two legal presumptions, that of survivorship and that of trust, has resulted in a confused body of case law. The matter is the subject of an Australian High Court decision.

[2.78] In *Russell v Scott* (1936) 55 CLR 440 a joint account was opened by an aunt and her nephew by means of the transfer of a sum of money from her private account into the new joint account. The nephew assisted his aunt in all business matters, but did not himself contribute to the account directly. Indeed, all funds which went into the account were from the aunt's investments. Withdrawals from the account were used solely for the needs of the aunt, although the mandate taken by the bank called for the signature of both before withdrawals could be made. It was found as a fact from statements made by the aunt that she intended that the nephew should take beneficially any balance in the account in the event of her death.

The court held that the nephew was entitled to the balance of the account and that the evidence of intention was sufficient to override any presumption of a resulting trust in favour of the aunt and her estate. During the course of their judgment, Dixon and Evatt JJ said (at 451):

> The right at law to the balance standing at the credit of the account on the death of the aunt was thus vested in the nephew. The claim that it forms part of her estate must depend upon equity. It must depend upon the existence of an equitable obligation making him a trustee for the estate ... As a legal right exists in the nephew to this sum of money, what equity is there defeating the aunt's intention that he should enjoy the legal right beneficially? Both upon

principle and upon English authority we answer, none. English authority is confined, so far as we can discover, to cases of husband and wife. But there is much authority to the effect that where a joint bank account is opened by husband and wife with the intention that the survivor shall take beneficially the balance at credit on the death of one of them that intention prevails, and, on the death of the husband, the wife takes the balance beneficially, although the deceased husband supplied all the money paid in and during his life the account was used exclusively for his own purposes.

On the other hand, in *Brophy v Brophy* (1974) 3 ACTR 57 the court held that where a joint bank account was operated by husband and wife but all the deposits were made from the wife's earnings and there was no evidence of an intention to make a gift of the money to the husband, the balance was held by him in trust for the wife: see also *Haythorpe v Rae* [1972] VR 633.

[2.79] The matter has been before the New Zealand High Court in *Taylor v National Bank of New Zealand* [1985] BCL 895.

About a week before his death W asked his wife to obtain forms for him to sign to change his trading and savings account to joint accounts. At first W did not sign the forms for the savings accounts because, it was said, he thought there was not much in them. The bank advised Mrs W that there was a substantial balance and that they should be converted to joint accounts if that was her husband's intention. Upon being informed of the true value of the accounts W signed the forms. The executors claimed the sums in the accounts but the bank refused to pay them out, claiming that they belonged to Mrs W by survivorship.

The court found that the forms did have the effect of converting the accounts to joint accounts, that W had the capacity to make the changes and that he intended the wife to be a joint account holder: see also *Edgar v Commissioner of Inland Revenue* [1978] 1 NZLR 590. There was also argument on behalf of the executors that there was a presumption of undue influence which could only be rebutted by showing that the bank had discharged its fiduciary duty by ensuring that the deceased formed an independent judgment after free and informed consideration. Prichard J held that there was no evidence that suggested that W did not exercise his own free and informed judgment: see also *National Westminster Bank v Morgan* [1985] 1 All ER 821 and the discussion of undue influence in Chapter 10.

[2.80] These disputes have all been between the surviving account owner and the estate of the deceased or heirs of the deceased. Ellinger argues that in spite of these cases, the bank may honour the survivor's cheques since the survivor is the legal owner of the account. He notes that it is common for the bank to obtain express authorisation at the time of opening a joint account, but that it may honour the cheques even in the absence of such an authorisation: Ellinger, op cit, p 232. See also Paget, op cit, p 171. Cf Weaver and Craigie, op cit, para [5.420].

WHEN ONE SIGNATURE FORGED

[2.81] When more than one of the account owners is required to sign cheques, there may be problems if the bank honours cheques on which the signature of one of the parties is forged or missing. There has been some confusion concerning the right of one party to recover from the bank in such a circumstance.

The problems have been caused by the decision in *Brewer v Westminster Bank* [1952] 2 All ER 650, a decision of the Queen's Bench Division in England. A joint account was operated by two co-executors. One of the parties drew over 450 cheques totalling some £3000 which he signed himself and forged the signature of the plaintiff. The plaintiff claimed that the money had been wrongly debited to the account. McNair J found in favour of the bank on the basis that no action could be maintained by the joint account holders unless each of them was in a position to sue. Since it was clear that the fraudulent party could not have sued, the action failed.

[2.82] The decision was much criticised and only a few years later the Supreme Court of Victoria refused to follow *Brewer* in *Ardern v Bank of New South Wales* [1956] VLR 569. The joint account holders were partners, but in other respects the facts appear to be identical to those of *Brewer*. Martin J held in favour of the innocent account owner apparently agreeing that when the bank contracts to honour joint drawings it is also agreeing with each party severally that it will not honour drawings which are signed by a single party.

The *Ardern* case also noted that the appropriate measure of damages is half the amount of the forged cheques, since the partners in that case were entitled to equal shares in the account. When the account is a trust account or where it can be established that all of the funds in the account were the property of the defrauded customer, such a reasoning would not apply.

[2.83] It now seems very unlikely that *Brewer* will be followed even in England. In *Catlin v Cyprus Finance Corporation (London) Ltd* [1983] 1 All ER 809 there was a joint account held by a husband and wife where the signature of both parties was required to operate the account. The husband made representations to the bank to the effect that he had his wife's authority to operate the account on his own and the bank then paid out funds on the strength of the husband's signature alone. The wife sued the bank. Contrary to most of the cases of this type, the husband was not joined as a party to the action. The court noted that the parties had, when opening the account, clearly expected that the bank would honour the obligation to require both signatures. The only way in which that obligation could be given legal effect is if the duty to refrain from paying on one signature was owed to both parties severally and it could therefore be enforced at the suit of the innocent account holder alone. The court refused to follow *Brewer* and it now seems unlikely that *Brewer* retains any authority at all. See also *Jackson v White and Midland Bank Ltd* [1967] 2 Lloyd's Rep 68.

COMPANY ACCOUNTS

[2.84]   A company is a separate legal entity which may sue and be sued in its own name. In Australia, the formation of companies, their powers and responsibilities are governed for the most part by the 'Corporations Law'. This was originally enacted as the Corporations Act 1989 (Cth). The constitutionality of the Corporations Act 1989 was challenged in *New South Wales v Commonwealth* (1990) 169 CLR 482. Those sections of the Act which purported to confer on the Commonwealth legislative power for the incorporation of trading and financial institutions were found to be *ultra vires* the power of the federal government and hence invalid.

By agreement with the states, the Corporations Legislation Amendment Act 1990 converted the Corporations Act into a law for the government of the Australian Capital Territory. It also created the 'Corporations Law' out of the existing interpretation and substantive provisions of the Corporations Act. Each state has an applications statute which adopts the 'Corporations Law' as set out in s 82 of the Corporations Act.

Because company law is intrinsically a complex and frequently changing body of law, there is little point in trying to cover detailed provisions in a general work of this kind. On the other hand, there are certain principles of company law which have not changed in more than a hundred years and are unlikely to be changed in the foreseeable future. The unchanging principles which are of interest to bankers are discussed in this section; references to the Corporations Law are used where appropriate.

By far the largest number of companies are companies which are limited by shares, that is, the liability of the shareholders of the company is limited to the nominal value of the value of the shares held. These are the only companies that will be dealt with in this book, but most of what is said concerning the relationship between a banker and a company customer applies to all types of company.

[2.85]   The formation of a company is a matter of some formality which culminates in the issue of a certificate of incorporation by the Commission: s 121. Perhaps the most fundamental concept is that a company is a legal person, separate and distinct from the shareholders, directors or employees. This fundamental principle was not fully recognised until the decision of the House of Lords in *Salomon v Salomon & Co Ltd* [1897] AC 22. In that case S owned 20,001 of the total 20,007 shares in the company. The other six were held by close family members. When the company failed, creditors of the company argued that S should be personally liable for the debts which he had incurred in the company's name. It was held that S was not liable for the debts of the company which was a separate individual legal entity in its own right.

This principle is given statutory recognition in s 123 which provides that upon the day of commencement of registration stated in the certificate of incorporation the company is capable of performing all the functions of a body corporate, is capable of suing and being sued, has perpetual succession, has a common seal and has power to acquire, hold and dispose of property. Subject only to the limitations of the Corporations Law or those imposed by its own 'constitution', a company may exercise the same powers and incur the same obligations as a natural person.

[2.86]   The certificate of incorporation is in some respects similar to a birth certificate of a natural person, but is even more important to those who would have dealings with the company, for the company does not exist before the issue of the certificate and the general rule is that a company is not bound by contracts made prior to its incorporation although the company may ratify the contract if it thinks fit: s 183(2). Section 183(5) permits the court to make orders against a company which has derived benefits from a pre-incorporation contract and s 183(4) imposes liability on the promoters who purported to execute the contract on behalf of the non-existent company if the company is not formed or if the company fails to ratify the contract after formation.

[2.87]   Although a company is a separate legal entity, it must clearly act through agents. Generally, the shareholders of a company do not have a direct say in the day-to-day running of the affairs of the company, but rather periodically elect a board of directors. This board of directors may, in turn, delegate many powers to individual directors or managers. It is this necessity for the company to act through agents which causes some of the difficulties which may appear in the banker-customer relationship. Historically, there were two problems which caused difficulty for anyone dealing with a company. The first was that the legal capacity of a company could be arbitrarily and artificially limited by the documentation required for the creation of the company. The second was that the power of the company's agents might be similarly limited. Both problems were exacerbated by the doctrine of constructive notice of the contents of registered documents.

[2.88]   The objects and powers of the company itself are circumscribed by the memorandum and articles of association. Under the Corporations Law, the memorandum and articles together have, subject to the Corporations Law, the effect of a contract under seal as between the company and each of its members, between the members inter se and between the company and each of the officers of the company: s 180(1). Every company must have a memorandum, but the articles are optional in most cases, a company having the option of accepting a set of model articles: s 125.

Roughly speaking, the first of these documents is the more important to the banker as it sets out the objects and powers of the company and the relationship of the company with the outside world. The articles govern the internal management of the company, a matter which will usually, but not always, be a matter of less importance to the banker. It is said that in the event of a conflict between the two documents the memorandum should dominate: see *Ashbury Railway Carriage & Iron Co v Riche* (1875) LR 7 HL 653.

The old rule was that the banker and everyone else who dealt with a company had to be certain that the transaction was within the powers of the company. A transaction which exceeded those powers, an *ultra vires* transaction, was void. The consequences were catastrophic: a loan made to a company which had no power to borrow was irrecoverable by the lender in an action for debt: *Cunliffe, Brooks & Co v Blackburn and District Benefit Building Society* (1884) 9 App Cas 857. Even worse, the money was not recoverable in an action for money had and received: *Sinclair v Brougham* [1914] AC 398.

[2.89]   Under the Corporations Law, the *ultra vires* doctrine is abolished: ss 164–6. A company has the power and legal capacity to do anything that a natural person may do: s 161. Exercise of powers in excess of that contained in the memorandum are a 'contravention' of s 151 but do not invalidate the transaction. A person who is dealing with a company may make certain assumptions, the most important of which is that in any dealings with the company the memorandum and articles of the company have been complied with: s 163(a). Lodgment of the memorandum and articles does not give constructive notice of their contents: s 165.

The problem of limited authority of agents is also addressed by the Corporations Law. Under s 164(3) a person who is dealing with a company is entitled to assume that a person who is named in registered documents as a director, principal executive officer or secretary has been duly appointed and has authority to exercise the powers and perform the duties customarily exercised or performed by an officer of the named type. The section also permits the person dealing with the company to rely upon the validity of certain documents and that the directors and other officers of the company are performing their duties to the company: see, for example, *Story v Advance Bank Australia Ltd* (1993) 31 NSWLR 722.

[2.90]   It is not possible for the party dealing with the company to rely upon these statutory assumptions in any of the following situations:

a) the party has actual knowledge that the assumed matter is incorrect: s 164(4)(a);

b) the party has a connection or a relationship with the company which is such that it ought to know that the matter being assumed is incorrect: s 164(4)(b); or

c) the party has actual knowledge of fraud or forgery by the company signatory: s 166.

The degree of knowledge required in (a) above is not entirely clear. It may be sufficient that the party is aware of facts even though not fully appreciating that these lead to the conclusion that the assumed matter is incorrect. Similarly, the party may be taken to 'know' if he or she deliberately closes their eyes to circumstances which should alert them to the fact that the assumptions are false.

[2.91] These fundamentals of company law have profound consequences for the banker who wishes to open an account for a company customer. First, any mandates taken from the company must be dated after the date of the issue of the certificate of incorporation. Second, the banker should inspect the relevant clauses of the memorandum and the articles of association, making copies at least of the relevant clauses. Bankers should take careful note of the borrowing powers of the company, the right to sign cheques and other negotiable instruments and the seal of the company and the correct method of affixing. Third, the banker should also see copies of the minutes of the directors' meeting which authorises the opening of an account and the names of the personnel who are authorised to operate the account.

Although the changes in the *ultra vires* rule and the assumptions of s 164 may save the banker from the worst consequences of dealing with an agent of a company in circumstances where the agent exceeds his or her authority, it is better to prevent these problems from arising rather than dealing with them after the fact: see, for example, *Bank of New Zealand v Fiberi Pty Ltd* (1994) 12 ACLC 48.

[2.92] There are a number of other issues which the banker must consider when dealing with a company customer. These include forming contracts with directors which may have an interest in the transaction, transactions which involve a company dealing in its own shares, the winding up of a company, and certain investigations which give inspectors the right to examine company accounts and override the duty of secrecy owed by a banker to the customer. Each of these will be discussed in later sections.

WHO IS A BANKER?

[2.93] Surprisingly, there is no precise definition of either 'banker' or 'the business of banking'. This might be no cause for concern except that banks and bankers are given special privileges by some statutes and are subject to special duties as a result of others. Because of the important economic function of banks they are from time to time more heavily regulated than other financial institutions. Bank records are subject to special laws regarding their production in court and to certain regulatory bodies: see [4.52].

Some of the older cases where the question was important were concerned with the Moneylenders Acts. This is no longer relevant in most Australian jurisdictions since the repeal of the Moneylenders Acts by general credit legislation in New South Wales, Queensland, Victoria, South Australia, Western Australia and the Australian Capital Territory.

Possibly the most important reason to determine whether any particular institution is or is not a bank is the prominence given to banks and bankers in the Bills of Exchange Act 1909 and in the Cheques and Payment Orders Act 1986. A cheque must, by definition, be drawn on a banker: Cheques and Payment Orders Act 1986 s 10; see Chapter 6. Bankers are given quite privileged statutory defences to certain actions which arise when a cheque is misappropriated: Cheques and Payment Orders Act 1986 s 95. If the Act is amended as foreshadowed to allow non-banks to issue 'cheques' then this will, of course, no longer be a problem.

The question of what is 'banking business' will remain important as new products such as smart cards are issued by organisations that are not 'banks'. Is the issue of smart cards 'carrying on some banking business'? If so, the issuer will require an exemption under s 11 of the Banking Act 1959.

It seems likely that failure to comply with the Banking Act does not invalidate contracts entered into with customers: *SCF Finance Co Ltd v Masri* [1987] 1 All ER 175.

DIFFICULTY OF DEFINITION

[2.94]   There is an historical reason for the difficulty in defining 'bank' and 'the business of banking'. Banking during the Middle Ages was largely the use of private fortunes in the lending and financing of trade projects. It was not until comparatively recent times that the deposit of funds by the wider community with a banker who was then expected to use the funds at his or her discretion for commercial lending was established.

This modern form of banking is said to have begun during the mid-seventeenth century when citizens began to deposit money and valuables with goldsmiths. The practice changed slightly when the goldsmiths' receipts began to circulate as a kind of informal currency. That development combined with the trend to return only a certain amount of gold, not necessarily the same goods which were deposited in the first instance, led directly to the development of 'fractional reserve' lending. The goldsmiths learned that it was most unlikely that more than a relatively small number of demands for return of valuables would be made at any one time. By lending through the issue of receipts, it was possible for the goldsmith, now called a banker, to lend more than the total amount which was actually held in reserve.

These banks were owned by individuals or by partnerships which often engaged in banking as a sideline to some other business. It is for this reason that the early habit was to refer to individuals as 'bankers' and to the 'business of banking', for a person carrying on such a business might be engaged in any number of enterprises.

In Australia and New Zealand, the current banking system consists of relatively few large banking corporations which carry on business through many branches. In these circumstances, it might be thought that the search for a definition is merely an academic exercise, but that would be a great mistake, for there are still a significant number of circumstances where the outcome of a dispute will be decided on the basis of whether or not one of the parties 'carries on the business of banking'. As more and more financial institutions seek their customers' deposits, often in the form of cheques made payable to the customer, the matter becomes of increasing importance.

SOME STATUTORY DEFINITIONS

[2.95]   The Bills of Exchange Act 1909 contains a number of provisions which are of immense importance to bankers. Unfortunately for the immediate purposes, the definition in s 2 is most unhelpful: 'Banker' includes a body of persons, whether incorporated or not, who carry on the business of banking.

The Cheques and Payment Orders Act 1986 requires that the drawee of a cheque must be a bank and the term 'drawee bank' is defined in s 3(1) to mean the bank upon which the cheque is drawn. A bank is defined in s 3(1) to include the Reserve Bank of Australia, any institution which is a bank within the meaning of the Banking Act 1959 and the various state banks which are recognised by the Constitution. These should cause no difficulty, but the Act goes on to include a fourth class within the definition, namely, 'a person ... who carries on the business of banking outside Australia'.

The Banking Act 1959 takes a descriptive point of view: 'bank' means a body corporate authorised under Part II to carry on banking business in Australia, and includes State Bank Limited, the Commonwealth Bank and the Commonwealth Development Bank: Banking Act 1959 s 5. Unfortunately, the problem does not disappear, for the same Act makes it an offence for anyone other than an authorised body corporate to 'carry on any banking business': ss 7 and 8, Pt II, Div 1.

A search of the Acts discloses no clues as to what the 'business of banking' might be. It is common knowledge that banks borrow money from depositors and lend money to customers and others. It is also well known that banks deal in foreign exchange, the discounting of bills of exchange and the facilitation of international trade through the operation of the documentary letter of credit system. But other organisations accept deposits and lend money. The banks are no longer the sole method of exchanging foreign currency and there are an increasing number of financial institutions which could never be mistaken for banks which issue and confirm letters of credit.

On the other side of the same coin, banks now seem to be branching out into businesses which have little to do with the traditional business of banking. It may be that the local branch bank also runs a travel service or acts as an agent for the collection of certain payments.

JUDICIAL DEFINITION

[2.96]   The High Court of Australia considered the question in *Commissioners of the State Savings Bank of Victoria v Permewan, Wright Co Ltd* (1914) 19 CLR 457 where it was held, by a majority, that the Commissioners of the State Savings Bank of Victoria were 'bankers' for the purposes of the Bills of Exchange Act 1909. This was in spite of the fact that the repayment of deposits was permitted only on the production of the depositor's passbook with the order for payment. The 'bank' neither collected nor paid its customers' cheques. It is to be noted that *Permewan Wright* preceded *Joachimson's* case, where there seemed to be more emphasis on the operation of the cheque account.

During the course of his judgment, Isaacs J said:

> The fundamental meaning of the term is not, and never has been, different in Australia from that obtaining in England ...

> The essential characteristics of the business of banking are, however, all that are necessary to bring the appellants within the scope of the enactments; and these may be described as the collection of money by receiving deposits upon loan, repayable when and as expressly or impliedly agreed upon, and the utilisation of the money so collected by lending it again in such sums as are required. These are the essential functions of a bank as an instrument of society. It is in effect a financial reservoir receiving streams of currency in every direction, and from which there issue outflowing streams where and as required to sustain and fructify or assist commercial, industrial or other enterprises or adventures. If that by the real and substantial business of a body of persons, and not merely an ancillary or incidental branch of another business, they do carry on the business of banking.

[2.97]   The passages cited above were quoted with approval by the High Court of Australia in *Australian Independent Distributors Ltd v Winter* (1965) 112 CLR 443. One of the issues was whether the Adelaide Cooperative Society had carried on the 'business of banking'. The court held that it had not since although the society accepted deposits from their members and the deposits were recorded in a passbook, the society lacked one of the 'essential characteristics', namely the power to lend money. This was interpreted to mean a general power to lend. Since the society was limited to the making of loans to its members rather than to the world at large, it could not be a 'bank': see also *Re Adelaide Cooperative Society Ltd* [1964] SASR 266.

[2.98]   The English Court of Appeal has also considered meaning of the 'business of banking'. In *United Dominions Trust Ltd v Kirkwood* [1966] 2 QB 431 Lord Denning referred to the *Permewan Wright* definition of banker and said of it and some other old cases (at 446):

> If that were still the law, it would mean that the building societies were all bankers.

> The march of time has taken us beyond those cases of fifty years ago. Money is now paid and received by cheque to such an extent that no person can be considered a banker unless he handles cheques as freely as cash ... Whereas in the old days it was a characteristic of a banker that he should receive *money* for deposit, it is nowadays a characteristic that he should receive *cheques for collection* on behalf of his customer. How otherwise is the customer to pay his money into the bank? It is the only practicable means, particularly in the case of crossed cheques ... Whereas in the old days he might withdraw [money] on production of a passbook and no cheque, it is nowadays a characteristic of a bank that the customer should be able to withdraw it by cheque, draft or order. [Original italics.]

Lord Denning thus identified three characteristics as usual characteristics of the business of banking. These characteristics had been proposed as a test by *Paget on Banking* as early as the 6th edition: *Paget on Banking*, 6th ed,

Butterworths, London, 1961, p 8. The characteristics are that a banker must: (1) conduct current accounts; (2) pay cheques drawn on him or herself; (3) collect cheques for his or her customers.

While Denning MR thought that these were the usual characteristics, Diplock LJ indicated that the three characteristics were essential characteristics: at p 465.

[2.99]   The difference between finding the characteristics to be usual as opposed to essential is important when evidence is given as to reputation. Lord Denning found that UDT was a banker on the basis of its reputation in the City of London as well as by the application of this three pronged test. He noted that the usual characteristics were not necessarily the sole characteristics, so that the evidence that UDT was considered by the financial community as a banker was, of itself, sufficient to establish it as such. Under Lord Diplock's view, the only relevant evidence would be that which established the essential three characteristics.

The difference might be important in the future as the 'business of banking' in the commercial sense changes. For example, it is possible that the cheque account could be replaced by an account operated by means of a plastic card for the majority of non-commercial customers. It would be most unfortunate if the 'business of banking' in the legal sense was unable to keep pace with such changes. The test based on commercial reputation is a valuable addition to a purely mechanical test which may soon be outdated.

[2.100]   The *UDT* case was considered in *Re Roe's Legal Charge; Park Street Securities Ltd v Albert William Roe* [1982] 2 Lloyd's Rep 370. The plaintiff lent the defendant £11,000 for the purposes of purchasing a leasehold. The defendant argued that the plaintiff was an unregistered moneylender within the terms of the Moneylenders Act 1900. The plaintiff claimed to be exempt as a 'banker' within the meaning of that Act.

The evidence showed that the plaintiff operated current accounts, paid cheques drawn on themselves and collected cheques for customers. The problem was that this type of business was a very small part of their total business and, indeed, was a very small business in terms of the major banking corporations since the plaintiff operated only 157 current accounts and 53 deposit accounts. The Court of Appeal held that the plaintiff was engaged in the business of banking. A similar result was reached in *London and Harrogate Securities Ltd v Pitts* [1976] 2 All ER 184.

[2.101]   Whether the characteristics be considered as usual or as essential, there seems little doubt that an institution authorised to carry on the business of banking under the Banking Act 1959 would be considered a bank for all purposes. In *Commercial Banking Co v Hartigan* (1952) 86 ILT 109, the organisation failed the *Kirkwood* test but was held to be a bank because of compliance with the Irish Central Bank Act and was licensed under that Act.

RANGE OF POSSIBLE TESTS

[2.102]   The Supreme Court of Canada has provided a valuable discussion of the various tests which might be applied to determine if a person or an organisation is carrying on 'the business of banking'.

The issue before the court in *Canadian Pioneer Management v Labour Relations Board* (1980) 107 DLR (3d) 1 was whether a company fell under legislation concerning labour relations; part of the determination of that issue involved the question of whether the company was a bank. Laskin CJC and Dickson J considered the question to be whether functionally the business of such a trust company was that of a bank. Their use of the word 'functionally' apparently meant that the company was or was not treated like a bank by the regulatory authorities, for they observed that although a trust company such as the one being considered carried on many activities also carried on by banks, it had not been brought within the federal regulating authority in relation to banking. Throughout the case, the meaning of the so-called 'functional' test seems to vary: see the summary given by Beetz J below.

The other members of the court, Beetz, Martland, Ritchie, Pigeon, Estey and Mcintyre JJ, disagreed. They considered that the functional test was, in the circumstances, inappropriate. They preferred what they referred to as the formal or institutional test. Under this test it is relevant to consider whether an institution holds itself out as a banker, and its reputation as such, a test very similar to that proposed by Lord Denning in the *UDT* case.

[2.103]   Beetz J provides a valuable survey of the possible means of defining the business of banking. They are:

- By a consideration of the nature of the relationship between the institution and its customers. This is the test which is implicit in the *Foley* and *Joachimson* line of cases which decide the formal legal relationship between the parties.

- By a consideration of the function of the institution. This approach in turn breaks into two parts, the economic point of view, that banks create credit, and the legal point of view, that banks operate current accounts and pay and collect cheques. The legal functional test is represented by the formal definition of banking given by Lord Denning in the *UDT* case.

- By a consideration of the way in which the institution views itself and is viewed by other institutions. Beetz J refers to this as the formal or institutional test, 'holding oneself out as a banker', or 'having a reputation as a banker'.

CHAPTER 3

THE CURRENT ACCOUNT

[3.1] There is no precise definition of a current account even though the vast majority of banking transactions, both by number and by value, are those which are through what is undeniably a current account. Chorley says (R S T Chorley, *The Law of Banking*, 6th ed, Sweet & Maxwell, London, 1974 p 167) that:

> The principal feature of such an account is the fact that the customer gets his money repaid from it, or any advances which he is receiving from his banker by way of loan; and this is so whether the repayment is to himself or to a third party.

The salient feature of the current account is that it may be used for third party payments by means of the cheque. In more recent times the current account may also be accessed by a debit card, either to withdraw cash from automatic teller machines or to make limited third party payments through electronic point of sale terminals: see [8.2]ff. Traditionally the account has been non-interest-bearing, but recent increases in competition between banks and other financial institutions are making inroads into this tradition both in Australia and overseas. But even where the account is interest-bearing, it will normally be at a rate which is far less than that which may be obtained from other investments. Were it not for the convenience of the third party cheque payment system and access to cash through ATMs, few customers would keep a current account in credit with the bank.

The current account is a widely used form of granting credit to customers, although there are indications that it is decreasing in importance in this role. When this occurs, the basic relationship of the banker and customer is reversed, the banker becoming the creditor and the customer the debtor. In most cases, the account continues to be operated in the usual way, the banker acting as the customer's agent for the collection and payment of cheques.

APPROPRIATION

[3.2] The fluctuating nature of the current account gives rise to some legal problems. For most purposes, it is sufficient to determine a net balance at some point in time. However, there are disputes which arise requiring a more sophisticated approach to the account. As an example, a security is taken by the bank on a certain date to secure an overdrawn account. If the customer continues to operate the account, does the security cover the full net balance? Or are the payments in to be treated in some way differently from the drawings out?

The word 'appropriation' refers to two different practical situations. First, it describes the situation in which a particular entry in an account is set against or matched with a transaction on the other side of the same account. Second, when there are several different accounts, it describes the process whereby the transaction is ascribed to one account or the other. Each raises different problems. It is convenient to consider the second meaning of the word first.

[3.3]   The law as to the appropriation of payments to different accounts is described in the following passage from *Deeley v Lloyds Bank Ltd* [1912] AC 756 at 783:

> According to the law of England, the person paying the money has the primary right to say to what account it shall be appropriated; the creditor, if the debtor makes no appropriation, has the right to appropriate; and if neither exercises the right of appropriation, one can look on the matter as a matter of account and see how the creditor has dealt with the payment in order to ascertain how in fact he did appropriate it. And if there is nothing more than a current account kept by the creditor, or a particular account kept by the creditor and he carries the money to that particular account, then the court concludes that the appropriation has been made; and having been made, it is made once for all, and it does not lie in the mouth of the creditor afterwards to seek to vary that appropriation.

Although the passage assumes that it is the debtor who is making the payment, it is clear that it is the paying person who has the primary right of appropriation. Even when the customer's accounts are all in credit, so that it is the customer who is the creditor and the banker who is the debtor, it is the customer that has the right to appropriate the payments of money in.

It is not necessary that the act of appropriation indicate that the payment in is to be credited to a separate account. The payer of the money may indicate that it is to be used only for a particular purpose. As an example, it may be that the customer wishes to be certain that a particularly important cheque will be met. He or she may deposit a sum of money with the instructions that it be used only for the purposes of meeting the cheque: see *W P Greenhalgh & Sons v Union Bank of Manchester* [1924] 2 KB 153; *Huenerbein v Federal Bank of Australia* (1892) 9 WN(NSW) 65.

[3.4]   Weaver and Craigie question whether it is necessary for the bank to accept certain types of appropriation: G A Weaver and R C Craigie, *The Law Relating to Banker and Customer in Australia*, Law Book Co, Sydney, 2nd ed, 1990, para [7.860]. There is no doubt that if the banker accepts the order in the example above, or if the banker merely fails to dissent, then any use of the deposit for any purpose other than the meeting of that cheque would be improper and would expose the banker to an action in damages. However, such an appropriation is very inconvenient for the banker since the normal banking operation is simply not organised to deal with such an appropriation. Unfortunately, Weaver and Craigie can only suggest that the banker threaten the customer with closure of the account if the customer insists on exercising the right to appropriate payments: Weaver and Craigie, op cit, para [7.860]. Presumably if the requested appropriation is 'unreasonable' then the bank would be entitled to refuse the request, but it is not at all clear what might amount to an 'unreasonable' request: see also Weerasooria, *Banking Law and the Financial System in Australia*, Butterworths, Sydney, 4th ed, 1996, p 538.

[3.5]   If the banker does accept the deposit on the conditions imposed, then he or she must see that the money is applied to the appropriate purpose. In *Huenerbein v Federal Bank of Australia* (1892) 9 WN (NSW) 65 the plaintiff had an overdrawn account with the defendant. He paid in a sum of money with instructions that it was to be applied to meet a certain cheque which would be presented. The cheque was dishonoured although the manager had been informed of the appropriation. The court held that the plaintiff could recover damages for wrongful dishonour.

However, the customer must indicate the desired appropriation with some certainty. In *Re Australian Elizabethan Theatre Trust; Lord v Commonwealth Bank of Australia* (1991) 30 FCR 491 the Australian Elizabethan Theatre Trust had reached an agreement with the Tax Commissioner whereby gifts made to it could still be tax deductible even though the donor expressed a 'preference' that the donation go to one of three other organisations. Before the appointment of a provisional liquidator for the Trust, money received from donors stipulating a preference had been deposited to the Trust's account with the Commonwealth Bank but there had been no express appropriation of the money so deposited.

Gummow J held that the money was not held in trust by the Trust on behalf of the nominated organisations since the language used by the parties, the nature of the transaction and the circumstances attending the relationship between them did not lead to the relevant intention. A significant factor was that the Trust did not 'earmark' the donations or segregate them in a separate bank account. There was no express trust or other equitable obligation since the 'preference' expressed by donors represented only a statement of motive or expectation importing no legal or equitable obligation on the part of the Trust.

[3.6]   As indicated in the quotation from *Deeley v Lloyds Bank*, if the customer does not appropriate the payment either to a special purpose or to a particular account, then the bank may appropriate the payment. In these days of preprinted deposit slips it is most unlikely that the deposit will not be appropriated to an account, so the problem is ordinarily confined to those circumstances where the bank receives a payment on the customer's behalf.

THE RULE IN CLAYTON'S CASE

[3.7]   The first type of appropriation problem arises when there is no express appropriation of payment. Since money is from time to time deposited into the account and, at the same time, regularly drawn upon by cheques, it is sometimes necessary to determine which of several competing claims will have priority when the account is not sufficient to satisfy all. The starting point for the discussion is *Devaynes v Noble: Clayton's case* (1816) 1 Mer 529 at 572; 35 ER 767 at 781.

Clayton maintained a current account with a firm of bankers in which the accounts were kept in the ordinary way, that is, transactions were recorded chronologically on a debit and credit ledger. One of the bankers died and the bank soon afterward failed. At the time of the partner's death, Clayton's account was in credit some £1700, that is, the firm of bankers owed him that amount of money. Between the time of the death and the failure of the firm, Clayton had continued to operate the account, drawing out more than the sum which had stood to his credit, but paying in an even larger sum than that withdrawn.

The issue was whether or not Clayton could recover anything from the estate of the deceased partner. If the drawings and deposits which occurred after the death could be treated separately, then the debt of £1700 was owed to Clayton jointly and severally by all of the partners and he could recover. If, however, the withdrawals, that is, the payment by the banker, had the effect of extinguishing by repayment the earlier debt, then Clayton could only prove in bankruptcy.

The court held that each payment out, went to pay off the earliest payment in. During the course of the judgment, Sir William Grant MR said (at (1816) 1 Mer 529 at 608; 35 ER 767 at 783):

> ... this is the case of a banking account, where all the sums paid in form one blended fund, the parts of which have no longer any distinct existence. Neither banker nor customer ever think of saying, 'this draft is to be placed to the account of the £500 paid in on Monday, and this other to the account of the £500 paid in on Tuesday'. There is a fund of £1000 to draw upon, and that is enough. In such a case, there is no room for any other appropriation than that which arises from the order in which the receipts and payments take place, and are carried into the account. Presumably, it is the sum first paid in, that is first drawn out. It is the first item on the debit side of the account, that is discharged, or reduced, by the first item on the credit side. The appropriation is made by the very act of setting the two items against each other. Upon that principle, all accounts current are settled, and particularly cash accounts.

LIMITS TO THE RULE IN CLAYTON'S CASE

[3.8]   *Clayton's case* has been described as a presumption rather than a rule of law. In the case of *Re Diplock* [1948] Ch 465, 554 it was said that the rule in *Clayton's case* is a 'rule of convenience based upon so-called intention'. In the same case, Lord Greene MR said that the rule does not extend beyond the case of a bank account, but that proposition should be considered with caution since there must be some rule of appropriation when there are running accounts kept between the parties.

The rule only applies when there is a current account between the parties. It does not apply when the accounts rendered make it clear that the payer intended to reserve the right to appropriate the payment to a different account. Finally, it is said that the rule does not apply to transactions which are effected on the same day, for in that case, the order of the transactions in the books is wholly accidental: per Lord Halsbury LC in *The Mecca* [1897] AC 286. Even though the Tasmanian case *Re Laughton* [1962] Tas SR 300 followed this 'same day' exception to the rule in *Clayton's case*, it may not necessarily be a general exception. After all, it may still be necessary to appropriate payments made within a single day to the discharge of some obligation in preference to others, and the rule in *Clayton's case* is not illogical if the parties have expressed no actual or implied intention as to appropriation.

Thus, in *Laughton's* case, a solicitor had become a bankrupt and the issue in the case concerned the trust account which contained money belonging to clients. The rule in *Clayton's case* was applied in order to determine the order in which the money belonging to various clients had been withdrawn, but concerning entries on any one day, the order of the entries was said not to be relevant. Consequently, if the balance was insufficient to meet the claims of these clients, their claims were met on a basis of proportionality. In the circumstances of the case, this seems like a fair enough division of the account, but it can scarcely be said to be any more logical than the rule in *Clayton's case*. The departure from the rule could have been justified by an appeal to the presumed intention of the parties, rather than elevating to a general principle that some other rule of appropriation necessarily applies when the transactions are same day.

[3.9] The rule does not operate so as to affect the rights of third parties. The classic example is a trustee who has mixed his or her own money with that held on trust. The presumption then is that any money withdrawn by the trustee is the money of the trustee, not that of the beneficial owner: see *Re Hallett's Estate* (1880) 13 Ch D 696.

The rule can be displaced by agreement between the parties. In modern banking practice, it is customary for banks to include a clause in a loan contract which has as its object the partial exclusion of the rule in *Clayton's case*: see Chapter 10.

OVERDRAFT ACCOUNT

[3.10] It is possible for a current account to have a debit balance; when that is the case, it is called an overdraft account. It is one of the most common methods of bank lending to meet business credit needs. When the overdraft is intended to be for a relatively long term, it will be customary for the banker to take a security interest from the customer. The use of overdrafts for lending and the taking of securities is discussed in Chapter 10.

There may be informal overdrafts which are not secured and may not even be arranged ahead of time. Although the banker is not bound to pay a cheque if there are insufficient funds in the account, he or she may choose to do so. The drawing of a cheque by the customer when there are insufficient funds to meet it is an implied request to the banker to grant overdraft facilities: *Cuthbert v Robarts Lubbock & Co* [1909] 2 Ch 226. It would seem in such a circumstance that the banker is entitled to charge interest even if no formal arrangements have been made, the right being based on the usage and uniform custom of bankers: *National Bank of Greece v Pinios Shipping Co No 1, The Maira No 3* [1990] 1 Lloyd's Rep 225; [1990] 1 All ER 78. The right to charge simple interest has long been recognised: *Deutsche Bank v Banque des Marchands de Moscou* (1931) 4 LDAB 293; *The Maira No 3* confirmed that the bank also had the right to add periodically the amount of the interest to the overdraft. The right does not terminate when the bank demands payment of the overdraft but can extend right up to the day of judgment: see *National Bank of Greece v Pinios Shipping Co No 1, The Maira No 3* [1990] 1 Lloyd's Rep 225 at 235; [1990] 1 All ER 78 at 90.

TRUST ACCOUNTS

[3.11] A trust account is an account which is held by one party who is bound by law to exercise his or her rights over the account for the benefit of some other person or persons. The person who holds the account is known as the trustee and the person for whose benefit it is held is the beneficiary or *cestui que trust*. There are certain circumstances where the person holding the account is not strictly speaking a trustee, but there is nevertheless a duty similar to that owed by a trustee arising in favour of some other person. Such a duty is known as a fiduciary duty and may arise in a variety of circumstances.

An example of a trustee-like relationship is an agency relationship. The situation was described by Lord Cottenham in *Foley v Hill* (1848) 2 HL Cas 28 at 35:

> Partaking of the character of a trustee, the [agent] — as the trustee for the particular matter in which he is employed as [agent] — sells the principal's goods, and accounts to him for the money. The goods, however, remain the goods of the owner or principal until the sale takes place, and the moment that money is received the money remains the property of the principal. So it is with regard to an agent dealing with any property; he obtains no interest himself in the subject-matter beyond his remuneration; he is dealing throughout for another, and though he is not a trustee according to the strict technical meaning of the word, he is quasi a trustee for that particular transaction for which he is engaged.

[3.12] The reason that trust accounts are important to the banker is that the banker owes certain duties of care to the beneficiary. A breach of this duty, however innocent, may result in the banker being held liable to the beneficiary. As regards the relationship between the account holder and the banker and between the banker and the third party, there is no reason to distinguish between trustees properly so called and those who owe a fiduciary duty similar to that of a trustee. All cases will be referred to as trust accounts.

There is one common case that bankers must be aware of, namely, that of executors and administrators of deceased estates. Such people are not initially trustees, but they become so after the completion of their administrative duties if they are still holding property to be distributed to survivors of the deceased. This conversion from executor or administrator may happen by force of events so that not even the parties are aware of the transformation: see *Attenborough v Solomon* [1913] AC 76; *Re Donkin (dec'd); Riechelmann v Donkin* [1966] Qd R 96. Weaver and Craigie suggest that bankers should treat all such accounts as trust accounts since the banker has no way of knowing when an executor or administrator has been surreptitiously converted into a trustee: Weaver and Craigie, op cit, para [5.300].

KNOWLEDGE THAT ACCOUNT IS A TRUST ACCOUNT

[3.13]   A bank cannot be held liable to the beneficiaries unless it knows that the account is a trust account: *Thomson v Clydesdale Bank Ltd* [1893] AC 282; *Bank of New South Wales v Goulburn Valley Butter Co Pty Ltd* [1902] AC 543. When an account is headed 'trust account', there is little difficulty in fixing the banker with knowledge that the account is indeed a trust account. The real problems arise when the account is not described as a trust account, but where the banker knows, or should know, that the customer holds some or all of the money in the account on trust.

When the account is described in other terms, the question is whether the facts are such that the banker should have been aware that the funds were held in trust. In one of the leading cases, *Re Gross; Ex parte Kingston* (1871) 6 Ch App 632, a county treasurer had two accounts at the bank, one of which was headed 'Police Account'. The court held that the heading on the account, together with the knowledge that the treasurer was a public official, was sufficient to make it clear to the bank that the account was a trust account. Consequently, when the official absconded the bank was unable to combine his personal account which was in debit with the 'Police Account' which was in credit.

RESPONSIBILITIES TO THE BENEFICIARY

[3.14]   Once the banker knows that the account is a trust account, it is necessary to bear in mind several conflicting duties which make the banker's lot an unhappy one. On the one hand, it is beyond question that there is a duty owed to the beneficiary. On the other hand, it is equally beyond question that the banker owes the customer/trustee the usual duty to honour cheques. Undue zeal in pursuing one of these duties will lead inexorably to a breach of the other.

The precise scope of the duty owed to the beneficiary is far from clear. It is said that the banker does not have a duty to supervise the account, but the cases are not always easy to reconcile. In particular, the banker should always be concerned if the trustee draws a cheque on the trust account for the credit of his or her personal account with the same bank. It has been held that the bank must show that the payment was proper and that failure to do so will result in liability to the beneficiaries: see *Rowlandson v National Westminster Bank Ltd* [1978] 1 WLR 798.

Although the business of banking exposes the banker to circumstances which are unique, it seems that the duty of a banker with regard to trust funds is the same as that of any other person. There are, broadly speaking, two situations in which the banker may be liable to the beneficial owner of the account. The first is when the banker receives a benefit, usually a payment or a reduction in an overdraft of the customer, from the trust account with the knowledge that the benefit is trust property. The second is when the banker knowingly assists in the misappropriation of the trust property whether or not receiving any direct benefit as a result. The first is often referred to as 'knowing receipt', the second as 'knowing assistance'.

KNOWING RECEIPT

[3.15]   If the banker receives a benefit from a payment which he or she knows, or should know, is trust property, then the banker will be liable to the beneficiary. But mere receipt is not enough, there must be 'knowledge' that it is trust property.

[3.16]   In *Thomson v Clydesdale Bank Ltd* [1893] AC 282 a stockbroker deposited into his own account a cheque payable to himself which represented the proceeds of sale of shares sold on behalf of clients. The clients had instructed the broker to pay the proceeds into certain other banks, so the action by the stockbroker was a breach of his fiduciary duty to his customers. At the time of the deposit, the broker's account was overdrawn. The broker became insolvent and his clients claimed to be entitled to have the amount of the cheque repaid to them by the bank.

The bank was aware that the cheque represented the proceeds of the sale of shares but did not know whether the money was in the broker's hands as agent or otherwise. Lord Herschell LC said (at 288):

> No doubt if the person receiving the money has reason to believe that the payment is being made in fraud of a third person, and that the person making the payment is handing over in discharge of his debt money which he has no right to hand over, then the person taking such payment would not be entitled to retain the money, upon ordinary principles which I need not dwell upon.

There was no evidence in the case that the banker had reason to believe that the money was being improperly dealt with. The mere fact that the customer was a stockbroker and that the cheque represented proceeds from the sale of shares was not sufficient to fix the bank with liability, for it is well known that a broker may make advances to his or her clients in anticipation of the amounts that will be received from the sale of shares. In such a case, it would be perfectly legitimate for the broker to pay the cheque into his or her own account.

[3.17]   It is not usually necessary for the banker to make inquiries as to the title of the money being paid into the account. Lord Herschell also said (at 287):

> It cannot, I think, be questioned that under ordinary circumstances a person, be he banker or other, who takes money from his debtor in discharge of a debt is not bound to inquire into the manner in which the person so paying the debt acquired the money with which he pays it. However that money may have been acquired by the person making the payment, the person taking that payment is entitled to retain it in discharge of the debt which is due to him.

The *Thomson* case would have had a different outcome if the stockbroker had first deposited the cheque into the 'client account' and later drawn a cheque on that account for the credit of his personal account. In that circumstance, the principle in the *Rowlandson* case would fix the banker with knowledge that the payment was suspect.

[3.18]   The banker does not receive a 'benefit' by merely applying ordinary banking charges to a transaction which is in breach of trust. In *Nimmo v Westpac Banking Corp* [1993] 3 NZLR 218 a director misappropriated an amount deposited in a trust account of the company. He transferred most of the amount into foreign currency and travellers' cheques with the defendant bank which charged the normal fees for such purpose but otherwise received none of the proceeds for its own benefit. The court held that the case was not of the 'knowing receipt' type.

TYPE OF KNOWLEDGE REQUIRED: 'KNOWING RECEIPT'

[3.19]   A detailed consideration of the type of knowledge which is required to fix liability in the 'knowing receipt' type of case may be found in *Westpac Banking Corporation v Savin* [1985] 2 NZLR 41. A company called Aqua Marine carried on a business of selling boats. It was found as a fact that three out of four boats sold were sold by Aqua Marine acting as agents on behalf of individual non-commercial boat owners. One of the boats sold belonged to Savin. Proceeds from the sale of the boat were paid by Aqua Marine into its trading account with Westpac at a time when the company was in difficulties and its account was heavily overdrawn. Savin claimed to be entitled to recover the amount from Westpac, arguing that Westpac knew that the money was held by Aqua Marine on trust for the owner of the boat.

Note that there were actually two facts which were required in order for the plaintiff to win: (1) that the bank 'knew' that the money it received was the property of the plaintiff; and (2) that the payment of the money into the overdrawn account of Aqua Marine was a breach of fiduciary duty on that company's part.

The court cited with approval a judgment of Peter Gibson J in *Baden, Delvaux and Lecuit v Societe General pour Favoriser le Developpement du Commerce et de l'Industrie en France SA* [1983] BCLC 325; (1982) [1992] 4 All ER 161; on appeal (1985) [1992] 4 All ER 700, where he itemised five separate types of knowledge: (1) actual knowledge; (2) knowledge which is obtainable

but for shutting one's eyes to the obvious; (3) knowledge obtainable but for
wilfully and recklessly failing to make such inquiries as an honest and reasonable person would make; (4) knowledge of circumstances which would
indicate the facts to an honest and reasonable person; and (5) knowledge
obtainable from inquiries which an honest and reasonable person would feel
obliged to make, being put on inquiry as a result of his or her knowledge of
suspicious circumstances.

Applying this taxonomy to the facts of the present case, Richardson J said
(at 54):

> While the bank would or might not have known in respect of a particular
> banking whether it was in respect of a boat sold ex stock or as agent for a prin-
> cipal, it knew throughout that 3 out of 4 sales were in the latter category. That
> actual knowledge of the bank was such that in receiving those cheques and
> applying them in reduction of the overdraft it must be concluded that it wil-
> fully shut its eyes to the obvious (type 2 knowledge) or, at least, that it wilfully
> and recklessly failed to ascertain and satisfy itself that the receipts were not in
> respect of 'on behalf' sales (type 3 knowledge). The only reasonable conclusion
> is that it had constructive notice of the breach of fiduciary duty on the part of
> Aqua Marine and must account to the plaintiffs for their property.

Richardson J, although noting that it was not strictly necessary in the
present case, expressed the view that 'knowledge' of any of the five types
would serve to fix the bank with liability in the case where the bank has
received money which is subject to a fiduciary duty. Under this approach, the
payment of a cheque from a trust account to a personal account would clearly
result in 'knowledge' of type 5 and so fix the bank with liability if it received a
benefit from the payment. In the common case where the payment is made to
reduce an overdraft in the customer's personal account, the bank receives the
benefit of the payment.

[3.20]   The knowledge required, regardless of the category into which it
falls, must be knowledge of an actual trust, not a claimed one. In *Carl Zeiss
Stiftung v Herbert Smith (No 2)* [1969] 2 Ch 276 an organisation referred to as
the 'East German foundation' commenced an action against a group known as
the 'West German foundation' claiming that property in England which
belonged to the West German foundation was held on trust for them. The
claim was by no means clear, but depended upon many hotly disputed issues
of both fact and law. The solicitors for the West German foundation had
received payments for costs and disbursements. These payments were made
from the funds which the East German foundation claimed to be trust funds.
The solicitors were, of course, fully aware of the allegations concerning the
fund.

The East German foundation then brought the current action against the
solicitors, claiming that they were constructive trustees of the amounts which
they had received from the fund. The English Court of Appeal held that the
action failed, since the knowledge was of an alleged trust only. It was said that
notice of a 'doubtful equity' could not be equated with notice of a trust.

KNOWING ASSISTANCE

[3.21] The 'knowing assistance' class of cases is more difficult for the banker, partly because of the uncertainty of what must be 'known' and partly because if the banker is found liable the result is more serious. In the knowing receipt class, the banker must return some benefit received but in the knowing assistance category the banker may have to account for funds which went to the benefit of some third party.

Perhaps the clearest statement of the difference between the two classes of case is that of Jacobs P in the New South Wales Court of Appeal in *D P C Estates Pty Ltd v Grey and Consul Development Pty Ltd* [1974] 1 NSWLR 443 (at 459):

> The point of difference between the person receiving trust property and the person who is made liable, even though he is not actually a recipient of trust property, is that in the first place knowledge, actual or constructive, of the trust is sufficient, but in the second place ['knowing assistance'] something more is required, and that something more appears to me to be the actual knowledge of the fraudulent or dishonest design, so that the person concerned can truly be described as a participant in that fraudulent dishonest activity.

The decision of the Court of Appeal in the *D P C Estates* case was overturned by the High Court of Australia in *Consul Development Pty Ltd v D P C Estates Ltd* (1975) 132 CLR 373 on the grounds that the plaintiff had not established that the defendant had actual, as opposed to constructive, knowledge.

[3.22] This basic principle was established in *Barnes v Addy* (1874) 9 Ch App 244 where the plaintiff attempted to shift losses to solicitors who advised trustees. The court noted that the basic principle is that (from the headnote):

> A stranger who acts as the agent of a trustee in a transaction legally within his power, but which leads to a breach of trust, is not to be held responsible as a constructive trustee unless some of the property passes into his hands, or unless he is cognisant of a dishonest design on the part of the trustee.

The reason as explained by Lord Selborne LC (at 252) is that no one could 'safely discharge the office of solicitor, of banker, or of agent of any sort to trustees' if the principles were disregarded.

[3.23] The question of 'knowing assistance' has been considered by the Privy Council in *Royal Brunei Airlines v Tan* [1995] 2 AC 378. The defendant was a director and shareholder in a travel agency. He redirected money held on trust by the company. The company became insolvent and the plaintiff/beneficiary sought recovery on the grounds of 'knowing assistance'. The facts were unusual in that there was no allegation of dishonesty on the part of the trustee. The Privy Council reviewed the cases on 'knowing assistance', noting that the cases are concerned with the liability of an accessory to a breach of trust.

After a careful review of the cases, the Privy Council concluded that liability of an accessory is based on the accessory's own dishonesty.

Consequently, there may be 'knowing assistance' by the accessory even where the trustee's breach is entirely innocent.

TYPE OF KNOWLEDGE REQUIRED: 'KNOWING ASSISTANCE'

[3.24]   The Privy Council attempted to clarify the state of mind necessary to incur liability as an accessory. In keeping with the view that liability of the accessory is based on dishonesty, it was held that nothing short of dishonesty would suffice. In particular, the Baden categorisation of degrees of knowledge is irrelevant in the 'knowing assistance' cases.

What is 'dishonesty'? According to the Privy Council, there is a strong subjective element since the actual knowledge of the defendant at the time is relevant. However, the standard must be objective, the question being to determine the behaviour of an honest person in the circumstances of the defendant. According to the Privy Council (at 390):

> Acting in reckless disregard of others' rights or possible rights can be a tell-tale sign of dishonesty. An honest person would have regard to the circumstances known to him, including the nature and importance of the proposed transaction, the nature and importance of his role, the ordinary course of business, the degree of doubt, the practicability of the trustee of the third party proceeding otherwise, and the seriousness of the adverse consequences to the beneficiaries.

[3.25]   Although the language of 'dishonesty' appears to give greater certainty in 'knowing assistance' cases, the application in practice will probably be little different from the position set out in the *DPC Estates* case. There is little doubt that actual knowledge by the accessory of a dishonest or fraudulent design on the part of the trustee will be 'dishonest'. Some of the earlier cases where a banker was found liable for 'knowing assistance' may need to be re-examined to determine if there was actual knowledge, but that is also true under the *DPC Estates* test.

The *Royal Brunei Airlines* principle, that an accessory may be liable even when the trustee's breach is innocent, is a welcome clarification of the law. It seems doubtful, however, that it will apply in many banking cases.

[3.26]   There have been some doubts as to the position of agents of trustees, the suggestion being that they may be in some way specially privileged when compared with those who deal as strangers with trustees. Sir Clifford Richmond suggested in *Westpac Banking Corporation v Savin* [1985] 2 NZLR 41 that this might be so in cases where agents act in relation to trust property purely in their capacity as agents. He said:

> So it can be argued that an agent who receives trust funds from the trustee will be within the first category ['knowing receipt'] only if he is setting up a title of his own to the funds which he has received and is not acting as a mere depository or merely as a channel through which money is passed to other persons.

This would, of course, be relevant to the banker who is collecting a cheque for his customer when the customer is acting in breach of trust, but can be of no assistance to the banker who receives trust funds in reduction of an overdraft or to the banker who knowingly assists in the misappropriation of the account funds.

TRACING ORDERS

[3.27]   There are circumstances where there is no question of the banker being directly liable as constructive trustee but where there is a claim by a third party that the money in the account actually belongs to them and not to the customer of the bank. There are procedures which may be followed by the claimant to 'trace' the money into the account in certain circumstances. These procedures are of only marginal interest to the banker in the ordinary course of things, since the dispute is really between the customer and the third party. In such a case, the usual course for the banker is to avoid the dispute entirely by interpleading, that is, paying the money into court and leaving the customer and third party to fight it out.

If for some reason, the banker chooses to become involved in the dispute, the conflict mentioned above is faced in its starkest form, for on the one hand there is the contractual duty to the customer to obey mandates and on the other hand the danger that by so doing the banker will become liable to the third party under the principles discussed above.

Often the major question is whether or not the money which is claimed is actually in the account. Assuming that it can be traced into the account and that it then becomes mixed with the customer's own money, under what conditions can it be said that the money has not been withdrawn by the customer and dispersed elsewhere? The outlines of the law on tracing may be summarised by consideration of two cases.

[3.28]   In *Re Hallett's Estate; Knatchbull v Hallett* (1880) 13 Ch D 696 Hallett was a solicitor who had mixed money which he held in a fiduciary capacity in an account with his own money. He had operated the account as a personal account for some time after depositing the 'trust' money. The court held that he must be treated as having made all of his drawings on the account from his own money since it would be contrary to his duty as a fiduciary to draw on the other funds. Thus the rule in *Clayton's case* is displaced when the account consists partly of private funds and partly of funds held in a fiduciary capacity.

However, when there is more than one beneficiary, as indeed there were in *Hallett's* case, then as between the beneficiaries, the rule in *Clayton's case* is applied to determine which of them is entitled to the 'trust' funds in the event that the account is not sufficient to cover all claims: see also *Re Laughton* [1962] Tas SR 300.

[3.29]   It is possible to follow misappropriated funds through several transactions. In *Banque Belge pour L'Etranger v Hambrouck* [1921] 1 KB 321 an employee of a customer of the bank obtained sums of money by fraud from his employer's bank account. He then paid them into his own account with another bank. Later, he withdrew sums of money from that account and made gifts of the amount to a friend. She in turn paid the money into an account with the London City and Midland Bank. The Banque Belge had been obliged to restore its customer's account to its original condition and now claimed to be entitled to the sums in the London City account. The London City bank interpleaded. The Court of Appeal held that the money could be followed through each of the transactions. The money was recoverable from the friend since she had given no consideration for it.

The law was clarified and summarised in *Re Diplock* [1948] Ch 465. In that case it was said that money could be equitably traced into a mixed fund if three conditions were satisfied. First, there must be a fiduciary relationship between the claimant and the person who received the money in the first instance. Second, the money must be identifiable. Third, the making of the tracing order must not work an injustice.

It may be that the first condition stated is too stringent. In *Chase Manhattan Bank NA v Israel British Bank (London) Ltd* [1981] 1 Ch 105, the court indicated that a tracing order would be available where the claimant had paid money by mistake. See also *Bankers Trust v Shapira* [1980] 3 All ER 353; [1980] 2 WLR 1274 where the funds were obtained fraudulently.

When the money is in the hands of an agent, the tracing order may be obtained against both the person who has received the money and the agent, but the order against the agent may only be obtained so long as the agent has not paid the money to the principal or to the principal's order. Thus, if the bank in *Hambrouck* had paid the money to the friend or paid a cheque drawn by her, then there would no longer be the possibility of obtaining the tracing order as against the bank. The bank would not have been liable to the plaintiff unless it was privy to the breach of trust, that is, unless it was a 'knowing assistance' type of case: *Gowers v Lloyd's and National Provincial Foreign Bank Ltd* [1938] 1 All ER 766.

BANKER AS TRUSTEE

[3.30]   In the cases which we have been considering, there has been a breach of trust. There is no protection for the beneficiary when there is not a breach of trust but the beneficiary nevertheless loses his or her money. An example is *Space Investments Ltd v Canadian Imperial Bank of Commerce Trust Co (Bahamas) Ltd* [1986] 3 All ER 75. The bank itself was a trustee of funds with powers, indeed duties, of investment. The bank had trust power to deposit with itself as banker and did so in good faith. The bank then unfortunately went into liquidation and the beneficiaries of the trust claimed priority over the general creditors of the bank, arguing that this was a 'knowing receipt' case. The court held that when the bank went into liquidation the beneficiaries were entitled to obtain the appointment of a new trustee, but on the insolvency of the bank which lawfully appropriated trust money to itself and credited the moneys to a trust deposit account, the new trustee could only rank as an unsecured creditor on behalf of the trust.

On the other hand, it has been said that a banker must exercise a high standard of care when acting as a trustee, a standard which is higher than that of an ordinary trustee: *Bartlett v Barclays Bank Trust Co Ltd* [1980] 1 All ER 139.

COMBINING ACCOUNTS

[3.31]   It is not at all uncommon for a customer to keep more than one account with a bank. The reason for this may be one of convenience, for example, the separation of business and household accounts, or it may be that the customer is required to keep a separate account for particular purposes as, for example, solicitors' trust accounts.

If the customer does keep two or more accounts, he or she has no right to expect that the bank will treat them as a single entity for the purposes of meeting cheques. If the account on which the cheque is drawn is insufficient to meet the cheque, then the bank may dishonour the cheque even though, taken together, the accounts have ample funds to meet the cheque: *Arab Bank v Barclays Bank (DCO)* [1954] AC 495; *Garnett v M'Kewan* (1872) LR 8 Ex 10. The bank may pay the cheque, of course, treating the cheque as a request for an overdraft on the account on which it was drawn: *Cuthbert v Robarts, Lubbock & Co* [1909] 2 Ch 226. Under certain circumstances, the bank may choose to treat the multiple accounts as a single account for the purposes of meeting the customer's cheque: see below [3.32].

The bank may also wish to treat the multiple accounts as a single entity when the customer is a net debtor of the bank and one or more of the accounts is in credit, since doing so has the effect of giving the bank a significant advantage over other creditors. Under certain circumstances, the bank may exercise this so-called right of combination. This section discusses the extent and the limitations on this right of combination.

COMBINATION

[3.32]   The law has been settled for some time that the banker has a general right to combine two of the customer's current accounts in a number of circumstances. What is not clear is the extent of this right when the accounts are not of the same type, for example, if one of the accounts is a normal cheque account and the other is, say, an account which is only used in connection with a credit card. Nor is the extent of the banker's right clear with regard to certain express or implied agreements.

[3.33]   The right to treat all of the customer's accounts as a single sum for some purposes is known variously as the right of combination, the right of set-off, the right of consolidation and, erroneously, as the exercise of the banker's lien. The source of the right is *Garnett v M'Kewan* (1872) LR 8 Ex 10.

The plaintiff banked with the London and County Banking Company where he kept accounts at two different branches. One of the accounts was overdrawn by £42.15.11, the other was in credit some £42.18.10. The plaintiff drew three cheques on the account which was in credit, the cheques totalling slightly more than £23. The cheques were dishonoured and the plaintiff received a letter informing him that the account in credit had been debited with the amount necessary to pay the overdraft at the branch which was overdrawn. The plaintiff sued for wrongful dishonour.

The court held that the bank was entitled to combine the accounts in that fashion without notice to the customer. It noted that there was no special agreement to keep the accounts separate, nor could the customer show that there was any course of business upon which he could rely to show an implied agreement in spite of the fact that the overdrawn account had been 'closed', that is, inoperative, for some four months before the bank took action. In *Garnett's* case, the accounts were combined without any notice being given to the customer. In the course of the judgment, Kelly CB said (at 13):

> In general it might be proper or considerate to give notice to that effect, but there is no legal obligation on the bankers to do so, arising either from express contract or the course of dealing between the parties. The customer must be taken to know the state of each account and if the balance on the whole is against him or does not equal the cheques he draws, he has no right to expect more cheques to be cashed.

In cases where the account is governed by the Code of Banking Practice, the bank is obliged to give the customer notice as soon as practicable after exercising any right of combination: 12.4; see [9.2]ff for a discussion of the Code.

Garnett v M'Kewan was approved by the Privy Council in *Prince v Oriental Bank Corp* (1878) 3 App Cas 325.

[3.34]   Although the bank has the right of combination, the bank is under no obligation to combine accounts in order to meet an outstanding cheque. *Garnett* itself is authority for the proposition where the accounts are held at different branches. The same principle applies even where the accounts are kept at the same branch: *Direct Acceptance Corp Ltd v Bank of New South Wales* (1968) 88 WN NSW 498.

The customer may, however, call for the bank to combine two separate accounts. This is merely a matter of transferring funds when the banker-customer relationship still exists, but it seems that in certain circumstances the customer has the right even after the termination of the relationship: see *Mutton v Peat* [1900] 2 Ch 79.

LIMITS ON THE RIGHT OF COMBINATION

[3.35]   Although *Garnett's* case affirms the right of the banker to combine accounts, the restrictions on the exercise of that right were ill-understood. The judgments in *Garnett's* case make it clear that the decision would have been different had there been an agreement to keep the accounts separate, but the form and content of the required agreement was unclear. After all, the mere fact of opening a second account might, it was argued, be evidence to show that the parties intended that the banker should forfeit the right of combination. That argument was destroyed in *Halesowen Presswork & Assemblies Ltd v Westminster Bank Ltd* [1971] QB 1 (CA); *National Westminster Bank Ltd v Halesowen Presswork & Assemblies Ltd* [1972] AC 785 (HL).

The company maintained an account with the bank which became overdrawn. In February 1968 this account, referred to as the No 1 account, was overdrawn by more than £11,000 and the bank had discussions with officers of the company concerning the state of this account. In April of that year, it was agreed that the bank should 'freeze' that account, with the result that it was to all intents and purposes a fixed loan, and should open a new account, the No 2 account, which would be maintained strictly in credit. It was agreed that the arrangement would remain in force for at least four months 'in the absence of materially changed circumstances'. Unfortunately, the following month the company gave notice to the bank that a meeting of creditors would be held to consider a winding-up petition.

Surprisingly, the bank did not terminate the two account arrangement and the No 2 account was allowed to operate normally. On the morning of 12 June, a cheque for more than £8000 was paid into the No 2 account; that afternoon, it was resolved at the creditors' meeting that the company should be wound up and the company liquidator claimed the balance in the No 2 account. The bank argued that it was entitled to set off the credit balance in the No 2 account against the overdrawn No 1 account.

The claim of the bank was upheld at first instance by Roskill J, reversed by a majority in the Court of Appeal, and restored by the House of Lords. In the House of Lords, it was held that the true meaning of the agreement was that it had been intended to be operative while the relationship of banker and customer existed and the company was a going concern. Accordingly, it had come to an end when the winding-up resolution had been passed and that accordingly, the bank was entitled to combine the accounts immediately.

Throughout the course of the case, there was agreement that the mere opening of two accounts could not suffice to imply an agreement. Lord Denning MR put it most succinctly (at 35): 'You have to find an agreement to keep them separate. The mere opening of the two accounts does not do it.'

[3.36] The facts of *Direct Acceptance Corporation v Bank of New South Wales* (1968) 88 WN (Pt 1) (NSW) 498 are very similar to the *Halesowen* case. A company had an account which was overdrawn by about £35,000. The account was 'frozen' by agreement with the bank and a new account opened for day-to-day operations. The agreement with the bank was made orally; there was, not surprisingly, a conflict of evidence over its exact terms. When a receiver was appointed to the company, the question arose as to whether the receiver was entitled to the credit balance or whether the bank was entitled to combine it with the overdrawn account.

The court found as a fact that the agreement was to freeze the account and that there should be no right of set-off. Macfarlan J also found that the appointment of a receiver does not necessarily mean the termination of the banker-customer relationship, so that the arguments which succeeded in the *Halesowen* case would be of no avail.

Although the 'mere' opening of multiple accounts will not deprive the banker of the right of combination without notice, even when the accounts are at different branches as in *Garnett's* case, when the accounts are of a sufficiently different nature they cannot be combined. The most common example is when one account is a current account and the second is a loan account which has been opened with a view toward longer term finance. The designation of the second account is a clear indication that the parties intended the accounts to be treated separately: see *Bradford Old Bank Ltd v Sutcliffe* [1918] 2 KB 833. In another case, the bank was unable to exercise the right of combination when one of the accounts was designated as a 'wages' account and the agreement of the customer with the bank was that the account should be reserved for payment of wages to the customer's employees: *Re E J Morel (1934) Ltd* [1962] Ch 21.

[3.37] These cases may clearly be explained on the basis of an implied agreement to keep the accounts separate, since combination of accounts would destroy the basis for opening the accounts in the first place. However, three of the four judgments in *Garnett's* case also suggested that the bank would have no right of combination if the customer's debt to the bank had been incurred through some business other than banking. As there are an increasing number of activities carried on by bankers, this last point could be significant. Weaver and Craigie suggest that a debt to a bank in relation to travel services might not be recoverable by combination of accounts: Weaver and Craigie, op cit, para [7.950].

Just as it is possible for the bank to contract not to exercise its right of combination, so any person may contract so as to forgo any right of set-off that may otherwise be available: see *Hongkong and Shanghai Banking Corp v Kloeckner & Co* [1989] 3 All ER 513.

TRUST ACCOUNTS

[3.38] One of the important consequences of the fact that the accounts must be held by the customer in a single capacity is that there is no right to combine a customer's personal account with an account which the banker knows to be a trust account.

The matter came before the English court in *Barclays Bank Ltd v Quistclose Investments Ltd* [1970] AC 567. The Rolls Razor Co was in serious financial difficulties. It had a large overdraft with Barclays Bank. In an attempt to trade out of difficulty, Rolls was attempting to borrow a sum of approximately £1,000,000. The proposed source of this loan suggested that, if Rolls could obtain independent financing to pay a declared dividend of some £200,000, the financing arrangements could go ahead. This smaller sum was obtained from Quistclose on the agreed condition that it would be used only for the purposes of paying the dividend. The amount was paid into a special account with Barclays, who knew of the loan and the purpose thereof. Unfortunately, Rolls went into liquidation before the dividend could be paid. The House of Lords held that such an arrangement made Rolls a trustee of the money for the benefit of the creditors to whom the dividend was payable. When the purpose of that trust failed, there was a resulting trust in favour of Quistclose. The consequences were that Quistclose was entitled to complete recovery of the money which Barclays had claimed was to be combined with the overdraft account.

If, however, the banker has no notice that one of the accounts is a trust account, then there is old authority to the effect that the right of set-off may be exercised. In *Union Bank of Australia Ltd v Murray-Aynsley* [1898] AC 693 the trust account was called 'No 3 Account' and there was no evidence that the banker knew that it was held in trust. The banker was held justified in having exercised the right of set-off: see also *T & H Greenwood Teale v William Williams Brown & Co* (1894) 11 TLR 56. The correctness of this decision is open to question, for there is no reason to permit the bank to benefit at the expense of the *cestui que trust* when it is still possible to unravel the transaction.

[3.39]   The converse situation came before the English Court of Appeal. In *Bhogal v Punjab National Bank, Basna v Punjab National Bank* [1988] 2 All ER 298 (CA) the bank became convinced that an account held by a third party was in fact a nominee account of the customer. The facts were that one A S B had opened an account with the bank and was the proprietor of a travel agency. Discussions had taken place between S and the bank regarding the opening of the account. All statements were sent to S but all withdrawals were made by cheques signed by A S B. Y B was another customer. Much of the money paid into Y B's account came from S's travel agency. Y B had signed withdrawal forms in blank and left them with S. The bank formed the view that A S B's and Y B's accounts were nominee accounts beneficially owned by S. They combined accounts and dishonoured cheques. In separate actions A S B and Y B sued the bank and obtained summary judgment for the amount of their deposits.

The court held that a banker is required to pay cheques drawn by a customer if he or she has funds belonging to the customer. The bank is not entitled without warning to refuse to honour a cheque when there is money in the account to cover it, merely on the basis of a suspicion that the account was held by the customer as a nominee for a third party who was indebted to the bank. Instead, clear and identifiable evidence is required before the bank could set off the credit in one account against the other. Implicit in the judgment is that the bank would have had the right of combination if it had been able to prove that the other accounts were held on S's behalf.

THE MATTER OF TERMINOLOGY

[3.40] Throughout the judgment of Roskill J in the *Halesowen* case, he referred to the banker's lien and the exercise of that lien over a credit balance. In so doing, he was employing the terminology which had been used in many of the old cases. However, both the Court of Appeal and the House of Lords said that this use of the word 'lien' is incorrect. Lord Denning MR said ([1971] 1 QB 1 at 33):

> ... the use of the word 'lien' in this context is misleading ... when a banker has a lien over a cheque belonging to a customer or its proceeds, it means that the banker can retain the cheque or its proceeds until the customer has paid the banker the amount of his overdraft; and the banker can realise the cheque and apply the proceeds in discharge *pro tanto* of the overdraft ... Seeing that the banker's lien is no true lien, in order to avoid confusion, I think we should discard the use of the word 'lien' in this context and speak simply of a banker's 'right to combine accounts'; or a right to 'set-off' one account against the other.

BANKRUPTCY ACT 1966 s 86

[3.41] Section 86 of the Bankruptcy Act makes it clear that the right of set-off extends beyond the customer's bankruptcy, provided only that the person claiming the right of set-off is not entitled to do so if he or she had, at the time of giving credit to the bankrupt, notice of an available act of bankruptcy committed by that person: s 86(2) and see [3.70].

The right of set-off provided by the Bankruptcy Act might be a saving factor for the banker. If there has been an agreement to keep the accounts separate, then there is no longer an inherent right of combination. However, the best view appears to be that it is not possible to contract out of the effects of s 86, so that the right to set off will arise upon the bankruptcy of the customer by virtue of that section even if there has been an agreement to keep the accounts separate: *National Westminster Bank Ltd v Halesowen Presswork & Assemblies Ltd* [1972] AC 785. Since the section applies to the winding up of a company, the same comments apply in that case: see [3.71].

On the other hand, if one of the accounts is money which is paid in for a special purpose then there is no mutuality within the meaning of s 86 and the accounts may not be combined: *Rolls Razor Ltd v Cox* [1967] 1 QB 552; *National Westminster Bank Ltd v Halesowen Presswork & Assemblies Ltd* [1972] AC 785.

[3.42] There may be other common situations in which there is no mutuality for the purposes of s 86. In *National Safety Council v Lloyds Bank* (1992) 10 ACLC 1042 there were three agreements for loans secured by mortgages over three different chattels. The company was forced into liquidation and the bank sold the securities, realising a surplus on two of them, but a deficiency on the third. The liquidator claimed the right to the surpluses, the bank claimed to be able to set off under s 86 of the Bankruptcy Act which applied by virtue of the Companies Code of the time. Vincent J held for the plaintiff liquidator on the grounds that the dealings were not mutual since the property subject to the respective mortgages was transferred for the sole purpose of securing amounts outstanding under the relevant cash advances. The result might have been different if there had been an 'umbrella' facility instead of three different transactions.

STATEMENTS AND PASSBOOKS

[3.43]   At one time, current account customers were furnished with a 'passbook' which was a written copy of the customer's account in the bank's ledger. At certain intervals, the passbook would be updated by the bank's clerks and handed to the customer for perusal. The intention was that the customer should examine the book for accuracy and inconsistencies and return it then to the banker, along with any complaint if the book showed what the customer believed to be an error.

Passbooks have been supplanted by bank statements. In modern form, these are computer-produced documents which are printed by the bank's high speed printers. They are sent to the customer at intervals but, unlike the passbook, it is not expected that they will be returned to the bank. There is, consequently, no means of systematically detecting statements which may have gone astray since there is no evidence in the hands of the banker to show that the customer ever received that statement.

There is some old authority that the passbook is the property of the customer, not of the banker. If this is correct, then *a fortiori* the same must be true of the statement: see *Akrokerri (Atlantic) Mines Ltd v Economic Bank* [1904] 2 KB 465 at 470. Note, however, that Australian practice is that the passbook contains clauses reserving property to the bank.

LEGAL EFFECT OF THE STATEMENT

[3.44]   The cases on passbooks and statements are usually concerned with the legal effect of the statement when the customer fails to note discrepancies in the account. The courts have refused to impose a duty on the customer to read the account and to discover and report forgeries: see Chapter 5. The major textbook writers have been very critical of this, noting that there are early authorities which appear to recognise the existence of the duty, at least to the extent that the passing to and fro of the passbook should be evidence of a stated and settled account: see Chorley, op cit, p 178. However, given the decisions in the *Tai Hing* case and the *Walpole and Patterson* case, it now seems that only legislative action could impose such a duty on the customer: *Tai Hing Cotton Mill Ltd v Liu Chong Hing Bank Ltd* [1985] 2 All ER 947; *National Bank of New Zealand v Walpole and Patterson* [1975] 2 NZLR 7.

ACCOUNT STATED?

[3.45]   An account stated is defined by *Halsbury* (3rd ed, vol 8, para 439) in the following terms:

> Where parties mutually agree that a certain sum is due from one to the other an 'account stated' is said to arise, and the law implies a promise on the part of the one from whom such a sum has been agreed to be due to pay the same, on which the other party may sue without being put to proof of the details or correctness of the account.

If the statement could be considered as an account stated, at least after a reasonable period of time during which the customer could raise objections to entries thought to be incorrect, then it would be binding on both the parties, subject to certain exceptions which need not concern us here. However, that would be the equivalent of imposing a duty on the customer to read and reconcile the statement, and this has been decisively rejected.

But that is not to say that the account statement is wholly without legal effect, for there are circumstances where it may be used as evidence in disputes between banker and customer.

EVIDENCE AGAINST THE BANK

[3.46]   The bank has a duty to its customer to keep accurate accounts and if the customer relies on the statement honestly then the bank may on occasion be bound by the entries made by it. *Lloyds Bank Ltd v Brooks* (1950) 6 LDAB 161, was an action to recover money paid by mistake: see Chapter 6 for a general discussion of the right to recover money which is paid under a mistake of fact or law. Due to an error of the bank, dividends payable to her brother were wrongly credited to the defendant's account. It was found as a fact that the money had been paid under a mistake of fact and that the defendant was not aware that she was receiving additional money to which she was not entitled.

Her defence was that the bank was estopped from reclaiming the money by virtue of representations made to her through the periodic statement of account sent by the bank. If she had known that she was not entitled to the money, then there could be no effective estoppel, for she would not have been relying on the representation.

The court held that the bank had a duty to the customer to keep her correctly informed as to the position of her account and not to authorise her or induce her by faithful representations contained in the statement of account to draw money from her account to which she was not entitled. It was also held that, since the representations amounted to a breach of duty, she had spent more over a period of time than she would otherwise have done, and that this represented the change in circumstance necessary to support the estoppel: see [6.29].

[3.47]   It is not every entry in an account which will bind the bank, for it is implicit in the *Brooks* judgment that the bank could have recovered had it discovered the error before the defendant had changed circumstances by overspending.

An enlightening example of a situation where the bank will not be bound is *British and North European Bank Ltd v Zalzstein* [1927] 2 KB 92. A fraudulent bank manager attempted to deceive auditors by manipulating some accounts. One of the accounts belonged to the defendant and was overdrawn; the manager credited the account with £2000 which was debited to another account and then later debited the defendant's account with the same amount, restoring the accounts to their original position. The customer knew nothing about these entries until after the accounts had been restored to their original position, but he claimed to be entitled to claim the £2000 credit but to disclaim the corresponding debit. In the course of the judgment, Sankey J said (at 97):

> ... it can [not] be ... asserted that an entry made in a passbook is in all cases conclusive and binding on the bank ... but each case must be judged on its own particular facts, although the customer starts with the advantage that prima facie it is an admission by the bank in his favour, which cannot in some cases be refuted.

EVIDENCE AGAINST THE CUSTOMER

[3.48] Although it was for some time hoped that some duty to examine the statement might be imposed upon the customer, it now seems that that hope is dead. It is hard to imagine circumstances in which the customer will be bound, or indeed, even seriously prejudiced, by the entries in the statement.

It is possible that Australian banks could resort to the American practice of doing business on the basis of written terms and conditions. It is common in such agreements for there to be a duty imposed on the customer to inspect the statement. In the event of a failure to make an objection the statement becomes, in effect, an account stated. A common form for these clauses is the so-called 'conclusive evidence' clause which attempts to make the statement, in the absence of prompt objection by the customer, conclusive evidence of the state of accounts between the customer and the bank.

At least in a commercial context, such clauses are not void as offending against public policy: *Dobbs v National Bank of Australasia Ltd* (1935) 53 CLR 643. However, in light of the Privy Council decision in *Tai Hing Cotton Mill Ltd v Liu Chong Hing Bank Ltd* [1986] AC 80, such a clause will not be effective unless it is sheeted home to the customer the intended importance of the clause (and the procedure required by the clause) and that the clauses are intended to have the effect of being conclusive evidence clauses.

STOPPING THE ACCOUNT

[3.49] English cases often talk of 'closing the account', but that expression is misleading. It does not mean the termination of the banker-customer relationship, but a situation where it becomes necessary for the banker to refuse to allow any further withdrawals from the account. This includes the need for refusing to meet any cheques drawn on the account even though in all other respects the cheque is one which should be met. In some cases, the banker should even refuse to permit any further deposits into the account. The present section will follow Weaver and Craigie in referring to the situation as 'stopping the account'. However, the reader should be aware that the terminology is not fixed.

DEATH

[3.50]   The duty and authority to pay the customer's cheques are terminated by notice of his or her death: Cheques and Payment Orders Act 1986 s 90(1)(c). While this does not have the uncertainty associated with mental incapacity, it is subject to some exceptions in s 90(2), namely that the bank may pay cheques which are presented for payment within 10 days of the receipt of notice of the customer's death. Previously, payees of outstanding cheques were required to prove in the deceased estate, a process which can take considerable time. The estate is protected, since the cheque may be countermanded by a person who claims that he or she is, or will be, entitled to administer the estate or a beneficiary of the estate: s 90(2)(b).

This rule has no bearing on the situation where the deceased is not a customer but only a signatory to an account, for example, a company director. However, it would be very prudent for the banker to consider taking new authorities from the customer.

The death of one of the parties to a joint account has been dealt with earlier (see [3.7]) except in one respect. If the account is overdrawn, then the banker should not permit further operation by the survivors, since the operation of the rule in *Clayton's case* would mean that cheques paid after the date of the death would be fresh advances for which the estate of the deceased would not be liable and any deposits would go to paying off the earlier advances, thereby having the effect of reducing the liability of the estate. The same caveat applies also to an overdrawn partnership account when one of the partners dies.

The only person who is entitled to demand payment of the account balance of the deceased customer is the executor of the estate or the administrator, as the case may be. In theory, the executor is entitled to the balance immediately, since the powers of an executor, unlike those of an administrator, arise immediately on the death of the testator: see [2.71]. But it is clear that a banker cannot safely part with the balance of an account merely because someone comes forward claiming to be the executor or the administrator. As long ago as *Tarn v Commercial Banking Co of Sydney* (1884) 12 QBD 294 it was said that 'Bankers are in a peculiar position and when asked to hand over large sums of money to persons claiming as executors of deceased customers, they are justified in requiring to be made safe by production of probate'.

BANKRUPTCY AND WINDING UP

[3.51]   The law of bankruptcy is that part of the law which provides for the orderly division of assets among the creditors of individuals under certain circumstances. The law of bankruptcy is wholly a creation of statute, the current governing statute in Australia being the Bankruptcy Act 1966 (Cth). (References to 'the Act' and to sections not otherwise identified are, in paragraphs [3.51] to [3.70] of this chapter, to the Bankruptcy Act.)

The early law of bankruptcy was directed at the punishment and imprisonment of defaulting debtors. Contrary to popular opinion, imprisonment was not one of the early methods for dealing with debtors, but rather was originally a means to 'encourage' the debtor to use assets which were not available to the creditor by means of the existing legal processes: A N Lewis, *Australian Bankruptcy Law*, 10th ed, Law Book Co, Sydney, 1994. Once introduced, imprisonment for debtors who would not pay their debts was quickly extended to imprisonment of those who could not pay their debts. There is no doubt that severe injustices occurred.

Even where there were legal processes available to the creditor to attach the assets of the debtor, there was no means for ensuring that the creditors were treated fairly inter se. A single creditor who was better informed or simply quicker off the mark could attach all available assets of the debtor, thereby satisfying his or her own debt and leaving nothing for the other creditors.

Modern bankruptcy law attempts to balance the requirements of several competing policies. First is the desire to see that the creditors are treated equally among themselves. Second, there is a public interest in relieving the debtor from a hopeless financial position and returning that person to a productive life. Third, the legislation retains the policy that fraudulent or dishonest debtors should be punished.

'Bankruptcy' is a term which is often used carelessly. A person may only be made a bankrupt by the completion of the strict process of law. It is a very serious matter to declare that a person is a bankrupt and the banker should take care not to claim that a person is such unless very sure that the process has been completed. Failure to exercise care may result in quite large damages for defamation: see [5.74].

'Insolvency', on the other hand, describes a state of affairs in which the debtor is unable to pay his or her debts as they fall due from his or her own money. There has been a gloss on the language, for it has been said that 'own money' in this context does not limit consideration to the resources immediately available but extends to those funds which the debtor might realise if given a reasonable opportunity to liquidate some assets: *Sandell v Porter* (1966) 115 CLR 666.

DEBTOR'S/CREDITOR'S PETITIONS

[3.52]   All bankruptcy proceedings begin with the presentation of a bankruptcy petition. The petition may be presented by the debtor personally (a debtor's petition) or it may be presented by a creditor or several creditors acting jointly (a creditor's petition). Because of the severe consequences of a bankruptcy, the right of a creditor to present a petition is limited by a requirement that certain conditions be fulfilled prior to the presentation.

[3.53]　Section 44 of the Act defines the conditions which are prerequisite to the filing of a creditor's petition. They are:

- The debt owing to the petitioning creditor, or the aggregate debt owing to the petitioners, must be at least $1000 in liquidated sums. This debt must be owing at the time when the petition is filed.

- The debtor must have committed an act of bankruptcy (as defined by s 40) within a period of six months immediately before the petition is filed.

- The debtor must have had some connection with Australia at the time of the commission of the act of bankruptcy. The necessary connections are of a residential and/or business nature: see s 43.

The first of these conditions is intended to prevent the filing of nuisance petitions by small creditors. Unfortunately, the amount has failed to be changed to take account of inflation and so is now entirely too small. The result is that the filing or threat of filing of a bankruptcy petition is, improperly, often used as a powerful device for the collection of debts.

[3.54]　The acts of bankruptcy are defined in s 40 of the Act. These are intended to be acts whereby it may be objectively determined that the debtor is in fact insolvent, or to indicate certain acts or transactions which evidence a desire to prejudice some or all of the debtor's creditors. So, for example, departing or attempting to depart from Australia with an intention to defeat or delay creditors is an act of bankruptcy, as is any disposition of property which would, if the debtor became bankrupt, be void against the trustee: ss 40(1)(c)(i) and 40(1)(b)(i).

These acts of bankruptcy might be very difficult to prove without full access to the debtor's private records. However, there is one act of bankruptcy which is very easy to prove, namely, failure to comply with a bankruptcy notice: s 40(1)(g). The bankruptcy notice is a formal document which demands that the debtor pay a judgment debt or as much of it as remains unpaid. The notice must be in the prescribed form and must state the consequences of non-compliance: s 41. The vast majority of creditor's petitions are based on this act of bankruptcy.

Following the presentation of a creditor's petition, a date is set for the hearing of the petition and, provided the court is satisfied that the basic conditions which entitle the creditor to petition are satisfied, will declare the debtor bankrupt. It is at this point and not before that the debtor becomes a bankrupt.

EFFECT OF BANKRUPTCY

[3.55]　Upon being adjudicated a bankrupt, the consequences for the debtor and all creditors is dramatic. Subject to a few minor exceptions, all of the debtor's property vests immediately in another person who has agreed to act as the registered trustee or, if there is no such person, in the person known as the Official Trustee. Furthermore, it is not just the property which is owned at the time of the adjudication, but includes any property acquired by the debtor on or after the date of the bankruptcy and before discharge: s 58(I).

The trustee also acquires all rights and powers to take proceedings with regard to any of the bankrupt's property, again dating from the 'commencement' of the bankruptcy.

DOCTRINE OF RELATION BACK

[3.56]   The 'commencement' of the bankruptcy is at a time which precedes the time of adjudication and may even precede the act of bankruptcy which gave the creditor the right to file a creditor's petition. The concept of the 'commencement' effectively gives a retrospective effect to the bankruptcy. Since such a retrospective effect is unusual in legal proceedings, it is worthwhile to pause for a moment to consider the reasons for its necessity in bankruptcy proceedings.

Long before a debtor becomes bankrupt, he or she will be aware that their financial position is difficult at best and hopeless at worst. If the trustee could only take the property which was available at the time of the adjudication, then the debtor would have the opportunity to plan for the event and take steps to safeguard some or all of his or her assets. This might be done, for example, by transferring assets to relatives or to trusted friends. But even if there is no attempt to alienate property, the natural course of business is for the debtor to pay the most pressing of the creditors. The result would be that some creditors would receive full satisfaction while others would receive nothing, a situation which is one that modern bankruptcy law was intended to prevent.

In order to facilitate the intent of the legislation, the basic principle is that all property vests in the trustee from the time of the earliest act of bankruptcy within a period of time. Consequently, any dealing by the debtor after that time is prima facie invalid, for the property does not belong to the debtor, but rather to the trustee. Similarly, any money which is paid to the debtor does not discharge the obligation for which it is paid, for it is paid to the wrong person; it should be paid to the trustee.

[3.57]   The problem with this scheme is that no one knows that the position has changed. Indeed, if no creditor takes advantage of the act of bankruptcy by filing a creditor's petition within the specified period, then the act of bankruptcy 'lapses' and all dealings with the debtor are perfectly valid. Because of this 'conditional' effect, there must be some provisions which save some of the normal transactions even when the debtor is later adjudicated a bankrupt.

In summary, the prima facie position is that transactions with the debtor which occurred after the commencement of the bankruptcy are void. Some, indeed many, may be shown to be valid, but it is on the person wishing to show that the transaction is valid to establish that the transaction falls within one of the protected categories. As we shall see, bankers are given some special consideration by the legislation.

[3.58]   The retrospective effect of the adjudication is called the doctrine of relation back. It is found in ss 115 and 116 of the Act. The commencement of the bankruptcy is calculated as follows:

- if the debtor has committed only one act of bankruptcy, then that must be the one which formed the basis for the creditor's petition. The bankruptcy commences at the time of that act;

- if the debtor has committed more than one act of bankruptcy, then the bankruptcy commences at the time of the first act which occurred within a period of six months prior to the filing of the creditor's petition.

It is important to realise that even though most creditor's petitions are based on the failure to comply with a bankruptcy notice, the other acts of bankruptcy mentioned in s 40 are very important, for they allow the commencement to be pushed back in time, possibly allowing the trustee to increase substantially the amount which is available for distribution to creditors generally.

EXCEPTIONS TO THE RELATION BACK DOCTRINE

[3.59]   During the six month period which precedes the filing of a creditor's petition, all transactions by the bankrupt are subject to be overturned. A banker is in the same position as anyone else who has had dealings with the debtor during this period, but the nature of the banker-customer contract makes the banker even more exposed, for in theory, all cheques written by the debtor which have been paid by the banker might have been paid improperly.

It is clearly intolerable that all such transactions should be overturned and the Act makes provisions for saving transactions in s 123. Section 123 deals with transactions which are concluded before the date of the bankruptcy. It is expressly made subject to the sections which deal with the giving of preferences. However, as long as the transaction does not fall into one of the preference categories, it will be safe from the trustee provided that the transaction took place before the date of the sequestration order, the person dealing with the debtor had no notice of the presentation of a petition against the debtor and the transaction was in good faith and in the ordinary course of business: ss 123(1) and 123(2). Merely having notice of an act of bankruptcy does not preclude reliance on the saving provisions: s 123(3).

Transactions which fall within the scope of s 123 are payments made by the debtor to any creditor, conveyances, transfers or assignments for valuable consideration, contracts or other transactions for valuable consideration and, importantly for the banker, any transaction to the extent of a concurrent advance made by an existing creditor.

Certain transactions made under or in pursuance of a maintenance agreement or maintenance order are also protected, but these are of relatively little interest to the banker.

The section probably does not protect the banker who pays a cheque of the person who later becomes a bankrupt. It is very unlikely that the banker could be considered as the agent of the debtor who is making a payment to the creditor: see [3.61] below. On the other hand, it is clear that a payment by the customer to the banker by way of a reduction of an overdraft would be protected by the section.

[3.60] The way in which the section may be used by the banker is illustrated by *Re Keever (A Bankrupt); Ex parte Trustee of Property of Bankrupt v Midland Bank Ltd* [1967] Ch 182. K had an account with the defendant bank which was overdrawn. After she had committed an act of bankruptcy, she received a cheque for an amount which was in excess of the overdraft. She paid the cheque into her account for collection. The cheque cleared on the day when K was adjudicated a bankrupt. The trustee in bankruptcy claimed the proceeds. The bank argued that it had a lien on the cheque on the day when it was paid in and that at that time the bank had no notice of the act of bankruptcy. The bank was held entitled to succeed.

[3.61] Section 124 is even more important to the banker. A payment of money or a delivery of property prior to the date of bankruptcy to, or in accordance with the order or direction of the debtor is a good discharge to the person paying the money or delivering the property provided the payment or delivery was in good faith and in the ordinary course of business. If the payment or delivery is after the date of bankruptcy, then there is an additional requirement that the payment or delivery be made without negligence.

The section is of the utmost importance to bankers, for in its absence, a banker who paid a cheque of a person who became bankrupt would be unable to debit the account if the payment was made after the commencement of the bankruptcy. An example of this is *Re Hasler* (1974) 23 FLR 139. After the date of becoming bankrupt, the debtor wrote two cheques which were paid upon presentation by the bank. The Official Receiver applied for an order that the bank pay the sum of the cheques to the Receiver. The bank pleaded that the transaction was saved by s 124.

The main issue in the case was whether the bank had paid without negligence. The evidence showed that branch managers were instructed to read bankruptcy information in a number of publications and, in particular, supplied branch managers with a particular publication which contained information that a Mr Hasler had a creditor's petition presented and later was adjudicated a bankrupt. The address given in the publication was different from the address which had been given to the bank.

The court held that the bank was liable for the amount. Of particular interest for bankers is that the approach taken by the court is that s 124 is analogous to the protective provisions of the Cheques and Payment Order Act

1986: see [7.69]. In order to show that a payment is 'without negligence', it must be shown that due regard was given to the interests of the general body of creditors.

[3.62] Section 125 imposes a duty on bankers. Where a bank finds that one of its customers is an undischarged bankrupt it must inform the trustee in writing. There must be no further payments out of the account except under the written instructions of the trustee or a court order: s 125(1). The prohibition on payments only applies if the bank has received an instruction from the trustee or a court order within one month. After that time the banker is entitled to act without regard to any claim or right the trustee may have in respect of the account: s 125(2).

AFTER-ACQUIRED PROPERTY

[3.63] It is not only the property held by the debtor at the commencement of the bankruptcy which vests in the trustee, but also, subject to certain exceptions, any property which is acquired by the bankrupt before discharge: s 58(1)(b). One of the consequences of this is that dealings by the debtor with the property are prima facie invalid. However, it is clearly necessary for the debtor to continue living and working and the Act makes provisions for saving certain transactions provided that they are completed prior to an active intervention by the trustee.

This is done in s 126. A transaction by a bankrupt with a person dealing with him or her in good faith and for valuable consideration, which relates to after-acquired property, will be protected provided that it is completed before any intervention by the trustee.

Perhaps because it is expected that the bankrupt will continue a fruitful relationship with a banker, the banker is given special treatment in s 126(2). The section deems certain transactions to be for value, namely, the receipt of any money, security, or negotiable instrument from, or in accordance with the order or direction of, a bankrupt by his or her banker, and any payment or delivery of a security or negotiable instrument made to, or in accordance with the order or direction of, a bankrupt by his or her banker.

It must be emphasised that there is nothing necessarily improper in an undischarged bankrupt carrying on a current account. One of the exceptions to the rule that the property vests in the trustee is that the bankrupts are entitled to use personal earnings for their own benefit.

VOIDABLE PREFERENCES

[3.64] The trustee has a right to recover assets which were used by the debtor to give a preference to one or more creditors. This is in keeping with the policy of bankruptcy law to treat all creditors fairly inter se. Section 122 applies to all transactions which occurred within six months before presentation of the petition which led to the debtor being adjudicated a bankrupt and to all transactions which occurred between the presentation of the petition and the date of bankruptcy.

If, at the time of the transaction, the debtor was insolvent and the effect of the transaction is to have the effect of giving the creditor a preference, priority or advantage over other creditors, then the trustee may recover the payment or the property from the creditor who has received a preference: s 122(1). However, the preferred creditor has a defence if it can be shown that the transaction was in good faith, for valuable consideration and in the ordinary course of business: s 122(2).

Transactions include a conveyance or transfer of property, the creation of a charge on property, a payment or an incurring of an obligation in favour of a creditor: s 122(1). Since the payment, etc, must be in favour of a creditor, there is no scope for the trustee to attack the giving of mortgages or other securities in exchange for a new loan.

[3.65]   The transaction need only have the effect of giving a preference. It is quite immaterial what was in the mind of either the debtor or the creditor: *Re Stevens* (1929) 1 ABC 90. Furthermore, it does not matter if the effect of the payment might be to forestall bankruptcy and hence possibly be of benefit to all creditors.

The transaction cannot have the effect of giving a preference, priority or advantage over other creditors unless the creditor's net position is improved. Thus, where a creditor already had an equitable mortgage, the execution of a legal mortgage did not amount to a preference: *Re Weiss; Ex parte White v John Vicars & Co Ltd* [1970] ALR 654. The result would be different if the new security gave the creditor greater rights, as for example, when a new bill of sale replaces one which would be void for want of registration: *Re Simpson* (1935) 8 ABC 234. Similarly, if a mortgage or other security is given partially in respect of existing indebtedness and partly to secure new loans, then it can only be avoided in so far as it relates to the existing indebtedness: *Burns v Stapleton* (1959) 102 CLR 97.

There is a problem of determining whether the payment amounts to a preference when there is a running account between the parties. The High Court has indicated that if a payment only forms a part of some wider ongoing set of transactions, then the trustee may recover only the amount by which the debit balance is reduced during the relevant period: *Richardson v Commercial Banking Co of Sydney* (1952) 85 CLR 110. It may be difficult in practice to know whether a particular payment is to be isolated or treated as part of a larger group: see, for example, *Queensland Bacon Pty Ltd v Rees* (1967) 115 CLR 266.

[3.66]   The High Court has considered and extended the 'running account' defence in *Airservices Australia v Ferrier* (1995–96) 185 CLR 483. Airservices Australia had been ordered by the Full Court of the Federal Court to repay some $10 million to the liquidator of Compass Airlines as voidable preferences. It came to this conclusion on the basis that the payments were each specifically appropriated to pay a specific overdue debt owed by Compass. The High Court took a broader view, holding that, although the issue of preference is to be decided objectively for each payment, that does not mean that the purpose of the debtor when making the payment is insignificant. Where the payment is part of a 'wider transaction' the payment will probably not be a preference, but where the sole purpose is to discharge permanently an existing debt, the payment will be a preference. The approach is to examine the business purpose and context of the payment under challenge.

In this approach, the 'running account' is merely bookkeeping evidence of the business purpose and context of the payments. If the relationship between the parties contemplates further debits and credits, then the way in which particular payments are appropriated by either the creditor or the debtor is not relevant. The point is illustrated by the High Court's decision that the final payment was a preference since the demand by Airservices was 'looking backwards rather than forwards; looking to the partial payment of the old debt rather than the provision of continuing services'. Note that the recovery of such payments in the event of a company winding up is now governed by s 588FA of the Corporations Law: see [3.71]ff.

[3.67]   Section 122 combines with the rule in *Clayton's case* to place bankers in a very privileged position. A security taken by a banker on Day 1 will, of course, only secure advances made on or after that day. But if the debt is by way of overdraft, then continued operation of the account will have, by virtue of the rule in *Clayton's case*, the effect of reducing the prior debt with the result that the debt is gradually converted from an unsecured to a secured debt. That this is indeed the effect was confirmed in *Re Yeovil Glove Co Ltd* [1965] Ch 148; but see [10.85].

Even if the transaction is prima facie voidable under s 122(1), the creditor may still have a defence if he or she received the payment or property in good faith, for valuable consideration and in the ordinary course of business: s 122(2).

'Good faith' must be proved by the creditor, but s 122(4)(c) provides that the creditor is deemed not to have acted in good faith if it can be concluded that he or she knew or had reason to suspect that the debtor was insolvent and that the effect of the transaction was to give the creditor a preference. Although the section is framed as one which establishes when the creditor is not in good faith, a creditor who shows that the circumstances do not lead to these conclusions will ordinarily succeed: *Re Beatty* [1965] ALR 291. Mere knowledge that the debtor has had cheques dishonoured is not a circumstance that necessarily disentitles the creditor from succeeding: *Queensland Bacon Pty Ltd v Rees* (1967) 115 CLR 266.

The court in *Queensland Bacon* also observed, rather confusingly, that suspicion that the debtor might be insolvent is not the same as suspicion that the debtor is insolvent: at 303.

It is probably more difficult for a bank to prove 'good faith' when the debtor is a customer since it will usually be the case that the banker has considerable knowledge of the customer's financial affairs. So, for example, in

Rees v Bank of New South Wales (1964) 111 CLR 210 the customer agreed that all of its business takings should be deposited to its overdrawn account. The bank knew that the customer was extended and that it could only meet cheques drawn in favour of trade creditors from the business takings and that, even then, the cheques were not always met. It was not conclusive that the bank believed that the stocks of the company exceeded its liabilities for that was only one of the criteria which was relevant. The bank was found to be not in 'good faith' within the meaning of s 122.

[3.68] The High Court in *National Australia Bank Ltd v KDS Construction Services Pty Ltd (in liq)* (1987) 62 ALJR 63 considered the question of voidable preferences in respect of a cheque deposited for collection. A cheque for about $102,000 was deposited by the company for collection for its No 1 account on 3 September. At the time, the account of the company was in overdraft in the sum of about $62,000, although withdrawals during the day left the approximate net credit at only $33,000. The next day, a cheque for $40,000 was drawn on the account in favour of two of the directors of the company and the proceeds of this cheque were deposited in the 'suspense account' of the manager. Nearly all of that amount was then withdrawn on the same day and credited to various of the company's accounts.

The liquidator of the company claimed the amount of the $102,000 was a payment to the bank which was a preference. The High Court held that the deposit of the cheque in those circumstances was not a payment, the bank being merely an agent for collection: see [7.67]. On the other hand, the bank did have a lien on the cheque: see [7.62]. Consequently, when the bank did receive the payment of the sum from the paying bank, that sum was in discharge of an existing security and so could not be a preference.

The effect of the decision is artificial. There is no doubt that had the company presented the cheque directly to the paying bank and then handed the proceeds to the appellant bank there would have been a preference within the meaning of s 122. Why should the result be different merely because the appellant acted as the agent for collection? Further, if the reasoning of the High Court is correct, then why isn't the deposit of the cheque which creates the lien a charge on property or an obligation incurred within the meaning of s 122?

FRAUDULENT DISPOSITIONS

[3.69] There is one category of transaction which is voidable no matter when it occurs. Section 121(1) provides that every alienation of property which is made with an intent to defraud creditors is voidable at the instance of any person who is thereby prejudiced.

Once again, the potential harshness of the section is tempered by s 122(2), which provides that nothing in s 122(1) affects the title of a person who has acquired an interest in the property in good faith and for valuable consideration. The section does not require that the interest be acquired from the debtor, so that if the debtor gives the goods to X who then sells them to Y, Y's title may not be impeached, provided that Y took in good faith.

SET-OFF AND MUTUAL DEBTS

[3.70]   The other section which is of special importance to bankers is s 86 which makes it clear that the banker's right of combination of accounts survives the customer's bankruptcy, provided that the banker does not extend further credit to the bankrupt after receiving notice of an act of bankruptcy. The House of Lords held that a similar section in the UK Bankruptcy Act 1914 was mandatory in the sense that it was not possible to 'contract out' of the provision.

WINDING UP

[3.71]   The winding up of a company is similar to the bankruptcy of an individual, but there are some differences which are of concern to a banker. First, the property of the company does not automatically vest in a trustee as in the case of an individual. The winding up of the company begins at the time of the presentation of a winding-up petition and the disposition of the property of the company is governed by the Corporations Law. In most respects, the disposition of property is under restrictions similar to those suffered by an individual upon the commencement of bankruptcy. In particular, Pt 5.7B, Div 2 of the Corporations Law makes certain 'antecedent transactions' voidable on the application of the liquidator if that application is made to the court within the times specified in s 588FE. A transaction is 'antecedent' if it is made prior to the 'relation-back day', usually the day on which the application for winding up is filed: s 9. Section 588FF empowers the court to make a variety of orders related to voidable antecedent transactions, and s 588FG provides the creditor with a number of defences which may save, or partly save, a transaction which would otherwise be impugned.

[3.72]   There are three main classes of voidable antecedent transactions. An 'unfair preference' is one which results in a creditor receiving more than the creditor would receive if forced to prove for the debt during the winding up: s 588FA(1). Where the transaction is one that forms part of a continuing business relationship, all transactions in the series may be taken into account and only the net position considered for the purposes of avoiding the transaction: s 588FA(1).

The second class of voidable antecedent transaction is the 'uncommercial transaction' described by s 588FB. These transactions are similar in all respects to those 'settlements' in bankruptcy which are made without valuable consideration. The third class is the 'unfair loan' which is a loan to the company where the interest or other charges are unreasonably high having regard to the commercial factors involved in the loan: s 588FD. (References to 'the Act' and to sections are, in the remaining paragraphs of this chapter, to the Corporations Law unless otherwise specified.)

[3.73]   Upon the commencement of a winding up, any disposition of the property of the company, other than one exempted by the Act, is void unless the court makes an order to the contrary, usually known as a validating order: s 468(1). Note that this section says 'void' and not 'voidable'. The position of the banker who allows the operation of a company's bank account after the commencement of the winding up has received attention in several cases, with somewhat inconsistent views.

[3.74]   The equivalent section of the old Act was considered in *Re Mal Bower's Macquarie Electrical Centre Pty Ltd* [1974] 1 NSWLR 254. The bank had paid cheques drawn by the company in favour of third parties and the issue was whether the bank could sustain a debit to the account for the amount of the cheques. Street CJ said (at 258):

> There is, in my view, great force in the bank's argument that the paying by a bank of a company's cheque, presented by a stranger, does not involve the bank in a disposition of the property of the company so as to disentitle the bank to debit the amount of the cheque to the company's account. The word 'disposition' connotes in my view both a disponor and a disponee. The section operates to render the disposition void so far as concerns the disponee. It does not operate to affect the agencies interposing between the company, as disponor, and the recipient of the property, as disponee ... The intermediary functions fulfilled by the bank in respect of paying cheques drawn by a company in favour of and presented on behalf of a third party do not implicate the bank in the consequences of the statutory avoidance prescribed by s 227.

[3.75]   On the other hand, the English Court of Appeal has taken a somewhat different view of the English equivalent. In *Re Gray's Inn Construction Co Ltd* [1980] 1 WLR 711 a payment by the company into its overdrawn account was held to be a disposition since it had the effect of discharging a part of the company's indebtedness to the bank.

The only safer course which may be followed by the banker is to stop all operations on the company's accounts following the presentation of the winding-up petition pending the obtaining of a validation order.

Winding up of a company differs from the bankruptcy of an individual in one final respect. At the termination of the winding up, the company ceases to exist.

RECEIVERS

[3.76]   A receiver is a person appointed either by the court or by a debenture-holder out of court. The second is by far the most common and is the only kind which will be considered in this section. Such a person derives his or her powers almost exclusively from the terms of the debenture. Receivers may be appointed by equity courts for a wide variety of purposes. We will be concerned here only with the appointment of company receivers, but many of the considerations are relevant in the broader context. Company receivers are regulated by the Corporations Law Pt 5.2.

The function of a receiver who is appointed by a debenture-holder is to exercise the powers given by the debenture to realise assets over which he or she has control in order to satisfy the debts owed to the secured creditors who were responsible for the appointment. The powers given may range from the mere power to sell the property over which the charge is given to, more commonly, wide powers of management of the business of the mortgagor company. In the older cases, it is only the first type which is known as a receiver, the other type being referred to as a receiver and manager or sometimes simply as a manager. In more modern cases, the term 'receiver' covers the field.

The appointment of a receiver is not a winding up: *Moss Steamship Co Ltd v Whinney* [1912] AC 254. The structure of the company remains intact and the directors remain in office with full powers and duties save that the disposition of the assets covered by the debenture and within the powers granted to the receiver is within the control of the receiver. In a modern debenture, the actual assets available to the directors following the appointment of a receiver will be virtually nil.

[3.77]   The debenture commonly contains a clause which provides that in performing his or her duties, the receiver shall be the agent of the company and that the company-mortgagor alone shall be responsible for all acts and defaults. Since the company has absolutely no say in the appointment of a receiver or of the acts performed by the receiver once appointed, the situation seems strange, but the effect of the clauses has been upheld with the result that there is no liability on the appointing mortgagee for acts or defaults of the receiver: *Gosling v Gaskell* [1896] 1 QB 669. Furthermore, as agent for the company, the receiver may dispose of assets of the company in the name of the company. Failure to include an express clause in the debenture will result in the receiver being deemed the agent of the appointing mortgagee: *Albert Del Fabbro Pty Ltd v Wilckens and Burnside Pty Ltd* [1971] SASR 121.

A company receiver is liable for debts incurred in the course of the receivership, possession or control for services rendered, goods purchased or property hired, leased, used or occupied: s 419. This liability exists, notwithstanding any agreement to the contrary (s 419(1)) and is without prejudice to any claim which the receiver may have to be indemnified by the company: s 419(1). Sections 432–4 describe the powers of a receiver, and s 424 permits the receiver to apply to the court for directions in relation to any matter arising in connection with the performance of his or her functions.

[3.78]   A winding-up order has consequences for the receiver. If the receiver is the agent of the company, the agency will cease, with the consequences that the receiver will no longer be able to make contracts or convey property in the name of the company: *Gosling v Gaskell* [1897] AC 575. In such a circumstance it appears that the receiver does not automatically revert to being an agent of the mortgagee but instead becomes and assumes the responsibilities of a principal: *Gosling v Gaskell* [1897] AC 575 at 581, 592. As a result, a receiver who purports to be making a contract without personal liability following a winding-up order will have no principal and cannot be held liable on the contract, but would be liable in damages for breach of warranty of authority. If, on the other hand, the receiver does not disclaim personal liability then he or she will be personally liable on the contract. Since the damages in either case are likely to be the same, it is clear that a receiver would be well advised to cease activities on the winding up or, alternatively, to obtain an indemnity from the mortgagee on whose behalf appointment was made.

GARNISHEE ORDERS

[3.79]   Garnishee orders allow a creditor to attach a debt which is owed to his or her own judgment debtor by a third party. Since every customer of a bank who has an account in credit is a creditor of the bank, it will be clear that bankers must be familiar with the consequences of garnishment proceedings. The usual form of garnishment proceedings is in two stages. A garnishee order nisi will be addressed to the third party debtor, the banker in the case we are concerned with, ordering the debtor to show cause why the amount owing by the debtor to the judgment debtor should not be made available for the purposes of satisfaction of the judgment debt. The order nisi is granted on the affidavit of the judgment creditor that he or she believes that there are moneys owing by the garnishee to the judgment debtor.

Provided that the garnishee does not show cause, the court will issue an order absolute which directs the garnishee to pay the judgment creditor directly rather than to pay the original debtor.

DEBT DUE AND OWING

[3.80]   A garnishee order nisi is expressed to attach debts owing or accruing due to the judgment debtor. The usual test for whether a debt is one which is owing is whether it is one for which the creditor could have immediately sued, whereas an accruing debt is a debt which is not yet actually payable but is represented by an existing obligation.

When the order is phrased in these terms, it may not be easy to know if the entire account should be frozen or only the amount of the judgment debt. This matter came before the House of Lords in *Rogers v Whiteley* [1892] AC 118. Whiteley ran a banking business and Rogers had an account there which was in credit some £6800. Rogers lost an action and became a judgment debtor for some £6000; the judgment creditor obtained a garnishee order nisi ordering that 'all debts owing or accruing due' to Rogers should be attached and the order was served on Whiteley. Meanwhile, Rogers had drawn a number of small cheques which totalled less than £800. The cheques were dishonoured and Rogers sued Whiteley for wrongful dishonour. The sole issue in the case was whether the order nisi attached the whole of the account, or only enough to cover the judgment debt. The House of Lords held that it was the entire balance that was attached. When the order nisi states the precise sum which is to be attached, the position is thought to be different: see Weaver and Craigie, op cit, para [6.390].

THE NEED FOR A DEMAND

[3.81] *Roger's* case clearly assumed that the relationship between the banker and customer was the ordinary debtor and creditor relationship. Following the decision of the English Court of Appeal in *Joachimson v Swiss Bank Corporation* [1921] 3 KB 110 doubts were cast upon the availability of garnishment procedures against current accounts. The argument was that Lord Atkin had made it clear beyond argument that the debt owing from a banker to the customer was not 'due and owing', but required a demand in order to become so. The case was not a garnishee case, but the court addressed the matter, arguing that a garnishee order nisi would itself amount to a demand sufficient to allow attachment. While that is a very practical solution, it is one which is singularly lacking in logic, a point observed by Atkin LJ (at 131).

[3.82] Most authors consider that current accounts have been the subject matter of garnishee proceedings for so long that it is extremely unlikely that the view of the majority in *Joachimson* would not be followed. However, in *Re ANZ Savings Bank Ltd; Mellas v Evriniadis* [1972] VR 690 the Victorian Full Court doubted that the proposition is correct. They observed that the dicta in *Joachimson* which held that the order nisi itself could be the demand necessary to make the debt 'due and owing' were, at the most, obiter because in the *Joachimson* case their Lordships were not dealing with garnishee proceedings. However, the court expressly left open the question since it was not then necessary to decide it.

Weerasooria criticises this decision (W S Weerasooria, *Banking Law and the Financial System in Australia*, 4th ed, Butterworths, Sydney, 1996, p 600) and argues that it failed to consider other authority. It would seem that regardless of the logic of the position, the better view is that current accounts are subject to garnishee proceedings.

SAVINGS ACCOUNTS

[3.83] Although the garnishee order nisi might serve as a substitute for the customer's demand when there is an attempt to garnish a current account, there has not been the same acceptance that the order can substitute for other conditions precedent which there might be on an account. The matter has been considered on several occasions with regard to savings accounts.

Savings accounts ordinarily require that a passbook must be presented together with a signed withdrawal slip before the customer is entitled to withdraw money from the account. In addition, some accounts have a requirement that a period of notice be given before withdrawal or before withdrawal of sums in excess of a certain amount. The question is whether the service of a garnishee order nisi may be treated as a substitute for these requirements.

[3.84]   After a series of false starts, it now seems clear that unless the terms and conditions of the deposit account are complied with concurrently and together with the service of the garnishee order nisi then the balance in the account cannot be attached. It has been so held by the Full Courts of three Australian states and also represents the position in England prior to legislative intervention: see *Bank of NSW Savings Bank Ltd (Garnishee) v Fremantle Auto Centre Pty Ltd (Judgment Creditor) and Poland (Judgment Debtor)* [1973] WAR 161; *Music Masters Pty Ltd v Minelle and the Bank of NSW Savings Bank Ltd* [1968] Qd R 326; *Re ANZ Savings Bank Ltd; Mellas v Evriniadis* [1972] VR 690; *Bagley v Winsome and National Provincial Bank Ltd* [1952] 2 QB 236.

[3.85]   The position is now different in New South Wales, the Northern Territory, Victoria, Western Australia, and in England. Although the legislation differs slightly in each of the jurisdictions, the thrust of each is that certain conditions are to be disregarded when determining whether an amount standing to the credit of the customer is attachable as being a debt 'due and owing': see, for example, (NSW) Supreme Court Rules Pt 46 r 10A. Matters to be disregarded include:

(1) a condition that a demand must be made before any money or share is withdrawn;

(2) a condition relating to the manner in which or the place at which any such demand is to be made;

(3) a condition that a passbook, receipt or other document must be produced before any money or share is withdrawn; and

(4) a condition that notice is required before any money or share is withdrawn.

MONEY CREDITED AFTER SERVICE

[3.86]   Money which is deposited by the judgment debtor following the service of the order nisi increases the debt owed by the banker to the customer, but can it be said that such moneys were 'owing or accruing due'? The question was considered by an English court in *Heppenstall v Jackson* [1939] 1 KB 585. The bank had been served with a garnishee order nisi in respect of a customer's account. Money had been deposited into the account following this service and the issue in the case was whether these later deposits were attached by the order. The court reviewed the earlier cases and came to the conclusion that it was clear that a garnishee order attaches only those debts which exist at the time that the order is made and served. Consequently, the general rule is that money deposited into the account after the service of the order is not attached. The general rule has been changed by legislation in some jurisdictions: see, for example, Federal Court Rules (Cth) O37 r 7(2); Supreme Court Rules (NT) r 71.02(b); Rules of the Supreme Court (Vic) Ch I r 71.02(b), 71.03(b).

Unfortunately, the case does not make clear the fate of money which might be deposited after the order is made but before it is served or the status of money which might be paid out by the bank between the time of making and service of the order. Perhaps some guidance may be taken from *Bank of NSW v Barlex Investments Pty Ltd* (1964) 64 SR(NSW) 274. The issue concerned the fate of a cheque for some £400 which had been deposited prior to the making of the garnishee order nisi, but which had remained uncleared at that time. There was a credit for the amount in the customer's account, but the deposit had been accepted with the customary condition that uncleared effects could not be drawn upon. The court held that the sum, being uncleared funds, was not part of the debt owed by the bank at the time when the order was made and so was not attached by it: but cf *Jones & Co v Coventry* [1909] 2 KB 1029 and *Universal Guarantee Pty Ltd v Derefink* [1958] VR 51.

MULTIPLE ACCOUNTS

[3.87]   When there is an overdraft account and a current account in credit, it appears to be ordinary banking practice for the banker to combine the accounts and to treat as attached only the surplus balance if any. It appears that this practice is followed irrespective of any agreement with the customer concerning notice. This is probably acceptable, but the banker would be advised to apply for a discharge or variation of the order nisi before taking such a course of action.

Weaver and Craigie consider the position where one of the accounts is a fixed loan account: Weaver and Craigie, op cit, para [6.480]. While there appears to be no definitive authority on the matter, those authors suggest that the matter is probably governed by the terms of the fixed loan agreement which related to the banker's right to combine. Since most lending agreements give the bank a right to combine accounts when an order nisi is served, the situation is similar to that of an overdrawn current account. Again, the safe course is to apply to the court for a discharge or variation of the order nisi.

ACCOUNTS IN WHICH THIRD PARTIES HAVE AN INTEREST

[3.88]   The money in the account must belong to the judgment debtor in order to be attachable. Since the judgment creditor takes subject to all equitable interests, it is not sufficient that the account be in the name of the judgment debtor. So, for example, if the money is held in trust, or if there has been a valid assignment of the account to some other party, even if the assignment is equitable only, then the account is not attachable by the garnishment procedure. As an example, in *Harrods Ltd v Tester* [1937] 2 All ER 236 the account of a married woman was garnished. Her husband brought evidence to the effect that he had supplied all of the money in the account and that the wife only signed cheques with her husband's consent. It was held that there was indeed a resulting trust in the husband's favour and the account could not be attached by the wife's creditors even though it stood in her name.

Following on from the same principle, it seems that a joint account cannot be attached in respect of a debt owed by one only of the account holders. In *Hirschorn v Evans; Barclays Bank Ltd, Garnishee* [1938] 2 KB 801; [1938] 3 All ER 491 the Court of Appeal held that the joint account of a husband and wife was prima facie the property of both and that as a consequence it was not available for attachment in respect of the husband's debt. On the same principle, the order nisi will be discharged when the account is a partnership account and the debt is that of one only of the partners: see *Hoon v Maloff (Jarvis Construction Co Ltd, Garnishee)* (1964) 42 DLR (2d) 770.

[3.89]   A factual situation which is, in a sense, the opposite of *Hirschorn's* case occurs when the account is in the name of one or several, but not all, joint debtors. In *Colburt (D J) & Sons Pty Ltd v Ansen; Commercial Banking Co of Sydney Ltd (Garnishee)* [1966] 2 NSWR 289 a judgment was obtained against four debtors by C. The debtors were trading under the name CCS. C then took out a garnishee order and served it on the bank where an account was kept under the name CCS, but the customers of the bank under that name were only two of the four judgment debtors. The bank objected to the garnishee order on the basis that it did not attach funds held by it. The Court of Appeal held that in the case of joint and several judgment debtors, the full amount of the debt is recoverable against any one or more of them and so the garnishee order operated to attach a fund held on behalf of only two of them.

CHAPTER 4

DUTIES OF THE BANKER

[4.1] The contract between the banker and the customer imposes a number of duties upon the banker, the most important of which is the duty to pay cheques (see [5.40]) and the duty of secrecy. In addition, the law imposes certain duties on the banker when the banker undertakes to provide additional services which are not, strictly speaking, required of the banker. This chapter discusses the standards required of a banker who chooses to give a 'banker's reference', who chooses to offer financial advice to customers and the special duty of a banker who has knowledge of special circumstances which call for greater than usual care.

THE DUTY OF SECRECY

[4.2] One of the terms of the banker-customer contract is that the banker is under a duty of secrecy in respect, at least, of the transactions which go through the account and any of the securities taken by the banker. The leading case is *Tournier v National Provincial & Union Bank of England* [1924] 1 KB 461. The facts were that the plaintiff had banked with the defendant for some time. His account became overdrawn and he agreed with the branch manager to repay the overdraft by weekly instalments of £1. His address was given as that of a firm with which he was about to enter employment.

Unfortunately, he failed to maintain the weekly payments. The manager telephoned the employer, ostensibly to obtain the home address of the plaintiff, but in the course of the conversation the manager informed the employer of the reason for attempting to contact the plaintiff. Just for good measure, he added that the bank suspected the plaintiff of gambling, since several cheques had named a bookmaker as payee.

It was alleged that as a result of this information the employer refused to renew the employment. The plaintiff claimed damages from the bank for breach of contract. He succeeded, the court holding that there was the duty of confidentiality mentioned above. Several members of the court suggested that the duty went further. For example, Lord Atkin said (at 485):

I further think that the obligation extends to information obtained from other sources than the customer's actual account, if the occasion upon which the information was obtained arose out of the banking relations of the bank and its customers — for example, with a view to assisting the bank in conducting the customer's business, or in coming to decisions as to its treatment of its customers.

[4.3] The duty of secrecy is not, of course, absolute. Bankes LJ attempted to define the major exceptions in *Tournier's* case. He said (at 473):

> There appears to be no authority on the point. On principle I think that the qualifications can be classified under four heads: (a) where disclosure is under compulsion by law; (b) where there is a duty to the public to disclose; (c) where the interests of the bank require disclosure; (d) where the disclosure is made by the express or implied consent of the customer.

These 'qualifications' to the duty of secrecy are not as clear cut as they may first appear. There are numerous factual situations which place the banker in the insidious position of being forced to choose between the contractual duty of secrecy which is owed to the customer and some other legal or moral duty which requires disclosure of the customer's affairs. The following discussion outlines the general principles.

For these purposes it has been held that disclosure to a company which is part of a group to which the bank belongs is a breach of the duty of confidentiality: see *Bank of Tokyo Ltd v Karoon* [1987] AC 45; *Bhogal v Punjab National Bank* [1988] 2 All ER 296. If, however, the account is one which is governed by the Code of Banking Practice, then a bank may disclose certain information to a 'Related Entity'. In all circumstances the bank may disclose information necessary to enable an assessment to be made of the total liabilities (present and prospective) of the customer to the bank and the Related Entity: Code of Banking Practice s 12.2(a). Provided the customer does not instruct the bank otherwise, the bank may provide any information at all to a Related Entity which provides financial services which are related or ancillary to those provided by the bank: Code of Banking Practice s 12.2(b).

DISCLOSURE UNDER COMPULSION BY LAW

[4.4] There is no doubt that any contractual duty of confidentiality is overridden by the duty of both parties to submit to other legal requirements. There is little authority on the matter, but Lord Diplock made the point clearly and forcefully in *Parry-Jones v Law Society* [1969] 1 Ch 1 when he said (at 9):

> ... [the] duty of confidence is subject to, and overridden by, the duty of any party to that contract to comply with the law of the land. If it is the duty of such a party to a contract, whether at common law or under statute, to disclose in defined circumstances confidential information, then he must do so, and any express contract to the contrary would be illegal and void. For example, in the case of banker and customer, the duty of confidence is subject to the overriding duty of the banker at common law to disclose and answer questions as to his customer's affairs when he is asked to give evidence on them in the witness box in a court of law.

Stephen J made the same point in *Smorgon v FCT* (1976) 134 CLR 473.

At least where the order relates to a criminal prosecution, the bank has no duty to inform the customer that some order has been made which obliges the bank to disclose account information. Even less is there a general duty on the bank to resist the making of such an order: see *Barclays Bank plc (trading as Barclaycard) v Taylor* [1989] 3 All ER 563; *Citibank Ltd v Federal Commissioner of Taxation* (1988) 83 ALR 144 at 156. The court in *Taylor's* case indicated that there might be an exception to these rules if the bank knew something relevant which was not apparent on the face of the application.

It was thought that the same rules applied to civil cases, but a recent decision of the Privy Council has cast doubts on the rule. In *Robertson v Canadian Imperial Bank* [1995] 1 All ER 824 Robertson was sued in an action for debt. The bank provided photocopies of Robertson's statement in response to a subpoena. The bank attempted to contact Robertson but was unsuccessful. The Privy Council held that the bank had a duty to use its best endeavours to inform the customer of the receipt of the subpoena. On the facts of Robertson, the bank had complied with its obligation.

The Privy Council also suggested that there might be a duty to object to disclosure of 'irrelevant' parts of the document requested. Lord Nolan suggested that there might be such an obligation, but noted that the matter was not in dispute in *Robertson*.

Robertson's case places an onerous duty on bankers, one which will serve little practical purpose. The customer will always object to the disclosure of account information, for the subpoena would not otherwise be necessary. If there is some policy reason that the customer should be notified, then the obligation should be upon the person requesting the subpoena rather than the bank or, alternatively, subpoenas and similar orders for disclosure should be made subject to the customer being notified. The Privy Council's suggestion that there might be a duty to object to the disclosure of 'irrelevant' material is even more objectionable. The bank is in no position to evaluate what might or might not be 'relevant' to the purpose for which the documents are subpoenaed. There is good reason to argue that *Robertson's* case should not be followed in Australia.

There must be a compulsion. Not every demand which comes from a government department falls into the exception. There can be no doubt that the power to compel disclosures is more widely granted by various Acts than was previously the case, and a complete list of the circumstances in which there is a compulsion by law would soon be out of date. There are, however, several circumstances which are common and unlikely to change in the near future.

BANKERS' BOOKS

[4.5]   The obligation of a bank to abstain from disclosing information as to a customer's affairs is qualified by the authority of the court to order, for special cause, production of the books or the appearance of an officer of the bank. Since there are many legal proceedings where the bank accounts of the parties will be important evidence, the possibility arises that bankers could suffer considerable inconvenience in being ordered to produce books and to testify.

Each of the Australian jurisdictions except New South Wales has legislation which controls the production of bankers' books in legal proceedings. The provisions are all based on the Bankers' Books Evidence Act 1879 (UK): Evidence Act 1971 (ACT); Evidence Act 1993 (NT); Evidence Act 1977 (Qld); Evidence Act 1929 (SA); Evidence Act 1910 (Tas); Evidence Act 1906 (WA); Evidence Act 1958 (Vic). The Evidence Act 1995 (NSW) has no special provisions.

The clear object of the statutes is to provide an orderly method of producing certain evidence by means of copies of the books in certain legal proceedings and to save bankers from being compelled to attend in those same proceedings. The legislation does not alter the rules of admissibility of evidence so if the original document would be inadmissible then the entry in the bankers' book relating to the document is also inadmissible: *Arnott v Hayes* (1887) 36 Ch D 731 at 737 per Cotton LJ; *Hart v Minister for Lands* (1901) 1 SR (NSW) 133.

[4.6] If the business records of a bank are sought in proceedings where the banker is not a party, then no officer of the bank may be compelled to produce any bankers' book if the contents could be obtained under the relevant legislation. Further, in the absence of special circumstances, no officer of the bank can be compelled to appear as a witness to prove any matter that is recorded in a bankers' book. Typical of the provisions is s 49 of the (now repealed) Evidence Act 1898 (NSW):

> 49. (1) A banker, or officer of a bank, shall not, in any legal proceeding to which the bank is not a party, be compellable — (a) to produce any banker's book, the contents of which can be proved under this Part; or (b) to appear as a witness to prove the matters, transactions and accounts therein recorded, unless by order made for special cause.

[4.7] In place of the right to compel the production of the books and to compel witnesses, the statutes provide that copies of the entries in a bankers' book may be used in evidence. Further, any party to legal proceedings may apply to the court to be granted an inspection order which allows them to inspect and to take copies of entries in a bankers' book which relates to the matters in question in the proceedings.

A copy of an entry in a bankers' book which qualifies under the legislation is prima facie evidence of such an entry and of the matters, transactions, and accounts therein recorded. The requirements for qualification vary somewhat between the various jurisdictions. There are three essential requirements in New South Wales. First, that the book was at the time of making the entry one of the ordinary books of the bank. Second, that the entry was made in the ordinary course of business. Third, that the book from which the copy is taken is in the custody and control of the bank. These matters may be proved by an appropriate officer of the bank. Proof may be by either oral testimony or by affidavit.

Where an entry does qualify under the legislation it may then be necessary to prove that the copy in question has been compared with the original and is correct. Details of the method of proof of conformity vary between jurisdictions.

[4.8] In all jurisdictions the court has the power to order that one of the parties to a litigation may inspect and take copies of certain banking records. Again taking the repealed New South Wales Act as a prototype:

> 50. (1) On the application of any party to a legal proceeding, the Court or the Supreme Court may order that such party be at liberty to inspect and take copies of any entries in a banker's book relating to the matters in question in such proceeding. (2) An order under this section may be made either with or without summoning the bank or any other party, and shall be served on the bank two clear days before the same is to be obeyed, unless the Court or the Supreme Court otherwise directs.

This power to order inspection of bankers' books is discretionary, and it has been said that it should be exercised with caution: see comments by Bowen LJ in *Arnott v Hayes* (1887) 36 Ch D 731 at 738. It should never be made merely to facilitate a 'fishing expedition' where there are only suspicions concerning the operation of an account, and where an order is made it should be restricted to entries which can be shown to be relevant: *Arnott v Hayes* (1887) 36 Ch D 731. In order to protect the confidentiality of the customer, the order may be made subject to conditions restricting the use of the information disclosed: *Bankers Trust Co v Shapira* [1980] 3 All ER 353.

[4.9] The statutes do not limit the power of the court to make orders to inspect accounts only to accounts held by the parties to the litigation, but it is unusual to grant an order to inspect third party accounts. The equivalent section of an older New Zealand Act was considered in *James v Mabin (No 3)* [1929] NZLR 899, where Adams J was faced with a request to make an order under the Act which would allow the inspection of an account of a person who was not a party to the litigation. He refused, saying:

> the power [of the compelling section] should seldom if ever be exercised except where the account sought to be inspected is in form or substance really the account of a party to the litigation, or is kept on his behalf, so that the entries in it would be evidence against him at the trial ... Further, I think that on such an application the party whose account is to be inspected ought to be heard.

Of course, this restraint is unnecessary when the account is in reality that of one of the litigants even though held in the name of some other party: *Ironmonger & Co v Dyne* (1928) 44 TLR 579.

An order may be made ex parte under the statutes even if there is no notice given, but it is better if notice is served on the person whose account is to be inspected. So, for example, in *R v Marlborough St Metropolitan Magistrate; Ex parte Simpson* [1980] Crim LR 305, the accused was prosecuted for living on the earnings of a prostitute. The court held that an order for the inspection of the accused's bank account could be made ex parte, but that notice should ordinarily be given.

In some cases the court may require evidence of the bona fides of the applicant and of the materiality of the inspection: see *Arnott v Hayes* (1887) 36 Ch D 731.

[4.10] An example of the operation of the Acts is demonstrated by *Bankers Trust v Shapira* [1980] 1 WLR 1274. Two men presented to the plaintiff bank in New York two cheques purportedly drawn on the National Commercial Bank of Saudi Arabia and made payable to one of the men. The bank paid $1,000,000 and then, on their instructions credited more than $700,000 to accounts of the two men at the London branch of the Discount Bank (Overseas) Ltd, which was the third defendant. The cheques were forged and the Saudi bank refused to pay.

The plaintiff bank claimed against the Discount Bank asking for injunctions to prevent any dealings with the funds in the accounts of the Discount Bank: see Chapter 12 for a discussion of Mareva injunctions. They obtained the injunction and then sought an interlocutory order that the Discount Bank should disclose and permit the plaintiff bank to inspect and take copies of certain documents relating to the accounts of the two men.

At first instance, they failed on the basis of the confidential banker-customer relationship, particularly since the two men who appeared to be responsible for the fraud had not been served with notice of the motion. The Court of Appeal allowed the appeal, holding that an order was justified even at the interlocutory stages of an action where the plaintiff sought to trace funds which in equity belonged to them and of which there was strong evidence that they had been fraudulently deprived and where delay might result in the dissipation of the funds before the action came to trial. Walker LJ made the special point that the plaintiff should be bound to undertake that such information would be used only for the purposes of the action and not for any other purpose.

[4.11] There are circumstances where the court should refrain from making an order under the Acts. It may be that an inspection order should never be made if it includes documents held in an overseas branch of the bank. In *MacKinnon v Donaldson Lufkin & Jenrette Securities Corporation* [1986] 1 All ER 653 the plaintiff claimed that the defendant had engaged in international frauds. The plaintiff sought orders under s 7 of the Bankers' Books Evidence Act 1879 (UK) against the defendant's bank for documents held at the bank's New York office. These orders were obtained at the first instance and the bank sought to have them set aside on the grounds that the 'international jurisdiction' of the court was exceeded and that the sovereignty of the United States was infringed.

Hoffman J agreed with the bank, holding that in the case of a foreign bank the court should have particular regard to foreign sovereignty since documents held by a bank concern many others and the bank itself owes a duty of confidentiality under the law of the country where the documents are kept: see also *Arhill Pty Ltd v General Terminal Co Pty Ltd* (1990) 23 NSWLR 545 at 553–4.

[4.12]   The term 'bankers' books' covers all of the usual records used in the ordinary business of the bank. The legislative definition provides that the term includes ledgers, day books, cash books and account books. In *Barker v Wilson* [1980] 1 WLR 884 the court held that microfilm records kept by the bank were within the scope of the English statute, a conclusion also reached in *State Bank of South Australia v Heinrich* (1989) 53 SASR 256. It would seem that computer records would also be included at least when in the form of a computer printout: see *Griffiths v Australia and New Zealand Banking Group Ltd* (1990) 53 SASR 256.

Both Australian and New Zealand courts have held that the manager's diary is an ordinary book of the bank and an entry made therein is made in the usual and ordinary course of business: *Elsey v Commissioner of Taxation* (1969) 43 ALJR 415; *R v William Bacon & Co* [1969] NZLR 228; *R v Smart* [1983] 1 VR 265. Similarly, the following have all been held to be subject to the legislation: a page from an official's day book: *Re L G Batten Pty Ltd* [1962] QWN 2; forms completed by a customer when opening an account: *R v Wilson* [1988] VR 673. In *R v Daye* [1908] 2 KB 333 it was held that a sealed packet was a document even though it was given to the banker on terms that it should not be delivered up except with the consent of the depositor.

On the other hand, letters and correspondence contained in the bank's files are not bankers' books: *Tubby Trout Pty Ltd v Sailbay Pty Ltd* (1992) 113 ALR 748. It has also been held that ordinary pay-in slips are not 'bankers' books': *Lever v Maquire* [1928] VLR 262.

OTHER STATUTES COMPELLING DISCLOSURE

[4.13]   There are additional instances where the bank may be compelled to allow inspection and disclosure of the customer's affairs. Possibly the most important and common in practice is the power given to the taxation authorities and that given to various authorities under the Corporations Law.

The Commissioner of Taxation is given powers by the Income Tax Assessment Act 1936 which will allow an officer authorised by him or her to take extracts from, or copies of, certain records and documents. There must be a written authority specifying the information or records required, signed by the Commissioner. In a High Court challenge to the legislation, Stephen J made the observation that the duty of secrecy owed by the banker to the customer was contractual only: *Smorgon v FCT* (1976) 134 CLR 473. It was, consequently, subject to the ordinary law and could not be raised as a defence against an express power conferred by statute.

Similarly, the duty to produce documents under the Corporations Law is not subject to legal professional privilege: *Citibank v FCT* (1988) 83 ALR 144; *FCT v Citibank* (1989) 85 ALR 588. However, under the taxation statute in force at the time, there was no duty on the bank to assist tax officers to locate documents, to deliver them to other offices or to facilitate their inspection: *O'Reilly v Commissioners of the State Bank of Victoria* (1983) 153 CLR 1. Following this decision, the statute was amended to require banks to provide reasonable facilities and assistance: see Income Tax Assessment Act 1936 s 263.

[4.14]   In *ASC v Zarro* (1991) 6 ASCR 385 the bank was required by the ASC Act to produce certain specified documents which related to the affairs of a company under investigation. The bank resisted the demand, claiming that the statute related only to documents which on their face showed that they related to the affairs of the company. This argument was rejected by the Federal Court which noted that it would be completely impossible for the ASC to fulfil its obligations if it were required in every case to detail the basis of the asserted connection between the documents sought and the corporations which were the subject of the investigation. The court also noted once again that any contractual duty of confidentiality must yield to the statutory requirement of disclosure.

SECTION 52 TRADE PRACTICES ACT

[4.15]   One very important 'law of the land' in Australia is s 52 of the Trade Practices Act 1974 which imposes a prohibition on misleading and deceptive conduct. The problem is that under certain circumstances silence and/or non-disclosure may be 'misleading or deceptive' for the purposes of s 52: *Henjo Investments Pty Ltd v Collins Marrickville Pty Ltd* (1988) ATPR 40–850. In *Kimberly NZI Finance Ltd v Torero Pty Ltd* [1989] ATPR (Digest) 46–054 French J, although declining to give a general rule, thought that silence could not be misleading conduct unless the circumstances gave rise to some reasonable expectation that if a relevant fact exists it would be disclosed.

Under what circumstances does s 52 call for the banker to disclose information which would otherwise be subject to the duty of confidentiality? One approach is exemplified by the decision in *Kabwand Pty Ltd v National Australia Bank Ltd* [1989] ATPR 40–950, where the Full Court held that failure to disclose details of a customer's affairs to a prospective purchaser of property could not be misleading or deceptive because the purchaser knew that the banker was under a duty of confidentiality and so there could be no reasonable expectation of disclosure.

This reasoning is not very satisfactory because of its circularity. There is no duty of secrecy if disclosure is under compulsion of law. There is compulsion if there is a 'reasonable expectation'. But, according to *Kabwand*, there is no 'reasonable expectation' because there is a duty of secrecy. There have been similar problems in deciding when a bank should disclose information to prospective guarantors: see [11.142]ff.

In other cases the court has found a duty to disclose under s 52 but there does not seem to have been a careful analysis of the competing interests: see, for example, *Crisp v Australia & New Zealand Banking Group* (1994) ATPR 41–294. The position is not a happy one for the banker, but it will not be solved until there is an authoritative analysis of the policy issues which balance the customer's right to have his or her affairs remain confidential with the rights of the other parties to be notified of matters in which they have a legitimate interest. For a fuller discussion, see A L Tyree, 'Section 52 and the Banker's Duty of Secrecy' (1990) 1 *JBFLP* 143.

DUTY TO THE PUBLIC TO DISCLOSE

[4.16]   Aside from the *Libyan Arab Bank* case (see [4.17]) the author knows of no reported case which examines the rights of a banker who has assumed responsibility to disclose the customer's affairs pursuant to a duty to the public. The category is by far the worst-defined of any of the four categories of exception. Chorley has suggested that one example might be where the customer's dealings indicated trading with the enemy in time of war: R S T Chorley, *Law of Banking*, 6th ed, Sweet & Maxwell, London, 1974, p 23. Bankes LJ in *Tournier* referred to a suggestion by Lord Finlay that 'Danger to the state or public duty may supersede the duty of the agent to the principal': *Weld-Blundell v Stephens* [1920] AC 956 at 965.

[4.17]   The 'public duty' category of disclosure was recognised by the English court in *Libyan Arab Foreign Bank v Bankers Trust Co* [1989] QB 728. The American President had issued decrees which had the effect of freezing bank accounts owned by Libyan interests. The defendant bank informed the Federal Reserve Bank of New York that 'it looked like the Libyans were taking their funds out of the various accounts'. In considering an action for breach of the duty of secrecy, Staughton J refused to accept that the disclosure was in the defendant's own interest or that there was implied consent.

However, Staughton J did accept that 'public duty' exception to the *Tournier* duty. On the assumption that the New York Federal Reserve Bank had a duty similar to that of the Bank of England in obtaining information from banks, he was prepared to reach a tentative conclusion that the exception applied in the case before him: at pp 770–1. However, it was not necessary for him to reach a final conclusion on the point.

The only sound advice which may be given is that the banker should exercise extreme restraint before disclosing information pursuant to any supposed duty to the public.

INTERESTS OF THE BANK

[4.18] There are several circumstances in which the bank's own interest will justify disclosure of at least some of the customer's account information. Weaver and Craigie note that the issue of a writ whereby the bank initiates legal action against the customer will necessarily contain confidential information: G A Weaver and R C Craigie, *The Law Relating to Banker and Customer in Australia*, 2nd ed, Law Book Co, Sydney, 1990, para [6.670].

Another common instance is a guarantor seeking information concerning the account of the primary debtor. The bank need not, and should not, volunteer information concerning the account (see [10.114]), but if the guarantor asks questions, he or she is entitled to frank and honest answers even though the guarantor is not generally entitled to see the whole detail of the account. The precise limits of disclosure are not entirely clear. They will be discussed in Chapter 10.

[4.19] There seems to be only one reported case which expressly mentions this exception to the *Tournier* rule. In *Sunderland v Barclays Bank* (1938) 5 LDAB 163 the defendant bank had dishonoured the plaintiff's cheques due to insufficient funds in the account, but the real reason was that the bank manager thought it unwise to grant her an overdraft since he was aware that the plaintiff was losing large sums gambling. She complained to her husband. He encouraged her to telephone the bank to demand an explanation. She did so and during the course of the conversation handed the telephone to her husband. He was told that most of the cheques drawn on the wife's account were in favour of bookmakers. She sued the bank claiming breach of the duty of secrecy.

The court held that the manager had impliedly or expressly received a demand to explain and that by handing the telephone to her husband the plaintiff had impliedly authorised the disclosure to him. However, even if there was no implied authorisation, the fact that a demand for explanation had been made meant that it was in the bank's own interest to explain to Dr Sunderland. The reasoning and the decision are far from satisfactory, for it is perfectly clear that Mrs Sunderland would not have expressly authorised such a disclosure. The explanation given to the husband disclosed more information than was necessary to protect the bank's interest. It is also difficult to see how the bank's interest in maintaining the goodwill of one customer, that is, Dr Sunderland, can authorise a breach of contract with another.

The final point of the *Sunderland* case is that Du Parcq LJ went on to say that even if there had been a breach of contract by the bank, he would award only nominal damages since the plaintiff had suffered little if any damage as a result of the breach.

[4.20] The latter point is important, for there are often breaches of the duty of secrecy when account information, often the balance, is given by telephone in order to verify that there are funds in the account which are sufficient to cover a cheque which is about to be written by the customer. If not expressly or impliedly authorised by the customer, there is no doubt that there is a technical breach of the duty of secrecy, but, provided the information is correct, there will seldom, if ever, be any damage to the customer as a result of the breach. If the funds are adequate to cover the cheque then the transaction will go ahead; if the funds are inadequate, then the customer is attempting to write a cheque for which there are inadequate funds. It can scarcely be imagined that the 'damage' suffered in the latter circumstance is such as to be attributable to the breach by the bank.

This should not be interpreted as condoning the giving of account information over the telephone. There may well be circumstances other than those mentioned above where real damage flows from such a breach. In such a case, there would be no doubt that the banker would be liable. Since there is no way of knowing ahead of time which type of situation is being dealt with, the only safe course of action for the banker is to refuse to give account information over the telephone unless the customer has given an express, preferably written, authorisation.

EXPRESS OR IMPLIED CONSENT BY THE CUSTOMER

[4.21]   When the customer gives an express consent to the release of information, there can be no complaint provided that the banker discloses only information which is correct and within the confines of the customer's consent.

Implied consent may only be inferred when the customer knows that the information is likely to be disclosed and submits to it. In other words, there can be no consent to the giving of information unless it can be shown that the customer is aware of the banking practice which gives rise to the disclosure.

BANKERS' REFERENCES

[4.22]   Bankers' references are memoranda from one bank to another detailing certain financial information about a customer of the advising bank. These references are usually given in response to a request from the reference-seeking bank which is itself ordinarily a response to a request for information from one of its own customers. The characteristic feature of the reference is that it is given by one bank to another but with the clear understanding that the information will be passed on to a customer of the receiving bank. Furthermore, it is often given without the knowledge of the customer whose affairs are being investigated.

This is clearly a violation of the usual duty of confidentiality and the question arises as to the legal grounds which justify the giving of the reference. In order to identify these grounds, it is now necessary to distinguish between those accounts to which the Code of Banking Practice applies, accounts to which the Credit Reporting Code of Conduct applies and accounts which are covered by neither. This latter category would include most 'commercial' accounts, and it is convenient to begin with these.

The most persuasive argument is that by opening an account, particularly a business account, the customer impliedly authorises the bank to provide a banker's opinion when requested by another bank.

[4.23]   The court in *Tournier's* case considered the question of bankers' references and their legal foundation, clearly favouring consent as the basis. Bankes LJ seemed to have contemplated express consent in this circumstance when he said (at 473) that the common instance of the exception 'is where the customer authorises a reference to his banker'. However, Lord Atkin clearly contemplated implied consent when he said (at 486):

> I do not desire to express any final opinion on the practice of bankers to give information as to the affairs of their respective customers, except to say that if it is justified it must be upon the basis of an implied consent of the customer.

If the customer has given the name of his or her banker in the course of business dealings, then it is relatively easy to find an implied consent to the disclosure of what would ordinarily be confidential information. The customer must clearly appreciate that the name of the banker is required precisely because the other party expects to make inquiries.

However, the position is not so clear when the customer has not provided such information and does not know of the inquiry into his or her affairs. The common opinion among bankers is that they are entitled to give a banker's reference, a reference which almost necessarily must disclose some of the confidential account information, without the express authorisation of the customer. The only way in which this practice may be justified is on the basis of implied consent and there can scarcely be any implied consent if the practice is unknown to the customer.

[4.24]   This in turn raises the question of whether the practice of bankers giving references is not only widespread but also widely known. Weaver and Craigie argue that the practice is probably as well known as several other practices which are undoubtedly incorporated into the banker-customer contract, for example, that an overdrawn customer is taken to assent to the charging of interest, that a customer who lodges a cheque for collection assents to the normal delays inherent in the clearing house rules, even though in each case it is extremely unlikely that the customer is aware of the details of the arrangements to which he or she has consented: G A Weaver and R C Craigie, *The Law Relating to Banker and Customer in Australia*, 2nd ed, Law Book Co, Sydney, 1990, para [6.680].

However, the argument is not entirely convincing. Even though the customer may never have had an overdraft, the general practice of charging interest on loans is well known. Similarly, although the customer may not be aware of the precise content of clearing house rules, anyone who writes cheques is aware that there are delays involved. By contrast, the practice of bankers' references is not obviously so well known among non-business customers.

There is a possibility that the position of commercial customers is different in this regard from the position of the ordinary customer. It seems less likely that a commercial customer could be unaware of the practice. Further, it may be that the practice, although not well known earlier, is now becoming so. In *Mutual Life and Citizens' Assurance Co v Evatt* (1968) 112 CLR 556 Kitto J noted 'the multitudinous inquiries of this kind that everyone knows are constantly made of bankers'. Similarly, in *Commercial Banking Co of Sydney Ltd v R H Brown*, the High Court expressed its view that it is banking usage in Australia to supply bankers' opinions. However, there is still room to doubt that the facts known to a High Court judge and to lawyers generally are necessarily known to 'everyone'.

Clearly, the best advice is to obtain an express consent from the customer where practicable before giving confidential information, whether to another banker or to a commercial firm. Ellinger suggests the practice employed by German banks is desirable. The customer is asked, at the time of the opening of the account, whether answers should be given in response to inquiries without explicit reference to the customer: see Ellinger, op cit, p 456. Note that this is far different from the common Australian practice of forcing customers to 'consent' in a standard form contract at the time of opening an account.

CREDIT REPORTING CODE OF CONDUCT

[4.25] Where the account is one which is governed by the Code of Banking Practice, s 12.11 commits the bank to compliance with any applicable requirements of a Credit Reporting Code of Conduct issued by the Commonwealth Privacy Commissioner under s 18A(1) of the Privacy Act 1988. Since a bank is a 'credit provider' for the purposes of the Act, this provision of the Code is merely reciting obligations imposed upon the bank by the general law: Privacy Act 1988 ss 6(1), 11B.

The Privacy Act applies in all cases where the customer is a natural person, but the relevant parts of the Credit Reporting Code of Conduct only apply where the reference relates to the subject's consumer creditworthiness. Under the Code, a bank may not give a banker's opinion to another bank unless it has obtained the subject's specific agreement to the disclosure for the particular purpose if the opinion contains information which relates to the customer's consumer creditworthiness: para 2.16. The present practice of banks is to obtain a general consent when opening new accounts. It seems doubtful if this is 'agreement' as contemplated by the Code, and a bank would be advised to obtain the express agreement of a customer before giving a banker's opinion in regard to the customer.

[4.26] The requesting institution also has obligations under the Credit Reporting Code. Before receiving a requested reference which relates to a subject's consumer creditworthiness, the requesting institution must be satisfied that the individual has agreed in the appropriate form: para 2.12. The requesting institution must also keep a record of the date on which the report was obtained, the identity of the credit provider giving the report, a brief description of the contents of the report and a note to the effect that the individual's specific agreement to disclosure has been furnished if required: para 1.14.

Individuals have a limited right of correction: if an institution has received a reference which relates to the individual's consumer creditworthiness and it subsequently appears that the information was incorrect because it relates to the wrong person, then the receiving institution is under a duty to advise the sending institution of the mistaken identity and to destroy the mistaken reports: para 2.15.

DUTY TO THE CUSTOMER

[4.27] Consent, whether express or implied, would only be to giving a fair and accurate report of the customer's financial position. If the report is favourable, it hardly seems possible that the customer could sustain any damage regardless of the accuracy, although the ultimate recipient of the advice might suffer losses: see [4.28].

If the report is unfavourable but accurate, then any damage suffered by the customer would most likely not be recoverable, for the customer would be forced to argue that but for the (accurate) report a more favourable (inaccurate) impression of the customer's financial position would have been given to the inquirer. In the words of Weaver and Craigie (op cit, para [6.690]), 'it seems unlikely that a plaintiff in this position would attract a great deal of sympathy from a court' since the damage suffered by the customer is caused not by the accurate report but by the customer's own actions.

There is undoubtedly a duty on the bank to exercise reasonable care and skill in the giving of the reference. If the customer suffers damages as a direct result of inaccurate information carelessly supplied by the advising bank, then there seems no reason why these should not be recoverable in an action for breach of contract.

The customer may also have an action in defamation if the report is unfavourable. In such a circumstance, the banker would need to plead justification, if the report is accurate, and qualified privilege if it is not. The defence of qualified privilege, although ordinarily available when there is a contractual duty, may not be available since there is, strictly speaking, no contractual duty for the bank to supply a banker's reference: see A L Tyree, 'Wrongful Dishonour, Defamation and Qualified Privilege' (1980) 8 *Australian Bus L Rev* 220–31 and J C C Gatley, *Gatley on Libel*, 8th ed, Sweet & Maxwell, London, 1981.

DUTY TO THE ULTIMATE INQUIRER

[4.28] The banker who is giving a reference concerning the financial affairs of a customer also owes a duty to the ultimate inquirer. Except in those cases where the inquirer is also a customer of the same bank, or possibly the same branch, the relationship between the banker providing the opinion and the inquirer will not be one of contract. This is important because in the usual case the banker may refuse to give an opinion, there being no general duty for the banker to give advice when asked. If, on the other hand, the banker does comply with the request for an opinion concerning one of the bank's customers, the bank is under a duty to the inquirer. The scope and range of that duty are still not clearly defined in law.

That some duty is owed is now beyond dispute, even when the ultimate inquirer makes that inquiry through another banker, as indeed will usually be the case. In *Hedley Byrne & Co Ltd v Heller & Partners Ltd* [1964] AC 465, the House of Lords considered a case where a written opinion was sent by Heller & Partners to the National Provincial Bank in response to a request from that bank which was itself a response to a request from Hedley Byrne & Co concerning the financial standing of one of Heller's customers. The reference was headed 'For your private use' and also contained an express disclaimer of liability. The House of Lords held that the relationship between the ultimate inquirer and the banker providing the information was such as to raise a duty on the banker to exercise care in providing the requested information.

[4.29]   The words 'For your private use' were also considered by the High Court of Australia in *Commercial Banking Co of Sydney Ltd v R H Brown & Co* (1972)126 CLR 337. The court rejected an argument from the bank that these words meant that no duty on the bank in favour of the ultimate inquirer could arise. This was because banking practice is such that the information was obviously sought for a customer of the inquiring bank who would rely upon the terms of the reference.

THE SCOPE OF THE DUTY

[4.30]   Prior to *Hedley Byrne*, it was accepted law that in the absence of contract or of some very special relationship, the duty of a person who made a statement which purported to be fact or who made a statement of opinion was merely to be honest in making the statement. Such a duty was owed to those whom the maker could reasonably foresee would rely upon it in a matter affecting their economic interest. But there was thought to be no duty to be careful unless the recipient of the information was in a relationship with the maker of the statement of a sort which was classified as fiduciary. *Hedley Byrne* thus expanded the class of people to whom the duty to be careful might arise.

The duty is a duty to be careful, that is, to give an answer which is accurate and honest based on the facts which are available to it at the time. There is not, in the absence of special contractual terms, a duty to go outside the information which is in the possession of the bank through its operation of its customer's account and financial affairs. Lord Diplock summarised the position in the Privy Council in *MLC v Evatt* [1971] AC 793 as follows (at 803–4):

> ... A banker giving a gratuitous reference is not required to do his best by, for instance, making inquiries from outside sources which are available to him, though this would make his reference more reliable. All that he is required to

do is to conform to that standard of skill and competence and diligence which is generally shown by persons who carry on the business of providing references of that kind ...

The reason why the law requires him to conform to this standard of skill and competence and diligence is that by carrying on a business which includes the giving of references of this kind he has let it be known to the recipient of the reference that he claims to possess that degree of skill and competence and is willing to apply that degree of diligence to the provision of any reference which he supplied in the course of that business ... If he supplies the reference the law requires him to make good his claim.

Although there have been some developments which cast doubt on the basis of the liability of parties making careless statements, it would appear that by any of the tests of liability a banker giving a gratuitous reference is under the duty of care expressed by Lord Diplock: see [4.33].

DISCLAIMER OF LIABILITY

[4.31]   The House of Lords in *Hedley Byrne* found that, although the defendant had been negligent, there was nevertheless no liability because of the disclaimer of liability. It may be too soon to find that it will always be sufficient to allow the banker to escape completely. Barwick CJ in the High Court of Australia in *Mutual Life and Citizens' Assurance Co Ltd v Evatt* (1968) 122 CLR 556 treated the matter as one which was still open in Australian law. Further, on the matter of disclaimers, he expressly said (at 570):

The duty of care, in my opinion, is imposed by law in the circumstances. Because it is so imposed, I doubt whether the speaker may always except himself from the performance of the duty by some express reservation at the time of his utterance. But the fact of such a reservation, particularly if acknowledged by the recipient, will in many instances be one of the circumstances to be taken into consideration in deciding whether or not a duty of care has arisen and it may be sufficiently potent in some cases to prevent the creation of the necessary relationship. Whether it is so or not must ... depend upon all the circumstances.

[4.32]   This view of the basis of the duty contrasts sharply with that of Lord Devlin in the *Hedley Byrne* case where he said (at 529):

I do not understand any of your Lordships to hold that it is a responsibility imposed by law upon certain types of persons or in certain sorts of situations. It is a responsibility that is voluntarily accepted or undertaken, either generally where a general relationship, such as that of solicitor and client or banker and customer, is created, or specifically in relation to a particular transaction.

It is thought that the view of the Chief Justice is to be preferred. It seems contradictory to say that the duty arises because it is assumed by the advice giver who, although giving advice, then declares that there is no responsibility. It would be better to view the disclaimer as only one component of the overall situation and to ask if it was reasonable, in all of the circumstances, for the inquirer to rely upon the advice given. In the context of the banker's reference, the parties clearly intend that the advice be given seriously and carefully and all parties treat the disclaimer of liability as a formality in the sense that both the giver and the receiver of the advice would be surprised at any suggestion that it justified any carelessness of the advising banker: see Ellinger, op cit, p 462 for a contrary view. Of course, no disclaimer will be effective to avoid liability for advice which is given fraudulently or recklessly: see *Commercial Banking Co of Sydney Ltd v R H Brown & Co* (1972) 126 CLR 337 and below [4.40]ff.

The House of Lords set aside a disclaimer clause as being contrary to the provisions of the Unfair Contract Terms Act 1977: *Smith v Bush* [1990] 1 AC 831. It may be that s 51AA and s 51AB of the Trade Practices Act could be used to mount a similar attack in Australia. See J Jackson, 'Tortious Disclaimers and Negligent Mis-statement: Reasonableness and Unconscionability' (1991) 65 ALJ 507 for an argument to the contrary.

WHEN DOES THE DUTY ARISE?

[4.33]   It is not every gratuitous giving of advice which will place upon the adviser the duty to take care in giving the advice. As indicated above, the important feature is that in all of the circumstances it is reasonable to find that the adviser assumed responsibility for his or her advice. In *MLC v Evatt* [1971] AC 793 an insurance company gave information concerning the financial status of a fellow subsidiary company. The plaintiff, who was a policy holder with the defendant company, sought advice concerning the financial stability of the subsidiary, believing that the defendant had greater information and/or better facilities for obtaining that information than had the plaintiff himself. As a result of negligently given information, the plaintiff invested in the subsidiary and lost the amount claimed in the action.

At one point in the judgment, it seemed that Lord Diplock was severely restricting the scope of the *Hedley Byrne* duty. He indicated (at 807) that the principle laid down in *Hedley Byrne* should 'be understood as restricted to advisers who carry on the business or profession of giving advice of the kind sought and to advice given by them in the course of that business'. However, he later made it clear that there was no such precise confinement of the duty (at 809):

> ... their Lordships would emphasise that the missing characteristic of the relationship which they consider to be essential to give rise to a duty of care in a situation of the kind in which Mr Evatt and the company found themselves when he sought their advice is not necessarily essential in other situations — such as, perhaps, where the adviser has a financial interest in the transaction upon which he gives his advice.

[4.34]   It is certain now that the Australian courts will not permit the severe narrowing of the duty as suggested by the first passage of Lord Diplock quoted above. In recent times, the High Court has held that there is a duty of care in circumstances where the person making the statement was not in the business of advice giving. In so doing, the court preferred the reasoning of its own decision in *Evatt* over that of the Privy Council.

[4.35] In *Shaddock & Associates Pty Ltd v Parramatta City Council* (1981) 150 CLR 225 the plaintiff, through its solicitor, had sought information from the defendant by telephone and by a standard form. The solicitor spoke by telephone to an unidentified officer of the defendant and was assured that there were no road-widening plans which might affect the property in which the plaintiff was interested. The standard form was an application for a particular certificate which also asked for the same information. Although the practice of the Council was to note road-widening proposals at the foot of the form, no such notation was made in this case. The plaintiff purchased the property on the strength of this information. It transpired that there were road-widening plans which concerned the property.

The High Court held that the Council was under a duty to the plaintiff to take care in the provision of information even though the defendant was not in the business of providing such information nor were they under any statutory duty to do so. The court held that there was no breach of the duty where the information was supplied by an unidentified officer and was not subsequently confirmed, but that there was a breach of the duty with respect to the request in writing.

An important point is that the High Court held that there was no significant difference between providing advice and providing information. The duty of care arises when the adviser knows or ought to know that the inquirer is relying on the answer and that the reliance is reasonable in all the circumstances.

[4.36] New Zealand courts have also made it clear that the test is one of reasonable reliance. In *Meates v Attorney-General* [1983] NZLR 308 the plaintiff shareholders of Matai Industries claimed, inter alia, that they had been induced by the negligent statements of the Prime Minister and other ministers of the Crown to establish the company to assist with the then government's regional development plans. Further, it appeared that, when the company was in financial difficulties, the Minister of Trade and Industry had assured the plaintiffs that if they acquiesced in the appointment of a receiver with a view towards avoiding retrenchments then their interests would be safeguarded and they would be indemnified against losses. As a result of these representations, the plaintiffs failed to take normal commercial precautions to safeguard their own interests.

The Court of Appeal held that there was a sufficient proximity to establish a duty of care even though the ministers were not in the business or profession of giving advice of the type which was given. They held themselves out as having special knowledge in the areas of their own portfolios and, in the case of the Prime Minister, of government policy. They knew when they undertook to give advice that the advice would be relied upon. Woodhouse P and Ongley J specifically noted the second part of Lord Diplock's speech quoted above and concluded (at 334): 'Thus the presence or absence of a "business or professional" element should be regarded as but a single instance of a test in those particular situations where it has actual relevance.'

[4.37]   In summary, it would seem that the duty of care will arise at any time when it is reasonable to assume that the banker is assuming responsibility for the advice given. That will always be the case when the advice is of the sort that is within the usual advice given by a banker, but the duty may arise when there are other factors which place the parties in a relationship which is close enough that the banker ought to know that his or her advice is being relied upon.

BANKER EXCEEDING AUTHORITY

[4.38]   It is not generally a defence for the bank to argue that its employee has exceeded authority. In *Compafina Bank v ANZ Banking Group and Bennet* (1989) Aust Torts Rep 80–546 a bank manager gave an unauthorised and unduly favourable letter of introduction and credit report. As a result of these reports, the plaintiff bank lent the customer some $5.5 million. On the facts, it was held that the manager was liable for fraudulent misrepresentation. The defendant bank was held liable for negligent misrepresentation since even though the manager acted beyond his actual authority, he was acting within his ostensible authority when giving the credit reference.

PASSING ON AN ADVICE

[4.39]   On the other hand, a bank may escape liability if it is in effect merely passing on a reference given by another bank. In *Cunningham v National Australia Bank* (1987) 77 ALR 632; 15 FLR 495 the plaintiff was a customer of the defendant bank. He asked the bank to seek a reference from W bank concerning customers of that bank. W bank produced a reference which indicated that its customers were satisfactory on all accounts. The defendant bank passed this on to the plaintiff with a note that the report was 'as good a report as you will get'. The report was, however, incorrect as the customers of W bank were insolvent at the time when the report was made. The court held that the defendant bank was not liable as it had merely acted as a conduit of the information. The note which the defendant added was merely a comment on the reference, not a comment on the creditworthiness of W bank's customer.

THE DUTY TO BE HONEST

[4.40]   Even before the *Hedley Byrne* case, a duty to be honest was acknowledged. A failure to observe the duty leaves the person making the statement open to an action in deceit. In order to maintain an action in deceit, it must be shown that the representation was: (1) false as a matter of fact; (2) made knowingly or recklessly, that is, with complete disregard as to its truth or falsity; (3) made with an intention that it should be relied upon by the recipient; and (4) that the recipient did in fact rely upon it and suffer damage thereby: see *Derry v Peek* (1889) 14 App Cas 337.

It is crucial to note that actual dishonesty must be proved. It is not sufficient to establish that the person making the representation is merely careless.

There are, thankfully, few cases where an action in deceit has been brought against a banker. Nevertheless, it is clear that such an action may be sustained against a banker who has given a fraudulent banker's reference.

[4.41] In *Commercial Banking Co of Sydney v R H Brown & Co* (1972) 126 CLR 337 the plaintiffs had for some years conducted business with a company known as Wool Exporters Pty Ltd. In late 1976, they entered into a contract with Wool Exporters to sell the clip on the sheep's back. Shortly before they were to deliver the wool, they were informed by their banker that there were rumours to the effect that Wool Exporters were in financial difficulties. This naturally caused the plaintiffs much concern and, at the request of the plaintiffs, their banker wrote to Wool Exporters' banker, the Perth branch of the Commercial Banking Co of Sydney, seeking a report on the financial position of Wool Exporters. The request was in the following terms (at 340):

> Confidential. Kindly favour us with your opinion as to the financial position, character, standing and occupation of Wool Exporters Ltd and say whether you consider them quite safe in the way of business for £ generally ...

The request was signed by the manager of the plaintiffs' bankers. In due course, the Commercial Banking Co of Sydney branch manager returned a banker's reference in the following terms (at 341):

> The Company is capably managed by Directors well experienced in the wool trade. The Company has always met its engagements, is trading satisfactorily and we consider that it would be safe for its trade engagements generally. This opinion is confidential and for your private use and without responsibility on the part of this bank or its officers.

The document was not signed, but it was conceded that the reply was that of the branch manager of the Commercial Banking Co of Sydney. The plaintiffs delivered the wool to Wool Exporters on the faith of the opinion. Shortly thereafter, Wool Exporters failed and the plaintiffs brought action against both their own banker and the Commercial Banking Co of Sydney.

As against their own bankers, the plaintiffs alleged negligence in failing to mention that the qualifying clause was a part of the report received from the CBC of Sydney. It was claimed that in the absence of knowledge of the qualifications they were in no position to assess the true value of the opinion for the purposes of making their decision as to whether or not to deliver the wool to Wool Exporters. In the Supreme Court of Western Australia, it was found as a fact that the qualifications had been communicated to the plaintiffs and so the plaintiffs' own banker had not been negligent. There is some reason to believe that if the finding of fact had been different then the outcome might also have been different.

As against the Commercial Banking Co of Sydney, the plaintiffs alleged not only negligence, but also that the opinion was fraudulently given. The Supreme Court found that this was the case, that the manager knew or ought to have known that the request was for one of the requesting banker's customers, that the customer was likely to enter into business arrangements with

Wool Exporters and that the report was likely to be relied upon by the ultimate inquirer. The court further held that the report was made with intent to deceive and with intent that it should be acted upon both by the receiving banker and the customer who had requested the information.

[4.42] The Commercial Banking Co of Sydney appealed to the High Court arguing that the effect of the disclaimer was to relieve it from liability and that the damages awarded were inappropriate.

As to the first, the High Court made it clear that Australian banking practice was such that, when a bank requested information concerning the credit of a customer from another bank, it is understood that the inquiring bank will communicate that information to its own customer. It was considered impossible to construe the disclaimer to mean that the information is to be used by only the inquiring bank for the purpose of giving advice to its own customer without communicating the actual reply. The court also made it clear that even if a *Hedley Byrne* type of disclaimer is adequate for shielding the bank against negligence when making a banker's reference, there is no disclaimer which will protect the giver of an opinion which is tainted by deceit.

As to the question of damages, the bank had argued that a failure of the plaintiff to deliver the wool to Wool Exporters would have been a breach of contract and that the damages awarded against the bank should reflect that fact. The court held that such a fact (if indeed it was a fact) would not avail the bank, since the losses suffered were a direct and foreseeable consequence of the fraudulent representation.

[4.43] Lord Tenterden's Act affects the right of the inquirer to bring an action in deceit: Statute of Frauds (Amendment) Act 1828 s 6. The Act, which is still in force in some Australian jurisdictions, is one of the peculiarities which were implemented in the English Statute of Frauds series of legislation; the Act is in force in Tasmania (Mercantile Law Act 1935 s 11), Victoria (Instruments Act 1958 s 128) and Western Australia (Law Reform (Statute of Frauds) Act 1962).

The Act is very badly drafted (see the comments of Salmon J in *Diamanti v Martelli* [1923] NZLR 663) but the essence of it is that no action may be brought against a person who makes a fraudulent representation concerning another person's credit unless such a representation is made in writing and signed by the person making the representation. Although the Act itself merely refers to 'any representation or assurance', the restriction to fraudulent representations is a judicial interpretation of long standing; see *Banbury v Bank of Montreal* [1918] AC 626. But further, the Act only applies to those representations which are for a particular purpose, namely, for the purpose of including the plaintiff to give credit to a third person.

Furthermore, since the Act requires that the representation be signed by the person to be charged, it is not possible to fix the bank with liability for a fraudulent statement which has been signed by the manager, since in making the fraudulent representation the manager is acting outside the scope of his or her authority. The manager who signs is, of course, liable. It is interesting to note that the reference given in the *R H Brown* case was unsigned but the defendant bank elected not to rely upon the defence which would undoubtedly have been available to it under Lord Tenterden's Act. It should be recalled that the bank may be liable for negligent misrepresentation even where the manager is acting outside the scope of his or her actual authority: see *Compafina Bank v ANZ Banking Group and Bennet* (1989) Aust Torts Rep 80–546 and above [4.38].

[4.44]   Lord Tenterden's Act was considered in *Diamanti v Martelli* [1923] NZLR 663 at 670 where it was said that:

> [The] Act applies only when the defendant's representations have been made for the purpose of inducing the plaintiff to give credit to the third person — that is to say, to trust the third person with the performance of some obligation towards the plaintiff as, for example, the repayment of money lent, or payment for goods sold and delivered.

Therefore the Act did not apply when the plaintiff made fraudulent representations which induced the plaintiff to apply and pay for shares in a company, since in that case they did not give credit to the company.

Lord Tenterden's Act has now been repealed by statute in all Australian jurisdictions except Tasmania, Victoria and Western Australia.

FINANCIAL ADVICE

[4.45]   The banker owes the customer a duty to be careful in the giving of advice, at least when it is advice which is of the type which bankers would give in the ordinary course of the business of banking or where the bank has advertised or otherwise held itself out as giving the advice in question. There has been conflicting opinion over the years as to whether the giving of financial advice is a part of the general 'business of banking'. Earlier cases thought not: see *Banbury v Bank of Montreal* [1918] AC 626; *Barrow v Bank of New South Wales* [1931] VLR 323. However, later cases have treated the question as one of fact to be decided in each case, and the fact that the bank assumes the task will usually be sufficient to give rise to a duty of care: see *Woods v Martins Bank Ltd* [1959] 1 QB 55; *Shaddock & Associates Pty Ltd v Parramatta City Council* (1981) 150 CLR 225.

The bank is not relieved of this duty merely because it has issued secret instructions to staff that they should not give financial advice: *Woods v Martins Bank Ltd* [1959] 1 QB 55.

[4.46]   Although the banker must exercise care and skill in giving financial advice, the liability for negligent advice will be limited by the knowledge which the banker has of the financial affairs of the customer. The point is nicely illustrated by *Box v Midland Bank* [1979] 2 Lloyd's Rep 391; [1981] 1 Lloyd's Rep 434. The plaintiff claimed damages from the Midland Bank for more than a quarter of a million pounds but was only awarded £5000.

The plaintiff was an engineer who was hoping to contract with a nationalised concern in Manitoba. In order to gain the contract, he sought finance from the Midland Bank, where he already had an overdraft of some £20,000. At a meeting with the branch manager he was assured that the finance would be forthcoming subject only to insurance from the Export Credit Guarantee Department and approval from the Head Office, but the manager also advised that there would be no difficulty concerning either of these. On the faith of these assurances, the plaintiff proceeded to extend his overdraft and mortgaged his own house to the bank as security. The loan failed to materialise because the ECGD would not give approval.

The plaintiff argued that the advice given had been negligent and that as a result he had not only borrowed more money but he had also lost the large profit which would have accrued from the Canadian contract. Lloyd J found that the advice had been negligent, and that as a result the plaintiff had overdrawn an additional £5000, an amount for which the bank was liable since it was an obvious consequence of the negligent advice. However, the other damages claimed by the plaintiff, and in particular the benefits of the Manitoba contract, were too remote to be recoverable unless it could be shown that the banker knew or should have known of the details of the business arrangements: see also *Royal Bank of Canada v Pampellonne* [1987] 1 Lloyd's Rep 218; *Rust v Abbey Life Assurance Co* [1978] 2 Lloyd's Rep 385.

[4.47] In the absence of special knowledge, the banker has no duty to consider the taxation aspects of transactions. In *Schioler v Westminster Bank Ltd* [1970] 2 QB 719 the plaintiff was a foreigner who was resident in England. Under the taxation laws in force at the time, she was not liable for income tax on any foreign dividends provided only that they were not received in the United Kingdom. In order to prevent this from happening, she opened an account with the defendant bank at the Guernsey branch. As a shareholder in a Malaysian company, she instructed that company to send her dividends to the Guernsey branch. For several years this arrangement proved satisfactory because the company remitted dividends in sterling. However, in mid-1968, the company began sending dividend warrants expressed in Malaysian dollars. There were no facilities in Guernsey for negotiating foreign currency drafts, and the defendant bank sent the draft to the branch office in England in accordance with the normal practice. The sum was subjected to a deduction of UK income tax and the Guernsey account credited only with the net sum.

The plaintiff claimed the bank to be liable for performing the contract negligently. The court dismissed the claim, Mocatta J saying (at 728):

> Unless special arrangements were made with a customer or special instructions given by him, bankers could not, in discharge of their contractual duties in crediting an account with a dividend, be obliged to consider the tax implications to the customer or consult him before acting in accordance with their ordinary practice. To hold a bank obliged to do this would come near to holding that a bank must gratuitously give its customers tax advice. To take

such a view would be to place an impossible and unreasonable burden on the banks generally.

High interest rates in Australia during the early 1980s led financial institutions, including banks, to suggest that larger borrowers consider foreign currency loans. The floating and consequential devaluation of the Australian dollar in December 1983 had the effect of making these foreign currency loans extremely unprofitable for the borrower. A great deal of litigation has ensued.

An early example of this litigation is *Lloyd v Citicorp Australia Ltd* (1986) 11 NSWLR 286. The plaintiff was offered a foreign currency loan of $2.5 million which was drawn in Swiss francs. He lost between $500,000 and $700,000 when the value of the Australian dollar against the Swiss franc fell. The loan was not 'hedged' and the plaintiff claimed that the defendant was negligent in failing to advise that the loan should be hedged and in failing to monitor the loan. Rogers J found that a duty of care was owed and that the standard of care was that which a reasonably careful and competent foreign exchange adviser would exercise having regard to the market and the commercial and financial background of the borrower. On the rather unsatisfactory evidence of the case, the defendant had met this standard of care: see also *McEvoy v ANZ Banking Group Ltd* [1988] Aust Torts Rep 80–151; *Cunningham v National Australia Bank* (1987) 77 ALR 632; *James v ANZ Banking Group* (1986) 64 ALR 347; *Kabwand v National Australia Bank* (1989) ATPR 40–950; *Adour Holdings Pty Ltd v Commonwealth Bank* (1991) ATPR 41–147.

If, as seems likely because of widespread advertising of advisory services, the giving of financial advice is a part of the modern business of banking, then the individual branch managers must be considered as having the (ostensible) authority to give such advice. Apart from being ordinary common sense, this view was recognised even in the *Banbury* case: see the comments of Lord Wrenbury in *Banbury v Bank of Montreal* [1918] AC 626 at 715.

DUTY TO QUESTION A VALID MANDATE:
THE SELANGOR DUTY

[4.48]   There are circumstances which should alert the banker that the customer's interest will be prejudiced by certain transactions. The duty of the banker in these circumstances is, at the minimum, to make inquiries to clarify the customer's wishes. The duty may extend to questioning a properly drawn mandate from the customer. Two cases illustrate the scope of the duty, both involving the account of a company customer.

In *Selangor United Rubber Estates v Cradock (No 3)* [1968] 2 All ER 1073, a company bank account was used to facilitate a fraudulent purchase of the company by means of using the company's own funds. In the 1960s there were a number of companies which found themselves with no business to conduct following the withdrawal of England from her former colonies. In such a situation, the company could be wound up and the assets distributed among the shareholders, but it was found that it was often slightly more profitable to sell the company as a 'shell'. Unfortunately, such a practice permitted the kind of fraud which was practised in the *Selangor* case.

Cradock had made a 'takeover bid' for the company and had obtained control of 79 per cent of the stock by making a bid of some £195,000. Cradock did not have the money to pay, but had devised a scheme whereby his agents would be elected chairman of the board of the company; following that, they could draw cheques on the company account. But in order to become chairman of the board, it was necessary to pay for the 79 per cent interest.

As part of the takeover deal, Selangor's banker, National, drew two bank drafts totalling some £232,000 in favour of the District Bank, which was Cradock's banker. The funds were to be placed in a new account in the name of the company. Directors of the plaintiff company, who were working in concert with Cradock, drew a cheque for almost the entire sum in favour of Woodstock Trust (with which Cradock was closely related) by way of loan; Woodstock then loaned the required sum to Cradock, who paid for the shares with it. Cradock thus gained control of the company and its assets by means of using the company's assets in contravention of s 54 of the Companies Act, the English equivalent of s 129 of the Companies Code, and in breach of the duty which a director owes to the company and its shareholders.

The fraud could not have occurred were it not for the act of the District Bank in honouring the cheque drawn in favour of Woodstock, a cheque which was obviously drawn by Cradock for purposes which were not in the best interests of the company. The court held that the bank should have known that the transaction was not in the customer's, that is, Selangor's, best interest and should have queried the transaction. Note that this is so even though the cheque in question was properly signed by directors of the company who were authorised to sign cheques, although the authority to sign cheques was, of course, restricted to those cheques which were appropriate company business.

[4.49]   On almost identical facts, Brightman J found the defendant bank to be liable both for breach of contract and as constructive trustee in *Karak Rubber v Burden* [1972] 1 WLR 602: see [3.24] for a discussion of the trust aspects of the two cases.

In both cases the court emphasised that although the bank was obliged to pay a cheque which was in proper form and backed by adequate funds, it did not follow that the duty was an unqualified duty to pay without inquiry. The bank is under a contractual duty to exercise such care and skill as would be exercised by a reasonable banker, a duty which included a duty to make inquiries in appropriate circumstances. In both cases, the court indicated that the circumstances surrounding the drawing of the cheque were so out of the ordinary course of business that a reasonable banker would have been placed on notice.

Brightman J noted that it was open to the banker to show that such inquiries would have yielded no useful information or would have produced answers which would have been acceptable to the reasonable banker. This is undoubtedly correct since if the answers would have been acceptable then the losses suffered by the customers would not have flowed from the breach of contract. Note that this is an entirely different question from that of the 'useless inquiry' when the bank is seeking a defence to an action in conversion, for in that situation, the bank is attempting to bring itself within the ambit of a statutory defence: see [7.132] for a discussion of the 'useless inquiry' when attempting to establish a defence under s 95 of the Cheques and Payment Orders Act 1986.

The general rule is probably that a banker should question a mandate when a reasonable and honest banker with knowledge of the relevant facts would consider that there was a serious possibility that the customer was being defrauded or that the funds were being misappropriated: *Lipkin Gorman v Karpanale and Lloyds Bank* [1991] 2 AC 548.

[4.50] That general rule does not clarify the matter, however, and the precise scope of the *Selangor* duty is far from clear. At the very least the banker should make inquiries if asked to pay cheques drawn on a company account by directors if there is any suspicion that the money is to be channelled to uses other than those for which the directors are authorised. The *Selangor* and *Karak* cases themselves have been criticised as placing too great a burden on the banker, a matter which will be discussed below: see [5.39]. This criticism was made in *Lipkin Gorman v Karpanale and Lloyds Bank* [1991] 2 AC 548 but the principle of the existence of the duty was reaffirmed: see also *Barclays Bank v Quincecare Ltd* [1992] 4 All ER 363.

The existence of a duty to question a valid mandate in certain circumstances has also been affirmed in Australian cases: see *Varker v Commercial Banking Co of Sydney Ltd* [1972] 2 NSWLR 967 (where the mandate had been altered but was treated as a valid mandate under the principle of *London Joint Stock Bank Ltd v Macmillan and Arthur* [1918] AC 777; see [5.24]); *Ryan v Bank of New South Wales* [1978] VR 555.

Whatever the scope of the *Selangor* duty, it is a difficult one for the banker since it creates a situation in which the banker is subjected to the pressures of two conflicting duties. On the one hand, there is an obligation to pay on demand a cheque which is properly drawn and for which there are adequate funds. On the other, there is a duty to delay payment and to make inquiries if the circumstances are such as to raise doubts in the mind of a reasonable banker. It should be noted, however, that the circumstances in both *Selangor* and *Karak* were very unusual and that the sums involved were quite large.

In the *Selangor* case, Ungoed-Thomas J also expressed the view that if there was a duty to question the mandate then failure to do so is not excused by a conviction that the inquiry would be fruitless: *Selangor United Rubber Estates Ltd v Cradock (No 3)* [1968] 2 All ER 1073 at 1118.

DUTIES TO THIRD PARTIES

[4.51]   There are a number of circumstances where a banker owes a duty to parties who are not customers. For example, a banker has a duty to certain third parties who are beneficiaries of trust accounts (see [3.14]) and a duty to strangers to be careful when giving bankers' references: see [4.21]. The duty which a banker owes to the holder of a cheque is imposed by statute: see Cheques and Payment Orders Act 1986 s 67. In Chapter 8 it will be suggested that a banker may owe a duty to third parties when those parties are payees in a direct debit or a direct credit transfer: see [8.54]ff and also *H H Dimond (Rotorua 1966) Ltd v ANZ Banking Group* [1979] 2 NZLR 739.

[4.52]   In most cases the duty owed to third parties appears to be governed by ordinary tort principles. In *Johns Period Furniture v Commonwealth Savings Bank of Australia* (1980) 24 SASR 224 blank bank cheque forms were stolen during a burglary of the North Adelaide post office in early February 1979. The defendant bank did not learn of the loss until about a month later. They took no steps to give any public warning about the cheque forms. In early May one of the cheque forms with a forged signature was given to the plaintiff to pay for goods. The bank refused to pay the cheque and the plaintiff brought an action in negligence claiming that the bank owed a duty to traders in the area to warn of the stolen cheques. The court rejected the claim on the basis that the plaintiff was not a member of any clearly ascertained class as required by the decision of the High Court in *Caltex Oil (Australia) Pty Ltd v The Dredge 'Willemstad'* (1976) 136 CLR 529.

The court particularly relied upon a quote from Gibbs J (at 555):

> In my opinion it is still right to say that as a general rule damages are not recoverable for economic loss which is not consequential upon injury to the plaintiff's person or property. The fact that the loss was foreseeable is not enough to make it recoverable. However, there are exceptional cases in which the defendant has knowledge or means of knowledge that the plaintiff individually and not merely as a member of an unascertained class, will be likely to suffer economic loss as a consequence of his negligence, and owes the plaintiff duty to take care not to cause him such loss by his negligent act.

See also *Capri Jewellers Pty Ltd v Commonwealth Bank of Australia* [1973] ACLD 152 where a cleaner stole blank bank cheque forms.

SAFE CUSTODY

[4.53]   The taking of goods and documents for safe-keeping is a banking service which is at least as old as the modern business of banking itself. It is the original ancillary service offered by bankers to their customers and it offers the oldest examples of the problems of defining the duty of a banker to the customer.

When valuable chattels are deposited for safe-keeping, it is customary for the customer to deposit them with the banker in a locked box and for the customer to retain the key. Documents will ordinarily be placed in a sealed envelope by the customer. In smaller branches, the goods deposited will be kept in the bank's general safe.

The law which defines the duty of the banker to the customer in such circumstances is a part of the law of bailment. The banker is the bailee of the goods or documents and the bailor is the customer. The essence of bailment is that the goods are deposited by the bailor with the bailee on the condition that they will be returned to the bailor in due course.

[4.54]   The problems that might arise with a bailment fall substantially into two categories. First, the goods might be damaged or lost while in the custody of the bailee. Second, the bailee might deliver the goods to the wrong person, either inadvertently or as the result of the fraudulent conduct of an employee or agent.

[4.55]   In the first case, that of damage or loss, the bailee is liable to the bailor only if there has been some negligence in the keeping of the goods. However, from a very early time the law recognised that there is a wide range of circumstances in which a bailment might arise and that the standard of care required of the bailor should vary accordingly. For example, a neighbour who, as a favour, agrees to store a household item while the bailor is on holiday is as much a bailee as the banker who agrees to receive very valuable items and keep them in the bank's strong room. Yet, the average person would expect very different standards of care of these two bailees.

The distinction which was drawn by the law was between a bailee who charged for the service provided, called a bailment for reward, and the bailee who performed the service without reward, called a gratuitous bailment. Much of the discussion to be found in some case law and texts concerns the question of whether a banker who takes goods or documents for safe custody is a bailee for reward even when there is no direct charge made for the service. For reasons which will become apparent, it is thought that the distinction is no longer relevant for a banker since the standard of care required is special to the situation of the banker.

STANDARD OF CARE

[4.56]   The first case to consider the standard of care applicable to banker bailees was *Giblin v McMullen* (1868) LR 2 PC 317. A customer left a box containing debentures with the bank for safe custody. The box was stored in the strong room of the bank together with boxes belonging to other customers and other securities belonging to the bank. Customers had access to the room during banking hours but were at all times accompanied by a bank clerk. The room had two iron doors which were opened by separate keys. These keys were in the charge of the cashier by day and at night one of them was left with the cashier and the other to another officer of the bank. The cashier of the bank took the debentures from the box and used them for his own purposes.

Surprisingly, the Supreme Court of Victoria and the Privy Council held that the bank had not been negligent since the bank was a gratuitous bailee and was not bound to exercise more than ordinary care.

[4.57] *Giblin's* case has been extensively criticised. There appeared to be no serious consideration of the vicarious liability of the bank, as bailee, for its employee's action, nor as a principal for the fraud of the agent acting within the scope of employment: see *Port Swettenham Authority v T W Wu & Co (M) Sdn Bhd* [1979] AC 580; *Morris v Martin & Sons Ltd* [1966] 1 QB at 735; *Lloyd v Grace Smith & Co* [1912] AC 716. Further, although the court held that there was no actionable negligence, the jury found expressly that the bank had been grossly negligent. In his discussion of the case, Chorley notes (p 246) that '... it may be doubted whether the decision would be the same at the present time'.

[4.58] *Giblin's* case was distinguished in *Re United Services Co (Johnston's Claim)* (1870) LR 6 Ch App 212. Johnston owned railway shares which he deposited with a banker for safe-keeping. They were stolen by the manager who obtained a transfer of the shares to his own name by means of several forgeries of Johnston's signature. When Johnston learned of the transfer, he brought suit against the railway company and succeeded in having the shares re-transferred to him, but he did not receive any costs in the action. The banker went into liquidation and Johnston sought to prove for the amount of his costs in the action.

The court held that the banker was a bailee for reward, distinguishing *Giblin* on the basis that the banker here had received a small commission for the safe-keeping of the shares. The court also found that the banker had been negligent, but the loss claimed by Johnston was, of course, too remote.

[4.59] If the distinction between a gratuitous bailment and a bailment for reward is still relevant, then there can be little doubt that the modern banker will be a bailee for reward since a fee is invariably charged for the safe custody service: see *Port Swettenham Authority v T W Wu & Co (M) Sdn Bhd* [1979] AC 580. Even if the bank does not charge a fee for the specific service, it seems that the bank is expecting to obtain some benefit from the service. In the case of a customer, it is at least arguable that the service is provided under the general banker-customer contract. If the bank provides the service to a non-customer, then it seems likely that it is expecting that the person at least consider becoming a customer: see also *Smorgan v Federal Commissioner of Taxation* (1976) 134 CLR 465 where Stephen J indicated that the fact that safe custody is a part of banking business supported the argument that banks are bailees for reward.

It seems more likely that the distinction between a bailee for reward and a gratuitous bailee is not relevant. The distinction was originally made for the purpose of defining different levels of care which the bailee must exercise. A more useful approach is to adopt the modern practice of defining the standard of care required to be that which is reasonable in all the circumstances. This approach was followed by the English Court of Appeal in *Houghland v R*

R Low (Luxury Coaches) Ltd [1962] 1 QB 694 and by Gibbs CJ in *Pitt Son & Badgery Ltd v Proulefco SA* (1984) 153 CLR 644 at 646.

If that represents the law, and it is suggested that it does, then the standard of care required is that of a reasonable banker in view of all the surrounding circumstances. The receipt of consideration and the amount of that consideration would merely be a factor which was to be considered in determining the appropriate standard of care.

WRONGFUL DELIVERY TO A THIRD PERSON

[4.60] The standard of care required of the bailee in the second circumstance, that of delivering the goods to the wrong person, is on a very much different footing, for although the standard of care to be exercised in taking care of the goods might vary with the circumstances of the bailment, the very minimum required of any bailee is that the goods be returned to the correct person.

Consequently, there is a very strict duty on the bailee to return the goods to the correct person. Delivery to the wrong person will result in liability in an action for conversion. In such an action, it does not matter that the wrongful delivery was made honestly and without negligence; the principle is very old: see, for example, *Stephenson v Hart* (1828) 4 Bing 476; 130 ER 851; *Hiort v London and North Western Railway Co* (1879) 4 Ex D 188.

This problem of delivery to the wrong person is not as rare as might be thought, for when the goods are deposited in joint names or in the name of a company or a partnership, it might be difficult for the banker to establish the right of some particular person to claim redelivery. When goods are being deposited in such circumstances, it is of the utmost importance for the banker to obtain express instructions concerning the identity of those who are authorised to collect the goods. The banker may retain the goods for a reasonable period of time in order to make inquiries: *Clayton v Le Roy* [1911] 2 KB 1031. If the banker is unable to determine unequivocally which of the competing claims are valid, then the only safe course of action is to interplead. This, in effect, is asking the parties to determine their dispute before a court.

BURDEN OF PROOF

[4.61] The best view is that where goods are damaged the onus is on the bailee to show that the loss was not caused by the negligence or misconduct of employee's or agents with whom the goods were entrusted for safe-keeping: see, for example, *Port Swettenham Authority v T W Wu & Co (M) Sdn Bhd* [1979] AC 580; *Pitt Son & Badgery Ltd v Proulefco SA* (1984) 153 CLR 644. However, a different view is that expressed by Zelling J in *WGH Nominees Pty Ltd v Tomblin* (1985) 39 SASR 117. In his view, the onus is on the plaintiff to prove negligence. However, when goods are lost there is an evidential onus on the bailee to point to circumstances negativing negligence on his or her part. In view of the fact that the bailee is almost always the party who has access to information concerning the circumstances of the loss, the former view seems preferable.

CHEQUES

[5.1] Banks are central to the payments system of Australia. Most payments other than those made with cash are by cheque or by direct credit and debit through the electronic funds transfer system (EFT). The cheque system could not function as a major method of payment without the infrastructure of the banks and the clearing house system. Although there is no logical reason why the participants in the clearing system must be banks, there is every reason to demand that the participants be financial institutions of outstanding stability, for the amounts payable at the end of the day may be very substantial.

Financial institutions other than banks are beginning to play a greater role in the payments system. Building societies and credit unions were in the forefront of developments in electronic funds transfer systems since they saw this as a means of breaking the banks' monopoly over the payments system. Many of these non-bank institutions entered into 'cheque agency agreements' whereby their customers could make third party payments from their non-bank accounts. The Cheques and Payment Orders Act 1986 (the CPOA) authorised certain institutions, including building societies and credit unions to issue 'payment orders', instruments which are similar in all respects to cheques save that they are drawn on non-bank financial institutions. The CPOA also regulates certain aspects of the cheque agency agreements: see CPOA s 100.

Non-bank financial institutions may now belong to the clearing system operated by the Australian Payment Clearing Association (APCA). In its initial response to the Wallis Inquiry, the government has announced that non-bank institutions will be permitted to issue cheques. In spite of this, it is thought that many of the smaller institutions may continue to use agency arrangements for clearing purposes. The agency arrangements may be cheaper for small institutions as well as protecting them from the financial exposure associated with being a full participant in the payment system.

This chapter will discuss the major paper-based method of payment, the cheque. Because of the similarities, the payment order will be considered alongside the cheque even though it is, in numerical terms, of much less importance than the cheque and is likely to disappear in the near future.

[5.2]   The structure of the Australian payments system has changed very rapidly in the last few years. In the first edition of this text it was reported that the cheque was responsible for almost 65 per cent of all debits to bank accounts in terms of actual numbers of transactions. Figures recently published by the Australian Payments Systems Council show how the cheque has declined in importance as a percentage of all non-cash payments. In 1980, cheques accounted for 85% of all such payments. In 1991, the figure was down to 60% and by 1996 had dropped to 43%.

By 1996, direct entry transfers accounted for 25% of all non-cash payments, credit cards for 13% and EFTPOS for 18%. It is to be expected that the use of the cheque will continue to decline as a percentage of all non-cash payments.

[5.3]   Cash is probably the most common method of payment, although figures are impossible to verify. Estimates are that 90 per cent of all payments are made in cash, but a great many of these are small transactions. At the end of 1986, there was about $600 in currency held per head of population: *The Australian Payments System*, The Australian Payments System Council, Sydney, 1987. By June 1997, that figure had risen to more than $1000 per head.

Since the early 1990s there has been a sharp rise in the amount of currency in circulation. The reasons for this are not entirely clear, but are probably due to a combination of factors. These would include the fall in interest rates during the period, the various effects of the Financial Transactions Reports Act 1988 and the convenience of obtaining cash through ATMs.

According to figures provided by the Reserve Bank of Australia, the vast majority of cash is held in notes of denomination $100 and $50. These two denominations account for almost 80 per cent by value of outstanding currency.

[5.4]   New payment mechanisms are being introduced. Various forms of 'computer money' such as the 'smart card' and 'digital cash' seem destined to make an impact on both cash and non-cash payments: see [8.86] for a discussion of 'computer money'. A new method of initiating direct credits will be introduced by the major banks in 1998. Known as B-Pay, the system will permit ordering direct credits by telephone, paper or computer. Payment in the B-Pay scheme may be made to any participating payee.

[5.5]   Although cheques have declined as a percentage of the total volume of non-cash payments, that does not mean that the cheque is becoming obsolete. The number of cheques written each year has remained constant. Australians continue to write a large number of cheques in comparison with the rest of the world. The continued existence of the cheque system would not be possible without the computerisation of the cheque clearing system, a development which began in the early 1960s and is continuing today.

The opportunities presented by developments in computers and communications were stifled by certain aspects of the law relating to the banks' duties in handling cheques. For this reason, the federal government appointed a committee to review the Bills of Exchange Act 1909 (Cth) (the BEA), the legislation which governed many aspects of cheques. This committee was appointed in 1962. The Cheques and Payment Orders Act 1986 is the legislative fruit of that committee's report.

In order to understand the new Act, it is necessary to conduct a short digression to consider the history of cheques, for most of the old cases on cheques and bills of exchange continue to define the rights and obligations of those dealing with cheques.

THE ORIGINS OF CHEQUES

[5.6]   Until the passage of the new Act, cheques were simply a special form of a bill of exchange. Indeed, a cheque still remains, legally, a bill of exchange in most cases although it is clear that the CPOA is to regulate the relationship between the parties if the instrument is a 'cheque' within the definition of the CPOA. This identification with bills of exchange is an historical accident which has caused a certain amount of legal difficulty, for the commercial role of cheques is entirely different from that of bills. This difference in function is one of the primary reasons for the introduction of the CPOA.

BILLS OF EXCHANGE

[5.7]   A bill of exchange is a written order from a creditor to his or her debtor ordering the debtor to pay some third party. The reason for the legal importance of bills is that our law has incorporated the ancient law merchant relating to bills of exchange: see BEA s 5(2). The result is that the rules governing transfer and the taking of bills are very much different from the usual rules of English property law. As a very general simplification, the rules governing the transfer of bills of exchange favour the innocent bona fide purchaser of a bill rather than the rights of the original owner: see Chapter 9 for a discussion of negotiability of cheques and bills of exchange.

This is exactly the reverse of the situation in sale of goods, where the rules of transfer favour the original owner and a purchaser generally takes the goods subject to any defect of title, a position which is summed up by the Latin phrase *nemo dat quod non habet*. The law of transfer of bills is one which favours commercial transactions, the law of transfer of goods is one which favours property rights.

[5.8]   The rules of law which govern the transfer of bills of exchange also reflect commercial practice in that they contemplate and encourage the transfer of a single bill to many different parties. The reasons for this have to do with the use of the bill to facilitate international trade. In the classical commercial transaction, the buyer of goods is a debtor who owes money to the seller/creditor. Since the parties are in different places, the seller orders the buyer/debtor to pay a third party. This third party would often be a banker or other financier who had places of business both in the place of the seller and of the buyer. The seller could then take the bill of exchange to the local place of business of the financier and transfer the bill in exchange for cash. The financier would transfer the bill to the place of business at the place of the buyer and the buyer would pay locally.

Needless to say, the financier charged fees for performing these services. In addition, it might be arranged that the buyer would not pay immediately but would receive credit. In such a case, the financier might wish to keep the bill until time for payment or, alternatively, transfer the bill on to other financiers. The person in possession of the bill at the time when payment was due would present the bill to the buyer/debtor for payment.

THE INVENTION OF CHEQUES

[5.9] An account kept with a bank is in law a contractual debt owed by the bank to the customer: *Foley v Hill* (1848) 2 HL Cas 28; 9 ER 1002. Nothing could be more natural for the commercial community than to enlist the aid of a known instrument, the bill of exchange, in order to transfer that debt to a third party. Holden argues that this developed out of a simpler system whereby the 'note' written by the customer was taken to the 'banker', at that time either a scrivener or a goldsmith, where the person named in the note was paid directly in specie: J M Holden, *The History of Negotiable Instruments in English Law*, University of London Press, London, 1955, Chapter VII.

The 'check' as it was originally spelled was so named because of the early practice of keeping a counterfoil or 'check' as a means of restraining alterations and forgeries. It seems that the modern spelling 'cheque' was introduced in 1828 by Gilbart, who explained in a footnote that 'Most writers spell it check. I have adopted the above form because it is free from ambiguity and is analogous to ex-chequer, the royal treasury': J W Gilbart, *Practical Treatise on Banking* (1828) as quoted in Holden, op cit. The new spelling is now the preferred one in all common law countries except the United States, which clings to the older tradition.

THE INCREASE IN USE AS A PAYMENT INSTRUMENT

[5.10] Whatever the historical origins of cheques, their use in daily commerce quickly increased. Holden notes evidence that in the first half of the eighteenth century, the customers of London banks made use to about an equal extent of banknotes and of cheques drawn on the accounts kept with a bank. By the last half of the eighteenth century, banknotes had virtually ceased to be issued. Holden gives several reasons: the cheque could be drawn for the exact amount of the debt; the cheque provided a permanent record of settlement; and their use made it unnecessary to keep large amounts of notes and coins: Holden, op cit, p 214.

THE DUAL NATURE OF A CHEQUE

[5.11]   Thus, it is something of an historical accident that a cheque came to be a special form of a bill of exchange. It is an unfortunate accident for banking law students and for our payment system, for the function of a cheque is much different from that of a bill of exchange. The primary purpose of a bill was, and is, to provide extended credit. The primary purpose of a cheque is to make a simple payment: see [10.6] for a further discussion of bills as credit instruments.

In order to fulfil the purpose of a bill, it is desirable that the bill be easily and readily transferable and that the person who is taking the bill may take it with confidence. In order to fulfil the purpose of a cheque as a payment instrument, it is desirable to provide a secure means of seeing that it reaches the intended payee and no other party and that, if it does fall into the wrong hands, payment should be difficult or, better, impossible to obtain. The two functions and their requirements are clearly incompatible.

THE MANNING COMMITTEE REPORT

[5.12]   Because of the phenomenal growth of the cheque system in the post-war years, the English banks sought and obtained the passage of legislation which would enable them to streamline some of their operations and, at the same time, shift some of the risks of the cheque system from themselves to their customers. In England, the result was the Cheques Act 1957. This was followed in New Zealand by an almost identical Act, the Cheques Act 1960.

In Australia, the response was to form the Committee to Review the Bills of Exchange Act 1909–1958, which was known as the Manning Committee after its chairman, the Honourable J K Manning, who was a judge of the Supreme Court of New South Wales. The Committee was appointed in April 1962 and reported in 1964. Its terms of reference were to consider the provisions of the Bills of Exchange Act and to recommend any alteration to the Act that might be thought desirable, but in particular, to consider whether any of the changes effected by the Cheques Act 1957 should be adopted in Australia.

REASONS FOR THE COMMITTEE

[5.13]   The 'streamlining' which was required may be illustrated by evidence which was given to the Committee by the Australian Bankers' Association. It was said that the number of cheques drawn each year was in excess of 300,000,000 and that 77 per cent of those were deposited directly to the credit of the account of the named payee, that is, they were simple payment instruments. It was said that there were approximately 1,000,000 cheques dishonoured each year and that half of these were for lack of indorsement or for irregular indorsement.

At the time, all cheques required the indorsement of the depositor, even if the depositor was the named payee of the cheque. The evidence of the bankers, with which the Committee agreed, was to the effect that much time was wasted in confirming indorsements in situations where they served little purpose and often, particularly in the case of 'irregular' indorsements, caused needless disruption to the orderly collection of cheques: see [10.109] for a discussion of 'irregular' indorsements. The irony of the situation is that the demand for indorsements was probably not legally necessary and had no significant legal consequences: see *Smith v Commercial Banking Co of Sydney Ltd* (1910) 11 CLR 667 and G A Weaver and R C Craigie, *The Law Relating to Banker and Customer in Australia*, 2nd ed, Law Book Co, Sydney, 1990, para [13.400].

MAIN RECOMMENDATIONS

[5.14] The most important recommendation of the Committee was that there should be separate Acts for cheques and other bills of exchange. The primary reason for this was the difficulty of determining which of the rules relating to bills of exchange were to be applied to cheques and to what extent. The Committee correctly pointed out that the drawer of a cheque is the person who is ultimately responsible for payment whereas it is the acceptor who is primarily liable on a bill of exchange and that this fundamental difference causes problems throughout in the application of the BEA to cheques.

The Committee further recommended that every cheque should be transferable, that is, it should not be possible for the drawer of a cheque to insert words which prevented the payee from transferring the cheque to some other party. The primary reasons given were that millions of cheques were transferred each year and that in many cases this was necessary because the payee did not have a bank account: see [6.77] and CPOA s 39.

The abolition of indorsements in certain circumstances was approved and certain statutory protections were recommended for banks to protect them against actions by holders and customers when losses were suffered due to the elimination of indorsements. It was perhaps unfortunate that risks associated with measures designed to make business easier for banks were placed on the individual customer, but the Committee made no analysis of any alternative: see [7.54] for a discussion of the role of indorsements when collecting and paying a cheque.

The other major recommendations of the Committee concerned the alteration of the method of presentment to allow for a scheme of 'truncation'. The widespread use of computers in the clearing process was only a few years old at the time and it was believed that, rather than physically transporting the cheque to the paying bank, it should be possible to merely transmit the information on the cheque. The idea is sound and the details of its implementation occupy a significant portion of the new Act: see [5.108].

The Committee's recommendations were generally well received by the commercial community, but received only minimal support from the government of the day. There were amendments to the BEA in 1971 which implemented the proposals concerning indorsements, but the remainder of the recommendations of the Committee were more or less shelved, even though the Committee had included a draft Bill in their report.

The Cheques and Payment Orders Act 1986

[5.15] Almost 20 years to the day after the Report of the Manning Committee, the Attorney-General's Department produced a draft exposure of a cheques Bill for public comment. That Bill lapsed when the government called new elections and the Bill, with some changes, was reintroduced as the Cheques Bill 1985. There was then further delay pending the outcome of representations to government by interested non-bank financial institutions who were eager to be given the statutory protection enjoyed by banks. These protections were then incorporated into the Bill as well as a new instrument, the payment order. A payment order is similar in all respects to a cheque save that the drawee is a prescribed non-bank financial institution. While it would have been possible to extend the definition of 'cheque' rather than introduce a new instrument, the government acceded to representations from the banks that 'cheques' were accorded a certain privileged status by the community because of the banks' financial stability. The resulting Bill became the Cheques and Payment Orders Act 1986 which received assent in December 1986. It was then subject to several relatively minor amendments and was proclaimed on 1 July 1987.

Relationship to BEA

[5.16] Rather curiously, the cheques sections of the BEA remain in place, but s 6(2) of the BEA now provides that the BEA does not apply to any instrument to which the new Act applies. This structure may have practical importance, for there are circumstances where an instrument may fail the definition of 'cheque' in the new Act, yet still be a bill of exchange drawn on a banker and payable on demand: see Chapter 9. For such instruments, the BEA will continue to govern.

Main criticism of the Act

[5.17] The Act makes few significant changes in the law of cheques. The most significant are those concerning presentment of cheques, the new provisions allowing for truncation, and, of course, the extension of statutory defences to non-bank institutions and 'cheques' drawn on such institutions. There are numerous minor changes to the wording of sections taken directly from the BEA and there are a few welcome clarifications of the existing law.

On the whole, however, the Act continues the existing complexity of the law by failing to separate the payment function of a cheque from the negotiable instrument function. This is particularly disappointing since the past 20 years have seen substantial developments in the understanding of the payments system, as well as developments in the payments system itself and the establishment of an Australian Payments System Council which monitors the system: see *The Australian Payments System*, Australian Payments System Council, Sydney, 1987 and the yearly reports of the APSC.

[5.18]   While the payments system has undergone substantial development since the Manning Committee reported, the use of bills of exchange and other negotiable instruments has also changed considerably. The Manning Committee report said (para 32): '... while bills of exchange are used in the conduct of most overseas trading transactions, cheques are used overwhelmingly if not entirely for local transactions.'

The distinction between local and overseas transactions is simply no longer appropriate. The bill of exchange has become a major instrument in local short-term money market financing: see [10.6] and G de Q Walker, 'The Australian Revival of the Bill of Exchange' (1978) 52 *ALJ* 244 for a discussion of the use of bills in the money market. The cheque, while still a very important payment mechanism, is by no means the only non-cash means of making payments.

In short, it is disappointing that after 30 years, the Act remains primarily an implementation of recommendations made which were appropriate for 1964 rather than addressing the payments system as it was in 1986. In part for this reason, the law continues to be complex and unsatisfactory.

THE DRAWER-DRAWEE CONTRACT

[5.19]   A cheque is an order from a person to a bank which orders the bank to pay a certain sum of money: s 10. The definition of a cheque will be discussed in greater detail later, but the question immediately arises as to why the bank should obey such an order. The answer, of course, is that it is contractually bound to do so. The duty of the bank to pay its customer's cheques, provided that certain preconditions are met, is one of the most important of the bank's obligations. From a commercial point of view, it is probably the major reason that banks are able to attract significant deposits from the public on terms which traditionally have offered no interest at all and still offer interest rates which are substantially below those available elsewhere.

The definition of 'cheque' in the CPOA does not require that the instrument be drawn by a customer of the drawee bank. It might seem difficult to imagine situations in which anyone other than a customer would draw such a cheque since the drawee bank will be under no contractual obligation to the drawer to honour the cheque: see [5.66]. However, various agency arrangements may be used to permit a smaller financial institution to gain access to the payment system through existing participants. So, for example, a small institution S might make an arrangement with bank B that allows customers of S to draw cheques on B. Although B is under no contractual obligation to the drawer to honour the cheque, it is under a contractual obligation to S to do so.

[5.20]   When the bank pays the cheque, the obligation is to pay the person named by the drawer the sum named by the drawer. Paying any other person or any other amount is a prima facie breach of the bank's contractual duty. Unless the bank can show that the breach is caused by a breach of the customer or is excused in some other way, the bank may not debit the account with the amount of the cheque. As a corollary to this duty on the bank, the customer is under certain contractual duties which are intended to safeguard the bank's position. It is convenient to discuss the customer's duties with regard to the cheque system before the duties of the bank.

DUTIES OF THE CUSTOMER

[5.21]   There are two fundamental contractual obligations owed by the customer. These are known as the *Macmillan* duty and the *Greenwood* duty after the landmark cases in which the existence and the extent of the duties were clarified.

THE MACMILLAN DUTY

[5.22]   The customer is under a duty to exercise reasonable care in drawing cheques so that the banker is not misled and forgery is not facilitated. This contractual duty has long been recognised, but the definition of its precise scope is surprisingly recent.

In *Joachimson v Swiss Bank Corporation* [1921] 3 KB 110 Lord Atkin referred to the duty of the customer to exercise care in framing the order to the bank (see [2.10]ff), but it was not until 1981 that the existence of the duty was placed beyond doubt in Australia by the decision of the High Court in *Commonwealth Trading Bank of Australia v Sydney Wide Stores Pty Ltd* (1981) 55 ALJR 574. In that case, the High Court overruled older Australian authority (*Colonial Bank of Australasia Ltd v Marshall* (1904) 1 CLR 632) and approved of the English decision in *London Joint Stock Bank Ltd v Macmillan and Arthur* [1918] AC 777 which was itself based on the older case of *Young v Grote* (1827) 4 Bing 253; 130 ER 764. The *Sydney Wide* case brought Australian law back into conformity with the law in other parts of the Commonwealth. This duty to exercise care in the drawing of cheques is known as the *Macmillan* duty.

In *Macmillan's* case, a confidential clerk was employed by the plaintiff firm of stockbrokers. As part of his duties, the clerk prepared cheques for the firm. The cheques required the signature of at least one of the partners. The clerk prepared a cheque which was made payable to the firm 'or bearer'. The amount of the cheque was not entered in the place for words, but in the place for figures was entered as £ 2 :0:0, leaving a space between the sterling symbol and the first 2 and between the 2 and 0. He took the cheque to one of the partners who signed it and returned it to the clerk. The clerk then added the words 'one hundred and twenty pounds' in the space for writing and altered the amount in figures by filling in the spaces accordingly. The cheque was presented to the defendant bank which paid it over the counter at the branch where the account was kept.

The firm sued the bank for breach of contract, alleging that the firm had ordered the payment of £2 whereas the bank had paid £120. They were successful at the first instance and in the Court of Appeal, but the House of Lords took the opportunity to clarify the contract between the parties. In one of the most important of all banking law decisions, the House held that the customer owed the bank a duty to exercise care in the drawing of cheques and that the alteration of the cheque was, in the circumstances, a direct result of the breach of that duty.

[5.23] The extent of the duty is to exercise those precautions which are ordinarily taken by prudent drawers of cheques. It is possible that the precautions which must be taken vary from time to time and from place to place as business practices change. The *Macmillan* cheque was a particularly gross failure to take care. In *Slingsby v District Bank Ltd* [1932] 1 KB 544 the court held that there was no breach of the duty when a cheque was drawn which left space between the name of the payee and the printed words 'or order'. A fraudulent solicitor added words after the name of the payee which allowed him to obtain payment of the cheque. The court held that there was no breach of the *Macmillan* duty since it was not a usual precaution to draw lines after the payee's name. It is clear from the judgment that the court considered that practices might change and that there would then be an obligation on the part of the drawer.

In the *Sydney Wide* case, the drawer of the cheque carried on business with a company called Computer Accounting Services. A fraudulent clerk of the drawer company made a cheque payable to CAS and obtained an authorised signature of the drawer. He then added an 'H' to the end of the writing and obtained payment of the cheque. The plaintiff drawer sued the bank claiming that there had been a breach of contract in that the wrong person had been paid. As mentioned above, Australian law at the time did not recognise a duty to exercise care when drawing a cheque. Nevertheless, the bank pleaded such lack of care as a defence and the case went to the High Court on the question of law. It is important to realise that the court was not concerned with the particular cheque, but only the existence of the duty. The court approved *Macmillan* but specifically refrained from deciding whether there had been a breach of the duty in the particular circumstances.

The effect of warnings

[5.24] It is possible that the bank may increase the level of care required of a customer by giving explicit instructions concerning the drawing of cheques. In *Varker v Commercial Banking Co of Sydney Ltd* [1972] 2 NSWLR 967, the bank manager had personally given the customer warnings about the way in which the cheques should be drawn. In addition, the inner cover of the chequebook issued by the bank carried the warning:

Commence figures, and the words of the amount with a CAPITAL letter, as near the left-hand edge as possible, leaving no blank spaces between the words.

The court held that these factors were such as to impose a duty on the customer to draw cheques carefully at a time when there was no such duty under the general law of Australia. By the same reasoning, it would seem that it would be possible to raise the standard required by means of explicit warnings.

However, it is not easy for the bank to impose a higher duty. Merely printing warnings in chequebooks will not alter the contractual relationship unless it can be shown by the bank that the warnings were actually brought to the attention of the customer and that the customer fully understood the consequences of failing to heed the warnings: *Tai Hing Cotton Mill Ltd v Liu Hong Hing Bank Ltd* [1985] 2 All ER 947; *Burnett v Westminster Bank Ltd* [1966] 1 QB 742; see [2.31]. It may be easier for a bank to impose a higher duty when the account is governed by the Code of Banking Practice: see [9.2]ff.

Subsequent negligence by the bank

[5.25] Suppose that the *Macmillan* duty has been breached, that is, the customer has drawn the cheque carelessly and the cheque has been altered as a result of the careless drawing. It might still be possible for the customer to prevent the bank from debiting the account if it can be shown that the bank was negligent in the payment of the altered cheque. The question came before the court in the remarkable *Varker v Commercial Banking Co of Sydney Ltd* [1972] 2 NSWLR 967.

The plaintiff had been injured in a road accident and could write cheques only with difficulty. At the time when Varker opened the account with the defendant bank, the assistant accountant emphasised the importance of drawing cheques carefully and warned that if he trusted any other person to fill in cheques that he should take care to see that the cheque was properly drafted by the other party. Varker drew several cheques on the account which were made payable to 'cash or bearer', none of which exceeded $200. The assistant accountant telephoned Varker to warn that cheques should not be drawn payable to 'cash or bearer' if they were in fact intended for a specific payee.

About two months after the opening of the account, a cheque was filled in by Varker's brother-in-law and signed by Varker. The cheque as drawn had the words 'one hundred and fourty' [sic] in the space where the amount was to be written in words and there was a space between the printed words 'the sum of' and the beginning of the written words. In the space for figures, the amount appeared as 140.00 but there was a space between the printed dollar sign and the handwritten figure '1'. The cheque was made payable to 'cash or bearer'. After Varker had signed the cheque, the brother-in-law inserted the word 'sixty' in the space for words and the figure '6' in the place for figures making the cheque for the amount 6140.00. He deposited the cheque for collection with his own bank and the defendant bank paid the cheque though the clearing house.

The cheque was negligently drawn and was a breach of Varker's contractual duty to the bank. However, the court also held that the payment was negligently made. This was because the cheque was in an unusual form, Varker had been warned about drawing cheques in favour of 'cash or bearer', the bank knew that Varker was a person who could be easily defrauded and the bank could have telephoned Varker about the cheque, as it had done occasionally in the past, but it did not. This negligent payment was a breach of the bank's contractual duty, for it is an implied term in every contract that the obligation be performed with appropriate care.

The issue in the case was whether this subsequent breach of contract by the bank precluded it from debiting Varker's account with the amount of the cheque. Macfarlane J held that it did, saying (at 976):

> ... if, subsequently to the breach of duty by the plaintiff there had been a breach by the bank of the duty which it owed to the customer in the very same transaction ... then the bank would not be able to maintain the debit.

[5.26] It has been said that *Varker's* case penalised the bank for taking special steps to warn Varker and to treat him as a special customer, since it was precisely that evidence which contributed to the finding that payment had been negligent. However, a better view is that once the bank knew of Varker's disability there was an obligation to see that his interests were protected, an obligation which was not discharged merely by one interview and a telephone call. If the bank had chosen to do nothing in such circumstances, it would have been even more negligent than it was.

THE GREENWOOD DUTY

[5.27] The second duty of the customer is to notify the bank of any forgeries known to the customer. Since the bank bears the risk of a forged drawer's signature, it would clearly be inappropriate to allow the customer to remain silent in those circumstances where the customer's knowledge may prevent further losses to the bank. As will be seen in the following, the duty is only to notify known forgeries and other account irregularities. There appears to be no duty to discover forgeries or other irregularities, even if this might be done easily by the customer: see [5.32].

In *Greenwood v Martins Bank Ltd* [1933] AC 51 the plaintiff's wife had forged a series of cheques on his account. When he discovered the forgeries, he threatened to notify the bank immediately, but she begged him not to, explaining that she had used the money to assist her sister in a legal action. The plaintiff did not inform the defendant bank of the forgeries. Later he found that the explanation was false and that she had continued to forge cheques on his account. He again threatened to notify the bank, whereupon she committed suicide. The husband brought the action to prevent the bank from maintaining the debit to the account for the amount of the forged cheques.

The court held that there had been a breach of duty by the husband in failing to notify the bank of the forgeries. Under legislation in force at the time, the plaintiff's liability for the torts of his wife came to an end upon her death so that the bank lost any right of recovery as a result of the plaintiff's breach. The bank was held entitled to maintain the debit for the amounts of cheques forged both before and after the plaintiff learned of the forgeries.

The *Greenwood* duty extends to notifying the bank of any unauthorised transaction on the account which is known to the customer: *West v Commercial Bank of Australia* (1935) 55 CLR 319.

The basis of the duty

[5.28]   The duty to notify is often phrased in terms of estoppel rather than in terms of contract. Indeed, the language of estoppel was used in *Greenwood's* case, where it was said that silence could raise an estoppel when there is an obligation on the party to speak. On this analysis, failure to notify of known forgeries estops the customer from denying the validity of the signature.

This analysis in terms of estoppel has caused difficulties. In *Brown v Westminster Bank Ltd* [1964] 2 Lloyd's Rep 187, the bank manager had visited an elderly woman customer in order to ascertain the validity of signatures on a series of cheques. The cheques were drawn in favour of Mr Carless, a servant who lived with her. She assured the manager that the cheques were genuine. In fact, they were forged.

The court held that she was estopped from denying the validity of the signatures. This is clearly correct as to the cheques which had been written after the visit of the manager, but the court held that the estoppel also extended to those cheques which were drawn before the visit. As to the argument that there could not have been any reliance by the bank on the representation prior to the representation being made, the court said (at 203):

> What were the facts which then existed and in relation to which the representation is then made? The facts that cheques which in truth were forged were represented as genuine ... the plaintiff is thereafter debarred from setting up the true facts ... by reason of the fact that the bank paid the future cheques, the bank has suffered detriment.

In truth, however, there must be seen to be two representations. The first is that the original cheques were valid. This was an express representation by the customer. The second representation was that future cheques would also be valid. This representation was implied. It was the second representation which was relied upon by the bank and the only representation in *Brown's* case which led to detriment. It may be possible for reliance on the first representation to cause losses, such as in *Greenwood's* case, but that was not the situation in *Brown*.

[5.29]   *Brown's* case was followed in *Tina Motors Pty Ltd v Australian and New Zealand Banking Group Ltd* [1977] VR 205 where a total of 54 forged cheques had been paid by the defendant bank. On two occasions the bank had questioned the signatures on the cheques before paying but had been informed by the plaintiff's manager that the signatures were genuine. Only one of the cheques had been paid before the representation. Crockett J held that the bank was entitled to succeed with regard to this cheque, citing the passage from *Brown's* case quoted above. Again, it is submitted that the correctness of the reasoning depends upon a construction and interpretation of the actual representation.

[5.30] A better analysis of these cases would be to rely upon the customer's contractual obligation to give careful consideration to the bank's request for information. The off-hand assurance that the signatures are genuine would be a clear breach of this contractual obligation and the damages could be assessed on usual contractual grounds. In *Greenwood's* case, this would lead to the same result, but in *Brown* and *Tina Motors*, the customer would succeed with regard to those cheques which were drawn prior to the request for information. For a view favouring the estoppel analysis, see T Damian, 'The Customer is Nearly Always Right: Banks and Unauthorised Cheque Payments', (1996) 7 *JBFLP* 277.

[5.31] Whether the analysis be by estoppel or by contract, it is clear that not every breach of the *Greenwood* duty will allow the bank to debit the account. In order to succeed, the bank must show that it has suffered some loss from the customer's breach of duty. For example, in *Fung Kai Sun v Chan Fui Hing* [1951] AC 489 the plaintiff discovered that some mortgage documents were forged. The defendant was not notified for some three weeks. The Privy Council dismissed the defendant's claim that they were prejudiced by being deprived of the opportunity to obtain restitution from the forger, there being no evidence to substantiate such a claim.

POSSIBLE OTHER DUTIES

[5.32] From time to time there are suggestions that the customer is required by the banker-customer contract to exercise some further duty for the purpose of protecting the bank's interests. Generally speaking, these additional duties fall into three categories. First, it is said that there is, or should be, a duty to exercise a reasonable effort to discover forgeries. Second, that there is, or should be, a limited duty (beyond that of exercising care in the drawing of cheques) to prevent forgeries, most notably by the exercise of care in the keeping of the chequebook. Finally, it is said that there is, or should be, some broader duty on the customer to organise business so that the bank's interest is safeguarded. Each of these alleged duties has been the subject of recent case law.

Duty to discover forgeries

[5.33] If there is a duty to discover forgeries, then at the very least that duty would require the customer to read the periodic statement which is sent by the bank and to notify the bank of any entries there which the customer believes to represent unauthorised debits.

[5.34] The question of a duty to read the statement was first canvassed seriously in *Kepitigalla Rubber Estates Ltd v National Bank of India Ltd* [1909] 2 KB 1010. The secretary of a company forged the signatures of two directors on a number of cheques over a period of time. At that time, the method of banking called for the customer to come to the bank from time to time to collect the 'passbook'. The passbook contained a statement of accounts as well as the cancelled cheques which had been paid by the bank since the last time that the customer collected the passbook. It was expected that the customer would reconcile the account stated in the passbook with their own accounts and return the passbook to the bank when so satisfied. In the *Kepitigalla* case neither the company's own books nor the bank passbook had been examined by the directors of the company for a period of more than two months, during which time the series of forgeries had occurred. Bray J held that the customer had breached no duty owed to the bank and that the bank was not entitled to debit the amount of the forged cheques. The case was followed a few years later in *Walker v Manchester and Liverpool District Banking Co Ltd* (1913) 108 LT 728; 29 TLR 492 where it was held that the fact that the customer did not examine the passbook did not entitle the bank to maintain the debit of the account for payment of forged cheques.

[5.35] The passbook has been replaced by the bank statement which is sent at intervals to the customer. The current practice would seem to favour the customer even more than the older practice since there is no way of knowing that the customer has even received the statement. *Kepitigalla* was approved by the New Zealand Court of Appeal in *National Bank of New Zealand v Walpole and Patterson* [1975] 2 NZLR 7 and by the Privy Council in *Tai Hing Cotton Mill Ltd v Liu Chong Hing Bank Ltd* [1985] 2 All ER 947. The principle would seem to be firmly established.

It should, however, be noted that there is no legal obstacle to imposing by contract a duty of discovery on the customer. Indeed, that is precisely what the bank attempted to do in the *Tai Hing* case: see below, [5.41]ff. Such agreements are often called 'verification agreements' and are phrased in terms which attempt to place upon the customer a duty to 'verify' the entries in the statement. The Privy Council in *Tai Hing* held that the agreements in that case were not brought sufficiently to the attention of the customer. Similar agreements have been held to be binding by Canadian courts: see, for example, *Arrow Transfer Co Ltd v Royal Bank of Canada* (1972) 27 DLR (3d) 81; *Columbia Graphophone Co v Union Bank of Canada* (1916) 34 DLR 743. However, Canada follows the common law in holding that there is no duty in the absence of an express contractual clause: *Canadian Pacific Hotels Ltd v Bank of Montreal* (1987) 40 DLR (4th) 385.

Duly to take care of the chequebook

[5.36] If there is no duty to discover forgeries, there might at least be a duty to prevent them. At the very lowest level, this would require that the customer take care of the printed chequebook which is supplied by the bank.

The most recent case which is directly on the point is *Westpac v Metlej* (1987) Aust Torts Reports 80–102. A partnership account required two signatures on cheques. One of the signatories adopted a practice of signing partnership cheques in blank and leaving them with Metlej for the addition of his signature when and as the cheques were needed. Metlej took the chequebook containing cheques with a single signature with him to a building site. When not actually using the chequebook, he would leave it in his lunch box in his car.

Three cheque forms containing the single signature were taken from the chequebook. The fact that these forms were missing was noticed on 6 December and the bank was notified on the morning of 7 December. The cheque forms were completed by some person unknown and the plaintiff's signature forged. The cheques were cashed over the counter on 7, 12 and 23 December for amounts which totalled $62,000.

In the New South Wales Court of Appeal, it was found that it was not necessary to decide the general principle of the existence of a duty since if there was such a duty the customer had not been in breach in the facts of the case before the court. This suggests that the standard required of the customer would be very low even if a duty is found to exist.

[5.37] The court also noted that Australian courts are not bound by the decision of the Privy Council in the *Tai Hing* case, but expressed little sympathy for the judicial imposition of duties on bankers' customers which the banks themselves could impose by contract if they so wished. It is clearly correct that Australian courts are not bound by the *Tai Hing* decision: *Cook v Cook* (1986) 61 ALJR 25. On the other hand, there is much to be said for maintaining uniformity in commercial law generally and in banking law in particular, so that a decision such as *Tai Hing* should be considered as very persuasive.

[5.38] Even if there is a duty to take care of the chequebook, it may be difficult to show that the breach of the duty is the cause of the loss. In several older cases, the court seemed to be of the opinion that leaving a chequebook with an unsupervised agent who then has the opportunity not only for committing the forgeries but also for concealing them, was behaviour which was too remote from the resulting loss to allow the bank to maintain the debit: *Bank of England v Vagliano Bros* [1891] AC 107; *Farquharson Bros & Co v King & Co* [1902] AC 325; *National Westminster Bank Ltd v Barclays Bank International Ltd* [1975] QB 654.

In *Metlej* itself, two members of the Court of Appeal adopted this view, holding that it had not been shown that the breach, if it was a breach, by the plaintiff was the cause of the defendant's loss. In the view of Priestley and Hope JJA, the cause of the loss was the defendant's failure to detect the forged signature on the cheques: see [6.45] for a discussion of the bank's duty to recognise its customer's signature.

Similar arguments attempting to impose a duty on the keeping of the company seal have been rejected. In *Bank of Ireland v Evans Charities Trustees in Ireland* [1855] 5 HL Cas 389 the bank was held unable to debit the account of a forged cheque where it was alleged that the loss was caused by the negligence of the customer in keeping the company seal.

Duty to organise business

[5.39]   As the reader may have guessed, the attempts to impose a more general duty on the customer have all failed. One of the earliest attempts was *Lewes Sanitary Steam Laundry Co Ltd v Barclay & Co Ltd* [1906] 95 LT 444; 11 Com Cas 255. The company's cheques required signature by the secretary and one other director. The secretary forged the name of one of the directors on several cheques and obtained payment. What made the case interesting was that the secretary had been convicted of forgery some years previously, a fact which was known to the chairman of the board of directors. The bank claimed that entrusting the chequebook to such a person was a breach of the customer's duty which was such as to allow the bank to maintain the debit.

The defence failed on the grounds that the harm complained of was not caused by the conduct of the officers of the company but by the fraud of the secretary. Note that on this analysis, it is theoretically possible that some 'negligence' on the part of the customer could be a defence for the bank, but given the facts of *Lewes* it is difficult to imagine what conduct of the customer would in fact have that result. The same decision was reached on similar facts in *Les Edwards & Son Pty Ltd v Commonwealth Bank* (SC NSW Giles J, 4 Sept 1990).

There is a curious inconsistency in the analysis of causation between cases such as *Macmillan* and *Lewes*. Why is the chain of causation broken by the fraudulent bookkeeper in cases such as *Lewes*, but not by the fraudulent actions of the clerk in *Macmillan*?

[5.40]   The existence of a general organisational duty came before the New Zealand Court of Appeal in *National Bank of New Zealand v Walpole and Patterson* [1975] 2 NZLR 7. A clerk had forged cheques over a period of six years and received payment from a branch of the defendant bank. At no time during the six years did any other responsible member of the plaintiff company examine the statements or accounts. It was alleged that the company had adopted a course of business which facilitated the commission of fraud.

The Court of Appeal held that the customer is under no duty to exercise reasonable care in the organisation of the general course of business to prevent forgeries by employees. The court said that the only type of negligence by the customer which will exonerate the banker is negligence in or immediately connected with the drawing of the cheque itself, that is, a breach of the *Macmillan* duty.

[5.41]   The Privy Council decision in *Tai Hing Cotton Mill Ltd v Liu Chong Hing Bank Ltd* [1985] 2 All ER 947 considered the matter in detail. The plaintiff company was a customer of each of the three defendant banks. The banks honoured a total of some 300 cheques having a total value of approximately HK$5.5 million. The cheques, which appeared to be signed by the company's managing director, were forgeries.

The forger was an accounts clerk employed by the company who was given total responsibility for the books of account of two of the five divisions of the company. He began to steal from the company almost immediately, stealing over HK$300,000 in the first year of his employment. The trial judge found that the clerk was trusted and that the accounting system in use by the company had ineffective means of internal control. There was no division of function which might have made the clerk's task more difficult. There was a failure to check or to supervise the reconciliation of the monthly bank statement with the cash books of the company. The frauds were uncovered after more than five years only when a newly appointed accountant 'entered upon the simple, though tedious, task which had not previously been undertaken, of reconciling bank statements with the company's account books': at 951.

The Privy Council held that there was no breach of any contractual terms of the banker-customer contract, that there was no breach of any duty owed in tort, and that there was no estoppel against the customer. The decision is not, of course, strictly binding on Australian courts but any decision to the contrary would be counter to decisions which have stood over a long period of time and through many changes in banking practice.

[5.42]   The New South Wales Court of Appeal in *Metlej* declined to decide if the *Tai Hing* decision represents the current Australian law. They found that if there is a duty to take care of the chequebook, then the duty was not breached in the case before them. Although strictly speaking *Metlej* is a case which is concerned with the care of the chequebook, the Court of Appeal clearly addressed the issue in wider terms when commenting on the *Tai Hing* case. See also *Canadian Pacific Motels Ltd v Bank of Montreal* (1987) 40 DLR (4th) 385.

In finding that there was no breach of any duty owed in tort, the Privy Council in *Tai Hing* adopted a principle that where there is a contract which sets out the obligations owed by the parties to each other that the contract should govern, and that it was not appropriate to search for other, broader, duties in tort. That broad statement of principle does not represent the current state of Australian law. In *Hawkins v Clayton* (1988) 62 ALJR 240 the High Court found that the duty of care owed by a solicitor to a client in respect of professional work transcends the duty imposed by express or implied terms of the contract between them.

[5.43]   There are, from time to time, suggestions that the attitude of the courts is changing with regard to the imposition of these duties. For example, in *Mercedes Benz (NSW) Pty Ltd v ANZ and National Mutual Royal Savings Bank*

Ltd (Supreme Court, NSW, Comm Div, 5 May 1992, unreported), Mrs R was appointed as paymistress of the plaintiff company. Due to a wholly inadequate method of supervision and audit she was able to continue accounts for employees which had left the company and also to establish accounts for non-existent employees, diverting deposits into these accounts for her own purposes. In the course of his judgment, Palmer AJ indicated that 'an important consideration of justice' was that he should never lose sight of the fact that the 'fons et origo' of the losses was the abuse of the position as between employer and fraudulent employee. In such a circumstance:

> If the employer has been lax in protecting his own interests from the fraud of his employee, can he reasonably require that third parties, with their own legitimate commercial pressures and concerns to attend to, be more vigilant in his interest than he himself?

But does this ask the correct question? Surely the 'requirement' is that the bank be vigilant in pursuing the business of banking. The 'lax' employer is not requiring the bank to look after his or her own interests, but rather to adhere to those standards which are required of banks paying and/or collecting cheques.

The reader should also note that the comments were made in the context of a case against the collecting bank, not the paying bank. For a more complete discussion of the *Mercedes Benz* case, see Tyree, 'Bad Business Makes Hard Cases: *Mercedes-Benz v NMRB*' (1992) 3 *JBFLP* 192 and '*Mercedes-Benz v ANZ and NMRB (Pt 2)*', (1992) 3 *JBFLP* 277. For a discussion of the duties of a collecting bank, see [5.105]ff and Chapter 7.

An appeal to the Court of Appeal was unanimously dismissed: *Mercedes-Benz (NSW) Pty Ltd v National Mutual Royal Savings Bank Ltd* (NSW Sup Ct CA, No CA 40583 of 1992, 1 April 1996, unreported).

[5.44]   Perhaps the comments in the *Mercedes-Benz* case encouraged bankers to have another try in their attempt to get the courts to impose additional duties on the customer. The argument was raised again in *National Australia Bank Ltd v Hokit Pty Ltd* (1996) 39 NSWLR 377. More than 530 cheques totalling more than $675,000 were forged by a bookkeeper, Mrs B, over a four- year period. The mandate called for cheques to be signed by a director of the company. Some of the cheques were signed in the director's name by Mrs B, but these signatures were authorised and the company did not claim for the amount of these cheques.

The court held that there was no breach of the *Greenwood* duty in failing to notify the bank of these 'forgeries' since the bank did not suffer any detriment from not being notified. Indeed, notification would have served no purpose since the signature, although technically a forgery, was authorised by the director. Although the bank claimed that it would have taken steps to avoid the risk of loss flowing from Mrs B's other forgeries, it offered no proof of such an assertion and so the claim for a *Greenwood* estoppel failed.

The bank also argued that the customer owed a duty to the bank to prevent forged cheques from being presented for payment; to establish business practices that would allow forgeries to be discovered within a reasonable time, and to carry out regular audits by directors or, if necessary, by experts.

These arguments were rejected both at first instance and in the Court of Appeal. The source of the duties could only be found in estoppel, in contract or in tort. The argument from estoppel foundered on the lack of evidence that the customer's action had caused the bank to act to its detriment. The argument that the terms should be implied into the banker-customer contract foundered for the same reasons that they failed in *Tai Hing*. The argument for broader tort duties failed since the bank was unable to establish the conditions for liability for economic loss, in particular, there was no assumption of responsibility nor was there any reliance by the bank.

Clarke JA also considered policy matters to be important. He referred to the importance of certainty in commercial transactions, commercial practice and, most importantly, that Parliament had recently had the opportunity to change the banker-customer relationship when it passed the Cheques and Payment Orders Act 1986 and did not do so. He also referred to the international nature of banking law and the undesirability of making Australian law out of step with those of its neighbours.

[5.45] The New Zealand court in *Walpole & Patterson* made an interesting suggestion that has never been seriously argued. Although the point was not pleaded, Richmond J suggested that a customer might be held liable vicariously for the fraud of the employee. It is not an answer that the fraud is against the employer: *Lloyd v Grace, Smith & Co* [1912] AC 716. The real issue is whether the fraud was committed in the employee's course of employment. In cases such as *Hokit*, *Tai Hing* and *Walpole & Patterson*, there is at least a strong argument that the employee was acting in the course of employment.

THE BANK'S DUTY TO PAY CHEQUES

[5.46] Recall that Lord Atkin said that the banker's obligation '... includes a promise to repay any part of the amount due against the written order of the customer addressed to the bank at the branch ...': *Joachimson v Swiss Banking Corporation* [1921] 3 KB 110 at 127. Although there is some doubt about 'written orders' that are not cheques, there is no doubt that there is a contractual duty to pay cheques drawn by the customer, a duty which is now partly defined by the requirements of the Act.

WHEN THE DUTY ARISES

[5.47] The duty to pay cheques is not, of course, an absolute duty. It only arises when certain preconditions are met. Indeed, in some cases there is a contractual duty to refuse to pay the customer's cheque even when the cheque is in a proper form and otherwise regular: see [5.89]. In general, the duty to pay arises when:

- the cheque is a proper mandate, that is, it is drawn in a proper form and signed by a person who is authorised to draw on the account;
- there are funds which are available to meet the cheque;
- there are no legal impediments to the bank's honouring the cheque; and
- the cheque is properly presented for payment.

The bank may refuse payment if any one of the conditions is not fulfilled. In certain circumstances, the bank must refuse payment. Each of these four conditions requires elaboration.

Cheque drawn in proper manner

[5.48]   A cheque is not merely an authority from the customer to the bank to make a payment, it is a mandate, that is, an order to make the payment. The obligation of the bank is to follow the terms of the mandate strictly. The reason for this strict rule is that the bank is acting as the agent of the customer in making payment. In particular, this means paying the right amount to the right person and if the bank fails in this obligation, then there is a prima facie breach of the banker-customer contract by the bank.

[5.49]   As a direct corollary of this obligation to follow the terms of the mandate strictly, there is an obligation on the customer to express the mandate carefully and clearly. One aspect of this duty on the customer is the existence of the *Macmillan* duty to draw cheques in a way which does not facilitate forgery. Another aspect is that a bank is not obliged to attempt to give effect to a mandate which is not clear and free of ambiguity. As Viscount Haldane expressed it in *London Joint Stock Bank Ltd v Macmillan and Arthur* [1918] AC 777 at 814: 'The banker, as a mandatory, has a right to insist on having his mandate in a form which does not leave room for misgiving as to what he is called upon to do.'

[5.50]   Thus, if the mandate is ambiguous, then the bank may refuse to pay. This could happen, for example, if the amount of the sum in words is different from the amount expressed in figures. Even though the Act provides in such a circumstance that the smaller of the two amounts is the sum which is ordered there is no contractual obligation to pay: s 15(2). No doubt the bank could rely upon s 15(2) if it wished to pay in spite of the ambiguous mandate. This is just an application of the general rule that if the mandate is ambiguous then a reasonable interpretation of the mandate by the agent will give the customer/principal no cause for complaint: *Ireland v Livingstone* (1872) LR 5 HL 395.

Funds available

[5.51]   There is no obligation on the bank to pay a cheque unless there is a sufficient balance in the account to pay the entire amount or unless overdraft arrangements have been made which are adequate to cover the amount of the cheque. Thus, in *Bank of New South Wales v Laing* [1954] AC 135 at 154 the Privy Council said:

... where the creditor is a customer and the debtor a bank on current account, the 'peculiar incidents' of that relationship govern the position and determine what the plaintiff must prove ... If the 'balance' falls short of [meeting the cheque] he fails altogether; another distinction which distinguishes the creditor-debtor relationship in the case of a customer and banker from that relationship in other cases.

[5.52]   The bank should ordinarily pay cheques in the order in which they arrive. A problem which seems to have concerned text writers more than bankers is the problem of two or more cheques arriving simultaneously where the account is sufficient to meet either but not both. The best legal advice appears to be to pay the smaller of the two on the theory that it is more serious to dishonour a small cheque than a larger one: see [5.70]; R S T Chorley, *Law of Banking*, 6th ed, Sweet & Maxwell, 1974, p 72; Hapgood, *Paget's Law of Banking*, 11th ed, Butterworths, London, 1996, p 330; *Westminster Bank Ltd v Hilton* (1926) 43 TLR 124; cf Ellinger and Lomnicka, *Modern Banking Law*, 2nd ed, Clarendon Press, Oxford, 1994, p 337. However, Weaver and Craigie claim that Australian practice is to pay the larger cheque: G A Weaver and R C Craigie, *The Law Relating to Banker and Customer in Australia*, 2nd ed, Law Book Co, Sydney, 1990, para [12.180].

There is occasionally difficulty in knowing precisely the amount of the 'funds available'. When money is paid into the account it is not 'available' until the bank has had a reasonable amount of time to complete the necessary internal accounting procedures: *Marzetti v Williams* (1830) 1 B & Ad 415; [1824–34] All ER 150; and see the discussion on clearing of cheques in Chapter 9.

[5.53]   When cheques are paid into the account, it is customary for the deposit slip to contain a note to the effect that the proceeds are not available for drawing upon until such time as the cheques have been cleared. In *Westminster Bank v Zang* [1966] AC 182 both the English Court of Appeal and the House of Lords held that such a notice was sufficient to negate any possible implied term to the contrary. As a consequence, the funds are not necessarily 'available' even if they have been posted to the account of the customer.

If there is an agreement with the customer that an overdraft is to be provided, then the bank is required to honour cheques to the limit of the overdraft: *Fleming v Bank of New Zealand* [1900] AC 577. If there is not an agreed overdraft limit, then the drawing of a cheque which exceeds the funds available amounts in law to a request for an overdraft by the customer: *Cuthbert v Robarts, Lubbock & Co* [1909] 2 Ch 226. Although the bank is not obliged to grant this request, it may do so and debit the account with the amount of the cheque.

[5.54]   Where the customer's account is in credit, but is inadequate to pay the cheque, may the holder of the cheque offer to pay the difference into the drawer's account? Opinion on the matter is divided, partly because of an ancillary question, namely, how does the holder know how much to pay in? There is a breach of the contractual duty of confidentiality if the bank discloses the state of the customer's account: *Foster v Bank of London* (1862) 3 F & F 214; *Tournier v National Provincial and Union Bank of England* [1924] 1 KB 461. It seems doubtful if the banker has the authority to accept payment into the customer's account from a stranger: see Chorley, op cit, p 71 and *Rekstin v Severo Sibirsko Gosudarstvennoe Akcionernoe Obschestvo Komseverputj and the Bank for Russian Trade Ltd* [1933] 1 KB 47. On the other hand, Ellinger says (op cit, p 337) that it is London banking practice to accept such payments, although he acknowledges that the right to do so is disputed.

No legal impediment to payment

[5.55] Even though the mandate is in proper form and the account has sufficient funds, there may be certain legal impediments which prevent the bank from paying the cheque. One of the most common of these is the garnishee order which, in effect, makes the debt owed by the bank to the customer payable to some third party: see [3.79].

Another increasingly common legal impediment is the Mareva injunction which has the effect of 'freezing' the account or part of it until such time as the injunction is discharged. Payment of cheques in defiance of the injunction is a contempt of court: see the discussion of Mareva injunctions at [12.1] and A L Tyree, 'Mareva Injunctions and the Banks', in M Hetherington, *Mareva Injunctions*, Law Book Co, Sydney, 1983.

- *Stale cheques*

[5.56] The Act itself contains several provisions which place impediments in the way of payment. A stale cheque is one which appears on its face to have been drawn more than 15 months earlier: s 3(5). By s 89 of the Act, the duty and authority of the bank to pay are terminated when the cheque becomes stale although that is subject to an agreement to the contrary made with the drawer of the cheque. The time of 15 months was chosen so as not to cause undue disruption around the first months of each new year when a number of cheques are inadvertently dated incorrectly.

- *Notice of death or mental incapacity*

[5.57] The duty and the authority of a bank to pay a cheque are also terminated by notice of the drawer's mental incapacity to incur liability on a cheque: s 90(1)(b). Given the serious consequences of a wrongful dishonour, the vague notion of 'mental incapacity' could cause the bank some difficulty.

The duty and authority to pay are also terminated by notice of the drawer's death: s 90(1)(c). While death does not have the degree of uncertainty which is associated with mental incapacity, it is subject to some exceptions in s 90(2), namely that the bank may pay cheques which are presented for payment within 10 days of the receipt of notice of the customer's death. Previously, payees of outstanding cheques were required to prove in the deceased estate, a process which can take considerable time. The estate is protected since the cheque may be countermanded by a person who claims that he or she is or will be entitled to administer the estate or a beneficiary of the estate: s 90(2)(b).

- *Countermand*

[5.58]   Perhaps the most common form of impediment to payment is the countermanded or 'stopped' cheque. Section 90(1)(a) revokes both the duty and the authority of the bank to pay a cheque once the cheque has been countermanded. The wording of the section is based on that of s 81 of the BEA. Note that there is no indication of who is entitled to give the countermand or how the countermand is to be communicated to the bank. The Explanatory Memorandum indicates that consideration was given to expanding the section to give guidance on these matters, but that in view of the considerable body of case law the BEA section was followed so as not to inadvertently affect any established rules of law: EM 418.

The right to countermand given by s 90 has effect notwithstanding any agreement to the contrary: s 6(2). The right given is against the bank only, that is, the consequence of stopping a cheque so far as the rights of the payee and other third parties are concerned is an entirely different question. These other rights are derived primarily from the provisions of the Act relating to negotiation: they are discussed in Chapter 9.

Although not explicitly required by the section, it is clear that the countermand must be at the branch where the account is kept: *London, Provincial and South-Western Bank Ltd v Buszard* (1918) 35 TLR 142.

A cheque drawn on a joint account may be countermanded by any one of the account owners, and it does not matter that the cheque is not signed by the person wishing to countermand payment: see *Husband v Davis* (1851) 20 LJCP 118; *Gaunt v Taylor* (1843) 2 Hare 413; 67 ER 170; see also *Twibell v London Suburban Bank* [1869] WN 127.

Method of stopping

[5.59]   It is in all cases a question of fact whether or not a particular cheque has been stopped. A countermand need not be in writing, although the bank may reasonably require that a written confirmation follow. It is thought that a telephone call which identifies the cheque with sufficient particularity will suffice to countermand the cheque. If the identification of the caller is not positive, it might be that the bank is under an obligation to make inquiries before making payment. This is not a happy position for the bank, since there is on the one hand a duty to the customer to comply promptly with the mandate and on the other the uncertain possibility that the mandate has been withdrawn.

[5.60]   In order to be effective, the countermand must be brought to the attention of a responsible officer of the bank. In *Commonwealth Trading Bank v Reno Auto Sales Pty Ltd* [1967] VR 790 the drawer of a cheque had given it to the payee during a weekend as payment on a second-hand motor car. The drawer changed his mind concerning the transaction and asked his wife to telephone the branch early on the following Monday and to place a stop order on the cheque. The wife spoke to an employee of the bank to whom she gave the message that the cheque should be stopped. The employee misunderstood the message, believing that the customer would call in to sign a stop payment notice before the cheque could be presented.

As a consequence, neither the manager nor any officer of the bank was notified of the telephone message. The cheque was presented later in the morning and was paid after being referred to the manager on the question of adequacy of funds. The court held that there had been no effective countermand. The employee was little more than a switchboard operator and communication to her could not be communication to the bank. Since the employee misunderstood the message, it may be that the message was ambiguous, in which case the outcome of the case would have been the same even if a proper officer of the bank had been contacted.

[5.61] If a countermand is effective, then the bank has no authority to pay the cheque and consequently cannot debit the account for the amount. This is obvious from s 90(1)(a), but the position has at times been confused by arguments concerning contractual damages. In *Reade v Royal Bank of Ireland Ltd* [1922] 2 IR 22 there was an effective countermand of a cheque which the drawer had given as a part-payment of a gambling debt. The bank argued that it should be able to debit the account with the amount of the mistaken payment since the drawer of the cheque had not acted to minimise his losses by pursuing the payee to recover the money. A further argument to the same effect was that the payee could not have enforced the cheque against the drawer since the debt was a gambling debt.

The court held that the bank had breached its contract and that the amount of the damages was the amount of the cheque. The case was appealed on the question of damages and the Appeal Court came to the same conclusion. The outcome is clearly correct, but the true position is simply that the bank had no right to debit the account, since its authority to pay the cheque had been withdrawn.

[5.62] When a bank mistakenly pays a cheque which has been stopped, it may be possible for it to recover the amount from the payee of the cheque in an action for money paid under a mistake of fact; this topic is discussed at [6.49]. In a very few cases, it may be possible for the bank to maintain the debit by virtue of an equitable principle known as the *Liggett* principle: see [7.43].

Time for stopping

[5.63] In order to be effective, the countermand must be given before the cheque is paid. This seemingly obvious proposition conceals a complex legal concept, namely, the time at which payment may be said to be completed: see [8.66]ff and R M Goode, *Payment Obligations in Commercial and Financial Transactions*, Sweet & Maxwell, London, 1983.

• *Cheque is properly presented for payment*

[5.64] There is no duty on the paying bank to pay a cheque which is not properly presented for payment. One of the major innovations of the CPOA is a detailed treatment of what constitutes due presentment for payment. Since presentment for payment is usually done by the collecting bank, the details are discussed at [5.109]ff.

HOW THE DUTY IS TO BE DISCHARGED

[5.65] Assuming that the preconditions for payment are present, the paying bank is under a duty to pay promptly. This rule follows from fundamental principles of agency, but the Act has placed an independent statutory duty on the paying bank.

[5.66] Section 67 of the Act provides that the drawee bank must either pay or dishonour a cheque which is duly presented for payment and that payment must be made as soon as reasonably practicable. The consequence of failing to do so is that the bank is liable to the holder of the cheque for the value unless it can show that the holder of the cheque has a defective title. As already noted, the duty to the drawer to pay promptly exists independently of the statute.

There is one peculiarity of the section. We noted earlier that there is nothing in the definition of a cheque which requires that it be drawn by a customer of the drawee bank. If a cheque were drawn by a non-customer, then the drawee bank should, of course, dishonour it, but if for some reason it fails to do so within a 'reasonable time' then it would appear that it is liable to the holder of the cheque. The holder of such a cheque would not have a defective title merely because the drawer was not a customer of the drawee bank. The result was probably not intended by the framers of the Act.

[5.67] Section 67(2) lists a number of factors which are relevant in determining whether or not the payment or dishonour was effected as soon as reasonably practicable. The most important of these factors are: (s 67(2)(c)) the means that were available to it for paying or dishonouring the cheque; (s 67(2)(d)) the relative speed, reliability and cost of those means; (s 67(2)(e)) the usage of banks in relation to the payment and dishonour of cheques. In the vast majority of cases, it will be s 67(2)(e), in the form of the clearing house rules, that determines whether the cheque was dealt with in a timely manner.

Recall that customers may claim the benefit of clearing house rules in the sense that the collecting bank may be obliged to use the rules to benefit their customer: *Riedell v Commercial Bank of Australia Ltd* [1931] VLR 382. On the other hand, both the Act and the general law make it clear that the customer must expect the usual delays associated with collection through the banking system: *Dimond (HH) (Rotorua 1966) v Australia and New Zealand Banking Group Ltd* [1979] 2 NZLR 739.

CONSEQUENCES OF FAILURE TO PERFORM THE DUTY

[5.68]   The bank may breach its duty to pay cheques in one of two separate ways. It may fail to pay a cheque when the preconditions for payment exist, or it may pay a cheque in circumstances when it should not. The first is called wrongful dishonour, and is the most common form of breach. Wrongful payment is discussed below: see [5.82].

Wrongful dishonour

[5.69]   A wrongful failure to pay gives rise to liability for breach of contract with the customer. When the cheque is actually dishonoured, it is common practice to write an 'answer' on the dishonoured cheque itself. Since the cheque together with the writing on it is returned to the collecting bank, the answer is 'published' within the legal meaning of the word and the bank may also be liable to the customer in defamation.

A wrongful failure to pay ordinarily occurs when the bank has failed to credit deposits made by the customer. This may happen because of customers with similar names or because the amount of a deposit is understated by a misplacement of the decimal point or an accidental transposition of figures. Another common cause is that the bank overlooks overdraft arrangements which have been made by the customer. In any case, the usual problem is that the customer has funds which are available to meet the cheque, but the bank mistakenly believes that the account is inadequate. It does not matter that the mistake made by the bank is innocent or reasonable. The action is for breach of contract and the contract calls for the bank to pay in certain circumstances, not merely to exercise care.

Damages for breach of contract

[5.70]   Damages are assessed in accordance with well-established principles of contract law, namely the banker will be liable for all damage which is foreseeable as a consequence of the failure to carry out the contractual promise. This includes not only damage which flows directly and naturally from the failure to perform the contract, but also includes damage which is reasonably foreseeable in the light of any special knowledge which might be known to the party in breach: *Hadley v Baxendale* (1854) 9 Exch 341; 156 ER 145.

It is clear that failure to pay a cheque may result in damage to the credit of the customer. Indeed, damage to credit is the fundamental loss which will be suffered by the customer and there is no doubt that the bank is liable for any such damage as may be proved. It is likely that recovery for other forms of damage which flow from the wrongful dishonour will require that special knowledge of the bank be shown.

For example, in *Evra Corporation v Swiss Banking Corporation* 522 F Supp 820; 673 F 2d 951 (1981), the plaintiff was required to make a payment of $26,000 under a charterparty. In failing to make the payment, the plaintiff forfeited his rights under the charterparty, damage which was assessed at about $2,000,000. Although the *Evra* case was framed in tort, the court applied the principles of *Hadley v Baxendale* and held that the loss was too remote. If the plaintiff had been able to show that the bank knew the importance of the payment then the results might have been different: see [8.64]ff.

• *Traders*

[5.71]   In certain cases, the damage to the credit of the customer is so obvious that it need not even be pleaded. This is so when the customer is a 'trader', a term to be considered below. The rule is an exception to the general rule of pleading and proving damages for breach of contract.

The rule dates from the decision in *Rolin v Steward* (1854) 14 CB 595 where the plaintiff was a merchant and shipowner whose cheque was wrongfully dishonoured by the defendant bank. It was said that there was no actual damage suffered since the cheques were met the next day. The jury awarded £500. Although that sum was reduced to £200 on appeal, the principle that in such a case the damage is so obvious that it need not even be pleaded was upheld.

• *Non-traders*

[5.72]   Unfortunately, later decisions have rendered the scope of the principle unclear. In *Gibbons v Westminster Bank Ltd* [1939] 2 KB 882 the defendant bank wrongfully dishonoured a cheque for about £19 drawn by the plaintiff in favour of her landlord. The court held that, as no special damages were pleaded or proved and the plaintiff was not a trader, she was entitled to nominal damages of 40 shillings only.

This decision was followed in a New Zealand case, *Baker v ANZ Bank Ltd* [1958] NZLR 907. The plaintiff was a substantial shareholder and a director of a company. The court held that, since she was not a trader and had not pleaded special damages, she was entitled to nominal damages of only £2 for each cheque which was wrongfully dishonoured. The *Baker* case was approved in *Hill v National Bank of New Zealand Ltd* [1985] 1 NZLR 736: see [5.77] for a further discussion of the *Baker* case.

• *The trader/non-trader distinction*

[5.73]   The restriction to traders makes little sense. There are certainly other sections of the community which are no less obviously damaged when a cheque is dishonoured. In *Magill v Bank of North Queensland* (1895) 6 QLJ 262 Griffith CJ expressed his view that the trader/non-trader distinction should not be followed, but it does not seem that his views have been followed in later cases.

The English Court of Appeal has now abolished the rule. In *Kpohraror v Wollwich Building Society* [1996] 4 All ER 119, the Court accepted the arguments outlined above, holding that a non-trader could recover damages for loss of credit without proving special damages. There is, in other words, a presumption of damage to credit in every case.

The decision is to be welcomed and should be followed in Australia. It may be that at the time of *Rolin's* case that traders were the only class whose credit would be obviously damaged by a wrongful dishonour, but many people today rely on credit ratings in the form of credit cards and other forms of consumer credit. Similarly, it does not seem reasonable to suppose that someone in the position of the plaintiff in *Baker's* case is not damaged by a wrongful dishonour. Since the damage is clearly recognised in the defamation action, it is artificial and arbitrary to continue to make the distinction in the award of damages for breach of contract.

Defamation

[5.74]   When a cheque which has been physically presented to the paying bank is dishonoured, it is customary to write an 'answer' on the cheque which gives a brief reason for the dishonour. When the cheque is then returned to the collecting bank, the answer is published in the legal sense and the paying bank is exposed to an action in defamation: *Baker v ANZ Bank Ltd* [1958] NZLR 907; *Hill v National Bank of New Zealand Ltd* [1985] 1 NZLR 736.

[5.75]   There can be no defamation if there is no publication to a third party. Thus, when the drawer of the cheque presented it himself for payment over the counter, it was held that there was no defamation because there was no publication to a third party: *Kinlan v Ulster Bank Ltd* [1928] IR 17 1. It has occasionally been suggested that the bank might rely on the defence of qualified privilege, but the better view seems to be that such a plea will fail: see A L Tyree, 'Wrongful Dishonour, Defamation and Qualified Privilege' (1980) 8 *Aust Bus L Rev* 220.

[5.76]   There are some answers on cheques which could scarcely be found to carry a defamatory meaning. 'Signature indistinct' or 'Words and figures differ' would be such examples. Even if the dishonour turns out to be wrongful, the words are simply not defamatory although the bank may still be liable for breach of contract.

[5.77]   The real problem arises when the cheque is dishonoured for lack of funds, for if the words convey that meaning, then there is a clear imputation that the drawer has defaulted as to the time for performance of the obligation to provide funds for payment of the cheque on presentment. Such an imputation is clearly defamatory since the test is whether the meaning 'tend[s] to lower the customer in the estimation of right thinking members of society generally': per Atkin LJ in *Sim v Stretch* [1936] 2 All ER 1237 at 1240. Usually, the only question in such cases is whether the words used are capable of carrying that message.

The most common phrases used when a cheque is dishonoured for insufficient funds are 'present again' and 'refer to drawer'. The phrases have had a mixed reception in the courts, occasionally being held to be incapable of defamatory meaning. However, it is thought that the analysis by the New Zealand court in *Baker v ANZ Bank* [1958] NZLR 907 is the correct one. Shorland J said:

... the answer 'present again' marked on a cheque conveys the meaning, inter alia, that the customer has insufficient credit in his account to meet the cheque on original presentation ... Whatever the answer 'present again' may imply as to prospects of future or later payments, it surely imports the clear intimation that the maker of the cheque so answered has defaulted as to time for performance of the legal and ethical obligation to provide for payment by the bank on presentation of a cheque issued for immediate payment. Written words which convey such meaning must, to my mind, tend to lower a person in the estimation of right minded members of society generally.

[5.78] The words 'refer to drawer', often abbreviated to 'R/D', have also had a mixed reception by the courts. In *Flach v London and SouthWestern Bank Ltd* [1915] 31 TLR 334, Scrutton J found that the words could convey no defamatory meaning but amounted only to a statement by the bank to the effect 'We are not paying; go back to the drawer and ask why'. In *Jayson v Midland Bank Ltd* [1968] 1 Lloyd's Rep 409, the jury found the same words to be defamatory and the Court of Appeal refused to disturb the finding.

Eichelbaum J considered the phrase 'R/D' in *Hill v National Bank of New Zealand Ltd* [1985] 1 NZLR 736. During the course of his judgment, he said (at 750):

... I have concluded that dishonour of a cheque remains a serious matter and that the majority of reasonable people would think that in all probability the bank had done so on good grounds founded on some circumstance discreditable to the drawer of the cheque.

Levine J, after a review of the cases, considered that the phrase 'refer to drawer' carried the innuendo that the drawer was insolvent: *Raatbye Corporation Pty Ltd v Westpac Bank* (SC NSW, (Levine J), 21 October 1994, unreported).

[5.79] If the *Baker* test is the correct one, and it is submitted that it is, then the search for an innocuous phrase to use as an answer on dishonoured cheques is a fruitless one. Either it will convey the information that the account is inadequate or it will not. If it does, then it is capable of a defamatory meaning. If it does not convey that meaning, then why use it?

[5.80] The defamation action can only succeed if the cheque has been wrongfully dishonoured, but not every case of wrongful dishonour will allow the plaintiff to succeed, for the essence of damage in a defamation action is damage to reputation. If the reputation of the customer is such that the words used by the bank cannot damage it, then there will be no liability. Thus, in *Ellaw Co Ltd v Lloyds Bank Ltd* (1934) 4 LDAB 455 the account of the plaintiff was being used for kiting operations and there had been a number of cheques which had been properly dishonoured. The court found that in the case before it the dishonour had been proper, but said that even if it had been wrongful only nominal damages would have been awarded.

On the other hand, the actions of the bank upon being notified of the wrongful dishonour may serve to increase the damages to which the plaintiff is entitled. In *Baker*, the court noted that the bank had offered no apology and no retraction, instead choosing to defend the case vigorously. This vigorous defence had the effect of exacerbating the defamation and damages were assessed accordingly.

Liability to the holder

[5.81] Prior to the passing of the CPOA, the paying bank may have had a duty to deal promptly with the cheque upon presentment and that failure to do so could give rise to liability in negligence: see the discussion at [5.66] and *HH Dimond (Rotorua 1966) v Australia and New Zealand Banking Group Ltd* [1979] 2 NZLR 739.

The CPOA seems to have strengthened the position of the holder. Section 67(1) of the CPOA places a duty on the paying bank to pay or dishonour the cheque as soon as is reasonably practicable. Failure to do so means that the drawee bank is liable to pay the cheque to the holder. This is substantially more favourable to the holder than the *Dimond* duty, since the holder need not prove any damage.

Wrongful payment

[5.82] The duty to pay cheques requires that the bank pay the proper amount to the proper person. Paying the proper amount will seldom cause any difficulties. If the words and figures on the cheque differ as to the amount to be paid, the proper amount is the smaller of the two: s 15(4), although the banker would probably be justified in refusing to honour an ambiguous instruction; see [5.48]ff.

Another possible way in which the wrong amount could be paid is if the amount in MICR figures is incorrectly coded on the cheque. If the coded amount is too small, then there is no doubt that the paying bank would make good the difference when the mistake is found. If the coded amount is too much, then the paying bank may recover the money as paid under a mistake of fact: see *Georgia Railroad Bank and Trust Co v The First National Bank and Trust Co of Augusta* 229 SE 2d 482 (1976); affirmed by the Georgia Supreme Court 235 SE 2d 1 (1977).

The bank may also pay the wrong amount when the cheque has been fraudulently altered: *London Joint Stock Bank Ltd v Macmillan and Arthur* [1918] AC 77; *Imperial Bank of Canada v Bank of Hamilton* [1903] AC 49; CPOA s 78, s 91.

- *Paying the wrong person*

[5.83] In contrast to the requirements of the BEA, the CPOA does not require that the order to pay be directed to or to the order of a specified person or to bearer: see Chapter 6 for a discussion of the form of a cheque. If, however, the order does specify such a person, then that person is known as the payee of the cheque.

If a cheque is expressed as payable to or to the order of a person specified in the cheque, then the duty of the bank is to pay that person or someone who is specified by that person, that is, to that person's order. The secondary order is by means of indorsements and the CPOA has seen fit to give the banks statutory defences to an action for breach of contract when the breach is caused by a forged indorsement. This defence will be discussed at [7.69].

[5.84] If a cheque is not payable to order, then it is payable to bearer and the duty of the bank is simply to pay whoever might be in possession of the cheque: s 22. This is important for the paying bank, since it is virtually impossible for the bank to pay a bearer cheque to the wrong person. It is for this reason that most preprinted cheques are in terms 'Pay ... or bearer'. A careful drawer will put a line through the 'or bearer' part of the printed cheque form and draw the cheque as payable to order.

A person is not a payee of the cheque unless the person is named or otherwise indicated with reasonable certainty in the cheque and is not a fictitious or non-existing person: s 19(1). Since it is common to order that cheques be paid to some office bearer, for example, 'Commissioner of taxation', the Act provides that the person who is the holder for the time being of the office shall be taken to be named in the cheque as payee: s 19(2).

* *Fictitious person*

[5.85] The phrase 'fictitious or non-existing person' which is used in s 19(1) has been the cause of some difficulty. Apart from certain philosophical difficulties, the meaning of 'non-existing person' is relatively clear, but what does 'fictitious' add to the meaning? How is it possible for the person in question to be 'fictitious' while still being an existing person?

The importance of the matter for the simple payment instrument is that, if the payee is fictitious, the cheque is to be taken as payable to the bearer of it: s 22. Thus, if a cheque that is made payable to 'John Jones' is stolen by Bob Brown and paid by the drawee bank, then on the face of it the paying bank is in breach of contract and may not debit its customer since it has paid the wrong person. However, if the bank can show that 'John Jones' is a fictitious or non-existing person, then the cheque is payable to bearer and the bank has not been in breach of contract.

[5.86] The confusion over the meaning of 'fictitious person' may be traced to the decision in *Bank of England v Vagliano Bros* [1891] AC 107. A clerk named Glyka forged bills of exchange. The instruments purported to be drawn by Vucina, a foreign agent of Vagliano's. The instruments were made payable to Petridi and were accepted payable at the Bank of England by Vagliano. Vagliano often accepted bills made payable to Petridi as they conducted a fair amount of business together. Glyka then forged an indorsement and presented the bills at the bank for payment which he obtained across the counter.

The case was simply disposed of by the law of agency. Since the bank was acting as Vagliano's agent for payment and was misled by the actions of the principal, the bank was entitled to an indemnity from the principal for any losses which were sustained as a result.

However, a great deal of the argument in *Vagliano's* case concerned the question of whether the payee was fictitious. Obviously there was a real person named Petridi; he was not non-existent. The House of Lords held that the payee was 'fictitious' in the sense that, although real, he 'has not and never was intended by the drawer to have any right upon [the bill] or arising out of it; and this is so though the bill (so called) is not in reality a bill but is in fact a document in the form of a bill manufactured by a person who forges the signature of the named drawer, obtains by fraud the signature of the acceptor, forges the signature of the named payee, and presents the document for payment ...': from the headnote.

[5.87]   In spite of that rather clear summary emphasising the intention of the drawer (Glyka), it was thought for some time that *Vagliano's* case had decided that a payee was 'fictitious' if he or she had no right to enforce the instrument: *City Bank v Rowan* (1893) 14 NSWLR 127; *Rutherford Copper Mining Co NL v Ogier* (1905) 1 Tas LR 156.

That misconception was laid to rest in *Vinden v Hughes* [1905] 1 KB 795. A clerk who was employed by the plaintiffs had as a part of his duties the drawing of cheques in favour of trade creditors. On a number of occasions he drew cheques in favour of known traders even though the plaintiffs owed these people no debt. After obtaining the signature of the plaintiff, the clerk would forge the indorsement of the named payee and pass them on to the defendant, who took them in good faith. They were then collected through the defendant's account and paid by the drawer's bank.

Once again, it is clear that the payee was not a non-existent person, but could he be treated as fictitious under the rule in the *Vagliano* case? One argument for the defendant was that the fraudulent clerk here was the 'drawer' in precisely the same way that Glyka was and that there was similarly no intention that the named (real) payee should ever obtain the money. The argument was rejected by the court. The 'intention' is the intention of the drawer of the cheque, that is, the plaintiff. Since it was clearly the intention of the plaintiff that the named payee should receive the proceeds of the cheque, the payee was not 'fictitious'. The defendant also argued that the payee was fictitious because he could not have enforced the cheque against the drawer. This was also dismissed, the court preferring the 'intention' test.

[5.88]   Byles sums up the effect of these cases as follows:

> ... in determining whether a payee is fictitious or not, the intention of the drawer of the bill is decisive. If he inserted the name as a mere pretence, to give colour to the instrument, the payer is fictitious notwithstanding that he in fact exists ... If on the other hand, the drawer intended his named payee to receive his money, the payee is not fictitious.

This begs the question of who is the 'drawer' since in both *Vagliano* and *Hughes* the fraudulent clerk 'authored' the instrument and in each case one of the signatures was real even though obtained by fraud. It seems that if the drawer's signature is forged, we are to look to the intention of the 'author'; but if the drawer's signature is real, we look to the intention of the drawer and the intention of the author is irrelevant. This scarcely has any logic to it and one can only deplore the state of the law in this situation: see Laskin CJC in *Royal Bank of Canada v Concrete Column Clamps (1961) Ltd* (1976) 74 DLR (3d) 26.

There is one thing that is clear from the cases and which is of the utmost importance to a banker who would rely upon the concept of the fictitious payee. When the section applies, the bill may be treated as payable to bearer not merely by the holder but by all who have any dealings with it. It is this feature, reinforced by s 22 of the CPOA, which provides the defence for a bank which has wrongfully paid the cheque to the wrong person.

- *Selangor*

[5.89]   Even when all of the preconditions for payment are satisfied, there are certain occasions when the bank should not pay the cheque without making some inquiries. If it fails to do so, it may find that it is unable to debit the customer's account.

The facts of *Selangor United Rubber Estates v Cradock (No 3)* [1968] 2 All ER 1073 have been discussed at [4.47]. The court found that the paying bank was in breach of its obligation to discharge its duties carefully even though the cheque was properly drawn. The surrounding circumstances should have made the paying bank question the validity of the payment.

The general rule is probably that a banker should question a mandate when a reasonable and honest banker with knowledge of the relevant facts would consider that there was a serious possibility that the customer was being defrauded or that the funds were being misappropriated: *Lipkin Gorman v Karpanale and Lloyds Bank* [1989] 1 WLR 1340; [1991] 2 AC 548. For a general discussion, see A L Tyree, 'Liability of a Bank which Follows its Customar's Mandate' (1992) 3 *JBFLP* 40.

THE DRAWER-PAYEE CONTRACT

[5.90]   The usual reason for drawing a cheque is to make a payment to the payee. It is drawn as a partial fulfilment of a contractual obligation between the drawer and the payee. When the debtor offers to pay by cheque and the creditor agrees to accept payment in that form, there are certain consequences for the contract between the two parties.

'PAYMENT' BY CHEQUE

[5.91]   First, 'payment' by cheque is not, strictly speaking, payment at all, that is, it does not unconditionally discharge the debt which gave rise to its drawing. This is manifested in at least two separate ways.

NOT AN ASSIGNMENT OF FUNDS

[5.92]   First, the cheque is not an assignment of funds held by the banker on behalf of the drawer. This is placed beyond doubt by s 88 of the Act which makes it clear that the drawing of a cheque does not of itself operate as an assignment. The debt owed by the banker remains owed to the drawer of the cheque, not to the payee.

One important consequence of this is that the payee has no right against the bank on the cheque itself. The only obligation owed by the bank to the payee is to deal with the cheque promptly: see [5.66] and *HH Dimond (Rotorua 1966) v ANZ Banking Group* [1979] 2 NZLR 739. A second important consequence is that the bank may not obtain a discharge of the debt owed to the customer unless the order in the cheque is strictly followed. The cheque is merely a mandate, not a transfer of rights.

From the payee's point of view, the fact that a cheque is not an assignment of funds means that he or she has no remedy against the bank if the bank refuses to pay for any reason. The only remedy in such a case is to proceed against the drawer of the cheque: see [10.58].

CONDITIONAL PAYMENT

[5.93]   Second, if the creditor does accept payment by cheque, then the payment which is effected when the cheque is delivered to the payee is conditional only. The condition to which the payment is subject is a condition subsequent, namely that the cheque will be met upon proper presentment for payment. If the cheque is so presented and paid, then the contractual time of payment as between the creditor/payee and the debtor/drawer is generally taken to be the time at which the cheque was delivered although that time may be altered by express or implied agreement: *Tilley v Official Receiver* (1960) 103 CLR 529; *Armco (Australia) Pty Ltd v Federal Commissioner of Taxation* (1947–1948) 76 CLR 584; *National Australia Bank Ltd v KDS Construction Services Pty Ltd* (1987) 62 ALJR 63.

As a consequence of this, when a cheque is dishonoured, the payee will generally have two causes of action against the drawer. The first is on the cheque itself and the second is the contractual right which gave rise to the original debt. The exercise of the former option will in almost all cases be the most advantageous. The obligations on the cheque are autonomous and separate from the underlying contract and the courts have shown themselves reluctant to do anything which would interfere with that autonomy. It will be rare that a counterclaim for unliquidated damages may be set up by way of defence to an action on the cheque itself: see, for example, *Nova (Jersey) Knit Ltd v Kammgarn Spinnerei GmbH* [1977] 1 WLR 713; *Mobil Oil Australia Ltd v Caulfield Tyre Service Pty Ltd* [1984] VR 440. Similar results may follow from the cancellation of a direct debit: see *Esso Petroleum Co Ltd v Milton* [1997] 2 All ER 593 and [8.9].

DELAYED PRESENTMENT

[5.94]   On the other hand, the condition is that the cheque will be met on presentment. Consequently, a failure by the payee to present the cheque will not result in a revival of the contractual debt. Similarly, if a cheque is misappropriated after it has come into the hands of a payee and payment is somehow obtained from the bank, then generally speaking the debt does not revive, for the conditions under which it was taken have been satisfied.

If the drawee bank fails before the cheque has been presented, then the above rule would mean that the drawer was liable for the full amount of the cheque to the payee, for the condition subsequent could not then be satisfied. The common law made an exception to this when the payee failed to present the cheque within a reasonable period of time. In that case the payee was considered to be in the same position as someone who has wasted a security given by the debtor and the debtor was completely discharged: *Polak v Everett* (1876) 1 QBD 669.

[5.95]   The CPOA provides for a division of risks: s 60. When a cheque is not presented within a reasonable time after delivery of the cheque to the payee and the drawee bank has become insolvent in the meantime, the drawer may assign to the payee the rights against the drawee bank. The drawer will then be discharged from liability to the extent of that assignment. Unfortunately, the section is not clear as to how to determine the 'extent of those funds'. Is it the face value of the sum assigned or is it the actual value which can be obtained from the assignment (which will usually result in a payment of far less)? The corresponding section of the BEA is no clearer and appears not to have been the subject of any decisions: B B Riley, *Bills of Exchange in Australia*, 3rd ed, Law Book Co, Sydney, 1976.

PRESENTMENT OF CHEQUE BY NON-BANKER

[5.96]   Although most cheques will be presented for payment by a collecting bank (see [5.106]), the CPOA provides for presentment by an individual. This is done by 'exhibiting' the cheque, in person, at the 'proper place' in relation to the cheque at a reasonable hour on a day on which the drawee bank is open for business at the place where the cheque is exhibited: s 63.

'Exhibited' apparently means to show the cheque. Section 3(7) indicates that 'exhibited' includes delivery of the cheque. The paying bank has the right to possession of the cheque (s 68(1)(a)), so that what is really required is that the holder of the cheque take the cheque to the 'proper place' during business hours, demand payment and hand the cheque over if payment is to be made.

The 'proper place' is defined by s 64. It is the drawee bank's place of business specified on the cheque. This, on a printed cheque, will always be the branch at which the account of the drawer is kept. If no place is designated on the cheque, then the 'proper place' is still the same, that is, the place of business of the branch of the drawee bank at which the account is maintained: s 64(b).

PAID CHEQUES AS EVIDENCE

[5.97]   One of the significant advantages of paying by cheque is that the cheque itself may be retrieved as evidence of payment. In the days when all cheques were required to be indorsed, this evidence was thought to be a consequence of the indorsement which showed that the cheque had been negotiated. In 1971, the BEA Amendments were introduced which dispensed with the need for indorsements in certain cases. At the same time, a section was introduced which extended the evidence rule to all order cheques. The CPOA continues this in s 113 to provide that an order cheque which has not been indorsed by the payee and which appears to have been paid by the drawee bank is evidence of the receipt by the payee of the sum ordered to be paid by the cheque. Why the section applies only to unindorsed cheques is a mystery.

CONTRACTUAL TERMS IMPLIED BY WRITING A CHEQUE

[5.98]   The obligations undertaken by the drawer of a cheque are partly those defined by the Act and partly those which are a part of the underlying contract which gave rise to the drawing.

UNDERTAKINGS IMPLIED BY THE ACT

[5.99]   Merely drawing a cheque imposes certain obligations on the drawer. The most important undertaking is that the cheque will be paid upon due presentment and that if it is dishonoured, the drawer will pay: s 71. Since this and other obligations are owed not merely to the payee but to any later holder of the cheque, they will be discussed in detail when the cheque is considered as a negotiable instrument: see [10.58].

UNDERTAKINGS IMPLIED BY CASE LAW

[5.100]   When the payee accepts a cheque as a conditional satisfaction of the debt and the debtor draws such a cheque, there are implied terms which are a part of the contract between them. According to Phillmore LJ in *R v Page* [1971] 2 QB 330, those terms are that the drawer of the cheque has an account with the drawee bank, that the drawer has authority to draw on the account for the amount of the cheque, and that the cheque, as drawn, is a valid order to that amount, that is, that in the ordinary course of events, the cheque will on its presentment be met.

Note that there is not an implied term to the effect that the drawer currently has the sum in the account. It may be that the drawer is relying upon an overdraft arrangement or that the drawer is anticipating the deposit of money to the account before the cheque could be presented for payment. On the other hand, a person who is not a customer of a bank but who draws a cheque on the bank is in breach of this implied term of the drawer-payee contract.

These implied terms may change with banking practice. The essential content is that the drawer has authority to draw the cheque and that the cheque will be met on presentment. Thus, if A has authority to draw cheques on the account of B, it is no breach of the implied terms that A gives such a cheque to C in payment.

DISHONOUR

[5.101] When a cheque which has been accepted as payment has been dishonoured, then the payee has an option of suing on the original contract or of suing the drawer on the cheque itself. The benefits of suing on the cheque itself are discussed in Chapter 9.

MEANING OF DISHONOUR

[5.102] The meaning of 'dishonour' is that the cheque has been duly presented for payment, the payment has been refused by the drawee bank and the refusal has been communicated by the drawee bank to the holder or the person who presented the cheque on the holder's behalf: s 69. Notice that there is no dishonour unless the cheque has been duly presented nor is there any dishonour unless there is communication of the refusal.

CONTRACTUAL CONSEQUENCES

[5.103] When the cheque has been dishonoured, the drawer is liable on the cheque whether or not he or she has notice of the dishonour: s 70. However, it seems as though the drawer is not liable if there has been no dishonour.

The Act seems to have inadvertently shifted some risks in these sections. Under the BEA, 'dishonour' included the situation where payment 'cannot be obtained'. The present Act holds the drawee bank liable to the holder in such a circumstance, that is, when there is no refusal but the payment is not made: s 67(1). The Explanatory Memorandum states that the end result under the Act is payment, whereas under the BEA there would be dishonour.

However, that explanation seems to assume the drawee bank is in a position to pay. If the bank has become insolvent, then the liability to the payee would be of little solace. Under the BEA, the risk of bank insolvency, assuming that the cheque was presented promptly (see [5.94]), was on the drawer of the cheque. Under the Act it is on the payee.

PROPERTY CONSEQUENCES

[5.104] When the cheque has been given in payment of the price in a contract for the sale of goods, then the dishonour of the cheque may have an effect on the rights of the parties to possession of the goods. Under s 41 of the Sale of Goods Act 1923 (NSW), the payee becomes an 'unpaid seller' within the meaning of that Act. The unpaid seller is given various rights of stoppage and of resale in certain conditions.

Furthermore, the title received by the drawer of the cheque will usually be voidable at the option of the seller. It is usually necessary for the seller to communicate to the buyer the intention to avoid the title, but when the buyer is a rogue who cannot be found it may be sufficient if the seller takes all reasonable steps to avoid the title: *Car and Universal Finance Co Ltd v Caldwell* [1965] 1 QB 131.

THE PAYEE-COLLECTING BANKER CONTRACT

[5.105]   When a bank is collecting a cheque on behalf of its customer, it is acting as an agent and so has the legal obligations of an agent. These are, inter alia, to follow the instructions of its principal and to act at all times in the best interests of its principal. In the case of collecting cheques, this means that the collecting bank must present the cheque for payment promptly and it would be liable to its customer for any losses suffered as the result of a breach of the duty.

PRESENTMENT OF CHEQUES

[5.106]   This common law duty has now been incorporated as part of the statutory duty of the bank. Section 66(1) provides that, except where there is no duty to present the cheque, where the holder of a cheque lodges the cheque with a bank, called the deposit bank, for collection, the deposit bank shall duly present the cheque for payment itself, or ensure that the cheque is duly presented for payment on its behalf as soon as is reasonably practicable and, if the deposit bank fails to do so, it is liable to the holder for any loss that the holder thereby suffers.

Section 66(3) sets out the factors to be considered when attempting to determine if the bank has fulfilled its duty to present promptly. As in the case of s 67, the most important factor appears to be the usage of banks in relation to the presentment of cheques. As in the case of the paying bank, regard shall also be had to the means that are available for duly presenting the cheque and the relative speed and cost of the available means: s 66(3)(b) and (c). Once again, it is clear that the clearing house rules will have an important role to play in determining if the collecting bank has fulfilled its duty to present promptly.

It is clear that if a holder of a cheque chooses to present the cheque for collection through the clearing system, then he or she must be taken to assent to the ordinary delays that accompany the chosen method of presentment: see *HH Dimond (Rotorua 1966) v ANZ Banking Group* [1979] 2 NZLR 739.

[5.107]   The relationship of the customer to the clearing house rules was considered in *Riedell v Commercial Bank of Australia Ltd* [1931] VLR 382 where it was held that although the customer of the collecting bank could not complain of reasonable delays involved in clearing house practice, the customer was entitled to the benefit of clearing house rules relating to the expiry of time for the return of the dishonoured cheque. This is merely a reflection of the fact that the bank is the customer's agent for the collection of cheques and an agent is obliged to use all best efforts to protect the interests of the principal.

METHODS OF PRESENTMENT

[5.108] Due presentment for payment by a collecting bank is effected by making a demand for payment of the cheque after the date of the cheque in accordance with the rules of s 62: s 61. It should be emphasised that it is impossible for a post-dated cheque to be duly presented for payment prior to the date on the cheque: see CPOA s 61(2).

PRESENTMENT OF CHEQUES BY A BANK

[5.109] The first attempt to provide a legal framework for truncation was the enactment of the Cheques and Payment Orders Act 1986 (Cth), ss 61 and 62. In fact, one of the great disappointments of the CPOA was that the main substantive changes in the law were restricted to the presentment of cheques. The remainder of the Act was (and is) a rewording and expansion of those sections of the Bills of Exchange Act which were applicable to cheques. Those sections which were specific to bills of exchange and promissory notes were omitted. It has been described as being drafted 'in line with modern preference for comprehensive, technical drafting' [A R Coleman, *The Cheques and Payment Orders Act 1988*, Longman Professional, Melbourne, 1987, p vii].

The sections which were intended to permit truncation were never put into practical effect. Following representations by banking interests, the Act was amended in 1994. Sections 61–68 were amended and several new sections were added in an attempt to clarify the truncation scheme.

[5.110] A cheque is 'duly presented' if a demand is made from payment in accordance with procedures established in ss 62, 62A or 63. A post-dated cheque is not 'duly presented' if the demand is made prior to the date of the cheque: see s 61(2).

[5.111] The amendments distinguish between a bank which is collecting a cheque which is drawn on another bank (called 'external' presentment by the Act) and collecting a cheque which is drawn on itself (called 'internal' presentment). 'Internal' presentment permits the bank to make demands of itself, to exhibit cheques to itself, etc. In the following discussion it will be assumed that the presentment is an 'external' one. The rules for 'internal' presentment are similar.

[5.112] Cheques may be presented by being 'exhibited'. The term is not defined in the Act but it seems that presentment by exhibition is the type of presentment with which we are familiar. This type of presentment may be either at the 'proper place' or a place that is a 'designated exhibition place': s 62(1)(c)(i). The 'proper place' is either the business address as specified on the cheque (if the cheque contains such a specification) or the place of business of the branch at which the account on which the cheque is drawn is maintained: s 64.

[5.113] By publishing a notice in the prescribed form a bank may specify a place as a 'designated place'. The place so specified will be a 'designated exhibition place' if the notice so specifies. In this rather roundabout way the decision in *Barclays Bank plc v Bank of England* [1985] 1 All ER 385 is overcome and cheques may be presented at the clearing house.

[5.114]   If the demand is not made by exhibition then it must be made at a designated place, at a designated time and (most importantly) made by a means of communication that is a designated means of communication: s 65 defines the relevant terms. Whatever the means of communication, the information required by the Act must be presented in a form which is 'intelligible to, or readily decipherable by, the drawee bank'.

[5.115]   The Act attempts to provide a complete code for truncated presentment without limiting the forms of communication which might be used. This necessarily results in sections which are too wordy and somewhat convoluted.

[5.116]   It is clear that in any truncation scheme the collecting bank must provide sufficient details of the cheque so that it can be unambiguously identified. The Act incorporates this observation as s 62(3)(1). The Act goes further in ss (4) by deeming that the cheque is adequately identified by indicating the sum to be paid, the cheque number, the account against which it is drawn and the proper place in relation to the cheque.

The scheme permits the drawee bank to seek more information about the cheque. To this end, the Act requires that the collecting bank provide as part of the demand a 'nominated place' where further inquiries may be made, the time at which such inquiries may be made and the means of communication which should be used: s 62(3A).

[5.117]   Subsection 5 gives the drawee bank the right to make requests of further particulars of the cheque or, if it so wishes, to request the collecting bank to exhibit the cheque of a copy of a specified kind, provided that the request is made at the nominated place, at the nominated time and using a nominated means of communication. The request must identify the cheque with reasonable certainty (ss 7) and the Act repeats the criteria for identification (ss 8).

Other subsections of s 62 spell out in similar detail the responsibilities of the collecting bank responding to requests and the responsibilities of the paying bank when asking for further information.

[5.118]   The section ends with ss 12 which is a 'fail safe' section intended to ensure that the truncation scheme has no unintended adverse consequences. The subsection declares that nothing in the scheme is to be taken to relieve the drawee bank of any liability to which it would have been subject in relation to the particular cheque if the cheque had been presented by exhibition.

[5.119]   The Act seems to provide a complete framework for a cheque truncation scheme without unnecessarily restricting the type of technology which might be used. This is obviously important since 'presentment' by computer communications might be the norm but imaging technology might be more suitable for answering requests from drawee banks.

These sections certainly exhibit the 'comprehensive, technical drafting' style mentioned above. It is impossible to read them without feeling that there has been a rather massive overkill for what should be a simple problem. On the other hand, there is much at stake and it is easy to be forgiving of institutions who wish to see that every possible problem is properly addressed. For an argument, now of historical interest only, that truncation could have been achieved without statutory support, see A L Tyree, 'Legal Aspects of Electronic Clearing and Settlement' in *Banking Law and Practice, Proceedings of the 13th Annual Conference of the Banking Law Association*, Surfers Paradise, 30 May 1996, p 289.

RIGHTS TO POSSESSION OF PAID CHEQUE

[5.120] Allowing the presentment of cheques by particulars raises the problem of rights to the possession of the paid cheque. Section 68 of the Act deals with this problem. While the original version of this section was straightforward, it was amended prior to proclamation by the Proceeds of Crime (Miscellaneous Amendments) Act 1987 which imposes obligations on institutions to keep copies of certain cheques, called 'relevant cheques', for a period of seven years after the date of the cheque. The amendments are poorly drafted and it is by no means clear when a bank must keep the cheque and when it must, or may, keep only a copy of the cheque.

When the cheque has been exhibited to the drawee bank either initially as part of the demand for payment or pursuant to a request to the collecting bank, the drawee bank has a better right to the possession of the cheque than the exhibitor: ss 68(1), 68(2). Once the drawee bank obtains possession of a relevant cheque, it must retain the cheque unless the drawer claims possession, in which case it must keep a copy of the cheque. In either case, the period for retention is seven years after the date of the cheque.

When the cheque is paid without being exhibited to the drawee bank and the cheque is in the actual possession of either the collecting bank or another financial institution (called the 'relevant financial institution' in the section), then 'the collecting bank or other financial institution, as the case requires, shall ... retain the cheque, or a copy of the cheque, on behalf of the drawee bank for a period of seven years after the date of the cheque'. Presumably, it is intended that the institution in possession of the cheque will retain the cheque, while the other will retain a copy. If that is what is intended, it might have been better said, for as it stands, it is possible that the only obligation is for all parties to retain a copy.

Throughout the section, a 'copy' is taken to include a document in which there is recorded the information contained in the cheque: s 68(9). Since a 'document' may be a computer record, it seems that the bank need retain only computer records of the cheque for the required period.

However, at any time during the period when a cheque or a copy of the cheque is retained by the 'relevant financial institution', the drawee bank may demand that the institution deliver the cheque or the copy of the cheque: s 68(4). Presumably, the section intends that when a copy is demanded it is necessary only to deliver a copy, not the copy. If the drawee bank exercises this right with regard to a relevant cheque, then it must retain a copy of the cheque for a period of seven years after the date of the cheque: s 68(3B).

RIGHTS OF THE DRAWER TO A PAID CHEQUE

[5.121] Unfortunately, the Act only provides that nothing in the section shall affect the rights to possession which the drawer of the cheque has against the drawee bank: s 68(5)(a). The Explanatory Memorandum states that the drawer of a paid cheque is entitled to the possession of the cheque, basing its comments on the authority of *Charles v Blackwell* (1877) 2 CPD 151 at 162: see EM para 332. The approach is unfortunate, since it is well known that certain of the Australian banks assert the right to possession of the paid cheque. It would have been a simple matter to clarify the position in the new Act rather than rely upon an English case which is more than 100 years old.

Section 65(5)(b) provides that nothing in s 68 shall be taken to affect any obligation that the relevant financial institution would have, apart from the section, to retain the cheque. This presumably is intended to clarify the matter referred to above, that is, that it might be possible for the institution to retain only a copy of the cheque and destroy the cheque itself, but once again the drafting is opaque.

A 'relevant cheque' is any cheque which is for a sum of $200 or more (at the present time) and which is not drawn by a public authority. Failure to retain the cheque or a copy of the cheque as required by the section exposes the financial institution to a fine not exceeding $10,000.

The drafting of the entire section is unfortunate and exemplifies the undesirability of making amendments in a piecemeal fashion by reference from another statute which appears to have been drafted by those lacking an intimate knowledge of the Act being amended.

CHEQUES II

NON-CONTRACTUAL RELATIONSHIPS

[6.1] The payee ordinarily has no contractual relationship with the paying bank and even if he or she is a customer, there is no contractual right for a particular cheque to be paid. Similarly, the drawer of a cheque will ordinarily have no contractual relationship with the collecting bank and even if he or she is a customer, the only contractual right concerns the payment of cheques, not the process of collection. There are, however, non-contractual relationships in each instance.

THE PAYEE-PAYING BANK RELATIONSHIP

[6.2] It has long been thought that the payee has no right against the drawee bank to obtain payment of a cheque. The reason for this view was that the drawee bank is not liable on the cheque, since it has not become a party to the cheque by signing, nor is there any contractual relationship with the payee which obliges the drawee bank to pay. Case law suggests that this may be simply another example of the confusion caused by a cheque being a form of a bill of exchange.

Thus, in *HH Dimond (Rotorua 1966) Ltd v ANZ Banking Group* [1979] 2 NZLR 739 the plaintiff was the payee of a cheque drawn on the defendant bank. The cheque was deposited with his own bank for collection and was processed by the Wellington Databank centre (the local clearing house) on 4 February. It was delivered to the defendant bank at about 9am the following morning and it was agreed between the parties that this delivery was the time of presentment. The place of the cheque on the Databank list indicated that the cheque would normally have been dealt with at about 2.30 in the afternoon, but sometime just before noon a receiver had been appointed to the drawer of the cheque and the receiver exercised the right of countermand.

The clearing house agreement allowed for the dishonour of cheques until 3pm following the debit in the branch bank. Accordingly, the defendant bank dishonoured the cheque and reversed the credit which had been made in favour of the plaintiff. The action against the paying bank was framed in negligence, claiming that if the cheque had been dealt with promptly when it was presented then it would have been paid. It was argued that in those circumstances the paying bank was not entitled to the full time allowed by the clearing house rules for dishonour.

The court held that when the cheque is presented for collection through a clearing house that the paying bank is given the time allowed by the rules. It was acknowledged that the cheque would have been paid earlier had it been presented at the counter on the morning of the 5th. However, the holder chose to present the cheque through the clearing house. In such a circumstance, he must have been taken to assent to reasonable clearing house rules.

[6.3]   The *Dimond* case itself is remarkable in that the court and the parties appeared to assume that the drawee bank owed a duty of care to the payee. Whether or not this is correct, the situation after the Cheques and Payment Orders Act 1986 would seem to be more favourable to the payee, for by s 67 of the Act, if the drawee bank fails to pay or dishonour the cheque within a reasonable time, then it may not dishonour and is liable to the holder of the cheque for the amount. Under the *Dimond* approach, it would be necessary for the payee to show that the negligence of the bank had been the cause of loss and the amount recoverable would have to be proved in evidence.

Payment under a mistake

[6.4]   As we have seen, when a bank mistakenly pays a cheque after the authority of the customer has been withdrawn or, in the case of a forged drawer's signature, when there was never any authority to pay, it will usually not be possible to debit the customer's account. In such circumstances, the bank may seek to recover the money from the person who has been paid.

In a slightly different situation, the bank pays on a cheque drawn by a customer in the mistaken belief that there are funds available to meet the cheque. In this case the bank has the right to recover from the customer, the cheque being taken as a request for an overdraft, but that right may be of little value if the customer has become insolvent. Again, the bank may attempt to recover money paid from the payee.

[6.5]   These are but examples of a wide variety of situations where one person pays another a sum which would not have been paid had the payer known the true facts. Of these situations and the legal framework which deals with them, Lord Wright has said (*Fibrosa Spolka Akcyjna v Fairbairn Lawson Combe Barbour Ltd* [1943] AC 32 at 61):

> It is clear that any civilised system of law is bound to provide remedies for cases of what has been called unjust enrichment or unjust benefit, that is to prevent a man from retaining the money or some benefit derived from another which it is against conscience that he should keep. Such remedies in English law are generally different from remedies in contract or in tort and are now recognised to fall within a third category of the common law which has been called quasi-contract or restitution ... Payment under a mistake of fact is only

one head of this category of the law ... the gist of the action is a debt or obligation implied or, more accurately, imposed by law.

But when is it 'against conscience' that a payee should keep the sum? If the holder of a valid cheque obtains payment of it before the drawer stops payment, then it is clear that he or she may keep the sum paid. Is it 'against conscience' for the payee to keep the sum even though the sum was obtained after the customer has withdrawn authority? Or because the bank, through its own mistake, paid the cheque without realising that funds were insufficient? Is it relevant that the payee has knowledge of the payer's mistake as, for example, when the payee of a cheque presents the cheque knowing that it has been countermanded?

[6.6] Payment under a mistake was considered by the High Court in *David Securities v Commonwealth Bank of Australia* (1992) 109 ALR 57. DS entered into an agreement with CBA which included an option of foreign currency loans. There was a clause in the agreement which provided that DS was to pay the bank with respect to certain tax liabilities. This clause was, unknown to either party at the time, avoided by s 261 of the Income Tax Assessment Act 1936. The bank commenced proceedings against DS claiming default under the agreement. DS counterclaimed for recovery of money paid to the CBA under the mistaken belief that the clause was valid.

Note that the mistake here was one of interpretation of a contractual clause. Such a mistake is one of law as opposed to one of fact. The distinction was important since it was long thought that there was a fundamental difference between mistakes of fact and mistakes of law. Under the law as understood, there was a potential right to recover money paid under a mistake of fact but no such right if the mistake was one of law: *Bilbie v Lumley* (1802) 2 East 469; 102 ER 448; *South Australia Cold Stores Ltd v Electricity Trust of South Australia* (1957) 98 CLR 65.

This distinction was based on some vague notion that the payer must be taken to know the law. Thus, in *Kelly v Solari* (1841) 9 M & W 54; 152 ER 24 it was said that 'The safest rule ... is that if the party makes the payment with full knowledge of the facts, although in ignorance of the law, there being no fraud on the other side, he cannot recover it back again': per Lord Abinger (1841) 9 M & W 54 at 58. The rule was never satisfactory. Apart from the occasional difficulty of distinguishing a mistake of law from one of fact, the rule simply makes no sense. The circumstances are, *ex hypothesi*, those in which the payee has no right to receive the money: see, for example, *Kiriri Cotton Co Ltd v Dewani* [1960] AC 192.

David Securities held that there is no such difference and that the rule precluding recovery of money paid under a mistake of law is no part of the law of Australia. The general principle is that a person will be entitled prima facie to recover money paid in the mistaken belief that he or she is under a legal obligation to make the payment or that the payee is legally entitled to receive the payment.

[6.7]   The right of recovery is based on the concept of unjust enrichment. 'Unjust enrichment' is not a subjective concept of what is unfair or unconscionable. There must be some factor such as mistake, duress or illegality. Where there is a mistake, be it of fact or law, there is no requirement that the person seeking recovery of the payment prove any 'unjustness' over and above mistake. The mistake itself is sufficient to give rise to a prima facie obligation to make restitution.

David Securities has been approved in *Baltic Shipping Co v Dillon* (1993) 111 ALR 389 and in *Winterton Constructions Pty Ltd v Hambros Australia Ltd* (1993) 111 ALR 649.

ELEMENTS OF THE CAUSE OF ACTION

[6.8]   The essential feature of the action is that the payment would not have been made save for the mistake. Some of the English cases have suggested that in addition to being the cause of payment, the mistake must be 'fundamental': see, for example, *Aiken v Short* (1856) 1 H & N 210; *Morgan v Ashcroft* [1938] 1 KB 49; *Norwich Union Fire Insurance Society Ltd v Price Ltd* (1934) AC 455. This requirement usually meant that the mistake was such that, if true, the fact would have made the payer legally liable to have made the payment. There seems little sense in such a requirement and the High Court so held in *David Securities*, adding (at 74):

> The notion of fundamentally is, however, extremely vague and would seem to add little, if anything, to the requirement that the mistake cause the payment.

'Mistake' includes those cases, like *David Securities* itself, where the parties are simply ignorant of the law as well as those cases where there is a positive but incorrect belief.

[6.9]   Although it is essential that the mistake caused the payment, it is not relevant that the mistake was caused by the negligence of the payer. Thus, in the landmark case of *Kelly v Solari* (1841) 9 M & W 54; 152 ER 24 an executrix received the proceeds of a life assurance policy from the plaintiff company. The company had negligently overlooked the fact that the life policy had been allowed to lapse by reason of a failure to maintain premium payments.

The Court of Exchequer allowed the recovery of the money, dismissing arguments that the company should not be allowed to recover since it alone had the means of discovering the true facts but had carelessly neglected to do so. However, the court did indicate that, had the company made an intentional decision to decline to investigate the currency of the policy, then the position would have been different, for in that case it would have appeared that the company intended to make the payment no matter what the true state of the facts might be.

[6.10]   In some of the earlier cases it was argued that the mistake must be 'between the payer and payee': see, for example, *National Westminster Bank Ltd v Barclays Bank Ltd* [1975] QB 654. There are obvious difficulties with interpreting the meaning of the concept, but in any case the notion has been abandoned in both England and Australia: *Barclays Bank Ltd v W J Simms, Son & Cooke (Southern) Ltd* [1980] QB 677; *Porter v Latec Finance (Queensland) Pty Ltd* (1964) 111 CLR 177.

[6.11] It has sometimes been said that a 'voluntary' payment cannot be recovered. Part of the problem is in assigning a sensible meaning to 'voluntary'.

If 'voluntary' merely means that the payer would have paid the money even knowing the true facts, then it adds nothing to the analysis. In that case, the mistake was not the operative cause of the payment and there are no grounds for the action.

In some of the earlier cases, 'voluntary' appeared to mean that, assuming the mistaken facts to be true, the payer is under no legal obligation to make the payment. The cases are confusing and inconsistent, mainly because it has never been clear to whom the obligation must be owed: see, for example, *Aiken v Short* (1856) 1 H & N 210; 156 ER 1180 and *Morgan v Ashcroft* [1938] 1 KB 49.

The question is important to the paying banker because the payment of a cheque is 'voluntary' if the requirement is that a legal duty be owed to the payee of the cheque. If, however, the duty may be owed to some third party, then the payment is not 'voluntary', for the banker owes a contractual duty to the drawer of the cheque.

[6.12] The meaning and effect of 'voluntary payment' was considered in *David Securities*. There it was said (at 70–1):

> The payment is voluntary or there is an election if the plaintiff chooses to make the payment even though he or she believes a particular law of contractual provision requiring the payment is, or may be invalid, or is not concerned to query whether the payment is legally required; he or she is prepared to assume the validity of the obligation, or is prepared to make the payment irrespective of the validity or invalidity of the obligation, rather than contest the claim or payment. We use the term 'voluntary' therefore to refer to a payment made in satisfaction of an honest claim rather than a payment not made under any form of compulsion or undue influence.

The majority indicated that 'voluntary' payments would not be recoverable on the policy grounds that the law should uphold bargains and enforce compromises freely entered into.

[6.13] Brennan J in dissent criticised this approach, arguing that it would include payments which were obtained under compulsion or duress. He argues that 'voluntary' must relate to the mind of the payer. Honest compromises would be protected under Brennan's argument by a rule that payment may not be recovered where the defendant payee 'honestly believed, when he learnt of the payment or transfer, that he was entitled to receive and retain the money or property' (at 92).

[6.14]   Prior to *David Securities*, it had been argued that the meaning of 'voluntary' adds nothing to the basic requirement that the mistake must be the cause of the payment. In *Porter v Latec Finance (Qld) Pty Ltd* (1964) 111 CLR 177 Barwick CJ said (at 187):

> There is some possibility of confusion when dealing with the subject matter of the recovery of payments said to have been made under mistake in speaking, as some of the cases do, of the payments being 'voluntary', as if a voluntary payment made to the wrong person could never be recovered. It is preferable in my opinion to test the matter by determining whether the mistake is fundamental to the transaction, properly identifying the transaction and the relationship of the mistake to it. Such a course is, I think, universally valid although as yet the subject of money paid under mistake is not fully exhausted by decision.

Note that Barwick here is using the word 'fundamental' merely in the sense of identifying the cause of the payment. His comments were followed in *Commercial Bank of Australia v Younis* [1979] 1 NSWLR 444.

It seems very unlikely that we have heard the last word on 'voluntary' payments. Whatever the meaning of the word, it is doubtful that rules of recovery may be based on whether the plaintiff did or did not 'want' to make the payment: for a good discussion of the issue, see P Birks, 'Modernising the Law of Restitution' (1993) 109 *LQR* 164.

MISTAKE OF FACT/LAW

[6.15]   As noted above, prior to *David Securities* a mistake of law was not grounds for recovery. In both New Zealand and Western Australia, legislation placed mistake of law on an equal footing with mistake of fact: Judicature Act 1908 (NZ) s 94A; Property Law Act 1969 (WA) s 124.

WHOSE MISTAKE?

[6.16]   The mistake must be on the part of the payer. It is not relevant that the payee was or was not mistaken: see, for example, *Westminster Bank Ltd v Arlington Overseas Trading Co* [1952] 1 Lloyd's Rep 211. This does not mean that the knowledge of the payee is irrelevant, for if the knowledge of the payee is such as to make the receipt of the money fraudulent, then he or she will not be able to retain the money, no matter what defence might be otherwise available. Ellinger argues that the knowledge of the payee is itself a basis for an action in restitution, but, as he acknowledges, the cases which he discusses involve the receipt of trust property: Ellinger and Lomnicka, *Modern Banking Law*, 2nd ed, Clarendon Press, Oxford, 1994, p 396.

In many, perhaps most, cases payment will be made by an agent. This will be the case, for example, when a teller makes a mistaken payment of a cheque which has been stopped by the drawer. Is the mistake of the agent sufficient to ground recovery by the bank? The rule is expressed succinctly by Lynskey J in *Lloyds Bank Ltd v Brooks* (1950) 6 LDAB 161 (at 164): 'If the hand that pays the money, even though it is only that of an agent, is acting under a mistake of fact, that payment is a payment made under a mistake of fact.'

This will be true even if some other agent of the bank had full knowledge of the facts, provided only that the agent with full knowledge is not aware of the payment being made on erroneous facts. In other words, the principal does not have the knowledge of all of its agents for these purposes: *Turvey v Dentons (1923) Ltd* [1953] 1 QB 218 at 224; *Secretary of State for Employment v Wellworthy (No 2)* [1976] ICR 13.

DEFENCES

[6.17] A complete review of cases concerning the recovery of payment under a mistake of fact was undertaken by Robert Goff J in *Barclays Bank Ltd v W J Simms, Son & Cooke (Southern) Ltd* [1980] QB 677, [1979] 3 All ER 522. He summarised his findings as follows:

(1) If a person pays money to another under a mistake of fact which causes him to make the payment, he is prima facie entitled to recover it as money paid under a mistake of fact.

(2) His claim may, however, fail if
  (a) the payer intends that the payee shall have the money at all events, whether the fact be true or false or is deemed in law so to intend;
  (b) the payment is made for good consideration, in particular if the money is paid to discharge, and does discharge, a debt owed to the payee (or a principal on whose behalf he is authorised to receive the payment) by the payer or by a third party by whom he is authorised to discharge the debt;
  (c) the payee has changed his position in good faith, or is deemed in law to have done so.

This statement was quoted with approval by the High Court in *David Securities* at 76 and must now be taken to cover payment under mistake of law as well.

[6.18] To this list must be added certain circumstances in which the payment was made to an agent. This circumstance will be of the utmost importance to a bank paying a cheque since the payment will very often be made not to the holder of the cheque but to the agent of the holder, the collecting bank: see [6.19]. There are also circumstances where a good defence might ordinarily be made, but there is some additional fault on the part of the defendant which will permit the plaintiff to recover: see [6.31]. Finally, there are some special rules which are thought to apply to payment on a negotiable instrument: see [6.42].

We have already discussed the meaning of the first defence, that the payer intended the payee to receive the money at all events: see [6.11].

Payment to an agent

[6.19] When money is paid by mistake not to the principal in the transaction but to an agent, the agent will not be obliged to refund the money if it has been paid over to the principal or if the agent has, in reliance on the payment, done something which has otherwise altered the relationship between the agent and the principal.

But this rule applies only if the agent receives the money purely as a 'conduit' to the principal. It has no application if the money is received by the agent payee as principal in his or her own right, nor if the receipt is in consequence of some wrongdoing to which the agent was a party. In these latter cases, liability to the payer will remain even if the agent has already accounted to the principal.

[6.20]   The principles are nicely illustrated by *Gowers v Lloyds & National Provincial Foreign Bank Ltd* [1938] 1 All ER 766. The plaintiffs were agents of the Crown who were charged with, inter alia, the payment of pensions to retired officers of the British colonial civil service. In order to collect the sums due, a pensioner would fill in forms which included a witnessed certificate to the effect that the pensioner was still alive. The forms were provided by the plaintiffs, but in most cases the pensioner would present the completed forms for payment through the pensioner's own bank.

The defendant bank acted as an agent for the collection of the pension of a customer named Gibson. For more than five years, forged forms and certificates had been forwarded through the defendant bank and paid by the plaintiffs. Neither the plaintiff nor the defendant bank was aware that Gibson had been dead for at least that amount of time. The plaintiffs sought recovery of the sums as money paid under a mistake of fact.

Although the plaintiffs were prima facie entitled to recover, the Court of Appeal held that they must fail since the defendant bank was innocently acting for a principal to whom they had passed on the money. Note that the actual principal was the rogue, not the person with whom the bank thought that it was dealing, but that did not alter the application of the general principle.

[6.21]   *Gower's* case was approved by the High Court of Australia in *ANZ Banking Group Ltd v Westpac Banking Corporation Ltd* (1988) 78 ALR 157; 62 ALJR 292. Acting under instructions from a customer, the plaintiff bank was to transfer about $14,000 for the credit of a customer of the defendant bank. Due to a clerical error, the sum transferred was about $114,000. The higher sum was credited to the account of the customer of the Westpac bank and allowed drawings of all but $17,000 against the account before it became aware of the error. The customer of Westpac agreed to repay, but was wound up after having repaid only $2500.

Most of the litigation concerned the amount which Westpac was obliged to repay. In the Supreme Court, Clarke J found that the plaintiff was entitled to the whole $100,000 less the $2500 which the customer had already repaid. The Court of Appeal reduced that sum to about $39,000. The High Court reduced the sum even further to $17,000 on the principle outlined in *Gower's* case. The different amounts awarded by the Court of Appeal and the High Court are attributable to different evidence concerning the amount actually paid over to the customer by Westpac.

Payment made for good consideration

[6.22] When a payment is made for good consideration, in particular when the receipt by the payee discharges a debt, then it can hardly be 'against good conscience' for the payee to retain the payment.

The defence may be illustrated by *National Mutual Life Association of Australasia Ltd v Walsh* (1987) 8 NSWLR 585. Because of the frauds of a third party, the defendant was paid substantial commissions by the plaintiff over a period of more than a year. Although the payments were made under a mistake of fact, Clarke J held that they were not recoverable. The defendant established that he had spent some 18 to 24 hours each week on work which was associated with the fraudulent claims. As a result of that, he was unable to seek other business. Further, but for the mistaken payments he would have sought other employment and other opportunities. Clarke J found that this constituted consideration moving from the defendant.

This is not entirely satisfactory since the 'consideration' provided by the defendant was nothing that was the result of a bargain between the parties. At the time of the *National Mutual* case the defence of 'change of position' was not fully recognised. There is little doubt that the defendant suffered a 'change of position' in reliance on the payments: see discussion of the 'change of position' defence at [6.25]ff.

Other problems with this defence of 'consideration' usually arise when the payment is made not by the debtor but by some third party, typically a bank. Such a payment is effective to discharge the debt only if the person who makes the payment has a personal obligation to make the payment, if the payer had actual or ostensible authority to do so or if the debtor later ratifies the payment expressly or by implication: see P Birks and J Beatson, 'Unrequested Payment of Another's Debt' (1976) 92 *LQR* 188.

[6.23] The principle may be illustrated by *Aiken v Short* (1856) 1 H & N 210; 156 ER 1180; 25 LJ Ex 321. The plaintiff bankers had taken an assignment of an interest in an estate as security for advances made to one Carter. It was later learned that Carter had given a previous assignment of the same interest to the defendants and that the first assignment had priority. The plaintiffs then made arrangements to pay off the debt owed by Carter to the defendants and so gain a first interest in the estate. It was then learned that Carter had no interest to assign.

In an action to recover the payment as money paid under a mistake of fact, the plaintiffs failed, in part because the payment had been made for good consideration. Carter owed the money to the defendant and the plaintiff was authorised by Carter to make the payment and so the debt was discharged. Although the payment was made under a mistake of fact, it could not be recovered.

[6.24] The High Court in *David Securities* affirmed that consideration may provide a defence to the action for money paid under a mistake and also clarified certain aspects of the defence. Where consideration may be 'apportioned' the defence may be partial, allowing the plaintiff to recover some, but not all, of the moneys paid. For these purposes, there is a total failure of consideration when the plaintiff has not received any part of that which was bargained for, and it is not directly relevant that he or she may have received some other benefit: at 78.

Change of position

[6.25]   Although Robert Goff J listed 'change of position' as a defence, it is by no means clear what the scope of the defence might be. It has long been recognised that 'change of position' is different from the defence of estoppel. This acknowledgment is clear from the wording of those Acts which have changed the common law. For example, the Western Australia Act reads:

> s 125(1) Relief, ... in respect of any payment made under mistake, whether of law or fact, shall be denied wholly or in part if the person from whom relief is sought received the payment in good faith and has so altered his position in reliance on the validity of the payment that in the opinion of the Court, having regard to all possible implications in respect of the parties (other than the plaintiff or the claimant) to the payment and of other persons acquiring rights or interest through them, it is inequitable to grant relief, or to grant relief in full.

[6.26]   In considering a similar New Zealand provision, the Court of Appeal noted that '[t]he only available defences to [an action for recovery of money paid under a mistake of fact] are true estoppel and s 94B of the Judicature Act ...'. This is a clear acknowledgment that 'change of position' is different from the general principle of estoppel. The early cases seem to confirm that it is necessary to establish a true estoppel and that change of position, by itself, is not a defence: *Baylis v Bishop of London* [1913] 1 Ch 127; *National Mutual Life Association of Australasia Ltd v Walsh* (1987) 8 NSWLR 585.

However, the High Court in *David Securities* has made it clear that change of position is a defence. In part, this is necessary in order to prevent injustice arising because of the court's analysis in terms of unjust enrichment. In the words of the court (at 80–1):

> ... a defence of change of position is necessary to ensure that enrichment of the recipient of the payment is prevented only in circumstances where it would be unjust. This does not mean that the concept of unjust enrichment needs to shift the primary focus of its attention from the moment of enrichment. From the point of view of the person making the payment, what happens after he or she has mistakenly paid over the money is irrelevant, for it is at that moment that the defendant is unjustly enriched. However, the defence of change of position is relevant to the enrichment of the defendant precisely because its central element is that the defendant has acted to his or her detriment on the faith of the receipt.

[6.27]   When has the defendant 'acted to his or her detriment on the faith of the receipt'? The High Court offered only a negative answer, noting that it is not a change of position where the defendant has simply spent the money received on ordinary living expenses.

Before the *David Securities* case, the conventional wisdom was that 'change of position' is merely one component in making out a defence of estoppel: see the comments of Clarke J in the *National Mutual* case. This position may no longer be maintained. It may be that 'acting to his or her detriment' may not necessarily mean the same thing when considered in the context of change of position as it does in the context of estoppel.

Estoppel

[6.28] Estoppel is a rule of evidence which prevents a party from asserting facts in certain circumstances. The essential elements of an estoppel are that a person has, by words or conduct, led another to believe that a certain state of affairs exists and that it would, in all the circumstances, be unfair or unjust to allow the first person to assert that the state of affairs does not exist.

The problem is to establish precisely when it is unjust to allow the representor to deny the state of affairs. It is usually said that the representee must have relied upon the representation and have acted upon it in some way to his or her detriment. It is clear that spending the money in reliance only upon the payment itself does not establish the estoppel. It seems that the reason for this is that the mere payment of money by the payer cannot be taken as a representation that the payee is entitled to treat it as his or her own: *R E Jones Ltd v Waring & Gillow Ltd* [1926] AC 670.

There must be some representation beyond the mere fact of payment before the defendant may rely upon an estoppel. This additional representation may be by express statement, action or conduct. If a person who is under some duty to speak is silent, then silence may itself amount to a representation which is sufficient to establish the estoppel: *Greenwood v Martins Bank Ltd* [1933] AC 51.

[6.29] After it is shown that there was a representation by the plaintiff to the effect that the defendant is entitled to treat the payment as his or her own, then the defendant must show that he or she has 'acted to his or her detriment' as a result of relying on the representation. Merely spending the money is not necessarily a change of position. What must be shown is that the payee would not have spent the sums in the absence of the payment and/or the representation.

In *Lloyds Bank Ltd v Brooks* (1950) 6 LDAB 161 the plaintiff bank made payments under a mistake of fact to the defendant over a period of time. In reliance upon the periodic accounts sent to her by the bank, the defendant spent sums which she would not otherwise have spent. The court held that the payments could not be recovered since the bank was under a duty to its customer to maintain accurate accounts. In breaching this duty, the bank made a representation to the defendant which was independent of the actual payment. The court also found that as a result of this representation, the defendant spent sums of money which she would not otherwise have spent and that this was a change of position sufficient to support an estoppel.

[6.30]   It may sometimes be difficult to identify the money spent by the defendant in a way which relates it to the money received. The English decisions show that it may not be necessary to be too precise. In *Avon County Council v Howlett* [1983] 1 All ER 1073 the defendant was overpaid by his employer over a period of time due to an error in computer programming. As a result of these overpayments, the defendant had forgone a claim for a social security benefit and had spent some money which he would not otherwise have spent.

It was found by the trial judge that the plaintiff had, in the circumstances, made representations to the defendant which were sufficient to found an estoppel. The main issue before the Court of Appeal concerned the fact that the defendant had been overpaid some £1007 but had only spent a smaller sum. Was it possible for the plaintiff to recover the unspent balance? The Court of Appeal said not, arguing (per Slade LJ at 1086):

> ... one has to postulate a situation in which the defendant was perfectly entitled to conduct his business affairs on the assumption that the relevant representations were true ... a defendant in the situation of the defendant in the present case may ... have either altered his general mode of living or undertaken commitments or incurred expenditure or entered into other transactions which it may be very difficult for him subsequently to recall ... He may even have done so, while leaving some of the particular moneys paid to him by the plaintiff untouched.

Note that this demonstrates a strange difference between the defence of estoppel and the other defences considered above. Both 'consideration' and 'change of position' would appear to allow the plaintiff partial recovery in certain circumstances. Estoppel, however, is an 'all or nothing' defence.

Fault of the defendant

[6.31]   It is well established that the defence of estoppel will fail if there is some 'fault' on the part of the defendant. Although the exact scope of 'fault' is unclear, it is certain that any fact which indicates that the defendant had notice that the representation was incorrect or knew of some material facts which would have made the payer recognise his or her mistake will disentitle the defendant from relying on the mistake.

The position was stated precisely by Lord Brampton in *George Whitechurch Ltd v Cavanagh* [1902] AC 117 at 145:

> ... no representations can be relied on as estoppels if they have been induced by the concealment of any material fact on the part of those who seek to use them as such; and if the person to whom they are made knows something which, if revealed, would have been calculated to influence the other to hesitate or seek for further information before speaking positively, and that something has been withheld, the representation ought not to be treated as an estoppel.

Although there does not appear to be any direct authority, the same analysis should apply when the defence is based on a change of position.

Delay in making claim

[6.32] An undue delay in making the claim for the return of the mistaken payment will provide a defence at least if the defendant has changed position. This will be true whether the delay was caused by negligence or by some other circumstance.

[6.33] The defence is illustrated by the facts of *General Accident, Fire and Life Assurance Corporation Ltd v National Bank of New Zealand* (1932) 51 NZLR 1289. An insurance company paid an insurance claim which arose from the destruction of a truck by fire. The truck was owned by a company, but the beneficiary was a bank which held a mortgage over the truck. Six months after the payment, the plaintiff discovered that there were false statements in the proposal and that the policy was void. However, another 12 months passed before they made a claim for recovery, by which time the company was in a financial position which precluded any recovery by the bank from the company. The court held that the plaintiff must fail since it had with full knowledge stood by while the bank's chance of recovery vanished.

APPLICATION TO MISTAKEN PAYMENT OF CHEQUES

[6.34] A bank who pays a cheque under a mistake may wish to recover the money from the payee, either because the bank is unable to debit the customer's account or, although the debit is able to be maintained, the right is worthless due to the customer's insolvency or for some other reason. There seem to be three different classes of case.

* Where the bank pays a cheque mistakenly believing that the account of the customer is adequate to cover the cheque.

* Where the bank pays a cheque mistakenly believing that there is authorisation to do so when in fact the cheque has been validly stopped by the customer.

* Where the bank pays a cheque believing it to be a valid mandate from the customer when it fact it bears a forged drawer's signature.

The bank's right to recovery has been complicated by the cheque's other function as a negotiable instrument. The law concerning the recovery of money paid by mistake on a negotiable instrument has been influenced by the need for certainty when dealing with such instruments. A view emerged which favoured finality of payment in those circumstances where there was some possibility of detriment to the person receiving payment.

[6.35] The modern trend is to bring the law concerning payment on a negotiable instrument more into line with the general law of recovery. As will be seen below, it is likely that the Act has, by removing the requirement of notice upon dishonour, completed this trend in the case of cheques. If that is correct, then problems of mistaken payments of cheques may be solved by the application of the general principles, although even here there remains some disagreement as to how those principles apply.

Insufficient funds

[6.36] When the bank pays a customer's cheque in the mistaken belief that there are sufficient funds, the payment is not recoverable from the payee. When the cheque is presented for payment the bank has the authority from its customer to pay the amount and to debit the account, the writing of the cheque being treated in law as a request for an overdraft: *Cuthbert v Robarts, Lubbock & Co* [1909] 2 Ch 226.

This factual situation thus falls squarely within the second category mentioned by Robert Goff J. The bank has followed a valid mandate and the debt owed by the drawer to the payee of the cheque is thus discharged and, according to *Simms'* case (see [6.38]), the bank is no longer entitled to recover.

On the other hand, the bank has clearly made a mistake and would not have paid the money had it known the true position of the account. It is extremely artificial to treat the payment as being the granting of an overdraft when the bank was never in a position to know that an overdraft is required. Ellinger argues that the question should remain open: op cit, p 415.

It seems likely that the view of Robert Goff J will prevail. While it is true that the bank has made a mistake, the fact that the bank has acted within its authority and has followed its mandate means that the debt owed by the drawer to the payee has been discharged: see [5.89]. As a consequence, the payee of the cheque has given good consideration and may resist the claim.

This analysis does not fit well with the High Court's view that consideration as a defence should focus on the payer. What consideration has the bank received for the payment? Perhaps it could be argued that it has 'received' the right to claim the payment from the drawer of the cheque and that this is what it bargained for.

Alternatively, and perhaps more transparently, it could be argued that the payee has, as a result of the payment, changed his or her position. Since the cheque has been paid, the payee no longer has a right of action on the original debt against the drawer of the cheque. Unfortunately, this argument has been rejected when applied to the 'cheque stopped' category of cases: see below [6.37]ff.

Cheque stopped

[6.37] When payment is made on a cheque which has been validly stopped, it now seems clear that the bank is prima facie entitled to recover, although the logic of the position is not entirely satisfactory. There have been several Australian and New Zealand cases which have allowed recovery: *Commercial Bank of Australia Ltd v Younis* [1979] 1 NSWLR 444; *Bank of New South Wales v Murphett* [1983] 1 VR 489; *Southland Savings Bank v Anderson* [1974] 1 NZLR 118; *KJ Davies (1976) Ltd v Bank of New South Wales* [1981] 1 NZLR 262.

[6.38]   The most thorough analysis has been made by Robert Goff J in *Barclays Bank Ltd v WJ Simms Son & Cooke (Southern) Ltd* [1980] QB 677. The facts were not extraordinary. A housing association drew a cheque on its account with the plaintiff bank in favour of a building company. There were, at the time, adequate funds available to meet the cheque. However, the following day a receiver was appointed to the payee company and the association gave immediate instructions to stop payment of the cheque. Due to an oversight, payment of the cheque was made by the plaintiff bank which then sought recovery from the receiver.

There is clearly a prima facie case for recovery, for if the true facts were known the bank would not have made the payment. As to the possible defences, the court held that there was no discharge of the debt (at 542):

> ... since the drawer had in fact countermanded payment, the bank was acting without mandate and so the payment was not effective to discharge the drawer's obligation on the cheque; from this it follows that the payee gave no consideration for the payment, and the claim cannot be defeated on [the second] ground.

As to the defence of change of position (at 542):

> ... there is no evidence of any actual change of position on the part of either of the defendants or on the part of the [collecting bank]; and, since notice of dishonour is not required in a case such as this, the payee is not deemed to have changed his position by reason of lapse of time in notifying them of Barclays' error and claiming repayment.

[6.39]   *Simms'* case has been criticised on several points. In particular, it has been said that since the cheque has been paid it is discharged and the payee no longer has any rights on the cheque. If that is correct, then the payee has only the action on the original debt, an action which is not nearly so advantageous as the action on the cheque: see R Goode, 'The Bank's Right to Recover Money Paid on a Stopped Cheque' (1981) 97 *LQR* 254. This would seem to be a clear 'change of position' which should entitle the payee to retain payment.

The argument was raised in *Bank of New South Wales v Murphett* [1983] 1 VR 489 but was rejected by all members of the Victorian Full Court. The attitude of the court was expressed bluntly by Starke J who said (at 493) that if '... this claim succeeds [the cheque] will in fact not have been paid'. That is a most curious comment, for the Act clearly defines payment in due course of a cheque and the consequences which flow from it: ss 78, 79. It is difficult to see how success in an action for the return of money has the effect of payment never having been made. The effect is to create a doctrine of revival of a discharged cheque, a doctrine that certainly receives no support from the Act itself.

[6.40]   A second criticism of *Simms'* case is that, although the bank lacked actual authority to pay the debt of its customer, it had apparent authority to do so. Since that is sufficient to discharge the debt, there is good consideration given by the payee and, as argued above, the payee has changed position. This argument does not appear to have been raised in any of the cases. It has been said that the consideration thus given by the payee is not one which was bargained for by the bank: see K G Nicholson, 'Recovery of Money Paid Under a Mistake of Fact' (1986) 60 *ALJ* 459, but that, even if correct, does not meet the 'change of position' argument.

The policy reason which is usually given for permitting bank recovery is that there is then no possibility of the payee or the bank customer being unjustly enriched, whereas if recovery is denied either the payee or the customer will receive a windfall at the bank's expense and the real dispute, that between the customer and the payee, will never be aired.

This argument is not convincing. Since the bank may not debit its customer's account it will be subrogated to the rights of the customer under the principle in *Liggett's* case: see [7.43] and R Goode, 'The Bank's Right to Recover Money Paid on a Stopped Cheque' (1981) 97 *LQR* 254. Thus, the 'real' dispute may be pursued but with a different plaintiff. Note also that there is a conflict between the mistake cases and the cases on the equitable relief available under the principle in *Liggett's* case: see the discussion at [7.54].

[6.41]   In summary, the cases seem to establish that the bank has a right to recovery money which it has paid when overlooking a stop payment order on a cheque. However, there are difficulties with the analysis of the cases and it is doubtful if the final word has been heard on the subject.

Forgery: the rule in Price v Neal

[6.42]   When one or more of the signatures on a cheque is forged, then the bank would not pay the cheque if it knew the true facts. Because of the statutory defence given to the bank when the forged signatures appear as indorsements, the bank will ordinarily attempt to recover from the payee only when it is the drawer's signature that is forged: see [7.54] for the position when there is a forged indorsement. At one time it was thought that the person making the payment might be taken to be making a representation that the signatures were genuine, but the modern trend is to assimilate the rules of such payments to those of the general payment under a mistake.

The problem dates to the old case of *Price v Neal* (1762) 3 Burr 1354; 97 ER 871. The plaintiff was the drawee of two bills of exchange of which the defendant was holder. The first bill was presented to Price for payment and it was paid promptly. The second bill was accepted by him and subsequently paid. It turned out that the drawer's signature on the bills had been forged although the defendant had acted throughout in good faith and without any knowledge of the forgeries. Price sought to recover the amounts paid as money paid under a mistake of fact.

The court held that the action must fail, but unfortunately for later applications gave a multiplicity of reasons. Lord Mansfield said first that it would not be unconscionable to retain money received as an innocent holder for value of a bill. Second, there was a duty on the drawee to make sure that the bills were valid before paying or accepting. Finally, if there was any fault or negligence on the part of either of the parties to the transaction it was that of the plaintiff, not that of the defendant.

[6.43] *Price v Neal* was considered in *Cocks v Masterman* (1829) 9 B & C 902; 109 ER 335 and again in *London and River Plate Bank Ltd v Bank of Liverpool Ltd* [1896] 1 QB 7 where it was explained that the importance of certainty in dealing with negotiable instruments required a harsh rule as to finality of payment. It is not necessary that there be any actual prejudice or damage to the payee if the amount of time which has elapsed is such that the holder's position may be, not necessarily is, affected. Recall that lapse of time may be a defence in all cases of mistaken payment, but the time factor may be critical when dealing with bills.

One of the reasons that this is of the utmost importance when dealing with bills of exchange is that the holder must give notice of dishonour in order to hold the drawer and previous indorsers liable: BEA s 53. Further, the time allowed for giving notice is short: BEA s 54.

[6.44] The rule in *Price v Neal* was first explained in terms of the need to give notice by the Privy Council in *Imperial Bank of Canada v Bank of Hamilton* [1903] AC 49. Although the drawer's signature was not forged, the cheque in question had been altered in such a way as to make it appear to be a cheque for $500 instead of the $5 for which it was drawn. The cheque so altered was void and the plaintiff bank sought recovery of the raised amount of the cheque which had been paid. The Privy Council allowed recovery, saying (at 58):

> There were no indorsers to whom notice of dishonour had to be given ... The rule laid down in *Cocks v Masterman* ... has reference to negotiable instruments, on the dishonour of which notice has to be given to some one ... who would be discharged from liability unless such notice were given in proper time.

Even under the BEA it is not generally necessary to give the drawer notice of dishonour in order to establish liability: BEA s 55(2)(c). Under the CPOA, it is not necessary to give notice to either the drawer or an indorser in order to establish liability: s 70. Consequently, it would seem that the rule in *Price v Neal* has no application to forgeries on cheques which are governed by the new Act, at least that part of the ratio of *Price v Neal* which presumes detriment by virtue of the need to give notice.

[6.45] But that still leaves open the possibility that payment is a representation that the signature is genuine. This question was considered by Kerr J in *National Westminster Bank Ltd v Barclays Bank International Ltd* [1975] QB 654. A customer of the plaintiff bank lived in Nigeria. In late 1971, while he was away, his house was broken into and various items taken. It was not noticed at the time that a cheque from the middle of a spare chequebook was one of the items taken. This came to his attention when he received a statement of account containing a debit item of £5000. He immediately notified the plaintiff bank of the forgery.

The cheque had been collected by the defendant bank which continued to hold the proceeds. The plaintiff sought recovery of the funds as money paid under a mistake of fact.

As to Lord Mansfield's suggestion that there is a duty on the drawee bank to know the signature of the drawer, Kerr J said (at 674):

> It seems to me ... that [the payee] can in the present case only succeed in raising an estoppel against the plaintiffs if the mere fact of a banker honouring a cheque on which his customer's signature has been undetectably forged carries with it an implied representation that the signature is genuine. I cannot see any logical basis for this. At most ... the paying banker is thereby representing no more than that he believes the signature to be genuine.

[6.46] Robert Goff J also considered the rule in *Price v Neal* in *Simms'* case, coming to the conclusion that it applied only when there was some need to give notice of dishonour.

If these cases are correct, then s 70 of the Act has the effect that the rule in *Price v Neal* may be disregarded so far as it affects the right of the bank to recover money which is paid on a forged drawer's signature or a forged indorsement. Under the rule in *David Securities*, the bank would have a prima facie right to recover the money from the payee.

THE DRAWER-COLLECTING BANK RELATIONSHIP

[6.47] Although there is no contractual relationship between the drawer of a cheque and the collecting bank, the collecting bank owes the drawer the duty to refrain from interfering with property of the drawer. The duty is breached whenever the collecting bank deals with a cheque which still belongs to the drawer but which has been misappropriated. In such circumstances, the collecting bank may be liable to the drawer in conversion. The collecting bank may have common law and statutory defences available to it in such circumstances. The action in conversion and the possible defences will be discussed in Chapter 7.

THE FORM OF THE ORDER

[6.48] The duty of the bank is to pay its customer's cheques and it is to the strict definition of 'cheque' that we now turn. It must be appreciated that the form of instruments such as cheques is of the utmost importance. One of the basic policies underlying the law of negotiable instruments is that the value of such instruments should be determinable quickly, certainly and cheaply. One of the important implementations of this policy is that, roughly speaking, the value of the instrument should be capable of determination merely by its form and 'if it looks right, it is right'. There are obvious limitations to the implementation of the policy, but it explains why the form of such instruments is so important in commercial law.

DEFINITION

[6.49]   By s 10 of the CPOA:

A cheque is an unconditional order in writing that — (a) is addressed by a person to another person (being a bank); (b) is signed by the person giving it; and (c) requires the bank to pay on demand a sum certain in money. An instrument that does not comply with this definition or that orders any act to be done in addition to the payment of money, is not a cheque.

For those readers who are familiar with the Bills of Exchange Act 1909 it will be immediately clear that the definition is very similar to the definition of a bill of exchange contained in section 8 of that Act. Perhaps the most notable difference, apart from restricting drawees to banks, is that the order need not specify a payee. The consequences of this are discussed below.

PARTIES TO THE CHEQUE

[6.50]   The term 'party to a cheque' means a person whose name appears on the cheque itself. The Act requires only two parties in the definition, the drawer, that is, the person who gives the order to pay, and the drawee, that is, the person to whom the order is directed.

THE DRAWEE: WHO IS A BANKER?

[6.51]   The drawee must be a bank and the term 'drawee bank' is defined in s 3(1) to mean the bank upon which the cheque is drawn. A bank is defined in s 3(1) to include the Reserve Bank of Australia, any institution which is a bank within the meaning of the Banking Act 1959 and the various state banks which are recognised by the Constitution. These should cause no difficulty, but the Act goes on to include a fourth class within the definition, namely, 'a person ... who carries on the business of banking outside Australia'. (See [2.93] for the definition of 'bank' and 'business of banking'.)

THE DRAWER

[6.52]   The drawer of the cheque, a term which is not defined by the Act, is the person who gives the order to the bank. There is nothing in the Act which requires that the drawer be a customer of the drawee bank, but if he or she is not, then the drawee bank owes the customer no duty to honour the cheque: see [2.15] for the definition of 'customer' and [5.66] for the consequences of a cheque being drawn by a non-customer. The bank may, however, owe some other party the duty to honour the cheque. This will be the case with so-called 'agency cheques': see [8.32].

FORMAL REQUIREMENTS

[6.53]   The form of an instrument must comply strictly with the requirements of the Act or it is not a cheque. This can have important consequences, for it may be that the instrument, although not a cheque for the purposes of the Act, will be a bill of exchange, in which case the BEA will govern the relationships between the parties, or it may not be a negotiable instrument at all, in which case the relationship between the parties will be governed by the general law.

As a simple example, an instrument which specifies that a certain sum is to be paid 'with bank charges' will probably not be a cheque, but will be a bill of exchange: CPOA s 15, BEA s 14 as amended by Bills of Exchange Amendment Act 1986. Such an instrument will still be a 'cheque' within the meaning of the BEA, but will be governed by the old regime rather than the new one. Similarly, a 'cheque' drawn on a party that is not a bank will be a bill of exchange, but it will not be a cheque.

The remainder of this section is an examination of the component parts of the formal definition of a 'cheque'.

AN 'ORDER'

[6.54] Section 11 of the Act provides that an order must be more than an authorisation or a request to pay. It has been said that the inclusion of words of courtesy will not invalidate an expression which is in all other respects an order to pay, but it must be said that the cases are by no means easy to reconcile. In *Little v Slackford* (1828) 1 Mood & M 171; 173 ER 1120 an instrument bearing the words 'Please let the bearer have £7 and place it to my account and you will much oblige me' was held not to be an order, whereas one drawn '[The drawee] will much oblige [the drawer] by paying to the order of [the payee]' was acceptable: *Ruff v Webb* (1794) 1 Esp 129; 170 ER 301. Since the use of preprinted forms is virtually universal, it is very unlikely that there will be serious problems with s 11.

Casino 'House cheques' signed by the defendant containing the words 'Payable to:' were held to be cheques in *Newham v Diamond Leisure Pty Ltd* (1994) 4 NTLR 111; 117 FLR 429. The majority of the Court of Appeal held that the words constituted more than a mere authorisation or request to pay.

'UNCONDITIONAL'

[6.55] One of the most fundamental formal requirements is that the order to pay should be 'unconditional'. The reasons for this have been explained in *Carlos v Fancourt* (1794) 5 TR 482 at 485:

> It would perplex the commercial transactions of mankind, if paper securities of this kind were issued out into the world encumbered with conditions and contingencies, and if the persons to whom they were offered in negotiation were obliged to enquire when these uncertain events would probably be reduced to certainty.

The policy is incorporated into the Act by s 12(1) which confirms that an order to pay on a contingency is not an unconditional order and it matters not that the event has in fact happened.

On the other hand, the cheque will usually indicate the account to be debited and it is useful and customary to write on the cheque itself an indication of the transaction which gave rise to the cheque. To place the matter beyond doubt, s 12(2) provides that the order may be unconditional even if the cheque includes one or both of these indications.

The reason for writing the transaction on the cheque is to increase the value of the paid cheque as evidence that the payment obligation of the transaction has been met. There have been attempts to go further and require the payee to sign a receipt attached to the cheque.

In such cases, it has been held that when the instruction is addressed to the drawee, then the order to pay is conditional; when the instruction concerning the receipt is addressed to the holder or to the world at large, the order to pay is unconditional. So 'Pay X on completion of the attached receipt' is a conditional order, but 'Pay X' together with a notice on the bottom of the instrument which says 'The attached receipt must be completed' is an unconditional order: see *Bavins Junr and Sims v London & South Western Bank Ltd* [1900] 1 QB 270; *Nathan v Ogdens Ltd* (1905) 94 LT 126; *Capital & Counties Bank Ltd v Gordon* [1903] AC 240.

Ellinger and Lomnicka suggest that instructions appearing above the signature risk being interpreted as a condition. They therefore recommend that any such instructions be below the signature, but they offer no authority for this analysis: p 309.

[6.56] It is a universal characteristic of traveller's cheques that they require a counter-signature by the person to whom the cheques are issued. The most common form of such an instrument is that the drawer instructs its overseas correspondent to cash the cheque against the customer's counter-signature. Does this requirement make the order 'conditional'? Goode argues that the requirement is for identification only and that, considering the policy of the requirement in the Acts, to hold that the order is 'conditional' is 'excessively technical': Goode, *Commercial Law*, Penguin, London, 1982, p 522. However, the 'excessively technical' approach seems to be ordinary in interpreting provisions relating to bills, and it is hard to see why the decision for a traveller's cheque would be different from that in *Bavins Junr and Sims v London & South Western Bank Ltd* [1900] 1 QB 270. Ellinger argues that the order is conditional and that traveller's cheques probably form a new species of negotiable instrument established by a general mercantile usage: Ellinger and Lomnicka, *Modern Banking Law*, 2nd ed, Oxford, 1994, p 331; Ellinger, 'Traveller's Cheques and the Law' (1969) 19 *University of Toronto Law Journal* 132.

ADDRESSED TO A BANK

[6.57] It is the essence of a cheque that it be drawn on a bank. Section 13(1) spells this out in detail. The order must be addressed to a bank and to no other person; it must be addressed to one bank only and that bank must be named or otherwise indicated with reasonable certainty.

While s 13(1) is a paragon of clarity, s 13(2) is poorly drafted and confusing. It says:

An order to pay may be an order to pay addressed to a bank notwithstanding that a person other than the bank on which the instrument containing the order is drawn, the payee or the drawer is specified in the instrument.

According to the Explanatory Memorandum, the purpose of the section is to make clear that the instrument may be a cheque even though the name of a non-bank financial institution also appears on the face of the instrument. Such would be the case in the so-called 'agency cheque': see CPOA s 100.

Again, the universal use of preprinted forms should mean that s 13 should cause little trouble in practice. The BEA allows for a bill to be drawn on more than one person; if an instrument is drawn in that way, it would appear to be a bill governed by the BEA. If both of the drawees are banks, then it may be that the instrument is a 'cheque' as defined in the BEA even though it is not a 'cheque' for the purposes of the CPOA.

[6.58]   Most traveller's cheques are not drawn on banks and are not, therefore, 'cheques' for the purposes of the CPOA. See [6.56] for an argument that they are probably not even bills of exchange.

SUM TO BE PAID

[6.59]   Since a bank must be prepared to pay on demand, it is clear that the amount to be paid should be stated accurately and clearly. Section 15(1) implements this policy by providing that the sum must be specified with 'reasonable certainty' in the instrument containing the order.

Where more than one amount

[6.60]   The only exception to this rule is where the instrument on its face specifies two or more different amounts to be paid. This may occur for a number of reasons ranging from simple mistake on the part of the drawer to fraud on the part of the holder of the cheque. In any case, s 15(2) solves the problem by decreeing that the amount to be paid is the smallest of the specified sums. This is a departure from previous law which gave priority to the amount expressed in words, a rule which has now been changed by the Bills of Exchange Amendment Act 1986 even for bills: BEA s 14(2), as amended.

Exchange rates

[6.61]   Cheques expressed in a foreign currency can cause problems in determining the amount. In the absence of any instructions to the contrary, the prevailing rate of exchange is used. However, the parties to the cheque may wish to express a fixed exchange rate or to determine the rate in some specified manner. Section 15(3) permits this practice as long as the rate is expressed on the cheque itself or can be ascertained from the instrument.

Placing an upper limit on the amount

[6.62]   Section 15 also addresses another common practice which might have caused trouble. As a means of limiting the opportunities for fraud, it is not uncommon for a preprinted cheque form to express a maximum sum for which the cheque may be drawn. Section 15(4) provides that such an instrument is to be taken to require payment of the lesser of the sums so specified.

Interest?

[6.63]   Section 14 of the BEA provides that a sum payable is a sum certain even though the sum is required to be paid with interest. The Cheques and Payment Orders Act does not contain any express provision on this matter. The Explanatory Memorandum explains that this reflects the desire to streamline as much as possible the processing of cheques by banks. Consequently, it was thought that an exact sum should be shown on every cheque.

It is not clear that the CPOA achieves that aim. The only requirement is that the sum be 'specified with reasonable certainty' on the cheque. The phrase might easily be found to include amounts such as '100 dollars together with 12 per cent interest from the date drawn'. Further, s 4(2) specifically retains the common law rules except in so far as they are expressly in conflict with the provisions of the Act. The BEA rule regarding interest was a codification of existing common law rules, so provided the sum with interest is specified with 'reasonable certainty' it would seem to be a sum certain within the meaning of the CPOA.

ON DEMAND

[6.64]   The order must be to pay on demand, but, subject to two qualifications, s 14(1) provides that an order is an order to pay on demand if it requires payment 'on demand', 'at sight' or 'on presentation'. Further, it is an order to pay on demand if no time at all is expressed for payment. It seems likely that the phrases used in s 14(1) are not exhaustive and that any phrase which imports a similar meaning would suffice.

The qualifications to s 14(1) are contained in s 14(2) and s 14(3). The order is not one to pay on demand if it requires, either expressly or by implication, payment otherwise than payment on demand. Possibly because this was thought to be somewhat less than helpful, s 14(3) gets to the heart of the matter. Without limiting the generality of s 14(2), the order is not one to pay on demand if payment is required at or before a particular time or where presentment is required at or before a particular time.

The Explanatory Memorandum accepts the recommendation of the Manning Committee that the drawer of a cheque should be required to accept the ordinary rules as to the time for presentment and payment and should not be permitted to impose conditions of this kind for his or her own greater protection at the expense of the payee or a holder. This seems another of those provisions which confuse the cheque as a payment instrument and as a negotiable instrument. There is, after all, no obligation on the payee to accept a cheque which is drawn in the way described, yet there may be perfectly legitimate reasons for the drawer wishing to see that the cheque is presented promptly. An example of the latter might be a drawer who is leaving the country; as things stand now, such a drawer could be forced to maintain an account for up to 15 months after drawing the last cheque.

Payment 'on demand' does not mean that the bank must hand over the money immediately. The bank must be permitted a reasonable time to check on the state of the account and to perform reasonable bookkeeping operations: G A Weaver and R C Craigie, *The Law Relating to Banker and Customer in Australia*, 2nd ed, Law Book Co, Sydney, 1990, para [12.580] and see [5.51].

DATE

[6.65]   Most preprinted cheques have a space provided for the drawer to enter the date. When the cheque is dated, there is a rebuttable presumption that the cheque was drawn on that day: s 16(1). On the other hand, a cheque need not be dated at all to be a valid cheque: s 16(2)(a).

Section 16 makes an important clarification to the law of cheques by recognising the validity of post-dated cheques. There has been some problem with post-dated cheques since it is obviously difficult to say that such an instrument is payable 'on demand'. Indeed, it is common ground that the bank should refuse payment of a post-dated cheque which is presented before the date on the cheque: *Brien v Dwyer* (1978) 141 CLR 378; 22 ALR 485; *Hodgson & Lee Pty Ltd v Mardonius Pty Ltd* (1986) 5 NSWLR 496.

For these reasons, and because they cause the banking community some problems, the Australian Bankers' Association made representations to the effect that post-dated cheques should be abolished. However, the evidence has shown that there is a strong desire in the commercial community to use such cheques and the CPOA has accepted this second course.

[6.66]   Not only is the post-dated cheque a 'cheque', but an attempt to obtain payment prior to the date on the cheque is not a 'presentment' of the cheque for payment: s 61(2). This has important ramifications for the parties to a post-dated cheque, since the drawer and others are not liable on the cheque if it has not been presented for payment: s 58.

Although the clarification provided by the CPOA is welcome, it seems that the law had probably reached the same conclusions in any case. The New South Wales Court of Appeal recently decided that a post-dated instrument could be a cheque under the old definition of the BEA: *Hodgson & Lee Pty Ltd v Mardonius Pty Ltd* (1986) 5 NSWLR 496; see also *Pollock v Bank of New Zealand* (1901) 20 NZLR 174; cf *Brien v Dwyer* (1978) 141 CLR 378.

It had also been concluded that a post-dated cheque could be validly negotiated between the date of its issue and its 'maturity' date: *Hodgson & Lee Pty Ltd v Mardonius Pty Ltd* (1986) 5 NSWLR 496.

ROLE OF THE DRAWER'S SIGNATURE

[6.67]   There is often confusion as to the meaning and effect of a signature on a cheque. Once again, this is partly due to the confusion caused by using a single instrument both as a simple payment device and as a negotiable instrument. The drawer's signature actually serves three different purposes. It is necessary for the creation of a 'cheque', it is necessary in order to establish the liability of the drawer in an action against the drawer by a holder of the cheque, and it is the device whereby the drawer gives a mandate to the paying bank.

FOR THE CREATION OF A 'CHEQUE'

[6.68] The drawer's signature is necessary for the creation of a cheque, for a 'cheque' is an order which is signed by the person giving it: s 10(b).

When the signature is forged or unauthorised, then the signature is wholly inoperative as that of the person whose signature it purports to be unless the signature is adopted or ratified or unless the person against whom it is sought to assert a right on the cheque is estopped from asserting the true position: s 32(1). Consequently, the paper with the forged drawer's signature is not a cheque of the person whose name has been forged.

However, s 32(1) appears to give a limited validity to the paper. The forged or unauthorised signature operates as the signature of the person who wrote or placed it on the cheque in favour of any person who takes the cheque or pays it without notice that the signature was forged or unauthorised. This provision has no counterpart in the BEA. It is unlikely that it will be of much practical importance.

TO ESTABLISH LIABILITY

[6.69] Second, the signature is necessary in order to establish that the presumed drawer is liable in an action on the cheque. Section 31 of the Act specifically retains the BEA and common law rules that, with certain exceptions relating to persons signing in business names and that of firms, a person is not liable on the cheque as drawer or indorser unless the person has signed as drawer or indorser.

Furthermore, s 32(1) states that an unauthorised signature which purports to be that of the drawer is 'wholly inoperative' as that of the person whose signature it purports to be unless it is possible to raise an estoppel against that person or the signature is adopted or ratified by the person. The only important exceptions to the rule are that banks may treat certain forged indorser's signatures as genuine for certain purposes: see [7.54].

AS A MANDATE TO THE BANKER

[6.70] The final role of the signature does not owe its existence to the Act, but rather to the banker-customer contract. The drawer's signature is the means whereby he or she gives the bank the mandate to make the payment and the authority to debit the account with the amount so paid. This role is explained by Kerr J in *National Westminster Bank Ltd v Barclays Bank International Ltd* [1975] QB 654 at 666:

> The common aphorism that a banker is under a duty to know his customer's signature is in fact incorrect even as between the banker and his customer. The

principle is simply that a banker cannot debit his customer's account on the basis of a forged signature, since he has in that event no mandate from the customer for doing so.

CROSSINGS

[6.71] Crossings were originally placed on cheques only by bankers in the process of clearing. In the original clearing houses, each banker had a box with his or her name marked upon it. The clerks from the collecting bank would leave cheques drawn on the banker in the box so marked, but in order to indicate the bank to which payment was to be made, the clerk would 'cross' the cheque, that is, write the name of the collecting bank between two transverse lines on the cheque.

As the practice became known to the general commercial community, it was recognised as a significant safeguard against fraud. If the name of the payee's bank was known to the drawer of the cheque, the cheque could be 'crossed' at the time of drawing. Since the collecting bank was likely to be small and to know most of its customers, it would be nearly impossible for anyone other than the named payee to have the cheque collected by the bank named in the crossing. Because of the practice of bankers, it would be impossible for the cheque to be collected by any other bank: see J M Holden, *The History of Negotiable Instruments in English Law*, University of London Press, 1955, Chapter VII.

When the name of the collecting bank was not known, it became customary to merely mark the cheque with two parallel lines, omitting the name of a particular bank. Sometimes the words 'Bank' or '& Company' were written between the lines. In all cases, the 'general crossing', as this form became known, was interpreted as an instruction that the cheque was only to be paid to another banker, that is, the cheque was to be collected by a bank and not to be paid over the counter: *Bellamy v Marjoribanks* (1852) 7 Exch 389.

Crossings were given statutory status by a series of Acts commencing with the Crossed Cheques Act 1856. This tradition was continued in the BEA and is now found in Pt III Div 3 of the Cheques and Payment Orders Act.

THE EFFECT OF A CROSSING

[6.72] The effect of crossing a cheque is that the crossing acts as a direction by the drawer to the drawee not to pay the cheque otherwise than to a bank: s 54.

This makes it clear that the crossing is part of the mandate to the banker. Consequently, if the banker pays contrary to the crossing, that is, pays the cheque over the counter, then the customer may resist the debit to the account. This is an important clarification to the previous law, for it was possible to argue that the bank owed only a duty to be careful: G A Weaver and R C Craigie, *The Law Relating to Banker and Customer in Australia*, 2nd ed, Law Book Co, Sydney, 1990, para [12.440]. While there is no doubt that payment contrary to crossing is negligence on the part of the bank, the action in negligence is less favourable to the drawer since he or she must plead and prove actual damage which flows from the negligence.

[6.73] The consequences may be illustrated by *Bobbett v Pinkett* (1876) 1 Exch D 368. A banker erroneously and (it was found) negligently paid a cheque to a banker other than the one named in the special crossing. In the course of the judgment, Bramwell B said (at 372): 'It is certain that the present plaintiff [the drawer] might have refused to allow [the drawee bank] to debit his account with the amount of the cheque ...'.

Amphlett B said (at 374):

> It cannot be denied that the crossing operated as a mandate to the drawee to pay the cheque to the bankers named and to no one else, and that the plaintiff might ... have declined to allow his account to be debited with the amount so paid contrary to his orders ...

The end result is somewhat strange, for the drawer is not the only person who is given authority to cross a cheque: s 56. It is a fiction to deem that a crossing added by someone other than the drawer is an instruction by the drawer.

RELATIONSHIP WITH S 93

[6.74] There is some tension between s 54 and s 93(2) of the Act. By s 93(2), if the crossing has been skilfully obliterated and the bank pays the cheque in good faith and without negligence contrary to the instructions in the (invisible) crossing, then the bank does not incur any liability by reason only of its failure to pay the cheque to a bank and is deemed to have paid the cheque in due course.

The effect of paying a cheque in due course is to 'discharge' the cheque, that is, to terminate all of the rights and liabilities on the cheque: s 82(1). This does not on the face of it prevent the drawer from complaining about the debit to the account, for that is a claim which is based on breach of the bank-customer contract and not on the rights and obligations of parties to the cheque. Nevertheless, the courts have held that when the section applies, the bank is entitled to debit the account of the drawer: *Charles v Blackwell* (1877) 2 CPD 151.

CROSSINGS AUTHORISED BY THE CPOA

[6.75] The CPOA restricts the number of valid crossings on cheques. It authorises a 'general crossing' but does not authorise the 'special' crossing, that is, the original form of crossings whereby the drawee bank was instructed to pay the cheque to a named bank.

The general crossing

[6.76] The Act authorises only the 'general' crossing, that is, the later development which was construed as an instruction to pay another banker. This is, according to s 53(1), where a cheque clearly bears across the front the addition of two parallel transverse lines with or without the words 'not negotiable' between, or substantially between, the lines. Nothing other than this is effective as a crossing of the cheque: s 53(2).

Several cases have considered marks on cheques which were claimed to be crossings. In *Mather v Bank of New Zealand* (1918) 18 SR (NSW) 49 it was said that:

> Nobody would argue that the lines must be geometrically parallel. Neither would anybody argue that they must run across the full width of the cheque, nor that they should be at some particular distance apart. The question in every case must be for the jury to say whether that which the drawer of the cheque has done can fairly be said to be a crossing within the meaning of the Act, and to indicate to the banker that the cheque is intended to be crossed.

This was applied in *Hunter BNZ Finance Ltd v C G Maloney Pty Ltd* (1988) 18 NSWLR 420 where the cheque in question had two parallel transverse lines running for only approximately one-quarter of the distance between the top and the bottom of the cheque. The cheque was held to be crossed since the lines were plainly seen as parallel transverse lines and clearly revealed their status as performing the function of crossing.

'Not negotiable'

[6.77]   The effect of the crossing with the words 'not negotiable' is not to make the cheque non-transferable. This is an unfortunate but widespread misconception, one that is clearly incorrect in view of s 39 of the Act, which specifically states that nothing written on the cheque can have the effect of making it non-transferable. The effect of the 'not negotiable' crossing is given in s 55: when the cheque is transferred by negotiation, the person taking the cheque does not receive, and is not capable of giving, a better title to the cheque than the title of the transferor. Negotiation of cheques is discussed in Chapter 9 and the details of the operation of this section in [9.28].

The Act further provides that the words 'not negotiable' do not have effect as a crossing if the words are placed on the cheque without being substantially between parallel lines. Recall that the effect of a crossing is to act as an instruction to the drawee bank not to pay the cheque except to another bank. Therefore, it is puzzling for the CPOA to say that the words 'not negotiable' do not have the effect of a crossing if not enclosed between parallel lines. The words do not direct the paying banker to do anything, nor does the CPOA place any special duty on the paying banker when the words appear. What are we to make of an instrument which has the words 'not negotiable' on it but not appearing between lines?

[6.78]   The words 'not negotiable' written on a bill of exchange which was not a cheque have been held to make the instrument non-transferable: *Hibernian Bank Ltd v Gysin and Hanson* [1939] 1 KB 483. The decision is doubtful since the bill was written in the form 'Pay X only'. However, if the CPOA applies to the instrument, then that interpretation is no longer open, for it is clear that nothing written on a cheque can have the effect of making it non-transferable: s 39. However, the *Hibernian* case does show that we should try to give some meaning to the words. The best approach appears to be to give the words the effect which is given to them when they are a part of a crossing, namely the meaning of s 55.

A second possible effect of the words may be to make it more difficult for the collecting bank to establish its statutory defence in an action for conversion: see [7.69] and *Commissioners of State Savings Bank of Victoria v Permewan Wright & Co* (1914) 19 CLR 467.

Who may cross

[6.79]   Section 56 authorises the crossing of a cheque by the drawer or by any other person in possession of the cheque. It would seem from the Explanatory Memorandum that it is intended that the possession need not be lawful. In any case, it would seem that there is little disadvantage to the drawer of a cheque if a crossing is added by some later party, even if that party is not in lawful possession of the cheque.

Multiple crossings

[6.80]   A person in possession may add a crossing to a cheque even if it already contains a crossing and may add the words 'not negotiable' to an existing crossing: s 57. Since only the simple crossing and the 'not negotiable' crossing are authorised by the Act, the right for a person to add a second general crossing is somewhat puzzling. It would have no further effect, but, on the other hand, there is no harm done. It seems unlikely that there will be large numbers of cheques in circulation each with large numbers of parallel transverse lines.

'Account payee only'

[6.81]   Although the Act specifically says that nothing else written on a cheque shall be a crossing, that does not mean that other notations are meaningless. The most common notation that is added by the drawer is the phrase 'account payee only' or some equivalent. The phrase is interesting because it is clearly directed at the collecting bank, since that is the only person who is in a position to know for whom the cheque is being collected. As such, it is a curious order, for it is given by the drawer of the cheque who will ordinarily have no contractual relationship whatsoever with the collecting bank. Why should the collecting bank be bound by such an order?

The courts and the banks themselves have shaped a rather curious answer to the question. The collecting bank is not contractually bound by the order, but it seems that the order does have some effect when the collecting bank is attempting to rely upon the statutory defence to conversion: see *National Bank v Silke* [1891] 1 QB 435. The statutory defence and the effect of the 'account payee only' notation will be discussed in Chapter 7.

The words 'account payee only' do not affect the negotiability of the cheque, at least in the sense that it may be transferred: CPOA s 39. The same result was reached before the Act: *Universal Guarantee Pty Ltd v National Bank of Australasia Ltd* (1965) 65 SR (NSW) 102; [1965] 2 All ER 98.

OTHER INSTRUMENTS

[6.82]   Two instruments are dealt with expressly by the Act which are not the subject of similar sections in the BEA. The first, bank cheques, are a familiar instrument to the commercial community, but the second, the payment order, is a new creation.

BANK CHEQUES

[6.83]   It is not usually wise to accept a personal cheque from a stranger since, as has been seen, the cheque is commercially no more valuable than the credit of the parties who have signed it. There is, however, a need for an instrument for making large value payments which is safer than cash. In Australia, that instrument is the 'bank cheque' or 'bank draft'. Although usage is neither a term of art nor uniform, it seems that the instrument is a 'bank cheque' when drawn by a bank on itself, and a 'bank draft' when drawn by one bank on another.

These are instruments which are drawn at the request of a customer by a bank either on itself or on another bank in favour of some named party. The named payee may take the instrument in confidence since it is drawn by a bank; the bank is protected since it may debit its customer's account at the time when the cheque is issued.

Although these are known as bank cheques, under the bills of exchange legislation there was some uncertainty as to their legal status since the Act required that the instrument be 'addressed by one person to another': *Fabre v Ley* (1973) 127 CLR 665.

APPLICATION OF ACT

[6.84]   The position of bank cheques has been clarified by s 5 of the Act. Since the operation of bank cheques is to some extent different from the operation of ordinary cheques, the section does not take the simple approach of declaring bank cheques to be cheques for all purposes. Generally speaking, the requirements as to form and certain requirements of presentment do not apply to bank cheques. All other sections of the Act apply 'unless a contrary intention appears'.

On the other hand, s 5(2) provides that nothing in the CPOA, apart from the statutory defences available to banks, shall be taken to affect any liability that a bank would, but for the Act, have in relation to a bank cheque or bank draft drawn by it.

DISHONOUR OF BANK CHEQUES

[6.85]   The commercial community generally treats bank cheques as having the same commercial status as cash. Consequently, it sometimes comes as a surprise to that community to find that bank cheques may be dishonoured and that the drawer of a bank cheque may raise defences in exactly the same way as the drawer of an ordinary cheque. This is of considerable practical importance because bank cheques in Australia are usually crossed not negotiable by the drawing bank.

The problem first came to light in *Sidney Raper Pty Ltd v Commonwealth Trading Bank of Australia* [1975] 2 NSWLR 227. Mr and Mrs J came from the United States with an American dollar 'cashier's check', an instrument that is equivalent to the Australian bank cheque. This was deposited with the defendant bank which established a US dollar account on behalf of Mr and Mrs J. Although the deposit slip indicated that the amount could not be drawn upon until the cashier's check was cleared, the defendant bank issued a bank cheque for an amount of £29,500 and crossed 'not negotiable' in favour of the plaintiff or bearer and debited the US dollar account of Mr and Mrs J for an equivalent amount of US dollars.

The bank cheque was given to the plaintiff who deposited it in their own trust account to the credit of Mr J. When it was presented to the defendant bank it was dishonoured. The reason for the dishonour was that the original American cashier's check had been dishonoured and the defendant bank claimed a total failure of consideration.

The New South Wales Court of Appeal held that the consideration given for the cheque had wholly failed, that the plaintiff had given no fresh consideration and that the ordinary rules of the Bills of Exchange Act applied to bank cheques. As a result, the plaintiff could have no better title than that of the bank's customers and the action must fail.

[6.86] *Sidney Raper* was considered in *Justin Seward Pty Ltd v Commissioners of Rural and Industries Bank* (1982) 60 FLR 51 where the plaintiff was a payee of a bank cheque drawn by the defendant on itself. The drawee bank was seeking leave to defend on the basis of a failure of consideration and payment under a mistake of fact. The basis of this defence was that the cheque had been drawn at the instructions of a customer of the bank. The amount of the cheque represented the balance of a deposit on a house which the customer was purchasing. The customer rang the bank and cancelled the instructions for the issue of the cheque, but the cheque was issued by mistake.

In granting leave to defend, the court affirmed the rule in *Sidney Raper* that the principles which apply to a bank cheque are no different from those applying to an ordinary cheque, but suggested that the mere fact that the bank knew that its cheques were used for the discharge of debts as if with cash and the practice of estate agents accepting them as such might bring about a relationship between the acceptance of the cheque and the liability of the bank's customer which is sufficient to satisfy the need for consideration.

[6.87] While the suggestion in *Justin Seward* was ingenious, the situation was clearly intolerable if bank cheques were to continue to be used to settle debts in lieu of cash. As a result of consultations between the banks and the Law Societies, the Australian Bankers' Association formally announced in May 1985 that it would dishonour bank cheques only in very restricted circumstances. Four of the circumstances cause no difficulty: where the 'cheque' is a forgery; where the cheque has been materially altered; where the cheque has been reported stolen or lost; and where there is a court restraining order which prevents the bank from honouring the cheque.

The fifth ground for dishonour concerns the situation where the bank has not received consideration for the cheque. The announcement states that such a cheque will not be dishonoured unless the holder has not given value or unless the holder was aware at the time of giving value that the funds against which the cheque was drawn would not clear. This means that if the bank wishes to issue a bank cheque before the funds have cleared, then it is at its own risk, not that of the unfortunate holder of the cheque. For the complete text of the banks' statement, see N Mainwaring, 'Dishonouring Bank Cheques', *Law Soc,* July 1985, pp 430–31: see also P Lane, 'When is a Bank Cheque Not a Bank Cheque' [1984] *Law Soc J* 88.

ACCEPTANCE OF CHEQUES

[6.88]   When the cheque was merely a particular kind of bill of exchange, it was legally possible for the drawee bank to accept a cheque. If it had done so, then it would have become the party primarily liable on the bill and the resulting instrument would be of substantially higher value than one in which the holder must rely only on the credit of the individual drawer. In some countries bank accepted instruments are in wide usage and serve the function which is performed by bank cheques in Australia. Such instruments are usually called 'certified cheques': see *Shapera v Toronto Dominion Bank* (1970) 17 DLR (3d) 122.

[6.89]   In Australia, the practice of bank acceptance of cheques, known as 'certifying' was common at one time but is now virtually unknown. As a result, the new Act does not provide for bank acceptance. If a bank were to 'accept' a cheque, it would appear that the effect is that the bank becomes liable as an indorser within the meaning of s 75. Such a commitment would, of course, have the effect of guaranteeing the cheque to a holder in due course so that it is still open to the commercial community to reinstate the 'certified' cheque as a safe means of payment. There is no apparent advantage of a certified cheque over the existing practice of using bank cheques, and it seem both unlikely and unnecessary that the existing practice should change.

[6.90]   There will probably be judicial resistance to finding that markings on a cheque are intended to guarantee payment. As an example, the cheque in *Southland Savings Bank v Anderson* [1974] 1 NZLR 118 had been marked as good for payment by the appellant drawee bank. Quilliam J held that the marking was only an indication by the bank's ledger department to the teller that there were sufficient funds. There was, consequently, nothing to prevent the customer from making a countermand. Quilliam J noted that the marking was different from the practice of marking cheques by way of an undertaking to another banker to whom the cheque is to be paid.

PAYMENT ORDERS

[6.91] The Act introduces a new instrument, the payment order (PO) which is similar to a cheque but drawn on a 'non-bank financial institution' (NBFI). The instrument is defined and many, but not all, of the sections of the Act which apply to cheques are made applicable to the PO. There are special provisions concerning the presentment and payment of POs.

The federal government has announced that it intends to amend the CPOA so that building societies and credit unions will be able to issue cheques. Although not expressly stated in the press announcement, this will presumably entail the repeal of the sections concerned with payment orders: see Treasurer — Press Release No 99, 27 August 1997.

[6.92] The definition given in s 101(1) of a payment order is similar in all respects to a cheque save that the drawee is a 'non-bank financial institution' rather than a bank and the instrument must clearly bear the words 'payment order' on the front of the instrument.

The definition of 'non-bank financial institution' is given in s 3(1) of the Act. It is a building society or credit union that is a registered corporation within the meaning of the Financial Corporations Act 1974. The Act allows the inclusion of other institutions with a catch-all provision which allows any other registered corporation within the meaning of the Financial Corporations Act 1974 to be prescribed, either individually or as a class of institutions, for the purposes of the CPOA.

In determining whether the form of an instrument satisfies the definition of a payment order, ss 11–15 and s 16(3) are to be applied as if the references to a bank were references to a NBFI and the reference in s 16(3) to a cheque were a reference to a payment order: s 102.

[6.93] Sections 103 and 104 together provide that the majority of the law applicable to cheques will apply, with certain redefinitions, to payment orders.

Section 103 provides that the rules of the common law (including the law merchant) that apply in relation to cheques apply, *mutatis mutandis*, in relation to payment orders. Rightfully concerned that such a sweeping provision might leave room for doubts, s 103(2) mercifully gives some hints as to how the rules applicable to cheques are to be altered. We are to agree that a member of a building society or a credit union shall be taken to be a customer of the building society or credit union, as the case may be.

The Act gives no directions for analysing the rights and obligations of the parties when the NBFI is not a building society or a credit union. Presumably the common law definition of 'customer' will apply: see [2.15].

[6.94]   Section 104 is an extraordinarily awkward section which makes certain sections of the Act applicable to POs, again with certain modifications and pretences. Those sections which do apply are subject to modifications which are set out in the Schedule to the Act. Further, the sections which apply are to be read as if any references to a cheque were references to a PO and any reference to a bank were a reference to a NBFI.

[6.95]   Not all sections of the Act apply to POs. Sections 10–15 and s 16(3) are excluded since the definition of a PO is given explicitly in s 101. For similar reasons, the sections concerning the duty of presentment and retention of cheques are not applicable, the equivalent duties being specifically dealt with in ss 105–112. Sections 97–100 which deal with the rights and liabilities of NBFIs in relation to cheques are not applicable to POs, the latter being dealt with specifically by ss 110–112.

[6.96]   Section 117, containing rules governing the conflict of laws for cheques, is excluded from applying to POs, apparently because it was believed that POs would have no overseas recognition or currency. While that is probably correct, commercial disputes reach the courts precisely because circumstances have arisen which are outside the contemplation of the parties and it seems remarkable that the law on POs is to be left to find its own way. One possible solution is that a PO probably fulfils the definition of a bill of exchange so that the conflicts provisions of s 77 BEA will be applicable.

[6.97]   The law for presentment of POs is in all respects similar to that for cheques. Presentment by particulars is provided for by s 106 when the party presenting the PO is a financial institution, that is, either a bank or a NBFI. When presentment is not by a financial institution, then presentment is only by exhibition: s 107. Sections 108 and 109 define proper places and designated places for presentment which are in all respects similar to the definitions of ss 64 and 65 for banks.

Section 110 defines the duty of the collecting institution to present the PO promptly. The duties are similar in all respects to those placed on institutions collecting cheques on behalf of customers. Section 111 defines the duty of the NBFI to pay or dishonour promptly and is similar in all respects to s 67. Section 112 describes the responsibilities of institutions to retain paid POs and is similar in all respects to the duties imposed by s 68 for cheques.

[6.98]   There are so many similarities between cheques and POs that anyone reading the Act begins to wonder why they have been treated separately. There is, however, one very significant commercial effect of the CPOA. Although the Act contemplates that any financial institution may present POs by particulars (see [5.109] for a discussion of presentment by particulars), it is only banks which are permitted to present cheques in this way since s 62 is not one of the sections which is incorporated by reference by s 104.

When a NBFI is collecting a cheque, its duties are defined by s 97 which requires it to 'ensure that the cheque is duly presented for payment on its behalf as soon as is reasonably practicable'. Of course, the NBFI could resort to the pre-clearing method of presentment, but the practical effect is to require that the NBFI enter into an agency arrangement with a bank. There is no indication in the CPOA as to why the competitive position of banks has been given this privileged status.

TRAVELLER'S CHEQUES

[6.99]   Traveller's cheques have been mentioned at [6.55] and [6.57], where it was concluded that the common form of traveller's cheque does not conform to the requirements of either the Bills of Exchange Act or the Cheques and Payment Orders Act. If traveller's cheques are negotiable it must be that they are a new form of negotiable instrument established by mercantile custom: see Ellinger and Lomnicka, *Modern Banking Law*, 2nd ed, Oxford, 1994, p 331; Ellinger, 'Traveller's Cheques and the Law' (1969) 19 *University of Toronto Law Journal* 132.

One of the reasons that traveller's cheques have enjoyed great popularity with travellers is that they have been perceived to be protected against loss since it is common that the issuer provides some degree of 'insurance' against loss. Although it is commonly believed that the issuer will replace traveller's cheques which are lost, recent English cases cast doubts on the extent of protection.

[6.100]   In *Braithwaite v Thomas Cook Travellers Cheques Ltd* [1989] 3 WLR 212, the customer purchased some 400 traveller's cheques worth £50,000. The contract of purchase contained a clause which provided that the issuer would replace any traveller's cheques which were lost or stolen, provided that '... [the purchaser has] properly safeguarded each cheque against loss or theft'. The plaintiff was carrying the traveller's cheques in a brown envelope which was in a plastic bag together with cigarettes he had purchased. Upon arrival in London he spent the evening socialising with friends, then travelled on the underground resting the bag on his lap and concealing it with a newspaper. He fell asleep and upon waking realised that he no longer had the bag. His claim for replacement was rejected by the defendant issuers.

The court held that the onus was on the plaintiff to show that he had satisfied a condition precedent to a right of refund. Applying an objective test of the 'ordinary member of the travelling public', Schiemann J found that the plaintiff had not properly safeguarded the traveller's cheques.

[6.101]   The facts were remarkably similar in *El Awadi v Bank of Credit and Commerce International SA Ltd* [1990] 1 QB 606 except that the contract of purchase provided that any claim for a refund of a lost or stolen cheque shall be subject to approval by the issuer and to presentation to the issuer of the purchaser's copy of this agreement.

There was no express provision requiring the purchaser to safeguard the traveller's cheques, nor any provision entitling the issuer to refuse a refund in case of carelessness on the part of the purchaser. However, the issuer argued that there must be an implied term to that effect. Hutchinson J rejected that argument, holding that there was no such implied term. It is interesting to note that he was prepared to find an implied term to the effect that the issuer was obliged to refund for lost or stolen traveller's cheques, for otherwise there would be no purpose to the transaction. The plaintiff succeeded on the basis of the interpretation of the contract. For a complete discussion, see Bilinsky, 'How Safe are Traveller's Cheques?' (1990) 4 *JBFLP* 271.

CHAPTER 7

MISAPPROPRIATED CHEQUES

[7.1] A cheque is misappropriated when it is acquired by a person who has no right to the cheque or when a person with a limited right to the cheque uses it for some unauthorised purpose.

A typical example of the first type of misappropriation occurs when a thief steals a cheque from the payee's mailbox. If the cheque is an uncrossed bearer cheque, then the thief may negotiate the cheque to a person who takes for value and in good faith and thereby becomes a holder in due course. Although the holder in due course obtains good title to the cheque, it will be appreciated that the thief is still a person who will be liable to the former holder of the cheque.

If the same thief steals a cheque which is an order cheque, then it will not be possible for the cheque to be negotiated unless an indorsement is forged. In such a case, of course, the person taking the cheque obtains no rights over it. As will be seen, if the cheque is further negotiated, then later 'holders' will have rights against the person who took from the thief, but not from any indorser prior to the misappropriation: see Chapter 9.

An example of the second kind of misappropriation is where a clerk has possession of a cheque for the purposes of mailing it to a creditor of the employer, but instead deposits it to the credit of his or her own bank account. In this section, we are concerned with the rights of the 'true owner' of the cheque against later parties who have dealt with the cheque. This will include all parties who later become 'holders' of the cheque as well as their agents, particularly when the agent is a collecting bank.

There is also a contractual aspect to misappropriation. In most cases, the paying bank will be paying the wrong person and possibly the wrong amount. That is, the drawer of the cheque has ordered the paying bank to pay X or order, but instead the bank pays to the order of some other person. This is a breach of contract and the drawer of the cheque has a prima facie right to demand that his or her account not be debited with the amount of the cheque.

REMEDIES

[7.2] As suggested above, there are essentially two legal actions which may arise when a cheque is misappropriated. The 'true owner' of the cheque may sue in the tort of conversion and the drawer of the cheque may have a claim against the paying bank for breach of contract.

It is customary to join the action in conversion with one for money had and received to the use of the plaintiff. Although these two actions usually stand or fall together, there are occasions where one will succeed and the other fail.

THE ACTION IN CONVERSION

[7.3] Conversion is: 'An intentional exercise of control over a chattel which so seriously interferes with the right of another to control it that the intermeddler may justly be required to pay its full value.' (JG Fleming, *Law of Torts*, 6th ed, Law Book Co, Sydney, p 49.)

An important aspect of the tort is that the 'intention' which is required is merely the intention to deal with the chattel. It is not necessary that there be an intention to interfere with the right of another's control. Thus, an entirely innocent person who takes a chattel from a thief is just as liable to the owner of the chattel as is the thief.

Further, it usually does not matter that the intermeddler is acting on behalf of a principal. An agent who collects a stolen chattel will be just as liable to the owner of the chattel as his or her principal is.

Finally, a bailee of a chattel, that is, someone other than the owner of the chattel who is in rightful possession of the chattel, becomes liable in conversion upon forming the intention to deal with the chattel in a way which is inconsistent with the rights of the owner.

RELEVANCE TO NEGOTIABLE INSTRUMENTS

[7.4] As will be gathered from the above quotation, the tort of conversion is primarily concerned with rights over chattels. Its importance for negotiable instruments derives from a series of nineteenth-century decisions which extended the remedy to rights over cheques and other negotiable instruments. Scrutton J traces the evolution of the remedy in *Lloyds Bank Ltd v Chartered Bank of India, Australia and China* [1929] 1 KB 40. He explains (at 55–6) that the tort applies to such instruments '… by treating the conversion as of the chattel, the piece of paper, the cheque under which the money was collected, and the value of the chattel converted as the money received under it'.

[7.5] In *Koster's Premier Pottery Pty Ltd v Bank of Adelaide* (1981) 28 SASR 355, it was held that an instrument purporting to be a cheque on which the drawer's signature had been forged could not be the subject of an action in conversion against the collecting bank. In holding that only cheques or other negotiable instruments could be the subject of an action in conversion, the decision followed Canadian authority to the same effect: *Arrow Transfer Co Ltd v Royal Bank of Canada* (1972) 27 DLR (3d) 81. However, *Koster's* case appears not to have considered a number of objections to the Canadian decision and to have overlooked English authorities which clearly contemplate the possibility that such an instrument may be the subject of an action in conversion: see A L Tyree, 'The Liability of Banks Collecting Forged Cheques' (1983) 11 *Aust Bus L Rev* 236 and see [7.51].

[7.6] In particular, the instrument in *Orbit Mining and Trading Co Ltd v Westminster Bank Ltd* [1963] 1 QB 794 was held not to be a cheque but that was no bar to the action in conversion. Indeed, the main point of dispute in that case was whether the bank was entitled to rely upon the statutory defence when collecting an instrument which was not a cheque. The instrument in *Slingsby v Westminster Bank Ltd (No 2)* [1931] 2 KB 583 was held not to be a cheque since it had been avoided by a material alteration. Far from holding that the action in conversion could not be maintained, the court in *Slingsby* held that the statutory defence was not available to the bank.

The decision in *Koster's* case emphasised the fact that the cheque in question was, as a forgery, a complete nullity. In addition to the objection noted above, the case against the bank may now be stronger since even a forgery has a limited validity as a cheque since the forged drawer's signature operates as the signature of the person who wrote or placed it on the cheque in favour of later 'holders': see CPOA s 32(1).

WHO IS ENTITLED TO MAINTAIN THE ACTION?

[7.7] It is generally said that the action in conversion may be sustained by the 'true owner' of the cheque. 'True owner' is a phrase which is used in the Act, for example, s 93, but is nowhere defined. It is a curious term, for what does the adjective 'true' add to the concept of 'owner'? The best explanation is that the phrase is intended to emphasise the dual nature of the cheque as, first of all a piece of paper which is capable of conversion, and second as a negotiable instrument with special rules for the determination of ownership. Since the physical piece of paper is subordinate, the 'true' indicates that we are to look not to the right to the piece of paper, but rather to the rights given to the parties under the Act.

Thus, one widely quoted passage reads (J Paget, *Paget's Law of Banking*, 8th ed, Butterworths, London p 348; this passage appears to be absent from later editions):

> ... the true owner, in the sense of the person who can support conversion for a bill, note, or cheque is the person who, taking into consideration the provisions of the Bills of Exchange Act, and recognising that the negotiable character of the instrument overrides the mere property in the chattel, is on that basis entitled to the property in and possession of the piece of paper.

There are some circumstances where it is clear, either on principle or on authority, who is the true owner of the cheque. If the drawer of a cheque, in the absence of fraud and intending that the payee should become entitled to the cheque, hands the cheque to the payee, then the payee becomes the true owner. If the cheque is indorsed, again in the absence of fraud, then the indorsee becomes the true owner of the cheque.

[7.8] Problems of establishing the identity of the true owner may arise where the drawer of the cheque is the victim of a fraud. In *Hunter BNZ Finance Ltd v Maloney Pty Ltd* (1988) 18 NSWLR 420 the plaintiff was induced by the fraud of one M to draw cheques in favour of a supplier. The cheques were handed to M by the plaintiff and later deposited in his account. On the question of whether the plaintiff was able to maintain an action against the collecting bank, the court held that title passed to the supplier when the plaintiff handed the cheque to M since that was the common intention of each. However, the title was voidable by reason of the fraud and was in fact avoided by the plaintiff bringing the action. The actions of the defendant amounted to conversion since the recission of title made the title void *ab initio*.

[7.9] This latter point is somewhat puzzling, and a different result was reached in *Citibank NA v Brown Shipley & Co Ltd* [1991] 2 All ER 690. A person claiming to represent a company with an account at the issuing bank telephoned the receiving bank with a request to make substantial foreign currency purchases. The caller then called the issuing bank with instructions to prepare bank drafts for the purpose of making the purchases. The issuing bank prepared the draft, then handed it to a person thought to be a messenger of the company. The 'messenger' had a letter purporting to confirm the telephone instructions but it was signed with forged signatures.

The draft was presented to the receiving bank. They checked the authenticity of the draft with the issuing bank. The receiving bank paid the fraudster, then presented the draft to the issuing bank for payment. The issuing bank claimed to have remained the true owner of the draft throughout, and sought to recover damages in conversion. The court held that the action failed. Title to the draft passed to the receiving bank (as in the *Maloney* case) and presentation of the cheque for payment could not be an act of conversion since the defendant had title to the cheque even though the title was a voidable one.

[7.10] In *Hunter BNZ Finance v ANZ Banking Group* [1990] VR 41, affirmed by the Full Court at [1991] 2 VR 407, it was said that the drawer of a bearer cheque remains the true owner after parting with possession in the event that the cheque does not reach the hands of the payee. Although that result is usually correct, it is probably a result of the intention of the parties rather than a rule of law.

[7.11] When the delivery is by post, then the time at which the payee becomes the true owner depends upon the agreement between the parties. There is a presumption that the post office is the agent of the sender so that the drawer remains the true owner of the cheque until such time as it is actually delivered to the payee: *Channon v English, Scottish and Australian Bank*

(1918) 18 SR (NSW) 30. The most common way in which the presumption is displaced is to show that the payee has expressly or by implication requested the drawer of the cheque to deliver by post. In that case, the post office is the agent of the payee and the payee becomes the true owner at the time of posting. However, no implied request will be found merely from the fact that the drawer has customarily sent cheques by mail or that it is generally customary that cheques be delivered in such a fashion.

[7.12] If the creditor agrees to accept payment by a cheque which is drawn in a certain form, then a drawer of a cheque that does not comply with that form remains the true owner until such time as the payee accepts the unauthorised form as payment. Thus, in *London Bank of Australia Ltd v Kendall* (1920) 28 CLR 401 cheques were left in a collection box at the office of the Commissioners of Taxation by the plaintiff. They were misappropriated from the office by a rogue and collected by the defendant bank. Since the cheques were not drawn in a form specified by the Commissioner as acceptable for payment, the plaintiff was still the true owner and entitled to maintain an action for conversion. Note that the plaintiff's debt to the Commissioner was not discharged by the cheques.

[7.13] The way in which the Act overrides the ordinary rules which determine the right to bring an action in conversion is graphically demonstrated by *Smith v Union Bank of London* (1875) 1 QBD 31. A cheque was delivered to the payee and indorsed by him in a way which made the cheque payable to bearer. The cheque was stolen and negotiated to a person who took the cheque under conditions which made him a holder in due course. It was held that the holder was the 'true owner' of the cheque and entitled to maintain an action in conversion even though his title was derived through a thief.

[7.14] There can be problems in establishing the identity of the true owner when there is an agent involved in the drawing of a cheque. In *Marquess of Bute v Barclays Bank Ltd* [1955] 1 QB 202 instruments were drawn payable to Mr D McGaw who was the farm manager of the plaintiff. The words 'for the Marquess of Bute' also appeared on the face of the instruments. The court held that the words were an essential part of the description of the payee and that it followed that the intention of the drawer was that the plaintiff should be the true owner. McGaw was merely an agent who was accountable to the Marquess. The *Marquess of Bute* case was approved in *International Factors Ltd v Rodriguez* [1979] QB 351; [1979] 1 All ER 17 (CA).

The *Marquess of Bute* case should be contrasted with the decision in *Australia and New Zealand Bank Ltd v Ateliers de Constructions de Electriques et Charleroi* [1967] 1 AC 86. Cheques were drawn payable to a Belgian company. A local company, acting as agent for the Belgian company, routinely deposited the cheques into its own account with the defendant bank, deducted its own expenses and entitlements and remitted the balance to the Belgian company. The court held that there was no conversion of the cheques since the local company had implied authority from the Belgian company to

deal with the cheques in this way. The basis for the finding of implied authority was that it was required by business efficacy.

[7.15]   Even when there is no indication on the face of the cheque that the
payee is being given the cheque as agent for a third party, the principal is the
owner of the cheque. Thus, in *Great Western Railway Co v London & County
Banking Co Ltd* [1901] AC 414 a cheque was made payable to one Huggins
who was a tax collector. During the course of the judgment Lord Davey said
(at 419):

> I am of opinion that Huggins never had any property in the cheque, which was
> handed to him only as the collector and agent of the overseers in payment of a
> debt alleged to be due to them. The appellants never intended to vest any
> property in him for his own benefit, but the property in the cheque was
> intended to be passed to his employer, the overseers, notwithstanding that it
> was made payable to Huggins' order. Huggins therefore had no real title to the
> cheque.

[7.16]   If an agent is drawing a cheque and performs his or her duty fraudulently or if the drawing of the cheque has been induced by fraud, then the
innocent principal, not the fraudulent agent, is the true owner of the cheque:
Smith and Baldwin v Barclays Bank Ltd (1944) 5 LDAB 370; *Midland Bank Ltd v
Reckitt* [1933] AC 1; *Morison v London County and Westminster Bank Ltd* [1914]
3 KB 356.

However, if the fraudulent agent is able to exchange the cheque for a bank
cheque which he or she has not the actual authority to receive, then the bank
cheque belongs to the agent, not to the principal. Presumably the same result
would follow if the cheque were exchanged for a chattel.

[7.17]   In *Union Bank of Australia Ltd v McClintock* [1922] 1 AC 240 McClintock was the manager of the plaintiff company who had authority to be a co-
signatory on cheques. There was evidence given to the effect that a common
method of making payments to trade creditors was for the company to draw
cheques payable to its own banker and to receive a bank cheque in exchange.
By such a course of action, accounts could be paid by cheque even when the
company's creditors would not accept the company's own cheques. It was
found as a fact that McClintock's authority to exchange company cheques for
bank cheques extended only so far as to obtain cheques for the company's
legitimate business. By a series of frauds, McClintock obtained cheques drawn
on the company account in favour of the company's bank and exchanged them
for bank cheques which he then misappropriated by depositing them in his
account with the defendant bank. The company sued the defendant bank for
conversion of the bank cheque and money had and received.

The action failed since the plaintiff was not the true owner of the bank
cheques. It would have been otherwise if it had been within the manager's
general authority to obtain bank cheques. Nor could the plaintiff claim title
by ratification, for they could not choose to ratify the action of the manager in
obtaining the cheques and then claim that he was not so entitled.

[7.18]   *McClintock* was followed in *Commercial Banking Co of Sydney Ltd v Mann* [1961] AC 1 on facts which are virtually indistinguishable. A fraudulent partner in a firm of solicitors drew cheques in favour of 'Pay bank cheque' and took them to the ANZ bank where the partnership account was kept. That bank issued bank cheques in favour of W according to the directions of the fraudulent partner. The cheques were paid into an account with the defendant bank. The plaintiff sued for conversion and for money had and received. The Privy Council held that the claim must fail since the authority of fraudulent partner extended only as far as to enable him to obtain bank cheques for the purpose of the partnership. Therefore, the plaintiff was not the true owner of the bank cheques. Nor could the plaintiff obtain title by attempting to ratify the partner's action for if he ratified at all, he ratified the dealing by the fraudulent partner and the appellant bank with the cheques, and, if he did not ratify, nothing had ever been converted that belonged to him.

Both the *McClintock* and the *Mann* case were challenged in *Lipkin Gorman v Karpanale Ltd* [1991] 2 AC 548; [1992] 4 All ER 512. The House of Lords declined the invitation to overrule the cases, but distinguished them on the basis that the draft in *Lipkin Gorman* was issued payable to the principal rather than to a third party. There was no doubt in such a case that it was the principal who was entitled to possession of the draft.

AGAINST WHOM MAY THE ACTION BE BROUGHT?

[7.19]   The action may be brought against anyone who intentionally interferes with the interest of the 'true owner'. That interest, of course, is the right to the cheque and to the proceeds from the cheque. Consequently, the collecting bank and the paying bank will ordinarily both be subject to an action in conversion once a cheque has been misappropriated.

There are arguments that the action in conversion may not be brought by the true owner of the cheque against the paying bank which pays some other person. The essence of the argument is that the paying bank neither appropriates the cheque nor destroys it, but rather obeys, or purports to obey an instruction for payment: see Ellinger and Lomnicka, *Modern Banking Law*, 2nd ed, Clarendon Press, Oxford, 1994, p 361. There are, however, a number of cases where the action for conversion has been explicitly or implicitly allowed: *Smith v Union Bank of London* (1875) LR 10 QB 291; (1875) 1 QBD 31; *Charles v Blackwell* (1877) 2 CPD 151; *Australia Mutual Provident Society v Derham*; *Bank of New South Wales v Derham* (1978) 25 ACTR 25.

[7.20]   Banks have available to them the same defences as any other defendant in a conversion action, but in addition the CPOA has seen fit to grant them special statutory defences which are not available to the public at large. The privileged position has existed since the passage of the Stamp Act 1853; the CPOA extends the privilege to building societies, credit unions and other prescribed non-bank financial institutions: see [7.140].

THE ACTION FOR MONEY HAD AND RECEIVED

[7.21] Whenever there is an action in conversion, it is customary for the plaintiff to make an alternative claim for a like amount as money had and received to the use of the plaintiff. The joinder of a claim for money had and received does not operate as a waiver of the tort so as to prejudice the claim in conversion although, of course, it will not be possible for the plaintiff to recover the full amount in both causes of action. The plaintiff is free to recover on either ground and defences appropriate to each of the actions are open to the defendant: *United Australia Ltd v Barclays Bank Ltd* [1941] AC 1.

The action for money had and received is a separate action. There may be times when it is in the interests of the plaintiff to waive the tort and proceed with the action for money had and received. If it is correct that an instrument which is not a negotiable instrument can only attract nominal damages in an action for conversion, then it may benefit the plaintiff to waive the tort. Thus, in *Bavins Junr and Sims v London and South Western Bank* [1901] 1 QB 270 the instrument was not a cheque due to technical deficiencies of form. After referring to the argument that only nominal damages would be available, the court said (per Vaughan Williams LJ at 278):

> ... in any case it seems to me to be clear that the plaintiffs are entitled to recover the amount received by the defendants upon the document as money had and received. Having received money by presenting the document which belonged to the plaintiffs they cannot in my opinion, if the plaintiffs choose to waive the tort, say that they did not receive the money on account of the plaintiffs ...

But see *Arrow Transfer Co Ltd v Royal Bank of Canada* (1972) 27 DLR (3d) 81 and *Koster's Premier Pottery Pty Ltd v Bank of Adelaide* (1981) 28 SASR 355 and see [7.51] where it was held that the action is not available where payment is made against a forged instrument.

It was originally thought that the claim was based on an implied promise by the person receiving the payment, but the obvious difficulties with such a fiction caused increasing discontent. Finally, the House of Lords acknowledged that the claim is a restitutionary claim based on the principle of unjust enrichment: *Westdeutche Landesbank Girozentrale v Islington Borough Council* [1996] 2 All ER 961; [1996] 2 WLR 802. The earlier approach, established in *Sinclair v Brougham* [1914] AC 398 is now discredited.

[7.22] There will be no waiver of tort unless the plaintiff clearly intends to make such a waiver. In *United Australia Ltd v Barclays Bank Ltd* [1941] AC 1 a cheque payable to the appellants was converted by M company and collected by Barclays. United Australia brought an action in debt against M but discontinued. A proof of debt lodged in the winding up of M was also rejected. United Australia then brought an action for conversion against the collecting bank. Barclays claimed that the bringing of the original action against M must be considered a waiver of tort. The House of Lords rejected the argument, holding that merely bringing an action is not waiver of tort. It is judgment and satisfaction in the first action which is a bar to the second.

Three members of the House (Lord Atkin, Lord Porter and Viscount Simon LC) indicated that in their view even if the tort had been waived as against M company that would not have the effect of waiving the separate action in conversion against the bank.

[7.23]   However, in *Clarkson Booker Ltd v Andjel* [1964] 2 QB 775 the Court of Appeal considered Lord Atkin's dictum and noted that it is always a matter of fact if the tort has been waived. It was said concerning election that the initiation of proceedings against one party is strong evidence of an election, although not conclusive.

THE ACTION FOR BREACH OF CONTRACT

[7.24]   When a cheque is misappropriated, it will most likely be paid to the 'wrong' person and, if altered, for the wrong amount. In the case of a cheque payable to bearer, it will almost always be paid to the 'right' person, at least in the sense that the bank will be following the order of its customer. However, when the cheque is payable to order, then payment will most likely be to some person other than that ordered by the drawer.

In either case, payment to the wrong person or for the wrong amount, the bank is guilty of a breach of the contract between it and its customer. Again, the bank has available to it all of the usual contractual defences which might apply, but in addition has special defences given to it by the CPOA: see [7.50].

DEFENCES

[7.25]   There are certain defences available to an allegation of conversion of a cheque that are not available when there is an allegation of conversion of a chattel. Some of these defences are available to all parties and depend upon the characteristics of negotiability. Others are available only to banks and non-bank financial institutions (NBFI's) and exist only because of the statute.

DEFENCES OF THE 'HOLDER'

[7.26]   A person who accepts a transfer by negotiation of a misappropriated cheque may or may not be a holder of the cheque within the meaning of the CPOA. If the cheque is an order cheque and the indorsement is genuine, then the taker will be a holder, but if the cheque has been stolen and the indorsement forged, then the taker cannot be a holder: see s 40 and the discussion in Chapter 9. If the misappropriated cheque is payable to bearer, then the taker will always be a holder.

DEFENCES WHEN TAKER IS A HOLDER

[7.27]   When a person takes a misappropriated cheque under conditions which make the taker a holder, then the liability of that person to a previous owner of the cheque will depend upon whether the cheque is taken under conditions which constitute the holder a holder in due course.

When the cheque is crossed 'not negotiable' then the holder can never be a holder in due course and the holder is subject to any defect in title no matter how far back it might have occurred in the chain of transfers. It is important to note here that the 'not negotiable' crossing imposes the full strength of the *nemo dat quod non habet* rule. Furthermore, although there was some early doubt, the defect in title may be traced through to the proceeds of the cheque as well as to the cheque itself.

[7.28] The situation is illustrated by *Great Western Railway Co v London and County Banking Co Ltd* [1901] AC 414. A rogue had obtained by fraud a cheque crossed 'not negotiable'. The rogue was the named payee of the cheque. He persuaded the defendant bank to collect the cheque on his behalf even though he was not a customer of the bank. The bank, in the circumstances, became a holder of the cheque although not a holder in due course.

It was argued on behalf of the defendant bank that the title of the rogue, being obtained by fraud, was a voidable title rather than no title at all. Consequently, it was argued, the title could not be avoided after a bona fide transfer without notice of any defect in the title. This, of course, was and is the normal rule which is applied to chattels: see Sale of Goods Act 1923 (NSW) s 27. The House of Lords held that the effect of s 55 is not merely to destroy the full negotiability of a cheque but to re-establish the full force of the *nemo dat quod non habet* rule. Consequently, the title obtained by the bank was still voidable at the option of the 'true owner'.

The defendant also argued that although the defendant received only a defective title to the cheque, their title to the proceeds was good. Lord Halsbury LC said (at 418):

> The supposed distinction between the title to the cheque itself and the title to the money obtained or represented by it seems to me to be absolutely illusory. The language of the statute seems to me to be clear enough. It would be absolutely defeated by holding that a fraudulent holder of the cheque could give a title either to the cheque or to the money.

FICTITIOUS PAYEES/BEARER CHEQUES

[7.29] It is sometimes possible for a person who takes a cheque to establish that he or she is a holder even though the cheque appears to be an order cheque with a forged indorsement. The key to this defence is the notion of the 'fictitious or non-existent' payee which was discussed at [3.81]. The logic of the defence is that if the payee or named indorsee is 'fictitious or non-existent' then the cheque, although it appears to be payable to order, is in fact payable to bearer. Consequently, it is not necessary for the defendant to rely upon the forged indorsement to establish title.

Vinden v Hughes [1905] 1 KB 795 provides an example of the way in which the defence operates, even though on the facts of that case the defence failed. A fraudulent clerk of the plaintiff drew cheques in favour of existing trade creditors and obtained the signature as drawer of the plaintiff. The clerk then forged an indorsement naming himself as indorsee and then further negotiated the cheques to the defendant who took without notice of any fraud and in good faith. The defendant argued that the cheques were in fact payable to bearer and he was thus a holder in due course who was entitled to resist the action in conversion. The court held that the payees were not 'fictional' so that the defence failed: see [5.87].

The CPOA has made some minor changes in the law. In *Orbit Mining and Trading Co Ltd v Westminster Bank Ltd* [1963] 1 QB 794 the English court held that a 'cheque' made payable to 'Cash or order' was not a cheque since there was no named payee. It also rejected the argument that 'Cash' should be considered as a fictitious or non-existing payee. Under the CPOA, such an instrument would be a cheque which, since no payee is named, would be payable to bearer: ss 10, 20 and 22 and see [10.19].

THE CHAIN OF LIABILITIES

[7.30] When a person takes an order cheque after an indorsement has been forged, then the person cannot be a holder, but may have rights against previous parties who also took after the forged indorsement. By s 74(2), the indorser effectively guarantees that he or she had good title to the cheque. The theory of the section is to throw the loss of a misappropriated cheque on the person who takes from the rogue, for it is only that person who has no recourse against earlier parties. In practice, that theory may be defeated if some of the parties are insolvent or cannot be found.

An individual, that is, a person who is not a bank or prescribed institution, who holds under a forged indorsement has no defence to an action in conversion. The true owner of the cheque remains forever the person who was the last holder of the cheque.

THE STATUTORY DEFENCES: GENERAL COMMENTS

[7.31] The above defences are available to all. A bank or a prescribed financial institution may rely upon the defences the same as anyone else, but in addition there are statutory defences available.

Statutory defences were first extended to banks by the English Parliament when the Stamp Act 1853 was passed. That Act placed a statutory duty on banks to deal with crossed cheques in accordance with the crossings and it was thought only fair that the bank should receive some protection if it carried out its duties in a careful way.

The statutory defences were later extended to cheques which were not crossed, the argument being that it was 'anomalous' that there should be the distinction between crossed and uncrossed cheques. The defences available include defences against both actions in conversion and actions for breach of contract.

Whatever the justification for such defences might have been in the early days, it is difficult to understand the justification for them in a modern Act.

The banks make large profits from the cheque system and there seems little reason why the risks inherent in the system should be placed upon those individuals who are unfortunate enough to have cheques stolen. A more rational approach would be for the risks to be borne equally by all users of the cheque system or, alternatively, by those who are demonstrably careless. There appears to have been no consideration given to reforming this part of the CPOA.

'WITHOUT NEGLIGENCE'

[7.32] The sections of the Act which give special defences to banks and other institutions all refer to the actions of the institution being 'without negligence'; in order to invoke the defence, the institution has the burden of showing that its actions fall within the test: *Commercial Bank of Australia Ltd v Flannagan* (1932) 47 CLR 461; *Hunter BNZ Finance Ltd v Maloney Pty Ltd* (1993) 18 NSWLR 420. In several of the older provisions in the BEA, the test was whether the action was in 'the ordinary course of business'.

The 'ordinary course of business' was less strict than the 'without negligence' test. Rather extraordinarily, it has been held on several occasions that a banker might be acting negligently yet still be within the ordinary course of business: *Carpenters' Co v British Mutual Banking Co Ltd* [1938] 1 KB 511; *Smith v Commercial Banking Co of Sydney Ltd* (1910) 11 CLR 667.

The meaning of 'without negligence' is discussed at [7.74].

'GOOD FAITH'

[7.33] In order to invoke the statutory defences, the institution must show that the actions were done 'in good faith'. Section 3(2) of the Act is: 'A reference in this Act to an act or thing being done in good faith is a reference to that act or thing being done honestly, whether or not the act or thing is done negligently.'

There is, thankfully, a paucity of cases in which the good faith of the banker has been questioned. Although it must be pleaded by the banker, its existence is essentially assumed by the court.

[7.34] One of the few times that there has been a serious challenge to the good faith of a bank was in *Lawrie v Commonwealth Trading Bank of Australia* [1970] Qd R 373. A fraudulent senior interviewing and investigating bank officer obtained a cheque from the plaintiff made payable to 'B T Clifford or bearer' and crossed 'Bank payee only'. The fraudulent officer had the cheque credited to the named account which was operated by him. The officer disposed of the proceeds of the cheque and the amount was debited to the plaintiff's account. The plaintiff sued in conversion and the defendant bank relied upon the statutory defences. The jury found that the officer had not acted within the scope of his apparent duty when he represented to the plaintiff that 'B T Clifford' was a customer of the bank who required a loan for bridging finance. As a result, the fraudulent conduct of the officer could not be attributed to the bank and it was held that the bank had acted in good faith. If the decision is correct, it is difficult to see how the bank could ever act otherwise than in good faith.

DEFENCES OF THE PAYING BANK

[7.35]   Even when there has been a wrongful payment by the paying bank, it may be possible that it will escape liability to the customer because of some defence available to it. As intimated above, these defences include statutory as well as common law defences.

COMMON LAW DEFENCES

[7.36]   The paying bank has available certain defences which are based on the contract which it has with its customer, the drawer of the cheque.

CUSTOMER'S BREACH OF CONTRACT

[7.37]   The customer's duty to draw cheques carefully has already been discussed: see [5.21]. If the customer has failed to draw the disputed cheque carefully and if the wrongful payment is a consequence of the customer's breach of contractual duty, then the bank has a defence to the contractual action and may debit the account for the amount of the cheque: *Commonwealth Trading Bank of Australia v Sydney Wide Stores Pty Ltd* (1981) 55 ALJR 574. If the wrongful payment is a result of an alteration of a cheque which was validly drawn by the customer, then there is little problem with establishing that the wrongful payment was caused by the customer's breach. The only cases where the defence has succeeded has been in those cases where the alteration was to the amount of the cheque. Although there is no theoretical reason that would prevent the defence from applying when the alteration is such that the name of the payee has been changed, it would be difficult to establish the defence since it may not be a breach of the customer's duty to leave blanks following the payee's name: *Slingsby v Westminster Bank Ltd (No 2)* [1931] 2 KB 583. However, the duty is to observe reasonable precautions and may change over time as commercial practice changes: *Commonwealth Trading Bank of Australia v Sydney Wide Stores Pty Ltd* (1981) 55 ALJR 574.

The defence may be defeated if the bank has been subsequently negligent in the payment of the cheque. This is so even if the fraud could not have happened but for the breach of contractual duty by the customer. This is the result of the decision in *Varker v Commercial Banking Co of Sydney Ltd* [1972] 2 NSWLR 967: see [5.25].

[7.38]   Section 91 of the Act gives the bank certain rights when the cheque has been 'raised'. Provided the cheque has been fraudulently altered so as to raise the amount and that the alteration is the only fraudulent material alteration of the cheque then the drawee bank may debit the account for the amount of the cheque as drawn if it has paid the cheque in good faith and without negligence: see [7.74] for the meaning of 'without negligence'. This is expressly stated to be without prejudice to any other rights that the bank may have against the drawer of the cheque.

The rights given by s 91 are extremely limited, and will usually be of little value. Cases involving raised cheques show that typically the amount of the altered cheque is an order of magnitude larger than the cheque as originally drawn, so that the right to debit the account for the original amount will be of small comfort if the bank is unable to make out the complete defence.

[7.39] Section 91 may be a restatement of a common law right. In *Imperial Bank of Canada v Bank of Hamilton* [1903] AC 49 the Privy Council held that a cheque which had been raised from $5 to $500 was a valid cheque for the amount of $5 although it was a 'forgery' as to the remainder. However, the reasoning in the case is far from clear so the clarification of s 91 is welcome.

The *Bank of Hamilton* case might still be relevant, since it is clear that s 91 does not apply when there are fraudulent alterations to the cheque in addition to the alteration to the sum. There is no reason, however, why the bank should not attempt to rely upon the *Bank of Hamilton* principle. Note that the Explanatory Memorandum para 422 indicates that s 91(b) protects the bank where there has been a prior fraudulent alteration; it is difficult to reach that conclusion from a plain reading of the section. For a brief history of the law of altered cheques, see E P Ellinger, 'Liability of Paying Bank in Respect of Cheques Altered Without Authority', *Oxford Journal of Legal Studies*, Vol 2, 1982, pp 459–65.

FORGERIES

[7.40] When there is a forged drawer's or indorser's signature, then the bank generally has very limited common law defences. In the case of the forged indorser's signature, this is not very important for the bank, for the statutory defence will most often apply: see [7.50]. In the case of the forged drawer's signature, the bank may not debit the account for the simple reason that the bank has no mandate from the customer to make the payment: see [6.67] and *National Westminster Bank Ltd v Barclays Bank International Ltd* [1975] QB 654.

However, if the customer has breached the *Greenwood* duty to notify the bank of known forgeries, then the bank may be able to establish a defence and so maintain the debit to the customer's account in spite of the absence of mandate: *Greenwood v Martins Bank Ltd* [1933] AC 51; *Brown v Westminster Bank Ltd* [1964] 2 Lloyd's Rep 187; *Tina Motors Pty Ltd v Australian and New Zealand Banking Group Ltd* [1977] VR 205.

Although there is no authority on the question, it would seem that the *Varker* principle would hold when the customer has breached the *Greenwood* duty, so that if the bank has been negligent in paying the forged cheque then it will not be able to rely upon the customer's breach as a defence: see [5.25] and *Varker v Commercial Banking Co of Sydney Ltd* [1972] 2 NSWLR 967.

Recall that there is no duty on the customer to take care of the chequebook or to organise his or her business in a way that protects the interests of the bank: *Tai Hing Cotton Mill Ltd v Liu Chong Hing Bank* [1986] AC 80; [1985] 2 All ER 947; *Westpac Banking Corporation v Metlej* [1987] ACLD 511; *National Bank of New Zealand v Walpole and Patterson* [1975] 2 NZLR 7 and the discussion at [3.20].

BEARER CHEQUES

[7.41] Payment will in almost all cases be to the person in possession of the cheque. Thus, if the cheque is payable to bearer, then the bank will have paid the person which was specified in the mandate from its customer. This is true even if the payment is made to the thief or the finder of the cheque, even though such a person would not be a holder in due course and, of course, would have no right to enforce the cheque against the drawer. If the bank pays without any knowledge of the defect in title, then the customer's mandate has been followed.

This seems correct in principle, although there was, surprisingly, some doubts about it before the CPOA. However, s 22(b) now provides that where a cheque is not payable to order, the cheque shall be taken to require the drawee bank to pay the sum ordered to be paid by the cheque to the bearer.

[7.42] However, this does not mean that the bank may escape all liability merely because the payment is to the bearer of a bearer cheque. It may be that there are some extraneous circumstances, or even circumstances apparent from the cheque itself, which should raise the suspicion of the bank and indicate to it that the cheque should not be paid without making inquiries. In other words, the fact that a cheque is payable to bearer does not absolve the bank from any of its other contractual duties: see [5.89] and *Selangor United Rubber Estates Ltd v Cradock (No 3)* [1968] 1 WLR 1555.

Recall that a cheque is payable to bearer if it is not payable to order and that a cheque is not payable to order if the payee or the last indorsee is not 'specified': ss 21, 22. Further recall that a person is not 'specified' if the person is a fictitious or non-existing person: see [7.29]. It may sometimes be possible for a bank to make out a defence based on these provisions even though it has paid the cheque to the wrong person.

THE EQUITABLE DEFENCE

[7.43] The law is generally intolerant of those who meddle in other people's affairs. Thus, a person who, without the authority of the debtor, pays another's debts will find that the debt is not discharged. The meddler will not be able to claim any repayment from the person whose debt has been 'paid'. The reasons for this are that the debtor might wish to dispute the debt, or wish to set it off against a counterclaim or would prefer to use his or her limited assets to discharge other more pressing claims.

This is exactly the position of a bank which has paid a cheque when its customer has withdrawn authority. We have seen that it will often be possible for the bank to recover the payment from the holder of the cheque as money paid under a mistake of fact: see [6.4]. However, there will be times when that person has either become insolvent or cannot be found. In either case, there is a sense that the customer of the bank has received a windfall, for the person who has received the money will not attempt to recover from the customer, yet the bank is unable to debit the customer's account.

[7.44]   Because of this possibility of an unfair windfall, there are certain circumstances where the person who pays the debts of another may take advantage of the payment even though the payment was made without the authority of the person concerned. As an example, recovery has been allowed under a right of subrogation of money lent by a bank to meet the necessities for a mentally disordered person's household: see *Re Beavan, Davies, Banks & Co v Beavan* [1912] 1 Ch 196.

In certain cases, the banker may take advantage of this 'equitable defence' in order to justify the debiting of an account for payment of cheques which are, strictly speaking, paid in circumstances where the banker has no mandate but where it would be manifestly unjust to allow the customer to keep the benefit of the payment.

[7.45]   The operation of the principle may be seen in *Liggett v Barclays Bank* [1928] 1 KB 48. The defendants negligently and contrary to instructions paid cheques of their customers, the plaintiff company, which had been signed by one director only. The cheques were drawn in favour of trade creditors of the company in payment for goods supplied to the company in their business. The court held that as the liabilities of the company had not been increased by the payments the defendants were protected from liability on equitable grounds. The bank was entitled to stand in the place of the creditors whom they had paid.

[7.46]   The scope of the principle is not entirely clear. In *Re Cleadon Trust* [1939] Ch 286 a director had paid some debts of subsidiary companies at the request of the secretary. The payment discharged a liability of the company, as the company was guarantor of the debts owed by the subsidiaries. There was a meeting which purported to confirm the arrangement, but it was invalid. All of the companies went into liquidation and the director sought to recover the amounts advanced, arguing that he was so entitled under the *Liggett* principle. The court held that there was not knowledge or acquiescence on the part of the company which would make it liable at common law under an implied contract and there was no equitable principle which imposed a liability on the company, in as much as it had never had anything to do with the transactions.

[7.47]   The equitable defence was allowed in a slightly different context in *Shapera v Toronto Dominion Bank* (1970) 1 7 DLR (3d) 122. The plaintiff made an attempt to stop a cheque, but although his description of the cheque which he wished to stop gave the correct payee and amount, the date described was 27 January instead of 26 January. The court held that it was not a valid countermand, but went on to say that even if it had been, the bank would be entitled to succeed under the *Liggett* principle. The court argued that the cheque went to discharge a valid legal obligation of the customer and it would be inequitable to permit the customer to recover its value and leave the bank in the position of having paid the customer's debt.

[7.48]   Shapera was followed in *Royal Bank of Canada v Huber* (1971) 23 DLR (3d) 209. A cheque in favour of the defendant was mistakenly paid by the plaintiff bank which overlooked a stop payment order of the drawer.

Huber had been notified of the stop payment order before depositing the cheques with the Toronto Dominion bank, but they were collected for his account and paid by mistake by the plaintiff bank. The company drawer of the cheques had not asked that its account be recredited, nor did the bank show any intention to do so. The court explained this as follows (at 211):

> It is not difficult to understand why the Bank has not admitted liability. There is no dispute, but that the moneys which Huber received were in payment of wages — a debt owed to him. Under these circumstances, if a claim were made by the Company against the bank for payment to it of the money paid out in contravention of the 'stop payment' order, it may be that the Bank would be entitled to equitable relief: see *Shapera v Toronto Dominion Bank* 17 DLR (3d) 122 ...

The court held that the defendant was entitled to retain the money, but the reasons are obscure (at 212): '... I am satisfied that the facts fully establish that it would be against equity, and good conscience to insist that the defendant return the money ...'.

[7.49]   After a careful consideration of the cases, Ellinger and Lee conclude that in order to make out the Liggett defence it must be shown that the customer owed a valid debt to the payee of the cheque, that this debt was discharged by the wrongful payment and that it would be unconscionable for the customer to retain the benefit of the payment: E P Ellinger and C Y Lee, 'The "Liggett" Defence: a banker's last resort' [1984] 1 *LMCLQ* 459.

There is a serious conflict between the *Liggett* line of cases and the *Simms* and *Murphett* cases on the repayment of money paid under a mistake of fact. These latter cases held that, when a bank pays a cheque overlooking a countermand, the debt owed to the payee of the cheque is not discharged since the bank has paid without authority. On the other hand, the operation of the *Liggett* principle clearly requires that the debt be discharged. If the *Simms* analysis wins out, as appears to be the case in Australia, then there will be no scope for the Liggett doctrine in this class of case: see A L Tyree, 'When rules collide: *Liggett* meets *Simms*' (1990) 1 *JBFLP* 213.

STATUTORY DEFENCES

[7.50]   For the paying bank, the statutory defences continue to distinguish between crossed and uncrossed cheques, but in either case the paying bank is offered sweeping defences against its customer both for actions in contract and in tort. The protection is further extended in the current Act to include payment by non-bank financial institutions of payment orders drawn upon them: see [7.140].

FORGED CHEQUES

[7.51] The sections of the Act which grant the statutory defences to the bank are all stated to be subject to s 32(1). That is the section which makes inoperative a forged drawer's signature unless there is an estoppel against the person whose signature it purports to be or unless the person has adopted or ratified the signature. Thus, nothing in the protective provisions alters the risks associated with cheques bearing a forged drawer's signature.

PAYMENT OF CROSSED CHEQUES

[7.52] Where a bank, in good faith and without negligence, pays a crossed cheque drawn upon it to a bank, the bank shall be deemed to have paid the cheque in due course: s 92. Payment in due course discharges the cheque with the result that all rights on the cheque are discharged: ss 79, 82. The meaning of 'without negligence' will be discussed at [7.74].

The section is not happily worded. Consider the case of a cheque which has been misappropriated by a rogue who has managed to obtain payment of the cheque under conditions which make s 92 applicable. If the cheque was delivered to the payee, then the payee may not bring any action against the drawer on the cheque since the cheque is discharged by the payment. It might be thought that this payment in due course is precisely the complaint of the payee, the true owner of the cheque. This is technically correct, but in *Charles v Blackwell* (1877) 2 CPD 151 it was said that if the cheque has been paid in due course then there could be no action in conversion by the true owner.

If *Charles v Blackwell* is correct on this point, then it would seem that the bank is safe from both an action for breach of contract by the drawer of the cheque and from an action in tort by the true owner of the cheque. As between the drawer and the payee, if the cheque has been delivered to the payee, then the deemed payment in due course will discharge the debt owed by the drawer. This, according to *Charles v Blackwell*, is because the payee agreed to take an instrument which would discharge the debt if the bank paid it in accordance with the existing law. Since payment by the bank within the conditions of s 92 is payment of that type, the payee cannot be heard to complain.

PAYMENT CONTRARY TO CROSSING

[7.53] When a bank disregards the crossing and pays the cheque otherwise than to a bank, the bank is liable to the true owner of the cheque for any loss that the true owner suffers as a result of the cheque being paid other than to a bank: s 93(1). This section is only concerned with the consequences of a bank paying contrary to the crossing; if the true owner may sustain an action in conversion, then the bank may be liable, subject to the statutory defences, even if it pays the cheque in accordance with the crossing.

In either case, the paying bank which disregards a crossing may find itself responsible to two different parties. The true owner of the cheque has rights against the bank either by virtue of s 93(1) or the ordinary action in conversion, and the drawer of the cheque may resist the debit of the account: see *Bobbett v Pinkett* (1876) 1 Exch D 368.

Section 93(1) is made subject to the defence available to the bank by s 93(2). If the cheque is a crossed cheque, but the crossing has been so skilfully obliterated that the cheque does not appear to be, or at any time to have been, a crossed cheque, then payment by the bank is deemed to be payment in due course of the cheque provided that it has been paid in good faith and without negligence.

FAULTY INDORSEMENTS

[7.54] If the cheque which is misappropriated is an order cheque, then the only way that the rogue may obtain payment is by forging an indorsement. This means, of course, that not only is the rogue not a holder, but neither can any later indorsee be a holder: see Chapter 9. As a consequence, payment to the apparent holder will not discharge the cheque under s 79. Further, payment will be contrary to mandate, for the drawer has ordered that the bank pay to the order of the named payee, whereas the bank has paid to the order of the rogue.

Perhaps the most valuable defence offered to paying banks is s 94 which virtually excuses the paying bank from being concerned in any way with indorsements on cheques. The section deals separately with the case of forged/unauthorised indorsements and those which are either absent or irregular. Defences are provided in the first situation, where the indorsement is forged or unauthorised, whether the payment is made to another bank or to some other party, whereas in the case of missing or irregular indorsements, the defence applies only if payment is made to another bank.

When the indorsement has been written or placed on the cheque without the authority of the person whose indorsement it purports to be and the bank pays the cheque in good faith and without negligence, then the bank does not incur any liability either by reason of the forged indorsement or by reason of its failure to concern itself with the genuineness of the indorsement: s 94(1). Further, the bank is deemed to have paid the cheque in due course: s 94(1)(d).

When the indorsement is missing entirely or is irregular, then the paying bank is excused only if payment is made to another bank. As will be seen, the CPOA does not entirely dispense with the need for banks to concern themselves with indorsements, but the effect of this section is to place the responsibility with the collecting bank when the payment is made through the clearing system. This makes good practical sense when the operation of the clearing system is considered: see [5.19]. When payment is made to another bank in good faith and without negligence, the effect is much the same as that in s 94(1), that is, the bank does not incur any liability by reason of the absent or irregular indorsement and the bank is deemed to have paid the cheque in due course: s 94(2).

[7.55]   The operation of these sections may be illustrated by the decision in *Bank of New South Wales v Derham* (1978) 25 ACTR 25. Derham and his wife were the joint payees of an order cheque drawn in their favour by an insurance company at their instructions. The instructions included an instruction to mail the cheque to the address of their insurance broker, one Volters. The cheque had a space on the front which was marked 'Endorsement of the payee'. In that space was forged the name 'C J Derham'. On the back of the cheque was written 'Pay W Volters'. Volters deposited the cheque with a branch of the ANZ bank and it was then paid by the defendant bank.

The indorsement was found to be forged, but it was also irregular since it was a single indorsement of a cheque with joint payees. There was also a missing indorsement for the same reason. The bank succeeded in raising the statutory defence against the plaintiff. Note that this was an action in conversion against the paying bank: see [7.3]. The drawer of the cheque had delivered a cheque in an appropriate form in accordance with the instructions of the payee. Consequently, the debt owed by the insurance company to the payee was discharged and the payee was the true owner of the cheque.

DEFENCES OF THE COLLECTING BANK

[7.56]   The collecting bank is exposed only to an action in conversion or for money had and received since there are no contractual relationships with any of the parties who are entitled to the misappropriated cheque. As mentioned above, there are few defences to an action in conversion. In the case of the collecting bank, there has been some confusion concerning its possible position as a holder of the cheque.

COMMON LAW DEFENCES

[7.57]   The bank is not, merely by being a bank, disqualified from any of the defences which could be used by an ordinary person being sued in conversion. The principal defence available is, of course, that the cheque has been taken under conditions that qualify the taker as a holder in due course.

HOLDER FOR VALUE

[7.58]   The problems which have arisen concern the issue of whether or not the bank has given value for the cheque. The confusion stems from the decision in *Capital and Counties Bank Ltd v Gordon* [1903] AC 240. A fraudulent clerk stole cheques which were drawn in favour of his employer, forged indorsements on them and paid them into his own accounts. Immediately the cheques were deposited, the clerk's accounts were credited with the amounts and he was in fact allowed to draw on the amounts so credited. The true owner of the cheques, Gordon, sued the collecting bank.

In the course of the judgments, it was necessary to decide if the bank had been collecting for itself or for its customer, the court believing that it was impossible that the answer could be 'both'. Weaver and Craigie express it well in saying that the House of Lords decision in holding that the bank was collecting for itself involved two propositions.

First, a bank is not collecting a cheque for a customer in any case where the bank is a holder for value of the cheque. Second, a bank is a holder for value of a cheque if it credits the account of its customer with the amount thereof before the proceeds of the cheque have been collected from the paying banker and this position prevails even though the fact of crediting the account has not been communicated to the customer: see G A Weaver and R C Craigie, *The Law Relating to Banker and Customer in Australia*, 2nd ed, Law Book Co, Sydney, 1990, at [15.360].

The effect of the finding in *Gordon's* case was that the bank was not entitled to rely upon the statutory defence. The bank's position is strengthened under the CPOA since it is made explicit that the defence applies when it 'receives payment of a cheque and, before or after receiving payment, credits a customer's account with the sum ordered to be paid by the cheque': s 95(1)(a)(ii).

[7.59]   The question of when the bank becomes a holder for value is still relevant, however, for there may be situations where the bank cannot rely upon the statutory defence. For example, the bank may not have collected the cheque 'without negligence' but still satisfy all of the requirements to be a holder in due course. In other cases, the issue is one which is outside the scope of the CPOA, for example, *National Australia Bank Ltd v KDS Construction Services Pty Ltd (in Liquidation)* (1987) 62 ALJR 63 where the issue concerned a preference in winding up. The problem is to determine those situations where it may be said that the bank has given value for the cheque.

It will usually be of little use for the bank to establish that it is merely a holder for value, for in order to defend against an action in conversion it must establish itself as a holder in due course. Except for the question of indorsements (see [7.66]), the bank must establish the same requirements as any other person to become a holder in due course: see [10.27]. This will often prove more troublesome than might be expected because of the requirement of completeness and regularity: see [10.105]. Cheques are not as a rule as carefully drawn as bills.

THE EFFECT OF CREDITING THE ACCOUNT

[7.60]   The second proposition of the *Gordon* decision places far too much importance on the bookkeeping processes of the bank. There is no reason to prevent a bank from conditionally crediting an account without being considered as a purchaser of the cheque. It is now recognised that the proposition is incorrect.

The true position with regard to crediting the account is now accepted to be that as explained by the court in *A L Underwood Ltd v Barclays Bank Ltd* [1924] 1 KB 775. A managing director misappropriated cheques payable to the company by paying them into his own account which was credited immediately with the proceeds although the director did not in fact draw upon the funds until the cheques were cleared. The Court of Appeal held that the bank was not a holder for value of the cheques, Scrutton LJ summarising the reasoning concisely (at 804):

> The cases where an agent for collection becomes a holder for value must turn on an express or implied agreement between bank and customer that the latter may draw against the cheques before they are cleared.

[7.61]   The consequences for banks in Australia is that the crediting of the account will be largely irrelevant in the determination of whether the collecting bank is or is not a holder for value. The reason for this is that (1) there will seldom be an express contract that the customer may draw against uncleared effects; and (2) since deposit slips carry warnings that the customer may not draw on uncleared effects it will not be possible to find an implied contract that he or she may do so: see *Westminster Bank Ltd v Zang* [1966] AC 182; see also the New South Wales Court of Appeal in *Sidney Raper Pty Ltd v Commonwealth Trading Bank of Australia* [1975] 2 NSWLR 227; *National Australia Bank Ltd v KDS Construction Services Pty Ltd* (1987) 62 ALJR 63.

This result seems correct in principle. The accounting which the bank chooses to adopt is purely an internal matter and should have no relevance to the question of whether the banker is or is not a holder for value. If the accounting methods are to be evidence of this, then it is likely that the bank will be inviting legislative interference in the accounting procedures, a situation which exists in the United States.

THE BANKER'S LIEN

[7.62]   The bank has a lien over a deposited cheque when the customer's account is overdrawn: see [10.93]. According to s 38, a holder who has a lien is conclusively presumed to have taken the cheque for value to the extent of the value of the lien. Is the banker who receives a cheque over which he or she has a banker's lien a holder for value?

[7.63]   In *Barclays Bank v Astley Industrial Trust* [1970] 2 QB 527 M Ltd had a large overdraft with the plaintiff bank. The plaintiff received five cheques totalling £2850 for collection to M's account and, on the faith of those cheques, paid two of M's cheques to an amount of £345. The cheques made payable to M were drawn by the defendant in respect of hire purchase transactions which were later found to be fraudulent.

The defendant stopped payment on the cheques and the plaintiff bank sued on the cheques, claiming to be holders in due course. It was held that the plaintiff had given value for the cheques by virtue of the banker's lien and by virtue of the fact that they had honoured two cheques which would otherwise have been dishonoured. Even though the cheques were delivered for collection, the bank still became holders for value and could sue on the cheques: see s 38.

[7.64] On the other hand, the High Court in *National Australia Bank Ltd v KDS Construction Services Pty Ltd* (1987) 62 ALJR 63 held that the banker-customer relationship was such that the mere existence of the lien was insufficient to constitute the banker a holder for value. The court explained the *Astley* case solely on the grounds that the bank there had agreed 'to treat the cheques as cash'. Throughout the *KDS* case, the court seems to assume that being an agent for collection and being a holder for value are mutually exclusive: see [7.67].

The analysis of the court is wholly dependent on the banker-customer contract and on the notion of payment by cheque. Section 32(3) BEA, the equivalent of s 38 CPOA is not mentioned in the judgment. It is hard to see why the plain words of the CPOA are insufficient to constitute the bank a holder for value. If the cheque is a bearer cheque, then the bank is a holder by virtue of its possession. If the cheque is an unindorsed order cheque, then the CPOA provides that the bank is to have rights which it would have if the cheque were indorsed: see CPOA s 96. It is to be hoped that if the matter arises again that the apparent conflict with the statute will be explained.

[7.65] Even if the lien is itself adequate to make the bank a holder for value, the situation must be such that the particular cheque is covered by the lien. In *Baker v Barclays Bank Ltd* [1955] I WLR 822 the bank collected a cheque made out in favour of a partnership for the account of one of the partners, Jeffcott. In reply to inquiries, Jeffcott led the bank to believe that he was holding the proceeds on behalf of Bainbridge, the other partner. Devlin J held that the bank could not be a holder for value since Jeffcott's explanation to the manager was inconsistent with his having given value for the cheques and the bank believed the cheques to be Bainbridge's money, so they could not be applied to reduce Jeffcott's overdraft: see [3.38].

UNINDORSED CHEQUES

[7.66] Although the bank will often be collecting cheques over which it has given value either by express agreement or by virtue of a banker's lien, just as often it will not be a holder since the cheque is an order cheque which has not been indorsed. The Act gives some help in s 96. If the cheque is lodged by the payee for collection for the payee and if the bank has either given value for the cheque or has a lien on the cheque, then the bank has such rights (if any) as it would have had if, before the lodgment of the cheque, the payee had indorsed the cheque in blank.

Indorsement 'in blank' is a concept which is used in the BEA and which seems to have found its way into this section by accident. By s 39(1) of the BEA, an indorsement in blank specifies no indorsee, and a bill indorsed in blank becomes payable to bearer. Presumably the Act intends the phrase to mean the same kind of indorsement. If so, the cheque becomes payable to bearer by virtue of s 21 and s 22.

The apparently peculiar clause 'before the lodgment of the cheque' is to overcome the legal difficulty posed by *Smith v Commercial Banking Co of Sydney Ltd* (1910) 11 CLR 667. In that case a bank requested the apparent holder of a bill to 'indorse' the bill by signing his name on the back. The High Court held that such a signature was not an indorsement for there was no intention to transfer property in the bill to the bank. The signature was merely for the purposes of identification.

When the bank has given value for the cheque or, it is submitted, where the bank has a lien on the cheque, s 96 has the effect of making the bank a holder to all intents and purposes. In particular, if all of the other requirements are satisfied, the bank will be treated as a holder in due course: see *Midland Bank Ltd v R V Harris Ltd* [1963] 1 WLR 1021 and *Westminster Bank v Zang* [1966] AC 182.

AGENT FOR COLLECTION AND HOLDER FOR VALUE

[7.67]   There still remains the question of the first proposition of the *Gordon* case, that a banker is either an agent for collection or a holder for value but cannot be both. The *Astley* case also held that a bank may be collecting for a customer and at the same time be a holder of a cheque. Milmo J said (at 538):

> I am unable to accept the contention that a banker cannot at one and the same time be an agent for collection of a cheque and a holder of that cheque for value. It seems to me that the language of s 2 of the Cheques Act 1957 negatives this proposition since it presupposes that a banker who has been given a cheque for collection may nevertheless have given value for it.

[7.68]   This analysis clearly depends upon the wording of the United Kingdom Act. Although that wording is slightly different from the wording of s 96, the same logic applies, for s 96 clearly contemplates that the cheque has been lodged for collection and that the bank has also given value for it.

On the other hand, the High Court in *National Australia Bank Ltd v KDS Construction Services Pty Ltd* (1987) 62 ALJR 63 seems to assume that the bank must be one or the other, although the point does not appear to have been expressly addressed. The court explains cases such as *Astley* solely on the grounds that there are special arrangements where the bank is treating the cheque as 'cash' or as 'property': at 66. In the *KDS* case itself, the court found that the relationship was inconsistent with the bank being a holder for value even though the bank had a lien over the cheque.

The view in the *Astley* case seems preferable on this point. Suppose that the customer is depositing a cheque for $1000 and at the same time wishes to draw cheques which will leave the account in overdraft $100. The bank agrees to the arrangement on the faith of the deposited cheque. According to the analysis in both *Astley* and *KDS*, the bank becomes a holder for value of the cheque. Can it really be said that it is not acting as an agent for collection at the same time?

STATUTORY DEFENCES

[7.69]   The bank's main defence against an action in conversion or money had and received is s 95(1). Where a bank in good faith and without negligence collects for a customer who has no title or a defective title, then the bank incurs no liability to the true owner of the cheque merely by the collection. Further, the section makes it clear that the bank may use the defence whether or not the account is credited before or after the actual receipt of the payment, thus overcoming any possible difficulties remaining from *Capital and Counties Bank Ltd v Gordon* [1903] AC 240: see [7.60].

NATURE OF THE SECTION

[7.70]   Much confusion will be avoided if it is recognised that s 95 places no new duty on the collecting banker. Quite the contrary, the collecting banker like everyone else is under a duty imposed by law to refrain from interfering with chattels and goods belonging to other people. The effect of s 95 is to provide a collecting banker with a defence which is not available to the general public.

This position requires some comment, for a number of influential textbooks and not quite a few judgments are in different terms. Thus, Paget comments that (p 330):

> The importation of negligence into this section is ... an anomaly; there can be no negligence without a duty. There is no contractual relation between the collecting banker and the true owner which gives rise to a duty on the part of the former to the latter ... The true exposition is that given by Denman J and the Court of Appeal in *Bissell & Co v Fox Bros & Co* [(1884) 51 LT 663]; the duty is a purely statutory one imposed on the banker in favour of the true owner and the negligence consists in the disregard of his interests. The assumption of this duty and liability to a stranger must be regarded as the price paid by bankers for protection under statute.

[7.71]   The truth is that the word 'negligence' in the statute is indeed an anomaly, but it is wrong to say that the statute imposes a duty. Without the statute the duty would still exist, but the banker would have no defence at all.

The use of the word 'negligence' has, however, undoubtedly had its effect. As will be seen below, the cases tend to analyse the behaviour of the bank in terms of a duty owed by a reasonable banker to the true owner of a cheque. On the other hand, in a true negligence action, the plaintiff must prove the negligence. When suing in conversion, the plaintiff need only prove that the conversion occurred; if the banker wishes to rely upon the section, it is up to the banker to prove that the collection was 'without negligence'.

Lord Wright expressed the position clearly in *Lloyds Bank Ltd v E B Savory & Co* [1933] AC 201 (at 229):

> Section 82 [the precursor to s 95] is therefore not the imposition of a new burden or duty on the collecting banker but is a concession affording him the means of avoiding a liability in conversion to which otherwise there would be

no defence. As it is for the banker to show that he is entitled to this defence, the onus is on him to disprove negligence.

[7.72]   The distinction has several very important practical consequences. In the first place, as a defence, it is for the bank to establish that it acted 'without negligence': *Hunter BNZ Finance Ltd v Maloney Pty Ltd* (1993) 18 NSWLR 420. Second, if it fails to establish that it so acted, there is no need for the plaintiff to show that the losses were caused by the bank's action: see *Savory & Co v Lloyds Bank Ltd* [1931] 2 KB 122; [1933] AC 201; *Hunter BNZ Finance Ltd v Maloney Pty Ltd* (1993) 18 NSWLR 420; Ellinger and Lomnicka, *Modern Banking Law*, 2nd ed, Clarendon Press, Oxford, 1994 p 512; and [7.132].

The question of whether the defendant bank acted without negligence is a question of fact for the jury.

RECEIVES PAYMENT FOR A CUSTOMER

[7.73]   The defence is available only when the banker 'receives payment for a customer'. The meaning of 'customer' has been discussed at [2.15], and, if the *Astley* case is correct, it is possible for a banker to be a holder for value and at the same time be receiving payment for a customer: see [7.67].

However, if the bank is acting purely as a discounter, that is, is actually purchasing the cheque or bill, then the statute will provide no defence if the banker takes under a forged indorsement. It will, of course, be very unusual for a banker to discount a cheque.

MEANING OF 'WITHOUT NEGLIGENCE'

[7.74]   Although the question of whether a banker has collected without negligence is a question of fact for the jury, there are a number of cases where there are judicial pronouncements on the meaning of the expression. And, although it is often said that it is incapable of a precise definition, there are a number of cases where the court has attempted to do just that. However, the statement of the Privy Council in the *Commissioner of Taxation v English Scottish and Australian Bank Ltd* [1920] AC 683 has become the classic pronouncement on the subject.

In that case, a man who called himself Thallon wished to open an account with the defendant bank. He gave as his address a well-known address in Sydney and signed the signature book. The account was opened with £20 in banknotes and Thallon was given a chequebook. No inquiries were made to check the authenticity of the address. On the following day, Thallon deposited a crossed bearer cheque for more than £750 which the bank collected for him. He withdrew the entire amount from his account soon thereafter and disappeared. The cheque turned out to be stolen, 'Thallon' was an assumed name and no such person lived at the address given.

The true owner of the cheque sued the bank for conversion of the cheque. During the course of the judgment given by the Privy Council, Lord Dunedin gave what has become the classic definition of 'negligence' for the purposes of the statutory defences available to the collecting bank (at 688):

... the test of negligence is whether the transaction of paying in any given cheque [coupled with the circumstances antecedent and present] was so out of the ordinary course that it ought to have aroused doubts in the bankers' mind, and caused them to make inquiry.

PRACTICE OF BANKERS

[7.75]   The reference to 'the ordinary course' suggests that the standard should be related to the business of banking. The practice of bankers has always been influential in determining whether the particular banker has acted without negligence, but it has never been guaranteed to automatically bring the banker within the protective provisions of the statutory defences.

For example, in *E B Savory & Co v Lloyds Bank Ltd* [1932] 2 KB 122; [1933] AC 20 1 there was evidence available that it was the practice of bankers which had a head office in London and branch offices elsewhere to accept cheques paid in at any branch for the credit of an account at any other branch. It was said that this was a practice which had been established for over 40 years. The House of Lords found the practice to be inconsistent with prudent precautions against known risks, Lawrence LJ referring to cases (at 144) 'where bankers, solely for the convenience of their customers, have adopted a system with an inherent and obvious defect which no reasonably careful banker could fail to observe'.

[7.76]   This approach by the courts is often criticised by commercial and banking interests, but when a case has come before the court it is one in which the commercial system demonstrably has failed to work and someone must then bear the losses. There is perhaps a natural tendency for the courts to shift losses to the party who is in the position to make changes in the way in which the practice is carried on rather than to let it fall on a party who must simply take the system as it is or leave it.

A further difficulty which is often experienced is that the 'practice of bankers' is often not as uniform as is thought. If the court is faced with conflicting evidence as to the practice of bankers, then there is little that can be done other than to base a decision on other principles: see, for example, *Ladbroke & Co v Todd* (1914) 30 TLR 433. It is not just the practice of an individual bank which is relevant, but the practice of bankers generally: *Rosenhain v Commonwealth Bank of Australia* (1922) 31 CLR 46.

Finally, since the concept of 'without negligence' is related to current practice, there will be variations from time to time in circumstances which qualify. This is nicely illustrated by the cases which define the duty of the bank when opening the account: see [7.83].

BANK RULES

[7.77]   Banks have books of instructions to staff which lay down procedures to be followed in various situations. It might be thought that a banker who has not followed the procedures laid down by the bank might have an uphill battle to establish that a cheque has been collected without negligence.

While that is indeed the case, it is by no means true that a failure to follow internal rules and procedures will necessarily be fatal to the s 95 defence.

In *Motor Traders Guarantee Corporation Ltd v Midland Bank Ltd* [1937] 4 All ER 90 Goddard J considered that the rules were evidence upon which the plaintiffs could rely, but that they were not entitled to demand literal performance. He said (at 96):

> The bank does not owe a duty to [the plaintiffs] to carry out this rule, that rule, or the other rule. Indeed, I doubt whether they owe their own customers the duty of carrying out all the rules which they may lay down as counsels of perfection. The question in every case is ... whether the particular acts which are done are enough to discharge the onus which is upon the bank ...

[7.78] On the other hand, the rules do offer some evidence of what may reasonably be expected. In *Orbit Mining and Trading Co Ltd v Westminster Bank Ltd* [1963] 1 QB 794 Harman LJ noted that even though the failure to comply with the rules 'does not convict the bank of negligence [sic] ... where the rules are not kept the matter needs close attention'.

Priestley JA considered the rules of the bank in *National Commercial Banking Co of Australia Ltd v Robert Bushby Ltd* [1984] 1 NSWLR 559, saying at 575 that 'I do not (and could not) use [the rules] to ground either any finding or admission of law against the Bank but as evidence that the practice of some banks involves them in taking what are, to their knowledge, legal risks ...'.

AMATEUR DETECTIVE

[7.79] In determining whether the circumstances are 'out of the ordinary course' the banker is not required to be unduly suspicious. In *Lloyds Bank Ltd v Chartered Bank of India, Australia & China* [1929] 1 KB 40, Sankey LJ said (at 73): 'In my view, a bank cannot be held liable for negligence merely because they have not subjected an account to a microscopic examination. It is not to be expected that the officials of banks should also be amateur detectives.'

On the other hand, in *A L Underwood Ltd v Bank of Liverpool* [1924] 1 KB 775 Scrutton LJ said (at 800): 'If banks for fear of offending their customers will not make inquiry into unusual circumstances, they must take with the benefit of not annoying those customers the risk of liability because they do not inquire.'

[7.80] A similar situation arose in *National Commercial Banking Co of Australia Ltd v Robert Bush by Ltd* [1984] 1 NSWLR 559 where the bank collected cheques for a businessman who enjoyed a good reputation in a small business community. After referring to the bank's rules on collecting third party cheques, Priestley JA noted (at 575) that the bank was 'as a practical matter ... prepared to take the risk where its right of recourse against its customer is assured'.

When a case actually goes as far as litigation, there is undoubtedly a tendency to apply rather stricter rules, so that it is at the banker's peril if he or she does not examine cheques which are paid in for collection. Again, it must be noted that this is not some new and onerous duty which has been placed upon the banking community, but rather is the precondition for taking advantage of a defence which no other part of the community may use.

CONSIDERATION OF EACH CHEQUE SEPARATELY

[7.81]   It is clear that the bank must establish that it collected each and every cheque without negligence. So, for example, when a large number of cheques were misappropriated and collected for the rogue by the State Savings Bank of Victoria, the High Court considered differences in the way in which the cheques were drawn, their amount and other details, holding that some of them had been collected 'without negligence' while others had not: *Commissioners of the State Savings Bank of Victoria v Permewan Wright & Co Ltd* (1914) 19 CLR 457.

FACTORS IN DETERMINING NEGLIGENCE

[7.82]   Although it is difficult to give general rules concerning the circumstances under which a banker will succeed in establishing that a collection was 'without negligence' for the purposes of s 95(1), it seems possible to identify factors which have influenced the courts in various cases. This is facilitated if the cases are classified according to the type of negligence considered. There are essentially three such categories, namely, negligence connected with the opening of the account, negligence which results from factors which are apparent on the face of the cheque, and negligence connected with facts known by the banker about the customer.

Negligence in opening of account

[7.83]   There is little doubt that the banker has an obligation to make certain inquiries concerning the customer at the time when an account is opened and that if these inquiries are not made it may prove impossible for the banker to rely upon the s 95 defence. Unfortunately, the scope of these requirements is by no means clear. Banking practice will be relevant but in this area more than any other it is difficult to identify a uniform practice among bankers or to ascertain that the practice is stable over time.

At first sight, it might seem that the circumstances of opening an account are far removed from later misappropriations of cheques. Indeed, that would be true when a customer has operated an account honestly for a period of years and then begins to misappropriate cheques. On the other hand, cheque frauds are almost impossible to perpetrate without access to a bank account and there are certain situations in which care taken in the opening of the account will prevent the frauds from occurring.

As an example of the latter situation, in *Commissioners of Taxation v English, Scottish and Australian Bank Ltd* [1920] AC 683 even a very perfunctory inquiry by the bank when opening the account for 'Thallon' would have revealed that he was not what he claimed to be. Surprisingly, the Privy Council found that the bank was entitled to rely upon the defence in that case, a case which has been criticised and upon which it would be very foolish for a modern banker to rely: see [7.74] for a discussion of the case.

[7.84]   It is likely that the decision in *London Bank of Australia Ltd v Kendall* (1920) 28 CLR 401 is a better guide to current practice. A man calling himself 'Howard' went to the head office of the defendant bank in Sydney, introduced himself to the assistant accountant and indicated that he wished to open an account. He claimed to be an indent agent from Adelaide and, in response to questions from the accountant, said that he had never had a banking account in Sydney but that he had been banking in Adelaide. The accountant made no further inquiries concerning the banking activities of the man, the accountant believing that such inquiries were unnecessary because 'the man appeared to be about 36–37 years of age, looked quite respectable and had the appearance of a businessman and spoke like an educated man'.

The account was opened, with the approval of the bank manager, with £5 in notes and four crossed bearer cheques. The cheques were stolen and the plaintiff, who was the true owner of one of the cheques, sued in conversion. The High Court of Australia held that the circumstance surrounding the opening of the account was one of the 'antecedent circumstances' to be taken into account for the purposes of deciding if the defendant bank had collected without negligence.

The court held that the bank did not collect without negligence. The customer was unknown to the bank, he had no credentials, he offered no information concerning his banking activities and opened the account with cheques that needed explanation. So far as his appearance was concerned, the court noted that it was plainly insufficient as a basis for opening an account. The transaction was such as to arouse doubts in the mind of an ordinary banker.

[7.85]   In *Ladbroke v Todd* (1914) 30 TLR 433 the plaintiffs were book-makers who had drawn a cheque in favour of a client payee. The cheque was crossed and marked 'account of payee only'. It was mailed to the client, but intercepted by a rogue who apparently forged an indorsement. The cheque was taken to the defendant bank where the rogue requested that an account be opened with the proceeds of the cheque. He explained that he had an account with another bank but that since the cheque represented the proceeds of gambling, he did not wish to pass it through that account as he feared that it would come to the attention of the authorities of the college at which he was an undergraduate.

The banker asked the rogue to sign the signature book and compared the signature with the indorsement on the cheque, but neither asked for referees nor checked the rogue's story with the other bank. The cheque was cleared specially the same day at the rogue's request and the proceeds withdrawn soon after. The court held that although the cheque had been collected for a customer the bank had not collected without negligence and so was liable for the proceeds of the cheque.

Since it is clear that failure to exercise care when opening an account may lead to a situation where the banker cannot rely upon the s 95 defence, it is necessary to ask what is required. On the one hand, we have the comments made above that the banker is not required to act as an amateur detective, but on the other that the banker must evidently make some inquiries.

[7.86] Diplock LJ has made an influential analysis of the banker's obligation to make inquiries and the scope that those inquiries must take if the banker is to be assured of the benefit of the s 95 defence. In *Marfani v Midland Bank* [1968] 1 WLR 968 one Kureshy was in possession of a cheque for some £3000 which had been drawn by his employer in favour of Eliaszade. Kureshy went to the defendant bank where he pretended to be Eliaszade and sought to open an account in the name of Eliaszade. Kureshy, pretending to be Eliaszade, gave the name of two referees and opened the account with a small cash deposit. The bank wrote to the referees, receiving a reply from only one of them, who was also a customer of the bank, and that reply was favourable. It was later learned that Kureshy had introduced himself to the referee as Eliaszade. The referee had in fact known Kureshy, under the name of Eliaszade, for only a short time.

On the day after opening the account, Kureshy paid in the cheque which was then collected by the defendant bank. Kureshy later withdrew all of the funds and left England. On the question of whether the bank had been negligent in opening the account, it was argued for the plaintiff that the bank should have taken steps to ascertain the true identity of Kureshy. This might have been done by asking for his passport or other documents of identification, by seeking the name of his employer or of previous bank accounts.

The court held that it was probably desirable that a banker should seek documentary identification of a new customer, but that in the present case where the customer was introduced by an 'apparently trustworthy referee' it is not always necessary. There was no point in asking about employment, for Kureshy had said that he was self-employed and there is no requirement that the banker should cross-examine the potential customer on such a matter.

[7.87] It was also argued that the bank had been negligent in failing to obtain both referees' reports and that in fact the bank had collected the cheque before receiving the one favourable report.

This latter point was a difficult one for the bank, primarily because of a statement made by Bankes LJ in *A L Underwood Ltd v Barclays Bank Ltd* [1924] 1 KB 775 (at 789):

> I feel satisfied that the obvious inquiry whether the company had not got its own banking account would have put a stop to the fraudulent system adopted by Underwood, and I do not think that it lies in the mouth of the appellants to say that an inquiry would have been useless.

[7.88] In the *Marfani* case, it is clear that the fact that the cheque was collected before the receipt of the referee's report made no difference whatsoever to the collection of the cheque, but it was not certain that seeking the second referee's report would have been pointless. All that could be said is that in all likelihood, the rogue would have made arrangements so that the report of the second referee would have been as good as that of the first. Cairns J said (at 977):

> In my opinion, if the bank can show that in all probability a particular precaution would have been unavailing, the failure to take that precaution is not such negligence as deprives them of the protection [of s 5]. The burden of proof on the bank is no doubt heavy, but I do not think that it can be so heavy as to require them to prove with certainty that the precaution would have been useless.

[7.89]   The need to pursue 'useless' precautions frequently arises in the context of the banker failing to make inquiries which are indicated in the circumstances. The matter is discussed in more detail at [7.132].

The apparently favourable opinion in the *Marfani* case should not cause bankers to believe that they may neglect the making of inquiries when opening an account, for a careful look at the judgments will convince the reader of how close the decision came to being for the plaintiff. Yet the standard of care exercised by the banker was considerably higher than is often the case. It is also important to note that there is not the slightest hint in *Marfani* that the circumstances surrounding the opening of the account is an inappropriate factor to consider when determining if the banker has collected without negligence.

On the other hand, the *Marfani* case is to be welcomed for its increased attention to the actual practice of bankers. Diplock LJ said (at 972):

> What facts ought to be known to the banker, that is, what inquiries he should make and what facts are sufficient to cause him reasonably to suspect that the customer is not the true owner, must depend upon current banking practice and change as that practice changes. Cases decided thirty years ago, when the use by the general public of banking facilities was much less widespread may not be a reliable guide to what the duty of a careful banker, in relation to inquiries and as to facts which should give rise to suspicion, is today.

[7.90]   *Marfani* was cited with approval by Palmer AJ in *Mercedes-Benz (NSW) Pty Ltd v ANZ and National Mutual Royal Savings Bank Ltd* (Supreme Court, NSW, Comm Div, (Palmer AJ), 5 May 1992, unreported). The plaintiff company had employed a Mrs R as paymistress. She perpetrated a number of frauds which involved, inter alia, the establishment of a number of bank accounts with NMRB in the name of former or non-existent employees. This fraud was made easier by virtue of an arrangement whereby NMRB provided Mrs R with a number of forms for the establishment of employee accounts. In order to reduce delay, the arrangement was that Mrs R would later pick up the card and PIN necessary to operate the employee's account.

Palmer AJ held that this procedure was not such as to disqualify NMRB from reliance on the statutory defence. In doing so, he purported to follow *Marfani*, noting that it was not negligent to open an account for a new customer if the bank relied on a reference from an existing and reputable customer. Palmer AJ seems to have been influenced by some notion of negligence on the part of the plaintiff (see [7.127]) for the argument would clearly be untenable if the plaintiff had been some other party. In essence, the result is that it is 'without negligence' to hand over the account opening procedure to an importer of luxury cars! For a fuller discussion, see Tyree, 'Bad Business Makes Hard Cases: *Mercedes-Benz v NMRB*' (1992) 3 *JBFLP* 192 and '*Mercedes-Benz v ANZ and NMRB* (Pt 2)', (1992) 3 *JBFLP* 277.

An appeal in the *Mercedes-Benz* case was unanimously dismissed by the NSW Court of Appeal. There was no satisfactory discussion of the above point: *Mercedes-Benz (NSW) Pty Ltd v National Mutual Royal Savings Bank Ltd* (CA 40583/92, 1 April 1996, unreported).

[7.91] The requirements of the Financial Transactions Reports Act 1988 for opening accounts will be relevant in any future cases: see [1.43]ff. Certainly a bank which follows the requirements can successfully defend a claim that it was negligent in opening an account. Where an account is opened and there is a failure to observe the procedures there will be evidence of negligence, although it might still be that the account is opened 'without negligence' if the failure in the procedures is minor.

Face of the cheque/facts known by banker

[7.92] Certain features of the cheque itself should put a collecting banker on inquiry. This includes not only the information which is directly discoverable from the cheque itself, such as apparent alterations to the cheque, but also information which may be combined with other information known to the banker which would then indicate that the transaction is outside the ordinary course of business. Examples of this latter kind of information might be that the cheque is drawn in favour of the customer's employer.

Once again, the exact metes and bounds of conduct which will disentitle the banker from relying upon the s 95 defence are not possible to state, but by examining a number of cases which have come before the court it is possible to establish some broad principles.

Indorsements

[7.93] One of the consequences of the historical identification of a cheque as a species of bill of exchange is the cheque is negotiated by means of indorsement. It has already been observed that the majority of cheques are never negotiated, but are sent directly to the payee and deposited directly into an account for collection. It was the practice of banks to require that the holder of the cheque indorse the cheque, usually in blank, upon paying in. It is not clear why this practice began or precisely what advantage the banks believed that they were obtaining, for it was held in more than one case that the application of the signature of the holder to the back of the cheque at the request of a bank teller did not amount to an indorsement: see *Smith v Commercial Banking Co of Sydney Ltd* (1910) 11 CLR 667.

This practice of requiring 'indorsements' upon paying in extended to the case where the cheque had not been negotiated. The consequential waste of time was a nuisance to all concerned and seemed to serve little purpose when the cheque had not been negotiated.

[7.94]   Prior to the amendment of the Bills of Exchange Act in 1971, collection of an unindorsed or irregularly indorsed cheque for anyone other than the payee was virtually conclusive evidence that the collection was not without negligence. The amendment inserted s 88D into that Act and forms the basis for s 95(2) of the CPOA. The effect of that section, which is rather clumsily worded, is that the bank need not concern itself with an indorsement if the cheque is an order cheque that has not been negotiated and if the name of the customer and the name of the payee are the same, or so close to the same as to be reasonable for the bank to have assumed that the customer was the person intended by the drawer to be the payee.

The restriction to order cheques is curious. Presumably the framers of the CPOA supposed that there was no need to have an indorsement on bearer cheques whether negotiated or not, but it would have done no harm to make the section general. Section 88D(3) BEA on which the section is based has no such restriction.

'Not negotiable'

[7.95]   Is the mere fact that a banker collects for someone other than the payee a cheque which is crossed 'not negotiable' without making inquiries sufficient to disentitle the banker from reliance on the s 95 defence? At first blush, the answer would appear to be 'no', since it is clear that such a cheque remains transferable.

However, doubt was first cast upon the simple answer by Lord Brampton in *Great Western Railway Co Ltd v London and County Banking Co Ltd* [1901] AC 414 when he said (at 422):

> I am not, however, quite so sure that it was altogether without negligence, for I must assume the manager at Wantage knew the meaning and legal effect of the crossing with the words 'not negotiable'. This point, however, does not appear to have been raised, and certainly there was no finding upon it at the trial.

Although the point was made obiter and with some diffidence, it seems clear that Lord Brampton thought that collection of a crossed 'not negotiable' cheque for a third party without inquiry might not be a collection which was made without negligence.

[7.96]   The notion has gained some currency in Australia. Griffith CJ in *Commissioners of the State Savings Bank of Victoria v Permewan Wright and Co* (1914) 19 CLR 457 said (at 467):

> In my opinion the words 'not negotiable' on a crossed cheque are a danger signal held out before every person invited to deal with it, and are equivalent to saying 'Take care: this cheque may be stolen'. I think, further, that they indicate that the drawer of the cheque ... intended that the person to whom it was

to be handed or sent should apply it to some specific purpose and no other. A reasonably careful man to whom such a cheque is tendered should therefore examine the cheque to see whether there is anything upon its face to indicate such a purpose. If there is not, it may be that he may safely rely on the honesty of the bearer; but, if there is, it is his duty to make inquiries and if he fails to do so he cannot claim to have acted without negligence.

Although this speech is often cited as reflecting the same views as those of Lord Brampton, it must be noted that the Chief Justice said something quite different. It is not just the crossing which should put the banker on inquiry, but the crossing together with some indication of a special purpose. In the *Permewan Wright* case the cheques in question were for the payment of customs duty and that many of them had 'duty' marked upon them.

The joint judgment of Gavan Duffy and Rich JJ reflect this distinction (at 484):

When we remember that such cheques are crossed cheques within the meaning of the protecting sections, we have difficulty in appreciating the suggestion that the banker should prima facie be more suspicious of customers paying in such cheques than of those paying in cheques crossed without the words 'not negotiable', though circumstances might call for suspicion in the case of one class of crossed cheque which would not call for it in another.

[7.97] It seems that there are few who would argue that if a 'special purpose' is apparent on the face of the cheque, then the banker ignores that purpose at the risk of being unable to rely upon the statutory defence. On the other hand, the 'pure' argument of Lord Brampton that the 'not negotiable' marking itself should preclude the collection without inquiry of the cheque for a third party has been severely criticised and seems to have little merit: see *Paget's Law of Banking*, 11th ed, Butterworths, London, 1996, p 455; Ellinger and Lomnicka, op cit, p 524.

[7.98] As a final point on the 'not negotiable' cheque, it may well be that the banker who collects such a cheque as the first transaction on an account might be well advised to take a higher degree of care. The High Court of Australia has considered the matter in *Savings Bank of South Australia v Wallman* (1935) 52 CLR 688. In a joint judgment, Rich, Dixon, Evatt and McTiernan JJ said (at 695):

There is, of course, no doubt that special vigilance is demanded when a new account is opened and a crossed cheque is tendered, particularly when it is marked 'not negotiable'. For it is evident that the purpose of opening a new account may be to obtain payment of a cheque dishonestly come by, and experience has shown that frauds are not uncommonly perpetrated in this manner.

Notice that the inclusion of 'not negotiable' in the above quotation adds nothing to the analysis. A rogue with a crossed cheque faces the problem of finding a bank account for deposit of the cheque whether it is marked 'not negotiable' or not.

'Account payee only'

[7.99] If the foregoing is correct, it is not every collection of a 'not nego-tiable' cheque for a third party which should put the banker on inquiry. It should be noted that the Manning Committee did not come to the same con-clusion, clearly believing that a 'not negotiable' cheque could not be collected 'without negligence' if it was collected without inquiry for someone other than the named payee: see para 77.

However, drawers of cheques clearly adopt a different view. It was for this reason that a 'crossing' of the form 'account payee' or 'account payee only' became customary. It is clearly an indication by the drawer that the cheque is only to be collected for the named payee. There is probably no difference in the meaning of the two different forms: see *Importers Company Ltd v Westmin-ster Bank Ltd* [1927] 2 KB 297 at 307.

[7.100] The 'crossing' is peculiar in several ways. First, it is clearly directed by the drawer to the collecting bank. But the drawer has no contrac-tual relationship with the collecting bank so why should that bank be obliged to follow the orders of the drawer? Second, the words 'account payee only' are in direct contrast to other parts of the cheque; what sense is to be made of 'Pay to X or order' together with the words 'account payee only'? Or even more ambiguous, 'Pay to X or bearer' together with the words 'account payee only'.

Third, it is clear that no matter what the drawer intended, that the cheque remained legally transferable as the law stood under the BEA and evidence given to the Manning Committee established that many cheques marked 'account payee only' are, in fact, paid to the credit of an account other than that of the named payee: see *National Bank v Silke* [1891] 1 QB 435; Manning Committee Report, paras 68 ff.

[7.101] The view of the Manning Committee was that: '... the crossing "account payee only" does not afford much if any greater protection for the drawer of a cheque than is provided by the present "not negotiable" crossing': para 78.

As a result of this view, the Committee considered that the 'account payee' crossing should receive no statutory approval. In the CPOA, s 53(2) declares that nothing written or placed on a cheque is effective as a crossing other than the general crossing and the 'not negotiable' crossing described in s 53(1), but s 54 describes the effect of a 'crossing' as a direction to the drawee bank. The words 'account payee' are clearly a direction to the collecting bank.

It is thought that the law concerning the 'account payee' and 'account payee only' markings on a cheque has not changed with the introduction of the new Act. The words have always been given force as a result of judicial interpretation combined with banking practice. There is nothing in the new Act which would challenge those interpretations. Indeed, the one peculiarity of the old law was the interpretation that a cheque marked 'account payee only' was still a transferable cheque, but this is now beyond doubt by virtue of s 39 which provides that nothing written on a cheque can make it non-transferable by negotiation.

[7.102] The meaning of the words 'account payee' and 'account payee only' have long been established. There is little doubt that a cheque so crossed requires the collecting bank to make inquiries when collecting for someone other than the named payee. The position is put strongly in *Paget's Law of Banking*, 11th ed, p 454:

> Conclusive evidence of negligence in the collecting banker is, without inquiry, to take a cheque marked with the words 'account payee', or 'account so and so', for an account other than that indicated.

One exception, recognised by Paget, is when the bank is collecting on behalf of a foreign bank which is in turn collecting for its customer. There is, of course, no way that the local bank could know the identity of the person for whom the cheque is being collected. Either such foreign collections must be at the risk of the local bank or an exception to the rule must be made. The law has chosen to make an exception: *Importers Co v Westminster Bank Ltd* [1927] 2 KB 297.

[7.103] It may be that the words have a broader effect at the time when the account is being opened. In *Ladbroke v Todd* [1914–15] All ER 1134, the words should have put the banker on inquiry even though the customer represented that he was the named payee: see [7.85].

How should a bank deal with a cheque which is drawn 'Pay X or bearer' yet which is crossed 'account payee'? In *House Property Co of London Ltd v London County and Westminster Bank* (1915) 84 LJKB 1846 Rowlatt J found that collection without inquiry of such a cheque for the account of a third party disentitled the bank from reliance on the statutory defence. The argument for the bank, dismissed as 'shallow' by the court, was that as the cheque was made payable to 'bearer' they had complied with the instruction to collect for the payee.

[7.104] The words may also be sufficient to put the bank on inquiry when they appear on only one of several cheques collected at the same time. In *National Commercial Banking v Robert Bushby* [1984] 1 NSWLR 559 there were two cheques deposited at the same time. One was crossed 'not negotiable' and made payable to the plaintiff or bearer, the second was payable to plaintiff or order and crossed 'not negotiable' and 'account payee'.

Priestley JA considered it 'elementary' that some inquiry should have been made before collecting a cheque marked 'Not Negotiable – Account Payee'. He also thought that (at 574):

> Had the cheque payable to the plaintiff or bearer been deposited independently of the other, the same comment would not apply to it with the same force ... [but] ... In the absence of explanation there was no reason why two cheques, which taken together appeared to be the property of a third party, should be deposited for credit to the trust account of an accountancy firm. Not

to make some inquiry, before collection of the cheques, appears to me to be negligence as that term is used in s 88D.

A number of factors were said by the bank to enable them to collect the cheques without negligence. These were that the account was a trust account, that the account was conducted in Katoomba where there was a comparatively small business community in which it was known that the reputation of the person who misappropriated the cheque was good and that the account had been conducted over a substantial period to the satisfaction of the bank. The Court of Appeal dismissed these arguments, holding (per Priestley JA at 574) that: '... whether taken singly or in combination, [these factors] do not seem ... to overcome the prima facie situation with which the bank was confronted when the cheques were deposited'.

There was an appeal to the High Court in an attempt to recover from the innocent partner of the accounting firm. The attempt failed. The High Court held that the innocent partner was not liable to the bank either through the operation of s 10 of the Partnership Act or because the firm had received the proceeds of the cheques to the use of the bank: see *National Commercial Banking Corporation of Australia Ltd v Batty* (1986) 160 CLR 251.

[7.105]   A decision of the New Zealand High Court has flown in the face of the perceived settled state of the law. In *New Zealand Law Society v ANZ Banking Group Ltd* [1985] 1 NZLR 280 one Calkin, a solicitor who was also a director of a company called Tina Colliery Ltd, obtained finance from a finance company for the purposes of purchasing two trucks by the company. Under the arrangement, the finance company was to become the owner of the trucks and let them to Tina Colliery under a hire-purchase agreement. The trucks were to be purchased from another company of which Calkin was also a director.

Calkin completed the hire-purchase proposals and turned them over to the finance company in return for two cheques representing the purchase price of the trucks. The cheques were drawn in favour of 'Tina Colliery Ltd or order', crossed 'not negotiable' and 'account payee only'. Calkin paid the cheques into his solicitor trust account and misappropriated the proceeds. The trucks were in fact owned by another finance company and Calkin had no authority or power to make the sale. The finance company made a claim against the Solicitors' Fidelity Guarantee Fund which was settled by the Law Society who were then subrogated to whatever rights the finance company might have had against the collecting banker.

In spite of the fact that there had been no inquiries made by the collecting banker, the court held that the collection had been without negligence. This appeared to be for the sole reason that there was evidence which established that current banking practice was to collect the proceeds of cheques for the credit of solicitor's trust accounts without making inquiries.

With respect, the decision is clearly out of step with settled law and the decision of the New South Wales Court of Appeal is much to be preferred.

The *New Zealand* case is also in conflict with recent authority which concerns the need to make inquiries which will be unlikely to yield useful information: see [7.132].

[7.106] In *Hunter BNZ Finance Ltd v Maloney Pty Ltd* (1993) 18 NSWLR 420, Giles J held that the 'account payee' crossing puts the collecting bank on inquiry even when the cheque appears to be regularly indorsed.

Relationship between the holder and other parties

[7.107] There are a number of cases where the relationship between the customer/holder and some other party on the cheque has been such as to raise the need for inquiry by the collecting banker. The most obvious of these is where the customer is the employee of either the payee or the drawer of the cheque. In either case, there is reason to suspect that the customer has misappropriated the employer's cheque. The matter is so serious for the banker that Weaver and Craigie recommend that when the cheque is drawn by the employer in favour of a third party or when drawn by some third party in favour of the employer the situation is so unsatisfactory that the banker should simply refuse to accept the cheque.

In *Bennett & Fisher Ltd v The Commercial Bank of Australia Ltd* [1930] SASR 26 the plaintiff's general manager had authority to draw cheques on the plaintiff's account. The manager drew and signed a cheque for £250 in favour of 'A or bearer' and crossed the cheque 'not negotiable'. The manager then deposited the cheque into his account with the defendant bank. Although the manager was well known and of good repute and had had an account with the bank for a period of years, the teller asked him what title he had to the cheque. The teller received an assurance from the manager that 'it was all right'. Over a year later, the manager drew several cheques in a similar form which were collected without any inquiry being made.

The Supreme Court of South Australia found that there was a conversion of the cheque in each case and that the bank had not acted without negligence since there had been no proper inquiry made as to the manager's title to the cheques.

[7.108] The cases are not restricted to employer-employee relationships. There are problems whenever the relationship is one which makes it possible for the customer to be misappropriating cheques and where the circumstances are such that the customer would not ordinarily be expected to be depositing cheques of that particular form.

The situation is not, however, always fatal for the bank. In *Orbit Mining and Trading v Westminster Bank Ltd* [1963] 1 QB 794 the customer of the bank was one of the signatories of instruments which were made payable to 'Cash or order'. The mandate from the plaintiff company called for two signatures to each cheque. The customer's co-signatory was going to be abroad for a period of time and was persuaded to leave a number of forms pre-signed. The customer deposited the instruments into his own account with the defendant bank. The Court of Appeal held that there was nothing to put the bank on inquiry since the banker did not know and, in the view of the court, could not be expected to know that the customer was employed by the plaintiff company.

[7.109]   The need for the bank to make inquiries will often depend upon the form of the cheque itself. Thus, in *Morison v London County and Westminster Bank* [1914] 3 KB 356 a clerk by the name of Abbott was authorised to draw cheques on the company's account. He drew some 50 cheques in fraud upon his employer Morison, an insurance broker who carried on business under the name Bruce Morison and Co. The cheques totalled more than £1800 and were all signed by Abbott in the form 'per pro. Bruce Morison & Co, H Abbott'.

The court at first instance held that the bank could not rely upon the statutory defence since the bank knew that Abbott was the manager for the firm and that, on their face, the cheques showed that there should be inquiries before collecting them for Abbott. The Court of Appeal reversed the findings on grounds that are now considered to be incorrect: see [7.121] and the doctrine of 'lulling to sleep'.

- *Director*

[7.110]   The position of a director of a company is, in some respects, similar to that of an employee. When a director is depositing what appears to be a company cheque into a private account, matters precisely similar to those which obtain for the employee situation must be considered.

This can be a matter of particular difficulty when the company is essentially a 'one person' company since it is so easy in such cases for the banker to overlook the legal distinction between the person and the company. Further, in such cases, there is no person to whom inquiries may be addressed since the director/owner of the company who is depositing the cheque into a personal account is unlikely to shed any light on the circumstances and the drawer of such a cheque, if in favour of the company, will be equally unlikely to interfere in the personal financial arrangements between the director and the company.

[7.111]   The difficulty is exemplified by *A L Underwood Ltd v Bank of Liverpool Ltd* [1924] 1 KB 775 where the sole active director of a 'one man company' appropriated company cheques for his own account. If the collecting banker had made the inquiry suggested by the court, it could only have been directed to the sole director of the company and there seems little doubt as to the nature of the reply. However, the Court of Appeal found that once the duty to make inquiry arose that the bank could not conjecture on the nature of the response: see [7.132] for a discussion of the 'useless inquiry'.

• *Fiduciary*

[7.112]   When the customer of the bank is known to be in a fiduciary relationship with another party, great care must be taken in the collection of cheques made payable to the principal or where the cheque is signed by the fiduciary on behalf of the principal. The standard example is *Midland Bank v Reckitt* [1933] AC 1.

Lord Terrington was the plaintiff's solicitor and authorised by an express power of attorney to draw cheques on the account of the plaintiff for the purposes of the plaintiff's financial affairs. The form of the document which conferred the power of attorney was broader than the actual authority: it authorised Lord Terrington to draw 'without restriction'.

Lord Terrington signed several cheques in the plaintiff's name and used them to reduce his own overdraft at the Midland Bank. The House of Lords held that the form of the cheque was sufficient to put the Midland Bank on inquiry and to give them notice that the cheque may not have belonged to their client. Notice that in this case, an inquiry to the paying bank to discover the form of the authority would probably have satisfied the collecting bank's responsibility.

The result will, of course, be the same where a trustee draws on a trust account and deposits the cheque into his or her own personal account: see, for example, *House Property Co of London v London County and Westminster Bank Ltd* (1915) 31 TLR 479; *Harrisons Group Holdings v Westpac* (1989) 51 SASR 32.

• *'Pay A and B or bearer'*

[7.113]   It is clear that a cheque which is crossed 'account payee' and made payable to more than one person should not be collected for the account of only one of the named payees: see [7.99]. It would seem dangerous to collect any order cheque for the account of one of a number of payees, but if the cheque is simply made drawn 'Pay A and B or bearer then there is at least an argument that the collecting bank may safely collect for the account of either A or B. Note that there would be no breach of contract by the paying bank in paying the cheque to either one of the parties. Indeed, the paying bank would probably be safe in paying to any bearer provided it has no external reasons to believe that the cheque is being used to defraud its customer: see the discussion of *Selangor United Rubber Estates Ltd v Cradock* [1967] 2 All ER 1255 at [3.81].

The question was before the court in *Moser v Commercial Banking Corporation of Sydney* (1973) 22 FLR 1 23. A cheque was made payable 'J & A Moser or bearer' and was crossed 'Bank Not Negotiable'. The plaintiff was at the time married to J Moser who took the cheque to the defendant bank and had it collected for his private account. Franki J held that the bank had been negligent in collecting the cheque for the account of only one of the payees without making inquiries (at 126):

... because unless there is some evidence to the contrary it seems clear that one payee was entitled to no more than a joint interest in the cheque ... it seems clear that the mere addition of the words 'or bearer' is not sufficient to justify the bank regarding the details concerning the payee or payees as of little or no consequence.

[7.114]   On the other hand, the fact that the cheque is a bearer cheque is not irrelevant to the question of whether the collecting bank has been negligent. In *Day v Bank of New South Wales* (1978) 19 ALR 32 there were two cheques which were misappropriated by a fraudulent real estate agent and collected by the defendant bank. The circumstances of the collection were similar for both cheques, save that the first was made payable 'F L Day or bearer' and the second was to 'Frank L Day' and the words 'or bearer' were struck out. Both cheques were crossed 'not negotiable'. The Supreme Court of South Australia found that the collection of the first cheque was not negligent, but that the banker should have questioned the indorsement of the other cheque and sought proof of authority. The court also expressed its opinion that contributory negligence is not a defence to an action for conversion: see [7.127].

Priestley JA referred to this in *National Commercial Banking Co of Australia Ltd v Robert Bushby Ltd* [1984] 1 NSWLR 559. Two cheques were deposited together by the rogue. One was an order cheque crossed not negotiable – Account payee only', the other a bearer cheque simply crossed 'not negotiable'. Priestley JA thought that it was 'elementary' that some inquiries should have been made, but that had the bearer cheque been deposited on its own (at 574), 'the same comment would not apply to it with the same force'. It is not clear whether he was influenced by the fact that it was a bearer cheque or that it lacked the 'account payee only' marking.

- *Public officials*

[7.115]   There are cases where cheques have been collected for the customer's private account when the cheques name a public authority as payee or when there is some other indication on the cheques that they are intended for such a purpose.

For example, in *Commissioner of the State Savings Bank of Victoria v Permewan Wright & Co Ltd* (1914) 19 CLR 457 a total of 58 cheques were misappropriated. Thirty-six of the cheques showed clearly that they were to be payable to the Customs Department; the remaining 22 were marked 'duty' or some such similar phrase. The High Court held that the banker had, by not making adequate inquiries, failed to establish the statutory defence with regard to the first class of cheque, but by a bare majority held that the second class of cheque did not sufficiently identify the intended purpose or payee and that the bank did collect these cheques without negligence.

In *Ross v London County Westminster and Parr's Bank Ltd* [1919] 1 KB 678, cheques were stolen by a quartermaster employed by an office established to collect the estates of soldiers killed in the war. The cheques were paid into the rogue's private account. Each cheque was drawn in favour of 'The Officer in

Charge, Estates Office, Canadian Overseas Military Forces'. The cheques were properly indorsed by the payee and then stolen by the rogue. The court held that the bank did not collect without negligence on the grounds that (at 686):

> It is not in accordance with the ordinary course of business that a cheque so drawn and endorsed should be used for the purpose of paying the debt of a private individual. It was highly improbable that the officer in charge of the Estates Office would hand to [the quartermaster] cheques in this form with the intention that the latter should pay them into his private account. It therefore seems to me that when [the quartermaster] presented these cheques with a view to having them credited to his private account a cashier of ordinary intelligence and experience should have been put on inquiry whether or not the credit ought to be made.

[7.116]   Merely asking the customer for an explanation in such a case is unlikely to discharge the duty of the bank, for as Dixon J said in *Commercial Bank of Australia v Flannagan* (1932) 47 CLR 461 at 467: 'to rely exclusively upon the agent's own explanation of his use of such a cheque is to encounter the risk, not to exercise care to avoid it.'

• *Partnerships*

[7.117]   A cheque made payable to a partnership should not be collected for the private account of one of the partners. The arguments which have been used to support the proposition are similar to those which concern the paying in of a company cheque to the private account of a director. In some ways, the banker is more exposed in the partnership context because it may be more difficult to know what inquiries to make and of whom. For example, in the situation encountered in *Baker v Barclays Bank Ltd* [1955] 1 WLR 822 it seems almost impossible to recommend an appropriate action on the part of the banker.

The plaintiff was in a partnership with Bainbridge. They operated a couple of confectionery shops under the name 'Modern Confections'. Although it was a partnership, each of the partners was more or less responsible for the running of one of the shops. There was no written partnership agreement.

Bainbridge misappropriated some cheques worth some £1160 which were payable to Modern Confections. They were paid into a personal bank account by Jeffcott who was innocently assisting Bainbridge in the commission of his frauds. The cheques were indorsed 'Modern Confections, pp G Bainbridge' and also indorsed by Jeffcott. The manager of the defendant bank noticed one of the cheques which had 'MC' as payee and asked Jeffcott to see him. Jeffcott said that Bainbridge was the sole proprietor of MC and that Jeffcott was assisting him in the financial side. Jeffcott also said that Bainbridge owed him £450 and that he hoped that, by his running the financial side, the debt could be reduced. The manager did not ask to see Bainbridge.

Devlin J held that the bank had not made inquiries which were sufficient to establish the statutory defence. There was, one might have thought, little to be gained from further questioning of Jeffcott, but the court held that this was not necessarily the case, for the focus of the inquiry could broaden during the course of an interview.

Also, it seems that the court considered that the bank should treat Bainbridge as a prospective customer since it was known that the money belonged to Bainbridge. In that case, the bank had a duty to interview Bainbridge. Again concerning the futility of such a discussion so far as learning of the misappropriation of the cheques, Devlin J thought that 'discussions of this sort may very well roam more widely': see [7.132] for a discussion of the need to pursue inquiries which may prove to be fruitless.

Although it was open to the bank to prove that nothing further could have been learned, they had not done so (at 838):

> ... if a bank manager fails to make inquiries which he should have made, there is at the very least a heavy burden upon him to show that such inquiries could not have led to any action which could have protected the interests of the true owner.

• *Circumstances of the account*

[7.118]   When should 'unusual' account activity place the banker on inquiry concerning collection of a customer's cheques? In the *Permewan Wright* case, Griffith CJ said (at 479):

> ... what might in the case of an account current in a commercial bank pass as an ordinary payment in of a cheque, subject to a business adjustment between the depositor and the drawer of the cheque, might well be so far out of the ordinary course of a savings bank deposit as to excite suspicion or raise a demand for inquiry in the minds of the officials.

It seems unlikely that the history of the account would ever be the sole factor which disentitled a banker from reliance on the s 95 defence, but it has often been mentioned as one of the circumstances to be considered. So, for example, in *Lumsden v London Trustee Savings Bank* [1971] Lloyd's Rep 114 the customer built an account to just under £900 during the first two months but there followed deposits totalling more than £5000 during the following five weeks. In view of the fact that the bank had failed to make proper inquiries concerning the customer's credentials at the time of the opening of the account, the court considered that this movement of the account should have put the bank on inquiry.

The timing of the deposits may also be a matter for concern. When a customer opens an account with a small cash deposit which is then followed swiftly by large deposits by cheques drawn in favour of third parties, then that is a factor which should put a collecting banker on inquiry.

[7.119]   The operation of the account was one of the factors considered in *Crumplin v London Joint Stock Bank* (1913) 109 LT 856; 19 Com Cas 69. The plaintiff was a stockbroker whose manager misappropriated cheques over a period of time. The cheques were all made payable to Davies, a customer with whom the plaintiff had done a few transactions. The clerk wished to speculate but, knowing that he could not do so in his own name, he fraudulently used the account of Davies. The clerk forged the indorsements on cheques which were then collected for his account by the defendant bank. Until the use of the account by the clerk, there had not been a large number of transactions on the account and nearly all of those transactions involved amounts of less than £30.

On the question of the general operation of the account the court said (at 78):

> The question in this case in my opinion comes down to a very narrow one — whether having regard to the nature and number of the cheques of this description that were paid into Rands' account and to the large proportion which the amount of those cheques bore to the amount of other cheques which were paid in to the credit of the account, those circumstances were such as ought to have put the bank on inquiry? In my opinion this case is very near the line.

[7.120]   The activity of the account was also a significant factor in *Nu-Stilo Footwear Ltd v Lloyds Bank Ltd* (1956) 7 LDAB 121. M was the secretary of the plaintiff company who opened an account under the name of 'E Bauer' with the defendant bank. When opening the account, M described himself as a 'freelance agent' who was only beginning in the business. He named himself under his real name as a referee and gave 'Bauer' favourable references when telephoned by the bank. He also wrote to the bank describing 'Bauer' as a fit and proper person.

M misappropriated some nine cheques which were drawn on the plaintiff's account and made payable either to himself or to third parties. The first cheque was for £172 and was deposited with the bank on the day following the opening of the account. There were no further deposits for a month when a cheque for more than £550 was deposited.

The case is interesting because the court found that there was no negligence in opening the account and that the first cheque was collected without negligence. However, the further cheques were 'out of harmony with the description of [M's] trade or prospects as revealed by him to the bank'. Because of this, the bank could not establish that the cheques had been collected without negligence.

The case was strongly criticised by the editors of the report, and Weaver and Craigie, op cit, pp 505–506 observe that it implies that the banker has a perfect, or at least a very long, memory and to 'engage in speculation as to the likely turnover and profitability of any businessman who may become a customer ...'.

The unusual activity of the account was also a factor in *Lloyds Bank Ltd v Chartered Bank of India, Australia and China* [1929] 1 KB 40; [1928] All ER 285.

Although the banker should be concerned with the occupation of the customer, there is clearly no general duty to be informed of changes in employment or in status: *Orbit Mining and Trading Co Ltd v Westminster Bank Ltd* [1963] 1 QB 794 per Harman LJ.

SOME POSSIBLE DEFENCES RELEVANT TO NEGLIGENCE

[7.121] There have been a number of cases where the collecting bank has argued that even though the collection has not been made without negligence, nevertheless the behaviour of the customer has been such that they should be entitled to the statutory defence or to some form of defence analogous to the defence of contributory negligence in a tort action based on negligence.

'Lulling to sleep'

[7.122] The argument that the banker may be 'lulled to sleep' by the customer began with the decision in *Morison v London County and Westminster Bank* [1914] 3 KB 356. The frauds committed by the clerk Abbott had extended over a number of years. Some of them were known to the owner, others to the staff employed by Morison. Indeed, some of the cheques had been the subject of an arrangement between Abbott and Morison whereby Abbott agreed to repay the sums involved. Abbott had been re-employed after the earliest frauds had been discovered. None of this had been communicated to the defendant bank. Note that this is not the *Greenwood* type of case for the defendant here is the collecting, not the paying, bank. Morison owed no contractual duties to the collecting banker: see *Greenwood v Martins Bank Ltd* [1933] AC 51 and the discussion at [5.21].

The court recognised that there was no contractual duty to notify the collecting bank, but nevertheless found in favour of the bank with regard to cheques which had been misappropriated later in the series of frauds. Buckley LJ in discussing these later frauds said (at 377):

> ... any suspicion which they ought to have had would have been lulled to sleep by the action of Morison himself. Such a sufficient time had then elapsed during which the customer had received back his passbook and his cheques, and had raised no question as to the validity of the cheques, as that the defendants were entitled to assume that there was no cause for suspicion or inquiry. Further, the court seemed to consider that the bank should be entitled to the statutory defence with regard to the later cheques since the circumstances there were merely repetitions of earlier ones which had gone unchallenged.

[7.123] The 'lulling to sleep' doctrine did not survive for long. In *Lloyds Bank Ltd v Chartered Bank of India, Australia and China* [1929] 1 KB 40 Scrutton LJ doubted the grounds of the decision in *Morison's* case, noting that it was inconsistent with the doctrine (at 60):

> ... that in order to act as an estoppel negligence must be the proximate cause of the loss. If my butler for a year has been selling my vintage wines cheap to a small wine-merchant, I do not understand how my negligence in not periodically checking my wine book will be an answer to my action against the wine-merchant for conversion.

[7.124]   The matter was taken beyond all doubt in *Bank of Montreal v Dominion Gresham Guarantee and Casualty Co* [1930] AC 659 when Lord Tomlin said (at 666): 'Neglect of duty does not cease by repetition to be neglect of duty. If there be any doctrine of lulling to sleep it must depend upon and can only be another way of expressing estoppel or ratification.' The defence was also rejected in *Bennett and Fisher Ltd v Commercial Bank of Australia* [1930] SASR 26; see also, *Wilton v Commonwealth Trading Bank of Australia* [1973] 2 NSWLR 644.

Chorley describes the situation best of all (at p 136): 'This theory of "lulling to sleep"' is ... not without its difficulties, since if the banker was already asleep during the earlier period it is really more a case of failure to awaken him than of lulling him to sleep.'

Exigencies of business

[7.125]   Generally speaking, it will not be open to the bank to plead that staffing problems or inadequacies are an excuse for a failure to consider the interests of the true owner of a cheque. The 'hard line' position on this is summarised by the statement of Pickford J in *Crumplin v London Joint Stock Bank Ltd* (1913) 109 LT 856; 19 Com Cas 69: 'It is no defence for a bank to say that they were so busy and had such a small staff that they could not make inquiries when necessary; they must take the consequences.'

A slightly softer line is taken by Bailhache J in *Ross v London County Westminster and Parr's Bank Ltd* [1919] 1 KB 678 in a statement which recognises that the standard to be applied may vary between various classes of employees of a bank:

> I recognise that the same degree of intelligence and care cannot be looked for in a cashier as in an official higher in authority ... I must, however, attribute to the cashiers and clerks of the department the degree of intelligence and knowledge ordinarily required of persons in their positions to fit them for the discharge of their duties.

[7.126]   Weaver and Craigie criticise this line of cases, noting that under modern conditions and pressures the courts' attitude is somewhat unreal when compared with the duties required of the customers. However, that once again seems to overlook that the statutory protection offered by s 95 is a privilege which is extended to bankers and to no other person. It scarcely seems unreasonable for the courts to require a relatively high standard for any banker who is seeking to throw the loss caused by the banker's own conversion onto the innocent owner.

The recent attitude of Lord Scarman in the *Tai Hing* case is also relevant here. Responding to arguments that the court should impose stricter standards on customers because of the nature of modern banking, he said (at 956):

> One can fully understand the comment of Cons JA [of the Hong Kong Court of Appeal] that the banks must today look for protection. So be it. They can increase the severity of their terms of business, and they can use their

influence, as they have in the past, to seek to persuade the legislature that they should be granted by statute further protection. But it does not follow that because they need protection as their business expands the necessary incidents of their relationship with their customers must also change. The business of banking is the business not of the customer but of the bank.

Contributory negligence by the customer

[7.127]   At common law, liability for conversion was very strict. Carelessness on the part of the person whose property was converted was simply not relevant to the question. Phrased another way, there was no obligation on an owner of property to take care of that property. Anyone interfering with the property did so at their peril: *E B Savory & Co v Lloyds Bank Ltd* [1932] 2 KB 122.

On the other hand, in a tort action for negligence, if the defendant could prove that the plaintiff had also been negligent in a way which contributed to the losses suffered by the plaintiff, then the defendant had a complete defence, the defence of contributory negligence. Even when the defendant had been grossly negligent and the plaintiff only slightly negligent, the defence was complete.

This unsatisfactory state of affairs was changed by state Acts which changed contributory negligence from a complete defence to a partial defence. The amount of damages to be awarded is reduced according to the degree of contribution from the plaintiff's own contributory negligence.

[7.128]   Although the Acts were thought to apply only in tort actions for negligence, the New Zealand Court of Appeal held that it applied also to other tort actions. In *Helson v McKenzies Ltd* [1950] NZLR 878 the plaintiff had carelessly left her handbag lying on a counter on the premises of the defendant shop. It was found by the staff who then passed it on to an impostor claiming to be the plaintiff. There was no doubt that the handing of the handbag to a stranger was conversion, but the amount of damages was reduced by virtue of the contributory negligence of the plaintiff.

[7.129]   The matter does not seem to have been tested in an action for the conversion of a cheque until the English decision in *Lumsden v London Trustee Savings Bank* [1971] 1 Lloyd's Rep 114. A fraudulent employee of the plaintiff firm of stockbrokers altered the employers' cheques and paid them into the account of the defendant bank. The fraud was made possible by the careless drawing of the cheques. Note that the careless drawing of the cheque may preclude an action against the paying bank, but there is no contractual obligation owed the collecting bank: see *London Joint Stock Bank v Macmillan and Arthur* [1918] AC 777 and the discussion at [5.21]. Donaldson J took the view that *Helson v McKenzies Ltd* [1950] NZLR 878 correctly stated the law and that the contributory negligence of the plaintiffs, which was assessed at 10 per cent, could be the basis for a reduction in the damages awarded.

Lumsden's case has not been very enthusiastically received. Chorley observes that the decision 'cannot necessarily be regarded as correctly stating the position unless and until confirmed by a higher court', a confirmation which was placed on a statutory footing in the United Kingdom by s 47 of the Banking Act 1979: see R S T Chorley, *Law of Banking*, 6th ed, Sweet & Maxwell, London, 1974, p 136.

[7.130] In Australia, the New South Wales Court of Appeal considered the matter in *Wilton v Commonwealth Trading Bank* [1973] 2 NSWLR 644. The case again concerned a fraudulent clerk who misappropriated cheques which were collected by the defendant bank. Samuels J examined the *Helson* and *Lumsden* cases in some detail and found that the reasons given were 'far from compelling' and refused to follow them. More recently, apportionment based on contributory negligence when the action is for the conversion of a cheque has been refused in Australia in *Tina Motors v ANZ Banking Group* [1977] VR 205 and in *Day v Bank of New South Wales* (1978) 19 ALR 32; see also *Grantham Homes Pty Ltd v Interstate Permanent Building Society Ltd v ANZ Bank* (1979) 37 FLR 191.

The Supreme Court of Victoria has also considered the question of contributory negligence. Noting the existing Australian authorities, the court found that it was not appropriate to re-examine the state of the law. The court also noted the desirability of maintaining a consistent approach in Australia to questions of liability on bills and cheques and that, if alterations were to be made, they must come from parliament. It was significant that the CPOA had not introduced any changes to the principle: *Australian Guarantee Corporation Ltd v Commissioner of the State Bank of Victoria* [1989] VR 617.

[7.131] The matter cannot, however, be considered as fully settled. In *Mercedes-Benz (NSW) Pty Ltd v ANZ and National Mutual Royal Savings Bank Ltd* (Supreme Court, NSW, Comm Div, (Palmer AJ), 5 May 1992, unreported) Palmer AJ expressed support for a 'principle' that comes very close to acknowledging contributory negligence as an ingredient in a conversion action. Palmer AJ cited with approval Holt CJ in *Hern v Nichols* (1701) 1 Salk 289; 90 ER 1154: '… it is more reasonable that he that employs and puts a trust and confidence in the deceiver should be a loser than a stranger.' Palmer AJ warned that such broad statements of principle 'do not provide a panacea for the resolution of all claims arising out of the frauds of employees' and that each case 'will ultimately depend upon its own facts and circumstances'. In his view, however, the principle does 'provide the light by which one is able to tell at least some of the wood from the trees'. For a full discussion, see Tyree, 'Bad Business Makes Hard Cases: *Mercedes-Benz v NMRB*' (1992) 3 *JBFLP* 192 and '*Mercedes-Benz v ANZ and NMRB* (Pt 2)', (1992) 3 *JBFLP* 277.

Giles J also doubted the existence of the rule against contributory negligence in *Commonwealth Development Bank v McDonald* (NSW SC, 7 Nov 1991, unreported). He noted that it had not been the subject of any authoritative High Court judgment. On the other hand, the defence was rejected by O'Keefe CJ in *Liquor Distributors Pty Ltd v State Bank of NSW* (SC NSW, (O'Keefe CJ), 28 March 1994, unreported).

For an analysis of various implementations of a contributory negligence rule, see Tyree, 'Contributory Negligence in Cheque Collections' (1994) 5 *JBFLP* 128.

Inquiries which would have yielded nothing

[7.132] Suppose that the circumstances are such as to put the collecting bank on inquiry, but that the only reasonable inquiries would be fruitless. Is it possible for the bank to use this fact as a substitute for making the inquiries? Or, put another way, has the bank collected the cheque without negligence if it can be shown that the only reasonable inquiries which could have been made would have yielded nothing?

There have been differing judicial views on the question. On one hand, there are views similar to that expressed by Bankes LJ in *A L Underwood Ltd v Barclays Bank Ltd* [1924] 1 KB 775 (at 789):

> I feel satisfied that the obvious inquiry whether the company had not got its own banking account would have put a stop to the fraudulent system adopted by Underwood, and I do not think that it lies in the mouth of the appellants to say that an inquiry would have been useless.

Similar expressions may be found in *E B Savory & Co v Lloyds Bank Ltd* [1932] 2 KB 122; *Baker v Barclays Bank Ltd* [1955] 1 WLR 822; *Lumsden v London Trustee Savings Bank* [1971] 1 Lloyd's Rep 114; *Hunter BNZ Finance Ltd v C G Maloney Pty Ltd* (1988) 18 NSWLR 420.

[7.133] The other view is that there must be some demonstrable connection between the failure to make inquiries and the loss suffered by the customer. Thus, Diplock LJ in *Marfani & Co Ltd v Midland Bank Ltd* [1968] 1 WLR 968 said (at 977):

> It does not constitute any lack of reasonable care to refrain from making inquiries which it is improbable will lead to detection of the potential customer's dishonest purpose if he is dishonest, and which are calculated to offend him and maybe drive away his custom if he is honest.

The most recent opinion of the English court is found in *Thackwell v Barclays Bank plc* [1986] 1 All ER 676. While acknowledging the view expressed by Diplock LJ in *Marfani*, the court relied on authority mentioned above to express the view that (at 684):

> ... I would hold that as a matter of law it is no answer for a bank who have been found guilty of negligence in the collection of a cheque to prove that, even had the question the omission to ask which constitutes such negligence been asked, a reassuring answer would have been given.

[7.134] The defendant bank in *National Commercial Banking Co of Australia Ltd v Robert Bushby Ltd* [1984] 1 NSWLR 559 argued that had there been an inquiry by the bank that the rogue would have been able to give answers which would have satisfied the bank and the bank's duty to make inquiries. Priestley JA said (at 575):

> I think that it is a complete answer to this submission to point out that it is simply not known 'what responses [the customer] would have made to an

inquiry from the Bank ... There is nothing in the evidence to indicate one way or the other whether he was a glib and confident person as well as being dishonest.

Priestley JA clearly contemplated that it was at least possible that the bank might show that the inquiries would have not protected the interest of the true owner of the cheque and so escape liability. However, the speculative nature of the exercise and the need to establish the likely answers of the various parties of whom inquiries might have been made make the task of the bank a very difficult one.

[7.135] Weaver and Craigie express the view that the *Marfani* approach is to be preferred as 'the more rational and less draconian of the two alternatives' and believe that it is the view which will prevail in Australia: Weaver and Craigie, op cit, p 323. By 'less draconian' they appear to mean that it favours the banker, for it is the other view which is less draconian to the customer whose cheque has been converted. In truth, it is submitted that the argument for a causal connection between the negligence and the loss is simply a confusion caused by the words 'without negligence' in the statutory defence. The tort is conversion, not negligence, and the defence is a privilege which is extended to bankers only at the expense of customers.

The question of the 'useless inquiry' arose in *Hunter BNZ Finance Ltd v C G Maloney Pty Ltd* (1988) 18 NSWLR 420. Although not convinced that an inquiry would have been useless, Giles J, after a thorough review of the authorities, expressed preference for the *Thackwell* view.

REDUCTION OF DAMAGES IN CONVERSION

[7.136] Just as the 'equitable defence' may protect the banker in certain circumstances where payments have been made to the plaintiff's benefit, so it may be possible to obtain a reduction in damages if it may be shown that part of the sums obtained by the conversion went to the plaintiff's use. However, it will not usually be easy to establish that the precise money which went to the plaintiff was the money which was obtained from the misappropriated cheques.

The problem for the banker is stated precisely by Scrutton J in *Lloyds Bank v The Chartered Bank of India, Australia and China* [1929] 1 KB 40 at 61:

> It seems to me clear that damages in conversion may be reduced by the return of the chattel converted; ... But when you come to the conversion of a cheque, it is not at all clear how the fact that one of the persons converting has after conversion paid to the plaintiff not the cheque converted, but some currency, not necessarily the currency derived from the cheque converted, can be treated without more as a reduction of the damages for the original conversion ... But whether any particular payment to the plaintiff by one of the wrongdoers reduces the damages for conversion must depend on the facts of each case, and cannot be settled by mere proof of receipt without more.

This was cited by Sellers J to deny a reduction in damages when the bank argued that M had drawn on the account to make some payments to the plaintiff: *Nu-Stilo Footwear Ltd v Lloyds Bank Ltd* (1956) 7 LDAB 121.

[7.137] The question came before the New South Wales Court of Appeal in *Associated Midland Corporation Ltd v Bank of New South Wales* [1983] 1 NSWLR 533. A cheque belonging to the plaintiff had been misappropriated by T and collected by the defendant bank. The peculiarity of the case is that T used the sums so obtained to pay M, the original payee of the cheque. The court held that in the circumstances, which were more complex than the brief summary given here, the payments made by the tortfeasor T to discharge a liability of the true owner of the cheque, the plaintiff, could be taken into account in determining the measure of damages in an action in conversion against the other tortfeasor, the bank.

The decision is in keeping with a general move to bring damages in conversion within the general principles that the purpose of damages is to compensate for actual losses. Since the plaintiff in this case suffered no actual losses from the conversion itself, there seems little reason to allow recovery of the amount of the converted cheque: see the discussion of Mahoney JA at 552. The case went on appeal to the High Court but the issue of damages was not discussed: *Associated Midland Corporation Ltd v Bank of New South Wales* (1984) 51 ALR 841.

[7.138] In *Hunter BNZ Finance v ANZ Banking Group* [1990] VR 41 the defendant argued that certain payments made should have the effect of reducing their liability. The court noted that the prima facie measure of damages is the face value of the converted cheques but that this might be reduced by payments made to the drawer of the cheque by the converter. However, for this reduction to apply the source of the payments must be shown, and it is relevant that the payments be made out of the proceeds of the conversion. Where the source of the payments is not clear or where it is clear that they are not made from the proceeds, there will be no reduction in the quantum of damages. An appeal on the quantum of damages was dismissed: [1991] 2 VR 407. See also, Luntz, 'Conversion of Finance Company Cheques' (1990) 1 *JBFLP* 190.

INSTRUMENTS TO WHICH THE DEFENCE APPLIES

[7.139] Section 95 provides a statutory defence to a bank which collects a 'cheque'. This expression will include a bank cheque by virtue of s 5, but suppose that the instrument is not strictly speaking a 'cheque' because of some technical deficiency of form. There are some judicial suggestions that the defence is not available.

The court found that the instrument in *Orbit Mining & Trading Co Ltd v Westminster Bank Ltd* [1963] 1 QB 794 which was in the form of a cheque but made payable to 'cash or order' was not a cheque under the BEA definition of 'cheque'. However, under the English Cheques Act 1957 it was possible for the collecting bank to rely on s 4(2)(b): 'Any document issued by a customer of a banker which, though not a bill of exchange, is intended to enable a person to obtain payment from that banker of the sum mentioned in the document.'

This section, incidentally, shows that the legislature believed that it is possible that a banker may be sued in conversion even though the instrument is not a negotiable instrument. Compare with the decisions in *Arrow Transfer Co Ltd v Royal Bank of Canada* (1972) 27 DLR (3d) 81 and *Koster's Premier Pottery v Bank of Adelaide* (1981) 28 SASR 355 and [7.5].

The problem is by no means purely hypothetical, since there is also authority for the proposition that the defence is not available when the cheque has been discharged by means of a material alteration: *Slingsby v Westminster Bank Ltd (No 2)* [1931] 2 KB 583, 586; *Bank of Ceylon v Kulatilleke* (1957) 59 Ceylon NLR 188. If that is correct, then the collecting bank is deprived of its statutory defence under conditions when it may need it the most.

The position of the bank may be strengthened under the CPOA since a material alteration no longer 'avoids' the cheque as provided by the previous legislation. By s 78(2) the cheque is 'discharged' by a fraudulent material alteration but, presumably, remains a cheque.

NON-BANK COLLECTIONS

[7.140]   For some time, building societies and other financial institutions have accepted cheques for deposit to the credit of their customer's account. Since the institutions are not banks, their liability for conversion was the same as that of any other member of the community.

The CPOA extends the statutory defences to 'non-bank financial institutions' as that term is defined in the Act: see Chapter 5. The CPOA also provides for a statutory duty to present the cheque promptly, but, as in the case of the duty on banks, the duty probably existed independently of the statute under the general law of agency.

DUTY TO PRESENT PROMPTLY

[7.141]   Section 97 provides that a non-bank financial institution which accepts a customer's cheque for collection shall ensure that the cheque is duly presented for payment as soon as is reasonably practicable. As in the case of a bank, in the event that it fails to do so, it is liable to the holder for any loss which the holder thereby suffers.

Section 97(3) sets out the rules to be used to determine if the institution has performed its duty of presentment. The rules are in all respects similar to the rules of s 67(2) and the comments made about that section apply here: see Chapter 5.

DEFENCE AGAINST CONVERSION

[7.142]   Institutions which are 'non-bank financial institutions' within the meaning of the CPOA have been given a statutory defence to conversion which is similar to that given to banks. Section 98 of the Act reproduces the first two subsections of s 95.

In applying the law concerning collection of cheques, one obvious problem is the definition of 'customer' for the purposes of NBFIs. The problem is partly solved by s 103(2) which decrees that members of building societies and of credit unions shall be taken to be customers of those institutions: see [2.15].

Since the need for indorsement is dispensed with when the name of payee is the same or similar to that of the customer, the CPOA gives non-bank financial institutions the same privileged status as banks with regard to rights over unindorsed order cheques for which the institution has given value. See the discussion of s 96 at [7.66].

CHAPTER 8

OTHER PAYMENT SYSTEMS

GIRO SYSTEMS

[8.1] If the legal nature of a cheque is reconsidered for a moment, it will be recalled that it is an order from the drawer of the cheque to his or her banker, an order to make a payment to a named person or to that person's order. When considered as such, it must be viewed as somewhat peculiar that the cheque, that is, the order, is then sent not to the banker, but rather to the intended recipient of the funds. Of course, the reason for this is the historical identification of the cheque as a species of negotiable instrument which is valuable in its own right quite apart from its value as an order to the banker.

If the order could be given directly to the banker, then many of the opportunities for fraud would simply disappear, for a significant number of cheque frauds involve the interception of the cheque between the time it leaves the drawer and the time when it should be received by the payee.

This simple idea of directing the order to the banker directly rather than through the payee is the basis for a system of payment which has been used successfully in European countries for some years. The system, which has also been successfully introduced into the United Kingdom, is known as the GIRO. Since the GIRO system is particularly easy to implement in a totally electronic form, it is expected that more and more payments will be made by GIRO-type payment orders. The bank clearing system already handles a significant number of such payments and the number may be expected to grow as the handling of cheques becomes more and more expensive.

GIRO SYSTEMS GENERALLY

[8.2] It is probably easier to describe the paper-based system of GIRO payments at the outset. Once the paper system is understood, the electronic form presents few new problems.

A typical GIRO payment requires the person who wishes to make the payment, the payer, to instruct his or her bank concerning the details of the payment to be made. In the typical implementation of the GIRO system, this is done by writing on a printed form the amount of the payment to be made, the account which is to be debited, the bank which is to receive the payment and the details of the account at that bank which is to be credited.

The terminology which is used in describing GIRO systems varies somewhat. The bank at which the transaction is initiated is usually called the paying bank or the transferring bank. The bank at which the account is to be credited is called the recipient bank. The person initiating the transfer of the type described in the preceding paragraph is called the payer and the person whose account is to be credited is the payee.

[8.3]   There are some variations on the basic transfer described above. In the UK, there are two separate GIROs in operation, one, the National Girobank, operated by the Post Office and a bank GIRO which is operated by the major trading banks. By agreement between the parties, it is possible to initiate the transfer from any one of the institutions participating in either of the GIROs. Further, the payment may be initiated by a person who does not maintain a bank account by lodging the appropriate sum with the transferring bank. This is a valuable feature for low income families who traditionally had to resort to more expensive forms of payment.

A further variation on the basic theme is the use of magnetic media to give instructions to the bank. This may be done, for example, by larger institutions which have a large number of relatively small payments to make on a periodic basis. The instructions for the transfers are encoded in a computer readable format on the magnetic media and delivered to the institution's bank which then makes the payments in accordance with the instructions. The use of such payment mechanisms to meet payroll obligations results in a substantial reduction in the number of cheques which must be used.

[8.4]   A more significant departure from the transactions described above is the possibility of the payee initiating the transaction. The obvious possibility for abuse means that strict controls must be implemented, but provided that this is done, the procedure may result in substantial savings in system costs. A typical use of this system of 'direct debit' is the payment of insurance premiums or of other regular payments which are likely to be of varying amounts. In such a situation, the standing order is not appropriate but the institutional payee may prepare instructions on magnetic media which are then delivered to the recipient bank.

[8.5]   Note that a GIRO system requires a system of clearing. It would be prohibitively expensive to arrange for actual cash movements to accompany each transfer order. Further, in a GIRO system, the method of settlement will almost certainly be by accounts held by the participating institutions with the central bank of the country.

For some years the Australian banks operated a tape clearing system known as CEMTEX (Central Magnetic Tape Exchange). Tapes prepared by each of the banks contained transfer orders from that bank to others. The

CEMTEX computers would take each of these tapes as inputs and 'unravel' the instructions to produce tapes which provided details of the orders which each bank was receiving. The CEMTEX system was closed when the number of banks became small enough that direct interchange was more feasible. The demise of CEMTEX was also hastened by the use of direct electronic messages between bank computers instead of recording the messages on tape. The CEMTEX system was the equivalent of the 'Bankers' Automated Clearing Service' (BACS) which operates in the United Kingdom: see Ellinger and Lomnicka, *Modern Banking Law*, 2nd ed, Clarendon Press, Oxford, 1994 p 432.

CREDIT TRANSFERS

[8.6]   The legal principles of the GIRO system are of general application. Many payments are made both domestically and internationally by methods which have the same functional and legal structure although they are not based on paper orders.

The basic transaction described above is called a 'credit transfer'. The transaction is initiated by the payer and is often described as 'pushing' the funds from the transferor to the transferee. The transferring bank advises, possibly with the assistance of an intermediary bank or other institution, the recipient bank of the transfer. The recipient bank then credits the account of the payee and notifies the payee of that fact.

The feature which distinguishes the general credit transfer from the corresponding transaction in a GIRO system is that there is no necessary need for an existing clearing system. Further, in many circumstances the method of settlement between the banks may be decided on a case-by-case basis. If the system is to handle a large number of payments with minimal error, then a sophisticated method of transmitting messages between banks is needed. This message system is at the heart of any modern funds transfer system.

[8.7]   In an international transfer, the recipient bank must be reimbursed in some way for the amount which is to be credited to the account of the payee. The most common way for this to be done is either through the crediting and debiting of accounts held by the transferring bank and the recipient bank on behalf of the other. Thus, an Australian bank may keep an account in American dollars with a New York bank. When a credit transfer is arranged on behalf of an Australian payer and a New York payee, the Australian bank will send the appropriate credit order to the New York bank but will also include an indication that the account held by the New York bank is to be debited. Alternatively, the Australian bank may indicate that the account held by it on behalf of the New York bank will be credited. In the language of international banking, the first arrangement is a debit of the 'nostro' account, the second is a credit to the 'vostro' account.

If the banks do not hold mutual nostro/vostro accounts then settlement will necessarily involve a third bank. This could be a bank at which both the transferring and the recipient banks hold accounts or it could be a more complex arrangement.

DEBIT TRANSFERS

[8.8] In a debit transfer, the transaction is initiated by the payee. In international transactions, the debit transfer will nearly always be accompanied by a bill of exchange or other negotiable instrument and the legal aspects of the transfer tend to be dominated by the law applicable to the instrument. However, there is no logical need for the instrument and a debit transfer may follow the general principles of the GIRO direct debit. Again, means of settlement between the participating institutions will need to be identified and agreed upon.

One of the reasons that the debit transfer is usually accompanied by a negotiable instrument is that there is a very fundamental commercial difference between the credit and the debit transfer. In the credit transfer, there is no need for any institution to concern themselves with the solvency of the payer. When the advice is received to credit the account of the payee, the payer has either placed the money with the transferring bank or that bank is willing to grant credit to the payer. In either case, the recipient bank is unconcerned with the financial position of the payer. Another way of putting it is that the solvency of the payer is relevant only to the initiation of the transaction. By contrast, the direct debit transaction relies upon the solvency of the payer to be completed. Until that time, it is possible that the participants may need to 'unwind' the transaction and so to rely upon the credit and the liability of prior parties to the transaction. When that occurs, the law relating to negotiable instruments makes the procedures more reliable and the liabilities more certain.

[8.9] The UK Court of Appeal in *Esso Petroleum Co Ltd v Milton* [1997] 2 All ER 593 has held that in modern commercial practice cancellation of a direct debit facility is similar to countermanding payment by cheque. It followed that set off could not normally constitute a defence to a claim following a cancelled direct debit. The majority of the court considered that the same principles applied as those in *Nova (Jersey) Knit Ltd v Kammgarn Spinnerei GmbH* [1977] 2 All ER 463. Whereas 20 years ago cheques were used to provide the commercial equivalent of cash, the modern mechanism for handling what are effectively cash sales on a large scale is the direct debit system. Both members of the court conceded that the principle requires further consideration and perhaps modification, but approved of the basic principle.

EFT SYSTEMS

[8.10] The term 'electronic funds transfer' refers to a number of related systems which have as their common characteristic the use of computer technology and as their common effect a reduction in the growth of the amount of paper which is involved in the payments system.

DOMESTIC EFT SYSTEMS

MICR CHEQUES

[8.11]   The earliest use of computers in the payment system was concerned not with the elimination of paper but with the efficient handling of it. Cheques are printed on forms which contain information which may be read by machines and processed by computers. The cheques are known as MICR cheques, the adjective being an acronym for magnetic ink character recognition, the strangely shaped numbers and letters which are now familiar to all bank customers.

When the MICR chequebook is issued to the customer, the MICR figures already on the cheque contain information which identifies the drawee bank and branch and the account information of the customer. In order to make possible machine handling and accounting, other information must be added to the cheque after it has been drawn. Consequently, the collecting bank adds MICR figures which identify the amount of the cheque, the branch of the collecting bank and the account for which the cheque is being collected. Because of the consequences of a mistake when this information is added, it is to all intents and purposes added twice and the results compared for conformity.

Since the deposit slips are also MICR coded, the procedure supplies enough information for the accounting and the clearing process to be completed by a single computer process. There is little doubt that the cheque system could not have achieved anything like the volume of cheques now processed without the aid of the MICR system.

MONEY TRANSFERS

[8.12]   On the other hand, processing the paper in the cheque system remains one of the most costly features of the system. In those circumstances where it is possible to dispense with the paper there are substantial opportunities for saving transaction costs. Direct messages between bank computers allow for both credit and debit transfers. Payers with suitable equipment who have large numbers of payments to be made on a regular basis are permitted and encouraged to use the system of credit transfers. Similarly, debit transfers are used when it is possible to make the appropriate safeguards against abuse.

ATMs

[8.13]   The use of electronic banking methods is often described as a move toward the 'cashless society', but the most common form of electronic banking has achieved its popularity not by eliminating cash but by making it easier to obtain. The automatic teller machine (ATM) is now familiar to most bank customers. It is operated by means of a card which contains machine readable information concerning the customer's account and a personal identification number (PIN). By inserting the card and keying the correct PIN, the user of the machine may make certain banking transactions, the most common of which is the withdrawal of cash from an account.

POS

[8.14] The final stage of development in an EFT system is to remove the need for cash entirely. In the point of service (POS) system, there is a computer terminal at the retail or service outlet which is connected directly with the computers of the bank or other service organisation which operates the system. By means of the card-PIN combination described above, the customer is able to order immediate payment to be made for the goods or services. The retailer or other service provider is assured of same day payment.

POS systems make large computing and communications demands and so are expensive to install. They are likely to be preferred by financial institutions because of the elimination of the float and they may be preferred by retailers if the cost of the transaction is not too large. It is difficult to see why they should be preferred by customers unless the costs of credit cards are increased so as to make the customer bear the costs of the extended credit which until recently has been available free.

INTERNATIONAL EFT SYSTEMS

[8.15] In the international transfer of funds, electronic devices are used in ways which are slightly different from the domestic applications. As in the domestic systems, the computers and other communications equipment function solely as a message transmission system. However, because of the need to solve individual problems of settlement the messages are more complex and, consequently, more likely to contain errors. The computer messages replace telex or postal messages only because of their speed or because of the system standardisation which reduces the possibilities and chances of error.

By far the most significant of these message systems is that operated by the Society for Worldwide Interbank Financial Telecommunications (SWIFT). All SWIFT messages are passed first to a regional 'condenser' and then by satellite to the central 'switch' in Brussels where they are stored (if required) and re-routed to their destination. They are received, again by a regional centre and then forwarded to the destination bank. Messages must contain prescribed information and be in a prescribed format. The SWIFT system is so reliable and inexpensive that it is sometimes used to transfer funds from one Australian bank to another in the same city.

ELECTRONIC CLEARING SYSTEMS

[8.16] There are several large EFT systems which function as clearing systems and sometimes as settlement mechanisms for certain types of payments. Payments handled by these systems are typically very large and are restricted to payments between participants of the system.

CHIPS/CHAPS

[8.17] The best known of these systems is the CHIPS system in New York. CHIPS is an acronym for Clearing House for Interbank Payments System. The operation of the CHIPS system was described in some detail in *Delbrueck v Manufacturers Hanover Trust Co* 464 F Supp 989 (SDNY 1979), affd 609 F 2d 1047 (2d Cir 1979).

The CHIPS system has a curious rule which will be discussed in more detail below. In certain circumstances, the transferring bank is entitled to call back an ordered credit transfer. The effect is to 'unwind' certain transactions. In such circumstances, the parties must consider that the effect of a CHIPS transfer is conditional until the time allowed for revocation has expired.

The CHAPS system (Clearing House Automated Payments System) in London operates in a fashion which is quite similar to the CHIPS operation, but the rules consider a credit transfer to be irrevocable once communicated.

BITS

[8.18]   The major Australian trading banks have recently installed the Bank Interchange and Transfer System (BITS). The BITS system differs from CHIPS and CHAPS in that it is a decentralised 'gateway' system. This merely means that each bank has its own computer which is connected to the other three and which serves as a message control centre. The advantages of this system are that there is no significant central administration or overhead and, since the communications are all bank-to-bank, the level of security is high.

BITS is designed to facilitate 'high value' transfers, currently defined as payments of $10,000 or more. Institutions other than the major trading banks are currently excluded from direct access to the network but may enter into agency arrangements with the participants.

Available information is somewhat confusing concerning the finality rules of the network. It is said that 'subject to prudential safeguard mechanisms, a [receiving bank] either credits the beneficiary's account or forwards the payment message to another member ...'. On the other hand, settlement 'is effected as usual through the Reserve Bank in accordance with the Australian Clearing House Association Rules': *BITS, The Bank Interchange and Transfer System, An Overview* prepared by the BITS Secretariat.

RITS

[8.19]   The Reserve Bank Information and Transfer System (RITS) is owned and operated by the Reserve Bank. Its purpose is to allow government securities to be transferred and settled simultaneously.

AUSTRACLEAR

[8.20]   AUSTRACLEAR is owned and operated by its shareholders which are the major participants in the money market. It is used for the registration and trading of money market securities. For a discussion of AUSTRACLEAR and its original trading rules, see Tyree, 'Commercial Bills' in Austin and Vann (eds), *The Law of Public Company Finance*, Law Book Co, Sydney, 1986, p 312.

THE CLEARING AND SETTLEMENT SYSTEM

THE CLEARING SYSTEM

[8.21]   It is estimated that there are some 900 million cheques drawn each year in Australia at the current time: *The Australian Payments System*, Australian Payments System Council, Sydney, 1987. This is some three times the number that were drawn 20 years ago when the government convened the Manning Committee to consider changes to the law of cheques. During most of the intervening years, the cheque was the only significant non-cash form of payment instrument and it was expected to remain the dominant form of non-cash payment for the foreseeable future if dominance is measured in terms of dollar value. However, the growth of EFT has been faster than envisaged and has eclipsed cheque payments; see *Payment Systems in Australia*, Bank for International Settlements, Basle, 1994; see also the annual reports of the Australian Payments Systems Council.

THE CONCEPT OF A CLEARING SYSTEM

[8.22]   The cheque could not have achieved such a position without the existence of a sophisticated clearing system. In the early days of the cheque, clerks from each bank would sort the cheques which had been lodged for collection with their bank into groups according to the bank on which they were drawn. Each of these bundles would then be taken to the appropriate drawee bank for payment.

It is said that it was the clerks themselves who first recognised the futility of this procedure and began to meet in some central location to exchange their bundles of cheques. At first these meetings took place on street corners, but they soon chose a more salubrious venue at a local public house. In 1773, the London bankers rented a central location to serve as the clearing centre.

CLEARING AS AN ACCOUNTING PROCEDURE

[8.23]   Clearing is essentially an accounting process. Where three or more banks have cheques drawn on each other, it is pointless that each should deliver the cheques drawn on the others and receive the full amounts in cash. It is far more sensible to exchange cheques drawn one on another and set off the amounts so that only the net figures need to be exchanged. In a perfect world, Bank A would have cheques drawn on Bank B which would precisely equal in value the cheques held by Bank B which were drawn on Bank A. In an imperfect world, the sums differ, but it is still sensible for the debtor bank to pay only the difference to the creditor bank.

Clearing must be distinguished from settlement. While clearing is essentially a sorting and accounting process, settlement refers both to the method of payment of the resulting net sums and the payment itself. In Australia, settlement has been effected by cheques drawn on special accounts kept by each bank with the Reserve Bank of Australia. The new payments system which is in the process of implementation will provide for other means of settlement, but the Reserve Bank is still a central player in the process: see [8.39]ff.

[8.24]   The most important factor in designing or evaluating a clearing system is the management of 'exposure'. This expression refers to the amounts owed by an institution to the totality of other institutions in the clearing system. The larger the 'exposure' the greater the problems should the institution fail to meet its payment obligations.

The failure of an institution in a clearing system is a catastrophic event, and the system must have means of managing the resulting chaos. Should there be some form of 'unwinding' of payments? Or is it better that the payments should stand with the losses shared by the institutions? Or should the payments stand with the losses falling on the receiving institution alone?

[8.25]   To illustrate the operation of the system, suppose that X orders the A Bank to make a payment to Y via Y's bank, the B Bank. This could either be a direct credit order, or it could be in the form of a cheque drawn by X on A Bank, payable to Y and deposited in B Bank. In the clearing process, A Bank has an obligation to B Bank. Suppose that A Bank fails before settlement.

In the 'unwinding' model, the obligation of A Bank to B Bank is cancelled, any obligation or payment to Y is cancelled, and the liability of X to make payment to Y is revived (if, indeed, it was ever extinguished). The risk of failure is on the customer-payer of the failed institution. Payment from X to Y cannot be considered to be absolute or complete until the settlement process is completed.

In the 'absolute payment' model, the payment by X to Y stands and the loss caused by A Bank's failure is born by B Bank in the first instance. Payment from X to Y is considered to be complete at the time when the order is accepted: see [8.66]ff. The problem with this model is that the total obligations incurred by A Bank to B Bank (and, of course, to all other institutions in the clearing system) may be very large, for it is not just the payment from X to Y which is in question but all of the payments ordered by customers of A Bank to customers of B Bank. The losses suffered by B Bank may be so large as to prevent B Bank from meeting its obligations. And so on.

[8.26]   These are not idle questions, for as the number of participants in the clearing and settlement system grow we can expect there to be failures from time to time. The Reserve Bank has a duty to depositors (see [1.12]ff) but there is no duty, and probably no power, to ensure that any individual institution survives bad management. The method of allocating losses of a financial failure should not expose other participants to risks so large or, more importantly, so unexpected, as to cause a domino effect resulting in the destruction of the financial system. In addition, the answer to these design problems will influence the time at which individual payments may be considered as final and binding: see the discussion of finality of payment at [8.66]ff.

NEW AUSTRALIAN SETTLEMENT STRUCTURE

[8.27]   Settlement may be by 'deferred net settlement' or by 'real time gross settlement' (RTGS). In the deferred net settlement system, payment instructions are 'exchanged' during the day and settled the following morning by calculating the net amounts due from or to each of the parties. Settlement is achieved by adjusting accounts held with the Reserve Bank. While net deferred settlement is efficient, it exposes the system to extreme dislocation should one of the parties fail overnight. The risk that an institution might fail before settlement of outstanding claims is known as 'settlement risk'.

RTGS permits significant reduction of settlement risk. Each payment is settled during the day as it is made. The clearing rules provide that a payment is not final until such time as settlement occurs.

[8.28]   Both netting and RTGS reduce certain risks inherent in the payments system. Netting the gross obligations between parties substantially reduces the exposure should one of the parties default. However, there are some reasons to doubt that netting could withstand a challenge from the liquidator of a failed financial institution. Netting agreements have the effect of giving participants preferential treatment over other non-secured creditors. This is precisely what bankruptcy and insolvency legislation was designed to prevent. The court in *British Eagle* held that a netting agreement was void as against public policy: *British Eagle & International Airlines Ltd v Compagnie Nationale Air France* [1975] 2 All ER 390; see A L Tyree, 'Legal Aspects of Electronic Clearing and Settlement' in *Banking Law and Practice*, Proceedings of the 13th Annual Conference of the Banking Law Association, Surfers Paradise, 30 May 1996, p 289.

[8.29]   Should a financial institution fail, its obligations under a net deferred settlement scheme may also be subordinated to s 16 of the Banking Act. This section provides that the Australian assets of the institution must be first applied to meet deposit liabilities: see the discussion at [1.15]ff. The so-called 'zero hour rule' of winding up also causes problems for a deferred net settlement system: see the discussion in A L Tyree, 'Legal Aspects of Electronic Clearing and Settlement' in *Banking Law and Practice*, Proceedings of the 13th Annual Conference of the Banking Law Association, Surfers Paradise, 30 May 1996, p 289.

[8.30]   Unfortunately, it is not feasible to entirely replace the deferred net settlement system. Where the payment system is concerned with large numbers of relatively small payments, real time gross settlement is simply not economical with today's technology.

The federal government has announced the introduction of legislation to remove the uncertainties inherent in the deferred net settlement scheme. Proposed legislation will validate netting arrangements in the payment system and subordinate depositors' claims to those of participating institutions. It is also proposed that certain payments may be 'unwound' in the event that the paying institution fails before settlement.

At the same time, a RTGS system for 'large' payments is being introduced. It should be operational in 1998.

The combination of a net deferred settlement system for low value payments, supplemented by risk-reducing legislation, and a RTGS system for large value payments will be a substantial improvement in Australia's payment system.

THE AUSTRALIAN PAYMENTS CLEARING ASSOCIATION

[8.31]   Until December 1993, clearing of cheques was done through the Australian Clearing House Association (ACHA). ACHA was owned by the major banks and membership of the clearing house was restricted to banks, although not all banks were members. The ACHA arrangement was unsatisfactory for several reasons, but the most important was that the exclusion of non-bank institutions became anomalous as credit unions and building societies became more 'bank-like' in their operations. Although the Cheques and Payment Orders Act 1986 authorised these institutions to operate cheque-like instruments, the exclusion from the existing clearing system made the instruments economically unattractive.

In their search for payment mechanisms to attract depositors, the non-bank institutions proceeded in two ways. The most important was their emphasis on electronic banking, the other was various 'agency' arrangements with clearing banks. Electronic banking is discussed in more detail in Chapter 9, but its increased use by both banks and non-banks led to pressures to have a single organisation which would oversee the clearing of both paper and electronic payments.

[8.32]   Two separate forms of agency arrangements developed. In the first, the institution keeps an account with the member bank and, in effect, allows their customer to draw on the institutional account. The amounts of these cheques are, of course, debited to the customer's account kept at the non-bank institution. These are known as 'agency cheques' and are the subject of regulation by the new Act: see CPOA s 100. In the second form of the arrangement, the cheque is drawn by the institution itself at the instructions of its customer. Again, the customer's account is debited with the amount of the cheque.

Although these agency arrangements appeared to work reasonably well, they have become less appropriate as the functional distinction between banks and other financial institutions has diminished. Building societies and credit unions must be expected to find it unsatisfactory that they must participate in the clearing system by making arrangements with a bank with which they are, in all other respects, competitors.

[8.33] The Australian Payments Clearing Association (APCA) was established in 1992 with a charter to reform the national payments clearing system. It is owned by the major banks, building society and credit union representative bodies and the Reserve Bank. As mentioned above, in December 1993 APCA took responsibility for clearing paper. The right to participate in the APCA paper clearing is effectively open to all financial institutions which offer cheque or payment order facilities to customers. Although fees are payable both for membership and for participation, the level of fees is not such as to constitute a barrier to entry, a charge often levelled at the old ACHA.

CATEGORIES OF MEMBERSHIP

[8.34] The right to participate in the new clearing system is open to all financial institutions which offer cheque or payment order facilities to their customers. Fees are payable, but these are non-discriminatory. Participants may do their own clearing and settling provided that acceptable settlement arrangements are made.

It is clear, however, that not all of the participants are of equal size. Some of them may have such low volumes that it is not economical for them to establish clearing procedures. Others may not wish to be exposed to the risk entailed in the clearing and settlement procedures.

To meet the needs of these parties, APCA has established three different levels of membership. 'Tier 1A' members are full participants which both clear and settle directly. 'Tier 1B' members appoint an agent to operate their clearing, but are responsible for their own settlement. 'Tier 2' members do not participate directly in either clearing or settlement but make agency arrangements with a Tier 1A member to handle both functions.

PAPER CLEARING

[8.35] Each capital city has a specified location where paper payments may be exchanged. The results of each of these 'local' exchanges is sent to the Reserve Bank where the results are collated. Settlement is still by cheque drawn on the Reserve Bank, but this will change when the PRESS system is implemented: see [8.39]. Payments cleared on a particular day must be settled by 9am on the following business day before the opening of the new day's clearing.

MICR CHEQUES

[8.36] In the mid-1960s and early 1970s the number of cheques drawn was increasing at an alarming rate. There was real and justified concern that the clearing system would not be able to maintain the standard of service which Australian customers had come to expect. The answer to the problem was to enlist the aid of computer technology in the clearing process.

The standard chosen was the 'magnetic ink character recognition' system. Following standard computer terminology, this is always replaced by the acronym, MICR, and cheques with the encoding on them are referred to as MICR cheques.

When the printed cheque is supplied to the customer, it comes with small figures at the lower left corner which may be read by the computer systems. The numbers identify the bank and branch at which the account is kept, the account number and the identifying number of the cheque itself.

[8.37] Ideally, of course, the amount of the cheque and the number of the account where it is to be deposited would also be printed on the cheque in a form which could be read by computer. That cannot be done since those items are not known until the cheque is drawn and then deposited for collection. Consequently, each cheque is subject to processing by the collecting bank which is charged with adding this information to the cheque. Because of the possibility of making a mistake in the amount and the consequences of such a mistake, the amount is checked by a 'proofing' device. Proofing is essentially just doing the same job twice and comparing the result.

The cheques so encoded may be processed by computer, along with other MICR paper such as deposit slips. The processing sorts the cheques into groups according to the drawee bank and performs the necessary accounting for the clearing.

'TRUNCATION'

[8.38] Although the MICR system has allowed the cheque system to grow far beyond the expectations of the participants, it must seem a strange system to an alien visitor. Why is it necessary to sort all the paper and transport it to the drawee bank? After all, the only information required by the drawee bank is the amount of the cheque, the identity of the bank which is collecting and the account to be debited. If it were possible to send only that information, then the cheque clearing system could be significantly streamlined and substantial savings realised.

The reason that the paper is transported to the drawee bank is, of course, the historical identification of a cheque with a particular form of a bill of exchange. It was thought, on the authority of *Griffin v Weatherby* (1868) LR 3 QB 753, that it was necessary to physically deliver the cheque to the drawee bank for there to be an effective presentment. Whether that is correct or not, the clearing house rules appear to have been drafted on that assumption and it is impossible to criticise the banks for failing to take a risk which, if the risk materialised, would result in enormous expenditure and potentially large liabilities: see *Barclays Bank plc v Bank of England* [1985] 1 All ER 385 which indicates that the English clearing rules require physical delivery of the cheque to the paying bank: see Tyree, 'Legal Aspects of Electronic Clearing and Settlement' in *Banking Law and Practice*, Proceedings of the 13th Annual Conference of the Banking Law Association, 1996.

The sending of information rather than the paper is called 'truncation'. Truncation could allow the cheque system to function much more efficiently and quickly, but, in spite of the provision for truncation in the CPOA, the advantages have not yet been judged sufficient to overcome the costs and the risks. The CPOA truncation scheme is discussed at [5.109]ff. The Act is currently being reviewed, and it is likely that changes will be made in the truncation provisions which will facilitate its introduction.

LOW-VALUE ELECTRONIC CLEARING

[8.39] 'Low-value' electronic funds transfer (EFT) refers to payments made by direct entry and by card-initiated transactions. As noted above, these payments now account for a large proportion of all payments by volume and a significant proportion by value.

BULK DIRECT ENTRY PAYMENTS

[8.40] Direct entry payments may be either direct credits or direct debits. Direct credits form by far the largest category. They are used in circumstances where a single payer has a large number of recurring payments to make, the most common examples being the payment of wages or government benefits. The payer processes the payment information in its own computers, passing the instructions to its bank in an agreed upon form. The paying bank then sorts the instructions according to the various receiving banks. These payment instructions must then be 'cleared' and the resulting sums settled.

Direct debit systems are similar, save that the processing is done by a single creditor who regularly receives large numbers of small payments. The most common example of these are insurance companies and health funds which receive authorisation from their customers to make regular debits to accounts held by those customers at various financial institutions.

[8.41] The bulk direct entry system is known as BECS (Bulk Entry Clearing System). The successful operation of a bulk direct entry system depends upon a system of account and institution numbering so that any institution may enter a code which identifies uniquely the destination account. Building societies and credit unions are now part of a national numbering system. Customers using direct entry systems may now provide only a single set of instructions, usually on a computer tape, which will allow payments to all three classes of institution.

Current practice still uses paper vouchers. These are returned to the payer when the account information is incorrect in the case of a direct credit or where there are insufficient funds in the case of a direct debit. Future plans call for the elimination of this paper in favour of direct electronic communications. Similarly, the use of tape to transfer payment information will be phased out as institutions upgrade their data processing facilities so that the instructions may be communicated 'on-line'.

Direct credit systems have the potential for shifting settlement risks away from the receiving institution. A bank receiving payment instructions could receive settlement funds before releasing credits to its customer's account. This is not done at present, but is contemplated as a future strategy.

RETAIL EFT PAYMENTS

[8.42] The retail EFT payment system does not fit into the general model of clearing and settlement. The existing systems are proprietary, being run either entirely by a single institution or in conjunction with one or two others. Where a cooperative structure exists, the accounting and settlement arrangements are governed by the private contract between the parties.

This may change in the future. The facilities offered by APCA would enable customers to use ATM cards in any machine. The use of a clearing system together with more sophisticated EFT terminals would allow customers to make third party payments.

HIGH-VALUE CLEARING — RTGS

[8.43] As discussed above, a real time gross settlement (RTGS) system provides for 'large' interbank payments to be settled by adjusting RBA Exchange Settlement Accounts on an individual basis as the payments occur. RTGS is scheduled to be introduced in May 1998. Since these 'large' payments account for a majority of all interbank payments, settlement risk will be substantially reduced by the introduction of RTGS: see the 1997 Annual Report of the Australian Payments Systems Council for an analysis of payment exchanges between direct clearers.

LEGAL QUESTIONS ARISING

[8.44] Regardless of the medium used to facilitate credit and debit transfers, the fundamental legal problems remain the same. Whether an international transfer is ordered by telex or by SWIFT, it may still be important to know the legal relationships between the payer and the various banks involved in the transfer. Some of the cases are concerned with the very difficult problem of determining precisely when it can be said that the payment is complete.

Although the legal problems are the same, the method of transfer used has made a difference to the importance the problem is likely to assume in a dispute. A postal transfer is probably used when the parties are not very concerned about the time of payment. However, when high interest rates prevail, a payer who is obliged to make a large payment may wish to retain the benefit of the amount until the last minute and so may choose to use a SWIFT transfer with the expectation that the payment may be made quickly once ordered. With a tighter timetable comes the occasional error and a legal problem which was at one time mainly of academic interest but may now become one of considerable practical importance.

PRELIMINARY OBSERVATIONS

[8.45] Before considering the particular legal problems involved in funds transfers, it is worth considering a few general comments concerning the relationships in a credit or debit transfer.

The first is that the law of contract will be relevant but not conclusive. We have already seen that the rules of the clearing house (a contract between the banks) may have an impact on a customer who is not party to the contract: *Dimond (HH) (Rotorua 1966) v Australia and New Zealand Banking Group Ltd* [1979] 2 NZLR 739; *Riedell v Commercial Bank of Australia Ltd* [1931] VLR 382. On the other hand, the clearing house rules cannot bind a customer who cannot be expected to have knowledge of the rules. So, for example, in *Barclays Bank plc v Bank of England* [1985] 1 All ER 385 Bingham J said (at 394):

> If it is to be said that the drawer loses that right [to have the cheque duly presented] as the result of a private agreement made between the banks for their own convenience, the very strongest proof of his [ie, the customer's] knowledge and assent would be needed, not only because of the general rule that an individual's rights are not to be cut down by an agreement made between others but also because, in this particular case, the rights of additional parties (such as indorsers) could be affected.

The inadequacy of a pure contract analysis is even clearer when there are overriding statutory considerations. As an example of this, the 'unwinding' and 'netting' rules to be used in the deferred net settlement system require, inter alia, amendment of the insolvency legislation in order to be effective against outside challenge: see the discussion at [8.28].

The second is that the law of agency is of overwhelming importance in the solution of any of the legal problems. Thus, in a credit transfer, it is clear that the transferring bank is acting as an agent for the payer. The transferring bank may then instruct the recipient bank directly or by means of some intermediary bank. It is difficult to see how the direct contractual relationships involved can be anything other than agencies. The difficulties will usually be to determine the scope of the agency and whether two particular parties are or are not in a contractual relationship. It will not always be easy to determine on whose behalf a bank may be acting in a particular transaction.

A third preliminary point is to note what should by now be obvious to the reader. Except for the operation of ATMs, the 'payment' that we are concerned with is not the transfer of cash. In all cases, the resulting changes effected by the transaction will be a change in institutional liabilities.

Thus, in the simplest case of the payer and the payee having accounts at the same bank, a credit transfer amounts merely to debiting the payer's account and crediting the payee's account with the same amount. The effect of the transfer has been to change the liabilities of the banker.

[8.46] When the transfer is more complex, there may be several such changes. In the international transfer where settlement is by accounts held by a third bank, then the institutional liabilities of all of the participating institutions are changed. The transferring bank's liability to the payer is reduced by the amount of the transfer, the recipient bank becomes liable to the payee for the amount and the third bank reduces its liability to the transferring bank and increases its liability to the recipient bank by the same amount.

It is important to keep the point in mind when discussing the time at which payment is made, for the answer to the question may depend upon the form of settlement and the identity of the parties to the dispute. That is, the time of payment between the payer and the payee might not necessarily be the time of payment as between the transferring bank and the recipient bank.

LEGAL NATURE OF TRANSFERS

[8.47]   A transfer of funds may be initiated in several ways. The payer may instruct his or her bank by means of a written or a printed form, by means of instructions coded on a magnetic medium, by means of direct input from a computer terminal using identifying codes or by means of direct input from an ATM using the plastic card and PIN. In all cases this amounts to a mandate to the banker and there seems little doubt that the banker is obliged to follow the mandate strictly and having done so has the authority to debit the account of the customer for the amount of the transfer.

The fact is, then, that the order to make a transfer looks very much like a cheque and the question arises whether an order to make a transfer may be a negotiable instrument.

NEGOTIABLE INSTRUMENTS?

[8.48]   There is no reason to suppose that transfer orders are treated as negotiable instruments by commercial custom. Consequently, the only way in which they could be considered as such is if they were to fall within the definition of a bill of exchange or a cheque. It is possible that electronic messages could be interpreted as being in writing since s 25, Acts Interpretations Act 1901 (Cth) provides that:

> 'writing' includes any mode of representing or reproducing words, figures, drawings or symbols in a visible form.

However, bills and cheques must be 'signed' as well, and the Acts Interpretation Act provides no assistance for electronic messages. This may change if 'digital signatures' are given legal status: see [8.90]ff.

As to those instructions which are in writing, the document must be an unconditional order. This will, of course, depend upon the actual form of the words used. It is said that the forms used in the United Kingdom cannot be construed as a formal order to the banker: E P Ellinger, 'The Giro System and Electronic Transfers of Funds' [1986] 2 *LMCLQ* 178.

When the order is in the form of a telex, the English Court of Appeal was prepared to hold that mere receipt of the telex message did not constitute payment since to do so would be to elevate the telex to the status of a negotiable instrument: *Tenax Steamship Co Ltd v Brimnes (Owners) (The Brimnes)* [1975] QB 929. This was approved by the House of Lords in *Mardorf Peach & Co Ltd v Attica Sea Carriers Corporation of Liberia* [1977] AC 850. Perhaps the best approach is simply to note that none of the parties conceive the orders to be negotiable instruments, that is, they are not negotiable instruments because of commercial custom regardless of whether they fit the formal definition of a bill of exchange. There is certainly no danger of a transfer order being mistaken for a bill even if the order fulfils the formal definition.

The matter is of more than mere academic interest, for if a transfer order is fraudulently issued or altered then the rights of the parties will depend solely on the law of agency and contract rather than on the law of negotiable instruments.

ASSIGNMENTS?

[8.49]   Chorley argues that the legal nature of the direct credit transaction is one of assignment of a debt: R S T Chorley, *The Law of Banking*, 6th ed Sweet & Maxwell, London, 1974. The argument is a natural one on a functional view of the transaction: at the beginning, a debtor D owes a debt to a creditor C; at the termination of the transaction, the recipient banker owes a debt to C, but D does not. At a functional level, a debt appears to have been transferred; in our law, the means of transferring a debt are limited. Since the entire transaction occurs by the issuing of instructions, it is natural to attempt the conceptual analysis by resorting to the law of assignment.

[8.50]   An assignment may be either an equitable assignment or a statutory assignment as prescribed in the various state Acts: see, for example, s 12 Conveyancing Act 1919 (NSW). The effect of an assignment is to transfer to the assignee all rights of the assignor: see Chapter 10. An equitable assignment need not take any special form so long as the intent to assign is clear, but for the present purposes it is essential to note that a mandate to pay is different from an assignment. The difference is clear as regards the legal concepts though the distinction may not always be an easy one to draw from the facts in a given case; compare *Ex parte Hall Ire Whitting* (1878) 10 Ch D 615 with *Re Williams* [1917] 1 Ch 1.

[8.51]   There are compelling arguments against considering the direct credit transaction as an assignment, the most telling of these being the contrast between the parties' intentions and expectations and the results of the assignment model. First, the payee would be in a stronger position than if he or she accepted a cheque, for he or she would be able to maintain an action directly against the banker in the case of a failure to credit. Second, the instructions to the paying banker would be irrevocable once the payee had notice of such instructions, for it is then that the assignment is complete; that this result cannot be contemplated by the paying banker is evidenced by the warning at the bottom of the monthly statement which warns that indicated credits may be later reversed. There is an additional argument against it being a statutory assignment. Section 130 of the Property Law Act 1952 has been held to be inapplicable to the assignment of part of a debt: *Williams v Atlantic Assurance Co Ltd* [1933] 1 KB 81; *Walter & Sullivan Ltd v Murphy & Sons Ltd* [1955] 2 QB 584. Yet the transfer of the whole account would be an extremely rare occurrence.

Dicta in an American case has held that a direct credit order is an assignment, but it should be noted that American law does not have the same restrictions on legal assignment of part of a debt: see *Delbrueck v Hanover Trust Co* 609 F 2d 1047 (1979).

These results, clearly not contemplated by any of the parties to the transfer scheme, seem to show conclusively that a credit transfer is neither an equitable nor a statutory assignment of funds. In truth, the law of assignments is not necessary to explain the credit transfer system. Much more in accord with the expectations of the parties is the simple agency model.

[8.52] This view seems to have been accepted by Webster J in *Royal Products Ltd v Midland Bank Ltd* [1981] 2 Lloyd's Rep 194. He said (at 198):

> [Credit transfers] are to be regarded simply as an authority and instruction, from a customer to its bank, to transfer an amount standing to the credit of that customer with that bank to the credit of its account with another bank, that other bank being impliedly authorised by the customer to accept that credit by virtue of the fact that the customer has a current account with it, no consent to the receipt of the credit being expected from or required of that other bank, by virtue of the same fact. It is, in other words, a banking operation, of a kind which is often carried out internally, that is to say, within the same bank or between two branches of the same bank and which, at least from the point of view of the customer, is no different in nature or quality when, as in the present case, it is carried out between different banks.

TRUST?

[8.53] Consider the position when a customer or some stranger places money or effects with the banker together with a request that the funds be transferred. Is the money or effects impressed with a trust? It is certainly true that moneys which are placed with a bank for a specific purpose may be impressed with a trust to the extent that if the purpose fails then the moneys are held in trust by the banker for the customer. When that happens, the moneys may not be retained against any amount owed by the customer to the banker: see, for example, *Re Kayford Ltd (in liq)* [1975] 1 WLR 279 and the discussion in Chapter 3.

However, it is thought that these cases depend on the fact that the funds originated not with the customer but with some other party intended to remain the beneficial owners of the funds even though the customer of the banker was the legal depositor. In *Re Kayford*, for example, the funds originated with customers of the company who paid for goods which were not then delivered. The funds so received by the company had been placed to the credit of a dormant deposit account.

Although the matter cannot be considered free from doubt, it is thought that the banker does not hold as trustee, but rather in the ordinary way is a debtor to the customer for the amount of the funds so deposited. Should the transfer fail for some reason, then the customer/payer is in the position of any other creditor of the bank.

LEGAL POSITION OF THE PARTICIPANTS

[8.54]   When considering the legal position of the participating banks in a funds transfer, it will be assumed that the foregoing is correct and that the order to transfer funds is neither a negotiable instrument nor an assignment of funds held by the banker on behalf of the customer.

TRANSFERRING BANK

[8.55]   As agent for the customer, the transferring bank is obliged to carry out its duties with an appropriate level of care and skill. Since it is following a mandate from the customer, it is obliged to follow the mandate strictly and will be prima facie unable to debit the account of the customer if it acts otherwise: see *Midland Bank Ltd v Seymour* [1955] 2 Lloyd's Rep 194, especially per Devlin J at 198. Of course, it also follows that the customer is under an obligation to give clear and unambiguous instructions. Although there does not appear to be any case law directly on the point, it would seem that if the transfer order is drawn in such a way as to facilitate a fraud to be perpetrated on the banker then the customer would be liable under the principles of *London Joint Stock Bank Ltd v Macmillan and Arthur* [1918] AC 777: see the discussion in Chapter 5.

When it is said that the banker must follow the mandate strictly, this must be taken to mean that the banker must transfer the amount which is specified in the mandate and the transfer must be to the proper person. It is not generally relevant how the transferring banker effects the transfer, provided only that it is done with the required degree of care and skill.

As in the case of cheques, the strict obligations on the banker impose a duty on the customer to give a clear mandate. In other words, there will be a *Macmillan* type duty on the customer. Generally, however, the distinction between a carefully given mandate and an unauthorised one is blurred in electronic systems, so that the principle has less scope for operation.

[8.56]   The point is illustrated by *Royal Products Ltd v Midland Bank Ltd* [1981] 2 Lloyd's Rep 194. The plaintiffs instructed the defendant bank to transfer funds to one of their own accounts with the B bank in Malta. It was their intention to later transfer the funds on to the N bank in Malta. The defendant bank effected the transfer by using their correspondent in Malta which happened to be the N bank.

One of the issues in the case was whether the defendant bank was precluded from debiting the account by virtue of the fact that they did not follow the mandate given by the customer, namely to transfer the funds to the B bank. The court held that the defendant bank had not been in breach of its mandate. In so holding, Webster J indicated that, when construing instructions for a money transfer, it is not necessary to give a legal implication to each detail of the order. It is sufficient that the transferring bank comply with the overall intent of the order and that the instruction be carried out with due care and skill.

[8.57] This is undoubtedly correct, but it should not be supposed that the customer is precluded from ordering that a transfer should occur in a particular way. If the plaintiffs had indicated to the defendant bank that they wished the funds to be transferred to the B bank without the use of correspondents or with the use of some particular method, there seems little doubt that the wishes would be respected by the court. In the *Royal Products* case, the real point is that it is not necessary to read each order in an attempt to divine some special wishes on the part of the payer, since in the ordinary course of events the precise path taken by the payment is quite irrelevant to the payer. It is, of course, open to the bank to decline a request for a transfer which it considers to be too onerous or which it cannot carry out.

[8.58] The fact that the way in which the mandate is carried out will usually be at the discretion of the bank means that these functions must be carried out with due care and skill. The essential steps involved in carrying out the mandate are that it must be timely and that if a correspondent is used, then that correspondent must be a choice which is both reasonable and reliable.

What amounts to a timely transfer will depend upon the circumstances. If the customer specifies a particular time then the bank would be prima facie in breach of its duties if the transfer is not made at that time. If there is no time specified, then the transfer must be made in a reasonable time, a time which will very likely depend upon the mode of transfer specified by the customer, if any. This is simply an application of the *Dimond* principle to a credit transfer system: see *Dimond (HH) (Rotorua 1966) v Australia and New Zealand Banking Group Ltd* [1979] 2 NZLR 739 and the discussion at [5.66].

The duty to provide a reasonable and reliable correspondent is expressed in part by the rule that the bank is liable for the default of its correspondent. The principle was originally developed and expressed in the context of documentary letters of credit. Whatever the scope of the duty when applied to funds transfers, it is unlikely to be a matter of practical consideration, for the banker-customer contract is very likely to contain a term which provides that the correspondent bank is employed at the risk and the expense of the customer. It seems very unlikely that such exemption clauses could be successfully challenged by a customer.

CORRESPONDENT BANK

[8.59] Although there seems to be no direct authority as to the position of the corresponding bank in a direct funds transfer, it seems that it would be the same as that of a bank which agrees to present a foreign bill for acceptance or for payment. If that is the case, then under the common law there is no privity of contract between the correspondent bank and the payer for whom the transfer is being made. In other words, the correspondent is the agent only of the transferring bank and not of the customer of that bank. The point may be of importance when the payer suffers losses caused by the negligence of the correspondent bank, for although the transferring bank is liable for the negligence of its agent, it is a liability which may be, and nearly always is, excluded by contract.

[8.60]   The situation may be illustrated by a consideration of the decision in *Calico Printers' Association v Barclays Bank Ltd* (1930) 36 Com Cas 71. Barclays acted on behalf of the plaintiff for the purposes of presenting a bill of exchange to the buyers of goods. Barclays in turn employed the A P bank as a correspondent for the purpose. The bill was dishonoured and the A P bank arranged for the goods to be stored in a warehouse but was guilty of 'a gross breach of the most elementary business precautions' in failing to have them insured. Barclays escaped liability by means of an exclusion clause and the A P bank was held not to be liable since there was no privity of contract with the plaintiff. This does not, of course, exclude the possibility that the correspondent bank may be liable in tort; the matter will be discussed below at [8.62].

THE RECIPIENT BANK

[8.61]   It is clear that the recipient bank is acting as an agent in a funds transfer, but it may not be clear for whom the bank is acting. As will be seen below, it is important that the recipient bank have the authority to receive the funds on behalf of the payee and in the absence of such authority the payment may remain incomplete.

In the 'standard' credit transfer where the payee nominates the recipient bank and the payer requests the transferring bank to make the transfer to that recipient bank, it is thought that the principles discussed above in relation to the correspondent bank apply and that there is no privity of contract between the payer and the recipient bank.

[8.62]   It is hard to see what facts could arise to change this basic conclusion. Even in the case where the payer requests the transfer without the consent of the payee, perhaps in the hope that the payee will accept the payment as timely even though the recipient bank is not authorised to receive it on the payee's behalf, there is no reason to suppose that the recipient bank is acting in any way on behalf of the payer. However, it must be acknowledged that the situation is less certain than might be hoped.

As we have already noted, there is unlikely to be any contractual privity between the payer and any of the participating banks other than the transferring bank. This assures the banks that there can be no contractual liability to the payer, but at the same time assures the payer that the banks may not rely upon contractual exclusion clauses in order to escape tort liability. This section examines the possibility that there could be such a liability.

[8.63] It is useful to consider briefly the types of loss which may occur when a funds transfer fails to go as expected by all of the parties. The United Nations Commission on International Trade Law (UNCITRAL) has classified the nature of the losses which may occur into four categories, namely, loss of principle, loss of interest, losses due to exchange rate fluctuations in international transfers, and consequential losses: UNCITRAL, *Electronic Funds Transfers*, A/CN.9/22 1, 1982. Any system of funds transfer must adopt rules which allocate losses of the first three types among the participating institutions. While these rules might be important for an individual institution, the actual liability rule merely shifts losses around within the system and so may not be particularly important in the long run.

Consequential damage is in a class all of its own. Much of the litigation as to the time of payment has concerned late payment made under contracts of hire which contained a clause making time of payment of the essence of the contract. In such a circumstance, a late payment which may result in no losses at all of the first three types may result in substantial contractual disadvantages to the party who was required to make the payment. In charterparties, these losses may be very high and the issue of liability of the system for such losses is an important one.

[8.64] As an example, consider *Evra Corporation v Swiss Banking Corporation* 522 F Supp 820, rev 673 F 2d 951(1981). The court at first instance allowed the plaintiff damages of approximately $2 million when the defendant bank negligently failed to make a $27,000 payment on the value date. The decision was reversed by the Court of Appeal on the grounds that the loss was not 'foreseeable'.

A reading of the *Evra* case shows that it will not automatically be resolved in the same way in Australia. The essence of the court's reasoning was twofold: a strict interpretation of the requirements of the second limb of *Hadley v Baxendale* (1854) 9 Exch 341 and an acceptance of the proposition that the standard of foreseeability in tort is the same as that required in contract. In the current state of law, both limbs of the argument could fail in an Australian court.

The strict interpretation of the requirements of foreseeability in *Hadley v Baxendale* is probably precluded by the House of Lords decision in *Koufos v Czarnikow Ltd (The Heron II)* [1969] 1 AC 350 which imposed a test of 'not unlikely' having regard to the knowledge of the parties at the time the contract was made as the measure of foreseeability required to impose liability. It is instructive to consider the factual situation in *The Heron II*. Owing to a contractual breach a cargo of sugar was delivered nine days late to the port of Basrah. The shipowner knew that the other party was a sugar merchant, but did not know that it was intended to sell the cargo immediately. The market dropped and the shipowner was held liable for the amount of the loss. Are the losses which were suffered in *Evra* less foreseeable than the losses in *The Heron II*?

[8.65] The second limb of the *Evra* argument would have little chance in Australia where it is generally accepted that whatever the tort test is for foreseeability, it is undoubtedly less demanding than the contractual test: *Overseas Tankship (UK) Ltd v Morts Dock & Engineering Co Ltd (The Wagon Mound)* [1961] AC 388; *Shirt v Wyong Shire Council* [1978] 1 NSWLR 631; *Mount Isa Mines Ltd v Pusey* (1970) 125 CLR 383.

Further, there is no problem which arises from the loss being purely economic, since it is clear that the problem fits comfortably within the *Caltex* test: *Caltex Oil (Australia) Pty Ltd v The Dredge 'Willemstad'* (1976) 136 CLR 529.

If this is correct, then it is not necessarily a very desirable outcome. Although it is right that there should be a duty on banks to use all care and skill in making the transfer, it is not obvious that the transfer system should bear all of the costs of mistakes, even when the mistake is caused by carelessness. If the payer chooses to become a party to a contract where such a minor default can have such major consequences, there is no obvious reason why that risk should then effectively be transferred to a banker who has no real relationship with the payer.

TIME OF PAYMENT

[8.66] The actual time at which payment is completed may be of importance in a number of circumstances. The customer may require that a transfer be completed at a particular time; failure to do so may result in substantial financial losses to the customer. One of the participants in the EFT system may fail; how are the losses to be spread throughout the system? The account of a customer may be attached or frozen in some way; which transactions have been completed?

As a preliminary point, it is important to note that even in a domestic EFT system there will be many transactions which are not 'instantaneous' for the purposes of this discussion. There are a number of transactions such as monthly credits or debits for payroll transactions and the like which are obviously delayed, but even in 'on-line' systems, the transactions may be held in suspense until some previously defined settlement or clearing time. In the jargon, the machines may be 'on-line' but the transactions are not 'real time'.

A further point to note in this context is that the problems are not all amenable to solution through the legal medium of contract. While inter-institutional problems may be solved by a multi-lateral agreement similar to the present clearing house rules for cheques and while institution-customer conflict may be regulated by the conditions of use imposed by the institution (subject to legislation such as the Credit Act and other consumer legislation), some of the issues involve parties who are not in direct contractual proximity.

This is obvious in the context of international transfers, but is no less true in domestic transfers.

As a final preliminary comment, note that there are at least two distinct problems. The first is to determine the time of payment as between the institutions. The second is to determine the time of payment as between the payer and the payee. These two problems may have different solutions.

[8.67] The reader should recall some of the fundamental terminology. 'Clearing' is essentially a bookkeeping process whereby relatively large numbers of transactions between relatively few financial institutions are amalgamated and set off against each other to minimise the required transfer of funds between the institutions: the terminology is taken from UNCITRAL, *Electronic Funds Transfers*, A/CN.9/22 1, 1982. In an ideal world, transfers from institution A to institution B would be exactly matched by transfers in the opposite direction so that no funds at all would need to be exchanged. In the real world, such perfect symmetry fails to occur: the required periodic transfer of funds is known as 'settlement'.

It is not generally appreciated that the 'exposure' of a financial institution in a payments system may be substantial. The CHIPS system in New York handles (1981 figures) more than 55,000 transactions a day with an average value in excess of $3 million: M Mayer, 'The Settlements Revolution' [1981] *Institutional Investor* 358. The result is that participants regularly clear items having a value well in excess of their total worth: J Revell, *Banking and Electronic Funds Transfers*, OECD 1983. Comparable figures do not seem to be available for a consumer-oriented EFT system, but since the obvious aim is to replace the paper-based system, the amounts will be large. As more and smaller institutions enter the payments system, failures must be expected and the time of payment becomes a question of fundamental importance.

At some point in time, the transfer of funds from the transferring bank to the recipient bank must be considered as final in the sense that the transferring bank can no longer stop or recall the transfer. It seems sensible to call this time the time of payment. Although there is no logical reason why the time of payment as between the transferor and the ultimate transferee need be the same, it is clear that the time of payment as between these parties cannot be earlier than the time of payment as between the two institutions. And, if the transferring bank cannot recall the transfer, it would seem that the same time might be the prima facie time of payment between the transferor and transferee. There may, however, be circumstances which would delay the time of payment as between the end parties. For an example, see *Awilco v Fulvia (The Chikuma)* [1981] 1 WLR 314; see [8.82].

AS BETWEEN INSTITUTIONS

[8.68] The existing law on the time of payment between institutions is concerned almost exclusively with credit transfers. The English courts appear to have established the rule that a credit transfer is complete when the recipient bank decides to accept the transferring bank's instructions to credit the account and the accounting processes (usually computer processes) are set in motion for so crediting. The case law is unsatisfactory and the proposition is offered with considerable hesitation; it cannot be said to be the ratio of any of the decided cases but is thought to be a fair distillation from all of them.

This rule is to be understood to apply only when there is no express contractual provisions which apply between the institutions. It is certainly possible to alter the basic rule by contract in much the same way that the clearing house rules determine the rights of participating institutions. The possible contractual alternatives will be discussed below.

[8.69] Since the rule is so uncertain, it is worth looking at several of the cases in detail. The cases arise in two quite different contexts. In the first, the payer wishes to stop the payment, usually because of some information concerning the solvency of the payee or because of some contractual dispute. In the second type of case, the matter arises because it is alleged that the payment has not been made in time with the result that the payer has lost some contractual benefit or has suffered some contractual loss.

[8.70] The reason for the distinction between the two types of case is that the first is concerned with the time of payment as between institutions. As agent for the payer, the transferring bank will reverse the transfer order if it can do so, that is, if the time of payment as between the institutions has not yet arrived. The second type of case concerns the time of payment as between the payer and the payee. In this section, we are concerned primarily with the first type of case.

[8.71] In *Momm v Barclays Bank International Ltd* [1977] QB 790 the plaintiffs were a German banking partnership. They entered into a contract with another German bank, Herstatt, which provided, inter alia, that Herstatt transfer to the plaintiff's account at the defendant's bank some £120,000 in sterling. The transfer was to be on the basis of 'value 26 June 1974' which meant that the payment had to be made on that date.

It happened that Herstatt also had an account with the defendant bank and intended to make the payment from that account, but that was not part of the contract between Herstatt and the plaintiff. Herstatt ordered the defendant to transfer the sum from Herstatt's account to the account of the plaintiff on 26 June.

The defendants approved the alteration of accounts on 26 June, even though this placed Herstatt's account in an overdrawn position. The decision to do so was made by an appropriate officer of the defendant bank. The accounts were processed by the defendant bank's computer that night. The next morning the defendant bank became aware that Herstatt had ceased trading. Upon receipt of this information, they informed the plaintiff, in response to an inquiry, that the transfer had not been made, 'due to the present position of Herstatt's accounts', and they took steps which resulted in the computer reversing the accounts.

When the plaintiffs learned of the bank's actions they sued, claiming a wrongful debiting of their account of the amount in question; the defendants claimed that the transfer would only have been complete upon the plaintiffs receiving notice of it, and that account entries do not constitute such notice. The defence was based on an interpretation of *Rekstin v Severo Sibersko Gosudarstvennoe Akcionernoe* [1933] 1 KB 47: see [8.74].

The sole issue in the case was whether the payment had become final. Kerr J thought that, as a matter of principle, when a credit transfer is to be effected by a bank on a given 'value date', then the position at the end of the day must be certain, that the bank could not delay its decision to credit until the next day. That principle, which is merely an application of the general principle that the banker must follow his or her instructions strictly, does not settle the matter, for the question still remains as to whether the bank in fact followed the instructions, in which case the plaintiff would win, or whether the bank did not do so, in which case the plaintiff could have no claim against the bank. If the bank failed to follow Herstatt's instructions, Herstatt as customer might have a claim against them but it by no means followed that the current plaintiff had such a claim.

[8.72]   Kerr J found for the plaintiff on the basis of the old case of *Eyles v Ellis* (1827) 4 Bing 112. He then went on to distinguish and explain *Rekstin v Severo Sibersko Gosudarstvennoe Akcionernoe* [1933] 1 KB 47, the main case relied upon by the defendant, reinforcing his view of that case by reference to Court of Appeal decisions in two shipping cases, *The Brimnes*; *Tenax Steamship Co Ltd v The Brimnes (Owners)* [1975] QB 929 and *Mardorf Peach and Co Ltd v Attica Carriers Corporation of Liberia* [1976] QB 835. The decision of the Court of Appeal in *Mardorf Peach* was reversed by the House of Lords ([1977] AC 850) but the principles relating to the time of payment do not seem to have been altered by the House of Lords. Each of these cases, together with the analysis of Kerr J and comment upon that analysis, will be discussed in turn. Note that *Momm* is a case which falls into the category of an institution attempting to reverse a transfer order. Although it is the payee who is the plaintiff in this case, the argument for the payee really concerns the right of the transferring bank to reverse the transfer order. As between the payer (Herstatt) and the payee, the precise time of payment is a matter of the utmost indifference.

Also note that *Momm* concerns a so-called 'in-house' payment, that is, the transferring and the recipient bank is one and the same. It may be that different principles are to be applied when there are different transferring and recipient banks, but some good reason must be made out for the difference.

[8.73]   In *Eyles v Ellis* the plaintiff was a creditor of the defendant. Both parties kept accounts at the same bank. On a Friday, the defendant debtor instructed the banker to transfer the sum owed to the account of the plaintiff. The banker did this by making the appropriate entry in his books, even though the defendant's account was then overdrawn. On that same day, the defendant wrote to the plaintiff to inform him that the transfer had been ordered, but the letter did not reach the plaintiff until Sunday. Kerr J observed, rightly it is submitted, that the sending of the letter cannot be notice. It is actual notice which is required. Meanwhile, on the Saturday the banker had failed. The court found for the defendant, observing that the plaintiff could have drawn for the sum and the banker could not have refused his draft.

Kerr J observed that 'the important feature of the case is that the payment was held to be complete when the payee's account was credited and before the payee had had any notice that this had happened'. He held that, on the facts, *Eyles v Ellis* was indistinguishable from *Momm*. It is not to be supposed that Kerr J was suggesting the above statement to be the ratio of *Eyles v Ellis*. It is important to notice a further feature of the case: the judgment of the court, given by Best CJ, clearly assumed that the bank had been given explicit authority to receive the money on behalf of the plaintiff. That this was indeed the case is evidenced by the fact that the transfer in question was a result of a complaint by the plaintiff that an earlier transfer had not taken place as it was supposed to have.

Also note that Kerr J refers only to the crediting of the payee's account. This in itself is not decisive of the time of final payment, since it has long been the custom of banks to credit the account of a payee of a cheque upon deposit while reserving the right to debit the account if the cheque is dishonoured upon presentment to the paying bank. Such a practice was held to be valid in *A L Underwood Ltd v Bank of Liverpool and Martins* [1924] 1 KB 775.

[8.74] There were two defendants in the *Rekstin* case. The first was a Russian trading organisation commonly referred to as 'Severo'. The second was a bank at which Severo had an account. The plaintiff was a judgment creditor of Severo. Severo devised a scheme to protect the contents of their bank account from a garnishee order. Severo ordered the bank to transfer the contents of their account to the account of the Russian Trade delegation, who had an account with the same bank. The Trade Delegation had diplomatic immunity. The order was made without the knowledge or consent of the Trade Delegation. Upon receipt of the order, a clerk of the bank made the necessary book entries to close the Severo account, and prepared a 'credit slip' which was preparatory to crediting the Delegation's account with the same sum. Before such a credit entry was made, the plaintiff served the bank with a garnishee order nisi in respect of the judgment against Severo.

The court held, inter alia, that the mandate from Severo to the bank to transfer the money to the account of the Trade Delegation was, in the circumstances, still revocable and was, in fact, revoked by operation of law upon receipt of the garnishee order nisi.

Counsel for Barclays in the *Momm* case attempted to define the ratio of the *Rekstin* case in terms of notice, asserting that transfer is incomplete until actual notice is received by the transferee. He might be forgiven for supposing that the line of argument would be readily accepted, for that seems to have been the accepted interpretation ever since the court explained the matter in those terms in *Continental Caoutchouc and Gutta Percha Co v Kleinwort Sons & Co* (1904) 90 LT 474. Kerr J, however, rejected this statement as the ratio of *Rekstin* on the grounds that it is inconsistent with the decision in *Eyles v Ellis*. He further observed that *Eyles v Ellis* was not mentioned in either the *Rekstin* case or the *Continental Caoutchouc* case.

Kerr J suggested that the basis of the *Rekstin* decision is one of two propositions: first, that there had been no final appropriation of the money to the credit of the Trade Delegation; second, '... the fact that the Trade Delegation knew nothing of the proposed transfer, that there was no transaction between Severo and the delegation underlying it, and that the delegation had accordingly never assented to its account being credited with these moneys'.

[8.75]   With respect, the first of these begs the question in that finality of the transaction is what the court had to decide in *Rekstin*. It is, on its own, wrong, or at least misleading, in that subsequent cases, as observed by Kerr J later on, clearly indicate that payment may be complete prior to the completion of internal accounting procedures when the bank has authority to receive the payment. In particular, the clerk had decided to act on the order. Payment would have been complete had the bank been authorised to receive the sum on behalf of the Trade Delegation.

The second basis given by Kerr J might be summarised by the proposition that the bank was not the agent of the Trade Delegation for the purposes of receiving this payment. As will be noted below, the House of Lords decision in *Mardorf Peach* shows that payment is not completed in such a situation. Indeed, on a commonsense approach, the bank in *Rekstin* was a complete stranger to the Trade Delegation in so far as this particular transfer was concerned. It is as though Severo had ordered a new account to be opened in the name of the Trade Delegation in some far off bank. That the Trade Delegation might have an account at the bank is clearly irrelevant.

If that is the true basis for the decision in *Rekstin*, then the case has little scope for practical applications in international funds transfers since it will usually be the payee who nominates the recipient bank. In such circumstances, the bank will always have authority to receive the funds.

[8.76]   The principles which may be drawn from *Momm's* case seem to be threefold:

1. If the receiving bank has no authority to receive the money on behalf of the payee, then the transfer may be recalled at any time prior to the recipient bank receiving that authority or actually parting with the funds to the payee: see *Rekstin*.

2. If the transfer order actually comes to the attention of the bank, semble in its role as receiving bank, then the transfer will be irrevocable from the time that it is decided to accept the transfer and, possibly, steps are taken to credit the account of the payee. Although the transfer in *Momm* was inhouse, the decisions which Kerr J considered to be of importance are

decisions which would be made by the recipient bank when the transfer involved more than one bank.

3. When a value date is specified, then the transfer may be recalled at any time prior to the value date; this is merely a consequence of the fact that the order is not merely one to transfer funds, but rather to transfer on a particular date. There may be situations where an estoppel could be raised against the transferring bank, but that is another question entirely. If the transfer does not actually come to the attention of officers of the recipient bank then the transfer will be irrevocable from the close of business on the value date; this would be the situation when the transfer is the result of a routine direct credit operation in a domestic EFT system.

[8.77]   It should be emphasised that the *Momm* rule is the rule which is applied when there are no contractual terms which prevent the transferring bank from recalling the order. Again, the important feature here is that the transferring bank is acting as agent. If the agent acts reasonably on the instructions of the principal, the payer, then the payer cannot change the instructions once the agent is committed.

[8.78]   This is illustrated admirably by the decision in *Delbrueck v Manufacturers Hanover Trust* 464 F Supp 989, American litigation which also resulted from the Herstatt collapse. The plaintiff had an account with the defendant bank in the United States. On 25 June the plaintiffs sent a telex to the defendant bank ordering them to transfer some $12.5 million, value date 26 June, to Herstatt's account with the Chase Manhattan Bank. Herstatt was closed by the German banking authorities at about 10.30am (New York time) on 26 June. About an hour later the defendant bank made the ordered transfers by keying the appropriate transfer instructions into the CHIPS computer which then credited the clearing house account of Chase and debited that of the defendant: see [8.17] for a discussion of the CHIPS system; the rules concerning reversals were changed as a result of this case. About half an hour after that, the plaintiffs telephoned and telexed the defendants in an attempt to halt the payment.

The plaintiffs sought to revoke the order and to recover the amount from Chase, but according to the CHIPS rules in operation at the time, the transfers were irrevocable once processed through the CHIPS system and Chase refused to return the funds. The plaintiffs sued in both negligence and in contract, but failed due to the fact that the transfer was irrevocable under the CHIPS rules. It was simply irrelevant for this purpose that the Herstatt account with Chase had not been debited until 9pm on the 26th. Note that if the question had been the time at which Herstatt was actually paid, then the time of crediting the Herstatt account may well have been relevant.

[8.79]   When all of the parties have agreed to some basic set of rules the time of payment may be determined by contract. There are, however, some fundamental conflicts which make such agreement difficult. In a credit transfer, the recipient bank will wish to delay acceptance of the item until such time as it is certain that the order is genuine and that it will be reimbursed for the payment order which it accepts. Consequently, it is in the interests of the recipient bank to delay the time of payment until there remains only a minimal risk that the bank will not actually receive settlement. On the other hand, a rule which gave effect to that policy would have the consequential effect of delaying the time of payment for all other purposes. The funds would presumably still belong to the transferor and not to the transferee and would be subject to legal process by the transferor's creditors. Since the transferor and the transferee may well be using an EFT system because of the speed and certainty of transfer, their desire will be that the time of payment should be as early as possible.

[8.80]   Probably the earliest time when payment might be considered complete is when notice of the transfer is received by the recipient bank. This is the rule used in the American FEDWIRE system, but there are certain features of that system which make the rule workable. Settlement between participants in a FEDWIRE transaction is made by the transfer of funds between the appropriate accounts held by the Federal Reserve and is guaranteed by that body. Consequently, both certainty of settlement and acceptability of the mode of settlement are assured. Furthermore, the FEDWIRE protocol authenticates the message before its receipt by the recipient bank: N Penney and D Baker, *The Law of Electronic Funds Transfer Systems*, Warren Gorham, Boston, 1980.

[8.81]   The next logical candidate is the time when the recipient bank makes the decision to accept the transfer. This is, of course, close to the rule which has been suggested in the English cases and may be appropriate for transfers when the mode of settlement is uncertain. One of the disadvantages of this rule is that evidence of the time of payment may be difficult to acquire. Further, the source of the evidence would be within the control of the recipient institution and that institution may have an interest in advancing or delaying the time of payment. Such was the case in *Momm* itself: Barclays wished to 'undo' an overnight transfer that left the Herstatt account substantially overdrawn. Herstatt ceased trading during the night. In a system with such a rule, 'acceptance' would be deemed to have accrued at some fixed time, probably the close of business for those payment orders which never actually receive consideration by bank personnel.

[8.82]   Some legal systems attach importance to the time of posting the account: the Uniform Commercial Code takes this approach. But the time of posting is, in the absence of legislative control, a matter solely for the internal bookkeeping of the institution. Consequently, time of payment rules which are based on the posting process must be accompanied by rules as to the practice of posting itself.

It will be immediately apparent that the form of any electronic clearing house rules as to the time of payment will depend very much on the financial integrity of the participants involved and the method of settlement proposed. In a system where settlement is virtually guaranteed, transmission or receipt of the payment message is an acceptable time for agreed payment. If either of these preconditions are weakened, the conflict mentioned above will tend to be resolved more in favour of some later time.

As between the transferor and transferee, it has already been noted that payment cannot be said to have occurred if the funds are not readily available to the transferee. There have been suggestions to the effect that payment is not complete until the transferee receives notice of the transfer: R S T Chorley, *The Law of Banking*, 6th ed, Sweet & Maxwell, London, 1974. Such a suggestion seems to be based on the notion that a credit transfer is some form of assignment of funds and has little to recommend it.

When the transaction is a debit transfer, a similar set of possibilities exists, but it is the transferring bank which must make the appropriate verification and decisions. The rules for time of payment are modified by substituting the decisions and the acts of the transferring bank.

AS BETWEEN PAYER AND PAYEE

[8.83] As between the transferee and transferor, the *Momm* rule must be further qualified by two fundamental principles. The first is that a debt owed cannot be discharged by means of a third party payment unless the party making the payment has the authority, either actual or ostensible, of the debtor to make the payment or unless the debtor subsequently ratifies the payment. For a detailed discussion, see P Birks and J Beatson, 'Unrequested Payment of Another's Debt' (1976) 92 *LQR* 188. The second principle is that the payment cannot be considered as complete until such time as the payee can utilise them without restriction: see *The Brimnes*; *Tenax Steamship Co Ltd v Brimnes (Owners)* [1975] QB 929 and the discussion below.

[8.84] In general, payment cannot be complete unless it is shown that the recipient bank is the agent of the payee with authority to receive the payment. A good example of the principle in operation is *Mardorf Peach & Co Ltd v Attica Sea Carriers Corporation of Liberia* [1977] AC 850. Payment was made by means of a bank 'payment order', a system of inter-bank accounting which banks considered the equivalent of cash transfers. The debtor's bank was distinct from the creditor's bank, that is, it was an 'out-house' payment. The Court of Appeal held that payment was complete when the receiving bank accepted the payment order and decided to act upon it, irrespective of the time required to complete the receiving bank's internal accounting processes. This decision was reversed by the House of Lords who found that the bank had authority only to receive payments which were within the contractual time. Since the payment was out of time and the owners rejected the payment as soon as it came to their notice, the payment was not effective.

The case shows dramatically the importance of identifying the parties when the time of payment is being discussed. There is no doubt that the payment as between the institutions was complete in the sense that the transferring bank could not recall the payment order, yet the payment to the payee could not have been completed at that time because of the lack of authority of the recipient bank.

[8.85] A second principle is that when payment is made by a funds transfer, the payment to the payee cannot be considered complete until such time as the payee has the unconditional right to the immediate use of the funds: see Edmund Davies LJ in *The Brimnes*; *Tenax Steamship Co Ltd v Brimnes (Owners)* [1975] QB 929. The effect of this principle is most effectively shown by the decision in *A/SAwilco of Oslo v Fulvia Sp A di Navigazione of Cagliari (The Chikuma)* [1981] 1 WLR 314.

Payment was due on 22 January and the day before the payers instructed the transferring bank to make the transfer. A telex message was sent on the due date and funds were remitted to the recipient bank but for some reason the 'value date' was shown as 26 January. Under Italian law the transfer was irrevocable and it was even possible for the payees to draw on the money on 22 January, but the importance of the value date was that no interest could accrue to the payees until the 26th; indeed, if they had exercised their right to draw on the fund, they would have been required to pay the recipient bank interest.

The House of Lords held that payment was not complete on the 22nd. Although payment by credit transfer was permissible even though the charterparty appeared to call for cash, the transfer had to be such that the payee had the equivalent of cash. A transfer which prohibited the payee from using the funds for investment purposes could hardly be said to be the equivalent of cash: see also A L Tyree, 'Electronic Funds Transfer in New Zealand', (1978) *NZUL Rev* 139; A L Tyree, 'Payment by Direct Credit', (1982) 10 *Aust Bus L Rev* 149. Note also that the same result would probably have been reached had the transfer been governed entirely by Australian law, for the transfer would be revocable by the transferring bank until the 'value date' and so could not be the equivalent of cash. Furthermore, the recipient bank may well lack the authority to receive the payment as a discharge of the contractual obligation when the 'value date' is later than the date on which payment is due. Of course, the 'payee' may ratify the bank's action even if it does not have authority to receive the payment: see *TSB Bank of Scotland plc v Welwyn Hatfield District Council and Council of the London Borough of Brent* [1993] 2 Bank LR 267.

COMPUTER MONEY

[8.86] Technical advances in computers and micro-chips have led to new forms of payment instruments. These are referred to generically as 'computer money'. There are two main forms, digital cash and smart cards. Digital cash will be used to make purchases 'on-line' on the Internet. Smart cards will be used to make small purchases at local merchants.

[8.87] Computer money, and Internet commerce generally, depends upon the concept of a 'digital signature'. The problem is that electronic messages pass through an unknown number of computers. They may be intercepted, redirected and easily changed. It is often said that commerce on the Internet requires a system that has 'message integrity' and 'authentication'.

Message integrity means that the message received may be verified as being unaltered from the message that was sent. Paper and ink messages have this quality as a consequence of the physical properties of the message medium. Indeed, it is one of the reasons that some contracts are required to be in writing.

Message authentication means that the message originates from the person who purported to send it. In ordinary commerce, we achieve message authentication by requiring a signature.

[8.88] Digital signatures are a method of applying the mathematics of cryptography to achieve both message integrity and message authentication for electronic messages. A message that has been digitally signed by the sender may not be altered without the alteration being apparent. The identity of the sender is established by comparing the digital signature with a 'public key' that is kept in a central register. For a detailed description of digital signatures, see A L Tyree, *Digital Cash*, Butterworths, 1997.

In order for the digital signature system to be workable on a wide scale, the appropriate signature registers must be established. The federal government has indicated that it will proceed to implement one of the most important of the recommendations of the Wallis Report, the establishment of 'certification authorities' that will be responsible for identifying individuals and certifying their digital signatures.

[8.89] Digital cash is designed to be used to make payments over the Internet. Because it is seen as primarily a low value payment mechanism, it is common to refer to a payment unit as a 'digital coin'. Note that although most payments will be small, there is nothing in the technology that restricts the value of a digital cash unit.

A digital coin is very similar to a banknote. It is a message digitally signed by the issuer. In its simplest form, the message specifies:

- the issuer;
- the value of the coin;
- the expiry date (if any);
- the serial number of the coin; and
- the Internet address of the issuer.

Since an electronic message may be freely copied even if it is digitally signed, there must be some method of preventing 'double spending' of the coin, and that is the reason for the serial number.

[8.90] The basic system operates simply. The would-be purchaser P contacts the coin-issuer I requesting the issue of coins of a certain value. I sends P the coins and debits P's account. P sends the coins to the Web merchant M in exchange for the goods or information to be purchased. M contacts I to ensure that the coin has not previously been spent. If it has not, then I adds the serial number of the coin to the 'previously spent' database and credits M's account.

There are disadvantages to the basic system. As described here, the merchant and the customer must have accounts with the same issuer. It is obviously a simple matter to extend this model with a 'clearing' system to include more financial institutions. There are also more complex implementations of the digital cash system that will allow the buyer to remain anonymous. In particular, the digital cash issuer will not be able to develop spending profiles of its customers: see A L Tyree, *Digital Cash*, Butterworths, Sydney, 1997.

[8.91] Smart cards are similar to credit cards in appearance but have a small micro-processor built in. This permits the card to act as a sophisticated 'electronic purse', maintaining its own account system. Smart cards may be used for many purposes, but when used in the manner described here, they are often referred to as stored value cards (SVC). A SVC may be either disposable or rechargeable.

Disposable cards are not much different to the special purpose magnetic stripe cards that have served as bus tickets and telephone cards. The main advantage of the SVC over these less sophisticated cousins is that the SVC has better security. It is difficult to alter the records on the card, and difficult to duplicate it.

[8.92] The rechargeable card is linked to an ordinary account. The card is 'charged' by transferring funds from the account through an ATM-like device. The funds are spent with a merchant by inserting the card into a special terminal that, in effect, transfers the funds from the card to the merchant terminal. Because there is no need for an on-line check for adequacy of funds the procedure is quick and inexpensive.

[8.93] Law enforcement agencies are concerned that computer money may be used in money transfer and laundering schemes. It is unclear to what extent the Financial Transactions Reports Act (Cth) 1988 applies to various forms of computer money, but it is clear that some amendment will be required: see A L Tyree, *Digital Cash*, Butterworths, Sydney, 1997. The potential for making off-shore payments also concerns the Australian Tax Office.

CONSUMER BANKING

[9.1] In the early days of banking it was only the elite and affluent or those in business who had current accounts. That has all changed, and with the change banks have had to come to grips with the problems associated with mass marketing of their products. Banks now recognise that 'consumer banking' has different problems from traditional banking. In recent years this has led to the introduction of an Electronic Funds Transfer Code of Conduct, the establishment of an Australian Banking Industry Ombudsman and, most recently, the Code of Banking Practice. These developments are discussed in this chapter along with a brief discussion of credit cards.

THE CODE OF BANKING PRACTICE

HISTORY OF THE CODE

[9.2] The success of the Electronic Funds Transfer Code of Practice sparked calls for a general code. A task force jointly chaired by Treasury and the Trade Practices Commission was established in 1992 for the purposes of drafting a code. The Task Force was established in response to recommendations of the House of Representatives Standing Committee on Finance and Public Administration following the report of its inquiry into Australian Banking: see the report, *A Pocket Full of Change*. The Task Force included representatives of the Attorney-General's Department and the Reserve Bank. The first draft of a code of practice was released to interest groups for comment in November of 1992.

The November, 1992 draft was revised in the light of comment by the interest groups and a second draft was released in June, 1993. It is not entirely clear what happened after this draft was released, but the Code as adopted by the Treasurer and the Minister for Consumer Affairs on 3 November, 1993 was written not by the Task Force but by the Australian Bankers' Association.

This development was not well received by consumer interests who claimed that the process had been 'hi-jacked' by the ABA: see comments in the *Sydney Morning Herald*, 4 November, 1993. There is little doubt that the resulting Code is less favourable to customer interests than the preceding drafts, but perhaps it can be expected that there will be greater adherence both to the spirit and the letter of the Code since it originated with the banks.

PURPOSE OF THE CODE

[9.3]   According to the Code itself, the purpose is to describe standards of good practice and service, to promote disclosure of information which is relevant and useful to customers, to promote informed and effective relationships between banks and customers and to require banks to have procedures for the resolution of disputes between banks and customers.

'Customer' in this context has a special meaning: a 'customer' is an individual who acquires a 'Banking Service' which is wholly and exclusively for his or her private or domestic use: Code of Banking Practice s 1.1; as to 'Banking service, see [9.8]. Although the service may be acquired jointly with another individual, any person who makes a written statement to the bank in relation to a particular banking service that the service is not acquired wholly and exclusively for private or domestic use is not a 'customer'.

MONITORING AND REVIEW

[9.4]   The Preamble of the Code contains provisions for monitoring and review. Primary responsibility for monitoring is placed on the Australian Payments System Council. The Council is given authority to obtain from the Reserve Bank consolidated information based on reports and information provided by the banks. The Council is to use this information to provide reports to the Treasurer on compliance with the Code and its general operation.

The Code obliges banks to provide yearly reports to the Reserve Bank on the operation of the Code and, in particular, the reports must contain information on the number of disputes which have been processed by both the internal and external dispute resolution procedures: Preamble, Code of Banking Practice. The precise information to be provided in the yearly reports must be determined by the Reserve Bank in consultation with the banks, but before such determination the Reserve Bank is to consult with the Australian Payments System Council.

The Preamble also calls for the Code to be reviewed at least every three years in accordance with the Objectives and Principles stated in the Code and having regard to the views of interested parties. There is no indication of who should conduct this review or of which interested parties should be consulted, but there is little doubt that the Australian Payments System Council in consultation with the Reserve Bank will play a major role in this exercise.

The Code also obliges banks to endeavour to ensure that their staff are aware of the provisions of the Code relevant to their duties and, in particular, of the procedures for handling disputes with customers of the bank. Although this is an important provision of the Code, it must be acknowledged that it is one of the most difficult given the large number of staff and the variety of banking services offered.

APPLICATION OF THE CODE

ADOPTION BY PUBLIC ANNOUNCEMENT

[9.5] The application of the Code to a bank is initiated by a public announcement by the bank that it adopts the Code: Code of Banking Practice s 1.3. Although the Code is voluntary, the Australian Bankers' Association assured the federal government that all of its member banks which offer retail banking services would endeavour to achieve full compliance with the Code by the end of 1994: Press Release No 142 by the Treasurer and Minister for Consumer Affairs, 3 November 1993. However, the 1996/97 Annual Report of the Australian Payments System Council identifies three banks which have still not adopted the Code as of October 1997.

From the date of the public announcement the bank is bound by the Code in respect of any banking service that the bank commences to provide to a customer. The bank is also bound by most of the Code in respect of any currently provided banking service provided that the individual to whom the service is provided would have been a 'customer' had the Code applied at the time when the individual first acquired the banking service: Code of Banking Practice s 1.3(b).

The sections of the Code which are excluded from this retrospective operation are those which were thought to be inappropriate because they relate to events which have already occurred. Since the Code does not apply in these circumstances the customer must have resort to the general law in the event of any dispute. As mentioned above, this law may lead to different results from that indicated by the Code. The excluded sections are ss 2.1, 2.2, 2.3 (sections concerned with the initial provision of Terms and Conditions), 7.1 (pre-contractual availability of Terms and Conditions), 11.2 (warnings in respect of foreign currency loans) and 17.1–17.7 inclusive (guarantee disclosure provisions).

[9.6] The provisions of the Code relating to privacy and confidentiality are expressly extended to include an individual who would have been a 'customer' if the Code had applied at the time when the individual acquired a financial service: Code of Banking Practice s 12.12. It is not clear why this section refers to 'financial service' rather than 'banking service': see [9.8].

LEGAL EFFECT OF THE CODE

[9.7] The Code is to be read subject to any Commonwealth, state or territory legislation and, to the extent of any inconsistency, the Electronic Funds Transfer Code of Conduct: s 1.4 Code of Banking Practice. The omission of any reference to non-statute law presumably means that the Code is to override non-statute law where that conflicts with the Code. Of course, in some circumstances it may not be possible for a non-statutory instrument such as the Code to override the general law, but where the non-statutory law merely defines implied contractual terms it seems as though the Code could prevail. It is argued below that in some circumstances customers are worse off under the Code than at general law.

The intention is that the Code should have contractual effect by means of incorporation into the Terms and Conditions of the various banking services. If that is the case then there is no doubt that the terms of the Code would override implied contractual terms which are inconsistent with the Code. It may be that a public announcement by the bank would give effect to the terms of the Code by virtue of s 52 of the Trade Practices Act 1974 even though the bank omits to include the Code as part of the Terms and Conditions of a banking service. Failure to include a statement that the Code applies is itself a breach of the Code (s 2.2), but it would scarcely be possible to argue that there has been a breach of contract.

SERVICES TO WHICH THE CODE APPLIES

[9.8] Many sections of the Code apply only to a 'Banking Service' acquired by a 'Customer'. We have considered the meaning of 'Customer' above. A 'Banking Service' is a deposit, loan or other banking facility which is provided by a bank to a customer, provided that the service is not one of a proscribed kind: Code of Banking Practice s 1.1. There are two (possibly three: see below) kinds of service which are explicitly excluded from the operation of the Code:

1. a service in relation to a bill of exchange;

2. a variation of a term or condition of a facility or a debt to the bank that arises as a result of a withdrawal of more than the amount by which an account is in credit without the approval of the bank.

As to the first point, presumably the expression 'bill of exchange' does not include a cheque since the Code defines an 'account' as including a cheque account or an account that may be accessed by cheque: Code of Banking Practice s 1.1.

The language of the Code is ambiguous in the second point. It is possible to read it as excluding two separate services, the first being the variation of a term or condition of a facility, the second being a debt that arises by means of an unauthorised overdraft: G A Weaver, 'The Code of Banking Practice' (1994) 5 *JBFLP* 60 seems to interpret it in the second way at p 61. Since the Code does not appear to regulate the variation of terms and conditions, the second reading may well be the correct one. This would be a serious deficiency in the Code, particularly when compared with the EFT Code: see [9.48]ff.

DISCLOSURE UNDER THE CODE

BANK MUST SUPPLY TERMS AND CONDITIONS

[9.9]   The Code requires that a bank provide to a customer in writing any Terms and Conditions which apply to an ongoing banking service provided to the customer. These Terms and Conditions must be supplied at the time of, or before the contract for the banking service is made except where it is impracticable to do so, in which case they must be provided as soon as practicable after the provision of the banking service.

The Code does not appear to oblige a bank to make Terms and Conditions of any banking service available to a non-customer or to a customer who has not acquired a particular banking service. Since one of the primary purposes of requiring disclosure is to allow the customer to make informed choices among competing banks and products, this seems to be an unfortunate weakness in the Code. It is also in contrast to the express requirement of cl 2.3 in the Electronic Funds Transfer Code: see [9.54]ff.

Form of the provided Terms and Conditions

[9.10]   The Code requires that the supplied Terms and Conditions should be distinguishable from marketing or promotional material, should be in English and any other language considered appropriate by the bank, clearly expressed, and be consistent with the Code itself: Code of Banking Practice s 2.1. The Terms and Conditions must also draw attention to certain general information on the operation of accounts which is required by other sections of the Code: see [9.16] and [9.17].

Content of provided Terms and Conditions

[9.11]   Where the Code requires that Terms and Conditions be supplied to a customer they must contain certain standard information. Perhaps most importantly the Terms and Conditions must contain a statement to the effect that the relevant provisions of the Code apply to the banking service provided, although there is no requirement to set out those provisions: Code of Banking Practice s 2.2. The supplied Terms and Conditions must also contain, where relevant to the particular banking service provided, the nature of all standard fees and charges which apply: Code of Banking Practice s 2.3(i). 'Standard Fees and Charges' are those fees and charges normally charged by a bank to its customers in respect of the banking service at a particular time: Code of Banking Practice s 1.1.

The provided Terms and Conditions must identify the method by which interest, if any, is calculated and the frequency with which it will be credited or debited, the manner in which variations in interest rates, fees and charges will be notified and, if appropriate, the fact that more than one interest rate might apply: ss 2.3(ii), (iii) and (iv).

[9.12]   The Terms and Conditions must specify any minimum balance requirement or other restriction on the deposit in or withdrawal of money from an account. In respect of term deposits the Code requires information on the manner in which payment of interest and principal will be made, the manner in which funds may be dealt with at maturity and the nature of any charge or variation to an interest rate resulting from early withdrawal: ss 2.3(v) and (vi).

Finally, the Terms and Conditions must specify the terms of repayment of a loan facility, the frequency of account statements, methods of altering or stopping a payment service and a general statement that interest rate information is available on request: ss 2.3(vii)–(x).

Cost of credit disclosures

[9.13]   The Code has an apparently broader disclosure requirement for cost of credit. The bank is required to make available to a customer, a prospective customer or to an appropriate external agency the interest rates and Standard Fees and Charges applicable to a banking service offered by the bank for use in the preparation of a comparison rate: Code of Banking Practice s 3.1. Unfortunately, the language is again ambiguous so that it is impossible to say if the Code requires disclosure to all of the named parties or only to one. So, for example, is it compliance with the Code for a bank to make the cost of credit information available only to an 'appropriate external agency'?

The question is probably a moot one since the credit legislation requirements of disclosure are generally more precise and will override the Code provisions.

Fees and charges disclosures

[9.14]   The Code requires a bank to provide to a customer, before or at the time of providing a particular banking service to a customer or otherwise on request by a customer, a schedule containing the Standard Fees and Charges which currently apply to the banking service: Code of Banking Practice s 4.1. Once again, there seems to be no obligation to provide this information to a person who is not yet a customer.

Payments services disclosures

[9.15]   Bank fees and charges which apply to certain, but not all, payment services must be disclosed to a customer to whom these services are provided. The payment services are: a direct debit or credit payment service, an automatic payment service and a service which provides access to an account by means of instruction via telephone or personal computer: Code of Banking Practice s 5.1.

There are two obvious problems with this section: there is no requirement that the information be provided to a person who is not receiving the service and, oddly, there is no requirement that fees and charges applying to cheque services be disclosed. The disclosure requirements for cheque accounts is treated in a separate section of the Code (s 6.2), but there is no mention there of disclosing fees and charges.

The disclosure required by the Code would not extend to 'computer money' systems unless the particular system provided access to an 'account' by telephone or personal computer. Many computer money systems do not operate through an 'account'.

Account operations disclosures

[9.16]   Certain account information must be provided both to customers and to prospective customers upon request. Where appropriate, the bank must provide information about account opening procedures, complaint handling procedures, the right to combine accounts, bank cheques, the advisability of a customer informing the bank promptly when the customer is in financial difficulty and the advisability of a customer reading the Terms and Conditions applying to the banking service in question: Code of Banking Practice s 6.1. The bank must also provide information concerning the bank's obligations regarding confidentiality of information: see [8.96].

[9.17]   With regard to cheque accounts, a bank must provide general descriptive information on the time generally taken for clearing a cheque and how a cheque may be specially cleared, how and when a cheque may be stopped and how a cheque may be made out so as to reduce the risk of unauthorised alteration. Information must also be provided as to the effect of crossing a cheque, the meaning of 'not negotiable' and 'account payee only' and the significance of deleting 'or bearer' when any of these expressions appear on a cheque. Finally, the bank should provide information on the dishonour of cheques, including post-dated and stale cheques: Code of Banking Practice s 6.2.

The cheque account information must be made available to any customer who opens a cheque account and to any other customer on request. There appears to be no obligation to provide this information to non-customers or to prospective customers. As noted above, there is no obligation to provide information as to the details of any bank fees or charges applying to the use of cheques as a payment service.

GENERAL PRINCIPLES OF CONDUCT

[9.18]   Part B of the Code is concerned with 'General Principles of Conduct'. These 'principles' cover a wide range of banker-customer interactions from the pre-contractual stage to the closing of accounts.

PRE-CONTRACTUAL

[9.19]   The Code requires that a bank have readily available any Terms and Conditions of any banking service currently offered to customers or to prospective customers: s 7.1. Curiously, the Code does not require that these Terms and Conditions be made available to prospective customers whether upon request or otherwise. The bank must disclose the existence of any application fee or charge and whether the fee or charge is refundable if the application is rejected or not pursued, but the Code is silent as to when this disclosure must be made: s 7.2.

It might be thought that the omissions referred to in the previous paragraph are trivial or accidental, but s 7.3 of the Code is precise in placing an obligation on the bank to disclose upon request any fee or charge which is levied by the bank for the provision of a bank cheque, a travellers' cheque or an inter-bank transfer.

OPENING ACCOUNTS

[9.20] The 'principle' which is applicable when opening an account is merely that the bank must provide upon request general descriptive information concerning the identification requirements of the Financial Transaction Reports Act 1988 and the options available under the tax file legislation: s 8.1. This is not an onerous requirement for the bank since the section specifically indicates that the provided information may be material made available by a government.

VARIATION OF TERMS AND CONDITIONS

[9.21] The bank must notify its customers where there is a new or changed government charge which is payable either directly or indirectly by a customer unless the change is publicised directly by the government: s 9.2. Notification may be either directly or by advertisement in the national or local media. Presumably the 'indirectly' in the section refers to the banking practice of passing on certain taxes such as the Financial Institutions Duty.

Where the bank itself wishes to make a change in any terms or conditions, the notification requirements vary in accordance with the importance of the change. If there is an intention to introduce a fee or charge (other than a government charge as above) or to vary the method by which interest is calculated or the frequency which it is debited or credited, the bank must provide written notice of the change to each affected customer at least 30 days in advance: s 9.1. This written notice is, unless otherwise agreed, properly given if sent to the customer's last recorded mailing address: s 9.4. Banks may require that their customers notify promptly of any change to the customer's name or address: s 9.4.

For all other variations, including a variation to Standard Fees and Charges or of an interest rate, the bank may notify the customer by advertisement in the national or local media no later than the day on which the variation takes place: s 9.3.

It is hard to say if these provisions make any change to the general law. On one hand, the bank may not implement a unilateral change in contractual terms: *Burnett v Westminster Bank Ltd* [1966] 1 QB 742. However, it seems likely that the bank's right to make some variation in fees without notice or by public notice is probably a term of the relationship at general law.

COMBINATION OF ACCOUNTS

[9.22]   The Code requires a bank to notify a customer promptly after exercising any right to combine accounts of the customer: Code of Banking Practice s 10.1. This is an improvement of the customer's position at common law where no notice of combination was required: *Garnett v M'Kewan* (1872) LR 8 Ex 10 and see [3.32]ff. The Code also requires that a bank comply with any applicable requirements of the Code of Operation for Social Security Direct Credit Payments: s 10.2.

FOREIGN EXCHANGE SERVICES

[9.23]   A bank which supplies a foreign exchange service to a customer, other than one supplied by credit or debit card or by travellers' cheque, must provide the customer details of the exchange rate and commission charges if known at the time, or details of the basis of the transaction otherwise: s 11.1(i). The bank must also give the customer an indication of when money sent overseas on the customer's behalf would normally arrive at its destination: s 11.1(ii).

When making a foreign currency loan in Australia a bank must give the customer a special warning in writing of the risks arising from exchange rate movements and must tell the customer of any available mechanisms for limiting such risks: s 11.2. In light of the decisions on foreign currency loans and bearing in mind that the Code only applies to 'consumer' banking, this section probably does not extend the bank's existing legal obligations. One would expect foreign currency loans to this class of customer to be a very rare event.

PRIVACY AND CONFIDENTIALITY

[9.24]   The sections of the Code which deal with privacy and confidentiality are less favourable to the customer than might be expected. In some cases the Code erodes a customer's common law rights, in others it does not go as far as we should expect in a modern Code. The privacy and confidentiality principles apply to a person who would have been a 'customer' if the Code had applied at the time that the individual acquired a banking service: s 12.12.

Tournier duties

[9.25]   The Code begins this subject by reciting the *Tournier* duties in a classic restatement. A bank which adheres to the Code 'acknowledges' that it has a general duty of confidentiality towards a customer except in the following circumstances:

> (i) where disclosure is compelled by law; (ii) where there is a duty to the public to disclose; (iii) where the interests of the bank require disclosure and (iv) where the disclosure is made with the express or implied consent of the customer: s 12.1.

[9.26] The Code weakens the customer's right to privacy by permitting disclosure of certain information to 'related entities'. The meaning of 'related entity' in the Code is the same as the meaning in s 9 of the Corporations Law. A bank may disclose to any related entity information necessary to enable an assessment to be made of the total liabilities (including prospective liabilities) of the customer to the bank and the related entity: s 12.2(a).

If the related entity provides financial services which are related or ancillary to those provided by the bank, the bank may release any information concerning the customer unless the customer instructs the bank to the contrary: s 12.2(b). The bank must inform new customers of this right, but there is no obligation to inform existing customers.

This section is a substantial erosion of the customer's existing common law rights where it has been held that disclosure to related companies is a breach of the duty: see *Bank of Tokyo Ltd v Karoon* [1987] AC 45; *Bhogal v Punjab National Bank* [1986] 3 WLR 414; [4.2]ff. It is also contrary to most modern thinking on privacy which requires consent before disclosure, not notification that privacy is desired.

Disclosure and correction of information held

[9.27] One of the keystones of modern privacy theory is that a person should have the opportunity to inspect information held about him or her and to request correction of incorrect information. This 'right of access' and the 'right of correction' are stated as Information Privacy Principle 6 in the Privacy Act 1988 (Cth) in Information Privacy Principles 6 and 7.

The right of access given by the Code is limited to 'customer information'. This is defined as the bank's record of the customer's address, occupation marital status, age, sex, accounts with the bank and balances and statements relating to those accounts: s 12.4. Provided this 'customer information' is readily accessible to the bank and may be lawfully provided, the Code requires the bank to provide it on request to the customer.

Somewhat confusingly, the Code provides that a bank need not reply with a request for customer information (which only needs to be provided if 'readily available') if the customer has not as clearly as possible identified the customer information requested and its likely location if known to the customer. The bank may recover its reasonable cost of supplying this readily available information: s 12.6. Any request for customer information must be dealt with in a reasonable time: s 12.7.

The Code generously provides that a customer may request correction of customer information held by the bank: s 12.7. Given the limited nature of 'customer information' this right is almost meaningless except in regard to the account information, and it scarcely requires a Code to give the customer the right to know about his or her own account information.

[9.28]   There is certain personal information which is so easily abused that many privacy laws prohibit its use. The Code begins by paying lip service to this principle in s 12.9: a bank may not collect, use or disseminate information about a customer's (i) political, social or religious beliefs or affiliations; (ii) race, ethnic origins or national origins; or (iii) sexual preferences or practices.

The Code then makes an exception to say that the bank may collect and use such information for a proper commercial purpose. Since the objection to collecting and using such information is that there is no 'proper commercial purpose', only the well-known improper ones, this section simply mocks the principle while purporting to honour it.

These sections of the Code are grossly inadequate to deal with reasonable customer expectations. A modern bank, not to mention its 'related entities' holds much more information on its customers, information which may be damaging to the customer if incorrect or if it falls into the wrong hands. It is disappointing that the Code appears to be trying to hold a line that is no longer reasonable or defensible.

Information security

[9.29]   The Code requires a bank to take reasonable steps to protect personal information held by it relating to a customer against loss and unauthorised access, use, modification or disclosure. The bank must require all staff with access to personal information concerning customers to maintain confidentiality concerning that information: s 12.10.

Banker's opinions

[9.30]   The Code requires a bank giving a 'banker's opinion' to comply with any applicable requirement of the Credit Reporting Code of Conduct issued by the Privacy Commissioner under s 18A(1) of the Privacy Act 1988. Under the Credit Reporting Code, a bank may not give a banker's opinion to another bank without the subject's specific agreement to the disclosure for the particular purpose if the opinion contains information relating to the subject's consumer creditworthiness: Credit Reporting Code of Conduct, para 2.16. The Credit Reporting Code also establishes certain responsibilities on banks which receive references: see generally the discussion at [4.25]ff.

Omissions

[9.31]   Save for the limited exclusion in s 12.9 and the requirement that a bank may not collect information by unlawful means, there is no limitation whatsoever on the kind of information that may be retained by a bank. There is no limitation on the manner and purpose of collection of information: cf Information Privacy Principle 1. There is no limitation on the solicitation of information from customers or any need to inform customers of the use to be made of solicited information: cf Information Privacy Principle 2. There is no obligation on a bank to enable a person, even a customer, to ascertain if the bank holds personal records relating to that customer: cf Information Privacy Principle 5. There is no general right of access to personal information, save for the very limited category of 'customer information': cf Information Privacy Principle 6. There is no general right of correction: cf Information Privacy Principle 7. There is no obligation on the bank to take any positive steps to ensure accuracy before use: cf Information Privacy Principle 8. There is no requirement that personal information be used only for relevant purposes, save for the offensive suggestion in s 12.9 that there might be a 'proper commercial' use of information named there: cf Information Privacy Principle 9. There is no requirement that a bank use personal information only for the particular purpose for which it was obtained: cf Information Privacy Principle 10.

PAYMENT INSTRUMENTS

[9.32] A bank may inform a customer of the advisability of safeguarding payment instruments and passbooks: s 13.1. It may require a customer to notify the bank as soon as possible of the loss, theft or misuse of any payment instrument: s 13.2. This last section seems to be a restatement, and possibly an extension, of the *Greenwood* duty: see [5.27]. It is noteworthy that banks impose a standard on customers that they choose not to meet themselves: see *Johns Period Furniture v Commonwealth Savings Bank of Australia* (1980) 24 SASR 224 and the discussion at [4.52].

A bank must inform the customer of the consequences arising from a failure to comply with any s 13.2 requirement, and must identify the means whereby the customer can notify the bank of any loss, theft or misuse of the relevant payment instrument: s 13.3.

STATEMENTS OF ACCOUNT

[9.33] Statements of accounts must be provided at least every six months for a deposit account unless (i) the account is operated by a passbook or similar document; (ii) there has been no customer initiated transaction during the six month period; or (iii) the account may be accessed by PIN and EFT card, in which case the EFT Code of Conduct applies to the account: s 14.1. The restriction to a 'deposit account' is unclear in this section. Presumably it is used in the usual sense of a non-cheque account. If that is the case, the exclusion of cheque accounts is peculiar.

PROVISION OF CREDIT

[9.34] When considering the provision of credit to a customer, the bank assesses whether, in the bank's view, the customer has or may have in the future the capacity to repay. It does this by considering a range of factors which it considers relevant to the question. Those factors may include (i) the customer's income and expenditure; (ii) the purpose of the banking service provided; (iii) a credit scoring method used by banks to determine acceptable risks; and (iv) the customer's assets and liabilities: s 15.1.

The only possible point of contention here is the use of credit scoring methods which are sometimes disliked by consumer organisations. There is, however, evidence that they are more reliable, and probably 'fairer' than judgments made by other means.

JOINT ACCOUNTS

[9.35]   A bank is required to give general descriptive information to customers opening a joint account: s 16.1. This must include information on (i) the method of withdrawing funds from the account, having regard to the instructions given by the customers; (ii) the procedures available for varying those instructions; and (iii) the nature of liability for indebtedness on joint accounts.

When accepting a customer's instructions to issue a subsidiary credit or debit card, a bank must provide general descriptive information to the primary cardholder about his or her liability for debts on the account. The bank must also inform the primary cardholder of the means by which a subsidiary card may be cancelled or stopped and the fact that this may not be effective until the subsidiary card is surrendered: s 16.2.

This last piece of information is extremely important since it appears that customers do not appreciate that the subsidiary card may not be easy to cancel: see the Report of the Banking Ombudsman 1992. However, the customer needs the information before applying for the card, not when the bank accepts instructions to issue.

GUARANTEES

[9.36]   There is probably no area of lending which causes more misunderstanding and disputation than guarantees. The reason is clear: the guarantor in a consumer loan is usually acting as a favour to the lender and derives no direct benefit from the arrangement. The guarantor will often have little understanding of the potential liability, and when the guarantee is called upon by the bank the guarantor is faced with real financial stress on top of the psychological stress of having been 'betrayed' by a friend or relative.

Application of Code

[9.37]   The Code does not apply when the guarantee is given in respect of a financial accommodation (i) provided to a public corporation or any of its Related Entities; (ii) provided to a corporation of which the guarantor is a director, secretary or member or any of its related entities; (iii) a trustee of a trust of which the guarantor or a corporation or a related entity of the kind referred to in (ii) is a beneficiary or one of a class of beneficiaries under the trust; and (iv) a partner, co-owner, agent, consultant or associate of any of the guarantor, a corporation or related entity referred to in (ii) or a trustee referred to in paragraph (iii). The relevant time is the time at which the guarantee is obtained. These sections of the Code do not apply unless the guarantor is an individual: s 17.1. The Code does apply to all other guarantees and indemnities obtained for the purpose of securing financial accommodation provided by the bank to a third party.

The clear intention of s 17.1 is to exclude guarantees which are security for 'commercial' loans. This is unfortunate, for it is not the nature of the loan, but the nature of the guarantee that has caused problems in the past. So, for example, many of the problems in recent years have been wives guaranteeing loans made to the family corporation where she is an officer of that corporation: see the discussion in Chapter 11. The Code does not apply to such a case.

Unlimited guarantees prohibited

[9.38]   If the Code does apply, the bank is restricted to taking guarantees which limit the amount of the guarantor's liability to a specific amount plus other liabilities (such as interest and recovery costs) that are described in the guarantee: s 17.2. This is a welcome change from guarantees which exposed the guarantor to liability for any amount which the bank chose to advance to the primary debtor.

Consent of the borrower

[9.39]   In an attempt to balance the bank's perceived duty of confidentiality to the borrower with the desirability of disclosure to the prospective guarantor, the Code calls for a bank to inform a prospective guarantor that certain documents will be provided if the borrower consents. If the borrower does not consent, the bank must inform the prospective guarantor and may not accept the guarantee without the agreement of the prospective guarantor to proceed in the absence of such consent: s 17.3. Of course, this also means proceeding in the absence of the information which would have been provided in the documents. This seems like a good solution to the conflict presented by the borrower's right to confidentiality and the guarantor's interest in full disclosure: see [11.136]ff for a discussion of guarantees.

Warnings and recommendations

[9.40]   A bank must warn in writing a prospective guarantor of the possibility of the guarantor becoming liable instead of, or as well as, the borrower: s 17.4(i). Provided the borrower consents, the bank should also provide the guarantor with a copy or summary of the contract evidencing the obligations guaranteed: s 17.4(ii).

The bank must also recommend that the prospective guarantor obtain independent legal advice: s 17.5. This, of course, is one of the factors which has always been of great importance in the 'guarantee' cases: see *Commonwealth Bank of Australia v Amadio* [1983] 57 ALJR 358 and the discussion in Chapter 11.

Post-guarantee information

[9.41]   Provided the borrower consents, the bank must send the guarantor (i) a copy of any formal demand sent to the borrower; and (ii) on request by the guarantor, a copy of the latest relevant statements of account provided to the borrower, if any: s 17.6.

Presumably the consent required by this section is the consent given by the borrower at the time when the guarantee is being sought: see s 17.3. The effect is somewhat curious, for the borrower must consent to providing the guarantor with statements of account which may disclose private information to the guarantor which goes beyond the need of the guarantor to track the general financial position of the borrower.

Discharge

[9.42]   A guarantor may extinguish his or her liability under the guarantee by paying any outstanding liability of the borrower (including any future or contingent liability) or any lesser amount to which the liability of the guarantor is limited by the terms of the guarantee: s 17.7.

General comment on guarantees

[9.43]   The Code is unlikely to have any serious effect on the position of guarantors. Most of the recent reported cases coming before the courts would have been excluded from the Code because of the character of the borrower. For those cases which do fall within the Code, the documents which must be provided to the prospective guarantor are of limited relevance and the ones which must be provided after the guarantee is obtained make no difference at all to the decision to enter into the guarantee. The requirement of the Code that a bank must recommend independent legal advice is a welcome clarification.

ADVERTISING

[9.44]   A bank must ensure that its advertising and promotional literature drawing attention to a banking service is not deceptive or misleading: s 18.1. This requirement does not extend the bank's obligation under the Trade Practices Act or the various Fair Trading Acts.

However, in any advertising in the print media and in any promotional literature that draws attention to a banking service and includes a reference to an interest rate, the bank must also indicate whether other fees and charges will apply and that full details of the relevant terms and conditions are available on application: s 18.2.

The requirements of this section are substantially less than that of existing consumer credit legislation: see, for example, Credit Act 1984 (NSW) s 121. The limitation to print media advertising is unsatisfactory. The section continues the general ambiguity in the Code as to whether Terms and Conditions are available on request or only upon application for the banking service.

CLOSING THE ACCOUNT

[9.45] Subject to the terms and conditions of the relevant banking service (i) a bank will close an account that is in credit upon request by the customer; (ii) may close an account in credit by giving notice that is reasonable in all the circumstances and repaying the amount of the credit balance; (iii) may charge the customer an amount that is a reasonable estimate by the bank of the costs of closure: s 19.1.

As to the right of the bank to close an account, this seems to be a re-statement of the existing position: see *Prosperity Ltd v Lloyds Bank* (1923) 39 TLR 372. As to the customer's rights, it may be more favourable to the bank since the previous law was unclear about termination when the terms and conditions called for the return of a passbook: Jamieson, 'Conditions Under Which the Banker-Customer Relationship is Terminated' (1991) *ALJ* 89. The Code unfortunately does not address the question of when the bank may close an overdraft account: see [2.25].

DISPUTE RESOLUTION UNDER THE CODE

INTERNAL PROCESSES

[9.46] Banks must have internal processes for handling a dispute between the bank and a customer. A 'dispute' exists when a bank's response to a complaint by a customer about a banking service provided to that customer is not accepted by the customer. The process must be readily accessible by customers without charge by the bank: s 20.1.

General descriptive information must be made available in branches. This must include information on (i) the procedure for handling disputes; (ii) the time within which the dispute will normally be dealt with by the bank; and (iii) the fact that the dispute will be dealt with by officers of the bank with appropriate powers to resolve the dispute: s 20.2.

If the customer requests resolution in writing or requests a response in writing, the bank must promptly inform the customer in writing of the outcome. If the resolution of the dispute is not acceptable to the customer, the bank must provide the reasons for the outcome and inform the customer of further action which may be taken, such as the process for the external resolution of disputes: s 20.3.

EXTERNAL PROCESSES

[9.47] A bank must have available for its customers an external and impartial process (not being an arbitration) for the resolution of disputes which are not resolved in a manner acceptable to the customer by the internal process. This external process must have jurisdiction similar to that of the Australian Banking Industry Ombudsman Scheme: s 20.4 and see [9.75]ff. The external process must apply the law, the Code and may also take into account what is fair to both the customer and the bank: s 20.5.

THE EFT CODE OF CONDUCT

BACKGROUND TO THE CODE

[9.48] Organised public discussion of the problems related to the electronic funds transfer system dates at least from the 10th International Trade Law Seminar in 1983: see A L Tyree, 'Electronic Funds Transfer: an Australian Perspective', *Proceedings of the 10th International Trade Law Seminar*, Canberra, 1983, p 129. The Campbell Committee of Inquiry into the Australian Financial System (1981) considered that there was reason for concern about the appropriate mix of obligations and liabilities in the consumer EFT system, but indicated that it had not undertaken enough work to provide a full assessment. It recommended that the federal government establish a task force with representation from governments and all interested parties to examine the need for legislation. The recommendation was never acted upon.

[9.49] The EFT issue was re-examined by the Martin Review Group on the Australian Financial System which reported in 1983. The *Martin Report* recommended that no legislation be undertaken. There was enough concern to recommend the establishment of the Australian Payments System Council. The Council, established in 1984, is charged with the oversight of the Australian payments system and, in particular, to consider the development of EFT standards. It is not clear what arrangements will be made for monitoring the Code when the APSC is abolished in accordance with the recommendations in the Wallis Report: see the discussion in Chapter 1.

At the same time as the establishment of the APSC, the federal government announced the formation of an inter-departmental Working Group under the chairmanship of Treasury to assess the operation of the EFT system. The working group was to also consider if formal arrangements were necessary to regulate the rights and obligations of the users and providers of EFT services.

[9.50] The report of the working group in October 1985 found that there was cause for concern and that financial institutions should be required to change their current practices, either by altering the conditions of use or, at the very least, by providing clear and honest information to users. The working group considered three options: legislation, an industry code of conduct and voluntary action by the financial institutions. Partly because the rhetoric of the day was 'let the market decide', the working group opted for the third of the options, conveniently overlooking the fact that it was the market which had produced the unsatisfactory results in the first place.

At the same time that the report of the working group was being finalised, a meeting of the Standing Committee of Consumer Affairs Ministers (SCOCAM) came to the conclusion that some government intervention would be necessary before any real changes could be expected. A draft code of conduct was prepared by Victoria and New South Wales and released at about the same time as the report of the working party.

[9.51] In an effort to forestall state legislation, the states, which had previously been pointedly excluded were invited to joint the working group. The second report of the working group appeared in September 1986. This report recommended adoption of a voluntary code known officially as the 'Recommended Procedures to Govern the Relationship between the Users and Providers of EFT Systems' but universally referred to simply as 'the Code'. This code, in terms identical to the code prepared by Victoria and New South Wales, was endorsed by the federal government and the state Consumer Affairs Ministers. The details and the operation of the Code are discussed below.

The Working Group was requested to undertake a monitoring role to see that the implementation of the Code proceeded smoothly. It was to report on that implementation in March 1988, but the report was initially delayed until late 1988 and finally appeared in mid-1989. The report found that some institutions had been slow to implement the Code and that there were inadequacies in complaint handling procedures.

[9.52] In December 1988 the Trade Practices Commission released a report *Finance industry code of conduce on electronic funds transfer services: An assessment by the Trade Practices Commission*. The thrust of the report was that there are significant shortcomings in both the Code and in its implementation. The report offers a number of recommendations for modifications of the Code and, most importantly, a specification of minimum, industry-based administrative and public reporting arrangements to support the modified Code.

The current Electronic Funds Transfer Code of Conduct is the result of this long process. While lacking the force of legislation it is supported by both the industry and the federal government. Any EFT dispute which falls within the jurisdiction of the Australian Banking Industry Ombudsman is governed by the EFT Code: see [9.73]ff. Card-issuers or their representative associations are responsible for reporting annually on compliance with the Code.

The Code has been subject to a further review, but at the time of writing the report has not been released. In light of technical developments in the payment system, particularly the development of smart cards and other forms of 'computer money', it is clear that major changes will be required: see the discussion at [8.89]ff.

APPLICATION OF THE CODE

[9.53] The Code applies to all transactions which are initiated by an individual through an electronic terminal by the combined use of an electronic funds transfer plastic card and a personal identification number (the PIN), or which are intended to be so initiated: EFT Code, cl 1.1. Recent technical developments will probably require modification of the Code. For example, some smart cards may have a 'lock' which prevents their use for large transactions except where the user provides a PIN. We are faced with the anomolous situation of some transactions being governed by the Code, while other transactions are not, even though the same card is used and the same account accessed. See the discussion of 'computer money' at [8.89]ff.

DISCLOSURE REQUIREMENTS

[9.54]   One of the earliest consumer complaints about the EFT system was that there was insufficient disclosure. The financial institutions would often refuse to show customers the terms and conditions of usage until the customer had applied for and been issued a card. The terms and conditions were often incomprehensible to the average user, and were found to be unfair where they could be understood. The liabilities of the cardholder were often found in the 'fine print'. The cardholder was often left with insufficient information about what to do when the card was lost or stolen, and there was seldom any information available about how to contest disputed transactions. The EFT Code addresses this problem at several levels.

Card-issuers must provide clear and unambiguous contracts for the terms and conditions of use of the cards: EFT Code, cl 2.1. The clauses in the terms and conditions which deal with the liabilities and the responsibilities of the cardholder must be simply stated and highlighted in the text, and the contracts must contain a warranty that the requirements of the EFT Code apply: EFT Code, cl 2.1.

Copies of the terms and conditions of use are to be available at all branches on request. They must in any event be supplied to the customer no later than (1) with the notice of acceptance of an application for EFT facilities; (2) with the initial issue of the card; or (3) with the provision of the PIN which allows the facilities to be used. Details of any charges, restrictions on use, and any available credit facilities must be provided before the first use of EFT facilities: EFT Code, cl 2.3(i)–(iv).

Procedures for reporting loss or theft of the card must be provided to all cardholders. This information must contain telephone numbers for reporting losses outside of normal business hours: EFT Code, cl 2.3(v). Finally, the card-issuer is responsible for providing documentation which explains the methods for activating an investigation of any complaint by the cardholder and the dispute resolution process of the issuer: EFT Code, cl 2.3(vi).

CHANGING TERMS AND CONDITIONS OF USE

[9.55]   When EFT was first introduced it was common for the terms and conditions to contain a clause to the effect that the card-issuer had the right to unilaterally and without notice change the terms of the contract. At the other extreme, consumer groups sometimes argued that the terms and conditions were like any other contract and so could not be unilaterally altered by either party. Neither position was reasonable. Some terms and conditions are clearly important and should not be altered without notice being brought to the attention of each individual cardholder, but others are less significant and may reasonably be changed by notice. It may be necessary to make rapid unilateral changes when the security of the system is in issue. The Code adopts a sensible classification and regime of alteration.

Where the changes are necessary to maintain the security of the system or of individual accounts, the issuer is given the authority to change the conditions of use unilaterally and without notice: EFT Code, cl 3.3. Certain changes require advance written notice of at least 30 days; such changes include (1) increased or imposed charges which relate solely to the use of EFT facilities; (2) increased liability for losses; or (3) variation of periodic transaction limits: EFT Code, cl 3.1. Other variations must merely be notified in advance through notices accompanying the periodic account statement, notices on terminals and in branches or through press advertisements: EFT Code, cl 3.2.

PAPER RECORDS

[9.56] Should EFT transactions be evidenced by paper receipts? If so, what information should the receipt contain? Is it necessary to issue a paper receipt at the time of the transaction or is it sufficient to issue them periodically? The Code takes a hard position on all of these questions in cl 4.

Unless the cardholder specifically chooses otherwise, a receipt must be provided at the time of each individual EFT transaction. It must contain sufficient detail so as to identify the transaction and, in particular, must identify the amount, time, date and type of the transaction. It must indicate which account has been accessed and also sufficient data to allow identification of the cardholder, the transaction and the terminal through which the transaction was conducted. If the transaction is a payment to a merchant then the receipt must contain the name of the merchant to whom payment is made. Where possible, a receipt for a transaction through an ATM should contain the balance of the account.

Clause 4.2 deals with the responsibilities of the issuer to provide periodic accounts. Cardholders must be given a statement of account on request. In any case, statements should be provided at least every six months, and cardholders must be given the option of receiving more frequent statements. The statement must provide certain information about each transaction including the amount and type, the date on which the transaction was credited or debited and the receipt number or other means of identifying the transaction. The statement must also identify any charges which relate solely to EFT transactions. It must include an address or telephone number for inquiries.

The Code forbids institutions from including clauses which would have the effect of imposing an obligation on the cardholder to inspect the statement: EFT Code, cl 4.4; see the discussion at [3.44]ff as to the general duty of the customer with regard to the statement of account.

LEGAL STATUS OF SIGNATURE

[9.57] The current means of transaction authentication in consumer EFT systems is the card-PIN combination. 'PIN' is the acronym for 'personal identification number'. On one view, the card-PIN combination is really just the substitution of one form of identification for another and in a sense this is correct when the transaction proceeds according to the expectation of the parties, but the situation is very much different when the transaction goes wrong, usually because of a misappropriation in the means of identification.

[9.58] The legal status of the signature on a cheque is not that it is a means of identification, but rather the mechanism whereby authority is granted to the banker to make a payment and to debit the account. Thus Kerr J in *National Westminster Bank Ltd v Barclays Bank International Ltd* [1975] 1 QB 654 said (at 666):

> The common aphorism that a banker is under a duty to know his customer's signature is in fact incorrect even as between the banker and his customer. The principle is simply that a banker cannot debit his customer's account on the basis of a forged signature, since he has in that event no mandate from the customer for doing so.

There is little doubt that the use of the card-PIN combination has the same legal effect when used by the rightful 'owner' (strictly speaking, the customer doesn't become the owner of the card since most conditions of use reserve the property in the card to the institution, the customer being entitled to the possession of the card only so long as the conditions of use permit).

[9.59] However, when the card-PIN is misappropriated by a rogue, the consequences to the customer are very different. Until the introduction of the Code, the usual conditions of use issued by the financial institutions threw the risk of all unauthorised use onto the customer at least until such time as the customer notified the institution of the loss of the card-PIN. For example, a typical condition read 'If the Card and PIN is lost or stolen the Customer must immediately notify the Bank. Until the Bank receives such notification the Customer shall be liable for all transactions conducted with the Card and PIN'.

LIABILITY FOR UNAUTHORISED TRANSACTIONS

[9.60] The change in the position of the customer under the pre-Code regime may be illustrated by considering the analogous situation of a forged drawer's signature on a cheque: the bank may not debit the account of the customer even if the customer has been careless in the keeping of the cheque-book: *Kepitigalla Rubber Estates Ltd v The National Bank of India Ltd* [1909] 2 KB 1010 and see the discussion in Chapter 5. The customer has no duty to discover forgeries or, generally speaking, to organise business affairs in such a manner as to guard against them: *National Bank of New Zealand Ltd v Walpole and Patterson Ltd* [1975] 2 NZLR 7; *Tai Hing Cotton Mill Ltd v Liu Chong Hing Bank Ltd* [1985] 2 All ER 947 and see the discussion in Chapter 5.

The Code provides for a limited cardholder liability for unauthorised use of the card. For the purposes of the Code, an unauthorised transaction is one which is carried out without the cardholder's knowledge and/or consent. If the cardholder has not been 'careless' in the sense defined below, then the liability is limited to $50, the balance of the account (including any prearranged credit) or the actual loss at the time of notification, whichever is the lesser: EFT Code, cl 5.5; but see [9.69] on the operation of the Code in practice.

[9.61] The cardholder may be 'careless' in two ways. First, he or she may mishandle the PIN by voluntarily disclosing to another person, by indicating the PIN on the card or by keeping with the card (without making a reasonable attempt to disguise the PIN) a record of the PIN. Second, the cardholder may be careless by failing to notify promptly the issuer of known misuse of the card or that the PIN has become known to another person or that the card has been stolen.

[9.62] When the customer has been careless he or she may be liable for substantially more than $50. When there is carelessness of the first type, the cardholder is liable for all loss not exceeding the lesser of: (1) the actual loss at the time the card-issuer is notified of the loss or theft of the card; or (2) the maximum amount the cardholder would have been entitled to access over the relevant period prior to notification of the loss or theft of the card calculated in accordance with the periodic transaction limit applicable to that cardholder's card or account(s); or (3) the balance of the nominated account(s) (including any prearranged credit). When the cardholder has been careless in notifying, the liability is similar save that the first limit is changed to the actual losses, which could otherwise have been prevented from occurring, in the period between when the cardholder became aware of the events described above (or should reasonably have become aware in the case [that the PIN has become known to another party or that the card has been lost or stolen]) and when the card-issuer was actually notified.

LIABILITY FOR SYSTEM MALFUNCTION

[9.63] The card-issuer is liable for losses which arise from system malfunction. The Code specifically makes the card-issuer liable for any direct loss caused by a malfunction within the EFT system: EFT Code, cl 6.1. If the customer is aware or should have been aware that the system or equipment was unavailable or malfunctioning, the card-issuer may limit responsibility to correcting any account errors and the refund of consequential fees or charges: EFT Code, cl 6.2. In other cases of system or equipment malfunction the Code forbids the card-issuer from denying 'a right to the cardholder to make claims for consequential loss or damage which may arise': EFT Code, cl 6.2. Further, the issuer may not avoid these obligations by reason only that they are a party to a shared system where the fault of some other participant may have caused the failure to meet the obligation: EFT Code, cl 8.1.

OTHER UNAUTHORISED TRANSACTIONS

[9.64] Clause 5 of the Code also deals with other forms of unauthorised transactions. The cardholder is not liable for any losses which are caused by the negligent or fraudulent conduct of employees of the card-issuer, those involved in networking arrangements or of merchants who are linked to the EFT system. The cardholder is not liable if the unauthorised transaction is effected by means of a card which is forged, faulty, expired or cancelled, or for any loss which occurs before receipt of the card and PIN. In any dispute concerning receipt of the card and PIN the cardholder has the benefit of a presumption that the item was not received. This presumption may not be rebutted by showing that the card and PIN was delivered by mail to the correct address, nor may there be any term in the terms and conditions of use which deems that such a delivery is receipt for the purpose of the Code. Most importantly, the cardholder has no liability for any unauthorised use which occurs after the cardholder has notified the card-issuer that the card has been lost or stolen or that PIN security has been breached.

PRIVACY

[9.65] Clause 10 of the Code establishes four privacy 'principles' for the guidance of card-issuers. Customer records are to be treated in the strictest confidence and electronic terminal access to details of a customer's account is to be restricted to employees and agents of the institution which maintains the account, the customer and any person authorised by the customer. An electronic terminal should be incapable of providing account information unless the appropriate card and PIN are used, except where the information is requested by an employee or agent of the institution which maintains the account. No information concerning the use of EFT services should be disclosed except with the consent of the customer or pursuant to a legal duty or responsibility. Card-issuers are not to use cameras to monitor transactions at electronic terminals unless a sign is displayed which indicates that transactions may be photographed.

Except for the prohibition of secret photography, the 'principles' probably add little to the bank's duty of confidentiality: see [4.2]ff. However, the Code also applies to non-bank card-issuers which may consider themselves to be outside the principles of *Tournier's* case. A careful reading of the decisions in the *Tournier* case shows that this belief is misguided: see A L Tyree, 'Does *Tournier* apply to building societies?' (1995) 6 *Journal of Banking and Finance Law and Practice*, p 206.

DISPUTE RESOLUTION PROCEDURES

[9.66] A code of conduct is no better than the means available to resolve disputes which may arise under the Code. One of the serious pre-Code problems was the lack of any suitable avenue for redress of complaints.

Clause 11 of the Code requires each card-issuer to establish appropriate procedures for investigating and resolving complaints concerning any matter covered by the Code. Although the Code does not require any specific procedure, it does establish minimum 'features' which are expected of an appropriate procedure. Failure to establish an appropriate procedure or failure by the card-issuer, its employees or agents to observe the procedures may result in the card-issuer being liable for the full amount of the disputed transaction. The card-issuer is required to keep records of complaints and their resolution for the purposes of the annual report to the federal government.

The card-issuer must establish a formal mechanism for the lodgment of complaints, and must publicise this mechanism through documentation provided to the cardholder. When a complaint is lodged, the cardholder is responsible for providing all information which is relevant to the complaint, and if the matter is not immediately resolved the cardholder must be advised in writing of the procedures for the investigation and resolution of the complaint.

[9.67] The normal rule is that an investigation should be completed within 21 days and the cardholder be notified in writing of the outcome. If more time is required, the cardholder should be notified in writing of this fact, and only in exceptional circumstances should the investigation fail to reach a decision within 45 days. Upon completion of the investigation, the cardholder is entitled to be advised in writing of the outcome together with reasons for the decision.

The Code requires that the decision be made on the basis of all relevant established facts and not on the basis of inferences unsupported by evidence. The Code establishes a minimum list of information which must be obtained from the cardholder in the event that the complaint refers to an unauthorised transaction. If the complaint concerns an unauthorised transaction the card-issuer must also refer to the systems log to establish if there was any malfunction at the time of the transaction.

If the investigation shows that the account was incorrectly debited (having regard to the liability provisions of the Code) the card-issuer must immediately correct the account and notify the cardholder in writing of the result. Where the result of the investigation shows that the cardholder is liable under the Code for at least part of a disputed unauthorised transaction, the card-issuer must provide the cardholder with the documents and evidence on which the decision is based.

[9.68] The procedures established by the institution must also provide written advice that any decision on a complaint is subject to appeal to the card-issuer's senior management upon request by the cardholder. The cardholder should also be advised of any external remedies available, including Consumer Affairs Departments, Small Claims Tribunals and, where applicable, the Australian Banking Industry Ombudsman.

THE CODE IN PRACTICE

[9.69] It is difficult to assess the impact of the EFT Code. There is little doubt that the disclosure provisions have resulted in dramatic improvements. The Terms and Conditions imposed by the Code are much fairer than those which were imposed by the institutions in the pre-Code days.

In the area of liability for unauthorised transactions, the situation has probably not changed much at least at the public level. The main reason for this is the assertion of the card-issuers that it is for the customer to prove that the institution is not entitled to debit the account: see [9.70]. This, is turn, is based on two assumptions. First, it is believed, or at least publicly asserted, that it is impossible to operate the machines without access to both the card and the PIN. Second, it is always assumed that when there is an unauthorised transaction, the only way that the user could have obtained the PIN is through the negligence of the cardholder. There is ample evidence to show that both assumptions are false. It is argued below that the legal burden of proof is on the card-issuer.

As to the infallibility of the computer network, there have been several well-publicised incidents of massive computer and/or software failure. In July 1987 the Westpac Bank system failed in a way that allowed cardholders apparently unlimited access to funds; in 1988 the Commonwealth Bank system failed in a way that confiscated all customers' cards: see A L Tyree, 'Who Pays? The Law and Electronic Funds Transfer' *Current Affairs Bulletin* Vol 65, No 9, August 1988, pp 23–8. The Westpac failure was acknowledged to be due to software error. The Commonwealth Bank failure was said to be through human error, but since the essence of good software design is to guard against human error, the difference is one of little importance.

The second belief is also publicly discredited. In 1987 a group of schoolboys in Perth were apprehended after manufacturing cards and obtaining PINs by observing cardholders through binoculars: Tyree, loc cit. If there is any negligence in such a situation, it must be that of the institution which installs machines in exposed positions.

BURDEN OF PROOF

[9.70] The cardholder is further disadvantaged by the insistence that the burden is on the customer to show that there was no negligence in the keeping of the PIN. It is submitted that this is incorrect. We can begin by observing that it is on the person claiming breach of contract to prove their case.

When a banker pays money, whether on a cheque or an EFT transaction, the money paid is that of the banker, not the customer; this principle is fundamental to modern banking law and is at least as old as *Foley v Hill* (1848) 2 HL Cas 28. The banker may debit the account of the customer only if the money has been paid in strict accordance with the customer's mandate or if the payment has been caused by a customer's breach of contract or if the banker has some other defence to wrongful payment: *London Joint Stock Bank Ltd v Macmillan and Arthur* [1918] AC 777; *Commonwealth Trading Bank of Australia v Sydney Wide Stores Pty Ltd* (1981) 55 ALJR 574.

Consider the unauthorised transfer. *Ex hypothesi*, the bank has not followed the customer's mandate. How then may it debit the account? There are no statutory defences analogous to ss 93 and 94 CPOA available to the bank. The only possibility is by showing that the customer has breached the banker-customer contract. Consequently, the burden of proof is on the bank.

WHAT MUST BE PROVED

[9.71] The EFT issuers do not seem to have a clear picture of what must be proved. If the institution is following the Code of conduct, then in order to maintain the debit for more than $50, the institution must show that the customer was careless in the keeping of the PIN within the meaning of cl 5.5(a) of the Code.

Clause 11.4 provides that decisions are to be made on the basis of all relevant established facts and not on the basis of inferences unsupported by evidence. In spite of this rule, most institutions regularly adopt the 'one-shot rule', inferring negligence from the fact that the transaction was completed without multiple attempts with the PIN.

Several arguments are advanced regularly which are either based on false information or are logically incorrect.

The most common argument is based on the reliability of the systems. The argument goes like this: it is not possible for an ATM to be used without a card and valid PIN. The likelihood of guessing a PIN is one in 10,000 if a four digit PIN is used and one in a million when a six digit PIN is used. The user has three opportunities to make a correct guess. Therefore, any unauthorised use of the ATM must be by someone who has access to the PIN and the only way in which that can happen is that the customer is careless within the meaning of s 5.5 of the Code.

The argument is incorrect at each step. The concept of infallibility of the ATMs has been discredited. It is possible to obtain PINs without any negligence on the part of the customer. The probability aspect of the argument is wholly misleading for the simple reason that we simply do not know how many attempts there are to guess PINs with stolen or forged cards. If there are a large number, then we may be virtually certain that some will succeed.

In fact, any argument which attempts to prove the liability of the individual cardholder on the basis of statistical information of the reliability of the EFT network is logically flawed. If a million or a billion or a trillion transactions are completed satisfactorily we still know nothing about the transactions that are disputed. Most airplanes arrive safely at their destination, but that is not proof, not even evidence, that there are no air crashes.

SUMMARY

[9.72] In the previous edition it was concluded that the rights of the card-holder are insufficiently protected. This is still formally the case, but informally there seems to have been a change. The institutions still assert their rights, but the existence of the Banking Ombudsman and the consequential improvement in the institutions' own dispute resolution structures means that a consumer with a good arguable case will probably succeed. In an area where proof is so difficult, where the opportunities for fraudulent claims are so obvious, this is probably the best that can be expected.

THE AUSTRALIAN BANKING INDUSTRY OMBUDSMAN

ESTABLISHMENT

[9.73] Motivated by a desire to improve public relations and to forestall any proposed legislation, the Australian Banking Industry Ombudsman was established in 1990 to provide a mechanism for the resolution of disputes between individual, that is, non-business, customers and banks. The scheme was modelled on a comparable scheme in the United Kingdom: see Burton, 'A Banking Ombudsman for Australia', (1990) 1 *JBFLP* 29. The scheme is a free service to customers provided to offset the prohibitive cost of litigation and the inadequate system of in-house dispute resolution in existence at the time.

In order to make the scheme credible, it must be seen to be independent of direct interference by the owners of the scheme, the banks. This is particularly so since the banks are, by definition, involved in disputes which come before the Ombudsman. In order to achieve both the independence and the appearance of independence, the Australian Banking Industry Ombudsman Limited, a company limited by guarantee is composed of a Board, a Council and the Ombudsman. The Board is the board of directors of the company. Its primary function is to approve funding and to make final decisions on changes to the Terms of Reference.

[9.74] The Council is composed of equal numbers of consumer and industry representatives. The stated role of the Council is to act as an intermediary between the Ombudsman and the banks. It also provides an advisory role to the Ombudsman in matters of policy and makes financial representations to the Board on the advice of the Ombudsman. It monitors the Terms of Reference, receives recommendations from the Ombudsman with respect to changes in the Terms of Reference and makes recommendations to the Board concerning amendments.

The structure has, for the most part, been successful in assuring the independence of the Ombudsman. Unfortunately, that appearance of independence was severely damaged when the Terms of Reference were changed to prohibit the Ombudsman from dealing with disputes related to the collection of third party cheques and the Ombudsman is no longer solely responsible for deciding if a case comes within the Terms of Reference.

Unfortunately, both of these changes were a direct response to cases either currently before the Ombudsman or which had recently been considered.

POWERS AND DUTIES OF OMBUDSMAN

[9.75]   The powers and duties of the Ombudsman are set out in the Terms of Reference. Under these Terms of Reference, the Ombudsman is required and authorised to consider disputes relating to the provision within Australia of banking services by any member bank to any individual.

A 'dispute' is a complaint over which a deadlock has been reached between the individual and senior management of the bank. 'Banking services' means all financial services provided by banks in the ordinary course of their business to individuals, including the use of credit cards overseas, and advice and services relating to insurance and investments and guarantees or charges given or created by an individual in favour of the bank to guarantee or secure any moneys owing to it by another individual under any advance or analogous facility.

Subject to certain jurisdictional limitations, the Ombudsman is required and authorised to facilitate the satisfaction, settlement or withdrawal of disputes by any means as seem expedient.

LIMITS ON OMBUDSMAN'S POWERS

[9.76]   There are some general limitations on the Ombudsman's powers which reflect the fact that the Scheme is intended to be for the resolution of consumer complaints rather than 'policy' matters or the business judgment of banks. Thus, under paragraph 17 of the Terms of Reference, the Ombudsman has no power to consider a complaint in so far as it relates to a bank's commercial judgment in decisions about lending and security, but this exclusion does not prevent consideration of disputes concerning maladministration in lending matters. A 'decision about lending or security' includes any decision (or the consequences thereof) concerning any advance or similar facility, guarantee or security. 'Commercial judgment' means the assessment of risk, of financial or commercial criteria or of character. 'Maladministration' means an act or omission contrary to or not in accordance with a duty of care owed at law or pursuant to the terms of the contract between the bank and the disputant: para 31(a). For the same reasons, the Ombudsman may not consider a complaint in so far as it relates to a bank's general interest rate policies.

[9.77]   The jurisdiction of the Ombudsman is also limited to hearing disputes where the amount claimed or which could be claimed does not exceed $150,000. This is extended to exclude claims where the complaint is part of a larger claim which the applicant has made or could make, or where the claim is related to another claim which could be made and the aggregate of all such claims exceeds $150,000: para 17.

The Ombudsman may only investigate complaints by an individual. 'Individual' includes a partnership or other unincorporated body of persons where the body is not composed entirely of bodies corporate but does not include unincorporated statutory authorities: para 31(a). The Ombudsman cannot investigate disputes where the complainant is a guarantor of a loan to a body corporate.

The Ombudsman is intended to be a kind of appeal structure. Consequently, the Ombudsman may not consider a complaint unless the senior management of the bank have had the opportunity to consider the complaint. The Ombudsman's jurisdiction arises when the bank advises that a deadlock has been reached or, if there is no such advice, three months after the complaint has been made. Recent research shows that the existence of the Ombudsman may have been responsible for a substantial improvement in the practice of banks' handling of customer complaints: Oborn, 'Procedures Adopted by Australian Banks for the Resolution of Customer Complaints and the Role of the Australian Banking Industry Ombudsman', (1992) 3 *JBFLP* 268.

TEST CASES

[9.78]   Since the Ombudsman is directed to apply the law in the resolution of disputes, it follows that there should be some mechanism for removing the complaint from jurisdiction when the law is uncertain. The Terms of Reference provide that the Ombudsman must cease to consider a complaint if the bank gives notice that the complaint involves issues which have important consequences for the business of the bank or for banks generally or which involve important or novel issues of law. Such a notice must be in writing and must include an undertaking that the bank will pay the applicant's legal costs in any court action which is undertaken in respect of the matter provided that the action is commenced within six months of the date of the notice. The Ombudsman must notify the applicant in writing of the receipt of the notice, the date of its receipt and the effect of the notice upon the complaint: paras 21, 22.

TIME LIMITS

[9.79]   Paragraph 20 of the Terms of Reference provide the 'statute of limitations' for the Scheme. The complaint to the Ombudsman must be made within two months of the bank informing the complainant of a deadlock provided that the bank also informs the complainant of the existence of the Ombudsman and the two month time limit. Except where the complaint is based on new evidence, the act or omission giving rise to the complaint must have occurred not more than six years before the applicant first makes a written complaint to the bank.

The Ombudsman may only consider disputes where the act or omission complained of occurred on or after 10th May, 1989 or, if it occurred before that date the applicant did not become aware of it, and could not with reasonable diligence have become aware of it until that date.

DISPUTES CONSIDERED BY OTHER BODIES

[9.80]   The Ombudsman is not intended to be an avenue of appeal from other bodies. Consequently, the Ombudsman may not hear a dispute which has already been the subject of proceedings before a competent court or tribunal where a judgment was given on the merits. Similarly, if the dispute is the subject of a completed investigation by a statutory ombudsman of any state: para 20.

When the dispute is the subject matter of any current proceedings before a court, tribunal, arbitrator or any other independent conciliation body, or is the subject of an investigation by a statutory ombudsman of any state, then the parties may consent in writing to the Ombudsman's consideration. If they do not so consent, the Ombudsman has no power to investigate.

PROCEDURE

[9.81]   Subject to the specific requirements of the Terms of Reference, the Ombudsman may decide upon the procedures to be adopted when considering disputes. In keeping with the informal nature of the process, the Ombudsman is not bound by any legal rules of evidence: para 15. The Ombudsman may take account of a bank's security measures of which he or she has knowledge notwithstanding that no disclosure of these measures has been or will be made to the applicant: para 8.

When making any recommendation or award the Ombudsman is required to do so by reference to what is, in his or her opinion, fair in all the circumstances. However, he or she is also required to observe any applicable rule of law or relevant judicial authority, and to have regard to general principles of good banking practice and any relevant code of practice applicable to the subject matter of the complaint: para 15. In determining the principles of good banking practice the Ombudsman must, if he or she considers it appropriate, consult within the banking industry. For an analysis of the effects of these sections, see Burton, 'A Banking Ombudsman for Australia' (1990) 1 *JBFLP* 29.

ACCESS TO AND DISCLOSURE OF INFORMATION

[9.82]   The Ombudsman clearly does not have the powers of a court to order disclosure, but the Terms of Reference give certain powers for disputes being considered: see paras 5, 6, 7A and 7. The Ombudsman may require any bank named in a complaint to provide information relating to the dispute which is in its possession unless the bank certifies that the disclosure of the information would place the bank in breach of its duty of confidentiality to a third party whose consent it had used its best endeavours to obtain.

There is no power to require that a claimant disclose information, but if either party does supply information it may be accompanied by a request that the information remain confidential. Such information may not be disclosed by the Ombudsman without the consent of the party giving the information, and the Ombudsman must return any such confidential documents to the supplying party upon the determination of the dispute. Any party to the dispute may examine information on the dispute which is held by the Ombudsman, except for information which is supplied on a confidential basis. Except in the case of information relating to a bank's security measures, the Ombudsman may not use undisclosed confidential information to reach a decision adverse to the party against whom the confidential information relates.

Subject to certain exceptions, the Ombudsman may not disclose information to any person (including a Board or Council member) from which it might be possible to identify the parties to a complaint: para 27. The exceptions to this rule are disclosure as required by law or by any competent authority or as reasonably required in connection with any legal proceedings instituted by or against the Ombudsman. The Ombudsman may also provide information to the Council Chairman or his or her authorised deputy, or to any employee, consultant, independent contractor or agent of the Ombudsman to the extent that the disclosure is reasonably required by the person for the purpose of performing the duties: para 27. The Ombudsman must also disclose to the relevant bank any threat to bank staff or property of which he or she becomes aware: para 28.

SETTLEMENTS, RECOMMENDATIONS AND AWARDS

[9.83]   Since the Scheme aims to arrive at agreed settlements, the Ombudsman may at any time seek to promote a settlement or withdrawal of the complaint: para 10. If the matter cannot be settled by negotiation then the Ombudsman may, at the request of either of the parties, make a recommendation for settlement or withdrawal provided that such a recommendation must be preceded by at least one month's notice. During the period of notice either party may make further representations to the Ombudsman in respect of the complaint. The recommendation must be in writing and supported by a summary of reasons: para 11.

If the negotiated or recommended settlement or withdrawal involves the bank in paying money or providing other valuable consideration, unless the bank otherwise requests or agrees then the proposal or recommendation must state that it is open for acceptance by the applicant only if it is accepted in full and final settlement of the subject matter of the complaint: para 12. There is no power to compel a complainant to accept a recommendation, but if he or she does so the bank has one month to accept or reject the recommendation. If the bank does not accept the recommendation then the Ombudsman has the power to make an award against the bank: para 13. The award must not be of a greater amount than is appropriate to compensate the complainant for the direct loss or damage suffered as a result of the act or omission which gives rise to the dispute: para 13. The award cannot be for an amount exceeding $100,000.

An award must be in writing and supported by reasons. The award must state that if within one month after its issue the complainant agrees to accept it in full and final settlement of the dispute, the award shall be binding on the complainant and the bank against which it is made.

Notice that the complainant need not agree to accept the findings of the Ombudsman although the bank must do so. The Ombudsman has no power to make any award against the complainant.

CREDIT CARDS

[9.84] One of the most significant features of retail banking over the past 20 years has been the emergence of the third party credit card as a major method of consumer payment. The third party card is a logical development of the two party cards which have been used by major retailers for many years. The two party card is little more than a token issued by the retailer which authorises the customer to purchase goods on short-term credit at the particular retail establishment. The third party card, by contrast, represents a complex commercial arrangement between the card-issuer, a significant number of merchants and a significant number of customers who are issued with the card.

The modern third party card which is issued by a bank provides not only a facility for purchasing goods on short-term credit, but also the ability to borrow cash to the limit agreed upon from the card-issuer without the need for any formalities.

BASIC OPERATION OF THIRD PARTY CREDIT CARDS

[9.85] The basic sequence of events when a third party credit card is used for the purchase of goods or services is that the customer tenders the card as a means of payment. The merchant takes an impression of the details of the customer's card which are embossed upon the card and fills in details of the purchase on a special form which is provided by the issuer. This form is in three parts. The customer receives a copy, one copy is retained by the retailer and one copy is delivered to the card-issuer. It is usually necessary for the customer to sign the form as well as produce the card. At an agreed time, the merchant's account is credited with the amount of the purchase less any agreed discount. The cycle is closed with the periodic statement to the customer who then pays the issuer the amount of the invoices or, depending upon the terms of the contract, pays a proportion of the charges and credit charges on the outstanding balance.

There are some advantages for each of the parties. The customer needs to carry less cash and the loss or the destruction of the card need not represent as great a loss as the loss of cash. The customer ordinarily obtains a period of free credit and receives a certain amount of accounting in the form of the monthly statement which may assist in his or her financial planning. On the other hand, it is thought that the ready availability of the means to purchase items may lead to an increase in 'impulse buying' which could have the effect of destroying any planning previously undertaken.

The merchant essentially eliminates the risks of bad debts, handles less cash which reduces the risks of theft and probably increases sales due to the above mentioned 'impulse buying' effect. The price which is paid for this is the agreed discount.

The card-issuer earns income from the discount agreed upon with merchants and by any interest charges paid by cardholders under revolving credit arrangements. When the issuer is a bank, there is a significant possibility of attracting customers who would not ordinarily keep a current account with the corresponding increase in low interest deposits. Against this must be weighed the large costs of establishing a scheme, for financial success of the third party credit card scheme depends upon the existence of a very large base of participating merchants and cardholders.

This basic scheme admits of two minor variations which may have legal effect. When the issuer is a bank or other financial institution, it is common to allow the cardholder to obtain cash advances against the card. Interest is charged from the date of the cash advance. Further, the cardholder is not normally required to pay all of the outstanding balance, but may elect to pay only a percentage each month provided only that the total credit does not exceed a prescribed limit.

The so-called 'travel and entertainment' cards differ from the financial institution card only in the requirement that all charges be paid at the end of the billing cycle. There is no provision made for the extension of credit beyond the single billing cycle.

The importance of this seeming minor distinction is that although the various state Credit Acts definitely apply to the financial institution type of credit card, they may not apply to the travel and entertainment cards: see Chapter 10.

THE LEGAL FRAMEWORK

[9.86]   A credit card is not a legal instrument in any way comparable with a bill of exchange; it does not carry with it any legal rights or obligations of itself. However, in order to use a credit card for the purchase of goods, there must be three basic contractual relationships established. First, there is a contract between the issuer and the cardholder which authorises the cardholder to use the card at authorised merchants in the way described above. Second, there is a contract between the issuer and the merchant which obliges the merchant to accept the card as payment for goods or services and obliges the issuer to reimburse the merchant when the card is so accepted. Finally, there is a contract for the sale of goods or services between the merchant and the cardholder by which the merchant accepts the card as a form of payment in lieu of legal tender.

Since not all jurisdictions have legislation similar to the Credit Acts and since some third party credit cards may not be regulated by the Acts in those jurisdictions where the Acts apply, the legal relationships will first be discussed as they exist under the general law. We will then consider the position in those jurisdictions where the cards are covered by the Acts: see [9.100].

THE CONTRACT BETWEEN THE MERCHANT AND THE ISSUER

[9.87]   Although the precise terms vary, it is common for contracts to contain terms which oblige the merchant to accept valid credit cards and to sell goods or services at the same price as when accepting payment by cash. The merchant usually agrees to obtain the cardholder's signature on the invoice form and to compare it with the signature on the card itself; there is ordinarily an obligation for the merchant to obtain express authority from the issuer before accepting the card for payment in excess of some agreed amount.

The merchant agrees to deposit the invoices within a specified period and to be credited with the face value of them less an agreed discount. This discount will vary with the type and size of the merchant's business, but the range appears to be between 1.25 per cent and 6 per cent. The merchant further agrees to accept certain debits to the account. This may happen in circumstances initiated by the merchant, for example, when the merchant gives a credit for goods returned, but the issuer usually reserves the right to make a debit to the account when there is a dispute between the cardholder and the merchant which relates to the specific transaction. The issuer also reserves the right to debit the account when the card is on a 'hot list' of cards which have been stolen, where the card is counterfeit or where the signature has been forged.

Sheppard J examined a typical 'Merchant Agreement' in *Cosmedia Productions Pty Ltd v Australia and New Zealand Banking Group Ltd* [1996] 434 FCA 1. The agreement provided, inter alia, that the merchant must obtain authorisation for any sale in excess of a specified 'floor limit'. The procedure is that the merchant telephones a number provided by the issuer and gives details of the proposed transaction. The merchant is then issued with an 'authorisation number' to be entered on the sales voucher.

Although the word 'authorisation' is used in the agreement, it is clear that an authorised transaction may later be reversed by the card-issuer. In the *Cosmedia* case, Sheppard J noted that the purpose of 'authorisation' is to 'facilitate the transaction' but the issuer does not guarantee that the merchant will necessarily be paid or, if paid, will be able to retain the payment.

THE CONTRACT BETWEEN THE ISSUER AND CARDHOLDER

[9.88]   The contract between the issuer and the cardholder is a standard form contract usually headed 'conditions of use' which is unlikely to be sighted by the customer prior to receiving the card. It is thought, however, that the first use of the card represents the cardholder's assent to the conditions of use. These conditions typically contain undertakings by the customer to reimburse the issuer for payments made by the issuer to merchants on behalf of the cardholder's use of the card, to notify the issuer in the event that the card is lost or stolen and not to raise against the issuer any defence or counterclaim which might have been raised against the merchant in respect of the transaction.

The conditions of use also contain clauses whereby the cardholder gives the issuer the authority to pay the merchant in respect of purchases made using the card.

There is ordinarily also a clause which places liability for all transactions initiated with the card, whether authorised by the cardholder or not, on the cardholder provided that the cardholder has not given actual notice to the issuer that the card has been lost or stolen, but current practice is to couple that with a 'ceiling' on liability, usually $50. There is also a clause which permits the issuer to vary the conditions of use without notice to the cardholder. It may be that the efficacy of this clause will need to be reassessed following the decision in *Tai Hing Cotton Mill Ltd v Liu Chong Hing Bank Ltd* [1985] 2 All ER 947: see [2.13]ff.

THE CONTRACT BETWEEN THE MERCHANT AND THE CARDHOLDER

[9.89]   There seems little change in the usual contract between the merchant and the cardholder. It remains a normal contract for the sale of goods save that the merchant looks to the card-issuer for payment of the price. The possibility of the issuer failing to meet that obligation is discussed below: see [9.93].

LEGAL PROBLEMS

[9.90]   There are few reported cases dealing with legal problems arising from the credit card system, probably because the system works well, and when it does not the amounts are relatively small so that the disputes may be resolved without litigation or the claim simply dropped. Since the use of the card usually involves a signature, the evidenciary problem that bedevils EFT systems does not arise. The only reported case in English law concerns the failure of the card-issuer, so that although the individual sums were small, the total sum involved justified litigation: *Re Charge Card Services Ltd* [1986] 3 All ER 289, discussed below.

The legal resolution of legal problems which do arise depends to some extent on the legal nature of the credit card transaction. There seem to be only two candidates. The transaction may be in the nature of an assignment or it may be similar to a letter of credit transaction.

[9.91]   In the assignment model, the theory is that the effect of the contractual relationships is that a debt is assigned by the merchant to the card-issuer. The debt is that owed by the cardholder and which arises from the transaction in question. The argument in favour of the assignment model is that the issuer pays the merchant a discounted value as would be expected. The contract between the card-issuer and the cardholder provides that the cardholder will not raise any of the defences against the issuer that he or she might raise against the merchant, a clause which would scarcely be necessary unless there were an assignment of the debt owed to the merchant by the cardholder.

[9.92] The second model of the transaction is that it is similar to a letter of credit transaction. Indeed, the plastic card does seem to have many similarities with the letter of credit. It is clear when the merchant accepts the credit card in lieu of payment that it is the credit of the card-issuer which is being relied upon. There is a clear analogy of payment against documents when the invoice is presented by the merchant. If it is the 'beneficiary' who pays the bank charges rather than the cardholder, that is no reason to change the legal analysis but is only a reflection of the difference between consumer and commercial practice. Similarly, it is argued that the clause which prevents the cardholder from raising contractual defences is merely a recitation of the fundamental position; in particular, it is not evidence that the true legal transaction is an assignment.

These models are merely convenient ways to fit the credit card into a familiar legal structure. It could be that credit cards are *sui generis* and that it is more fruitful to address problems as they arise rather than by reference to a predetermined model.

FAILURE OF THE CARD-ISSUER

[9.93] The nature of the legal transaction takes on importance when the card-issuer does not pay. Such was the case in *Re Charge Card Services Ltd* [1986] 3 All ER 289. The card issuing company, Charge Card Services Ltd, issued cards which were available for use at garages which had entered into an agreement with the issuing company. The cards were used by cardholders in the way described above. Because Charge Card Services Ltd normally paid the participating garages well before they were themselves paid by cardholders, they entered into an arrangement with Commercial Credit Services Ltd whereby debts owing or to become owing from cardholders were assigned to Commercial Credit.

At the time of liquidation, there was some £3 million due to the company from cardholders. The liquidator was directed to collect all sums due and at the time of the litigation had collected more than £2 million after allowing for the costs of collection. The issue in the case was whether this entire sum was to go to Commercial Credit or whether the garage owners who had not been paid at the time of the liquidation were entitled to claim the sums due them.

Note that the only way in which the garage owners could claim is if they had a right to claim directly from the cardholders. Thus, counsel for the garage owners argued that when cardholders filled their tank with petrol that they contracted to pay the price displayed on the pump and if they chose to pay by card it was conditional payment only, much as if they chose to pay by cheque. Counsel for Commercial Credit argued that the cardholder never became liable to the garage to pay for the petrol if they chose to accept the garage owner's standing offer to accept the credit card in lieu of cash and that the only obligation on the customer was to pay Charge Card. The garage owner must look to Charge Card to recover payment.

Millet J held that there were no grounds for the conditional payment argument. He held that the essence of the agreement was that the supplier and the customer had for their mutual convenience each arranged to open an account with the same company, Charge Card, and agreed that any account between themselves might, if the customer wished, be settled by crediting the supplier's account and debiting the customer's account with the company. Furthermore, the court held that the customer's liability to the garage owner was discharged at the latest when the owner's account was credited, not when he or she was paid.

These features were enough to displace any presumption that payment by card was conditional. Quite the contrary, they supported a conclusion that it was not meant to be conditional payment only. Further, since Charge Card had undertaken to guarantee its obligation to reimburse the garage, it was clear that the garage owner considered himself to be giving credit to the company, not to the customer.

Re Charge Card Services Ltd was followed in *Customs and Excise Commissioners v Diners Club Ltd* [1989] 2 All ER 385; [1989] 1 WLR 1196.

The Merchant Agreement in *Cosmedia* also specified that the bank would accept all valid sales transactions and credit the account of the merchant 'on the basis that the debt due to the Merchant is extinguished'. This clause in the Merchant Agreement provides very strong evidence that payment by credit card is intended by the parties to be final payment: see *Cosmedia Productions Pty Ltd v Australia and New Zealand Banking Group Ltd* [1996] 434 FCA 1.

[9.94] The result should be compared with the situation where an issuer of a documentary letter of credit has failed to make the payment called for. The normal position is that the seller of goods may then have recourse to the buyer, and if the buyer has already put the issuer in funds then he or she may have to pay twice: *W J Alan & Co Ltd v El Nasr Export & Import Co* [1972] 2 QB 189: see the discussion in Chapter 11. The difference may be explained by the commercial differences of the two arrangements. In a letter of credit payment, it is usually the buyer who selects the paymaster and the transaction is usually a 'one off sale'. There is no room in the letter of credit transaction for the argument that the buyer could choose to accept the seller's 'standing offer' to be paid by tender of the card rather than in cash. Furthermore, the continuing nature of the credit card arrangement means that the merchant has a much greater say in the choice of acceptable credit card.

UNAUTHORISED CARD USE

[9.95] As noted above, the contract between the card-issuer and the cardholder will most likely make the cardholder liable for all unauthorised use of the card until such time as the cardholder notifies the issuer that the card has been lost or stolen subject to a nominated ceiling on cardholder liability. Since the conditions of use currently place a relatively low ceiling on the liability, there is unlikely to be much scope for cases to arise.

If the conditions are changed to those similar to the conditions of use for EFT cards, then it is likely that problems of significant magnitude will arise. Apart from the possibility of challenging the imposition of unlimited liability as being 'unconscionable' under the Trade Practices Act 1974 or comparable state legislation (see [11.164]), there is the possibility that the cardholder might escape liability if there is fraud or negligence on the part of the merchants involved in the unauthorised use of the cards.

[9.96]   In *Gulf Refining Co v Willlams Roofing Co* (1945) 186 SW 2d 790 the plaintiff was a card-issuer who issued a number of cards to the defendant for use by the defendant's employees. The defendant typed across the face of the cards 'Good for Truck Only', but one of the cards fell into the hands of a rogue who made over 200 purchases with the card before the unauthorised use came to the notice of the defendant who then notified the plaintiff. One of the clauses in the conditions of use purported to make the cardholder liable for all purchases made with the card prior to notification.

The rogue was not driving a truck at the time when the fraudulent purchases were made and there was evidence given that some at least of the merchants knew that the rogue was not entitled to the use of the card. The court held that the plaintiff could not recover, noting that the merchants could not have recovered directly from the defendant and that the plaintiff could not then be in a better position.

The decision seems to be based on some variant of the assignment model with its consequences that the issuer takes the debt subject to equities, although the court did not spell out the background reasoning for its findings.

CHARGE BACKS

[9.97]   Credit card-issuers may retain the right to 'charge back' transactions. For example, in the *Cosmedia* case, a clause in the Merchant Agreement provided that the bank might charge back any invalid sales transaction, any transaction where the cardholder disputed liability for any reason or where the cardholder asserted a claim for a set-off or a counterclaim. The Agreement further identified unauthorised transactions as a particular form of 'invalid sales transaction': see *Cosmedia Productions Pty Ltd v Australia and New Zealand Banking Group Ltd* [1996] 434 FCA 1.

The right to charge back a transaction is clearly a valuable method of preventing the card-issuer from becoming involved in merchant-cardholder disputes over faulty goods or services. When used in that context, it is a valuable consumer remedy and is unexceptional in its operation. However, the charge back mechanism has also been used in circumstances where the merchant has become insolvent. For example, newspaper reports indicated that ticket holders of the failed Compass Airline received full refunds if they had paid by credit card. Ticket holders who paid by cash were, of course, in the position of unsecured creditors of the airline.

The card-issuer could withhold payment from the trustee under the merchant contract since there is a 'counterclaim'. However, for those payments already made to the merchant, the issuers right to reclaim the money paid would be merely a contractual right. There is no obvious reason why the issuer should obtain any priority over the general unsecured creditors.

Does the cardholder have a right to require the issuer to exercise its right of charge back? The answer depends upon whether the issuer is the agent of the cardholder for the purposes of making the payment. If the issuer is the agent, then the agent is obliged to use its rights in the interests of the principal. This is similar to the principle established in *Riedell v Commercial Bank of Australia Ltd* [1931] VLR 382 where it was held that the customer may obtain certain of the benefits of the clearing house agreement.

However, it is submitted that the better view is that the card-issuer is not the agent of the cardholder. If, as argued above, payment by credit card is final payment, then this is inconsistent with the issuer being the agent for payment. The terms of the Merchant Agreement clearly contemplate that the debt owed by the cardholder is extinguished, so that the issuer is not paying on behalf of the cardholder but on behalf of itself.

CRIMINAL LIABILITY

[9.98]　　There may be criminal liability for improper use of both credit and debit cards. Section 29B of the Crimes Act (Cth) provides penalties for offences related to imposing or endeavouring to impose 'upon the Commonwealth or any public authority under the Commonwealth by any untrue representation, made in any manner whatsoever, with a view to obtain money or any other benefit or advantage ...'. This section has been used to convict cardholders of Commonwealth Bank cards who have used the cards fraudulently: *R v Evenett* [1987] 2 Qd R 753; *R v Baxter* [1988] 1 Qd R 537; (1987) 84 ALR 537.

These cases have been extended to obtain convictions when a debit cardholder improperly obtains money from an ATM. In *Kennison v Daire* (1986) 160 CLR 129 the defendant had closed his account with the Savings Bank of South Australia, but had retained his card. He approached an ATM which was 'off-line' and was able to obtain a withdrawal of $200 since in the 'off-line' state the ATM was not in communication with the main bank computers and so unable to determine if the defendant maintained an account. The ATM was programmed so as to allow the withdrawal of up to $200 provided that the PIN keyed in matched the PIN encoded on the card.

The defendant was convicted of larceny, but appealed on the basis that the bank, by programming the ATM in the way which it did, must be taken to have consented to the withdrawal. That argument failed since it was clear that the bank did not consent to the withdrawal of money by a former customer whose account was closed.

[9.99]   More interestingly, it was argued that had the appellant approached a human teller in the bank and obtained the money either by writing a cheque or by presenting the card or by any other lawful means, then the bank must be considered to have consented by virtue of the authority of the teller to pay out the money of the bank. So, it was argued, an ATM must be taken to have similar authority to make decisions on the basis of its programming.

The High Court rejected the 'authority' argument, holding that a machine could not be taken to have the same authority as a human teller. The court said (at 132): 'The machine could not give the bank's consent in fact and there is no principle of law that requires it to be treated as though it were a person with authority to decide and consent.'

If this statement is restricted to the facts of the *Kennison* case then it is unobjectionable, but it cannot be taken out of that context for it is clear that there are certain 'decisions' which are within the scope of the machine's 'authority'. Thus, if a person with an account presents a card to an ATM and requests a withdrawal which would place the account in overdraft, then there seems every reason to suppose that if the machine is so programmed as to allow an overdraft then the overdraft is properly granted. This should be so even if the conditions of use of the debit card specify that the card should not be used to obtain overdrafts. Even in a normal transaction, if the machine cannot make decisions to allow withdrawal then how does the bank claim the right to debit the account?

The distinguishing feature of the *Kennison* case is that there was no account and it is clear that a machine, or probably a human teller, has no authority to permit the withdrawal.

CARD DISTRIBUTION

[9.100]   When credit cards were first introduced into Australia they were sometimes distributed by mail to parties who neither sought them nor wanted them. This unsolicited distribution was seen as undesirable and the Trade Practices Act 1974 was amended to regulate card distribution; similar provisions are included in the state Fair Trading Acts. The regulation is of both 'credit cards' and 'debit cards'. A 'credit card' is any article of a kind commonly known as a credit card or any similar article intended for use in obtaining cash, goods or services on credit. A 'debit card' is an article intended for use by a person in obtaining access to an account held by the person for the purpose of withdrawing or depositing cash or obtaining goods or services: s 63A(3).

The Act prohibits sending such cards to any person except in two circumstances: (1) the person has requested the card in writing and the person making the request is the person who will be under a liability for its use; or (2) the card is sent in renewal or substitution of a card previously sent. The first prohibition is framed in a way that prevents children or spouses from requesting 'second' cards on the account of the person who has primary liability for the account.

The Act also prohibits the 'conversion' of credit cards into debit cards and vice versa except in response to a written request from the cardholder: s 63A(2A).

[9.101]   The contract between the card-issuer and the cardholder is a 'credit contract' for the purposes of the Consumer Credit Code. See [11.47] for a brief discussion of the consequences of a contract being regulated by the Code.

CHAPTER 10

NEGOTIABLE INSTRUMENTS

NEGOTIABILITY

[10.1] Cheques are not only instruments for the simple payment of debts, they are also negotiable instruments, a role that is in some ways in direct conflict with the role of a simple secure payment device. Historically, the cheque is a negotiable instrument by virtue of the identification with the bill of exchange, but the Manning Committee Report and the Cheques and Payment Orders Act 1986 have confirmed its negotiability.

THE CONCEPT OF NEGOTIATION

[10.2] The essence of a negotiable instrument is that the debt which is represented by the instrument should be easily, cheaply, and freely transferable. Negotiable instruments were originally developed for the purposes of extending credit and obtaining payment in international sales transactions. In the form of bills of exchange and promissory notes, they now play a significant role in the mobilisation of short-term capital.

In either role, it is of the essence that the instrument should be freely transferable and that the person who is entitled to the instrument for the time being, the 'holder', should be able to obtain payment of it. In the case of a cheque, this means that the holder should at any time be able to obtain payment from the drawee bank for it is the debt owed by the bank to the drawer of the cheque which is the debt which is represented by the cheque.

In order to facilitate this easy transferability, the usual rules about the transfer of property do not apply to negotiable instruments. The rule *nemo dat quod non habet* which is so fundamental to the common law of property is the exception rather than the rule in negotiable instruments law. The fundamental position in the latter is that a bona fide purchaser for value with no notice of defect of title will get good title, even if the transferor has a defective title or, in some instances, no title at all.

This concept conflicts with the use of a cheque as a simple payment device. When a drawer of a cheque wishes to pay a debt by cheque, it is usually his or her intention that the cheque be used to pay the debt and for no other purpose. Most cheque users would be stunned to find that their cheque might be intercepted by a thief who, because of the rules of negotiable instruments, may give good title to some other party who may be able to claim payment from the drawer. And the original debt for which the cheque was drawn might still be undischarged!

ESSENTIAL FEATURES OF NEGOTIABILITY

[10.3]   The word 'negotiable' must be treated with care, for the complete meaning of the word is not always clear. Even the Bills of Exchange Act uses the word in several different senses. There is no 'correct' usage, but there are three characteristics that seem to be essential: B B Riley, *Bills of Exchange in Australia*, 3rd ed, Law Book Co, Sydney, 1976. Note that each of the characteristics is unusual when compared with the transfer of chattels.

METHOD OF TRANSFER

[10.4]   The first characteristic is that the transfer of the rights embodied in a negotiable instrument are transferred by delivery and, in some cases, indorsement. 'Indorsement' is the old spelling of 'endorsement' and it has been retained in the Cheques and Payment Orders Act 1986. It signifies the writing on the instrument, usually on the back, of the name of the person who is transferor. The addition of the indorsement will usually make the indorser a surety for payment as well as transferring the right to the payment. The process of transfer by indorsement and delivery is called 'negotiation'.

TRANSFEREE ABLE TO SUE IN OWN NAME

[10.5]   A second characteristic of a negotiable instrument is that the person who is entitled to the instrument, called the holder, may sue in his or her own name. This is an important exception to the common law doctrine of privity of contract, for it is not necessary to sue the person from whom the holder took the instrument. The holder may recover from any party who is liable on the instrument. The holder may choose to sue any one or all of the parties who are liable on the instrument.

TRANSFER FREE OF EQUITIES

[10.6]   Finally, the holder who takes an instrument which is in a proper form, who takes for value and without any notice of defects in the transferee's title may take 'free of equities', that is, it is possible in the ordinary course of transferring rights in a negotiable instrument to pass a better title to the transferee than is held by the transferor.

DISTINGUISH TRANSFERABILITY

[10.7]   It is important to distinguish transferability from negotiability. Every cheque is transferable by negotiation, that is, by indorsement (where required) and delivery: CPOA s 39(1). The CPOA is so determined on this point that s 39(2) says that every cheque is transferable notwithstanding anything that is written on the cheque and, in particular, the crossing of a cheque does not affect the transferability of a cheque by negotiation: s 39(3). Other negotiable instruments may be drawn so as to be non-transferable, but an instrument in that form is of little commercial value: see [10.6] and *Hibernian Bank Ltd v Gysin and Hanson* [1939] 1 KB 483; [1938] 2 KB 384.

On the other hand, not every cheque is negotiable in the sense of having all three of the characteristics of negotiability. In particular, and most importantly for those who wish to use the cheque as a simple payment instrument, it is possible to revive the *nemo dat* rule in regard to cheques with the addition of the 'not negotiable' crossing: s 55. Such a cheque remains transferable, but the transferee takes no better title than that of the transferor. As will be seen, this is important protection for the drawer, but other factors, namely the privileged statutory protection given by the statute to the financial institutions, make it quite insufficient: see Chapter 7.

COMPARISON WITH TRANSFER OF A DEBT BY ASSIGNMENT

[10.8]   The negotiable instrument is not the only method known to our law for the transfer of debts. Both legal and equitable assignments may be used for the same purpose. It is instructive to compare the two methods, negotiable instrument and assignment, to see why the assignment is wholly inappropriate both as a payment mechanism and as a financial device.

SUE IN OWN NAME

[10.9]   The holder of a cheque may sue in his or her own name: s 49(1). This is also true of a legal assignee of a debt, but it is not possible to make a legal assignment of a part only of a debt: *Re Steel Wing Co Ltd* [1921] 1 Ch 349 and see [10.72]. This makes the legal assignment useless as a payment device. A part of a debt may be the subject of an equitable assignment, but in that case the assignee of the debt must join the original debtor in an action to recover: *Durham Bros v Robertson* [1898] 1 QB 765. Recall that s 88 of the CPOA provides that the drawing of a cheque is not, of itself, an assignment of funds.

CONSIDERATION PRESUMED

[10.10]   The consideration for a negotiable instrument is presumed: CPOA s 36; BEA s 35. Thus it is not ordinarily necessary to plead and to prove that consideration has been given. This is, of course, in contrast to the usual rules of pleading and of debt recovery. It is one of the features that allows for simple summary procedures to be used by the holder of a negotiable instrument.

There are also certain extensions to the concept of consideration which give the holder of an instrument an advantage in certain cases.

NOTICE TO ORIGINAL DEBTOR NOT REQUIRED

[10.11] It is not necessary for the holder to give notice to the original debtor either for the purpose of making that debtor liable on the instrument or for establishing the priority of the holder over other claimants. By contrast, notice to the debtor is an essential component of a legal assignment and is necessary in order to establish priority in an equitable one: see [10.72] and *Dearle v Hall* (1823) 3 Russ 1; 38 ER 475.

TRANSFER FREE OF EQUITIES

[10.12] Finally, the assignee of a debt, whether legal or equitable, takes subject to all equities and rights of set-off. So, for example, if the original debt was tainted by fraud, then the debtor may plead that fraud against the assignee even though the assignee of the debt was not party to the fraud and had no knowledge of it. Again, if the original debt represented the price paid for goods, it may be that the assignee can be met by a partial defence that the goods failed to meet contract specifications, even though the assignee was not part of the original transaction and has no knowledge of the goods or of the breach.

By contrast, the holder of a negotiable instrument will, under certain circumstances, take the instrument free of equities. There have even been cases where the holder of the instrument has been successful even though the holder is the supplier of the goods which are alleged to be defective: see *Nova (Jersey) Knit Ltd v Kammgarn Spinnerei GmbH* [1977] 1 WLR 713. Similar results may follow where a direct debit is cancelled: see *Esso Petroleum Co Ltd v Milton* [1997] 2 All ER 593 and [8.9].

SUMMARY JUDGMENT

[10.13] The assignee of a debt must sue for breach of contract if the debt is not paid. All of the defences mentioned above may be raised by the defendant. By contrast, the holder of a bill of exchange must only plead that he or she is a holder and that the signature of the defendant is on the bill in a position which makes the defendant liable. The plaintiff is then entitled to summary judgment for the face value of the instrument unless the defendant can obtain the leave of the court to defend. This will not be granted lightly, for the rule is that negotiable instruments are to be treated as cash unless there are exceptional circumstances. As one court has said '[the] rule of practice is thus, in effect, pay up on the bill of exchange first and pursue claims later': *Ceborah SNC v SIP (Industrial Products) Ltd* [1976] 1 Lloyd's Rep 271 at 276.

This approach has been confirmed by a decision of the New Zealand Court of Appeal in *International Ore & Fertilizer Corporation v East Coast Fertiliser Co Ltd* [1987] 1 NZLR 9. ECF had contracted to purchase goods on c&f terms from the appellant. As part of this contract, they had accepted a bill of exchange. On arrival, the cargo was contaminated and there was deficiency in the documents. The buyer rejected the goods and sought leave to defend on an action on the bill of exchange on the basis of a total failure of consideration. The court referred approvingly to English principles on bills, namely (1) bills are to be treated as cash even between immediate parties; (2) except for a total or liquidated partial failure of consideration, a breach by the plaintiff of the underlying contract does not afford a defence, even between immediate parties; (3) a counterclaim for unliquidated damages cannot be put forward as a set-off. Under the circumstances, it was arguable that the buyers were entitled to reject the goods and the case is then one of total failure of consideration so that leave to defend was granted.

TYPES OF NEGOTIABLE INSTRUMENTS

[10.14] Aside from Australian notes and coins, there are only three payment instruments in use in Australia which are fully negotiable. They are the bill of exchange, the promissory note and the cheque. The cheque has been discussed at length in previous chapters.

These are not the only financial instruments which are negotiable. The CPOA itself includes dividend warrants, that is, a warrant issued by a company to enable a shareholder to obtain dividends from the company's bank: CPOA s 118; Chappenden and Bilinsky, *Riley's Bills of Exchange in Australia*, 3rd ed, 1976, Law Book Company, Sydney, p 236. Other instruments which have been held to be negotiable include short-term bearer securities issued by foreign or domestic governments, bearer debentures issued by corporations, some government and corporate bonds, warehouse certificates, and negotiable certificates of deposit: see Burton, 'Bills of Exchange and other Negotiable Instruments' in *Halsbury's Laws of Australia*.

Although it is not certain, it seems likely that travellers' cheques are also negotiable instruments: see Frohlich, Travellers' cheques and the Law in Australia', (1980) 54 *ALJ* 388 and *El Awadi v Bank of Credit and Commerce International SA Ltd* [1990] 1 QB 606. For a contrary view, see Bilinsky, 'How Safe are Travellers' Cheques?', (1990) 4 *JBFLP* 271.

Certain instruments are known to lack some essential feature of negotiability even though they are easily transferable. These include share certificates, bills of lading, storage receipts and money or postal orders: see Burton, 'Bills of Exchange and other Negotiable Instruments' in *Halsbury's Laws of Australia*. It should also be noted that receipts, IOUs and debentures which either create or acknowledge an indebtedness are not negotiable even though there may be a significant market for them: *Thomas v Hollier* (1984) 53 ALR 39 at 50 per Brennan J; *Gillard v Game* [1954] VLR 525.

Bills of exchange

[10.15]   Instruments similar to bills of exchange are very old. It is said that Arab traders used instruments very similar to bills during the eighth century. The instruments could be transferred by indorsement and the payee had rights exercisable against the acceptor and, in the event of default, against the drawer: W S Holdsworth, *A History of English Law*, 7th ed, Sweet & Maxwell, London, 1956. During the sixteenth and seventeenth centuries, the bill of exchange was the primary instrument used to facilitate both international and domestic trade: J M Holden, *The History of Negotiable Instruments in English Law*, University of London Press, London, 1955.

Although bills developed from the custom of merchants, the definition of a bill of exchange is now governed by statute. Section 8(1) BEA provides that:

> A bill of exchange is an unconditional order in writing, addressed by one person to another, signed by the person giving it, requiring the person to whom it is addressed to pay on demand, or at a fixed or determinable future time, a sum certain in money to or to the order of a specified person, or to bearer.

This is, of course, very similar to the definition of a cheque which was discussed in [6.49]. The primary differences are that the bill need not be drawn on a banker, need not be payable on demand and that the money must be payable to or to the order of a specified person or to bearer. Thus, a non-cheque which requires payment to 'cash or order' is not a bill of exchange since it does not specify a payee: *Orbit Mining and Trading Co Ltd v Westminster Bank Ltd* [1963] 1 QB 794.

[10.16]   The economic function served by bills and promissory notes is much different from that of a cheque. The primary purpose is to provide a secure legal mechanism for an extended period of credit: see the discussion of accommodation bills at [6.49]. For this reason, it is common for bills and notes to be drawn payable at some future time.

Other aspects of the definition of a bill of exchange are similar to the definition of cheque in the CPOA and the discussion in Chapter 6 applies.

Bills of exchange may be 'accepted' by the drawee. By accepting the bill, the drawee acknowledges that he or she is willing to comply with the order to pay: s 59. Since the bill may be negotiated prior to acceptance, the drawer of a bill undertakes, by the act of drawing the bill, that the bill will be accepted when duly presented for acceptance: see [10.51] and BEA s 60(1)(a).

Promissory notes

[10.17]   While the definition of a bill of exchange requires at least two parties, the drawer and the drawee, the promissory note requires only one. Section 89(1) BEA provides:

> A promissory note is an unconditional promise in writing made by one person to another, signed by the maker, engaging to pay, on demand or at a fixed or determinable future time, a sum certain in money, to or to the order of a specified person, or to bearer.

As there must be an 'order' in the case of a cheque and a bill of exchange, so must there be a promise in order for an instrument to be a promissory note. The words used must indicate an undertaking to pay, not merely an acknowledgment of a debt. Thus, an IOU is not a promissory note: *Akbar Khan v Attar Singh* [1936] 2 All ER 545.

Promissory notes have an interesting history as negotiable instruments. Although they were apparently widely used and treated as negotiable instruments by the commercial interests of the day, Lord Holt held that they were not negotiable at common law: *Buller v Crips* (1703) 6 Mod 29. This was evidently intolerable, for in 1704 an Act was passed which overcame the difficulty: 3 & 4 Anne, c 8.

THE METHOD OF NEGOTIATION

[10.18] The Acts specify the way in which an instrument is transferred by negotiation. In each case an instrument is 'negotiated' when it is transferred from one person to another in such a way as to make the transferee a holder of the instrument: CPOA s 40(1); BEA s 36(1).

BEARER INSTRUMENTS

[10.19] A bearer instrument is negotiated by delivery: CPOA s 40(3); BEA s 36(2). As a result of these definitions, bearer instruments may circulate like cash. There is no requirement that the transferor be a person who is entitled to the instrument. Under both Acts, the person in possession of a bearer instrument is the holder: CPOA s 3(1); BEA s 4.

There is, however, a difference in the definition of 'bearer' instrument in the two Acts. Under the CPOA, a cheque is a bearer cheque if it (or the last indorsement) does not name a specific payee: CPOA s 20 and s 21. The BEA definition is that a bearer bill is one which is expressed to be payable to bearer or on which the last indorsement is an indorsement in blank: BEA s 13(3) and see [10.109] for a discussion of the forms of indorsements. In either case, if the named payee is 'fictitious or nonexisting', then the instrument may be treated as payable to bearer: CPOA ss 19, 20 and 21; BEA s 12(3). Thus, an instrument which is 'Pay Cash or order' may be a valid cheque and, if so, is a bearer cheque. It cannot be a valid bill of exchange since it does not order payment to a person or order or to bearer: *Orbit Mining and Trading Co Ltd v Westminster Bank Ltd* [1963] 1 QB 794.

Bearer instruments are very insecure. If a bearer instrument comes into the possession of a thief, the thief is a holder of the instrument. If the thief delivers the instrument to some third party, that party becomes a holder and, if certain requirements are satisfied, may become a holder in due course who is entitled to enforce the instrument against all parties liable on it. Bearer instruments may circulate like cash.

ORDER INSTRUMENTS

[10.20]　Order instruments are much safer. An order instrument may only be negotiated by indorsement of the holder and delivery: CPOA s 40(2); BEA s 40(3). It is important to note that the indorsement must be made by the holder. The holder of an order instrument is the payee or an indorsee who is in possession of the instrument: CPOA s 3(1); BEA s 4.

To understand the effect of this arrangement, consider again the case of an instrument which falls into the hands of a thief, only now suppose that it is an order instrument. The thief is not the holder, being neither the payee nor an indorsee. If the thief delivers the instrument to some third party, that party does not become a holder; this is so even if the thief forges the name of the true owner of the instrument, for the instrument has not been indorsed by the holder.

There is a very important point to note about indorsements. Indorsement of an instrument serves two very distinct purposes. The first is that an indorsement is essential for the negotiation of an order instrument. Second, the indorsement is essential to make the indorser liable on the instrument. It is for this second reason that a bearer instrument will often be indorsed even though the indorsement is not necessary for the instrument to be transferred by negotiation.

CONVERTING BEARER INSTRUMENTS TO ORDER INSTRUMENTS

[10.21]　Because the bearer instrument is so easily negotiated, a holder of a bearer instrument may wish to convert it into an order instrument. When that is done, it may not be negotiated without his or her signature, a valuable safeguard. The situation is different for bills and cheques.

CONVERTING BILLS

[10.22]　Although the BEA provides an express method of converting an order bill to a bearer bill by means of an indorsement in blank, there is no express provision which allows the conversion of a bearer bill to an order bill. What is the effect of indorsing a bearer bill in a way that orders payment to or to the order of a particular person? In *Miller Associates (Australia) Pty Ltd v Bennington Pty Ltd* [1975] 2 NSWLR 506 Sheppard J suggested that it is not possible by indorsement to change the character of a bearer instrument and that a bill drawn payable to bearer always remains so payable.

Ellinger regards this view as questionable: Ellinger and Lomnicka, *Modern Banking Law*, 2nd ed, Clarendon Press, Oxford, 1994, p 616. He argues from two sections of the BEA. First, by s 39(4) the holder may convert an indorsement in blank into a special indorsement by writing above the indorser's signature a direction to pay the bill to or to the order of himself or some other person. Although the section only applies when the bill is a bearer bill by virtue of a blank indorsement, it shows that there is nothing in the policy of the BEA which prevents the conversion of a bearer bill to an order one. Second, s 13(5) provides that where a bill 'either originally or by indorsement, is expressed to be payable to the order of a specified person, and not him or his order, it is nevertheless payable to him or his order at his option'. There is certainly no assumption here that a bill which is originally drawn payable to bearer is immutable. The better view seems to be that conversion to an order instrument is possible. This may be done by the payee striking out the 'or bearer'.

CONVERTING CHEQUES

[10.23] The CPOA expressly provides for the conversion of a cheque which is originally drawn as a bearer cheque. Unfortunately, it does not seem to provide the kind of protection for the holder that might be wished, particularly when the holder is the original payee of the cheque. Section 23 provides that the bearer cheque may be converted by indorsing the cheque so as to require the drawee bank to pay the sum to or to the order of a specified person or persons and, in addition, clearly indicating on the front of the cheque that the cheque is payable to order. The most common way of dealing with the front of the cheque would be, of course, to strike out the words 'or bearer'.

This is the only way in which the payee is authorised to convert a bearer cheque into an order cheque. The reason that it is unsatisfactory is that it requires the payee to indorse the cheque. The payee may legitimately wish to convert the cheque to an order cheque without indorsing in favour of some third party at the time of the conversion.

[10.24] An indorsee of a bearer cheque is in a better position. When the last or only indorsement does not specify an indorsee, the holder may add to or alter the indorsement so that the cheque is expressed to require the drawee bank to pay the sum to or to the order of a specified person or persons: s 23(2). In particular, the holder may make the cheque payable to his or her own order.

Of course, many payees will simply strike out the 'or bearer' thinking that this has the effect of converting the cheque to an order cheque. The alteration has the effect of changing the duty of the drawee bank since originally the duty was to pay any holder, but in altered form the duty is to pay only the payee or to the order of the payee. Consequently, it would appear that the alteration is a material alteration within the meaning of the Act. However, this does not result in the cheque being discharged since the alteration is not done fraudulently: s 78(2) and see [10.84] for a discussion of the rights of the parties when there is a material alteration of a cheque.

Most printed personal cheque forms are in 'or bearer' form. It is not a 'conversion' of the cheque to strike out the 'or bearer' at the time of drawing the cheque.

THE RIGHTS OF THE HOLDER

[10.25] The holder of an instrument has one very valuable right, namely, he or she may sue on the instrument in his or her own name: CPOA s 49(1); BEA s 43(1)(a). This is not to say that the holder will necessarily succeed, for the other parties to the instrument may have defences.

ESTOPPELS IN FAVOUR OF THE HOLDER

[10.26] The holder of a cheque or other negotiable instrument obtains certain procedural advantages. By the act of indorsement, an indorser is estopped from denying to any subsequent indorser or to the holder that the instrument was a valid and undischarged instrument at the time of indorsement and that the indorser had a good title at that time: CPOA s 74(1)(b); BEA s 60(2)(c).

Suppose that the instrument is not a cheque or a bill of exchange at all by virtue of failing to fall within the appropriate definition. Is the indorser of such an instrument precluded from denying that the instrument is a valid instrument? The question was left open in *Chamberlain v Young and Tower* [1893] 2 QB 206, but the logic of the situation is clear since the Act only applies to cheques. Why the CPOA does not address the matter is a mystery, particularly in view of s 74(2) CPOA: see [10.32] below.

THE HOLDER IN DUE COURSE

[10.27] The full benefits of negotiability descend upon the holder who is a holder in due course.

DEFINITION

[10.28] The holder in due course is a holder to whom the instrument has been transferred by negotiation and, at the time when the holder took the instrument, it was complete and regular on the face of it. Further, the holder must have taken the instrument in good faith, for value and without notice of any dishonour or of any defect in the title of the transferor of the instrument: CPOA s 50(1); BEA s 34(1)(b). If the instrument is a cheque, then in addition, it must have been negotiated while it was not stale, and did not contain a 'not negotiable' crossing: s 50(1)(a). If the instrument is a bill, then it must have been taken by the holder before it became overdue: BEA s 34(1)(a). The 'defect' in the title may be that the transferor had no title at all; this is made express by the CPOA in s 50(1). Although the BEA does not expressly state it, the position is thought to be the same.

[10.29] Both Acts specify certain instances of defective titles. Section 50(2) CPOA deems that the taker has notice of a defect in title if the holder took the cheque with notice that the transfer is in breach of faith or under circumstances amounting to fraud. The section makes it clear that these are not to be taken as the only instances of defective title.

Section 34(2) BEA provides that the title is defective when the bill or the acceptance is obtained by fraud, duress, or force and fear, or other unlawful means, or for an illegal consideration, or when it is negotiated in breach of faith, or under such circumstances as to amount to fraud.

'Fraud' in this context indicates action amounting to common law fraud, so that the giving of a 'fraudulent preference' within the meaning of the Bankruptcy Act 1966 is not fraud which would prevent a holder from being a holder in due course: *Osterreichische Landerbank v S'Elite Ltd* [1980] 3 WLR 356.

[10.30]   In both the CPOA and the BEA, the language of the section clearly indicates that the examples of defective titles are not exhaustive: see *Stenning v Radio and Domestic Finance Ltd* [1961] NZLR 7.

One important effect of the definition is that the payee of the instrument cannot be a holder in due course when the instrument is first delivered, for the instrument has not been transferred by negotiation: *R E Jones Ltd v Waring and Gillow Ltd* [1926] AC 670. It may be that the payee can become a holder in due course of the instrument if he or she later takes the instrument by negotiation: see *Jade International Steel Stahl und Eisen GmbH & Co KG v Robert Nicholas (Steels) Ltd* [1978] 3 All ER 104 at 109 and [13.20].

Under s 50(1) CPOA it is impossible to become a holder in due course of a cheque which is crossed 'not negotiable'. Under the BEA, it was possible to become a holder in due course of such a cheque, although the main benefit, that of a better title than the transferor, was not available. The scheme of the CPOA seems more sensible.

BENEFIT OF BEING A HOLDER IN DUE COURSE

[10.31]   A holder in due course has substantial and important rights. A holder of a cheque who is a holder in due course holds the cheque free from any defect in the title of prior indorsers as well as from mere personal defences available to the drawer and prior indorsers against one another: s 49(2)(a). The holder in due course may enforce payment of the cheque against any person liable on the cheque: s 49(2)(b).

The wording of s 43(1)(b) BEA is slightly different: the holder in due course holds the bill free from any defect of title of prior parties, as well as from mere personal defences available to prior parties among themselves, and may enforce payment against all parties liable on the bill. It seems doubtful if there is any significant difference in the effect of the different wording: cf A R Coleman, *The Cheques and Payment Orders Act 1986*, Longman Professional, Melbourne, 1987, p 70.

As an example of the kinds of defence which do not concern the holder in due course, a bill may be enforced against an acceptor who accepted the bill under the mistaken belief that an attached bill of lading was genuine: *Guaranty Trust Co of New York v Hannay & Co* [1918] 2 KB 623.

The holder in due course may get a better title than that held by the transferor. By s 49(3) CPOA, if the title of a holder is defective and the holder transfers the cheque by negotiation to a holder in due course, then the holder in due course receives a good and complete title to the cheque. Section 43(1)(2)(a) BEA is to the same effect.

ESTOPPEL OF THE INDORSERS

[10.32]   The Acts also provide the holder in due course with valuable procedural protections. An indorser, by the act of indorsing the instrument, is estopped from denying to a holder in due course the genuineness and regularity, in all respects, of the drawer's signature and all previous indorsements: CPOA s 74(1); BEA s 60(2)(b).

It will be recalled that there can be no such thing as a holder, let alone a holder in due course, of an order bill which was transferred by a forged indorsement. In order to make the estoppels of s 74(1) CPOA effective, s 74(2) CPOA provides that the estoppels are to extend in favour of a person who, but for a forged or unauthorised signature being placed on a cheque, would be a holder in due course. The BEA does not contain an equivalent provision, but it has received this interpretation. Indeed, the estoppels would be completely inoperative without such an interpretation.

The effect is that an indorser of an instrument is essentially guaranteeing the validity of certain aspects of the instrument at the time when he or she adds the indorsement.

ESTOPPEL OF THE DRAWER

[10.33]   The Acts also provide for certain estoppels against the drawer, but the wording of the sections differ.

The CPOA section on the estoppel of the drawer is so badly drafted that it is difficult to ascribe any meaning at all to it. Section 72 reads: 'The drawer of a cheque, by issuing the cheque, is estopped from denying to a holder in due course that the cheque was, at the time when the cheque was issued, a valid cheque.'

The problem is one of circularity. If the instrument is not a cheque, then the CPOA, and hence the section, does not apply, whereas if it is a cheque then it would appear to be unnecessary. Further, the section does not even provide an evidentiary advantage to the holder, for it is always open to the drawer to argue that the CPOA does not apply to the instrument in question. The only way for the holder to show that the Act does apply is to show that the instrument is a cheque.

The Explanatory Memorandum explains that the section was intended to overcome some perceived difficulties in the equivalent BEA section which estops the drawer from denying to a holder in due course the existence of the payee and the capacity of the payee to indorse: BEA s 60(1)(b); EM paras 350–4. There is little doubt that the purpose served by the BEA section is obscure, but the new section is no better.

ESTOPPEL OF THE ACCEPTOR

[10.34]   The acceptor of a bill is estopped from denying to a holder in due course that the front of the bill is what it appears to be. This includes the existence of the drawer, the validity of the drawer's signature and the drawer's authority. If the bill is drawn to the drawer's order, the acceptor may not claim that the drawer had the capacity to indorse. If the bill is payable to the order of some third person, then the acceptor may not deny the existence of the payee and the capacity of the payee to indorse. In any of these cases, the drawer may argue that the actual indorsement is invalid.

The policy of this section is that the acceptor is only concerned with the drawer and the payee of the bill. In many cases, these will be the only parties appearing on the bill when the drawee is asked to accept. By accepting, the acceptor takes responsibility that these parties are what they appear to be, but this responsibility extends only to a holder in due course.

DERIVING TITLE FROM A HOLDER IN DUE COURSE

[10.35]   The rights of a holder in due course would be sharply diminished if he or she were unable to negotiate the instrument to a person who would acquire similar rights, yet if it becomes known that the instrument is affected by fraud or some other defect, it is clear that the person who takes the instrument cannot themselves become a holder in due course. The Acts deal with this problem by declaring that a holder who derives title through a holder in due course and who is not a party to any fraud, duress or illegality affecting the instrument has all of the rights of a holder in due course against the drawer and all indorsers prior to the holder in due course: CPOA s 52; BEA s 34(3). If the instrument is a bill of exchange, then the rights are exercisable against the acceptor: BEA s 34(3). There is no requirement in these sections that the holder be a holder for value.

[10.36]   The way in which this section may be of benefit to a holder is seen in *Jade International Steel Stahl und Eisen GmbH & Co KG v Robert Nicholas (Steels) Ltd* [1978] 3 All ER 104 at 109. The holder of a bill of exchange was actually the named payee and so could not be a holder in due course in that context. However, the holder was also an indorsee of the bill, having taken it from a holder in due course. The court held that the acceptor of the bill could not raise personal defences against the holder since the holder had all of the rights of the holder in due course from whom the bill had been taken.

LIABILITIES OF PARTIES

[10.37]   Liabilities of the parties to an instrument are arranged so as to facilitate the fundamental objects of negotiable instruments. In so far as possible, it should be possible to assess the worth of the instrument by inspection. The value of the instrument should depend upon the creditworthiness of the names contained therein and the taker should be able to rely upon the credit of any person who became an earlier party to the instrument.

Of course, all parties expect that the instrument will be paid on due presentment for payment. Due presentment is to the drawee if the instrument is a cheque or a demand bill, to the acceptor if the instrument is a time bill of exchange. To give effect to this expectation and to allocate the risks of it not happening, the Acts also provide that becoming a party to an instrument entails certain promises to later parties and specifies the consequences of these promises being broken.

Basic concepts of liability

[10.38]   Before looking at the detailed implementation of this scheme, we shall discuss several fundamental principles of liability on the instrument.

No liability without signature

[10.39]   The first is that a person cannot be held liable as an indorser, drawer or acceptor unless the person has signed the instrument in the appropriate capacity: CPOA s 31; BEA s 28. The principle is subject to several exceptions, none of which need concern us here. Problems occasionally arise when an agent signs a cheque on behalf of a principle, for it is not always clear in what capacity the signature is being placed on the cheque.

Person signing as agent

[10.40]   The Acts attempt to define the liabilities of a person who signs as agent or in a representative capacity. There are minor differences in detail. Provided the person signing a cheque is in fact signing on behalf of a principal, adds words to the signature which indicate that fact and the principal is named or otherwise indicated on the cheque itself, then the person signing is not personally liable on the cheque: CPOA s 33(1).

The corresponding section in the BEA is similar, but does not require that the principal be named: BEA s 31(1).

[10.41]   The complementary problem is when the signature is accompanied by words which indicate that the person signing is doing so in the capacity of an agent, but there is some defect in the agency arrangements. If the person signing a cheque does not in fact sign on behalf of the principal or if that person is not named then the signer of the cheque may be held to be personally liable on the cheque: CPOA s 33(2).

If the instrument is a bill which is not a cheque, then s 34(1) BEA provides that the mere addition to the signature of words which describe the signer as an agent or as filling a representative character does not exempt the signer from liability. The BEA also requires a construction which is most favourable to the validity of the instrument when attempting to determine if the signature is that of the principal or that of the agent by whose hand it is written: s 31(2). In operation, the two different approaches most likely produce the same results: see *Bondina Ltd v Rollaway Shower Blinds Ltd* [1986] 1 All ER 564 (CA) and below [10.44].

[10.42] The safest course for the principal is to require the agent to sign 'per pro', an abbreviation which indicates that the signature is affixed by procuration, that is, with the authority of the principal whose name actually appears. Thus, if the agent A signs on behalf of the principal P, then the appropriate form is 'P per pro A': Hapgood, *Paget's Law of Banking*, 11th ed, Butterworths, London, 1996, p 391. The reason that this is safe is that the signature operates as notice that the agent has limited authority to sign for the principal and the principal is not bound by the signature unless the agent is acting within his or her authority: see *Slingsby v District Bank Ltd* [1932] 1 KB 544. This position has been specifically included in s 34 CPOA.

[10.43] In *Muirhead v Commonwealth Bank of Australia* (1996) 139 ALR 561, the Queensland Court of Appeal had to consider documents in the form of bills of exchange. The forms were signed by Mrs M only under printed words 'For and behalf of GAR & SS Muirhead'. It was not disputed that Mrs M had actual authority to sign for both, but it was argued that the signature did not bind the husband since it did not comply with s 97(1) BEA since his signature was not 'written thereon by some other person'. The court noted that the section did not actually require that the signature be written, only that it was 'sufficient' if it was. In Australia, 'signature' does not preclude signature by agent, whether written in the name of the agent or the principal. In signing her name, Mrs M clearly confirmed the words 'For and on behalf of GAR & SS Muirhead'. She was adopting and authenticating those words by adding her own signature. In so doing, she 'signed' her own name but also that of her husband.

COMPANIES

[10.44] A company cheque must necessarily be signed by an agent of the company, usually a director. The problems which arise concern the nature of the director's signature and the situations under which the person who signs may be held personally liable on the cheque.

In *Bondina Ltd v Rollaway Shower Blinds Ltd* [1986] 1 All ER 564 (CA) the plaintiffs were payees of several cheques which had been dishonoured. The cheque was on a company account and used a printed form which contained the company's name and account information. It was, as the court noted, of a form which would be taken by any ordinary person to be the cheque of the company and of no one else. The company was in liquidation and the plaintiff sought to contend that the defendant was personally liable on the cheque, arguing that although the defendant had signed the cheque he had merely added 'words to the signature describing the signer as an agent' and so could be personally liable on the cheque under the English equivalent of s 31 BEA.

The argument was rejected, the court holding that the director adopts all of the printing and writing on the cheque, not merely the name of the payee and the amount. Consequently, the cheque was deemed to be drawn on the company's account and the director was not personally liable on it merely because he placed his signature on it. The argument seems general enough to cover any case where an agent signs and where the instrument clearly indicates the name of the principal: see [10.41] above.

The name and Australian Company Number (ACN) of a company must appear whenever the company is made party to a negotiable instrument or letter of credit, whether or not the company is carrying on business under a different business name: Corporations Law s 219; a person who signs without the correct name and ACN is liable to the holder unless the amount is paid by the company: Corporations Law s 219(6).

NO LIABILITY WITHOUT PRESENTMENT FOR PAYMENT

[10.45]   The second basic principle of liability is that the promises and the liabilities are conditional. In the ordinary course of events, a drawer or indorser has no liability until the cheque has been duly presented for payment: CPOA s 58; BEA s 60. When the instrument is a bill of exchange which requires acceptance, then the bill must be presented for acceptance before the liability of the drawer or indorser arises unless presentment for acceptance is excused: BEA s 60. When the instrument is a bill, there is the further requirement that the requisite proceedings be taken on dishonour: BEA s 60 and see [10.69]. It is not necessary to present the bill in order to hold the acceptor liable, but if the bill is not presented for payment, the holder may have costs awarded against him or her in any action to enforce the bill: see Riley, op cit, p 114. In extraordinary circumstances, liability can arise without due presentment. Because of the different functions served by cheques and bills of exchange, the rules which excuse presentment are slightly different. One of the welcome features of the CPOA is that these rules are clarified for cheques.

[10.46]   Section 59 CPOA details the circumstances in which presentment is not necessary. Presentment is dispensed with where the cheque cannot, with the exercise of reasonable diligence, be duly presented. This section is based on an interpretation of s 5 1(2)(a) of the BEA: see the Explanatory Memorandum. However, since presentment for payment now consists only of making a demand for payment, it may be more difficult to know when the cheque 'cannot' be presented. When presentment is dispensed with, the drawer and all indorsers are liable on the cheque even though it has not been duly presented for payment.

The drawer of a cheque is made liable in a wider range of circumstances. Section 59(b) CPOA provides that presentment is dispensed with where the drawee bank is under no contractual obligation to the drawer to honour the particular cheque and the drawer had no reason to believe at the time of issue that the cheque would be paid if duly honoured: CPOA s 59(b)(i). Drawers of bills are under a similar liability: s 51(2)(c). It is thought that these sections are of relatively limited application because of the dual requirement. It may be fraudulent to issue a cheque when there is no expectation that it will be met on presentment: *R v Page* [1971] 2 QB 330.

[10.47]   The drawer of either a cheque or a bill is also liable in the absence of due presentment if the drawer has waived the right to presentment. The waiver may be either express or implied: CPOA s 59(b)(ii); BEA s 51 (2)(e). Section 17(1) CPOA authorises the drawer by express stipulation written on the cheque to waive his or her right to presentment.

An indorser of either a cheque or a bill will be liable in the absence of due presentment where the indorser has expressly or by implication waived the right to presentment: CPOA s 59(c); BEA s 52(2)(e).

[10.48]   Section 51(2) BEA lists a number of circumstances where presentment is excused entirely. These include a section similar to that in the CPOA which excuses presentment where after the exercise of reasonable diligence presentment cannot be effected: BEA s 51(2)(a). It is not entirely clear if presentment is excused when it is obvious that no amount of diligence would suffice: see Riley, op cit, p 117.

Presentment of bills is also excused in several circumstances which do not generally apply to cheques. Thus, if the drawee is fictitious (s 51 (2)(b)) and, as regards an indorser, where the bill was accepted or made for the accommodation of that indorser and he has no reason to expect that the bill would be paid if presented: s 51(2)(d) and see [10.7] for a discussion of accommodation bills.

[10.49]   Delay in making presentment is also handled differently under the two Acts. A cheque is payable on demand and the ordinary expectation is that it should be presented for payment reasonably promptly. Section 60 CPOA deals with the consequences of delay in presentment: see the discussion at [5.94].

Bills, on the other hand, are usually expected to be presented at the time specified in the bill. Section 51(1) BEA provides a general rule which excuses delay in making a presentment for payment. Delay is excused when it is caused by circumstances beyond the control of the holder, and not imputable to his or her default, misconduct or negligence. When the cause of the delay ceases to operate, presentment must be made with reasonable diligence.

INCHOATE INSTRUMENTS

[10.50]   What should be the effect of a person signing a blank form which is then either delivered to another person for completion or is placed in a desk drawer or safe with explicit instructions that it should be used only for a particular purpose?

If the form is not completed then it is not a cheque or bill. Problems arise when an agent who is intended to fill out the instrument for a particular purpose uses the form for a different purpose or for the specified purpose but for an unauthorised amount. It may also happen that the signed form is stolen and filled in by a thief who, of course, has no authority at all.

We are concerned here with the rights of the payee or of a person who takes such an instrument by negotiation. When the instrument is a cheque, the rights of the paying bank against the drawer are defined by the contractual relationship defined by the *Macmillan* duty.

[10.51] It is clear that a form signed by a drawer is a dangerous instrument, and it seems reasonable that a person who lets such a dangerous instrument loose on the world should be responsible for his or her actions. The Acts do not adopt such a harsh approach, with the result that it is possible that a person who would otherwise be a holder in due course may be met with a valid defence. The distinction drawn by the Acts is between a drawer who 'delivers' the instrument and one who does not.

If the instrument is signed by the drawer and delivered to another person in order that the instrument may be completed, then any person who is in possession of the instrument is prima facie deemed to have the authority to complete the instrument in any way the person sees fit: CPOA s 18(1); BEA ss 25(1) and 25(2).

If the holder is not a holder in due course, then the completed instrument is not enforceable against the drawer or any indorser who became a party to the instrument prior to its completion unless the instrument is completed within a reasonable time and strictly in accordance with the authority given: CPOA s 18(2); BEA s 25(3). Reasonable time is, of course, a question of fact: CPOA s 18(3); BEA s 25(3).

When the holder of the completed instrument is a holder in due course then there is a conclusive presumption that it has been completed within a reasonable time and in accordance with the authority given: CPOA s 18(4); BEA s 25(3). The CPOA clarifies the issue further by stipulating that, as regards a holder in due course, it is conclusively presumed that the instrument was delivered to another person in order that it might be filled up as a complete cheque: s 18(4)(a).

NO LIABILITY WITHOUT DELIVERY

[10.52] These sections might be thought to solve the problem of the signed but incomplete instrument, but they must be read with the sections of the Acts which are concerned with delivery of the instrument.

Any contract arising out of the drawing or an indorsement of a cheque or a bill is incomplete and revocable until the delivery of the instrument: CPOA s 25; BEA s 26(1). In order to make a drawer, indorser or acceptor liable on the instrument, it must be shown that it was delivered by that person and that the delivery was for the purpose of giving effect to the drawing, indorsement or acceptance of the instrument: CPOA s 26; BEA s 26(1). There is an exception that an acceptance is complete when the drawee gives notice to the person entitled to the bill: BEA s 26(1).

There are conclusive presumptions in favour of a holder in due course that delivery was made for the purposes of completing the contract and rebuttable presumptions in favour of other holders: CPOA s 28; BEA s 26(2). Section 28(3) CPOA declares that nothing in s 28 affects the operation of s 18(1) or s 18(4), subsections dealing with the authority of agents to complete inchoate instruments. Notice that the presumption is about the purpose of the delivery, not that delivery was made.

'DELIVERY' AND INCHOATE INSTRUMENTS

[10.53] There are two circumstances which must be differentiated. In the first, an incomplete instrument is delivered to an agent for the purposes of the agent completing the instrument in a specified way. In the second, the instrument is left in an incomplete form with an agent for safe-keeping but where the agent has no actual authority to complete the instrument until instructions are received. In each case, the liability of the drawer or the indorser will be questioned when the agent exceeds his or her authority.

The point of the distinction is that the presumptions of s 28 CPOA and s 26 BEA in favour of the holder or the holder in due course are only that the purpose of the delivery was to give effect to the drawing or the indorsement. There is no presumption in these sections that a delivery was made to an agent for the purpose of completing the instrument for the purpose of CPOA s 18 or BEA s 25.

[10.54] The last circumstance is illustrated by *Smith v Prosser* [1907] 2 KB 735. The defendant left South Africa on overseas business. He left two of his agents a power of attorney and two documents which were lithographed forms of promissory notes. These documents were not filled in except for the defendant's signature in the place for the maker of the notes. The arrangement was that the documents should be in the custody of the agents until such time as the defendant should issue instructions for the documents to be issued as notes for the purposes of raising funds. No such instructions were ever issued, but one of the agents apparently misappropriated the documents, which were purchased by the plaintiff under conditions which would have made him a holder for value of the notes. The English Court of Appeal held that the defendant was not liable since the notes had not been 'issued'.

DELIVERY OF BEARER CHEQUE

[10.55] When the instrument is a bearer cheque, then there is no possibility of a delivery for conditional purposes. Section 29 CPOA declares every such delivery as effective to transfer the cheque by negotiation, whether or not the holder delivered the cheque for that purpose. There is no comparable section in the BEA, but the same results would probably follow in any practical situation since the person in possession is a 'holder' under the definition of s 4.

THE CHAIN OF LIABILITIES

[10.56]   The scheme of the Acts is to set up a 'chain' of liabilities. Each person who becomes a party to an instrument by drawing, accepting or by indorsing becomes responsible not only to any holder but also to any person who is further down the 'chain'. In the event that the drawee/ acceptor fails to pay the instrument, the holder may have redress against any of the previous parties who have signed the instrument. If one of these parties is forced to pay the holder, that party may in turn have recourse against any person who indorsed the instrument prior to his or her own indorsement. The process only ends when the drawer is forced to pay, for the drawer is the person who is ultimately liable on the instrument.

THE ACCEPTOR

[10.57]   If the instrument is a time bill of exchange, then it should be presented for acceptance by the drawee. If it is accepted, then the acceptor, by the act of acceptance, promises that he or she will pay the bill 'according to the tenor of his acceptance': BEA s 59(a). The holder of the bill may refuse to accept any acceptance other than an unqualified one; if the drawee refuses to give an unqualified acceptance, the holder may treat the bill as dishonoured by non-acceptance: BEA s 49(1). The acceptor is thus the person who is primarily liable on the bill. Other parties are only called upon to pay if the drawee defaults, either by refusing to give an unqualified acceptance or by refusing to pay at the time specified by the bill.

THE DRAWER

[10.58]   The drawer of a bill which requires acceptance undertakes that on due presentment the bill will be accepted: BEA s 60(1)(a). Section 46 of the BEA sets out the requirements which must be met in order that the bill be duly presented.

The drawer of either a cheque or a bill undertakes that, on due presentment for payment, the instrument will be paid according to its tenor as drawn: CPOA s 71(a); BEA s 60(1)(a). Due presentment of a cheque has been discussed at [5.106]ff; due presentment of a bill for payment is governed by BEA ss 50, 51.

In the event that a cheque is dishonoured or if it cannot be presented then the drawer will 'compensate' the holder of the cheque or any indorser who has been compelled to pay: CPOA s 71(b). The compensation will ordinarily be the value of the cheque together with interest which is payable in respect of the sum: CPOA s 76. The rate of interest is set from time to time by the Regulations. It should also be noted that the amount recoverable is deemed to be liquidated damages: CPOA s 76(3).

When a bill is dishonoured, the liability of the drawer is similar to that of the drawer of a cheque, but the liability only arises if 'the requisite proceedings on dishonour are duly taken': s 60(1)(a). The 'requisite proceedings' are discussed at [10.69].

THE INDORSER/INDORSEE

[10.59] By indorsing a cheque, an indorser undertakes that on due presentment the cheque will be paid according to its tenor as indorsed by the indorser and that if the cheque is dishonoured or if presentment is impossible then the indorser will compensate the holder or any subsequent indorser who has been compelled to pay: CPOA s 73. The indorser of a bill makes similar promises, again subject to the requirement that the requisite proceedings on dishonour are duly taken: BEA s 60(2)(a). The indorser of a time bill also guarantees that the bill will be accepted: BEA s 60(2)(a).

Note that the indorser promises to pay the instrument according to the 'tenor' as it was when he or she indorsed. In the event of a material alteration, this may be different from the promise of the drawer. No person undertakes to pay on terms different from those appearing on the instrument at the time when the person signs the instrument.

Further, the promise of the indorser differs from that of the drawer in that the indorser promises only to compensate subsequent indorsers who have been compelled to pay. An indorser who is compelled to pay may, of course, have recourse to previous indorsers and/or the drawer of the instrument.

STRANGER SIGNING THE INSTRUMENT

[10.60] There are times when a person signs an instrument but he or she is clearly neither the drawer, an indorser, nor, if the instrument is a bill, the acceptor. The reason for such a signature is to 'back' the instrument, that is, to lend the credit of the person signing so that the instrument becomes more valuable. The person so signing is said to be a stranger to the instrument.

Unfortunately, it is not always apparent from the instrument itself why the stranger signed the instrument or to whom the stranger intended to be liable. The Acts deal with this problem in slightly different ways.

[10.61] If the instrument is a cheque, then s 75 of the CPOA governs the position of the stranger. If the stranger intended to become liable, then s 75(1) provides that, save for several sections concerned with delivery, the Act applies *mutatis mutandis* to the person as if the person were an indorser and the person's signature were an indorsement. If the holder is a holder in due course, then the stranger is conclusively presumed to have signed the cheque intending to become liable; the presumption is rebuttable if the holder is not a holder in due course: CPOA s 75(2).

[10.62] The BEA limits the benefits to a holder in due course. Section 61 BEA provides that where a person signs a bill otherwise than as drawer or acceptor, he or she thereby incurs the liabilities of an indorser to a holder in due course. Arguments that the benefit of the section should extend to holders other than a holder in due course were rejected in *H Rowe & Co Pty Ltd v Pitts* [1973] 2 NSWLR 159.

[10.63]   There are reasons why a person might sign a cheque but not intend to become liable on the cheque. In *Miller Associates (Aust) Pty Ltd v Bennington Pty Ltd* [1975] 2 NSWLR 506; [1975] 7 ALR 144 a person who made the highest bid at an auction offered the selling agent a bearer cheque by way of payment which was drawn by a company in his favour. The cheque was crossed 'Not negotiable'. The purchaser wrote on the back of the cheque 'Pay [the agent]' and signed his name. The company stopped payment on the cheque and the agent sued the purchaser as indorser of the cheque. Sheppard J held that the cheque remained a bearer cheque in spite of the form of the indorsement and, on the facts, the signature was not an indorsement but an authority to the agent's bank to collect the cheque and pay the proceeds into the agent's account. The purchaser was not, therefore, liable on the cheque.

[10.64]   There is no objection to such a result as between immediate parties, but the intention of the person signing should not be relevant so far as later holders are concerned. The CPOA deals explicitly with this problem by providing that as against a holder in due course, the person is conclusively presumed to have signed the cheque intending to become liable: CPOA s 75(2)(a). If the holder is not a holder in due course, then the stranger is presumed to have signed intending to become liable, but the presumption is rebuttable: CPOA s 75(2)(b). These presumptions do not apply if it is apparent on the face of the cheque that the person did not intend to become liable on the cheque. This might be, for example, if the person makes it clear that his or her signature is in a representative capacity only or where the form of the cheque makes it clear that the person was signing only in a representative capacity: see *Bondina Ltd v Rollaway Shower Blinds Ltd* [1986] 1 All ER 564 and the discussion at [10.44].

In *Miller Associates* it seemed that the court considered that the fact that the cheque was a bearer cheque was itself sufficient to make clear that the person signing did not intend to become liable. If that is the argument in the case, then it must be questioned, for the most obvious reason to ask the payee of a bearer instrument to 'indorse' the instrument is to add the credit of the payee to that of the drawer.

[10.65]   The problem of the stranger who signs an instrument was considered in *H Rowe & Co Pty Ltd v Pitts* [1973] 2 NSWLR 159. The plaintiff had supplied goods to a company of which the defendant was a director. The company accepted a bill of exchange drawn by the plaintiff and made payable to the plaintiff. However, the plaintiff also wished to have the credit of the defendant. This was achieved by requesting the defendant to 'indorse' the bill. The bill was then indorsed by the plaintiff to another holder. When the bill was dishonoured, the plaintiff reimbursed the holder and sought to recover from the defendant.

The plaintiff was not a holder in due course since he took the bill following notice of the dishonour. The plaintiff was thus not entitled to the benefits of s 61 BEA nor would he be entitled to the conclusive presumption of s 75(2)(a) CPOA if the instrument were a cheque. The technical problem was that the plaintiff, as drawer, would ordinarily be liable to any indorser who was required to pay. The plaintiff was thus faced with the problem of circular action: if the defendant was held liable to pay as indorser, then the defendant could in turn claim from the plaintiff. However, the court considered evidence which allowed it to conclude that it was the intention of the parties that the defendant should be liable as an indorser without recourse to the drawer.

While the outcome of *Rowe v Pitts* is clearly correct, it shows the importance of drawing bills in a form which will avoid, if possible, any later litigation. In *Rowe v Pitts* itself, the litigation could have been avoided by requiring a bill to be drawn on the company by Pitts payable to his own order, accepted by the company and then indorsed by Pitts to Rowe. In such a situation, Rowe would have been a holder in due course and Pitts would have been a genuine indorser. Even when Rowe re-took the bill after dishonour by the company, he would have been an indorser forced to pay and so able to recover from Pitts as a previous indorser and drawer. This would have achieved the obvious intention of the parties, namely, to make the company primarily liable and Pitts a guarantor (in effect) of the company's liability.

[10.66]   The problems of *Rowe v Pitts* would be overcome by the European concept of the 'aval'. An 'aval' is, in effect, a guarantor of the acceptor of a bill and becomes liable to all parties to the bill equally with the acceptor. It does not matter whether the party claiming compensation from the 'aval' became a party before or after the name of the 'aval' was added to the bill. The concept of an 'aval' in English law was rejected in *Steele v M'Kinlay* (1880) 5 App Cas 754.

In the absence of some concept similar to an 'aval' the next best solution is that extrinsic evidence may be used to establish the liability of a backer of a bill to prior parties and to subsequent parties who do not qualify as holders in due course. This solution has the support of both the High Court and a judge of the New South Wales Supreme Court, although the High Court support is dicta only: *Durack v West Australian Trustee Executors and Agency Co* (1946) 72 CLR 189 at 208 per Starke J; *Miller Associates (Aust) Pty Ltd v Bennington Pty Ltd* [1975] 2 NSWLR 506 at 510 per Sheppard J.

It might be possible to argue that the 'backer' is an actual guarantor. The action in such a case is not on the bill, but rather a direct action on a guarantee. In those jurisdictions where the Statute of Frauds is in operation, the signature itself on the instrument is not enough to satisfy the requirement of writing: *G & H Montague GmbH v Irvani* [1990] 1 WLR 667.

OBLIGATIONS OF THE HOLDER

[10.67] Division 5 BEA is headed 'General Duties of the Holder' and although it is common to speak of the obligations of a holder, the term is not strictly correct. The holder of an instrument may destroy it or frame it for public display without thereby being in breach of any obligation owed to any other party. The term is merely a convenient shorthand to describe the actions which must be performed by the holder if he or she wished to receive payment or to enforce the instrument against other parties.

Because of the different economic functions of cheques and bills, the Acts differ markedly in the obligations imposed upon the holder.

DUTIES OF THE HOLDER OF A CHEQUE

[10.68] The only obligation on the holder of a cheque is to present the cheque for payment within a reasonable time. None of the parties to a cheque become liable on the cheque until the holder presents the cheque for payment: CPOA s 59. Section 60(2) CPOA provides that due presentment of a cheque for payment will not suffice to make an indorser liable on the cheque unless the presentment is effected within a reasonable time after the indorsement. Delay in presentment does not affect the liability of the drawer unless the drawee bank becomes insolvent: CPOA s 60(1) and [5.94].

Section 60(3) CPOA identifies factors which are to be considered in determining whether the cheque has or has not been presented within a reasonable time. Regard is to be had to the usage of the trade and of banks in relation to the presentment of cheques and to the particular facts of the case: CPOA s 60(3)(b). This latter factor is expanded to include the nature of the particular cheque and the cause of the delay in presenting the cheque: CPOA s 60(3)(c). The section also provides that regard shall be had to the fact that it is reasonable to expect a cheque to be presented promptly, a confusing instruction that does not seem to add much to the other requirements: CPOA s 60(3)(a).

The holder of a cheque is not obliged to give notice of dishonour to either the drawer or to any indorser. A person who is the drawer or an indorser is liable on a cheque that has been dishonoured following proper presentment whether or not the person has been given notice of the dishonour: CPOA s 70.

DUTIES OF THE HOLDER OF A BILL

[10.69] The holder of a bill of exchange must be concerned with presentment for acceptance, presentment for payment and with the giving of notice in the event of dishonour.

A bill may be payable either on demand or at a determinable future time: s 8(1). It is payable on demand if expressed to be payable on demand, or at sight, or on presentation or if no time for payment is expressed in the bill: BEA s 15. It is payable at a determinable future time if expressed to be payable at a fixed period after date or after sight or on a fixed period after the occurrence of a specified event which is certain to happen even though the time of happening may be uncertain: BEA s 16.

'Sight' here means either acceptance or protest for non-acceptance, for it is not just the physical act of showing the bill to the drawee, but some legal indication that the bill has been presented to the drawee.

[10.70]   Only two forms of bill must be presented for acceptance. If a bill is payable some fixed period after sight then it is important that the bill be presented for acceptance. Section 44 provides that such bills must be presented for acceptance in order to fix their maturity. A bill must also be presented for acceptance if the bill specifically requires that it be so presented: s 44(2). It is only these two types of bill which must be presented for acceptance, although it will often be to the advantage of the holder of the bill to obtain the acceptance of the drawee in order to increase the value of the bill: BEA s 44(3).

This brings us to the obligation of the holder. If the bill is one payable after sight, then the holder must either present the bill for acceptance or negotiate it within a reasonable time: BEA s 45(1). Failure to do so has drastic results, for the drawer and all indorsers prior to the holder are discharged unless the circumstances are such that the holder has some excuse under the Act: BEA s 45(2). The rules for presentment and excuses for non-presentment for acceptance are given in s 46 BEA: see Riley, op cit, p 109.

If the bill is not accepted when properly presented, then the holder must treat it as dishonoured by non-acceptance, that is, notice must be given to the drawer and each indorser: BEA s 47. Again, failure to comply with the requirement has catastrophic results for the holder since the holder 'shall lose his right of recourse against the drawer and indorsers': BEA s 47.

[10.71]   Unless otherwise excused, a bill must be presented for payment. If not duly presented for payment, once again the drawer and indorsers will be discharged: BEA s 50(1). The only way in which a bill may be presented for payment is by physically presenting the bill to the drawee. Section 50(2) BEA sets out the time and place where various types of bills must be presented: see Riley, op cit, pp 114 ff.

If the bill is not paid after being duly presented for payment, then the holder is obliged to treat the bill as dishonoured. This means giving notice to the drawer and each indorser. It should come as no surprise to learn that the penalty for failing to give timely notice to any party is that the party is discharged: BEA s 53. The rules as to notice of dishonour are given in s 54. These rules will not be discussed here in detail except to note that the time allowed for notice is very short and that it often happens that parties are unfairly excused from liability merely because notice fails to reach them within the stringent time constraints imposed by the BEA.

TERMINATION OR ALTERATION OF LIABILITIES

[10.72]   There are a number of events which may terminate or alter the actual or potential liability of the parties. The most dramatic event is the discharge of the instrument itself which terminates all rights and obligations on the instrument, but it is also possible that individual parties are discharged from all further liability or from liability to certain parties.

DISCHARGE BY PAYMENT IN DUE COURSE

[10.73]   The most common way in which an instrument is discharged is that it is paid in due course by the drawee: CPOA s 78(1); BEA s 64(1). Payment in due course means that the instrument is paid to the holder in good faith and without notice of any defect in the holder's title: CPOA s 79; BEA s 64(1). In the case of a bill, payment must be made at or after the maturity of the bill: BEA s 64(1). 'Defect in title' includes a complete absence of title by the holder, a situation which may occur, for example, when the instrument is one which is payable to bearer and the holder is a finder or a thief.

However, payment must be made to a 'holder'. As discussed previously, a person in possession of an order instrument following a forged indorsement is not a 'holder', and payment to that person is not payment in due course.

RENUNCIATION OF RIGHTS

[10.74]   There are other less common ways in which an instrument may be discharged. The holder of the instrument is the only person who may maintain an action on the instrument, so if the holder wishes to renounce his or her rights, then why should anyone object? The Acts provide that the instrument is discharged if the holder absolutely and unconditionally renounces his or her rights against the person primarily liable on the instrument. This is the drawer of a cheque (CPOA s 78(1)(b)) or the acceptor if the instrument is a bill, in which case the renunciation must be after the maturity of the bill: BEA s 67(1).

It is obviously dangerous to leave such a instrument in the hands of the holder. The Acts adopt different solutions to the problem. Under the CPOA, the renunciation does not discharge the cheque unless it is completed by delivery of the instrument to the drawer for the purpose of giving effect to the renunciation. The BEA requires that the renunciation be in writing or that the bill be delivered up to the acceptor: BEA s 67(2). In the event that the bill finds its way into further circulation, the rights of a holder in due course who has no notice of the renunciation are not affected: BEA s 67(3).

INTENTIONAL CANCELLATION

[10.75]   Another way that the holder may indicate his or her intention to abandon any rights on the instrument is to cancel the instrument. Provided the cancellation is not made by mistake, an intentional cancellation of the entire instrument will discharge the instrument if the cancellation is apparent from the instrument itself: CPOA ss 78(1)(c), 80(1); BEA s 68(1). In the case of a cheque, the instrument may be cancelled by an intentional cancellation of the drawer's signature if the cancellation is apparent: CPOA s 78(1)(c).

Some care must be taken in cancelling a cheque. In an old case, *Ingham v Primrose* (1849) 7 CB(NS) 82; 141 ER 145 an acceptor of a bill of exchange handed it back to the drawer for the purposes of having the bill discounted and the proceeds handed over. The drawer failed to have the bill discounted and returned it to the acceptor who tore the bill in half and threw the two pieces into the street. The drawer then retrieved the pieces, pasted them together and negotiated the bill. It was held that the acceptor was liable on the bill to a holder in due course. It is difficult to know how important the case is since at the time it was common to tear bills in half and mail each half separately as a security precaution. The court mentioned that the appearance of the bill was consistent with its having been divided for the purpose of safe transmission by post.

ALTERATION

[10.76] Since negotiable instruments are paper and ink, they are subject to alteration by parties who have access to the instrument. Alterations may be trivial and innocent, such as a holder writing in a correction to the way in which his or her name has been spelled, or they may be major and fraudulent, such as an alteration in the amount payable.

The common law differentiated between minor alterations and ones which were 'material'. Minor alterations had no effect, but the effect of a 'material' alteration was that the alteration provided a complete defence for any party liable on the instrument except the party who made or assented to the alter-ation: *Scholfield v The Earl of Londesborough* [1895] 1 QB 536. This was so even if no party was actually disadvantaged by the alteration.

When is an alteration to an instrument so serious that the rights of the par-ties should be affected? There seem to be only two general approaches to answering the question. In the first, we could attempt to enumerate all of the changes that might be made to an instrument and then to identify which of those is 'material'. In the second, we could identify some general principle which could be applied to determine if any particular alteration is significant.

[10.77] The BEA effectively chooses the first approach. Although the list provided by the BEA is not exhaustive, s 69(2) provides that any alteration of the date, the sum payable, the time of payment, the place of payment, and, where the bill has been accepted generally, the addition of a place of payment without the acceptor's assent. This 'listing' approach may cause hardship. In *Heller Factors Pty Ltd v Toy Corporation Pty Ltd* [1984] 1 NSWLR 121 a date was changed in a form which was actually beneficial to the defendant, but it was held that the alteration was, under the clear terms of the BEA, a material alteration which 'avoided' the bill: see [10.84] for further discussion of the effects of a material alteration.

[10.78]   The CPOA chooses the second approach. An alteration is 'material' if it alters, in any respect, a right, duty or liability of the drawer, an indorser or the drawee bank: s 3(8). It seems that the result in *Heller Factors* would be different if the instrument were a cheque governed by the CPOA.

The CPOA approach leads to a curious problem. Most of us would think that the alteration of the name of the payee would be one of the most serious alterations possible even on a bearer cheque. Is it a 'material alteration' under the CPOA? The cheque is, after all, a bearer cheque, so that the duties and liabilities of the parties are not altered so far as the cheque itself is concerned. However, the duty of a drawee bank paying the cheque might be altered under some circumstances. The argument is tenuous and the position is unsatisfactory.

The Acts also differ in the effects of an alteration. Under the BEA, a materially altered bill is 'avoided' but there are savings in favour of a holder in due course. Under the CPOA, a cheque is only discharged if the cheque is fraudulently and materially altered by the holder: s 78(2). Once again, savings are made for innocent holders: see [10.84] for further discussion of the effects of a material alteration. Note that s 78(2) also applies to bank cheques: s 5.

OTHER FORMS OF DISCHARGE

[10.79]   The BEA also provides that a bill is discharged if the acceptor of the bill is or becomes the holder of the bill in his or her own right at or after its maturity: s 66. This would be an unusual occurrence, so that it is not surprising that there seems to be little authority on the matter: see *Nash v De Freville* [1900] 2 QB 72 where the section was argued as a defence but rejected on the facts.

Wrongful payment by a banker of the instrument may also have the effect of discharging the bill or the cheque provided certain preconditions may be established by the banker: BEA s 65; CPOA s 92; see [7.50]. Certain bills known as 'accommodation bills' may be discharged when payment is made by 'the party accommodated': see [10.7].

[10.80]   These are the only forms of discharge specified by the BEA, but the CPOA adds a final subsection to s 78 which is somewhat puzzling. It provides that nothing in s 78 affects the discharge of a cheque otherwise than in accordance with the section. The Explanatory Memorandum gives no guidance as to the purpose of the subsection. The Explanatory Paper which accompanied the 1984 Bill mentions cl 102, but this concerns discharge by material alteration, a matter which in the CPOA was included in s 78. Coleman suggests that the intention is to preserve all other means whereby contractual rights may be extinguished at general law, for example, by agreement between parties or by mutual release: Coleman, op cit. If that is so, then it seems unnecessary in light of the general savings of s 4 CPOA and of the sections regarding renunciation and cancellation discussed above.

[10.81] The general effect of the discharge of the instrument will be that all rights on the instrument are extinguished. It is as though the instrument is 'born' when it is issued and 'dies' when discharged. There are, however, some exceptions which act as safeguards for innocent parties who might be unaware of the discharge.

Discharge by payment in due course

[10.82] The simplest case is discharge by payment in due course. In such a case, there are no parties who require safeguarding, and all rights on the instrument are simply and finally extinguished. This is made explicit in the CPOA: s 82(1). Although not explicit in the BEA, the result is the same: see *Harmer v Steele* (1849) 4 Exch 1; 154 ER 100.

Discharge by renunciation

[10.83] When the instrument is discharged by renunciation of the holder's rights against the person who is primarily liable on the instrument (see [10.56]), then there is at least the possibility that the instrument might be placed in circulation again. Of course, a person who takes the instrument cannot be a holder, since the instrument has been discharged, but it is clear that such a person should be protected in certain circumstances.

The Acts deal with the situation by providing that if the instrument comes into the hands of a person who would, but for the discharge, be a holder in due course then that person may enforce payment of the instrument as if the instrument had not been discharged: CPOA s 82(2); BEA s 67(3).

In the case of a cheque, the renunciation of rights is not complete until the cheque is delivered to the drawer, so it seems that there should be little scope for the operation of this section for cheques. Since the renunciation of rights on a bill may be in writing without the delivery of the bill, it is more likely that the instrument could return to circulation.

Discharge by alteration

[10.84] Innocent parties are much more likely to require protection when the instrument is discharged by material alteration since the reason for making the alteration will often be fraudulent. The Acts handle the problem somewhat differently.

If the instrument is a cheque, then s 82(3) CPOA gives certain rights to persons who would, but for the discharge, be holders and greater rights to persons who would, but for the discharge, be holders in due course.

A 'holder' of a cheque which has been discharged by alteration may enforce the cheque according to its tenor as altered against the person who made the alteration, against any person who authorised or agreed to the alteration and against any person who indorsed the cheque after the alteration was made: CPOA s 82(3)(a). The section is peculiar in that it appears to give the 'holder' the right to enforce the cheque against a person who may not be a party to the cheque!

If the alteration is not apparent, then a 'holder in due course' of the discharged cheque may enforce payment of the cheque according to the original tenor of the cheque as though the cheque had never been discharged: CPOA s 82(3)(b). This provision essentially reproduces the rights of the 'holder in due course' of an altered bill which are found in s 69 of the BEA. Although there is no express protection in the BEA for the holder who is not a holder in due course of a bill, the same result is achieved by the estoppels against the indorsers: see [10.32].

[10.85]   Section 69 BEA has caused difficulty because of the concept of an 'apparent' alteration. The fundamental problem is that no one in their right mind would take an instrument which has been 'apparently' altered and, if they were to do so, it is very unlikely that they could be a holder in due course. It is difficult to imagine an instrument which has been 'apparently' altered which would still be complete and regular on its face.

[10.86]   The problem is well illustrated by the leading Australian case of *The Automobile Finance Co of Australia Ltd v Law* (1933) 49 CLR 1. A promissory note was made on a printed form and signed by the maker of the note. The handwriting on the rest of the note was not that of the maker and, at the time of making the note, nothing was written after the printed words 'Payable at'. The payee of the note, without authority, filled in the place of payment in handwriting which was clearly distinguishable from that on the remainder of the note and using ink which was a different colour. The note was then negotiated to the appellant who was a holder in due course.

The High Court held that the alteration was not apparent. In order to be 'apparent', it must be obvious that some revision of the text has taken place and its appearance must be consistent with the revision having occurred after the completion of the instrument. It must be obvious that the text was put there as an addition or a substitution. In the words of Starke J (at p 12), the alteration must:

> ... be visible or apparent, as an alteration or change in the very words or figures originally written or printed in the document ... It is not enough to say that a prudent businessman would be put upon inquiry, or that his suspicions would be aroused by the form of the document. The alteration may be by addition, interlineation, or otherwise, but it must be visible as an alteration, upon inspection.

[10.87]   The English courts have developed a slightly different test. In *Woollatt v Stanley* (1928) 138 LT 620 it was said (at 620): 'An alteration in a bill is apparent within [s 69 BEA] if it is of such a kind that it would be observed and noticed by an intending holder scrutinising the document, which he contemplated taking, with reasonable care.'

Under either formulation of the test for an 'apparent alteration', it is difficult to see how the taker could satisfy the requirements to become a holder in due course: see [10.28].

DISCHARGE OF AN INDORSER

[10.88] It is possible that only certain indorsees of the instrument are released while the instrument itself remains undischarged. However, it is clear that if an indorser is discharged, then all subsequent indorsers must also be discharged, for they became parties to the instrument on the basis that the credit of the first mentioned indorser would be available to them. This scheme is implemented in ss 83–86 of the CPOA and in ss 67 and 68 BEA.

WHEN AN INDORSER IS DISCHARGED

[10.89] An indorser is discharged in three different circumstances. First, if the holder of the cheque absolutely and unconditionally renounces his or her rights against the indorser in writing and signed by the holder: CPOA ss 83(1)(a) and 84; BEA s 67(3). Second, an indorser is discharged if the holder intentionally cancels the indorser's signature, the cancellation is apparent from the cheque itself and the cancellation was not made under a mistake of fact: CPOA ss 83(1)(b) and 85(1); BEA s 68(2) and 68(3). There is a presumption that any cancellation was made intentionally and not under a mistake of fact: CPOA s 85(2); BEA s 68(3).

Finally, an indorser is discharged if he or she would have had a right of recourse against any indorser discharged by either of the two previous means: CPOA s 83(2); BEA s 68(2).

EFFECT OF DISCHARGE OF INDORSER

[10.90] The basic effect of the discharge of an indorser is that all rights on the cheque against the indorser are extinguished: CPOA s 86(1); the BEA does not explicitly define the effect of discharge, but the result appears to be the same. However, just as in the case of the discharge of the entire cheque, it is necessary to add some protection for innocent parties who later become holders of the cheque in the belief that the discharged indorsers are still liable. It is not necessary to provide any protection when the indorser is discharged by cancellation of signature, since in that case the cheque itself notifies the holder of the release.

When the indorser is discharged by a renunciation of rights by the holder, or when a subsequent indorser is discharged by a renunciation of rights against a previous indorser, then a person who takes the cheque without notice of the renunciation may enforce the payment as if the discharge had never occurred: CPOA s 86(2); BEA s 67(3).

TRANSFER TO DRAWER OR INDORSER

[10.91] It sometimes happens that an instrument will be transferred by negotiation to a person who is already liable on the instrument. Unless some special provision is made, the possibility of circular actions arise. Thus, suppose that A is either a drawer or an indorser and B is a person who has indorsed the instrument after A has become a party and the instrument is then transferred by negotiation back to A. If A attempts to enforce the instrument against B and succeeds, then B will in turn be entitled to enforce the instrument against A.

In order to avoid such circumstances, the Acts provide that when the instrument is negotiated back to a person who is already liable as drawer or as indorser, then the person may further transfer the instrument, but is not entitled to enforce payment against any person to whom the first mentioned person was previously liable: CPOA s 47; BEA s 42. Notice that the bar against enforcement is not against all intermediate indorsers, only those indorsers to whom the person was previously liable.

Further, the CPOA gives the person authority to make certain alterations to the cheque which have the effect of making explicit these changed liabilities. If the person is the drawer, then he or she may strike out any indorsements that the cheque may have. If the person is an indorser, then he or she may strike out his or her own indorsement and any subsequent indorsements. The BEA contains no equivalent provision, but the 'striking out' would amount to a cancellation of the indorsement, a right which is given to any holder by s 68(2) BEA.

PAYMENT BY DRAWER OR INDORSER

[10.92] There are various circumstances where one of the parties to an instrument might wish to 'pay' the holder. An example of this might be when it is known that the instrument would be dishonoured upon presentment but it is in the interests of one or more parties to the instrument to limit the damage to credit which results from dishonour. This is not really 'payment' of the instrument at all, for only the drawee may pay the instrument, but the use of the term does not seem to cause undue difficulties.

If an instrument is 'paid' in this way, then it is desirable that the person paying should be subrogated to the rights of the holder of the instrument. Since the role of the drawer of a cheque and of a bill are different, the Acts deal with the problem slightly differently.

If the drawer of an order bill which is made payable to a third party pays the bill then the drawer may enforce the bill against the acceptor, but may not re-issue the bill: BEA s 64(2)(a). If a bill payable to the drawer's order is paid by the drawer, or if any bill is paid by an indorser, then the party paying is remitted to his or her former rights as regards the acceptor or antecedent parties, and may strike out his or her own indorsement and again negotiate the bill: BEA s 64(2)(b).

Section 87(1) CPOA provides that a cheque which is paid by the drawer or the indorser is not discharged and, if the cheque is an order cheque and the person who has paid the cheque is not an indorsee, then he or she has the right to demand that the holder indorse the cheque so as to make the person who has paid a holder.

The section does not apply to the drawer of a bank cheque when that drawer is also the drawee bank: s 87(2). Such a payment is evidently considered to be an ordinary payment by the drawee and no protection is required or desirable.

THE ORDER OF INDORSEMENTS

[10.93]   Perhaps surprisingly, there are a number of cases in which the basic dispute has been the result of indorsements being placed on the instrument in an incorrect order. This may happen most easily when one party is indorsing as a 'backer' of an instrument: see [10.60]. The Acts provide that indorsements are presumed to be in the order in which they appear, but the presumption is rebuttable: CPOA s 48; BEA s 37(e); *Rowe & Co Pty Ltd v Pitts* [1973] 2 NSWLR 159.

OTHER STIPULATIONS

[10.94]   It is possible for an indorser to limit or to negative his or her liability by an express written stipulation on the cheque: CPOA s 17(2); BEA s 21. The most common form of such a limitation is the indorsement 'sans recourse'. This permits the indorser to transfer the cheque by negotiation but without attracting any liability to later holders of the cheque.

The BEA extends the right of limiting liability to the drawer of a bill. The drawer of a cheque has no such right under the CPOA. The scheme of the CPOA is to place the drawer of a cheque in a position which is analogous to that of an acceptor of a bill. Consequently, the Act does not permit the drawer to negative or to limit his or her liability on the cheque.

VARYING RIGHTS BY AGREEMENT

[10.95]   It has always been accepted that 'immediate' parties to an instrument may alter the rights and liabilities as between themselves. 'Immediate' parties in this context means drawer and payee or indorser and indorsee. This right is not expressed in the BEA, but the framers of the CPOA thought that it was desirable to include an express provision to that effect:

> s 6(1): Subject to subsection (2), nothing in this Act shall be taken to prevent 2 or more persons negating, inverting or otherwise altering, by agreement, their rights, duties and liabilities in relation to one another under this Act.

The problem with this is that there are clearly certain sections of the CPOA which are not suitable for alteration by agreement between parties. For example, it is obviously unsuitable that the parties should be able to alter s 5, which provides that the Act applies to bank cheques. The CPOA attempts to deal with this problem by enumerating the sections of the Act which are unalterable. This enumeration is done in s 6(2).

It seems unfortunate that the Act has adopted this approach, for the Explanatory Memorandum explains in considerable and effective detail the deficiencies of the enumeration approach in the context of the definition of 'material alteration'. The same problems will undoubtedly occur here.

It is easy to find examples which appear anomalous. Suppose that, because of the competition in banking that is so often mentioned by the banks, one bank chooses to waive its rights of protection under the CPOA. Unfortunately, those rights are contained in ss 90–95 which cannot be altered. Suppose that customers of a particular bank do not care about their cheque being presented as soon as reasonably practicable, perhaps being offered cheaper bank charges as an inducement. This cannot be done, since s 66 is not alterable.

Real life disputes have shown themselves to be much more inventive than the minds of text writers in the construction of bizarre fact situations. It seems safe to predict that the future of s 6 is one of substantial amendment.

SPECIAL PROBLEMS OF TRANSFER/NEGOTIATION

[10.96]   Because of the rights enjoyed by a holder in due course and because of the limited number of defences open to an indorser or a drawer, resisting a claim on an instrument often involves arguments over technicalities of form. In this section we discuss a number of issues which may arise when an instrument is transferred by negotiation, issues which, although technical in nature, can have a decisive outcome in an action on an instrument.

BECOMING A HOLDER IN DUE COURSE

[10.97]   There is a rebuttable presumption that every holder of an instrument is a holder in due course: CPOA s 51(1); BEA s 35(2). However, if in an action or proceeding on an instrument it is admitted or proved that the drawing, acceptance, issue or transfer of the instrument is affected by fraud, duress or illegality, then the holder is not entitled to this presumption unless and until he or she proves that value was given in good faith for the instrument at a time after the alleged fraud, duress or illegality: CPOA s 51(2); BEA s 35(2).

These sections are slightly misleading, for it is possible for a holder to prove affirmatively that he or she is a holder in due course by showing that value in good faith was given before the alleged fraud, duress or illegality. In other words, it is not necessary for the holder to rely on the presumption if he or she has the means of proving that the requirements of the definition of holder in due course are satisfied: *Barclays Bank Ltd v Astley Industrial Trust Ltd* [1970] 1 All ER 719; Riley, op cit, p 94.

If it is necessary for the holder to prove the status of holder in due course, then it is of course necessary to prove each part of the definition of holder in due course: CPOA s 50; BEA s 34(1).

GOOD FAITH

[10.98] A holder in due course must take the instrument in good faith. An act or thing is done in good faith if the act or thing is done honestly, whether or not it is done negligently: CPOA s 3(2); BEA s 96. Blundering and carelessness are not in themselves a lack of good faith, but the facts could be so bizarre that the court could infer a lack of honesty. As described by Lord Blackburn in *Jones v Gordon* (1877) 2 App Cas 616 at 628–9:

> [a person who] ... honestly blundering and careless, and so took a bill of exchange or a bank-note when he ought not to have taken it, still he would be entitled to recover. But if the facts and circumstances are such that a jury, or whoever has to try the question, came to the conclusion that he was not honestly blundering and careless, but that he must have had a suspicion that there was something wrong, and that he refrained from asking questions, not because he was an honest blunderer or a stupid man, but because he thought in his own secret mind 'I suspect there is something wrong, and if I ask questions and make further inquiry, it will no longer be my suspecting it, but my knowing it, and then I shall not be able to recover', I think that is dishonesty.

CONSIDERATION

[10.99] A holder in due course must have taken the instrument 'for value'. 'Value' means valuable consideration as defined in the Acts: CPOA ss 3(1) and 35; BEA ss 4 and 32(1).

Valuable consideration for an instrument may be constituted by any consideration which is sufficient to support a simple contract: CPOA s 35(1)(a); BEA s 32(1)(a). In the ordinary case where the instrument is given as payment of a debt, the consideration for the instrument is the agreement to accept the instrument in payment in lieu of the cash which it is the right of the creditor to demand: *Spencer v Crowther* [1986] BCL 422; *Belo Nominees Pty Ltd v Barellan Nominees Pty Ltd* [1986] 3 WAR 140.

[10.100] For negotiable instruments, there is an extension to the normal rule of consideration. The Acts provide that an antecedent debt or liability may also provide good consideration for a instrument: CPOA s 35(1)(b); BEA s 32(1)(b). This is so whether the instrument is payable on demand or at a future time; post-dated cheques are specifically included: CPOA s 35(2); BEA s 32(1)(b).

It must be appreciated that the antecedent debt or liability must have been one owed by the payee; third party debts or liabilities are not within the scope of the section unless the discharge of this liability may be taken to imply some obligation on the part of the payee. Phrased another way, an antecedent debt or a liability can constitute valuable consideration for a cheque if and only if there is some relationship between the receipt of the cheque and the antecedent debt or liability: *Oliver v Davis* [1949] 2 KB 727.

[10.101] In *Walsh, Spriggs, Nolan and Finney v Hoag & Bosch Pty Ltd* [1977] VR 178, a vendor of land owed a sum to a real estate agent for commission on the sale. A cheque was drawn by the solicitors of the vendor for the amount of the commission and made payable to the plaintiff. There was a dispute concerning the sale and the solicitors stopped payment of the cheque at the instruction of the vendor. In an action on the cheque, the defendant solicitors pleaded lack of consideration. The Full Court of the Supreme Court of Victoria held that an antecedent third party debt could constitute adequate consideration for a cheque provided only that there is a relationship between the receipt of the cheque and the antecedent debt. Because both the drawers and the payee of the cheque intended the cheque to be a conditional payment of the antecedent debt, there was sufficient relationship with the antecedent debt so as to constitute consideration for the cheque: see also *Oliver v Davis* [1949] 2 KB 727; [1949] 2 All ER 353; *Belo Nominees Pty Ltd v Barellan Nominees Pty Ltd* [1986] 3 WAR 140.

[10.102]   A holder who has a lien on an instrument is conclusively presumed to have taken the instrument for value: CPOA s 38; BEA s 32(3). These sections are most valuable for a bank which is collecting a cheque for its customer, for if the customer's account is in overdraft, then the bank has a lien on the cheque to the extent of the overdraft: see *Brandao v Barnett* (1846) 12 Cl & F 787; 8 ER 1622; *Bank of New South Wales v Ross, Stuckey and Morawa* [1974] 2 Lloyd's Rep 110; *Barclays Bank Ltd v Astley Industrial Trust Ltd* [1970] 2 QB 527.

[10.103]   The Acts make a further extension to the concept of consideration for a negotiable instrument. In effect, once a holder gives consideration for an instrument, then every later holder is to be considered as having given consideration as against the drawer, the acceptor and any indorser who became an indorser before the time of consideration being given: CPOA s 37; BEA s 32(2). Thus if A draws a cheque in favour of B and gives it to B as a gift, if B indorses the cheque to C as a gift and C indorses the cheque to D for value, then D and every later holder of the cheque is deemed to have given value for the cheque as against A, B, and C.

[10.104]   The Acts make certain presumptions as to consideration. The drawer and each indorser of a cheque are presumed to have received value for the cheque unless the contrary is proved; the presumption includes the acceptor in the case of a bill: CPOA s 36; BEA s 35(1). There is doubt as to whether the presumption of these sections is relevant if the holder is required to establish that he or she is a holder in due course. The Explanatory Memorandum states that it is not, but the argument seems directed at the presumptions that every holder is presumed to be a holder in due course. There seems no reason to suppose that the presumption of value does not apply when the holder is attempting to establish that he or she is a holder in due course, but it must be admitted that the matter is not entirely clear.

Complete and regular

[10.105]   In order to become a holder in due course, the holder must have taken an instrument that is 'complete and regular on the face of it'. An instrument is complete if it is not lacking in any material particular. An instrument is not regular if there is something on it which puts the taker on notice that something may be amiss. 'On the face of it' includes the back, with the consequence that the indorsements must be 'regular': *Arab Bank Ltd v Ross* [1952] 2 QB 216. Even prior to the CPOA, a cheque was not irregular solely by reason of being post-dated: Riley, op cit, pp 47–8.

An instrument is not regular if an indorsement is irregular. Regularity of indorsements is solely a matter of form. It is possible for an indorsement to be regular yet be completely invalid for the purposes of making the transferee a holder. Such would be the case if an indorsement was forged. On the other hand, it is possible that the indorsement is valid for the purposes of transferring the instrument by negotiation, yet be irregular because it is not in the appropriate form: *Arab Bank Ltd v Ross* [1952] 2 QB 216, especially per Lord Denning at 226–7.

[10.106] In *Arab Bank v Ross Ltd* [1952] 2 QB 216 the defendant had made two promissory notes payable to 'Fathi and Faysal Nabulsy Company' as a part-payment for some shares. The notes had been indorsed in favour of the plaintiff bank. The defendant later learned that the bank had a charge over the shares which ranked prior to his claim. He alleged fraud, partly on the basis that the payees of the notes were also directors of the bank. Fraud could only be raised against the plaintiff bank if it was not a holder in due course of the notes.

The indorsement to the bank was in the form 'Fathi and Faysal Nabulsy' with the word 'Company' omitted. The court held that the indorsement was valid in the sense that it was effective to transfer the notes by negotiation and thereby constitute the bank as holder. However, the indorsement was irregular since the omission of the word 'Company' was sufficient to give rise to reasonable doubt whether the payees and the indorsers were one and the same entity. Since the indorsements were irregular, the bank could not be a holder in due course and the defence of fraud could be raised by the defendant. On the facts, the defence failed.

NOTICE OF DEFECT IN TITLE

[10.107] Each of the Acts lists circumstances in which the title of the transferor is 'defective'. In each case, the list is not exhaustive.

The CPOA defines a person's title to a cheque as defective when it is obtained by fraud, duress or other unlawful means or for an illegal consideration: s 3(3). Section 3(4) provides that s 3(3) is not to be taken to limit by implication the circumstances in which title is defective. Section 50(2) deems a holder to have notice of a defect in title if the holder takes the cheque with notice that the transfer is in breach of faith or under circumstances amounting to fraud.

Section 34(2) BEA arrives at similar results: the title of the transferor is 'defective' if he or she obtained the bill or the acceptance of the bill by fraud, duress, or force and fear, or other unlawful means, or for an illegal consideration, or when it is negotiated in breach of faith, or under such circumstances as amount to a fraud.

[10.108]   The English Court of Appeal has held that 'fraud' means common law fraud. In *Osterreichische Landerbank v S'Elite Ltd* [1980] 3 WLR 356 the drawers of a bill of exchange were insolvent at the time of drawing the bill. They later negotiated the bill to the plaintiff bank, which knew of their insolvency. In the circumstances, the negotiation was a 'fraudulent preference' within the meaning of the Bankruptcy Act. However, the court found that there was no defect of title and that the acceptor had no defence to an action on the bill.

REQUISITES OF VALID INDORSEMENTS

[10.109]   In order to transfer an instrument by negotiation, the indorsement must be written or placed on the instrument itself and it must be an indorsement of the entire instrument: CPOA s 41(1); BEA s 37(b). Thus, it is impossible to 'split' the sum of the instrument into parts, some of which are transferred and some of which are not. Similarly, it is not permissible to indorse the instrument to two or more indorsees severally, although there is no prohibition against joint indorsees: CPOA s 43; BEA s 37(b).

When an instrument is made payable to or is indorsed to two or more persons jointly, then if they are not partners each must indorse the instrument in order to transfer the instrument by negotiation. The exception to this is when one or more of the parties has the authority to sign for the others: CPOA s 43; BEA s 37(c).

[10.110]   Each of the Acts contains a provision for 'extending' the instrument in the event that there is no longer any room for further indorsements. The extension is known as an 'allonge' and it is provided that an indorsement which is written or placed on an allonge shall be taken to be written on the instrument itself: s 41(2). The use of an allonge is very unusual in Australia. In some foreign legal systems, the first indorsement on an allonge must begin on the cheque itself and continue on the allonge. This is an obvious precaution against fraud and is to be highly recommended, although neither of the Acts impose such requirement.

No particular form of signature or formula is required in order to make a valid indorsement. A simple signature is sufficient provided only that it is written on the instrument itself: CPOA s 41(3); BEA s 37(a).

PAYEE MISDESCRIBED

[10.111]   Recall that the requirements of regularity of indorsements are strict: see [10.108]. Yet, it often happens that the payee or indorsee of a cheque is misdescribed. For example, the person's first name may be spelled incorrectly or his or her initials may be incorrect. If the person indorses with his or her usual signature, then the indorsement may well be irregular within the *Arab Bank* test. The Acts provide for a procedure in such a case.

The person who is misdescribed may indorse the instrument by indorsing in accordance with the designation or spelling in the instrument: CPOA s 44; BEA s 37(d). If this is done and the instrument is a cheque, the person must then add his or her proper signature: CPOA s 44. Under the BEA, the person may, if he or she thinks fit, add the proper signature: BEA s 37(d). Any person taking an instrument from a payee or an indorsee who is misdescribed should insist upon this procedure being followed, for otherwise the taker may find that he or she is not a holder in due course.

CONDITIONAL INDORSEMENTS

[10.112]   Indorsements are sometimes made where the transferor wishes the transfer to occur if and only if some condition is fulfilled. Some examples might be 'Pay to the Order of Jane Doe on the condition that she marries my son' or 'Pay to the Order of John Smith on the condition that he is not yet insolvent'.

Both Acts permit these so-called conditional indorsements, but severely restrict the operation of the condition. The CPOA spells out the effect in some detail. In the first place, the transfer by negotiation is complete whether or not the condition is fulfilled: s 45(a). Second, a drawee bank paying the cheque is entitled to disregard the condition and pay the cheque either to the conditional indorsee/holder or to any subsequent holder whether or not the condition is fulfilled: s 45(b). Finally, the condition is to be ignored for the purposes of determining whether a holder is a holder in due course: s 45(c).

[10.113]   The BEA is less verbose. The condition may be disregarded by the payer, and the payment to the indorsee is valid whether the condition is fulfilled or not: BEA s 38.

This does not mean that the condition is without any effect whatsoever, but the extent of its operation is by no means clear. The immediate indorsee is probably bound by the condition: *Laney v Gates* (1935) 35 SR (NSW) 372. It is thought that the indorsee under a conditional indorsement holds any proceeds in trust for the indorser if payment is obtained while the condition is not satisfied: see G A Weaver and R C Craigie, *The Law Relating to Banker and Customer in Australia*, 2nd ed, Law Book Co, Sydney, 1990. The Explanatory Memorandum observes, correctly that the same arguments should apply as between the conditional indorsee and the person who takes from the conditional indorsee and so on, so that any holder may be responsible to the previous one if the condition is not fulfilled. Unfortunately, after noting the uncertainty, the framers of the CPOA chose to ignore it.

OTHER KINDS OF INDORSEMENTS

[10.114]   The BEA recognises several kinds of indorsements which are not authorised by the CPOA. By s 37(f), an indorsement 'may be made in blank or special. It may also contain terms making it restrictive'.

Although the CPOA does not define 'indorsement in blank', it uses the term in ss 96 and 99. Presumably it means the same as it does in the BEA, namely that the indorsement specifies no indorsee: BEA s 39(1). In such a case, the CPOA indirectly provides that the instrument is payable to bearer: ss 20, 21 and 22. The BEA explicitly provides that the bill becomes payable to bearer: s 39(1).

[10.115]   A 'special' indorsement specifies the person to whom, or to whose order, the bill is payable: BEA s 39(2). All of the provisions of the BEA relating to a payee apply, with the necessary modifications, to an indorsee under a special indorsement: s 39(3). The blank indorsement may be converted to a special indorsement by writing above the indorser's signature a direction to pay the instrument to the order of the holder or to some other person: BEA s 39(4). Although the CPOA does not refer to 'special indorsement', the same effect is achieved by ss 20, 21 and 22.

[10.116]   A restrictive indorsement has no counterpart in the CPOA. An indorsement is restrictive which prohibits the further negotiation of the bill, or which expresses that it is a mere authority to deal with the bill as thereby directed and not a transfer of the ownership thereof: s 40(1). The section gives several examples of the latter type of restrictive indorsement: 'Pay D only', 'Pay D for the account of X' and 'Pay D or order for collection'.

A restrictive indorsement gives the indorsee the right to receive payment, to sue any party that the indorser could have sued, but no power to transfer his or her rights as indorsee unless expressly authorised by the indorsement: BEA s 40(2). If the indorsement does authorise further transfer, then later indorsees take subject to the same rights and liabilities as the indorsee under the restrictive indorsement: BEA s 40(3).

[10.117]   The CPOA does not recognise restrictive indorsements in any form. If a cheque were to be given a restrictive indorsement of the first type, the type purporting to restrict negotiation, then it would be of no effect because of the CPOA's strict insistence on unfettered transferability: s 39.

It is not clear what effect a crossing such as 'Pay D or order for collection' would have on a cheque. On the one hand, there is nothing which would prevent the taker of the cheque from being a holder in due course within the meaning of s 50, yet the terms of the indorsement must provide a defence for the indorser in the event that the indorsee attempted to recover. In addition, if the indorsee under the restrictive indorsement negotiated the bill further, it would be hard to argue that the taker has no notice of a 'defect in title'; at the very least, it is clear that the indorsee is attempting to negotiate the cheque in breach of faith: see CPOA s 50(2).

TRANSFER OF ORDER INSTRUMENT WITHOUT INDORSEMENT

[10.118] Sometimes the holder of an instrument will transfer it to a second party while withholding the indorsement until such time as some further condition is fulfilled. If the cheque is an order instrument, then the transferee is not a holder since he or she is neither the payee nor the indorsee. The transferee becomes a holder only when there is a transfer by negotiation, and that occurs when the indorsement is added to the instrument: *Day v Longhurst* (1893) 62 LJ Ch 334.

Until the time of negotiation, the transferee is merely in the position of an assignee of a chose in action and will be affected by any notice of fraud, duress or illegality which comes to his or her notice prior to obtaining the indorsement. Thus, in *Whistler v Forster* (1863) 14 CBNS 248; 143 ER 441 the defendant was the drawer of a cheque in favour of G. G transferred the cheque to the plaintiff, but did not indorse it at that time. It was found as a fact that G had obtained the cheque by fraud and that the indorsement was not added to the cheque until such time as the plaintiff had notice of the fraud. It was held that the plaintiff could not be a holder in due course.

[10.119] The CPOA attempts to formalise these relationships in s 42, but the section is not well drafted. It purports to apply 'where the holder of a cheque payable to order, without indorsing the cheque, delivers the cheque, for value, to another person in order to transfer the cheque by negotiation'. Presumably what is meant is that there is an intention to transfer title to the cheque, not merely hand it over for safe-keeping or for some other very limited purpose.

If the section applies, then the person who takes delivery of the cheque obtains, by virtue of the delivery, the same title in the cheque as that of the transferor and, in addition, acquires the right to have the holder indorse the cheque. The section does not specify how this right is to be enforced, but it has long been established that a court may make such an order: *Walters v Neary* (1904) 21 TLR 146.

[10.120] The BEA is less verbose: the same conclusion obtains when the holder of a bill transfers it for value without indorsing it. The section does not apply unless the transferor intended to transfer the whole of his or her rights in the bill: *Good v Walker* (1892) 61 LJQB 736.

TRANSFEROR BY DELIVERY

[10.121] An instrument which is payable to bearer does not require an indorsement in order to be transferred by negotiation although the transferee may sometimes be able to insist on an indorsement for the purposes of adding the credit of the transferor to the cheque. If there is no indorsement, then the transferor is, of course, not liable on the cheque either to the immediate transferee or to any later holder: CPOA s 31; BEA s 28.

This does not mean that the transferor has no obligations at all to the transferee, for just as the law relating to the sale of goods has imposed some responsibility on the seller for the quality of the goods, the Acts make the transferor of a bearer instrument responsible for certain deficiencies.

[10.122] A holder of an instrument payable to bearer who transfers it by negotiation without indorsement is known as a transferor by delivery: CPOA s 77(1); BEA s 63(1). The transferor by delivery is not liable on the instrument since he or she has not indorsed it: CPOA s 77(2); BEA s 63(2). However, the transferor by delivery warrants to the transferee for value that the instrument is what it purports to be, that the transferor has the right to transfer the instrument by negotiation and that the transferor is not, at the time of the transfer, aware of any fact that renders the instrument valueless: CPOA s 77(3); BEA s 63(3).

The warranties given by a transferor by delivery, although valuable to the transferee in some circumstances, are by no means a substitute for an indorsement, since an indorsement is in effect a warranty of payment. In particular, the warranty imposed by the Acts is not a warranty that the drawee will pay the instrument, remain solvent or that the drawer will pay the instrument or remain solvent.

It is important to notice that the warranty is that the transferor is not, at the time of the transfer, aware of any fact which renders the instrument valueless. Presumably, it would be a good defence for the transferor to show that the transferor was ignorant of any defect in the bill, even if that ignorance is the result of negligence: see Riley, op cit, p 151.

[10.123] There are circumstances, however, where there may be liability on the warranties even though there is no liability on the indorsement. In *Commercial Bank of Australia Ltd v Barnett* [1924] VLR 254 the defendant introduced a third party to the plaintiff bank. The third party wished for the plaintiff bank to collect some cheques for her, which the plaintiff agreed to do provided that the defendant would also indorse the cheques. It turned out that the cheques had been misappropriated and the plaintiff bank repaid the true owner of the cheques.

The defendant could not be liable on his indorsement since the cheques were not dishonoured and there was no liability under the BEA s 63 because the defendant was not a transferor by delivery. Cussen ACJ considered that the defendant was liable on the common law warranty that the 'cheques were what they purported to be' and that he, as an indorser, had a right to transfer them.

OVERDUE AND/OR DISHONOURED INSTRUMENTS

[10.124] When an instrument has been in circulation for too long or if it has been dishonoured, then the Acts in effect make the assumption that there is something wrong. The consequence is that a person taking such an instrument cannot become a holder in due course.

A cheque is in circulation for too long when it becomes stale, that is when it appears on its face to have been drawn more than 15 months previously. By s 46(1) CPOA, where a stale cheque is transferred by negotiation to a person, that person takes the cheque subject to any defect of title affecting the cheque at the time when the cheque became a stale cheque and does not receive a better title than that of the transferor, nor is the new holder capable of giving a better title than that which he or she has obtained. Note that the defect in title is that which affected the cheque at the time of its becoming stale, not that at the time of the transfer in question. There is a presumption that all transfers of a cheque occurred before the cheque became stale, but the presumption is, of course, rebuttable: CPOA s 46(3).

[10.125] It is more complex to determine when a bill has been in circulation for too long. Part of the reason for this is that bills serve widely differing economic functions. The BEA provides that a demand bill is overdue when it appears on the face of it to have been in circulation for an unreasonable length of time: s 41(3). Unnecessarily and unhelpfully, the section goes on to say that 'What is an unreasonable length of time ... is a question of fact'. The section does not appear to have caused any problems, probably because it is unusual to have a demand bill which is not a cheque.

For bills which are not payable on demand, s 19 BEA provides rules for determining the time of payment. The basic time for payment is the last day of the time of payment fixed by the bill: s 19(1). If the bill is payable at a fixed period after date, sight or the happening of some event, the day of payment is found by excluding the day of the event and including the day of payment: s 19(2)(b). Of course, it is possible that a bill payable a fixed time after sight might be dishonoured by non-acceptance. In that case, time begins to run from the date of noting or protesting for non-acceptance: s 19(2)(c). In all cases, a 'month' means a calendar month: s 19(2)(d). Non-business days are given special treatment by s 98.

As in the case of a stale cheque, if an overdue bill is negotiated, it can only be negotiated subject to any defect of title affecting it at its maturity and no person who takes it can acquire or give a better title than that of the transferor: BEA s 41(2).

CHAPTER 11

LENDING

GENERAL PRINCIPLES OF LENDING

[11.1] Although lending to customers is an important part of the business of banking, the normal relationship of banker and customer does not include any contractual terms related to lending by any means other than overdraft. In general, lending by the banker to a customer is the subject of a separate and explicit contract which is more often than not in writing.

The banker has few statutory or other legal privileges when engaged in the business of lending. Aside from the banker's lien discussed at [11.123] and a few provisions in the Bills of Exchange Act, bankers are in the same legal position as any other credit provider.

In the past, banks have been under direct restrictions as to lending practices. The Reserve Bank of Australia is given power to determine certain policies in relation to lending. Whenever it is satisfied that it is necessary or expedient to do so in the public interest, it may give directions as to the classes of purposes for which advances may or may not be made. The power is one of policy only, and the Bank is prohibited from giving directions with respect to an advance made or proposed to be made to any particular person: see Banking Act 1959, s 36(1).

TYPES OF LENDING

[11.2] Traditionally, lending by Australian banks has been short-term loans provided by way of overdraft. Even in the case of housing finance where the parties expected that the loan would continue for a number of years, the legal form was that of an overdraft which was repayable 'on demand'. With the onset of deregulation as well as the other economic changes which have occurred over the last 20 years, this pattern is no longer as inflexible as it once was.

This text is not concerned with the principles of good lending, although such a topic is of the utmost importance to the practising banker. We are concerned here only with the legal aspects of lending, practice being relevant only in so far as it affects or is affected by the law related to lending. Further, in a general text of this type, we can only provide a survey of the law. There are significant textbooks on the law of securities and of guarantees. In these chapters we provide only an overview.

SECURED/UNSECURED

[11.3] One distinction which must be drawn is that between secured and unsecured loans. An unsecured loan is a contract between the lender and the borrower whereby the lender advances money and the borrower promises to repay that money together with any interest and charges which might be agreed upon terms which are agreed. The only remedy which the lender has in the event of default is the action for breach of contract, although since the amount claimed will usually be for a liquidated sum the default summons procedure may be used. The problem with an unsecured loan is that in the usual case of default by the borrower he or she is unable, as distinct from unwilling, to repay the loan. A right of action against such a person is worthless.

A secured loan, by contrast, requires in addition to the above that the borrower provide the lender with an interest in some property. In the event of default, the lender may seek to recover the amount due from the property rather than directly from the borrower. Since the lender has an interest in property, that interest will not generally be affected by the insolvency of the borrower, so that recovery might be possible even when the borrower is unable, as distinct from unwilling, to pay.

OVERDRAFTS

[11.4] An overdraft facility is nothing more than a current account on which the banker has approved arrangements which allow drawings to a certain limit which will leave the account in debit. Generally, the overdraft is repayable upon demand: see the discussion at [2.47] concerning the meaning of repayment 'on demand'. The account is operated like a normal cheque account with interest being charged on the amount that the account is actually overdrawn. In addition, there may be establishment fees and penalty interest if the limit is exceeded.

Substantial overdrafts should be arranged ahead of time, but if the customer writes a cheque of a size which would, if honoured, result in the account being overdrawn, then this amounts in law to a request by the customer for an overdraft which the banker may or may not grant: *Cuthbert v Robarts, Lubbock & Co* [1909] 2 Ch 226.

[11.5] The banker has, in the absence of any agreement to the contrary, a right to combine the overdraft account with any other current account belonging to the customer whether that credit account be with the same or a different branch. An agreement which precludes combination may be relatively easily implied but does not follow from the mere fact of more than one account being opened by the customer: see [3.34].

[11.6] Right to repayment 'on demand' does not mean that the facility may be terminated without any notice at all to the customer. The customer must be given reasonable notice, and the bank may not refuse to honour cheques which are outstanding at the time when the notice is given: see, for example, *Rouse v Bradford Banking Co Ltd* [1894] AC 586; *Dawson v Bank of New Zealand (No 2)* (1884) 5 LR (NSW) L 386. Further, as in the case of the banker's right of combination, the right to claim repayment of an overdraft on demand may be altered or abrogated by an express or implied agreement to the contrary: *Williams and Glyn's Bank v Barnes* [1981] Com LR 205.

The latest edition of Paget suggests that there might be an obligation to pay outstanding cheques (that is, cheques drawn before notice in the honest belief that the facility was available) even if the limit of the overdraft has already been reached: see Paget, op cit, p 167, citing *Williams and Glyn's Bank v Barnes* [1981] Com LR 205; *Johnston v Commercial Bank of Scotland* (1858) 20 D 790; *Buckingham & Co v London and Midland Bank* (1895) 12 TLR 70. Lord Herschell in *Rouse v Bradford Banking Co* [1894] AC 586 suggested that the bank is obliged to honour cheques put into circulation before notice, but he qualifies it by saying that they must be within the limits of the overdraft.

The argument that cheques must be met even if they exceed the overdraft has some merit. The customer may have been planning to put the account in funds to meet the outstanding cheques so that, in the absence of notice that the facility was being cancelled, they would have been honoured on presentment.

[11.7] An overdraft may be a secured loan. Taking a mortgage to secure an overdraft is, contrary to what was thought at one time, not inconsistent with the relationship of banker and customer nor does it alter in any way the bank's right to charge and compound interest: *National Bank of Australasia v United Hand-in-Hand and Band of Hope Co* (1879) 4 App Cas 391.

The banker's right to repayment 'on demand' is, of course, matched by a right in the customer to repay the overdraft without notice and with payment of interest to the day of repayment only.

[11.8] The banker has a right to charge interest on overdrafts, a right which derives from the usage and custom of bankers. The bank not only has a right to charge interest on overdrafts, but may charge it at a variable rate which reflects the rates of the financial markets: *Re City and Country Property Bank Ltd* (1895) 21 VLR 405; *South Australian Banking Co v Horner* (1868) 2 SALR 109.

[11.9] Banks compound interest on overdraft accounts by periodically adding the interest to the outstanding balance. Interest is then computed on the increased balance during the next period. The right to compound interest in this way has long been recognised: *Bevan, ex parte* (1803) 9 Ves 223; 32 ER

588; *Fergusson v Fyffe* (1841) 8 Cl & Fin 121; [1835–42] All ER 48; *Yourell v Hibernian Bank Ltd* [1918] AC 372; *National Bank of Australasia v United Hand-in-Hand and Band of Hope Co* (1879) 4 App Cas 391 3.10.

At one time, it was thought that this right was limited to certain forms of mercantile accounts, but this restriction is no longer recognised: see *National Bank of Greece SA v Pinios Shipping Co No 1 (The Maira)* [1990] 1 AC 637, overruling, on this point, the English Court of Appeal in *Deutsche Bank und Disconto Gesellschaft v Banque des Marchands de Moscou* (1931) 4 LDAB 293. The basis for permitting the bank to charge compound interest on a loan is based on a fiction. The fiction, constructed to avoid the effects of the usary laws, is that the loan is considered repaid and then readvanced at each rest period: *National Bank of Greece SA v Pinios Shipping Co No 1 (The Maira)* [1990] 1 AC 637; *Deutsche Bank v Banque des Marchands de Moscou* (1931) 4 LDAB 293; *Paton (Genton's Trustee) v IRC* [1938] AC 341.

[11.10]   The right to charge interest and to compound it periodically does not cease when the bank demands repayment. The right continues until the debt is repaid or a judgment is obtained, whichever occurs first: *National Bank of Greece SA v Pinios Shipping Co No 1 (The Maira)* [1990] 1 AC 637. This may lead to a windfall for the bank if it is able to invoke escalation clauses which permit it to charge higher interest after default. Further, the decision appears to be based on the principle that the demand should not affect the manner in which the account is maintained. This may lead to problems where the loan does not call for periodic payments.

[11.11]   May the bank claim the compound interest from a guarantor? There is no account to be debited with the periodic interest accrued. Unless the guarantee instrument calls for the periodic payment of interest by a guarantor after demand has been made under the guarantee, the bank's right of charging interest might be limited to simple interest.

[11.12]   The right of bankers to charge compound interest on overdraft accounts was recognised by the High Court in *Bank of New South Wales v Brown* (1982) 151 CLR 515. However, it also noted that the character of the amount owed as interest does not change merely because it has been 'capitalised'. The case concerned an amount owed to the plaintiff bank. Under the appropriate section of the Bankruptcy Act, interest could not exceed 8 per cent. The bank argued that when the interest was capitalised and debited to the account, it lost its nature as interest and so the section did not apply. The High Court disagreed, holding that the rights of third parties given by the Bankruptcy Act could not be altered by agreement between the banker and customer.

TERM LOANS

[11.13]   Although lending by way of overdraft may fit comfortably into the usual banker-customer relationship, loans for a fixed period must be much more thoroughly documented. As mentioned above, the banker is in a position no different from any other lender for this type of transaction.

Functionally, the primary difference from an overdraft arrangement is that the loan is no longer repayable upon demand. Indeed, a demand for repayment before the contractual termination date would be a breach of contract by the bank. Further, while the loan agreement remains in force, the bank has no right to combine the loan account with any account which might be in credit unless there is a term in the loan agreement which expressly grants the bank the right of combination in the circumstances: *Bradford Old Bank v Sutcliffe* [1918] 2 KB 833.

COMMERCIAL/FINANCIAL BILLS

[11.14] In certain circumstances, the bank may be willing to lend to a customer but may not wish to advance cash by way of loan or overdraft. One method of 'lending credit' to the customer is by way of a 'line' of credit, usually through the mechanism of financial bills of exchange. A bill which bears the acceptance or the indorsement of a bank is known as a 'bank bill' and is obviously a very valuable item on the bill market. In establishing a bill line, the bank will agree to accept bills drawn on it by the customer up to the limit agreed upon. The customer may then discount the bank bill in the commercial market. The bank charges an 'acceptance fee' which together with the discount from the face value of the bill represents the interest which the customer will pay for the funds.

This arrangement allows the bank to 'lend its credit' to the customer. A related arrangement is a 'discount line' in which the bank agrees to discount bills drawn by the customer. As far as the customer is concerned, this is very much like a loan in that he or she receives money directly from the bank and is obliged to repay funds to the bank at a particular time. From the banker's point of view, however, the bill provides a hedge against liquidity pressures since the banker reserves the right to sell the bill on the market at any time.

Generally speaking, bills are for periods of 90 or 180 days. Since the customer is likely to need funds for a longer period of time, the line of credit usually provides that the bills may be 'rolled over', that is, new bills will be drawn at the time of maturity of the original set. In this way, the borrower is assured of longer term finance, although the interest rate will vary with the market.

[11.15] The use of a bill of exchange in the lending transactions may lead to certain legal problems. In the usual case, the bank is the acceptor of the bill and therefore the party who is legally the primary debtor on the bill, but it is the customer, usually the drawer of the bill, who is functionally the primary debtor. It might be expected that the law would reflect this economic distinction and s 33 of the BEA attempts to do this through the concept of an 'accommodation party'.

An accommodation party to a bill 'is a person who has signed a bill as drawer, acceptor or indorser, without receiving value therefor, and for the purpose of lending his name to some other party': BEA s 33(1). The BEA then makes certain provisions which give effect to the agreement between the party accommodated and the accommodation party. Thus, an accommodation party is liable on the bill to a holder for value and it is immaterial whether, when the holder took the bill, he or she knew that the other party was an accommodation party: BEA s 33(2).

Although the heading of the section refers to 'accommodation bill or party', the section itself defines only accommodation party. The term 'accommodation bill' is usually used to refer to a bill where the acceptor is an accommodation party, but commercial usage does not appear to have any inflexible rule.

The matter is not one of mere terminology for s 64(3) implements the remaining legal framework of the commercial function of the accommodation facility. It provides that 'where an accommodation bill is paid in due course by the party accommodated, the bill is discharged'.

[11.16]   Is the bank an 'accommodation party' within the meaning of the BEA when it accepts a bill under an acceptance facility agreement? Can it be said that it accepts the bill 'without receiving value therefor' when it receives the acceptance fee? Ellinger argues that the acceptance fee is not consideration for the acceptance of each individual bill. As evidence, he notes that the fee would be payable even if no bills were ever accepted: Ellinger and Lomnicka, *Modern Banking Law*, 2nd ed, Clarendon Press, Oxford, 1994, p 628. The argument is only partially convincing, for it is also clear that there would be no acceptance if the fee were not paid, so that the fee must be at least partly the consideration for the acceptance of each bill. Further, s 33 does not refer to the value being directly related to the instrument but rather to the acceptance.

[11.17]   Case law on the subject is not conclusive. In *Re Securitibank Ltd* [1978] 1 NZLR 97, the New Zealand Supreme Court held that the bills in question were not accommodation bills, but the fee payable was more complex than a simple acceptance fee. Ellinger argues that this distinguishes the case: Ellinger, op cit, p 628. The bills in *KD Morris & Sons Pty Ltd v Bank of Queensland Ltd* [1980] 54 ALJR 424 are referred to as 'accommodation bills', but it is clear that the term was being used in its commercial rather than its legal sense.

In spite of these problems, it must be agreed that to hold that the bills drawn under an acceptance facility are not accommodation bills leads to strange commercial results. The drawer of the bill is obliged to put the acceptor into funds to meet the bill. If instead he or she pays the bill directly to the holder can it be imagined that the acceptor may then be sued for the amount on the bill?

There may be a way around the problem. In *Cook v Lister* (1863) 32 LJCP 121 Willes LJ said (at 127):

> In each case with reference to bills of exchange, if a question arises who is the principal debtor, prima facie the acceptor is the principal debtor; and then, in order, the drawer and the indorsers, as their names appear upon the bill. But the court is bound to test the evidence to show that in any case the person who is not the principal debtor on the face of the bill is, in fact, the principal debtor; and if he is the principal, he is the agent to pay for all those debtors subordinate to him including the acceptor.

Cook v Lister was decided before the Act, but the logic of the argument remains intact. If that is so, then the commercial 'accommodation bill' would be discharged by payment by the drawer even if the bill is not a legal 'accommodation bill' within the meaning of the BEA.

[11.18] A customer who wishes to borrow money from a bank using the mechanism of a 'bill line' may be required to give security in precisely the same way that he or she would be expected to provide security in a normal loan. Problems have sometimes arisen where a party to the bill has been forced to pay and the party holding the security for payment is either not liable on the bill or has become insolvent. The person who has been asked to pay may argue that he or she is entitled to the security, that in some sense the security 'runs with the bill'.

[11.19] In *Ex parte Waring* (1815) 19 Ves 346; 34 ER 546 an indorser was forced to pay on an accommodation bill where the drawer and the acceptor were both insolvent. The drawer had been required to give securities to the acceptor to guarantee the payment of the bill. These were not securities held by the acceptor for the general liability of the drawer, but rather securities specifically appropriated to cover the acceptor's liability on the bill. The court held that the indorser was entitled to be subrogated to the securities. The same result has been reached when the security was one given by the acceptor to a prior indorser who had become insolvent: *Commissioners of State Savings Bank of Victoria v Patrick Intermarine Acceptances Ltd (in liq)* [1981] 1 NSWLR 175. For other cases on subrogation, see *Re New Zealand Banking Co* (1867) LR 4 Eq 226; *Ex parte Dever; Re Suse (No 2)* (1885) 14 QBD 611; *Powles v Hargreaves* (1853) 3 De GM & G 430; 43 ER 169; *Royal Bank of Scotland v Commercial Bank of Scotland* (1882) 7 App Cas 366; *Re Standard Insurance Co Ltd (in liq) and Companies Act 1936* [1970] 1 NSWR 392.

[11.20] In *Scholefield Goodman & Sons Ltd v Zyngier* [1986] AC 562 the security was given by a person associated with the acceptor of the bill. The security was given to the payee of the bill and was for both the acceptor's obligation to the payee on the bill and for other obligations as well. In the event, the drawer was forced to pay on the bill. The court held that he was not entitled to realise the securities: see also *D & J Fowler (Aust) Ltd v Bank of New South Wales* [1982] 2 NSWLR 879; *Maxal Nominees Pty Ltd v Dalgety Ltd* [1985] 1 Qd R 51.

[11.21] Where there is a right of subrogation, it arises at the time when the party becomes the holder of the bill by paying it. That is also the time for determining competing claims to the securities: *Westpac Banking Corp v AGC (Securities) Ltd* [1983] 3 NSWLR 348; *McColl's Wholesale Pty Ltd v State Bank of New South Wales* [1984] 3 NSWLR 365.

STANDBY CREDITS AND PERFORMANCE BONDS

[11.22] A second way in which the banker might 'lend credit' is through the use of standby letters of credit and/or performance bonds. These will be discussed in detail in Chapter 12, but the basic idea is that the banker promises to some third party that payment will be made under certain circumstances. As an example, a foreign purchaser of Australian technology may be concerned that the vendor may not be able to deliver. Such a failure may expose the foreign importer to substantial expenses, either directly or by way of damages for breach of contract for further supply. One way in which the dilemma is sometimes solved is for an Australian bank to issue a performance bond in favour of the foreign purchaser. If there is a failure by the Australian supplier, the foreign purchaser may call upon the bank to pay a sum which will protect against the possible losses.

The arrangement works because the creditworthiness of the Australian bank, which may be easily assessed, has been substituted for the creditworthiness of the Australian supplier. The latter may either be difficult for the foreigner to assess or may be unsatisfactory if it has been assessed. In this sense, the bank has 'lent credit'. Of course the banker will treat the issuance of a performance bond in much the same way as a loan. The customer must promise to put the banker in funds should the bond be drawn upon and the banker will need to assess the ability of the customer to fulfil this promise. The banker will take appropriate securities to guard against the possibility of insolvency.

Although the performance guarantee is most often used in connection with the supply of goods or services as in the above example, it can be used in purely financial transactions. The credit of the guaranteeing bank may be used to assist in the acquisition of finance in (commercially) the same manner as the acceptance of the bank on a bill of exchange.

LETTERS OF COMFORT

[11.23] When making a loan to one of a group of companies, the prudent course for the lender is to take a guarantee from the parent company and, if possible, from all the companies in the group. It is only in this way that the lender can be certain that assets of the group will be available to meet the obligations of the legal borrower.

Unfortunately, what is prudent for the lender is not always acceptable to the parent company. A variety of commercial reasons may make a guarantee unattractive. The parent company may not wish to incur legal liability or it may wish to avoid having a contingent liability showing on its balance sheets.

The compromise position is the letter of comfort. Although the term is not one with a fixed legal meaning, a letter of comfort is some form of assurance from a third party, usually a parent company, to a lender which represents that some fact is true, that the third party is aware of the loan or that the third party agrees to a certain conduct in the future.

[11.24]   Ellinger has classified letters of comfort into three basic types: see Ellinger 'Letters of Comfort' [1989] *JBL* 259. At the one extreme, the parent company may give an undertaking to maintain its shareholding or other financial commitment in the subsidiary. A second type of letter calls for the parent to use its influence to see that the subsidiary meets its obligation under the primary contract. The weakest form of the letter of comfort is a confirmation that the parent is aware of the contract with the subsidiary, but without any express indication that the parent will assume any responsibility for the primary obligation. Although Ellinger classifies 'letters' it is clear that a single letter may contain paragraphs of the different types.

A letter of comfort may have legal effect even though it is not a guarantee. The liability of the guarantor for the primary debt arises by the default of the primary debtor. But there may be other contractual promises, the breach of which would have the effect of allowing the lender to recover damages equivalent to the debt. The question in each case is to determine the legal effect of the terms of the letter.

The legal problem that arises from a letter of comfort is the determination of the extent of legal obligations, if any, undertaken by the author of the letter.

[11.25]   As an example, in *Banque Brussels Lambert S A v Australian National Industries Ltd* (1989) 21 NSWLR 502, Rogers J considered the effect of a letter of comfort that contained paragraphs of all three of the types identified by Ellinger. The defendant argued that the letter did not create a binding contract, basing its argument on the decision of the English Court of Appeal in *Kleinwort Benson Ltd v Malaysia Mining Corp Bhd* [1989] 1 All ER 785.

The basic facts of the *Banque Brussels* case were that the defendant held 45 per cent of the issued capital of the holding company that owned 100 per cent of the borrower. The bank required the letter of comfort, in a form satisfactory to it, as a condition of the loan. The defendant had previously refused to give a guarantee. The disputed letter of comfort was the negotiated compromise.

The letter contained three paragraphs. The first was a 'confirmation of awareness' paragraph. It was agreed by both parties that the paragraph had no promissory effect.

The second and third paragraphs were disputed, and the second paragraph was actually in two parts. In the first part the defendant 'stated' that it would not be their intention to reduce their shareholding in the borrower and in the second that they 'would' provide the bank with 90 days' notice of any decision to dispose of any shareholding.

The second disputed paragraph, the third paragraph of the letter, was in the following terms:

> We take this opportunity to confirm that it is our practice to ensure that our affiliate [the borrower] will at all times be in a position to meet its financial obligations as they fall due. These financial obligations include repayment of all outstanding loans within thirty (30) days.

Rogers J noted that there were two closely related questions. Was there an intention to create legal obligations and, if so, were the terms of the letter of a sufficiently promissory nature to be held to be contractual?

Rogers J found that at least the second part of the second paragraph was promissory and that the third paragraph was undoubtedly so. The court heard evidence establishing that the defendants knew that the plaintiff regarded the obligations as binding.

[11.26]   In interpreting letters of comfort, a court will invoke a presumption that in commercial dealings an agreement is intended to create legal relations: see *Rose & Frank Co v J R Crompton & Bros Ltd* [1925] AC 445. The presumption may be rebutted if the intention to so rebut is expressed with sufficient clarity. It is also necessary to consider the distinction between an undertaking as to the future and a mere statement of present intention. Statements of present intention need merely be true at the time that they were made, but an undertaking as to the future will be interpreted as a promise. Where a statement has a promissory effect it will not easily be found to be void for uncertainty: *Banque Brussels Lambert S A v Australian National Industries Ltd* (1989) 21 NSWLR 502; *Kleinwort Benson Ltd v Malaysia Mining Corp Bhd* [1989] 1 All ER 785; *Biotechnology Australia Pty Ltd v Pace* (1988) 15 NSWLR 130; A L Tyree, 'Southern Comfort' (1989–90) 2 JCL 279.

TYPES OF BORROWER

[11.27]   The banker must be aware of the different legal characteristics of borrowers, for different types of securities may be taken, different forms of guarantees may be needed and different loan structures may be used depending upon the class into which the individual borrower falls.

PRIVATE

[11.28]   In terms of numbers, the majority of bank lending is still to individual customers, either for 'private' purposes such as the purchase of a house or a vehicle or for business reasons. Since it is highly unlikely that the banker would even be contemplating a loan which would be used for an illegal purpose, there is little in the way of legal problems involved in such a loan provided the borrower has contractual capacity.

Minors

[11.29]   Until relatively recently, any person under the age of 21 was considered in law to be 'an infant' and so in need of special protection. At common law, this protection was provided by the rule that most contracts with infants were voidable at the option of the infant. Exceptions were contracts for 'necessaries' and contracts which were made for the benefit of the infant. Unfortunately, the development of case law left considerable uncertainty in the meaning of these terms: see D J Harland, *The Law of Minors in Relation to Contracts and Property*, Butterworths, Sydney, 1974. The age at which a person attains full contractual capacity is now 18 in all states and territories.

Most other contracts are valid unless and until the infant chooses to avoid them. The repudiation must be made before the infant receives benefit from the contract. Thus, in *Steinberg v Scala (Leeds) Ltd* [1923] 2 Ch 452, an infant was allotted shares in a company. Although she received no dividends and did not participate in the company in any way, the court held that she could not repudiate the contract and recover the money paid since the allotment of the shares had conferred a benefit to her under the contract.

In some jurisdictions, certain contracts with infants are void. In Victoria and Tasmania all contracts for the repayment of money lent or to be lent, payment for goods other than necessaries are 'absolutely void': Supreme Court Act 1958 (Vic); Infant's Relief Act 1875 (Tas). These contracts cannot be enforced even if the person purports to ratify them upon attaining full age. Because of these provisions, the banker should avoid allowing any account with a minor to run into overdraft.

[11.30] In New South Wales, the Minors (Property and Contracts) Act 1970 provides that a contract is binding on a minor if it is for the benefit of the minor at the time of entering the contract and if the minor does not, by virtue of being a minor, lack the necessary understanding: ss 18 and 19. The meaning of 'benefit' is not defined in the Act: see Harland, op cit. Since it is uncertain when a loan to a minor would be for the benefit of the minor, it is probably best to avoid such loans unless guaranteed by someone of full age.

The Act makes an important change in the law in relation to guarantors of loans to minors. Although generally a guarantor is not liable unless the principal debtor is liable, the Act provides that a guarantor of full age of a minor's obligation is bound by the guarantee to the same extent as if the minor were of full legal capacity: s 47 and see [11.162].

The court is given power to adjust the rights of the parties when a minor chooses to repudiate a contract: s 37. This power should allow the court to avoid the worst hardships of the older common law rules.

[11.31] South Australia has also implemented legislation which alters the rights and obligations of minors entering into contractual relations. The Minors' Contracts (Miscellaneous Provisions) Act 1979 (SA) does not abolish the common law rules, but does ameliorate some of the harshness of those rules concerning the repudiation and ratification of contracts. A contract may be ratified by the minor upon the attainment of full age if the ratification is in writing: s 4. As under the New South Wales Act, a guarantor who is of full age may not escape his or her obligations merely because the minor had no liability by virtue only of being a minor: s 5.

Under the South Australian Act, the minor may enter into a binding contract provided the prior approval of a court is obtained by either the minor or any party to the proposed contract: s 6.

Code of Banking Practice

[11.32]   Where the purpose of the loan is entirely for the individual's private or domestic use the Code of Banking Practice will apply: Code of Banking Practice, s 1.1. See Chapter 10 for a discussion of the obligations under the Code.

BUSINESS BORROWERS

[11.33]   Different forms of business association will give rise to slightly different concerns when the banker is lending for the purposes of the borrower's business activities.

Sole traders

[11.34]   There are no legal problems associated with lending to sole traders, although as will be seen at [11.85], there may be a problem with obtaining proper security over stock in trade.

Partnerships

[11.35]   The basic legal characteristics of partnerships have been discussed above in Chapter 2. Recall that a partnership is the relation that exists between persons carrying on a business in common with a view to profit and that such a circumstance may arise without any formal intention on the part of the parties to become partners. A single partner may bind the firm but this is so only if the purpose is that of the firm or apparently that of the firm. The death, bankruptcy or insanity of a partner will dissolve the partnership. A partner who dies or becomes bankrupt is liable for the partnership debts, but the debts of the private estate have a prior claim.

Since the banker is not generally in a position to monitor any of these possible changes, it is wise to make express provision for liabilities for loans to partnerships. This is usually done by expressly making each of the partners jointly and severally liable for the loan and by taking joint and several guarantees from each of the partners.

Finally, when notified of any change in the partnership, the banker should rule off any overdraft account so as to prevent the operation of the rule in *Clayton's case* causing a loss of the bank's rights against any of the parties: see [3.7] for a discussion of the rule in *Clayton's case*. If it is desired to carry on arrangements with the newly constituted partnership, a new account should be opened and new documentation taken.

Companies

[11.36] The legal aspects of lending to a company differ from those of individual lending in two major ways. First, the company must always act through agents, giving rise to questions of authority and capacity of the parties which the bank must deal with. Second, the securities which may be taken from a company differ from those which are taken from an individual: see [11.111]ff.

Further, although the company is a separate legal entity, there are many companies which are virtually alter egos of one (or a small number of) individual(s). Consequently, a loan to such a company will usually be accompanied by a taking of guarantees and/or securities from the individuals 'behind' the company.

• *Agency problems*

[11.37] Even though the company has the power to borrow and to give securities and even though the loan is for a proper purpose, a banker deals with the company not as an abstract legal entity but rather with directors and other individuals who are acting as agents of the company. But these individual agents do not have unlimited power to commit the company by signing contracts on the company's behalf. The agency problem is to determine the extent to which the company may be bound by an agent even though that agent is acting beyond his or her actual powers.

The relationship of such directors to outside third parties is the subject of s 164 of the Corporations Law, but it is worth considering the position reached by the common law courts before the passing of those amendments.

[11.38] The basic position was discussed in *Royal British Bank v Turquand* (1856) 119 ER 886 and is known as the rule in *Turquand's* case. There it was said that every person is deemed to have notice of the contents of the company's memorandum and articles of association but that it is not necessary for a person dealing with a company to inquire into the internal workings of the company to verify that an agent of the company is acting within the actual limits of authority. Phrased another way, a company will be bound by the acts of an agent if the act is one which would have been within the usual scope of an agent in the position of the agent who was actually dealt with.

This was not as favourable to the banker as might first be thought. For example, if the power to borrow which was granted in the memorandum or the articles was a power which could only be exercised by the passing of a general resolution, then the banker had to be certain to sight the resolution before granting the loan, for if there was no resolution then the director or other agent was not acting within the scope of the authority which they would have possessed had they been the actual agent of the company. On the other hand, if the resolution was sighted, then under the rule in *Turquand's* case, it was not necessary for the banker to inquire into the formal regularity of the resolution, as for example, ascertaining that a quorum was present at the meeting where the resolution was passed or that the proper rules of order were followed at the meeting.

[11.39] Suppose though, that the person with whom the banker is dealing is not even an agent. For many years this remained a confused area of law, but the decision by the English Court of Appeal in *Freeman and Lockyer v Buckhurst Park Properties (Mangal) Ltd* [1964] 2 QB 480, particularly the judgment of Diplock LJ, has clarified the matter considerably. The defendant company was formed for the purpose of buying a particular property and making a quick resale. The property was purchased, but the resale did not eventuate, so that the directors of the company were concerned merely to dispose of the property as advantageously as possible.

One Kapoor was a director of the company who was conducting the business of the company with the knowledge and approval of the other directors. Professing to act on behalf of the company, he instructed the plaintiffs to render certain services, namely the conduct of a planning application and appeal relating to the property. The payment for those services was the subject matter of the suit. The trial court found that the plaintiffs had intended to contract with the company, not with Kapoor personally. It was also found that although Kapoor had never been formally appointed as managing director he had been acting as such and that this was known to the board of directors.

In a comprehensive review, Diplock LJ summarised the position by concluding that there were four conditions which must be satisfied in order to entitle a contractor to enforce the contract against the company when it was entered into on behalf of the company by an agent who lacked actual authority to do so. In *Freeman and Lockyer v Buckhurst Park Properties (Mangal) Ltd* [1964] 2 QB 480 at 505–6 he said that it must be shown that:

(1) a representation that the agent had authority to enter on behalf of the company into a contract of the kind sought to be enforced was made to the contractor;

(2) such representation was made by a person or persons who had 'actual' authority to manage the business of the company either generally or in respect of those matters to which the contract relates;

(3) [the contractor] was induced by such representation to enter into the contract, that is, that he in fact relied upon it; and

(4) under its memorandum or articles of association the company was not deprived of the capacity either to enter into a contract of the kind sought to be enforced or to delegate authority to enter into a contract of that kind to the agent.

Since the implementation of the Corporations Law the fourth paragraph is no longer relevant since the doctrine of *ultra vires* no longer applies.

[11.40] The rule in *Turquand's* case was considered by the High Court in *Northside Developments Pty Ltd v Registrar-General* (1990) 170 CLR 146. Without authority, one director and his son purported to execute a mortgage over certain company assets. The son signed as 'secretary', a position which he did not hold. The High Court held that the company was not bound by the mortgage. There was no representation by the company that the son was the secretary, and the director had no actual or apparent authority to bind the company with such a representation.

[11.41] The Corporations Law provides some assistance for persons dealing with companies. Section 164 provides that such a person may, subject to exceptions discussed below, make certain assumptions and those assumptions will have the effect of binding the company.

The first assumption is that at all relevant times the memorandum and articles have been complied with. Second, if the person claiming to represent the company is named in returns lodged with the Commission as a director, principal executive officer or a secretary of the company, then it may be assumed that he or she has been duly appointed and has the usual powers which attach to the relevant position.

Third, if the person is held out by the company to be an officer or agent, then it may be assumed that he or she has been duly appointed and has authority to exercise the powers and perform the duties of the relevant position. Fourth, persons dealing with officers or agents of the company who have authority to issue documents may assume that the officer or agent has authority to warrant authenticity of documents.

Fifth, it may be assumed that a document has been duly sealed by the company if it appears to be sealed by the company and the sealing is attested by two people the first of which the person dealing with the company is entitled to assume is a director and the second of which he or she is entitled to assume is either a director or a secretary of the company.

Finally, every person dealing with a company is entitled to assume that the directors and other officers and agents of the company are properly performing their duties to the company.

[11.42] While s 164 is a very welcome clarification to the law of dealing with companies, it probably does not take the position of the banker much beyond what it was under the older regime. This is because the banker will usually have an actual copy of the memorandum and articles and so will be taken to know their contents. A person is not entitled to make a s 164 assumption if he or she has actual knowledge that the matter he or she would be entitled to assume is not correct: s 164(4)(a).

[11.43] It might be thought that the simple solution is for the banker to cease calling for a copy of these documents, but that is a course which may not be open, for s 164(4)(b) provides that the person may not make the assumptions if: 'his connection or relationship with the company is such that he ought to know that the matter that ... he would be entitled to assume is not correct.'

[11.44] The 'connection or relationship' described by s 164(4)(b) is not confined to 'insider' relationships such as a company director, shareholder or employee. Further, the 'connection of relationship' need not be based on a history of prior dealings, but may arise by knowledge gained during the course of a single transaction: *Bank of New Zealand v Fiberi Pty Ltd* (1994) 12 ACLC 48; *Story v Advance Bank Australia Ltd* (1993) 11 ACLC 629; (1993) 31 NSWLR 722.

Given the duty that banks have toward their customer, the banker might be a person whose 'relationship with the company' excludes him or her from the benefits of the section in most cases. If that is so, then the matter is right back to the basic principles established by Lord Diplock in *Freeman and Lockyer v Buckhurst Park Properties (Mangal) Ltd* [1964] 2 QB 480.

- *Statutory prohibitions*

[11.45] The banker should also be certain that there are no statutory restrictions on the company's borrowing powers. In particular, recall that a company is generally forbidden from providing financial assistance for the purchase of its own shares: see Corporations Law s 205 and *Selangor United Rubber Estates v Cradock (No 3)* [1968] 2 All ER 1073; *Karak Rubber Co Ltd v Burden (No 2)* [1972] 1 All ER 1210 and the discussion at [4.47].

Unincorporated associations

[11.46] The problems of lending to unincorporated associations relate directly to the previous discussion concerning the lack of a single legal identity for such organisations. There is no identity apart from the individuals, so special care must be taken that the individuals involved understand precisely the scope of their liability: see the discussion in Chapter 2.

THE CONSUMER CREDIT CODE

[11.47] The Consumer Credit Code commenced operation on 1 November 1996. The Code is a result of an intergovernmental agreement known as the Uniform Credit Laws Agreement of 1993. Under this agreement, Queensland has enacted the Consumer Credit (Queensland) Act 1994 which includes the Consumer Credit Code. Other states are obliged to either adopt the 'template legislation' or to pass alternative legislation which is consistent with the Queensland legislation. 'Consistent' in this context means that anything which is lawful under the Code must also be lawful under the alternative legislation, the purpose being to allow lenders to use the same procedures and documentation in all jurisdictions. Uniformity in regulations, of vital importance if uniformity of documentation and procedures is to be achieved, is obtained by the same 'template' method.

The Consumer Credit Code replaces the various existing Credit Acts. Although these Acts were intended to provide a uniform legal structure, they failed to so, the result being that lenders were forced into uneconomic and inefficient practices. The Consumer Credit Code was scheduled to begin full operation on 1 September 1995, but difficulties in drafting the regulations delayed implementation for more than a year.

[11.48]   The Code applies to any provision of credit where the debtor is a natural person or a strata corporation, the credit is provided wholly or predominantly for personal, domestic or household purposes, a charge is made for providing the credit and the credit is provided in the course of a business of providing credit or as a part of or incidentally to any other business of the credit provider: s 6(1). Investment by the debtor is not for a personal, domestic or household purpose: s 6(4). The Code also applies to 'credit contracts' which is any contract for the provision of credit of the type just described: s 5.

[11.49]   There is no general exemption for banks or any other class of financial institution. There are, however, certain classes of loans which are excluded from the operation of the Code, and these classes include certain types of loans which are traditionally made by banks. So, for example, the Code does not apply where credit is extended without prior agreement between the parties, the Code explicitly giving as an example the case of a cheque account becoming overdrawn where there is no agreement for overdraft facilities: s 7(2). The Code does not apply to the provision of credit arising out of a bill facility, although it is noted in the Code itself that the Regulations may provide for application of the Code to such a facility: s 7(5). This possibility forestalls any attempt to circumvent the Code using artificial structures. The Code does not apply to certain forms of 'short-term' credit, defined by the Code as credit limited by the contract to a total period not exceeding 62 days: s 7(1). Section 7 enumerates other general exemptions from the operation of the Code.

[11.50]   The Code applies only the 'purpose test' to determine if a transaction is to be regulated. The former Credit Acts imposed a 'monetary test' which generally excluded loans of more than a prescribed value. As a result, it would appear that housing loans which are made for non-investment purchase of housing will now be regulated by the Code.

[11.51]   The Credit Acts imposed a penalty of automatic forfeiture of interest where certain requirements of the Acts had been breached. Although there were provisions for application to reduce this forfeiture when the breach was insignificant, the financial institutions lobbied to have the provisions removed. The Code has rejected the concept of automatic forfeiture, substituting a regime of simple civil penalties when there has been a breach of 'key requirement'. The concept of a 'key requirement' differs depending upon whether the credit contract is a continuing arrangement or otherwise: s 100.

For non-continuing contracts, the civil penalty may be activated when there has been non-disclosure of various types in the credit contract or when there has been an excessive obligation imposed by the contract on the debtor at the time when the contract is entered into: s 100(1). Where the contract is a continuing one, the civil penalties may also be imposed when there is non-disclosure of certain information in the periodic statement of account: s 100(2). The Code contains provisions which are intended to allow 'systemic' contravention to be dealt with in a single jurisdiction: see ss 108, 109.

A debtor may apply to have the transaction reopened on the grounds that it is unjust: s 70(1). 'Unjust' includes 'unconscionable, harsh or oppressive': s 70(1). The Code provides a 'shopping list' of factors which are to be taken into account in determining if a transaction is unjust: s 70(2).

[11.52] The Code also applies to certain mortgages and guarantees. These are discussed at [11.119] and [11.140] respectively. For a more detailed discussion of the Code, see J Owens et al, *The New Consumer Credit Code*, Butterworths, Sydney, 1994; see also A Beatty, A Smith and A Barclay, *Annotated Consumer Credit Code and Regulations*, Butterworths, Sydney, 1997.

SECURITIES FOR ADVANCES

[11.53] When a loan is made, the borrower promises to repay the amount loaned together with any interest agreed upon. In the absence of unusual circumstances such a promise is enforceable in a court of law. If the creditor is forced to take such proceedings and if successful, there are procedures for ultimately recovering the debt from the property of the debtor.

But suit is both expensive and unsatisfactory and the truth of the matter is that most defaulting debtors would prefer to pay their debt but cannot because of their financial position. In such a circumstance, obtaining a judgment against the debtor will usually be of no value, for there is no property left from which to satisfy the debt.

It is for this reason that creditors may prefer to take a security from the debtor as well as the contractual promise to repay. A general definition of security' is notoriously difficult to formulate, but in all cases there is some right of the creditor to reclaim the debt, or part of it, from property which is 'reserved' for that purpose.

SECURITIES GENERALLY

[11.54] Perhaps the best formal definition of 'security' is that given in E Sykes, *The Law of Securities*, 5th ed, Law Book Co, Sydney, 1993, pp 12–13:

> an interest, not being an interest arising from a trust, in property which is either owned by another person or in which another person has incomplete or inchoate rights capable of maturing into full ownership, by virtue of which interest certain rights are exercisable in relation to that property in order to obtain payment or performance of an obligation by that other person either consensually provided for or provided for by implication of law or validly directed by some third party to be paid or performed.

As usual, the word 'security' is used in a narrower sense by lawyers than by the commercial community as a whole. There are at least three other ways in which the word is used in commercial practice. First, 'security' may refer to the property over which the security is given. Second, 'security' may refer to documents of various kinds, including notes and bills, share certificates, bonds and a whole host of others. Third, 'security' may refer to a guarantee by a creditworthy third party.

A guarantee given by a third party is not a security under the definition given by Sykes. A guarantee is merely a contractual promise given by some third party which makes that party liable in the event of a default by the debtor. However, because the guarantee is functionally so closely related to the concept of a security interest, the topic is covered in this chapter.

LEGAL AND EQUITABLE SECURITY INTERESTS

[11.55]   A distinction must be drawn between legal and equitable security interests. The definition is purely operational: a legal interest is one which, prior to the enactment of the Judicature Act (UK) 1873, would have been recognised by a court of common law; an equitable interest is one which, at the same time, would have been recognised only by a court of equity.

The distinction remains important for us today because of the fact that the Judicature Acts did not merge the two related legal systems into a single legal system, but rather merged the administration of each system of law into a single court system.

PRIORITIES WHEN MORE THAN ONE INTEREST

[11.56]   The distinction between legal and equitable interests has a number of consequences, but the most important for existing purposes is the problem which arises when there are competing security interests in the same item of physical property. It must be emphasised that there is nothing improper or fraudulent in this. A borrower may give a mortgage over property to lender A and then give a second mortgage over the same property to lender B.

If the borrower is unable to pay and the lenders have to realise the security, the question arises as to how the proceeds from the property should be distributed. Suppose that lender A had provided $1000 and lender B had provided $500. If the property realises more than $1500, then there is no problem. If it realises less, then the general rule would be that lender A takes the whole $1000 (if there is that much) and lender B takes whatever is left and has only an action on the contract of loan to recover the residue. This is a very simplified example since there are matters of interest due and costs of the sale of the property to take into account.

The problem becomes more difficult when the security interests given to A and to B are of substantially different types. Suppose, for example, that the borrower gives lender A a mortgage over some jewellery, but then later pledges the jewellery to B, that is, gives B the right to possession of the jewellery until such time as the debt may be repaid. Both A and B believe that they should be entitled to the 'first bite' of the money which might be realised from the sale of the jewellery in the event of the borrower's default.

This is a problem in priorities between competing security interests. These problems are generally very difficult and call for expert advice, but, subject to many exceptions, the basic rules which establish priorities depend upon first identifying the nature of the security as either legal or equitable and then:

1. if both interests are legal, then the one which has been created first in time should have priority;

2. if both interests are equitable, then the rule is the same, that is, the interest created first in time should have priority;

3. if the first interest is a legal one and the second is equitable, then the legal interest has priority;

4. if the first interest is equitable and the second is legal, then the equitable interest has priority unless the legal interest was taken by the creditor without notice of the existence of the already existing equitable interest, in which case, the legal interest has priority.

[11.57]   The fourth rule is a slightly simplified version of the priority rules, for the time at which the subsequent creditor must be without notice is the not the time of taking the legal title, but the time of making the advance: see *Taylor v Russell* [1892] AC 244. It seems that this applies only to fixed equitable charges: see Goode, *Legal Problems of Credit and Security*, Sweet & Maxwell, London, 1982.

This allows for a strange sequence of events as follows: Suppose that A lends to B, taking an equitable interest in some of B's property. Later C lends to B, also secured by an equitable interest over the same property. Later C learns of A's prior interest which, of course, gives A priority if the security must be realised. C then takes steps to acquire a full legal interest in the secured property. C then has priority over A who has been 'squeezed out'. The effect is called a *tabula in naufragio*; it would seem to be restricted to the situation where C's equitable interest is a fixed, as opposed to a floating, interest: see *Taylor v Russell* [1892] AC 244.

Again, it must be noted that these rules are general only and are subject to many exceptions and modifications. Nevertheless, they provide the starting point for any solution to a priority problem; consequently, the distinction between legal and equitable security interests is of great importance in priority problems.

Equitable security interests are also important because they are relatively easy to create. It may happen that the formalities necessary to create a legal interest have not been properly completed, so that the legal interest is not created, yet the procedures are adequate to create a similar equitable interest. In some of the cases, it seems that an equitable interest has almost been created by 'accident' for it is sometimes sufficient for the court to find an 'intention' in the behaviour of the parties which will create the equitable proprietary interest.

CONSENSUAL SECURITIES

[11.58]   Most security interests are created by the agreement of the parties. Such security interests are called consensual securities. However, it is also possible for a security interest to arise by operation of the law, that is, that the proprietary interest vests in the creditor by virtue of some set of circumstances regardless of the intention or even the knowledge of the parties. Most of the security interests which are of interest to the banker will arise by agreement between the parties, but one very important interest, the banker's lien, is a non-consensual security: see [11.123] for a discussion of the banker's lien.

Consensual securities will be examined first. The creation of these is, in contrast to so much of the banker-customer relationship, a very formal process. The contract which creates the security interest is usually a preprinted form used by the banker and contains many detailed and arcane clauses. Although they differ in detail from bank to bank, the contracts used by banks differ from those in general use in two ways. First, the contracts often call for the repayment of the loan 'on demand': see [2.47].

The second peculiarity of bank forms is the detail and scope of the definition of moneys to be secured. The forms usually contain many clauses which attempt to define explicitly virtually every conceivable situation in which the banker might advance money to the borrower or to someone associated with the borrower together with any interest or charges which might be due. All are purported to be secured by the interest being granted by the borrower to the banker.

[11.59]　　The length and scope of bank forms has been the subject of judicial criticism. In *Richards v The Commercial Bank of Australia* (1971) 18 FLR 95 a bank mortgage was given by a husband and wife who were referred to in the document as 'the mortgagor'. It was argued, unsuccessfully, by the bank that the document should be interpreted so as to secure the husband's liability under a guarantee which was given by the husband alone. During the course of the judgment, Fox J said (at 99–100):

> It surely is a sad commentary on the operation of our legal system that a borrower should be expected to execute a document which only a person of extraordinary application and persistence would read, which, if read, is virtually incomprehensible and which, in any event, has a legal effect not disclosed by its language.

See also the criticism by Higgins J in *Houlahan v ANZ Banking Group Ltd* [1992] 110 FLR 259 where he referred to 'incomprehensible legal gobbledygook', a single sentence of some 57 lines.

[11.60]　　Apart from special interests created by statute, there are only three types of consensual security interest known to our law. The pledge is the actual or constructive delivery of possession of an asset which is made with the intention that the creditor retain possession until the obligation is discharged. The mortgage is the transfer of ownership of the asset upon the express or implied condition that the ownership be transferred back to the debtor when the obligation is discharged. The charge, known only to equity, transfers neither ownership nor possession but allows the creditor to satisfy the obligation out of the proceeds of the property.

A reservation of interest in an asset may serve the same function as a security interest. In a hire-purchase arrangement, the seller of the asset retains the legal title to the asset until such time as the buyer has completed the payment obligations under the contract. The arrangement is functionally, but not legally, the precise equivalent of a mortgage. In both, the creditor is the owner of the asset while the debtor gains possession. It seems that it is not possible to retain an equitable interest while transferring legal ownership; an attempt to do so has been interpreted as a total transfer to the debtor followed by a grant back of the equitable interest sought to be retained: *Re Bond Worth Ltd* [1980] Ch 228; [1979] 3 All ER 919; cf *Len Vidgen Ski & Leisure Ltd v Timaru Marine Supplies (1982) Ltd* [1986] 1 NZLR 349 where the contract purported to retain 'ownership'.

Legislation in some states has attempted to rationalise the various forms of security interest. In particular, the Credit Acts have abolished the concept of hire-purchase in those circumstances where the Acts apply: see [11.120].

MORTGAGOR'S RIGHT TO DEMAND DISCHARGE

[11.61] In the earliest concept of a mortgage, the mortgagor had no right to have the property reconveyed prior to the time stipulated in the contract. There is a long history of decisions which gradually gave the mortgagor more rights, but the matter is now dealt with by the statutes.

The most important of these is the right to redeem the mortgage at any time prior to the exercise by the mortgagee of the power of sale. Any term in the mortgage which purports to limit or to remove the mortgagor's right of redemption is void save that the mortgagee may stipulate for the payment of all outstanding principal together with all interest that would accrue up to the contractual date when the final payment would be due: see *Kreglinger v New Patagonia Meat and Cold Storage Co Ltd* [1914] AC 25. Since this amounts to payment of interest after repayment of the principal, there is generally little incentive for the mortgagor to take advantage of this right. Many mortgages include a term which gives the mortgagor the right to obtain an early discharge by giving a specified length of notice and/or paying a relatively small amount of extra interest. Of course, even without the express term, the way is open to negotiate with the mortgagee for an early discharge.

Of course, the mortgagor is entitled both contractually and under the statutes to have the mortgage discharged provided that the payment is made on the due date.

The procedure for obtaining a discharge of a registered mortgage is simple. On the production of any document signed by the mortgagee and duly attested which purports to discharge the mortgage, the registrar is bound to enter upon the register a notation that the mortgage is discharged. The mortgage is discharged at the time of registration of the discharge.

SECURITY OVER REAL PROPERTY

[11.62]   Security interests may be taken in real property, in chattels and in choses in action. Each is governed by a fundamentally different set of legal rules. The remainder of this section will examine the taking of security interests over real property.

LEGAL ASPECTS OF MORTGAGES OVER REAL PROPERTY

[11.63]   The best way in which to understand the nature of a mortgage over land is to consider the form of the mortgage which existed prior to the introduction of the Torrens system of title registration. Under the so-called 'old system' or 'deeds system', a purchaser of land could obtain valid title only by having the land conveyed by the true owner of the land. In order to determine that the seller was the true owner, it was necessary to establish that the previous seller was the true owner and so on right back to the original Crown grant. Such an investigation of ownership is expensive and uncertain, with the result that title to land was subject to attack by the discovery of some defective link in the chain of title.

OLD STYLE MORTGAGES

[11.64]   In this context, a mortgage of land took the form of a conveyance of the land coupled with a contractual promise that the lender, the new owner of the land, would convey it back to the borrower when the borrower complied with the terms of repayment of the loan. To anyone who was not privy to the contract of loan, the transaction looked like a sale of property; there are still echoes of this procedure in the Sale of Goods Acts in those sections which provide that the Acts do not apply to transactions which, although in the form of a sale, are intended to be by way of security: see, for example, s 4(4) Sale of Goods Act 1923 (NSW).

THE RIGHT OF REDEMPTION AND SECOND MORTGAGES

[11.65]   One of the main problems with the old form of mortgage was the strict interpretation which the common law placed on the contractual promise to reconvey. If the borrower was in default by even a day, then the lender no longer could be held to his or her promise. Furthermore, even in the absence of default the only rights left to the borrower were contractual ones; the common law recognised no property interest remaining in the borrower following the conveyance.

This intolerable situation was remedied by the courts of equity which recognised the 'right of redemption'. By ordering specific performance of the contract to reconvey, and by a willingness to make such an order even when the borrower had been in default, the equity courts created a new property interest which remained with the mortgagor of the property. This equitable property interest was, and is, known as the 'equity of redemption'.

It was soon realised that this equity of redemption was itself a valuable property right which might be mortgaged as security for advances from other lenders. When this was done, the transaction became known as a 'second mortgage'. The second mortgage is an equitable one since it is a mortgage, a conveyance, of property recognised only by the courts of equity.

These developments were not without their problems, for the rights and obligations of the parties were complex and confused, depending as they did upon two separate but interlocking systems of law. When ownership of land was put on the more certain footing of a system of registration, it was also necessary to change the form of the mortgage and to define more precisely the relationships between the mortgagor, the mortgagee and the land.

OTHER FORMS OF EQUITABLE MORTGAGES

[11.66] Before considering the Torrens land registration system, it should be noted that the second mortgage is not the only form of an equitable mortgage. Under the deed system, an equitable mortgage could be created by the deposit of title deeds with the lender, by an informal attempt to create a legal mortgage and in certain other ways that need not concern us now. As will be seen, the importance of the equitable mortgage has been diminished by the introduction of the Torrens registration system, but it is by no means obsolete.

THE TORRENS SYSTEM OF LAND REGISTRATION

[11.67] The deficiencies of the deeds system led to the introduction into Australia of the Torrens system of land registration. The warning given earlier concerning the extent of the coverage of this section needs to be repeated here. The following material is the barest of outlines of the workings of the Torrens system. It is not intended and should not be used as a substitute for a textbook on the law relating to land tenure. The following descriptions focus on freehold property; certain property held on a lesser tenure from the Crown is also included in the Torrens system.

The touchstone of the Torrens system is indefeasibility of title: registration as the registered proprietor is conclusive evidence of ownership subject only to certain exceptions related to a person who becomes a registered owner by means of his or her own fraud. It is not necessary for the registered owner to prove that previous transfers were valid.

[11.68] Each parcel of land which is registered under the Torrens system is issued with a certificate of title. The original of this certificate is always retained by the titles office in the district where the land is located and a copy of the certificate is issued either to the registered owner or to the first registered mortgagee. As will be seen, this copy of the certificate is important and can play a role similar in some respects to the old deeds of title.

[11.69] Most major dealings with the land are required to be registered with the appropriate titles office. These dealings are recorded on a public register by notations on the original certificate of title. Consequently, an inspection of the public register will reveal details about the previous dealings with the land as well as any existing outstanding interests in the land which require registration. This public register is considered so important that everyone is deemed in law to know the contents of it.

Dealings with the land are entered on the register together with the precise time of registration. As will be seen, mortgages over the land have priority determined not by the rules mentioned above, but by time of registration. It is possible to change the priority of two registered mortgages by agreement among the interested parties which may then be registered.

[11.70] The Torrens system has a compensation system built into it for two reasons. First, the indefeasibility principle means that occasionally someone who would have remained the owner of land under the deeds system will lose ownership to an innocent registered owner. The system provides for a type of insurance payment to the deprived owner in such a circumstance. Second, it is possible that ownership of land could be lost through some error in the titles office. The system provides for compensation to be made by the Crown in certain circumstances.

Torrens land mortgages

[11.71] As noted above, when the deeds system was replaced with the registration system, the law related to mortgages was also rationalised. It was no longer necessary that a mortgage should be a formal conveyance of the property, since the interest could be placed on the register and the rights and obligations of the parties defined in the legislation. The end result is a clarification and simplification of the relationships established when land is mortgaged.

Under the provisions of the various Real Property Acts, a mortgage has effect as a security but does not operate as a transfer of the land. A registered mortgage is more in the nature of a charge than a mortgage although, of course, the interest is legal rather than equitable. Any mortgage is a registrable instrument and should be registered for reasons which will become apparent.

Note, however, that an unregistered mortgage is not a legal nullity; it may affect not only the immediate parties but third parties as well since it may form an equitable mortgage: see [11.72]. Further note that the distinction between legal and equitable mortgages, although blurred, is still relevant. For example, a mortgage document which purports to create a mortgage over Torrens system land is a valid equitable mortgage from the time of its creation even though the mortgagee does not have the legal rights provided by the statute until such time as the mortgage is placed on the register.

Equitable mortgages

[11.72] Under the old system of land transfer, an equitable mortgage could be created merely by the mortgagor depositing the title deeds with the mortgagee. Provided that the parties intended to create a security interest by these actions, the court would hold that there was indeed an equitable mortgage created: for a modern discussion, see *Re Molton Finance Ltd* [1968]

Ch 325. The nature of the transaction has been succinctly stated by Pape J in *Re Nairn's Application* [1961] VR 26 at 28:

> The nature of an equitable mortgage by deposit of title deeds is not in doubt. The deposit of title deeds as security for the payment of a debt is regarded as an imperfect mortgage which the mortgagor is entitled to have perfected, or as a contract for a legal mortgage which gives to the party entitled all such rights as he would have had if the contract had been completed. By the deposit the mortgagor contracts that his interest in the property comprised in the deeds shall be liable for the debt and binds himself to do all that is necessary to effect the vesting in the mortgagee of such interest as a mortgage should create.

It seems common for a lender to take a completed memorandum of mortgage together with the certificate of title. Even if the lender chooses not to register the mortgage, there is an equitable mortgage created and it is not necessary for the lender to enter a caveat on the title for the mortgage to remain good. There may be circumstances when a failure to lodge a caveat will be held against the equitable mortgagee: see *Abigail v Lapin* [1934] AC 491. Note that no change in ownership can take place without the production of the duplicate certificate of title except in extraordinary cases. If it becomes necessary for the lender to resort to the security for repayment of the loan, the mortgage may be registered at any time in order to take advantage of the powers of sale given to a registered mortgagee: see *J & H Just (Holdings) Pty Ltd v Bank of New South Wales* (1971) 45 ALJR 625.

Although convenient because of the simplicity, unregistered equitable mortgages suffer from some disadvantages. They are liable to be defeated by any prior equitable interest, although such defeat is by no means certain. An unregistered equitable mortgage is also subject to defeat by fraudulent dealings by the owner provided it is possible for the owner to provide some plausible explanation for the absence of the duplicate certificate of title. Finally, the mortgagee has no general power of sale. This last is not overly important since in the common form the lender has taken the certificate, and a memorandum of mortgage is no impediment to registration with its consequential statutory power of sale.

Registered mortgages

[11.73]   A registered mortgage may be either a legal or an equitable mortgage in form, but since registration amounts to notice and since the rights and powers of the parties are the same, the distinction is of little practical importance. The essential features of a registered mortgage are that certain rights and obligations are implied by the statute into all mortgages except in so far as they are expressly varied or negatived by the parties to the mortgage. There are, in addition, statutory powers of sale given to the mortgagee and powers of redemption given to the mortgagor.

A bank mortgage will ordinarily be a long and comprehensive document which defines the rights and obligations of both sides. Basic obligations of the mortgagor will be to repay the principal and interest on the agreed terms and to keep the property in good repair and insured. The mortgagee undertakes to allow the mortgagor to remain in possession and to discharge the mortgage according to the terms of the agreement when the debt has been repaid.

REMEDIES

[11.74] The mortgagee's main rights arise upon default by the mortgagor. There are three essentially separate remedies in the event of the borrower defaulting on the loan. The course of action which the mortgagee takes will depend upon all of the circumstances of the case with particular attention given to the financial position of the borrower and the value of the security interest.

Suit on the 'personal covenant'

[11.75] If the amount of the default is small in comparison with the total value of the security or if the debtor has significant assets apart from the property which has been mortgaged, it is always possible for the lender to ignore the mortgage and to sue on the promise of repayment which is an essential part of every form of memorandum of mortgage. Successful suit places the lender in the same position as any other judgment creditor, so that if the debtor still refuses to pay then the creditor may proceed to move against any of the debtor's assets, not merely against the property which was mortgaged. Of course, if the debtor has no other assets, then such a course will be fruitless.

Enter and take possession

[11.76] The various state Acts allow the mortgagee to enter into possession of the mortgaged property upon default by the debtor. For reasons which will become apparent, this is not a course which will ordinarily appeal to the banker except in extraordinary circumstances.

It is important to recognise that taking possession does not necessarily mean taking physical possession of the property, although this is allowed by the statutes. More common is that the mortgagee assumes management and control of the property, taking any rents or other income from it. This may be done, for example, by giving formal notice to any tenant to pay rent directly to the mortgagee.

The reason that this is not a popular option with mortgagees under normal conditions is that the mortgagee is required to account to the mortgagor and assumes a responsibility toward the mortgagor to manage the property reasonably. Although not allowed a free hand in the management of the property, the mortgagee in possession is none the less responsible for it and may under some circumstances be unable to quit the property when it suits.

Mortgagee sale on default

[11.77] The mortgagee's power of sale is the most drastic and most effective remedy. In the usual case, the memorandum of mortgage will contain an express power of sale. In the case of a registered mortgage, this is not necessary, since there is a power of sale given to the mortgagee by the Acts, but in the case of an unregistered equitable mortgage, there would be no power of sale in the absence of an express contractual term. For reasons which will become clear, it is advisable for the holder of an unregistered equitable mortgage to register the mortgage before exercising any power of sale.

In no case may the power of sale be exercised without compliance with the sections of the Real Property Acts which are designed to protect mortgagees from losing their property if there is any other alternative. Under these Acts, no power of sale, whether expressed in the memorandum or given by the statute, may be exercised unless the mortgagee has served the mortgagor with a notice giving the details of the alleged default and allowing the mortgagor a period of at least one month from the receipt of notice to remedy the default.

[11.78] The precise scope of the mortgagee's duty to obtain a fair market price is not entirely clear. On the one hand, it has been said that the mortgagee is not like a trustee for the mortgagor, but the Privy Council has said that it is the duty of a mortgagee to behave 'as a reasonable man would behave in the realisation of his own property': *McHugh v Union Bank of Canada* [1913] AC 299 at 311; *Alexandre v New Zealand Breweries Ltd* [1974] 1 NZLR 497. It is certainly clear that the mortgagee may not act fraudulently or sacrifice the property at a patently low price.

A Queensland case has held that damages may be awarded against the mortgagee in certain circumstances for failing to exercise the power of sale: see *Highton Enterprises Pty Ltd v BFC Finance Ltd* (Qld CA, 21/12/94).

Priorities

[11.79] We have already discussed the basic rules of priority among mortgages of various kinds. These rules apply, but need some amplification in situations where the security is taken over Torrens land. The general law of mortgages applies to Torrens land but will operate subject to the provisions of the Real Property Acts.

- *Torrens: priority by registration*

[11.80] Because of the importance of the register when the subject matter is Torrens land, the differences between a legal and an equitable interest are obscured if the competing interests are registered. In that case, since registration constitutes notice to the world of the interest, there can be no such thing as a later legal interest created without notice of a prior equitable one. In effect, then, the priority of interests is determined entirely by the time of registration.

- *Other: normal rules of priority*

[11.81] When one of the interests is unregistered, the registered interest will gain priority even if it is registered with notice of the existence of the unregistered interest. If both interests are unregistered, then it would seem that the normal rules concerning priority of interests apply.

• *Second and subsequent mortgages*

[11.82]   The possibility of a mortgagor giving subsequent mortgages has a special importance to the banker, for the operation of the rule in *Clayton's case* works, in this instance, against the interest of the banker unless some steps are taken to safeguard his or her interest.

The question which arises concerns the priority of the mortgagees when both have made advances to the debtor after the creation of the second security interest. If the first mortgagee has the right to claim priority for advances made after this time, it is said that the advances are 'tacked' onto the first security interest. So, for example, A takes a security interest over B's property which is expressed to constitute a security for present and future advances. A lends B $1000. Later, B grants a security interest to C in return for a loan of $500. Assuming that A has the security interest with the greater priority, then, if the security must be realised, A takes the first $1000 and, if there is sufficient, B takes the next $500. But now suppose that A lends a further $500. Is A entitled to the first $1500? Or is A entitled to the first $1000, B the next $500 and then A the following $500?

[11.83]   The situation is illustrated in *Hopkinson v Rolt* (1861) 9 HL Cas 514. A lender took a floating charge to secure advances already made to the debtor but also expressed to cover all future advances. The charge agreement also contained a clause by which the borrower agreed not to grant any further encumbrances on the property. In fact, the borrower did grant further charges over the same property and the question before the court was whether the lender had the right to 'tack' advances made to the borrower which were advanced after the creation of the second encumbrance.

The court held that there was no right to tack future advances which were made after the first mortgagee had notice of the creation of the subsequent security interest, but that advances made before having such notice could be tacked. In terms of the above example, A is entitled to first claim for the entire $1500 if and only if the $500 advanced by A to B was made without notice of C's security interest. The holding is known as the rule in *Hopkinson v Rolt* (1861) 9 HL Cas 514.

The rule applies to a mortgage of Torrens land: *Matzner v Clyde Securities Ltd* [1975] 2 NSWLR 293. In this context, registration of the second interest does not provide notice of that interest to the first mortgagee, for there is no duty on the registered first mortgagee to continually search the register: *Nioa v Bell* (1901) 27 VLR 82; *Queensland Trustees Ltd v Registrar of Titles* (1893) 5 QLJ 46.

[11.84]   It might be thought that the situation would be different if A was under a contractual or other obligation to make the further advances to B, but a later case established firmly that this was not the situation. If the borrower does in fact grant a subsequent security over the same property, then the lender is relieved of any obligation to make the further advances: *West v Williams* [1899] 1 Ch 132.

The importance of this to the banker is that the interaction of the rule in *Hopkinson v Rolt* and the rule in *Clayton's case* may work to erode the priority of the first security entirely. If the first security is for a loan by way of over-draft, then payments into the account will discharge the earlier debt (which is the one in which the banker has priority) whereas later advances will rank behind the second security in priority. The result is that if the account is a normal working overdraft the banker gradually loses all priority to the subse-quent security interest.

There is a simple remedy. Immediately upon receiving notice of the creation of the subsequent security, the banker should stop the overdraft account at once. If it is desired to continue making advances to the customer, then a new account must be opened, but understood to be on terms whereby the security for the advances is substantially inferior to the original arrange-ments. This course of action is the only way in which the banker may retain the priority for the advances made prior to the creation of the subsequent security interest.

There have been several Australian cases which have allowed tacking in certain circumstances. In *Matzner v Clyde Securities Ltd* [1975] 2 NSWLR 293 the first mortgagor made further advances after receiving notice of the subse-quent mortgage. The subject matter of the securities was a building under construction and it was found as a fact that the advances were made for the purposes of completing the construction, a result which was to the benefit of all concerned. The court allowed the further advances to be tacked to the first mortgage. See also *Network Finance Ltd v Deposit & Investment Co Ltd* [1972] QWN 19.

SECURITIES OVER CHATTELS

[11.85]   A banker who is contemplating a loan to a modern business may find that the land belonging to or leased by the business represents a very small part of the total value of the business. If the business is one of manufac-turing, for example, then the primary assets of the business are likely to consist of the raw materials used in the manufacturing process, the machinery used to manufacture the goods and the final product prior to sale. There may also be substantial assets in the form of debts owed to the manufacturer. Again, if the business is primarily one of retailing, it is likely that the major assets will consist of stock and debts owed to the business.

The point of this is that much commercial lending is to businesses which are able to offer substantial security over chattels, for example, the raw mate-rials and machinery, and over choses in action, for example, debts owed to the business. Lenders must be familiar with the broad outlines of the law relating to security interests over chattels and choses in action.

Unfortunately, the law of both subjects is complex. The reader must be warned that any real life legal problem in this area is likely to demand the attention of experts. What this section attempts to do is to equip the reader to recognise the likely areas of difficulty so that problems may be avoided where possible and referred to the experts at the earliest available opportunity when not in fact avoided. The discussion begins with a consideration of security interests in chattels.

HISTORICAL PROBLEMS OF SECURITIES OVER CHATTELS

[11.86] It is possible today to create security interests in chattels which are conceptually identical to the mortgage of deeds system land, but it was not always so. A consideration of the problems perceived by the early common law will assist in an understanding of the modern problem of chattel securities.

The early common law generally refused to allow the creation or transfer of an interest in chattels unless the interest created or transferred was accompanied by a transfer of possession. Since the mortgage is the transfer of the legal title to the lender while the borrower retains possession, it would have been prohibited under this rule of the early common law. The rule is at least as old as *Twyne's* case (1600) 3 Co Rep 80b; 76 ER 809 and may be considerably older.

The justification for the rule was that to allow such transactions would be an invitation to fraud. Chattels, it was argued, are different from land in that there is no way to prove ownership. Whereas a would-be purchaser or mortgagee of land could rely upon the title deeds to determine the true owner of the land, there was no comparable method of establishing existing interests in chattels. Consequently, a person in possession of a chattel could mortgage it first to one then to another, always representing that the chattel was unencumbered.

The rule in *Twyne's* case survived for some 200 years. Since few legal rules survive intact for so long a period, it must be presumed that it worked well enough for the commercial necessities of the time. Indeed, some have speculated that it was only with the rise of the Industrial Revolution and the subsequent movement of wealth from land to other forms of assets that the rule in *Twyne's* case began to inhibit commercial transactions: see Gilmore, *Security Interests in Personal Property*, Little, Brown and Company, Boston, 1965. Whatever the cause, legislation was introduced all over the common law world at about the same time to allow the creation or transfer of interests in chattels without the need to also transfer the possession of the chattels.

THE SYSTEM OF REGISTRATION

[11.87] The legislation, represented in Australia today by the various state Acts, for example, Bills of Sale Act 1898 (NSW), sought to overcome the 'fraud problem' by a system of registration. Interests could be created, but they must be registered or suffer from certain deficiencies. Some of the legislation made unregistered interests totally invalid, but more usual was that the interest would be invalid only in certain circumstances or against certain parties.

The aims of the legislation are clearly stated in the UK Bills of Sale Act 1882 (Sykes, op cit, p 441):

> ... avoiding the social evil that resulted from an owner of chattels being able to present to those giving him credit a fictitious appearance of prosperity whereas all his property, though still in his possession, might be disposed of by secret dispositions.

It must be said at once that the legislation has not, from a commercial point of view, been very successful. Documents which are registered are published by various trade papers and the resulting publicity has been damaging to the credit of the borrower. Registration fees and various forms of stamp duty are sometimes onerous. The result is that many arrangements, some very artificial, have been devised to avoid the legislation. The system is uncertain and unpredictable as a result.

Further adding to the problem is that the legislation is very badly drafted, resulting in what one commentator has referred to as 'the quagmire of chattel securities': S A Riesenfeld, *The Quagmire of Chattels Security in New Zealand*, Legal Research Foundation, School of Law, University of Auckland, Auckland, 1970. As will be seen, one of the results of this is that chattel mortgages form only a fraction of the interests used when it is desired to take a security interest in chattels.

WHICH INSTRUMENTS REQUIRE REGISTRATION?

[11.88]   The first feature of the Acts is that they require the registration not of interests, but of documents. The precise nature of the documents which must be registered varies, but the common format requires the registration of documents which include 'bills of sale'. The actual definitions and requirements vary among jurisdictions, but there are three main categories of documents which require registration.

First is the 'assurance of chattels' by which is meant the transfer of the legal or equitable title to the chattel. Second is the 'declaration of trust', an expression which may not extend the definition much beyond the notion of an equitable assurance of the chattel. In any case, the term probably does not include the so-called letter of trust which is used by bankers in documentary letter of credit transactions: *Re David Allester Ltd* [1922] 2 Ch 211; and see the discussion in Chapter 12.

The third general category of document may be described briefly as a power to seize. These are instruments which embody agreements to the effect that the creditor has the power to seize, and usually to sell, certain chattels belonging to the debtor in the event of default.

New South Wales has a further class of instrument which falls within the registration requirements, namely, 'any agreement ... by which in equity any charge or security is conferred over personal chattels to be acquired after the date of the agreement'.

An example of this type of instrument is found in *Shears & Sons Ltd v Jones* [1922] 2 Ch 802, where the debtor agreed in writing that he would execute an instrument at a later date if the debt had not been paid by that time. Such an agreement gives an immediate right in equity and so is a document which requires registration within the meaning of the NSW Act although it may not fall within the first three categories of document.

All Acts contain a list of documents which are exempted from the definition, and hence from the requirement of registration. The most important of these are those which evidence the transfer of chattels in the ordinary course of business of any trade or calling, any mortgage or charge given by a company and certain types of hire-purchase agreements. It is unlikely that hire-purchase agreements would fall within the requirements for registration in any case; see Sykes, op cit, p 678.

The Acts apply only to written instruments. An oral agreement to create a security interest may be perfectly valid and, provided there is no contemplation of executing an instrument at a later time, is untouched by the Act: *New Zealand Serpentine Co Ltd v Hoon Hay Quarries Ltd* [1925] NZLR 73. Of course, purely oral agreements are not to be encouraged because of the evidentiary problems.

CONSEQUENCES OF REGISTRATION

[11.89]   It is fundamental to an understanding of the Acts to recognise that registration of an instrument does not give the agreement any force greater than it could have had under the general law. Phrased another way, if the agreement itself does not confer either legal or equitable rights, then registration will be wholly irrelevant. Consequently, in order to solve any problem involving chattel securities, it is necessary to consider the rights of the parties just as though the Acts did not exist, then consider what modifying influences the Act might have upon those rights.

Registration of the document is not, in the absence of a special provision in the relevant Act, notice to the world either of the existence of the document or of its contents: *Joseph v Lyons* (1884) 15 QBD 280.

CONSEQUENCES OF FAILURE TO REGISTER

[11.90]   A failure to register has different consequences in the different Acts. In some, the security has no validity against third parties until registered. This is the case, for example, in Victoria and for traders' bills in New South Wales. This approach seems to be in keeping with the general principles of the Acts.

In other jurisdictions, the Acts make the security invalid against certain parties but it retains its full or partial validity against others. The New South Wales Act is typical in the list of three classes of persons against whom the security interest is invalid in so far as the chattels concerned are still in the possession or apparent possession of the grantor. The parties listed are the assignee in bankruptcy of the grantor, the assignee or trustee acting under an assignment for the benefit of creditors of the grantor, and any sheriff or similar person who is seizing the chattels on behalf of an execution creditor.

One might have thought that, having regard to the purposes of the Acts, the bona fide purchaser of a chattel from a mortgagee who has no notice of an unregistered instrument would be protected against the interests of the mortgagor, but this is not generally true.

In those jurisdictions where a time is given for registration, the security has full effect until the expiration of that time even though it is not registered: *Marples v Hartley* (1861) 30 LJ QB 92 (NS). This leads to the possibility of 'rolling over' instruments in order to avoid the registration requirements, that is, executing a new instrument every 20 days. In theory, the existing instrument should always have full force despite the lack of registration. Surprisingly, the practice was held to conform to that theory in an old New South Wales case but it is very much doubted that a modern Australian court would come to the same conclusion: *Lyons v Cohen* (1877) Knox 92.

The reader should note that declaring the instrument to be void does not necessarily mean that the grantee under the instrument loses his or her interest. As an example, if the secured creditor has already exercised the right of seizure granted by the instrument and sold the goods then it is no longer necessary to rely upon the instrument. One case has referred to the instrument as being 'spent' so that the rights of the claimants to the chattels or to the proceeds thereof no longer depend upon the instrument: see *Price v Parsons* (1934) 54 CLR 332.

A similar result is thought to follow as regards hire-purchase agreements. The argument is that if the hire-purchase instrument is declared void then the result is not that the owner of the legal title loses his or her interest, but rather that the debtor loses the right of possession which is granted by the instrument: see R M Goode, *Commercial Law*, 2nd ed, Penguin, 1995 and Sykes, op cit.

LEGAL AND EQUITABLE SECURITIES OVER CHATTELS

[11.91]   Because of the registration requirements, there is often a desire to create security interests in chattels which do not fall within the definition of 'instrument'. The remainder of this section examines the major characteristics of the various security interests which are commonly used in commercial financing.

Chattel mortgages

[11.92]   A chattel mortgage is similar in concept to the mortgage of deed system land. A legal mortgage is the transfer of the legal title to the mortgagee, possession of the chattel remaining with the mortgagor. No particular form is necessary to create a legal mortgage, a simple contract being sufficient to transfer the title. It is not necessary that the contract be in writing: *New Zealand Serpentine Co Ltd v Hoon Hay Quarries Ltd* [1925] NZLR 73.

It is also possible to grant an equitable mortgage over a chattel. One method of so doing is to contract to grant a legal mortgage: *New Zealand Serpentine Co Ltd v Hoon Hay Quarries Ltd* [1925] NZLR 73. Another is, as with the mortgage of land, to attempt to create a legal mortgage but to fail due to lack of compliance with some formality, an unusual occurrence since there are generally no formalities required.

In either case, if the transfer of title, be it legal or equitable, is reduced to writing, then the resulting document is an example of an instrument which requires registration.

It is a peculiarity of the Acts — one of the consequences of the poor drafting — that the Acts apply only to documents, not to transactions. Thus, a perfectly valid chattel mortgage may be granted orally and the Acts have nothing to say about it: *New Zealand Serpentine Co Ltd v Hoon Hay Quarries Ltd* [1925] NZLR 73. It is valid against all third parties if it is a legal mortgage and against third parties who take a later legal interest with notice if it is an equitable mortgage.

This is not to suggest that the taking of oral chattel mortgages is to be condoned as good business practice, for the problems of evidence alone suggest that such a course would not be prudent. The vagaries of the Acts, together with the aforementioned ill effect on the borrower's credit which may result from the registration of document, dictate that the taking of chattel mortgages is not much favoured as a means of obtaining a security interest in commercial financing transactions.

Mortgages over future chattels

[11.93]   It is sometimes desirable for the lending banker to make a loan to a customer which is to be used specifically for the purchase of some chattel. In such a case, it would be desirable that the lender should have a security interest in the chattel when it is acquired. At common law, not surprisingly, such an arrangement was considered merely a contract whereby the borrower agreed to execute a mortgage in favour of the lender at some time after the chattel was acquired. If such a mortgage was never formally executed, then the lender had no proprietary interest in the chattel. The remedy, if any, lay in contract.

However, in the great case of *Holroyd v Marshall* (1862) 10 HLC 191; 11 ER 999 the equity court argued that a purported mortgage of a 'future' chattel, although it clearly could not have any immediate proprietary effect, operated as a contract to assign title when the chattel was in fact acquired by the borrower. As a result of that contract and the operation of equity, the equitable title passed to the lender at the instant that the chattel was acquired. This is summarised, imprecisely, by saying that it is possible to give an equitable mortgage over future goods, but it must be remembered that no proprietary interest can be acquired by the lender until such time as the borrower/mortgagor actually acquires the chattel.

[11.94]   The analysis of competing claims may be confusing. In *Broadlands Finance Ltd v Shand Miller Musical Supplies Ltd* [1976] 2 NZLR 124 a person completed two separate security documents which related to the purchase of musical instruments. The first was an instrument by way of security with the appellant which specified that the money lent was to be used for the purchase of the musical instruments. This instrument was registered by Broadlands Finance. The second instrument was an agreement whereby it was provided that the respondent was to retain legal title in the instruments until such time as the full amount of the purchase price was paid. This document was not registered, although it was of a form which should have been registered under the Chattels Transfer Act 1924 (NZ).

Although much of the argument concerned the effects of s 24 and of purchase money securities, a moment's reflection should convince the reader that the Act has little to say concerning the rights of the parties. Since legal title at all times vested in the respondent musical company, the instrument which was completed with the finance company could never have had the effect contemplated by the parties, for the debtor never had any legal title to pass nor did the finance company ever acquire the legal title from any other source. Indeed, the debtor never had any rights in the chattels beyond a right to possession granted by the instrument executed between himself and Shand Miller.

Pledge

[11.95]   The pledge is, in a sense, the opposite of a mortgage. Whereas, in a mortgage, the grantor assigns his or her title to the creditor while retaining possession, in a pledge the owner, while retaining title, grants the creditor the right to possession. The pledgee has the right to retain possession of the chattel until such time as the obligation secured is discharged. In the event of default, the pledgee has the right to sell the chattel pledged and to recover the debt from the proceeds. If there is a surplus from the sale then the pledgee must account to the debtor; if there is a deficiency then the debtor remains liable for the excess.

In order to create a pledge, there must be a transfer of possession from the pledgor to the pledgee which results in the exclusion of the pledgor's rights to deal with the chattel: *Official Assignee of Madras v Mercantile Bank of India Ltd* [1935] AC 53. The delivery may be actual delivery, as when the pledgor hands jewellery to the pledgee, or it may be constructive, as when the pledgor hands the pledgee keys to a warehouse where the goods are stored.

The nature of a pledge was considered by Ormiston J in *Australia and New Zealand Banking Group Ltd v Curlett Cannon and Galbell* (1992) 8 ACSR 95. A deposit of goods with the Customs authorities was described in the documents as a 'pledge' even though there was no debt or other obligation owing at the time. Ormiston J held that a pledge may be created to secure obligations other than a loan or a monetary debt. He also found that a pledge may be made to secure a future debt or one which already exists at the time when the goods are deposited, that is, the deposit of the goods for security need not be contemporaneous with the creation of the secured obligation.

The pledge comes to an end when the pledgor returns possession to the pledgee, unless the return is temporary and for a particular purpose. An example of this might be that the pledgor is to ship the goods or to sell them on behalf of the pledgee. This occurs so often in commercial transactions that it will be examined in more detail in Chapter 12.

Since the debtor parts with the possession of the goods, it is clear that the pledge does not pose the 'social evil' which was the concern of the Bills of Sale Acts. The pledge is not a transaction which is covered by the definitions in the various Acts and no registration is required whether the pledge is created orally or in writing: *Re Vital Learning Aids Pty Ltd and the Companies Act* [1979] 2 NSWLR 442.

Use of the pledge as a commercial security

[11.96]   At first glance, the pledge seems ill suited as a security device for commercial dealings. While the pledge of some personal item for a personal loan might make some sense, both to the lender and the borrower, it is hard to imagine that a business borrowing commercial funds could part with possession of the chattels which form some of the major assets of the business.

Such a view overlooks both commercial ingenuity and legal adaptability. In the case of the pledge, there are two factors which make it a viable commercial security, namely, the role which may be played by constructive delivery and those situations, common in international trade, where there are documents of title to the chattels.

•   *Constructive delivery*

[11.97]   If the goods are lying in the warehouse of some third party, then the pledge is easily effected by constructive delivery. The usual method is for the customer to sign a transfer order addressed to the warehouse which directs the warehouse to hold the goods to the bank's order. This transfer order, together with the warehouse receipt which acknowledges that the goods are being held on behalf of the borrower, are handed to the lender who then produces them to the warehouse to have a new receipt issued. The process is called 'attornment' and the warehouse is said to 'attorn' to the lender: see *Official Assignee of Madras v Mercantile Bank of India Ltd* [1935] AC 53; *Dublin City Distillery Ltd v Doherty* [1914] AC 823.

This procedure is enough to create a pledge and to give the lender the right of sale in the event of default, but it is common for lending bankers to require that the borrowing customer also sign a further document which expressly authorises the lender to sell in the event of default. There is no harm in this provided that the proper order of execution is observed, for it has been held that if the memorandum giving the power of sale is executed first, then the document is a bill of sale and must be registered: *Ex parte Hubbard; Re Hardwick* (1886) 17 QBD 690; *Charlesworth v Mills* [1892] AC 231. If the memorandum is executed after the constructive delivery, then the document merely evidences the transaction, the pledge, and does not require registration: see *Ex parte Hubbard*; *Re Hardwick* (1886) 17 QBD 690.

When the goods are stored on the borrowing customer's own premises, the problem is more difficult. It seems that any document issued by the customer which purports to grant delivery or transfer to the lending banker is likely to be construed as falling within the Chattels Transfer Act and so require registration. In the leading case, *Dublin City Distillery Ltd v Doherty* [1914] AC 823 the owners delivered documents of this sort to the 'pledgee', but the House of Lords held that it could not amount to a constructive delivery and that the documents were bills of sale. The House appeared to be of the view that the delivery orders and the like which are excepted from the definitions of a bill of sale only include such as operate through the intervention of a third party who is in the possession of the goods.

This attitude places a considerable obstacle in the path of those who would pledge goods in the circumstances. There are two solutions, neither entirely satisfactory. In the first, the goods are left in the customer's possession and hypothecated to the bank, a procedure to be discussed at [11.84]. The second is for the customer to place the goods in a separate area of his or her premises which are then isolated in some way. The banker is then granted a lease over this area so that the goods are indeed in the possession of the banker. This method has been used frequently in the United States where a large body of case law has arisen which is concerned with the degree of control which the banker must have over access to the area where the goods are kept: see J R Peden, *Stock-in-Trade Financing*, Butterworths, Sydney, 1974. Because of these uncertainties and because of the legal and practical problems which may arise due to the bank being a lessee of the isolated premises, the method has never gained great popularity in Australia or New Zealand.

These constructive delivery methods are appropriate for creating a pledge when the goods are 'domestic' goods. However, possibly the greatest use of the pledge as a security for money advanced is in the area of international trade. In such a case, there will nearly always be a bill of lading which is, inter alia, a document of title to goods. When there is a bill of lading, the pledge of the document is the same as a pledge of the goods and is a device much used, particularly in connection with the operation of documentary letters of credit. This is discussed in detail in Chapter 12.

- *Charge/hypothecation*

[11.98] Hypothecation is a method of granting an equitable charge over chattels. The essence of an equitable charge is that there is no intention that title, either legal or equitable, should pass to the creditor either immediately or at any time in the future. Nor is there any intention that possession should pass. An equitable charge is sometimes described as the 'shadow cast upon the property by the debt'; although neither title nor possession passes, there is no doubt that the creditor receives a good equitable proprietary interest in the goods: D McLauchlan, 'The Concept of "Charge" in the Law of Chattel Securities' (1975–77) 8 *VUW L Rev* 283.

In the case of hypothecation, the charge is created by a letter of hypothecation, sometimes also called a letter of lien. Since the effect of such a document is to create a security interest while leaving the debtor in possession of the chattels, there is a very real danger that such documents may be caught by the definition of a bill of sale, so that it is vital that standard wording be used. If properly worded, letters of hypothecation fall within the exception of documents 'used in the ordinary course of business as proof of the possession or control of goods': see *Ex parte North Western Bank*; *Re Slee* (1872) LR 15 Eq 69 and *Re Hamilton Young & Co*; *Ex parte Carter* [1905] 2 KB 772.

Although hypothecation is often used, there are several warnings which should be mentioned. The first is to repeat that it is not easy to say when the wording of a document purporting to grant the charge will be held to be a bill of sale. The second is to note that the security obtained is an equitable one. Since the goods are left in the possession of the borrower, there is more opportunity for fraudulent dealing. In the event that some third party obtains a legal interest in the goods without notice of the hypothecation, then that interest would defeat the equitable charge. Such would not be the case if the banker were able to obtain a pledge of the goods.

SECURITIES OVER CHOSES IN ACTION

[11.99]   The early common law took the same attitude towards choses in action that it did toward chattels: it was not possible to give a security interest in choses in action. The reason, however, was slightly different. The common law treated that prototypical chose in action, the debt, as merely another form of contractual obligation. Since the general rule was that neither the benefit nor the obligation of a contract could be assigned it was not possible to create security interests in debts or other choses in action: *Lampert's* case (1613) 10 Rep 40b; 77 ER 994.

As we have come to expect, equity took a different point of view and allowed the creation of interests in debts which were enforceable by an action in equity. There were, however, substantial procedural difficulties which made the equitable assignment of debts a less than satisfactory mechanism for the creation of security interests: *Fitzroy v Cave* [1905] 2 KB 364.

In order to understand the procedure, consider the following example. Suppose that D owes C a sum of money by virtue of some contractual obligation. It may be that the sum is not immediately due but that C wishes to obtain some funds immediately. C borrows from E and wishes to use the sum owed him by D either as a security for the loan or, alternatively, it might be intended that E should obtain repayment directly from D. At common law, the assignment of the debt to E could not be made and, furthermore, if D did pay E, such a payment would not amount to the discharge of the debt owed to C.

In the equitable procedure to enforce the assignment, E must sue C in a court of equity and obtain an order that C should sue D in a court of law to recover the debt which would then be held in trust for E. This, aside from being a clumsy procedure, meant that E's claim was subject to any defences that D might be able to raise against C.

The procedure has been simplified in several ways. First, the Judicature Act (UK) 1873 introduced a statutory form of assignment of debts and other choses in action. In Australia, this has been incorporated in various state and territorial Acts: Conveyancing Act 1919 (NSW) s 12 and the various Judicature Acts. Second, the procedure for enforcement, even if the assignment does not comply with the statutory requirements and is therefore only an equitable assignment, now calls only for the original creditor, C in the above example, to be joined as a party to the proceedings. If C does not wish to proceed against D as a plaintiff, then E may join D as a defendant in the action.

ASSIGNMENT OF DEBTS

[11.100]   Many enterprises have the majority of their assets not in land or in chattels but in choses in action. One common asset is the debt which is owed to the enterprise and any system of law which is to satisfy the demands of modern commerce must allow the use of these assets as security for loans. In our law, this is done by means of the assignment or by means of the bill of exchange. The use of the bill for this purpose is discussed at [11.13]. Here the use of the assignment is further discussed.

Legal assignment

[11.101]   As mentioned above, debts and other choses in action are now assignable at law. A mortgage of a debt takes the same form as an old style mortgage of land, that is, there is an assignment of the debt to the lender with provisions that the debt should be reassigned. In order to make a legal assignment, the Acts require the following:

1. the assignment must be for the whole of the debt; it was held from an early time that the statutes did not apply to the attempted assignment of a part of a debt: *Forster v Baker* [1910] 2 KB 636; *Re Steel Wing Co Ltd* [1921] 1 Ch 349.

2. the assignment must be absolute and not by way of charge only; this does not mean that there can be no provision for reassignment, only that the original assignment must be absolute: see *Tancred v Delagoa Bay and East Africa Railway Co* (1889) 23 QBD 239.

3. express written notice must be given to the original debtor, D in the above example.

4. the assignment will be subject to all equities which would have taken priority over the rights of the assignor if the Judicature Acts had not been enacted. That is, all defences available to the debtor against the assignor and all rights of set-off which would be available to the debtor in respect of claims which arose prior to the debtors receiving the notice which

completes the statutory assignment: *Roxburghe v Cox* (1881) 17 Ch D 520.

Perhaps the only requirement which requires further comment is the second. Consider two forms of purported assignment. First, 'I hereby assign to Smith the debt due me from Jones until such time as the building is completed'. Second, 'I hereby assign to Smith the debt due me from Jones. When the building is completed, Smith promises to reassign the debt to me'. The first is not an absolute assignment; the second is, even though it contains a provision for reassignment: *Durham Bros v Robertson* [1898] 1 QB 765.

The rights of the assignee are that he or she may sue in his or her own name and that upon payment of the debt by the original debtor to the assignee, the debt is duly discharged.

Equitable assignment

[11.102]   The statutory provisions have not replaced the procedures available for an equitable assignment of debts or other choses in action: *William Brandt's Sons & Co v Dunlop Rubber Co Ltd* [1905] AC 454. There may well be an equitable assignment where the subject matter is inappropriate for a legal assignment or where the procedures required by the statute have not been carried through. Thus, there would be an equitable assignment of a portion of a debt when made for valuable consideration: *Re Steel Wing Co Ltd* [1921] 1 Ch 349. Also, there may be an equitable assignment when the original debtor is not notified in writing but the assignee may find that priority is lost if some other party gives notice of a later assignment to the debtor: see the rule in *Dearle v Hall* (1828) 3 Russ 1; 38 ER 475 and the discussion at [11.103].

In order to enforce an equitable assignment of a legal chose in action against the original debtor, it is necessary to join the assignor as a party to the proceedings: *Durham Bros v Robertson* [1898] 1 QB 765.

In order to create a valid equitable assignment, no special form of words is required as long as the meaning is plain: *Tailby v Official Receiver* (1888) 13 App Cas 523. The assignment may be made orally except in those cases where writing is required by some special rule of law.

Priorities: the rule in Dearle v Hall

[11.103]   Although a legal assignment requires that notice be sent to the debtor, there is no such requirement for the valid creation of an equitable assignment. It is, however, desirable that such notice should be given for two reasons. First, if the debtor has no notice of the assignment, the debt may be discharged by the debtor making payment to the original creditor, that is, the assignor of the debt. Once notice has been given to the original debtor, he or she disregards the notice at their peril, for if payment is made to the original creditor after receiving notice of the assignment, then the debtor may still be liable to the assignee as well: see, for example, *Brice v Bannister* (1878) 3 QBD 569.

The second reason for giving notice to the debtor is to establish priority in the event that the creditor/assignor makes further assignments of the debt. As in the case of multiple mortgages of real or personal property, there is nothing necessarily improper in making several assignments. But priority amongst assignees is determined in a slightly different way. It is the assignee who first gives notice to the debtor, provided that at the time of taking, his or her assignment has no notice of any assignment previously made, who has priority. The rule is based on the argument that 'perfection' of a security interest in chattels requires the taking of possession (or the registration of documents) and that the closest analogy when dealing with debts is to give notice to the debtor. The rule is known as the rule in *Dearle v Hall* (1828) 3 Russ 1; 38 ER 475, the case in which it was first clearly stated.

CHARGES ON ACCOUNTS

[11.104]   When the debt to be assigned consists of a bank account, the principles are the same as the assignment of any other debt. The only problem arises because sometimes the lending banker wishes to take a security interest in an account held by the customer with the lending bank. Since the lending banker is the debtor here, there can hardly be an assignment of the debt to the banker-debtor.

[11.105]   Can the bank take a charge over the account of one of its customers? The arrangement is strange, since the account is a debt owed by the banker to the customer. Millet J in *Re Charge Card Services* [1987] Ch 150 held that such a charge was 'conceptually impossible'. The matter was not discussed in the Court of Appeal. Doubts about the correctness of the view were expressed by Browne-Wilkinson VC in *Welsh Development Agency v Export Finance Co* [1991] BCLC 936 and on appeal in the same case by Dillon LJ at [1996] Ch 245.

The House of Lords has finally settled the issue in the UK by holding that such a charge is a valid charge: *Morris v Rayners Enterprises Incorporated*, 30 October 1997. The argument advanced by the House is purely pragmatic: commercial interests want and use such a charge and, since other jurisdictions have legislated to make it valid, it can hardly be 'conceptually impossible'.

It is unclear whether Australian courts will follow the House of Lords. There are at least two Australian decisions that have held explicitly that there is no charge or mortgage created: *Broad v Commissioner of Stamp Duties* [1980] 2 NSWLR 40; *Estate Planning Associates (Australia) Pty Ltd v Commissioner of Stamp Duties* (1984) ATR 862.

STOCKS AND SHARES

[11.106]   It is possible to take a legal mortgage over shares in companies, but often the transfer of title to the mortgagee is not suitable due to the expense, the restriction on the transferability of shares or for some other reason. It is far more usual to take an equitable mortgage.

The creation of the equitable mortgage is, of course, a very simple matter. The customer deposits the certificates with the bank and executes a memorandum of mortgage which contains the contractual terms of the arrangement. These terms would ordinarily include a power of sale and an irrevocable power of attorney which would enable the banker to transfer the shares in the event of a default.

The primary disadvantage of the equitable mortgage of shares is that common to most equitable interests, that it may be subject to some prior, and undiscoverable, equity. If, for example, the customer-borrower is a trustee of the shares then the deposit of them may constitute a breach of trust. If that is so, it is likely that the beneficiaries will have priority over the interest of the equitable mortgagee: see *Coleman v London County and Westminster Bank Ltd* [1916] 2 Ch 353.

LIFE POLICIES

[11.107] A policy of life insurance is a frequently used security, particularly for personal loans. A legal mortgage over the policy may be taken by complying with the forms specified in the 5th Schedule of the Life Insurance Act 1945. Bankers customarily use their own form of assignment which gives the bank the right to make premium payments and debit the customer's account in the event that the customer fails to maintain regular premium payments. There may also be other clauses permitting the bank to deal with the policy in a number of ways.

The Act requires that the insurance company be given a formal notice of the assignment. When the assignee complies with the terms of the Act he or she may sue in their own name and, in addition, acquire priority over any other assignees who have not given notice, provided only that there is no notice of the prior assignments at the time of taking the assignment. This is merely a statutory version of the rule in *Dearle v Hall*: see [11.103].

The usual form of the equitable mortgage is by now familiar to the reader. A deposit of the policy with the banker is accompanied by a memorandum of mortgage whereby the banker is granted a power of attorney to deal with the policy in whatever ways might be thought suitable. The equitable mortgage suffers the usual deficiencies of an equitable security.

[11.108]   Holden (in R S T Chorley, *Law of Banking*, 6th ed, Sweet & Maxwell, London, 1974, pp 316–17) lists three disadvantages of life policies as securities. None are very likely to arise in the usual course of things, but the banker should be aware of some of the problems which can arise.

First, if the customer failed to make complete disclosure to the insurance company at the time of application, then the insurance company may not be liable on the policy. This is due to the fact that insurance contracts are contracts of utmost good faith, *uberrimae fidei*. Such a contract may be avoided if the proposer failed to disclose material facts, and this is so even if the non-disclosure is innocent. Since the disclosures are made in the insurance proposal long before the policy is ever made and the banker will never see that proposal, it is a risk which the banker cannot possibly guard against.

Second, if the customer dies as a result of a criminal act committed by himself or if he dies by his own hand, then the policy may not be enforceable: see *Beresford v Royal Insurance Co Ltd* [1938] AC 586. It should, however, be noted that the scope of this rule is by no means clear and that expert advice should be sought immediately in the event that the insurance company indicates that it does not intend to accept liability on the basis of any act of the insured.

Finally, Holden suggests that there is a risk that the person who has taken out the policy has no insurable interest in the life insured. As Holden admits, it is difficult to see how such a circumstance could arise when a policy is offered to a banker as a security for a loan, but if there is any doubt whatsoever, the proper course is to request the insurance company to formally admit that such an interest exists. This would form the basis of an estoppel in the event of any dispute.

BOOK DEBTS

[11.109]   When the borrower is engaged in a trade or business, it may be that there are regularly occurring debts owed which the banker would like to take as security. These are usually called 'book debts'; although there is no precise legal definition in the term, it clearly contemplates debts which arise in the course of the business being pursued by the borrower. *Halsbury* gives the following definition (3rd ed vol 2 para 773; cf 4th ed vol 3A para 661 n 2):

> By 'book debts' are meant all such debts accruing in the ordinary course of a man's trade as are usually entered in trade books, but to constitute a book debt it is not necessary that the debt should be entered in a book.

'Book debts' have also been described as debts which in the ordinary course of business would be entered in a well-kept trade book: see *Shipley v Marshall* (1863) 14 CBNS 566; *Blakey v Pendlebury Property Trustees* [1931] 2 Ch 255.

There would appear no reason why future book debts cannot be assigned in the sense that future chattels may be under the doctrine in *Holroyd v Marshall* (1862) 10 HLC 191; 143 ER 567, that is, that a purported assignment of future debts operates as a contract to assign the debts when they come into existence. When they do so come into existence the equitable title in them is passed immediately provided only that they are sufficiently identifiable: see Sykes, op cit, p 714 and *Tailby v Official Receiver* (1888) 13 App Cas 523.

Consequently, there appears to be nothing to prevent a banker from taking an assignment of all present and future book debts as a means of securing an advance.

Generally, the assignee banker will not bother to give notice to each individual debtor, and this is particularly so when the business is a trade in which the debts are individually small, even though numerous. As long as the loan is being serviced satisfactorily, the debtors will pay the customer–borrower as usual as the debts fall due. There will usually be a term in the assignment which authorises the borrower to collect these debts and to hold the proceeds for the use of the banker.

There is one point that is relevant to the discussion below concerning the registration of such documents as bills of sale. In the event of default, the banker will need to gain access to the books of the borrower in order to determine those debts still outstanding which may be collected by the assignee banker. Consequently, the assignment document should contain a right for the banker to seize the books. But the books are chattels and there is then no doubt that the document is a bill of sale.

COMPANY SECURITIES

[11.110] When the borrowing customer is a company, very different types of securities may be taken. It is still possible to take mortgages of real property and of chattels and assignments of debts. However, there is in addition a form of security which is peculiar to companies, namely the so-called 'floating charge'.

FLOATING CHARGES

[11.111] A floating charge has been judicially defined in the following terms by Lord Macnaghten in *Governments Stock and Other Securities Investment Co Ltd v Manila Railway Co Ltd* [1897] AC 81:

> A floating security is an equitable charge on the assets for the time being of a going concern. It attaches to the subject charged in the varying condition in which it happens to be from time to time. It is of the essence of such a charge that it remains dormant until the undertaking charged ceases to be a going concern, or until the person in whose favour the charge is created intervenes. The chargee's right to intervene may of course be suspended by agreement. But if there is no agreement for suspension, then the right may be exercised, whenever he or she pleases after default.

[11.112] In *Re Yorkshire Woolcombers Association Ltd* [1903] 2 Ch 284 at 294–5 Romer LJ set out three characteristics of a floating charge in language which was less figurative and seemed more precise:

> I certainly do not intend to attempt to give an exact definition of the term 'floating charge,' nor am I prepared to say that there will not be a floating charge within the meaning of the Act, which does not contain all the three characteristics that I am about to mention, but I certainly think that if a charge has the three characteristics that I am about to mention it is a floating charge. (1) If it is a charge on a class of assets of a company present and future; (2) if that class is one which, in the ordinary course of the business of the company, would be changing from time to time; and (3) if you find that by the charge it is contemplated that, until some future step is taken by or on behalf of those interested in the charge, the company may carry on its business in the ordinary way as far as concerns the particular class of assets I am dealing with.

[11.113] Although the floating charge is described as an 'equitable charge', it does not 'attach' to any particular asset of the company. The company is free to deal with the assets in the ordinary course of business. When the company ceases to be 'a going concern' or when certain other circumstances occur, the charge is said to 'crystallise'; it then converts into a fixed charge which attaches to all of the assets which were previously under the umbrella of the floating charge.

Crystallisation will ordinarily occur when some event causes the de facto cessation of business. The most common such event is the appointment of a receiver or a liquidator or the intervention of the lender who holds the floating charge.

[11.114] Sometimes clauses are inserted in floating charges which specify that the charge will crystallise upon the occurrence of certain other events. Such a clause is known as an 'automatic crystallisation clause'. It would appear that such a clause will be effective if it is properly worded: see *Stein v Saywell* (1969) 121 CLR 529; *Re Manurewa Transport Ltd* [1971] NZLR 909; and D R Magarey, 'Charges' in *The Law of Public Company Finance*, (eds R P Austin and R Vann), Law Book Co, Sydney, 1986.

The reason that automatic crystallisation clauses are included is to provide a greater degree of security for the lender. Until the charge is crystallised, an execution creditor may gain priority over some of the assets of the company; in a typical case, it would be the more valuable assets. Once the charge has crystallised, it is, of course, a fixed equitable charge and therefore protects the assets from execution creditors and all others with merely an equitable interest in the goods. However, automatic crystallisation clauses are somewhat uncertain in their operation and may have effects that neither of the parties desire.

As an example, it might be that only a minor default could trigger the crystallisation clause, perhaps without the parties even being aware of it. Such an example might be a short delay in furnishing information or documents which the charge requires to be produced. In such a circumstance, the charge holder has the choice of taking some steps to formally reverse the crystallisation or of simply ignoring it, leading to a 'decrystallisation' by agreement or estoppel. As Goode points out, such a course of action may have effects beyond what is expected since a court may conclude that the entire clause should be ignored as failing to express the intention of the parties: R M Goode, *Legal Problems of Credit and Security*, Sweet & Maxwell, London 1982, p 41.

It seems that the courts have a slight tendency to read down automatic crystallisation clauses. In particular, the standard clause which declares that all moneys secured shall become due and payable in the event of issue of execution against the company does not have the effect of causing automatic crystallisation: see *Heaton and Dugard Ltd v Cutting Bros Ltd* [1925] 1 KB 655. On the other hand, it would appear that a clause which specifically stated that the charge would crystallise upon the issue of a writ of execution would have the effect of crystallising the charge and establishing the priority of the charge holder over the interests of the execution creditors: see *Stein v Saywell* (1969) 121 CLR 529; *Re Manurewa Transport Ltd* [1971] NZLR 909; and D R Magarey, 'Charges' in Austin and Vann, op cit.

Floating charges must be registered under the Corporations Law. Failure to do so renders them void against a wide range of other creditors.

SUBSEQUENT CHARGES

[11.115] The company is, in the absence of agreement to the contrary, free to create further floating charges. These will, in the ordinary course of things, rank in the order of their creation. A crystallisation of one of the charges would be an event which would mean that the business is no longer a going concern and would result in the simultaneous crystallisation of all.

The very nature of a floating charge is to leave the assets free for the company to use in the ordinary course of business. One activity which is very much in the ordinary course of business is the granting of mortgages, either legal or equitable, over various assets of the company. Subject to what is to be said in the following paragraphs, a fixed charge over the assets of a company will have priority over the interest of the floating charge holder, provided that the fixed charge is created prior to crystallisation. This is so whether the fixed charge assumes the form of a legal mortgage, an equitable mortgage or a fixed equitable charge. It is so whether or not the person taking the fixed charge has notice of the equitable interest, for it is based not on notions of notice, but on the basic nature of a floating charge.

This is not a situation which is dear to the heart of a lender who is contemplating the taking of a floating charge. Generally speaking, the risk of allowing the company to carry on business aside from the giving of securities is enough of a risk to the integrity of the security. For this reason, it has become common to insert a so-called 'restrictive clause', also called a 'negative pledge', in the document which evidences the floating charge. The restrictive clause purports to prohibit the creation of any mortgage or charge which ranks equal to or ahead of the floating charge. The effect which has been given to these clauses is not entirely logical, but is well established. If the person taking the fixed charge, whether legal or equitable, has notice of the restrictive clause, then the attempt to create a prior ranking interest will fail. Notice that it is the restrictive clause itself, not the existence of the floating charge, which must be brought to the notice of the person.

Since the floating charge will in the ordinary course of events be registered, it must then be asked if registration is notice to the entire world. The question needs refinement, for the courts have consistently held that registration is notice of the existence of the floating charge, but not of the restrictive clause: see *Wilson v Kelland* [1910] 2 Ch 306; *Dempsey v Traders' Finance Corporation Ltd* [1933] NZLR 1258. However, these cases were decided in jurisdictions where it was not required to register a copy of the relevant clauses, so the result under the Australian Codes could be different: see D R Magarey, 'Charges' in Austin and Vann, op cit.

[11.116]   A lender who takes a 'purchase money' security may gain priority over the floating charge even if the money is lent with notice of the restrictive clause. In this case, the money is lent specifically for the purchase of a particular item and the theory is that the debtor acquires the property with charge in favour of the lender already attached, that is, the only property which is ever acquired by the debtor is the property subject to the charge in favour of the lender of the purchase money security: *Re Connolly Bros Ltd (No 2)* [1912] 2 Ch 25. The operation of this principle is, however, unpredictable: see *Church of England Building Society v Piskor* [1954] Ch 553; *Capital Finance Co Ltd v Stokes* [1969] 1 Ch 261; *Re Bunbury Foods Pty Ltd* [1985] WAR 126.

There is a further point about subsequent charges. One of the reasons for inserting automatic crystallisation clauses is to prevent subsequent charges from gaining priority over the floating charge. The argument is that a clause such as that in *Re Manurewa* causes the charge to crystallise when there is an attempt to create the later charge. Since the later charge is then created after the crystallisation, it cannot, if it is equitable, have priority.

This analysis is challenged by R M Goode, *Legal Problems of Credit and Security*, Sweet & Maxwell, 1982, who argues at p 37 that:

> In accordance with normal principles of agency law, a person who (i) had dealings with the company in relation to the charged assets prior to crystallisation or (ii) knew of the floating charge, is entitled to assume the continuance of the company's dealing powers, despite crystallisation, until he has notice that the charge has crystallised.

[11.117]   In *Re Manurewa*, Speight J held that the subsequent chargee had notice not only of the prior floating charge, but also of the restrictive clause, so that the floating charge holder would have had priority whether or not the automatic crystallisation clause was held to be effective. The clause would, however, protect the floating charge holder from subsequent actions by unsecured creditors attempting to levy execution on the assets of the company which were comprised in the floating charge.

DEBENTURES

[11.118]   The modern company will often need to borrow more than may be comfortably supplied by a single borrower. One common approach to the problem is to find large numbers of small investors. The problem is to devise a security which will operate so as to provide equal protection for all of these small investors; it would be absurd that a small investor who lends on Monday should have priority over one who lends on Wednesday. The method used is the issue of 'debenture stock'. The word 'debenture' is one of those legal terms which seems to have a shifting meaning. At its widest, it can mean any document which creates or evidences a debt, but here its use will be restricted to the documents which are used in the way to be described.

The solution to the problem is to create a trustee who is granted the floating charge over the designated assets of the company. The beneficiaries of this trust are the smaller investors who share in proportion to the amount of their investment.

From the banker's point of view, the most difficult problems arise when he or she becomes one of the investors. The most likely situation is that the banker will be a significantly larger investor than members of the general public and would like to have substantial control over the manner in which the loan is supervised. If the banker is a party to the original trust deed, then this may be possible to arrange. Particular care is exercised in such cases to ensure that the banker may dictate to the trustee the precise limits of the bank's security interest.

Debenture deeds have become very long and complex documents and a banker considering investment where debenture stock is to be used as the security would be well advised to seek specialist advice.

SECURITIES AND THE CREDIT CODE

[11.119]   If the transaction is one to which the Consumer Credit Code applies, the relationship between the parties may be altered in several ways. With one exception, the hire-purchase arrangement, the Code does not attempt to define the form of the security. It is still necessary to look to the common law and the rules of equity to determine if a security interest exists. Once a security interest is determined, it may then fall within the operation of the Code and, if so, certain consequences follow.

The Code applies to any 'mortgage' which secures an obligation under a credit contract or a related guarantee provided the mortgagor is a natural person or a strata corporation: s 8(1); see [11.140] as to related guarantees. If the 'mortgage' secures other obligations the Code applies to the 'mortgage' to the extent that it secures obligations under the credit contract or related guarantee: s 8(2).

A 'mortgage' includes any interest in, or power over, property securing obligations of a debtor or guarantor. It also includes a credit provider's title to land or goods subject to a sale by instalments and a statutory mortgage of the type discussed in [11.120]: Sch 1, definition of 'mortgage'. This would seem to include the normal non-possessory security interests discussed above, as well as incorporating sales where title is reserved. The statutory mortgage referred to relates to a hire-purchase arrangement, but does not include a 'pure' lease, although leases are caught by a different part of the Code: see [11.120].

HIRE-PURCHASE AND LEASE ARRANGEMENTS

[11.120]   Hire-purchase agreements are dealt with by the Code in a manner similar to that of the superseded Credit Acts. Any contract for the hire of goods whereby the buyer has a right or obligation to purchase the goods is to be regarded as a sale of the goods by instalments: s 10(1). A debt is deemed to have been incurred and credit provided: s 10(2). If, under these assumptions, the contract would be a credit contract, then the Code provides for a number of 'translations' which then bring the arrangement within the regulatory scheme of the Code. In particular, the property in the goods passes under the contract to the hirer either on delivery or on the making of the contract, whichever is later: s 10(3)(d). Further, a mortgage containing the terms and conditions set out in the Regulations is deemed to have been entered into between the hirer and the supplier as a security for payment of the goods: s 10(3)(f). Any provision in the contract which enables the supplier to take possession or dispose of the goods to which the contract relates is void: s 10(3)(g).

Where the buyer has neither an obligation nor a right to purchase the goods, the Code does not transform the arrangement into a sale but, unlike the Credit Acts, the Code regulates consumer leases in circumstances precisely analogous to the regulation of hire-purchase arrangements: see Pt 10. Consumer leases are subject to most of the same requirements as a consumer hire-purchase arrangement, but certain leases are excluded: see s 149.

RELATED MORTGAGES

[11.121]   Where a security interest falls within the definition of 'mortgage' (see [11.119]) the Code will apply if the obligation secured is a credit contract or a related guarantee: see [11.119], [11.140]. It is convenient to call such a mortgage a 'related mortgage'.

A related mortgage must be in writing and signed by the mortgagor: s 38(1). It must describe and identify the property mortgaged: s 40(1). With some exceptions, it is not permitted to mortgage after-acquired or future property, and any attempt to do so will be void: s 41(1); see s 41(2) for the exceptions.

A related mortgage may not secure an amount that exceeds the sum of the liabilities of the debtor under the credit contract together with reasonable enforcement expenses: s 45(1). A mortgagee is never allowed to recover more than would have been recoverable under the underlying credit contract: s 45(1).

'Third party' mortgages, that is, a mortgage where the mortgagor is primarily responsible and liable for the debts of another person, are not permitted under the Code: s 44. A mortgage which purports to secure such a debt is void and the mortgagee may be compelled by a court to discharge the mortgage: ss 44(3), 44(4).

PROTECTION OF INNOCENT PURCHASERS

[11.122]   New South Wales, Victoria and Western Australia now provide for limited protection of third party purchasers for certain classes of goods. The Registration of Interests in Goods Act 1986 (NSW) provides that a purchaser of a motor vehicle which is the subject of a 'registrable interest' may take free of the interest in two circumstances. Where the purchase is from a dealer, the purchaser takes free of any registrable interest; notice is irrelevant: s 9(3). For all other purchases, clear title is obtained only by a purchaser who has no actual or constructive notice of the registrable interest: s 9(4). A purchaser who does not obtain a search certificate is on notice of any registered interest. A purchaser who does obtain a search certificate is on notice of those interests identified in the certificate and any interests of which the purchaser has actual notice. The term 'registrable interests' includes security interests arising from bills of sale, hire-purchase and lease agreements.

The Chattel Securities Act 1987 (Vic) provides for a register of certain interests, but the bona fide purchaser for value without notice obtains a good title in a wider range of circumstances. The Chattel Securities Act 1987 (WA) is similar to the Victorian statute: see S W Cavanagh and S Barnes, *Consumer Credit Law in Australia*, Butterworths, Sydney, 1988.

THE BANKER'S LIEN

[11.123]   The banker's lien is a right conferred by law on the banker to retain certain documents as security for debts due from the customer. It is a right which exists without the necessity for any express agreement, although may be abrogated by express or implied agreement. The right of lien exists even if the customer is unaware of such a right.

MAIN FEATURES

[11.124]   The main characteristics of the banker's lien flow from the law merchant and have been accepted into the existing law of banker and customer. As a result, the lien attaches in the absence of agreement to the contrary and whether the customer knows of the lien or not: *Brandao v Barnett* (1846) 12 Cl & F 787; 8 ER 1622.

GENERAL LIEN

[11.125]   One exceptional characteristic of the banker's lien is that it is a general rather than a particular lien. The distinction may be most readily made by example. A mechanic's lien gives a repairer the right to hold the item repaired until the owner tenders the amount of the specific repairs for which the item was brought to the repairer. If the owner of the object also owes the repairer for work performed in the past, the repairer has no right to demand that those sums be paid before releasing the object. The mechanic's lien is a particular lien. By contrast, the documents held under a banker's lien may be retained until all relevant sums owing the banker are repaid: see [11.135]. This right to retain the documents as security for the whole of the customer's indebtedness is summarised by saying that the banker's lien is a general lien: *Re Keever* [1967] Ch 182.

POWER OF SALE

[11.126] The banker's lien has another unusual characteristic, namely that it carries with it the power of sale and recoupment from the proceeds. This is such an unusual characteristic of liens that the banker's lien has been described as in the nature of an implied pledge: see *Brandao v Barnett* (1846) 12 Cl & F 787; (1846) 8 ER 1622; Holden, *Securities for Bankers' Advances*, 7th ed, Pitman, London, 1986.

This power of sale is not particularly important in the case of negotiable instruments which are encompassed by the lien since the banker will either be able to deal with these as holder or as agent for collection, but when the securities consist of other documents, the power of sale may become an important method of realisation: see BEA s 32(3) and CPOA s 96.

The precise scope of the power of sale is not clear. It may be that it is restricted to those documents and securities in which title may be passed by delivery or, at least, by some method which may be exercised by the bank by its own means: see *Gellibrand v Murdoch* (1937) 58 CLR 236 where it was said that the bank had no power to dispose of shares although it could retain them under a lien until payment of the debt.

Where the power of sale exists, it may be exercised on default if a fixed time for the repayment of the debt has been nominated. If no time has been fixed, then the bank may sell after request for repayment has been made and a reasonable notice of intention to sell has been given: see *Australia and New Zealand Banking Group Ltd v Curlett, Cannon and Galbell Pty Ltd* (1992) 10 ACLC 1292.

DISTINGUISH THE RIGHT OF SET-OFF

[11.127] The lien does not attach to the credit balance in a current account since that sum is in law a debt owed by the banker to the customer. The banker's remedy is the right of set-off: see [3.44] and *National Westminster Bank Ltd v Halesowen Press work and Assemblies Ltd* [1972] AC 785.

It is generally thought that money cannot be the subject matter of a lien. That it possibly could is traced to a speech by Lord Hatherley in *Misa v Currie* (1876) 1 App Cas 554. This seems wrong in principle, for either the money would not be identifiable or, if it were, would be paid in for some specific purpose which would exclude the possibility of the banker's lien. The correct analysis is probably that Lord Hatherley was referring to the right of set-off. As was noted [3.43], the terminology was often used rather carelessly prior to *National Westminster Bank Ltd v Halesowen Presswork and Assemblies Ltd* [1972] AC 785.

DOCUMENTS ATTACHED BY THE LIEN

[11.128] The banker is not entitled to a lien over all documents in his or her possession which belong to the customer. The precise scope of the documents to which the lien attaches is not entirely clear.

'ALL SECURITIES DEPOSITED WITH' THE BANKER

[11.129]   In *Brandao v Barnett* (1846) 12 Cl & F 787; (1846) 8 ER 1622, the court suggested that the lien could be exercised over 'all securities deposited with' the banker. While it is generally agreed that this is far too wide, there is no consensus on precisely which class of documents are subject to the lien. On the most narrow view, the lien attaches only to instruments which are fully negotiable. On the widest view, it attaches to all securities which are ordinarily dealt with on behalf of the customer other than those which are deposited for safe-keeping.

The correct view is almost certainly somewhere between, for the lien has been held to apply to share certificates and various other non-negotiable documents: see *Re United Service Co; Johnston's Claim* (1870) LR 6 Ch App 212; *Misa v Currie* (1876) 1 App Cas 554. Doubts have been expressed as to whether the lien attaches to documents of title to land: see *Paget's Law of Banking*, 11th ed, Butterworths, 1996 at pp 523–5. However, in *McLaughlin v The City Bank of Sydney* (1914) 18 CLR 598 the Privy Council held that deeds were encompassed by the lien. Similarly, in *Dale v Bank of New South Wales* (1876) 2 VLR (L) 27 it was held that a banker may have a lien over title deeds which the customer had deposited in the ordinary course of business, but not over deeds deposited for safe custody only. The problem is unlikely to be common in practice since the usual reason for the deposit of title deeds is to create an equitable mortgage: see [11.72]. In that case, the relationship is governed by the express contract of the mortgage and there is no room, or need, to consider the banker's lien.

By far the most important application of the lien in practice is in the non-controversial case of negotiable instruments. The most common example is the lien over cheques which have been deposited by the customer who has an overdrawn account. The fact that the cheques have been deposited for collection does not evidence an intention which is inconsistent with the operation of the banker's lien: *Bank of New South Wales v Ross* [1974] 2 Lloyd's Rep 110; *Akrokerri (Atlantic) Mines Ltd v Economic Bank* [1904] 2 KB 465.

In *National Australia Bank Ltd v KDS Construction Services Pty Ltd* (1987) 163 CLR 668 the High Court (at 678–9) suggested that the position might be different where the bank is a 'mere' agent for collection:

> The existence of the lien is not affected by the fact that the bank receives the cheque as an agent for collection, so long as the bank is not a mere agent for collection.

This extract was considered by Giles J in *Duke Finance Ltd (in liq) v Commonwealth Bank of Australia* (1990) 22 NSWLR 236. He noted that '… it is not easy to discern what their Honours meant by the sentence under consideration', but concluded that it did not mean that a bank which was an agent for collection but not also a holder for value did not have a lien. This conclusion is, of course, supported by the actual decision in *KDS Construction* as well as by the reasoning in *Barclays Bank Ltd v Astley Industrial Trust Ltd* [1970] 2 QB 527.

The lien extends only to securities which belong to the customer, at least when the securities in question are not fully negotiable instruments: *Cuthbert v Robarts, Lubbock & Co* [1909] 2 Ch 226. Securities deposited with the banker, for whatever reason, which do not belong to the customer may not be retained by the banker.

The lien does not attach to securities which are delivered to the banker for a special purpose other than the general purpose of collection. This is merely an application of the general principle that the lien may be excluded by express or implied agreement: see [11.132]. If the special purpose for which the securities are deposited is inconsistent with the operation of the lien, which is usually the case, then there is an implied agreement that the banker will not benefit from the right of lien. So, for example, securities received by the bank for safe custody are not attached by the lien: see *Brandao v Barnett* (1846)12 Cl & F 787; (1846) 8 ER 1622; *Hamilton v Bank of New South Wales* (1894) 15 LR (NSW) L 100.

QUA BANKER

[11.130]   The banker's lien only attaches to those documents which have been deposited with the banker in his or her capacity as banker. Thus, as mentioned above, the lien does not attach to those documents which are given to the banker for safe-keeping, for safe-keeping is not, strictly speaking, a part of the banker-customer relationship. The document must be some document which is ordinarily dealt with by bankers and it must have been left with the banker for the purpose of being dealt with in that way. Again, the main example is a bill of exchange which has been delivered to the banker for collection; the bill is a document with which bankers, in their role as bankers, deal, and leaving it with a banker for collection is leaving it to be dealt with in the usual way.

MAY BE EXCLUDED BY EXPRESS AGREEMENT

[11.131]   The lien may be excluded by an express contract between the customer and banker or by circumstances which are inconsistent with a lien. Thus, for example, money paid in for the express purpose of meeting a bill which has been accepted by the customer payable at the bank is not subject to a lien even if money could be the subject matter of a lien; nor can it be subjected to the banker's right of set-off. Again, a bill or other negotiable instrument which is handed to the banker solely for safe-keeping is not subject to the banker's lien.

Documents handed to the banker for collection might be thought to be given for a special purpose which is inconsistent with the operation of the banker's lien, but it has consistently been held that as collection is part of the ordinary business of banking that the lien attaches: *Misa v Currie* (1876) 1 App Cas 554; *National Australia Bank Ltd v KDS Construction Services Pty Ltd (in liq)* (1987) 62 ALJR 63. This may be so even if the collection is on behalf of a correspondent bank and the collecting bank knows that it is being collected on behalf of the correspondent's customer: *Johnson v Roberts* (1875) LR 10 Ch

App 505. This last decision seems wrong in principle, for generally the lien does not attach when the depositor is not the beneficial owner of the documents.

Perhaps the most difficult problem here is the situation where securities are handed to the banker as security for a particular liability but are allowed to remain in the banker's custody when that particular liability is discharged. There is little authority on the matter, but in *Re London and Globe Finance Corporation* [1902] 2 Ch 416 the court held that in such a circumstance, in the absence of evidence to the contrary, the documents had become subject to a general lien at least as regards future advances. There is some older authority that it would not encompass existing indebtedness: see *Re Bowes; Earl of Strathmore v Vane* (1886) 33 Ch D 586.

However, there is no doubt that in the event that the security must be realised in order to recover the debt, any surplus proceeds are available to the banker, either by way of the banker's lien or, more correctly, the right of set-off: see *Johnson v Peppercorne* (1858) 28 LJ Ch 158; *Re London and Globe Finance Corporation* [1902] 2 Ch 416. It is very peculiar that the immunity which attaches to the securities themselves do not extend to the proceeds, but the law is clear on the matter.

CREATION AND TERMINATION OF THE LIEN

[11.132]   Although the lien may be excluded by agreement between the parties, it is not a consensual security. The fact and the time of its creation and duration are matters of law and not of agreement between the parties.

TIME OF ATTACHMENT

[11.133]   Whatever the range of documents to which the lien might attach, the time of attachment is when the documents have come into the banker's hands in his or her capacity as banker, that is, in the course of the banker's business. The most common example of this is the cheque which has been paid in for collection by a customer who has an overdraft: *National Australia Bank Ltd v KDS Construction Services Pty Ltd (in liq)* (1987) 62 ALJR 63.

But the fact that the banker has a lien over a cheque or a bill deposited for collection does not affect the banker's duty of actually collecting the instrument. Of course, this is no disadvantage to the banker, for in the ordinary course of things, receiving the proceeds for the instrument will either go to reduce an overdraft or into an account over which the banker has the right of set-off.

Note also that where the banker is a holder of a cheque over which there is a banker's lien, then the banker may be a holder for value to the extent of any such lien: see CPOA s 96. In certain cases, therefore, the banker may be in a position to pursue remedies ordinarily available to a holder for value. As an example where the banker was able to take advantage of this status, see *Barclays Bank Ltd v Astley Industrial Trust Ltd* [1970] 2 QB 527.

[11.134] Like any other lien, the rights of the creditor are determined when he or she parts with possession. However, as noted above, in the most important example of the banker's lien, negotiable instruments, the normal way in which the lien will be terminated is by the collection of the instrument by the banker, in which case the right of the lien is replaced by the right of set-off.

DEBTS ENCOMPASSED BY THE LIEN

[11.135] In the absence of an express agreement to the contrary, the lien can only be exercised when the debt owing from the customer to the banker is one which has arisen out of the banker-customer relationship. An Australian example will illustrate the principle: a customer of the bank, A, had an overdraft with the bank which the bank wished to have reduced or secured. As a security for the overdraft, A gave the bank a bill of exchange which had been accepted by W. Later, A's overdraft was paid off. However, the bank had discounted another bill which had been accepted by A; since it was clear that A owed the bank the amount of the accepted bill, the bank claimed to be able to retain the bill accepted by W under the banker's lien. The court held that the lien did not attach, for the debt did not arise from the banker-customer relationship: see *Commercial Bank of South Australia v Wake* (1880) 14 SALR 31.

GUARANTEES

[11.136] A guarantee is not a 'security' in the same sense that the word has been used in this section of the book, for it is not an interest in property. Nevertheless, the need for a guarantee often arises in precisely those circumstances where a security interest might be taken instead, and bankers often speak informally of a guarantee being a security. For these reasons, it is customary in banking law texts to include guarantees in the discussion of security interests.

NATURE OF A GUARANTEE

[11.137] A guarantee is a promise by which one person, called the guarantor or the surety, undertakes to answer for the present or future obligation of another, called the principal debtor. The promise is made to the creditor of the principal debtor. It is a conditional promise of the form 'if the principal debtor defaults, then I will honour the obligation'. There can be no guarantee if there is no principal debtor and if there is no cause of action which has accrued against the principal debtor, then there is none against the guarantor, although, as will be seen, there may be circumstances where the principal debtor may escape liability even while the guarantor cannot.

It is important to distinguish a contract of guarantee from one of indemnity. While the distinction is quite clear in theory, it may be very blurred when considering an individual case. The essence of a contract of indemnity is an unconditional promise by one person to another that the obligation of a third party will be discharged. It is a promise of the form 'If you lend $1000 to A, then I will see that you are paid'. A guarantee, on the other hand, would have the form 'If you lend $1000 to A and A does not pay you, then I shall'.

The difference between the guarantee and the indemnity is brought sharply into focus when the principal debtor has some defence which negates or reduces liability. If the agreement is a guarantee, then the surety also escapes liability for there is no liability on the guarantor until the principal debtor fails to meet his or her obligation: see *Turner Manufacturing Co Pty Ltd v Senes* [1964] NSWR 692. However, if the agreement is an indemnity, then the 'surety' remains liable, for the liability under an indemnity is a primary liability which exists independently of the liability of the principal debtor: see, for example, *Yeoman Credit Ltd v Latter* [1961] 2 All ER 294.

The court will look to the substance of a promise to determine if it is a contract of guarantee or one of indemnity. The words used are not in themselves conclusive as to the nature of the contract.

There is no reason why a guarantee cannot be made to cover a continuing series of transactions such as might be found when the principal debtor is a banker's customer operating an overdraft. In such a case, the sum being guaranteed is not only a fluctuating amount, but the debt itself is one which is constantly changing, due to the rule in *Clayton's case*. For obvious reasons, guarantees taken by bankers are normally of the continuing type.

REQUIREMENTS OF A GUARANTEE

WRITING

[11.138]   Contracts of guarantee were included in the Statute of Frauds which required certain contracts to be evidenced in writing, failing which they were unenforceable. The requirement of writing now varies in different jurisdictions, but for the reasons outlined below, all guarantees taken by banks will be in writing so there is little reason to dwell upon the matter.

CONSIDERATION

[11.139]   A contract of guarantee, like all other contracts not under seal, must be supported by consideration. It is common to state in guarantees that the consideration is the continuation of financial accommodation already given or the present granting and subsequent continuation of financial accommodation by the bank to the principal debtor at the request of the guarantor. Since that constitutes consideration moving from the promisee (the banker), it is sufficient to support the contract: *Colonial Bank of Australasia v Kerr* (1889) 15 VLR 314.

If the formula used states that there was some form of request, then the banker should take care to see that the guarantor actually makes such a request. In *Reid Murray Holdings Ltd v David Murray Holdings Pty Ltd* (1972) 5

SASR 386 evidence was given that there was no such request and that there was no intention that the named consideration should exist. The guarantee was only saved by virtue of the fact that it was given in the form of a deed.

The problem of consideration becomes even more troublesome when the guarantee is only intended to cover existing advances and no other advances are contemplated or covered by the guarantee. In such cases, the proper consideration is that the banker gives the principal debtor extra time or, alternatively, defers suing the principal debtor on the debt at the request of the debtor: see, for example, *Colonial Bank of Australasia v Kerr* (1889) 15 VLR 314.

Care must be taken when the consideration is a promise to defer taking action against the principal debtor. In *Clarke & Walker Pty Ltd v Thew* (1967) 41 ALJR 139 the promise was 'not to sue or take any proceedings against' the principal debtor. During the currency of the guarantee, the creditor served a notice to pay and indicated that in lieu of payment the creditor would present a winding-up petition. There was no payment, but instead of presenting a winding-up petition, the creditor claimed on the guarantee. The guarantor pleaded total failure of consideration. The High Court held on the facts that the promise was to refrain from taking proceedings in a court, but there was no dispute that the defence would have been good had the meaning been that argued by the guarantor.

GUARANTEES UNDER THE CREDIT CODE

[11.140]   A guarantee is subject to the Consumer Credit Code if it guarantees or secures obligations under a credit contract which is regulated by the Code and if the guarantor is a natural person or a strata corporation: s 9(1); see also [11.47] for a discussion of the Code. Where the guarantee also guarantees other obligations it will be subject to the Code to the extent that it guarantees obligations under a credit contract: s 9(2). It is convenient to call such guarantees 'related guarantees'.

A related guarantee must be in writing and signed by the guarantor: s 50(1). A minimum disclosure requirement calls for the guarantor to be given a copy of the credit contract which is being guaranteed and a document in a form to be prescribed with informs the guarantor of his/her rights and obligations: s 51. An important provision gives the guarantor a 'cooling off' period so that the guarantor may withdraw at any time before credit is provided: s 53.

A guarantor cannot be liable for more than the amount of the credit contract to which the guarantee relates, plus a sum which represents the reasonable expenses of enforcement: s 55(1). Where the principal debtor is a minor, the guarantee cannot be enforced unless it contains a prominent statement to the effect that the guarantor may not be entitled to an indemnity against the minor: s 55(3).

A guarantor may apply to have the transaction reopened on the grounds that it is unjust: s 70(1). 'Unjust' includes 'unconscionable, harsh or oppressive': s 70(1). The Code provides a 'shopping list' of factors which are to be taken into account in determining if a transaction is unjust: s 70(2).

AVOIDANCE OF GUARANTEES

[11.141]   There are a number of circumstances where the surety may escape liability under the guarantee. Some of these arise merely from general contractual principles and some due to the special nature of a guarantee. Of the latter kind, some may be avoided by the creditor if the guarantee agreement is properly drawn. It is to guard against these 'escape routes' that bank guarantees are lengthy and complex documents.

The modern bank guarantee form is a very lengthy document. Part of the reason for this length is the necessity, from the banker's point of view, to include clauses which will define when the guarantor may or may not take action to terminate the guarantee. As noted by Weaver and Craigie, many of the modern cases on the subject are of interest only to legal draftspeople since they turn entirely upon the wording of some clause in the particular document before the court.

The law is generally very protective of guarantors, many of whom have little or nothing to gain by entering into the guarantee and everything to lose. Clauses which purport to detract from the rights which guarantors might otherwise enjoy are construed strictly against the bank (which is always the party responsible for the form of guarantee), particularly those clauses which attempt to deny the guarantor the rights to terminate the guarantee and so to limit his or her liability: *Dunlop New Zealand Ltd v Dumbleton* [1968] NZLR 1092.

In the following paragraphs we will examine the most common situations where guarantors have escaped liability. In some of these cases, it has traditionally been possible to protect the creditor's interest by careful drafting of the contract of guarantee.

The effect of many of these clauses must now be reconsidered in the light of the Trade Practices Act 1974, the state Fair Trading Acts and, in New South Wales, the Contracts Review Act 1980. It may be that clauses which overprotect the bank's interest will be struck out as 'unconscionable': see, for example, *Westpac Banking Corporation v Sugden* (1988) NSW Conv R 55–377, an action brought under the Contracts Review Act 1980 (NSW), and the discussion at [10.145].

PRE-CONTRACTUAL CIRCUMSTANCES

Misrepresentation/non-disclosure

[11.142]   A contract of guarantee, like any other contract, is liable to be avoided by the misrepresentation of a material fact, even if the misrepresentation is made innocently: *MacKenzie v Royal Bank of Canada* [1934] AC 468, 475; *Commercial Bank of Australia Ltd v Amadio* (1983) 151 CLR 447. But although misrepresentation may avoid the contract, a mere failure to disclose information which would obviously be relevant to the guarantor's decision will not avoid. The normal rule is that a contract of guarantee is not a contract *uberrimae fidei*, that is, one of the utmost good faith, and that generally the creditor is not obliged to disclose information to the would-be guarantor: *Davies v London and Provincial Marine Insurance Co* (1878) 8 Ch D 469; *Commercial Bank of Australia Ltd v Amadio* (1983) 151 CLR 447.

Thus, in *Cooper v National Provincial Bank Ltd* [1945] 2 All ER 641 the plaintiff had guaranteed an overdraft of Mrs R, a customer of the defendant bank. The plaintiff claimed to be released from the guarantees on the grounds that the bank had failed to inform him of several facts which, had they been known to the plaintiff, would have resulted in his refusal to enter into the guarantee. The relevant facts were that the principal debtor's husband was an undischarged bankrupt who had authority to draw upon the account and that there was information known to the bank that the husband had in fact used the account improperly in the recent past. The argument of the bank was that there was no legal requirement for them to disclose this information and that, indeed, to do so would be a breach of the banker's duty of secrecy concerning the affairs of the customer.

The court in *Cooper's* case upheld the bank's argument concerning the duty to disclose, thereby reaffirming the principle that a guarantee is not a contract *uberrimae fidei*. The point as to the duty of secrecy is less certain: see Holden in Chorley, p 335, fn 30. Probably the correct approach is that the banker has an implied authority to disclose relevant account and other information if the surety is one which has been proposed by the principal debtor, but not if the surety is one of which the debtor is unaware. To be on the safe side, the banker should probably seek the customer's consent or, alternatively, decline to answer the inquiries.

[11.143] In any case, it is clear that if the would-be guarantor does ask a direct question of the banker concerning the account, then it must be answered truthfully and accurately. The precise scope of the information which the proposed guarantor is entitled to receive, in the absence of express authority from the principal debtor, is by no means clear. It would seem that the guarantor may ask from time to time the amount for which he or she is liable, but again Holden argues that if the total debt of the principal debtor is larger than the amount of the liability of the guarantor, the guarantor should not be told the amount of the total debt but only the liability under the guarantee: Holden, *The Law and Practice of Banking*, Vol 2, Pitman, 1986.

The surety is not entitled to examine the customer's account activity or to be given a copy of the statement: *Ross v Bank of New South Wales* (1928) 28 SR (NSW) 539. In the event that the surety does demand information concerning the account or other matters which appear to infringe upon the customer's right of confidentiality, the banker should decline to answer unless the customer is present and/or gives his or her authority to disclose the information sought by the surety.

Misrepresentation may also attract the operation of s 52 of the Trade Practices Act 1954. In *Nobile v National Australia Bank Ltd* (1987) ASC 55–580 a bank represented to an intending guarantor that the principal debtor was in a satisfactory trading position. The guarantor was thereby induced to enter the contract of guarantee. The court held that the contract could be set aside under s 52 of the Trade Practices Act 1974 on the grounds that the bank engaged in misleading conduct. The manager of the bank who made the statement believed it to be true and there was no evidence to suggest that the statement had been made negligently, but that is not relevant under s 52 proceedings. The plaintiff also succeeded under the general principles of undue influence: see [11.146].

Cases where disclosure required

[11.144] Although the guarantee is not a contract *uberrimae fidei*, there are certain circumstances in which information should be brought to the attention of the proposed guarantor even if the banker is not explicitly asked. Lord Campbell set out the general rule in *Hamilton v Watson* (1845) 12 Cl & Fin 109; (1845) 8 ER 1339:

> I should think that this might be considered as the criterion whether the disclosure ought to be made voluntarily, namely, whether there is anything that might not naturally be expected to take place between the parties who are concerned in the transaction, that is, whether there be a contract between the debtor and the creditor, to the effect that his position shall be different from that which the surety might naturally expect; and, if so, the surety is to see whether that is disclosed to him. But if there be nothing which might not naturally take place between these parties, then, if the surety would guard against particular perils, he must put the question ...

It is not easy to find examples of situations where the banker has a duty to disclose under the rule in *Hamilton v Watson*. In one case, the court indicated that there might be a duty to disclose where the account to be guaranteed was not really that of the person in whose name it appeared, but rather belonged to an undischarged bankrupt: *Cooper v National Provincial Bank Ltd* [1946] KB 1. However, there have been cases where the banker suspected that the customer was defrauding the guarantor, yet non-disclosure was held not to invalidate the guarantee: *National Provincial Bank of England Ltd v Glanusk* [1913] 3 KB 335; *Royal Bank of Scotland v Greenshields* [1914] SC 259. It seems difficult to imagine circumstances which would fit more precisely into the category of cases defined by Lord Campbell. At best, then, it can be said that the situation is a very uncertain and unhappy one for the banker, for in a case which appears to fall within the rule in *Hamilton v Watson*, a failure to disclose might invalidate the guarantee while disclosure of the customer's affairs might be a breach of the banker's duty of secrecy.

[11.145] Disclosure may also be required when the banker is aware, or possibly should be aware, that the proposed guarantor is acting under a misapprehension as to the truth of a material fact. If the banker allows the contract of guarantee to be concluded in such circumstances, it may be that his or her silence will amount to a misrepresentation allowing the guarantor to escape liability: *Royal Bank of Scotland v Greenshields* [1914] SC 259.

Silence in some circumstances may also be 'misleading or deceptive' conduct within the meaning of s 52 of the Trade Practices Act 1974; see the discussion at [4.15].

Undue influence and unconscionable conduct

[11.146]   There are circumstances where it is incumbent on the banker to do much more than merely disclose certain information to the guarantor. It is sometimes necessary to see that the intending guarantor is capable of making a free and informed opinion concerning the advisability of proceeding with the guarantee. In the absence of doing so, there will be a presumption that the banker has exercised undue influence on the guarantor with the result that the guarantee may be set aside or the banker may be required to pay damages. The conditions under which this duty will arise are usually ones where the bank knows of some special relationship between the guarantor and the principal debtor or where the bank itself is obtaining a benefit from such a relationship.

[11.147]   There are some situations where the relationship between the parties is such that if a transaction occurs which confers a benefit on the 'dominant' party, then the law will presume that that party exercised some undue influence on the other in order to effect the transaction. The precise list of relationships which fall into this category includes, among others, parent and child, solicitor and client, trustee and beneficiary. In such a circumstance, there is a burden of proof on the dominant party to show that he or she did not exercise undue influence.

The presumption of undue influence is of concern not only for the parties directly concerned, but also those third parties who might also benefit from the transaction. In *Bank of New South Wales v Rogers* (1941) 65 CLR 42 a niece had resided with her uncle since the death of her father. She sought advice from the uncle on all matters related to business. She mortgaged virtually the whole of her property in order to secure advances made by the bank to the uncle.

The court summarised the law relating to such situations (at 51, 52) as follows:

> ... creditors cannot improve their security ... by instigating or inducing [debtors] to obtain further security for their debts from near relations or persons under their influence and not in a situation to resist their importunity. The inference of undue influence operates not only 'against the person who is able to exercise the influence', but 'against ... every person who claimed under him with notice of the equity thereby created, or with notice of the circumstances from which the court infers the equity'. But ... it would not operate against a person who is not shown to have taken with such notice of the circumstances
> ...

Since it was found that the bank had notice of the special relationship between the uncle and the niece, there was an onus on it to prove that the niece had given the security free from any undue influence, that she had given it freely and with a full understanding of the consequences of her actions. Since she had obtained no independent advice, it was virtually impossible for the bank to show this and the security was set aside.

[11.148] The relationship of husband and wife requires some special mention. At one time there was a presumption of undue influence when the wife acted as guarantor or in some other way was disadvantaged by the husband's business dealings: see *Yerkey v Jones* (1939) 63 CLR 649.

Merkel J considered the applicability of the *Yerkey v Jones* presumption in *Gregg v Tasmanian Trustees Ltd* (1996) 143 ALR 328, holding that the principle has been replaced by the *Amadio* doctrine. He was of the opinion that the legal, sociological and factual framework which gave rise to the *Yerkey v Jones* presumption no longer existed in Australia. He went on to hold, however, that the law will continue to protect persons in relationships in which one party reposes trust and confidence in the other since, in principle, such relationships may give rise to a position of special disadvantage within the *Amadio* principle. He further thought that relationships involving emotional dependence or influence could fall within the *Amadio* principle. He suggested, as examples of such relationships, that between wife and husband, parent and child and unmarried partners of either sex.

[11.149] Generally speaking, there is no presumption of undue influence merely because the parties are married: *Bank of Montreal v Stuart* [1911] AC 120; *MacKenzie v Royal Bank of Canada* [1934] AC 468. However, the relationship is such that it may require only a small amount of evidence to turn the tables and raise the presumption of undue influence. If it can be shown that the creditor requested the wife's guarantee of a debt owed by her husband, that there was not a proper explanation of the significance of the guarantee and that the husband insisted that she give the guarantee, then the guarantee may be set aside, but the burden of proof is on the person attempting to avoid the guarantee: *Dunlop New Zealand Ltd v Dumbleton* [1968] NZLR 1092. It would seem that the same principle would apply when the husband is guaranteeing the debt of the wife.

[11.150] The question has recently been the subject of two House of Lords decisions. In *Barclays Bank plc v O'Brien* [1993] 3 WLR 786 it was reaffirmed that there is no basis for providing special protection to wives in relation to surety transactions.

However, where (1) a wife offers to stand surety for her husband's debt; and (2) the transaction is not to her financial advantage; and (3) the transaction carries with it a substantial risk of the husband committing a legal or equitable wrong entitling the wife to set aside the transaction, that the creditor is put on inquiry and has constructive notice of the wife's rights unless it takes reasonable steps to ensure that her agreement to stand surety is properly

obtained. Since there was actual undue influence by the husband in the
O'Brien case, the wife had the right to set aside the transaction against him
and against all third parties with notice of the circumstances giving rise to her
equitable right.

The House of Lords emphasised that the same principles are applicable
when one co-habitee stands surety for the other's debts and the creditor is
aware that the surety reposes trust and confidence in the principal debtor.

The New South Wales Court of Appeal has expressed preference for the
O'Brien approach over the views of the High Court in *Yerkey v Jones*: see *Akins
v National Australia Bank* (1994) 34 NSWLR 155.

[11.151]   In *CIBC Mortgages PLC v Pitt* [1993] 3 WLR 802 the principles
were reaffirmed even though the conclusion was different. A joint loan was
made by the plaintiff to a husband and wife. There was nothing to indicate to
the plaintiff that this was anything other than a normal advance to husband
and wife for their joint benefit. It was found that the husband had exercised
actual undue influence over the wife. As a result of that undue influence, she
was entitled as of right to have the transaction set aside without any proof of
manifest disadvantage. This right did not extend to the plaintiff unless it
could be shown that the husband was acting as agent of the plaintiff in
obtaining the wife's agreement (which he clearly was not) or unless the plaintiff had actual or constructive notice of the undue influence. Unlike the
O'Brien case, there was nothing in the circumstances of the case to put the
plaintiff on notice since here it appeared that the wife was obtaining benefit
from the transaction.

[11.152]   The previous paragraphs have been concerned with the position
of a banker who gains a benefit from a guarantee which has been made under
circumstances where the principal debtor is in a special relationship with the
guarantor. The question to be examined now is whether the relationship of
banker and prospective guarantor is ever such that a presumption exists that
the banker has exercised undue influence over the guarantor. In other words,
should the relationship of banker and prospective guarantor be added, at least
in some circumstances, to the list of relationships which are fiduciary in
nature.

The story begins with a decision of the English Court of Appeal in *Lloyds
Bank Ltd v Bundy* [1975] QB 326; [1974] 2 Lloyd's Rep 366. Bundy and his
son both banked at the same branch of Lloyds Bank. The son was engaged in
business and maintained some company accounts at the branch. He sought
advances from the bank and it was suggested that his father could act as
guarantor. At the time of making the first guarantee, the bank manager suggested that Bundy should take legal advice. This Bundy did and entered into a
guarantee which was secured by a charge over his farm.

Some years later, the son wished to obtain further advances and his father
was again approached about the possibility of increasing his liability. On this

occasion, the father did not seek independent advice, nor was it suggested that he do so.

Although it is possible that the case could have been placed in the category of case which we have been discussing, the court instead held that the bank had breached a duty of care owed directly to Bundy, namely the duty to ensure that he obtained independent advice so that he was able to make a free and informed decision. After reviewing the cases in which transactions had been set aside due to the exercise of undue influence, Denning MR explained the origin and scope of the duty in the following terms ([1975] QB 326 at 339):

> ... I would suggest that through all these instances there runs a simple thread. They rest on 'inequality of bargaining power'. By virtue of it the English law gives relief to one who, without independent advice, enters into a contract upon terms which are very unfair or transfers property for a consideration which is grossly inadequate, when his bargaining power is grievously impaired by reason of his own needs or desires or by his own ignorance or infirmity, coupled with undue influence or pressures brought to bear on him by or for the benefit of the other.

The result was that both the guarantee and the charge over the property were set aside. Note that it is not entirely clear that the bank did in fact take advantage of Bundy or that he was significantly misled as to the state of his son's finances or the import of the documents which he was signing. Further, although Lord Denning's formulation of the duty is very wide, that Bundy was in fact a customer of the bank, not a stranger.

Bundy's case was applied and approved in *Daly v Sydney Stock Exchange Ltd* (1986) 160 CLR 371.

[11.153]   *Bundy's* case caused considerable consternation in banking circles, for it seemed to place a very heavy burden on the banker who would like to take a guarantee or some other form of security from a third party. The concern was not eased when *Morgan's* case came before the Court of Appeal.

In *National Westminster Bank v Morgan* [1983] 3 All ER 85 a wife signed a legal charge to a bank in order to secure a loan made to her husband. She had full knowledge of the circumstances, in the sense that she understood the nature of the charge and that she was indeed guaranteeing the loan to the husband, but she hoped it was the way of saving her home from being taken from her as the result of proceedings for possession which were being brought by a previous mortgagee.

The Court of Appeal held that a relationship of confidentiality could exist where one party relied on the guidance or advice of the other party who stood to benefit by the transaction. If the transaction was not at arm's length, then a presumption of undue influence might be raised, whereupon the party giving the advice would have to rebut it by showing that the other party had formed an informed and free independent judgment. The party relying on the other's guidance did not have to show that the resulting transaction was manifestly disadvantageous to himself or herself before the presumption could be invoked.

In this formulation there need be no special relationship between the parties. It was enough that the wife relied upon the advice of the bank and that the bank stood to benefit. Since that was enough to raise the presumption of undue influence it was over to the bank to prove that the wife had entered into the transaction freely and with a full understanding of her position. Since she had not received independent advice, the bank failed in discharging this burden. The Court of Appeal set aside the charge.

The case went on appeal to the House of Lords which reversed the findings of the Court of Appeal [1985] 1 All ER 821; [1985] 2 WLR 588. According to the House, in order to raise the presumption of undue influence when the parties are not in a special relationship, it is necessary to show that the transaction had itself been wrongful in that it amounted to one in which an actual unfair advantage had been taken of another person; it is not enough in this situation to argue that there might have been an unfair advantage taken. Since it was clear in *Morgan's* case that the bank had not in fact taken an unfair advantage and since there was no special relationship involved, the bank was able to rely upon the charge.

[11.154] Before the House of Lords decision in *Morgan's* case, the court considered *Cornish v Midland Bank plc* [1985] 3 All ER 513. The plaintiff customer signed a second mortgage in favour of the bank without appreciating, and without being informed by the bank, that it was so worded as to secure not only a loan of £2000 for renovations to a farmhouse jointly owned by the plaintiff and her husband, but also secured unlimited further advances made to the husband. The branch manager led the wife to believe that the borrowings secured by the mortgage would not exceed the amount of the renovations. The bank in fact made further advances to the husband which were secured under the mortgage. When the farmhouse was sold, the proceeds barely covered the first and second mortgagees and sale expenses.

At first instance, the court held, on the basis of *Bundy* and the Court of Appeal decision in *Morgan*, that the bank had been negligent in explaining the effect of the mortgage and that the mortgage should be set aside on the ground of undue influence. The husband was held liable to indemnify the bank for an amount of over £11,000. This indemnity was on the basis that if the mortgage was set aside, then the debt owed by the husband still existed.

When the House of Lords reversed the *Morgan* case, it was natural that the bank should appeal the *Cornish* case. The Court of Appeal agreed that the decision could no longer be sustained on the *Bundy-Morgan* line of reasoning, but then went on to hold that when the bank undertook to advise as to the nature and effect of the mortgage there arose a duty to do it carefully. The bank here had been negligent in this explanation. However, setting aside the mortgage was an equitable remedy which was not available unless the plaintiff could show undue influence. Under the House of Lords test in *Morgan*, that meant that the customer must show, at the very least, that the bank had taken unfair advantage so that there was raised a presumption of undue influence. It was impossible for the customer to show that unfair advantage had in fact been taken, and therefore no presumption of undue influence.

This did not mean that the bank succeeded, only that the remedy of setting aside the mortgage was not available. The plaintiff was still entitled to damages for the harm which had been caused by the negligent explanation of her responsibility under the mortgage. These damages were assessed so that the plaintiff was in the same position as if the mortgage had been set aside.

However, since the mortgage had not been set aside, the debt owed by the husband was discharged. It could not be argued that the bank was entitled to be indemnified by the husband, since the losses were caused by its own negligence and he had no part to play in that matter.

[11.155] The distinction between the *Morgan* case and the *Cornish* case is that in the former the advice, although technically incorrect, was not negligent. Although the charge in the *Morgan* case was formally wider than advised, the bank did not intend to enforce the charge to the extent of the husband's indebtedness and, in fact, was only seeking to enforce the security in respect of the re-financing agreement of which the wife was adequately and correctly informed.

It might be thought that the bank could avoid the problem by declining to give any advice whatsoever, since it appeared to be the undertaking of this responsibility which gave rise to a duty of care. The question of whether the bank actually has a duty to undertake this explanation was argued during the case, but was clearly not necessary for the decision.

However, Kerr LJ addressed the problem of whether it is incumbent upon the bank to undertake to give advice in the first place, concluding (at 522, 523):

> I think that I would have inclined to the view that in the circumstances of this case the bank owed a duty to the plaintiff, as the bank's customer, to proffer to her some adequate explanation of the nature and effect of the document which she had come to sign. If expert evidence had been called as to the standard practices of banks in situations such as the present, I think that this would have supported the conclusion that bankers themselves recognise that their proper professional standards would not be consistent with mere silence on their part in such situations.

On a strict view, the statement must be considered as obiter, but representing as it does the carefully considered statement of a senior member of the court, it seems likely to be an accurate statement of the law. Consequently, it seems safe to suppose that there is a duty to explain to a customer and that the explanation must be done without negligence. It is not clear to what extent the duty to explain might extend to a guarantor who is not a customer.

[11.156] In Australia, at least, the duty to explain will arise when the banker is aware that the guarantor is under some special disability which will make him or her vulnerable in the particular transaction. In *Commonwealth*

Bank of Australia v Amadio (1983) 57 ALJR 358 the bank knew that the business of the principal debtor was in financial difficulties and they sought a mortgage from his parents, the respondents in the case, as security for the debt owed to the bank. They were an elderly couple who read little English; they believed that their son's business was a growing and profitable concern and that their liability under the proposed guarantee would be limited to $50,000. They signed the mortgage, in the presence of the bank manager, without reading it. The bank sought recovery under the mortgage of more than $200,000. The High Court of Australia set the mortgage aside.

The court considered that the respondents were under a special disability due to their age and restricted knowledge of the language. In such a case, the court considered that it should look to the conduct of the party attempting to enforce the dealing, holding that the facts known to the bank were such as to raise in the mind of any reasonable person a very real question as to the respondents' ability to make a judgment in their own best interests. The bank had a duty in these circumstances to make inquiries.

[11.157]   In *Nobile v National Australia Bank Ltd* (1987) ASC 55–580 (see [11.180]) the court also found for the guarantors on the basis of the *Amadio* principle. The guarantor was under a 'special disability' since there was no real equality between the guarantor and the bank. This disability was sufficiently evident to the creditor to make it prima facie unfair to take the guarantee since there was no evidence available to the bank manager that the guarantors had received any independent advice. This was sufficient to place the onus on the bank to show that the transaction was fair, just and reasonable. This could not be done because the guarantee was procured, in part, by the erroneous representation of the state of the debtor's trading position.

When the 'special disability' exists, it is not enough that the banker takes all steps to explain the effects of the contract if the other party does not in fact understand the terms. In *Westpac Banking Corporation v Clemesha* (29 July 1988, SC (NSW), (Cole J), No 18226 of 1987, unreported) the defendant had given a mortgage to secure the borrowing of the husband of her former daughter-in-law. Cole J came to the conclusion that she did not understand that the bank could exercise a power of sale if the borrower defaulted, even though he accepted that the bank officer took steps to see that the defendant was fully informed. As a result of the close relationship between the borrower and the mortgagor, the defendant was under a special disability vis-a-vis the borrower and this extended to the bank. See also the decision of the High Court in *Stern v McArthur* (1988) 1 ALR 463 and the discussion above of *Barclays Bank plc v O'Brien* [1993] 3 WLR 786 and *CIBC Mortgages plc v Pitt* [1993] 3 WLR 802.

[11.158]   In the cases considered so far, there has been no direct threat on the part of the banker which is intended to force the guarantor–mortgagor into the contract. Needless to say, such a situation would arise rarely. As an example, in *Public Service Employees Credit Union Cooperative Ltd v Campion* (1984) 56 ACTR 74 the defendant entered into a contract of guarantee as a result of the plaintiff's administrative officer threatening to bring a prosecution against the defendant's son for an alleged fraudulent misappropriation of $1000. Kelley J held that the guarantee was not enforceable since the threat amounted to undue pressure on the defendant which was the equivalent of undue influence.

[11.159] Where one of the parties alleges that there has been undue influence by means of a misrepresentation, the burden of proof is on the bank to show that it did not have constructive notice of the misrepresentation. In *Barclays Bank plc v Boulter* [1997] 2 All ER 1002, the wife had pleaded all the necessary facts to establish that her husband had misrepresented the degree of the guarantee that she signed. She did not, however, explicitly plead constructive notice. The Court of Appeal held that explicit pleading was unnecessary since the burden was on the bank.

[11.160] The lesson for the banker in all of this is clear. In any situation where there might be a possibility of undue influence or where there is a duty to explain the effects of a guarantee or similar security to a customer, the banker should ensure that independent advice is obtained by the party proposing to give the security. When the debtor is a person who might unduly influence the proposed giver of the security, then this advice should be given in the absence of the debtor. Since this merely amounts to good business practice as well as good law, it should cause little hardship to the banker.

THE CREDITOR–PRINCIPAL DEBTOR CONTRACT

[11.161] In the absence of express clauses in the guarantee, the guarantor may use certain aspects of the contract between the creditor and the principal debtor as a defence to a claim on the guarantee. Some of these defences may be avoided by clauses in the contract of guarantee.

Principal debtor under a disability

[11.162] Subject to certain important qualifications, the basic rule is that when the contract with the principal debtor is void or unenforceable, the guarantor cannot be held liable under the guarantee. This rule follows logically, if somewhat harshly, from the basic notion that there can be no guarantor if there is no principal debtor. In those jurisdictions where the contractual capacity of minors is still governed by the common law, the rule could be applied to allow a guarantor to escape liability where the principal contract was void due to the infancy of the principal debtor even when all parties knew at the time of contracting that the principal debtor was under age: *Coutts & Co v Browne-Lecky* [1947] 1 KB 104, followed in *Robinson's Motor Vehicles Ltd v Graham* [1956] NZLR 545.

This rigid application of the principle is so harsh that it is not surprising that courts have occasionally sought to circumvent the result. After all, presumably one of the reasons that the bank sought the guarantee was precisely because of the minority of the borrower, and one of the reasons that the guarantor was willing to guarantee was to assist the minor to obtain the loan.

[11.163]   The way around the problem is to construe the 'guarantee' as being an indemnity, for, as already noted, an indemnity imposes a more severe obligation on the surety and the fact that the principal debtor is suffering from some contractual incapacity will not in any way assist the surety to escape liability. This approach seems to have gained some sympathy from the courts. In *Yeoman Credit Ltd v Latter* [1961] 1 WLR 828 Harman LJ said (at 835):

> Where all concerned know that the first promisor is an infant, so that as against him the promise cannot be enforced, the court should incline to construe the document signed by the adult (the second promisor) as an indemnity, for that must have been the intention of the promisee and the second promisor. Both know that the first promise has no legal validity; it may be that both hope that the first promisor will honour his engagement, but with the knowledge that he cannot be obliged to do so it must have been their intention that the promise of the adult promisor should have an independent validity. Otherwise the whole transaction is a sham.

[11.164]   Bankers have sought to avoid the problem by including in their forms of guarantee a clause to the effect that, even if the moneys guaranteed are not recoverable from the principal debtor by reason of that person's contractual incapacity, the guarantor shall nevertheless be liable for the sum as a principal debtor on the basis of an indemnity. The efficacy of such a clause does not appear to have been tested in court. Recall that the terms used by the parties are not conclusive; see *Total Oil Products (Aust) Pty Ltd v Robinson* [1970] 1 NSWR 701.

In New South Wales and South Australia, the problem with minors is now eliminated. Section 47 of the Minors (Property and Contracts) Act 1970 (NSW) and s 5 of the Minors' Contracts (Miscellaneous Provisions) Act 1979 (SA) provide that a guarantee shall be enforceable against the surety to the extent that it would have been if the minor had at all material times been a person of full age. However, presumably the principle in all of the 'minors cases' applies to other forms of contractual incapacity, so the cases are by no means irrelevant.

Although it seems that the guarantor will escape liability if there is no liability on the principal debtor, it seems that there is no right to rely upon any set-offs or partial defences which may have been available to the principal debtor: see, for example, *Covin v Bandag Manufacturing Pty Ltd* [1983] 1 NSWLR 237.

Variation in the principal contract

[11.165]   It is a basic rule that a material variation of the contract between the banker and the principal debtor will result in the discharge of the guarantor from all liability, and it does not matter that the variation may have been beneficial to the guarantor unless it is patently obvious that the variation either is beneficial to him or immaterial: *Dan v Barclays Australia Ltd* (1983) 46 ALR 437; *Dunlop New Zealand Ltd v Dumbleton* [1968] NZLR 1092.

Since the basic rule is so strictly construed, once again we find that many forms of guarantee contain clauses designed to circumvent it. Such clauses must be carefully drawn if they are to be effective. In *National Bank of Nigeria Ltd v Oba M S Awolesi* [1964] 1 WLR 1311 the Privy Council held a guarantor to be discharged when the banker opened a second account for the principal debtor through which all later transactions passed. The action was held to be a substantial variation of the principal contract which was unknown and detrimental to the surety, in spite of the fact that the guarantor had agreed to guarantee all advances, overdrafts and liabilities of the principal debtor. The case is solely one of construction, but shows the need for care in drafting the clauses which purport to limit the rights which the guarantor might otherwise enjoy.

[11.166]   The problem of breach of contract by the creditor is closely related to the problem of variation in the principal contract. The High Court in *Ankar Pty Ltd v National Westminster Finance (Australia) Ltd* (1987) 70 ALR 641 found that, when the creditor breached a condition of the debtor-creditor contract, the surety was released. There was no need for the surety to rescind the contract of guarantee or for breach of an essential term because the circumstances of the surety's liability no longer existed.

Extension of time to the debtor

[11.167]   At first sight, it may seem strange to argue that an extension of time to the principal debtor can possibly result in the discharge of the guarantor, yet upon reflection it will be seen that the result is correct. During the extended period of time, it is quite possible that the financial position of the principal debtor will deteriorate even further from the circumstances which forced the granting of extra time in the first place: *Nisbet v Smith* (1789) 2 Bro CC 579; 29 ER 317; *Bolton v Buckenham* [1891] 1 QB 278; *Deane v City Bank of Sydney* (1904) 2 CLR 198. Since, as will be seen, the guarantor has a right of recourse against the debtor, it will be in the interest of the guarantor to pay while the principal debtor still has substantial assets rather than wait until the last minute when the principal debtor has no assets whatsoever.

Since the guarantor also has rights against co-sureties, the same principle applies and a guarantor may be discharged when extensions of time are give to a co-surety.

In either case, it is of the utmost importance to the banker to include clauses which will allow the extension of time and any other indulgence which the banker believes to be in the best interests of both the bank and the customer. It is well known that such an extension is often the difference between successful recovery of a loan and the total or near total loss through the customer's insolvency.

Release of the debtor

[11.168]   It is clear that, in the absence of express provisions, the release of the principal debtor by the creditor has the additional effect of releasing the surety: *Perry v National Provincial Bank of England Ltd* [1910] 1 Ch 464. It may seem extraordinary to think of the banker releasing the debtor, but there are situations which amount to an implied release, the most common being that in which the customer enters into a voluntary composition with his or her creditors outside of bankruptcy. This would ordinarily discharge the surety: *Ex parte Smith* (1789) 3 Bro C C 1 but it seems that a proper clause in the guarantee will prevent this.

In *Perry v National Provincial Bank of England Ltd* [1910] 1 Ch 464 the efficacy of such a contractual term was precisely in point. During the course of the judgment, Cozens-Hardy MR said (at 473):

> It is said ... there can be no right as against the surety, because by reason of this arrangement with Perry Brothers you [the creditor] have released Perry Brothers, and there can be no suretyship after the release of the principal debtor. But I think the answer to that is that it is perfectly possible for a surety to contract with a creditor in the suretyship instrument that notwithstanding any composition, release, or arrangement the surety shall remain liable although the principal does not.

Payment

[11.169]   Payment of the debt by the principal debtor extinguishes any potential liability of the guarantor. The only problems that have arisen in these cases is where the payment is properly made, the guarantor discharged, but then the payment is set aside by the operation of some other law, most typically as being a preference under some equivalent of the Bankruptcy Act 1966. It has been held that, on the wording of the particular guarantee in question, the liability of the guarantor did not revive: *Commercial Bank of Australia Ltd v Carruthers* (1964) 6 FLR 247. The court did, however, note that it was a simple matter for the bank to include a clause which would have led to the opposite result. Most bank guarantee forms now include such a clause.

Change in the constitution of the debtor

[11.170]   A change in the constitution of the debtor terminates the guarantee as to any future advances: *Wright v Russei* (1774) 3 Wils K B 530; *Myers v Edge* (1797) 7 TR 254. Consequently, when the principal debtor is a group which might change its legal identity by a change in its membership, the lender runs a risk of finding the guarantors inadvertently discharged. Once again, the difficulty is overcome by a standard clause to the effect that the guarantor remains bound notwithstanding any change in the constitution of the principal debtor.

Death, etc, of the debtor or guarantor

[11.171]   The death of the principal debtor causes the guarantee to 'crystallise'. It is clear that the principal debtor will not be receiving any further advances from the banker. Any outstanding cheques should be returned unpaid. The CPOA gives the banker authority to pay cheques which were drawn prior to the customer's death and presented within 10 days: s 90(2). However, unless there is an express clause in the guarantee, it is thought that the guarantor would not be liable for the amount of these payments.

The death of the guarantor does not automatically terminate the guarantee. If the banker makes advances after the guarantor's death but before receiving notice of it, it appears that the banker is entitled to call upon the estate for the additional sums: *Bradbury v Morgan* (1862) 1 H & C 249; (1862) 158 ER 877. Notice of the death of the guarantor does terminate the agreement and again 'crystallises' the liability under the guarantee to the amount for which he or she was liable at the time when the banker received notice of the death: *Coulthart v Clementson* (1879) 5 QBD 42.

Again, clauses in the standard form of bank guarantee modify this position. The usual clause calls for continuing liability until the expiration of a fixed period of time, typically three months, following the receipt of a notice in writing of the personal representatives' intention to determine the guarantee.

It is thought that notice of mental illness of the guarantor operates in the same way as notice of his or her death, but there is little authority on the matter: *Bradford Old Bank Ltd v Sutcliffe* [1918] 2 KB 833.

THE CREDITOR–GUARANTOR CONTRACT

[11.172] A breach of any condition of the contract of guarantee will provide a complete defence for the guarantor. Thus, in *Ankar Pty Ltd v National Westminster Finance (Australia) Ltd* (1987) 70 ALR 641 the appellant had guaranteed performance of the lessee of some machinery. The lessee fell into arrears and assigned their rights under the lease. Under the contract of guarantee, the respondent was required to notify the appellant if the lessee fell into arrears or if there was to be an assignment of rights under the lease. Neither of these were done. The High Court held that there had been a breach of condition of the contract and therefore the surety was discharged. Deane J considered that the breach was such that the obligations of the surety never arose so that it was unnecessary for the appellant to rescind the contract. The respondent's argument was that only a breach going to the root of the contract could discharge the surety, but this argument was rejected.

Ascertainment of liability

[11.173] Under the normal rules of guarantee, the guarantor is not liable unless the principal debtor has defaulted. This has the potential of raising difficult evidentiary problems. In a bid to avoid these problems, standard bank guarantee forms usually contain a 'conclusive evidence' clause which provides that a certificate signed by an appropriate bank officer is conclusive evidence of default by the principal debtor for the purposes of establishing the liability of the guarantor. The effectiveness of these clauses was upheld by the High Court in *Dobbs v National Bank of Australasia Ltd* (1935) 53 CLR 643.

These clauses must now be considered to be of doubtful validity: see the discussion of *Westpac Banking Corporation v Sugden* (1988) NSW Conv R 55–377 at [11.182].

Limitation of the guarantor's liability

[11.174] There is no reason why a guarantee may not be limited either in duration or in amount. A limitation as to duration causes no difficulties beyond those of interpretation; it is necessary to spell out precisely the obligations of the parties. As an example, it may be difficult to ascribe a clear meaning to a phrase such as 'this guarantee shall cease to have effect two years after the date thereof': see R M Goode, *Legal Problems of Credit and Security*, Sweet & Maxwell, London, 1982.

In the case of a limitation of amount, the problem is more difficult. It is understandable that the guarantor will wish to limit the amount of total liability. There are two separate ways in which this might be done. First, the guarantor may guarantee only a certain amount of the debt. Second, there may be a guarantee of the whole of the advance, but with a limit on the liability. As an example, the first form is 'I hereby guarantee $5000 of the $10000 that you are to loan to D'. The second form is 'I hereby guarantee the entire amount that you are to loan to D, subject to my liability being limited to $5000'.

[11.175] It may seem that there is little difference in these forms, but they have quite different legal consequences. Suppose that the banker does in fact lend D the amount of $10000 and that D then defaults. The banker may then turn to the guarantor under either of the above formulae and demand the payment of $5000. However, under the second formula, the guarantor is not permitted to prove in the bankruptcy of the principal debtor in competition with the banker unless the guarantor has paid the full amount of the principal debtor's indebtedness, even though that amount is greater than the amount for which the guarantor agreed to be liable. Indeed, the banker is entitled to prove for the full amount of the principal debtor's debt even though having received a part of the sum from the guarantor. It is only if the total amount recovered by the banker, from both the guarantor and the dividend in the bankruptcy, exceeds the amount of the debt that the guarantor has any rights to recover: *Re Sass*; *Ex parte National Provincial Bank of England Ltd* [1896] 2 QB 12.

The situation is similar with regard to the guarantor's right to have resort to any securities given to the banker to secure the debt. If the second form of guarantee is used, the guarantor has no right against the securities until the whole debt is paid. If the first form is used, then the guarantor is entitled to share in the benefit of the securities.

The form used by bankers is, of course, the second one. Weaver and Craigie give the following as an example (at para [23.160]):

> This guarantee is to be security for the whole of the moneys hereby secured but nevertheless the total amount payable hereunder by the guarantor shall not exceed the sum of $ together with interest for a period of twelve months and the costs charges and expenses of obtaining or attempting to obtain payment from the guarantor.

Where the upper limit was left blank, the Full Court of the Supreme Court of New South Wales has held that the guarantee was for an unlimited amount: *Caltex Oil (Aust) Pty Ltd v Alderton* (1964) 81 WN (Pt I) (NSW) 297.

[11.176] It is also customary that the forms used by bankers contain a clause to the effect that a certificate signed by certain officials of the bank which states the balance of the principal and interest owed by the customer shall be conclusive evidence of the customer's indebtedness for the purposes of the guarantee. This 'conclusive evidence clause' has been upheld by the High Court of Australia in *Dobbs v National Bank of Australasia Ltd* (1935) 53 CLR 643. However, that was a commercial case and it now appears that it may be possible that these clauses could be challenged in appropriate cases under the Contracts Review Act 1980 (NSW) or under the 'unconscionable conduct' provisions of the Trade Practices Act 1974 (Cth) and related state legislation: see *Westpac Banking Corporation v Sugden* (1988) NSW Conv R 55–377 and the discussion at [11.182].

Notice of determination

[11.177] Most bank guarantees are, as previously noted, continuing guarantees. The guarantor is, under ordinary conditions, entitled to terminate the guarantee as to future advances at any time by notice to the banker: *Beckett v Addyman* (1882) 9 QBD 783. Of course, such a notice does not relieve the guarantor of any liability which existed at the time of notice and the terms of the guarantee may very well call upon the guarantor to pay what is then due under the guarantee.

In the event that the guarantor gives such a notice of determination to the banker, the banker should stop the account immediately to prevent any possible erosion of rights against the guarantor through the operation of the rule in *Clayton's case*. It is, of course, possible to open a new account for the principal debtor on terms to be arranged. The important point is that payment into the new account will not reduce the advances which were secured by the guarantee.

[11.178] Most forms of guarantee used by bankers specify that the guarantee may only be determined by a specific period of notice, typically three months. The object of such a clause is clearly to allow the banker and customer to make mutually satisfactory arrangements. It is not at all clear whether the banker may, after receipt of the notice, continue to make voluntary advances during the intervening period. The position where the contract is governed by the Credit Acts is discussed at [11.183].

On the one hand, the point of giving notice is to allow the guarantor the opportunity to limit his or her losses, and it is hard to see how the banker is prejudiced by being unable to rely upon the guarantor. On the other hand, to allow the guarantor to withdraw from any further liability may prejudice the principal debtor who may already have made plans which will call for finance which was fully and fairly expected to be forthcoming. The only advice which may be given is to express the rights and obligations as clearly as possible in the form of guarantee.

The notice of determination may also cause a problem when there is more than one guarantor. In *Kalil v Standard Bank of South Africa Ltd* [1967] 4 SA 550 (AD) the particular wording of the guarantee stated only that the guarantee was in force until the bank should receive notice 'from us' terminating the arrangement. The court held that one of the guarantors, acting alone, could give notice of termination in relation to his own liability.

Release of securities/co-sureties

[11.179] It is common practice for the banker to take securities from the creditor in addition to the guarantee. It may be that from time to time the banker may wish to realise some of the securities, to exchange them for other more appropriate securities, or even to release some of them so that the principal debtor may deal with them free of encumbrance. Under the general law, many, perhaps most of these actions would result in a discharge in whole or in part of the guarantor: *Carter v White* (1883) 25 Ch D 666; *Dale v Powell* (1911) 105 LT 291. This flows logically from the fact that the guarantor would be prejudiced by such actions, possibly losing rights against securities. The same result flows from the release of any co-sureties and for the same reason: *Ward v National Bank of New Zealand* (1883) 8 App Cas 755.

The general law result may be avoided by the inclusion of an appropriate clause in the form of guarantee and such clauses are routinely found in bank guarantee forms.

Unconscionable conduct: Trade Practices Act 1974

[11.180] The scope of unconscionable conduct has probably been extended by ss 52 and 52A of the Trade Practices Act 1974 and, where appropriate, the corresponding provisions of the state Fair Trading Acts. Section 52 provides that 'A corporation shall not, in trade or commerce, engage in conduct that is misleading or deceptive or is likely to mislead or deceive'. The Fair Trading Act 1987 (NSW) s 42 and similar statutes in other states repeats the section replacing 'corporation' with 'person'. The wording of the Commonwealth statute is due to concerns about the constitutional power necessary to enact the legislation.

Section 52A was introduced in the 1986 amendments. It provides that 'a corporation shall not, in trade or commerce, in connection with the supply or possible supply of goods or services to a person, engage in conduct that is, in all the circumstances, unconscionable': s 52A(1). The state Fair Trading Acts are similar, but 'corporation' is replaced by 'supplier' and 'person' is replaced by 'customer'; all states and territories save Queensland have enacted Fair Trading Acts (called the Consumer Affairs and Fair Trading Act 1990 in NT). It is not clear if 'customer' here means the same as it does for the purposes of the Cheques and Payment Orders Act 1986, but in view of the fact that the bank will always be a corporation, the Trade Practices version can be relied upon in any case.

Section 52A(2) provides a 'shopping list' of factors which may be considered by the court when determining if conduct has been 'unconscionable'. These include, but are not limited to, inequality of bargaining power, whether the customer is required to comply with conditions which are not reasonably necessary for the protection of the legitimate interests of the supplier, whether the customer was able to understand the documents, whether there was any undue pressure or influence on the customer by the supplier or a person acting on behalf of the supplier and the possibility of alternative supplies of the goods or services which might be available to the customer at lower costs.

Contravention of s 52 may give rise to an action in damages, but s 52A contraventions do not: s 82. However, the court may make orders varying the contractual rights of the parties if it is found that there is 'unconscionable' conduct which has prejudiced the customer: s 87. It is thought that the approach of the courts will be similar to that adopted under the Contracts Review Act 1980 (NSW), although s 52A deals with conduct whereas the CRA deals only with contracts: see [11.179] and J Goldring, 'Certainty in Contracts, Unconscionability and the Trade Practices Act: The Effect of Section 52A' (1988) 11 *Syd L Rev* 514.

There may not be a great deal of difference between actions brought under ss 52 and 52A and those which rely only upon the general law, particularly *Amadio's* case: see [11.156]. For example, in *Nobile v National Australia Bank Ltd* (1987) ASC 55–580, the court found that the contract should be set aside under s 52 and under the *Amadio* principle. Strictly speaking, it seems that the court must find some 'special disability' to raise the *Amadio* principle, but in practice it may be that any consideration of the factors of s 52A(2) which gives rise to a conclusion that the supplier acted 'unconscionably' would also allow the finding of a 'special disability'.

Contracts Review Act 1980

[11.181]   In New South Wales a guarantee may come within the scope of the Contracts Review Act 1980. In contrast to the Trade Practices Act 1974, the Contracts Review Act is directed not at conduct, but at contracts which are unjust or unconscionable.

The Act provides no protection for those contracts which are entered into in the course of or for the purpose of a trade, business or profession other than a farming undertaking: s 6(2). The section was considered by Rogers J in *Australian Bank Ltd v Stokes* (1985) 3 NSWLR 174. Two people had formed a company for the purposes of engaging in a business activity. When the company wished to borrow money, the two were asked to guarantee the loan and to give security. Rogers J held that the collateral transactions were not 'in the course of or for the purposes of a business carried on by them' and so not precluded from the operation of the Contracts Review Act 1980.

The Act gives the court wide powers to reopen the contract in the event that the contract is found 'to have been unjust in the circumstances relating to the contract at the time it was made': s 7(1). It is not necessary to make a formal application to obtain the benefits of the Contracts Review Act 1980; it is available as a general defence. When such a defence is available, the application of the defence on the merits should not be determined on a motion for summary judgment: *Commercial Banking Co of Sydney Ltd v Pollard* [1983] 1 NSWLR 74.

A contract may be unjust because of the way in which it operates or because of the way in which it was made but it will not be considered unjust simply because it was not in the interests of one of the parties to make the contract or because the party received no independent advice: *West v AGC (Advances) Ltd* (1986) 5 NSWLR 611.

[11.182]   The mere fact that contractual terms have been in use for a long time will not save them from the consequences of the Act. In *Westpac Banking Corporation v Sugden* (1988) NSW Conv R 55–377 Brownie J held that several standard clauses in a guarantee were unjust under the provisions of the Contracts Review Act 1980 in the circumstances since they were not reasonably necessary for the protection of the legitimate interests of the bank. The guarantees were signed by the guarantors without 'knowing the meaning of [the] complex provisions, and were told nothing of them'.

The clauses found to be unjust in the circumstances provided that:

- the bank may, without affecting the liability of the guarantors, release any security held;

- the guarantee was not prejudiced by any other security or guarantee or by the bank losing any security or failing to recover any of the moneys secured;

- a certificate was conclusive evidence of the facts;

- the guarantee was binding upon a guarantor upon execution notwithstanding that another guarantor failed to execute the document.

Brownie J noted that the 'conclusive evidence' clause went far beyond what was reasonably necessary for the protection of the bank. It seems that he would have accepted a clause which referred to 'prima facie evidence'. The case is important for showing that mere long use in the industry will not prevent a finding that the clause is unjust.

Reopening contracts of guarantee

[11.183]   A guarantor may apply to have the transaction re-opened on the grounds that it is unjust: Consumer Credit Code s 70(1). 'Unjust' includes 'unconscionable, harsh or oppressive': s 70(1). The Code provides a 'shopping list' of factors which are to be taken into account in determining if a transaction is unjust: s 70(2). The Credit Acts contained similar provisions for re-opening.

The courts will continue to be reluctant to re-open contracts when the relative strength of the parties is approximately equal or when the weaker party has received independent advice prior to entering into the contract. However, when these requirements are not satisfied, then the credit provider must expect to have the contract scrutinised closely.

[11.184]   In *Murphy v Esanda Finance Corporation Ltd* (1988) ASC 55–650 the tribunal said that 'a lender who fails to protect itself and the borrower by requiring the borrower to supply evidence showing that it is at least probable that the borrower has the ability to repay the instalments, runs a very real risk that this Tribunal will decide the contract is unjust'.

The borrower had approached the parent bank for a loan which was refused, the bank noting that the behaviour of the prospective borrower was unstable. The bank suggested that he approach the finance company. Although the absence of independent legal advice does not automatically lead to the conclusion that a contract is unjust, the unstable behaviour pattern should have indicated to the finance company that independent advice was required. The tribunal applied s 145 of the Credit Act 1984 to decide that the contract was unjust. The contract was varied and the total amount financed and the credit charges were substantially reduced.

There is a strange contradiction in the tribunal's decision, for although they strongly criticised the sharing of information between the bank and its finance company subsidiary, the knowledge of the bank concerning the debtor's limited mental capabilities was apparently imputed to the finance company. *Murphy's* case has since been reversed by the Supreme Court on the basis of certain procedural inadequacies.

GUARANTOR'S RIGHTS AGAINST THE OTHER PARTIES

DEBTOR

[11.185]   When the guarantor has paid any amount to the creditor, he or she acquires an immediate right of action against the principal debtor. The right of action does not arise until such time as the guarantor has actually paid: *Re Fenton; Ex parte Fenton Textile Association Ltd* [1931] 1 Ch 85. The guarantor also has the right to prove in the principal debtor's bankruptcy for any amount which he or she has paid under the guarantee, but as noted above, this right is usually circumscribed by standard clauses in the contract of guarantee which prohibit the guarantor from proving in competition with the bank. Further, if the guarantor is sued by the creditor, the guarantor may join the principal debtor as a third party to the proceedings.

CO-SURETIES

[11.186]   Just as the guarantor is entitled to an indemnity from the principal debtor when obliged to pay the creditor, so he or she is also entitled to look to any other sureties in the event that he or she has paid more than his or her 'fair' amount. What constitutes the 'fair' amount is a matter of some complexity when there are multiple co-sureties, some of whom may have paid sums to the creditor, some of whom have different limits of liability, and some of whom may have taken advantage of the rights of subrogation to securities: see, for example, *Re Arcedeckne* (1883) 24 Ch D 709; *Knight v Hughes* (1828) 172 ER 504.

The right of contribution arises whether the guarantors are bound jointly, jointly and severally, or severally, and whether they even knew of the existence of other guarantors, at the time of entering into the guarantee, provided only that the guarantee is respect of the same debt. The High Court has indicated that it is wrong to take too technical an approach in determining payment by a surety when that surety has supplied money. So, when the surety had provided money directly to the principal debtor who then paid the creditor, the court was prepared to find, by a majority on the facts, that the money had not been provided as a loan but to be applied in payment of the debt: *Mahoney v McManus* (1981) 55 ALJR 673.

RIGHTS TO SECURITIES

[11.187]   In general, if the guarantor pays off the entirety of the debt, then he or she is entitled to be subrogated to all of the rights previously enjoyed by the bank in respect of the debt. As a natural consequence of this rule, the guarantor is entitled to the benefit of all securities for the debt which are held by the bank. This entitlement extends to all securities received from the customer, whether received before or after the making of the guarantee and irrespective of whether the guarantor knew of the existence of the securities at the time of entering into the guarantee: *Forbes v Jackson* (1882) 10 Ch D 615. The right extends to securities given by third parties: *Duncan, Fox & Co v North & South Wales Bank* (1880) 6 App Cas 1.

Recall that this right of subrogation is usually restricted somewhat by the clause which ensures that the right of the guarantor does not come into existence until the entire debt owed by the principal debtor is paid, not the amount for which the guarantor might be liable.

When the creditor bank holds securities, it might be thought that the guarantor could force the banker to resort to those securities before calling on the guarantor, but such is not the case. In spite of some earlier confusion, it is clear that the creditor has the right to sue the guarantor without resorting to the securities: see *Duncan, Fox & Co v North and South Wales Bank* (1880) 6 App Cas 1, dictum of Lord Watson at 22. In *Ewart v Latta* (1865) 4 Macq 983 it was said:

> Until the debtor [ie, the guarantor] has discharged himself of his liability, until he has fulfilled his own contract, he has no right to dictate any terms, to prescribe any duty, or to make any demand on his creditor. The creditor must be left in possession of the whole of the remedies which the original contract gave him, and he must be left unfettered and at liberty to exhaust those remedies, and he cannot be required to put any limitation upon the course of legal action given to him by his contract by any person who is still his debtor, except upon the terms of that debt being completely satisfied.

Once again, it will be found that most bank guarantee forms contain clauses which are intended to put the matter beyond doubt.

CHAPTER 12

INTERNATIONAL BANKING

THE MAREVA INJUNCTION

INTRODUCTION

[12.1] The Mareva injunction is a judicial development which was devised to meet a very specific problem, namely, that between the time of the initiation of a suit and the time when final judgment is obtained and, if necessary, execution issued, the debtor may take steps to remove assets from the jurisdiction of the court. Any resulting victory for the plaintiff will be a hollow one if there are no assets against which the judgment may be enforced. Some American and European jurisdictions solve this problem by means of a prejudgment attachment of the defendant's property, but there is no general procedure available for this in Australian law.

The unusual name is derived from the name of the second case in which the injunction was granted: *Mareva Compania Naviera SA v International Bulk Carriers SA* [1975] 2 Lloyd's Rep 509. The first case was *Nippon Yusen Kaisha v Karageorgis* [1975] 3 All ER 282. This discussion of the Mareva injunction is necessarily incomplete. For a more detailed treatment, see H J W Hetherington (ed), *Mareva Injunctions*, Law Book Co, Sydney, 1983; Ough, *Mareva Injunctions*, Butterworths, London, 1987; Hoyle, *The Mareva Injunction and Related Orders*, Lloyds of London, London, 1989.

DEFINITION

[12.2] The Mareva injunction restrains a defendant by him or herself or by his or her agents or servants or otherwise from removing from the jurisdiction or disposing of or dealing with those of his or her assets that will or may be necessary to meet a plaintiff's pending claim. The order is ordinarily made in a very wide form, at least in the first instance, and has the effect of 'freezing' the assets of the defendant pending the outcome of the litigation.

PURPOSE

[12.3]   The situation in which a Mareva injunction may be granted and the purpose of the injunction is well illustrated by the *Mareva* case itself. The action was brought by the owners of a ship against the charterers in respect of unpaid hire charges. Prior to obtaining judgment, the owners sought an injunction of the kind now known as the Mareva injunction. Lord Denning described the plight of the shipowners in *Mareva Compania Naviera SA v International Bulk Carriers SA* [1975] 2 Lloyd's Rep 509 at 511:

> There is money in a bank in London which stands in the name of these time charterers. The time charterers have control of it. They may at any time dispose of it or remove it out of this country. If they do so, the ship owners may never get their charter hire. The ship is now on the high seas. It has passed Cape Town on its way to India. It will now complete the voyage and the cargo will be discharged. And the ship owners may not get their charter hire at all. In the face of this danger, I think this Court ought to grant an injunction to restrain the defendants from disposing of these moneys now in the bank in London until the trial and judgment in this action.

[12.4]   Between 1975 and 1980, it was not entirely clear that the courts of Australia and New Zealand would follow the lead given by the English courts. However, the prolonged litigation between the American citizen Nelson Bunker Hunt and BP Exploration Co (Libya) Ltd raised the question in these jurisdictions: *BP Exploration Co (Libya) Ltd v Hunt* [1976] 3 All ER 879; [1982] 1 All ER 986. BP Explorations had obtained a judgment of some A$30 million against Hunt. Hunt was a resident in the American state of Texas but had assets in many parts of the world, including Australia and New Zealand. He indicated an unwillingness to satisfy the judgment or to provide security for its satisfaction. BP instructed solicitors in various jurisdictions to seek injunctions restraining Hunt from removing or dealing with assets in those jurisdictions pending registration of the English judgment under the procedures available for enforcement under reciprocal enforcement legislation.

Although there was considerable argument concerning the source of the jurisdictional power to grant the injunction, Barker J in the New Zealand court relied on s 16 of the Judicature Act 1908 which says: 'The Court shall ... have ... all the judicial jurisdiction which may be necessary to administer the laws of New Zealand.'

Barker J granted the injunction and noted that (*Hunt v BP Exploration Co (Libya) Ltd* [1980] 1 NZLR 104 at 118):

> The court has to approach modern problems with the flexibility of modern business. In former times ... it would have been more difficult for a foreign debtor to take his assets out of the country. Today, vast sums of money can be transferred from one country to another in a matter of seconds as a result of a phone call or a telex message. Reputable foreign debtors of course have nothing to fear; the facts of the reported *Mareva* cases indicate that the jurisdiction is wholesome; the sheer number of Mareva injunctions granted in London indicates that the jurisdiction is fulfilling a need.

By the mid-1980s courts in all Australian states had granted Mareva injunctions although there have been some doubts expressed about the jurisdictional basis of the power; see, for example, Ormiston J in *Deputy Commissioner of Taxation (Vic) v Rosenthal* (1984) 16 ATR 159.

The High Court considered the question in *Jackson v Sterling Industries Ltd* (1987) 162 CLR 612. The court considered that the jurisdictional basis for granting a Mareva injunction is founded on the risk that the defendant will so deal with assets that any judgment given by the court will be rendered ineffective, thus having the effect of impairing the effective administration of justice.

REQUIREMENTS FOR GRANTING

[12.5]   The early cases put limits on the circumstances in which a Mareva injunction would be granted, but one by one the requirements seemed to have been relaxed. Thus, it soon became clear that it is not necessary for the defendant to be foreign: *Prince Abdul Rahman v Abu-Taha* [1980] 3 All ER 409. It is sufficient that there is a threat that the assets will be dissipated within the jurisdiction: *Z Ltd v A-Z* [1982] 2 QB 558; [1982] 1 All ER 556 (sub nom *Z Ltd v A*). And it would appear that the applicant for the injunction need not even have an existing cause of action against the other party so long as it seems likely that there will eventually be such a cause of action: *Turner v Sylvester* [1981] 2 NSWLR 295.

[12.6]   Concerning the circumstances in which a Mareva injunction should be granted, Kerr LJ has made the following suggestions (*Z Ltd v A* [1982] 1 All ER 556 at 572):

> It follows that in my view Mareva injunctions should be granted, but granted only when it appears to the court that there is a combination of two circumstances. First, when it appears likely that the plaintiff will receive judgment against the defendant for a certain or approximate sum. Second, when there are also reasons to believe that the defendant has assets within the jurisdiction to meet the judgment, in whole or in part, but may well take steps designed to ensure that these are no longer available or traceable when judgment is given against him.

The Mareva injunction should not be granted if there is little likelihood of the defendant removing the assets from the jurisdiction. In *Etablissement Eseffa International Anstalt v Central Bank of Nigeria* [1979] 1 Lloyd's Rep 445 the court refused to grant the injunction against the defendant bank for the simple reason that it was not believed that there was a danger that the bank would remove assets.

The Mareva injunction is usually granted as an interlocutory order, but it is possible to obtain the injunction after judgment and before execution: *Orwell Steel (Erection and Fabrication) Ltd v Asphalt and Tarmac (UK) Ltd* [1985] 3 All ER 747.

[12.7]   An Australian court has held that the Mareva injunction should not be used to restrain persons who are not party to the proceedings. In *Bank of Queensland Ltd v Grant* (1984) 54 ALR 306 the plaintiff had succeeded in an action against the first and second defendants. The bank learned that the second defendant planned to go abroad and was planning to transfer his interest in the matrimonial home to his wife, from whom he was separating. The bank sought an injunction to restrain the wife from registering her title.

Clarke J refused to grant the injunction. He also observed that although Mareva injunctions have occasionally been granted against banks to prevent them from dealing with funds of their customers, the court may lack jurisdiction to make such an order. The proper course of action is to seek an order against the defendant only and to make an ancillary order that notice of the injunction be given to the bank: see [12.12] for the effect of receiving notice of a Mareva injunction.

Similarly, if an application for an injunction includes assets which appear on their face to belong to a third party, the request should be refused unless there is some good reason for supposing that the assets are in truth those of the Mareva defendant. Where, as will usually be the case, it is the defendant who is claiming that the assets belong to someone else, the court is not obliged to accept the claim without inquiry although it may do so: see *SCF Finance Co Ltd v Masri* [1985] 2 All ER 747.

Foreign assets pose particular problems in considering whether to grant a Mareva injunction. The prevailing attitude has been that there is jurisdiction to grant a Mareva injunction which includes foreign assets but that the power should be used sparingly. The most thorough discussion of the problem has been by Staughton LJ in *Republic of Haiti v Duvalier* [1990] 1 QB 202. There it was said that relevant factors in deciding to grant an injunction which includes foreign assets are: (1) the plain and admitted intention of a defendant to move assets out of the reach of courts of law; (2) the resources obtained and the skill shown in doing so; and (3) the magnitude of the sums involved: see also *National Australia Bank Ltd v Dessau* [1988] VR 521; *Ballabil Holdings Pty Ltd v Hospital Products Ltd* (1985) 1 NSWLR 155.

EFFECTS OF A MAREVA INJUNCTION

[12.8]   The granting of a Mareva injunction affects all who know of it, for it would be a contempt of court to assist in violating the terms of the injunction by dealing with the assets of the defendant in any way which is inconsistent with the terms of the injunction. This is obviously of importance to bankers and others who deal with or have a claim to the assets of the Mareva defendant.

NOT A PROPRIETARY INTEREST

[12.9]   The granting of a Mareva injunction does not give the creditor or anyone else a lien on the assets of the debtor. The point was directly in question in *Cretanor Maritime Co v Irish Marine Management; The Cretan Harmony* [1978] 3 All ER 164; [1978] 1 Lloyd's Rep 425. The owners of a ship sought an injunction against the charterers. The charterers had only one asset within the jurisdiction, a certificate of deposit with the First National City Bank of

London. This asset was property which was covered by a floating charge given by the charterers to the Ulster Bank prior to the time when the injunction was sought. After the injunction had been granted, the Ulster Bank appointed a receiver under the terms of the floating charge. The question for the court was whether the terms of the injunction precluded the receiver from dealing with the certificate. The court held in favour of the receiver. During the course of the judgment Buckley LJ said ([1978] 1 Lloyd's Rep 431 at 431):

> It seems to me ... that it is not the case that any rights in the nature of a lien arise when a Mareva injunction is made. Under such an injunction, the plaintiff has no rights against the assets. He may later acquire such rights if he obtains judgment and can thereafter successfully levy execution upon them but until that event his only rights are against the defendant personally.

[12.10]   This view was reaffirmed and extended in *Iraqi Ministry of Defence v Arcepey Shipping Co SA (Gillespie Bros Ltd Intervening)* [1980] 1 All ER 480. In that case a Mareva injunction had been obtained which 'froze' the assets of the defendant. The defendant applied to be permitted to use part of the funds to pay a debt which fell due during the currency of the injunction. The court held that the defendant should be entitled to make the payment even though there was some argument that the debt might not be enforceable because of breaches of the Money Lenders Act. The decision is clearly correct if one accepts that the purpose of the injunction is to prevent the fraudulent removal or dissipation of the assets of the defendant. To hold otherwise would mean that the granting of the injunction would override the provisions of the Bankruptcy Act 1966. If the payment was a preference then it could be unwound in the event of a bankruptcy or a liquidation. The fact that it was not enforceable was largely irrelevant, the court observing that business people frequently pay debts which are technically unenforceable.

The same line of argument has resulted in the defendant being permitted to use assets for the purposes of meeting legal costs. This is important since the financial position of the defendant will often be such that the solicitors will require payment in advance: see the comments of Rogers J in *Riley McKay v McKay (No 2)* [1982] 1 NSWLR 264.

[12.11]   A Mareva injunction will not be granted when there would be a consequential unjust interference with the rights of third parties to carry on their normal business. This has most often arisen when the injunction applied for would, if granted, have the side effect of preventing ship's cargo or the ship itself from leaving the jurisdiction. Thus, in *Gilfoyle Shipping Services Ltd v Binosi Pty Ltd* [1984] 2 NZLR 742 the plaintiff sought a Mareva injunction to prevent the defendant from dealing with fuel in the ship's bunkers. If the injunction had been granted, there would have been considerable hardship on the owner of the ship and the ship's crew, the latter being mainly of Greek nationality. Barker J refused the injunction even though it meant the assets of the defendant would literally be 'going up in smoke' as the ship sailed for Australia the next day.

The *Gilfoyle* decision was a direct application of the English decision in *Galaxia Maritime SA v Mineralimportexport; The Eleftherios* [1982] 1 All ER 796 where the court similarly considered the welfare of the crew of a ship to be a significant factor in refusing the injunction: see also *Bank of Queensland Ltd v Grant* (1984) 54 ALR 306.

THE EFFECT ON THIRD PARTIES

[12.12] The effect of a Mareva injunction on third parties, particularly third party bankers, was discussed in *Z Ltd v A* [1982] 1 All ER 556. The case arose from an alleged fraud on a non-English company. Telex and cable orders were forged which resulted in the transfer of some £2 million to London banks and which then reached the hands of the conspirators. When the fraud was discovered, the company sought and obtained a Mareva injunction from Bingham J which prevented any dealings with the defendants' assets except in so far as they exceeded the disputed £2 million. By a prompt use of orders for specific discovery, interrogatories, injunctions and Anton Piller orders, the plaintiffs were able to recover £1 million; there then followed a settlement whereby a 'good deal of the balance' was recovered: see *Z Ltd v A* [1982] 1 All ER 556 at 560. In spite of this settlement, the five London clearing banks and one other defendant sought and obtained leave to appeal with a view toward clarifying the position of third parties when receiving notice of a Mareva injunction.

The Court of Appeal held that a third party will be liable if, having notice of the terms of the injunction, he or she knowingly assists in the disposal of any of the assets of the defendant whether or not the defendant has knowledge of the injunction. One obvious consequence of this view is that the banker should, upon receiving notice of the injunction, freeze all accounts known to belong to the defendant as well as other assets held on his or her behalf: see *Z Ltd v A* [1982] 1 All ER 556 at 562 and 567. The basis for the liability is that the third party who 'knowingly assists in the disposal of [the assets] ... will be guilty of a contempt of court, for it is an act calculated to obstruct the course of justice': *Z Ltd v A* [1982] 1 All ER 556 at 563.

The banker's obligation to honour the defendant's cheques is discharged because to do so has now become an unenforceable illegal obligation or, alternatively, it must be taken that the customer has only authorised the banker to do that which is lawful: *Z Ltd v A* [1982] 1 All ER 556 at 563 and 572.

[12.13] From these principles, the court extracted a set of guidelines which is intended to assist in the drafting and the interpretation of Mareva injunctions. The guidelines proposed divide into two groups, the first aimed at applicants who are seeking Mareva injunctions which might affect third parties and the second describing the obligations imposed on the third parties who have received notice of the injunction. Since the banker may often be in either position, both sets of guidelines are given here.

Matters to be considered at the time of seeking and making the injunction include the following.

1. The plaintiff should normally be required to give an undertaking to indemnify against any liability incurred and to pay any expenses reasonably incurred in complying with the terms of the injunction.

2. The plaintiff should identify third parties upon whom it is intended to serve notice of the injunction. This, presumably, will enable the court to insert terms intended to protect the third parties from unreasonable obligation. It is not intended that this should preclude the giving of notice to other third parties if additional information is obtained.

3. If possible, the plaintiff should identify assets held in the hands of third parties. The ability to make such an identification will probably be the exception rather than the rule in the case of assets held by the bank, since the bank owes a duty of secrecy to its customer which should preclude it from voluntarily disclosing either the existence or the extent of the defendant's assets held: *Tournier v National Provincial and Union Bank of England* [1924] 1 KB 461. In this circumstance, the power of the court to order the defendant or the third party bank to make discovery in proper cases is of the utmost importance: see *A J Bekhor & Co Ltd v Bilton* [1981] 2 All ER 565.

4. If the injunction is intended only to restrain dealings with the defendant's assets up to a maximum amount, the order should contain terms which state clearly that the 'maximum sum part of the order does not include assets known or believed to be in the hands of a third party'. This is a matter of particular concern to the banks, since without such a term they are left in the position of being in possible breach of the order if they allow dealings with the account (and those dealings involve assets which are within the terms of the injunction) and in possible breach of contract with the customer if they do not permit dealings (and the defendant has adequate assets elsewhere).

5. If it is thought desirable to allow the defendant normal living expenses or, presumably, an operating account for any reason whatsoever, the order should indicate the sum to be allowed, but should not state the purpose for which the sum is to be used. The bank should open a special account for the defendant, placing the account in funds in accordance with the amounts mentioned in the injunction. It is no concern of the bank to inquire as to the actual use of the account.

[12.14]   The obligations on the bank when receiving notice of the injunction include:

1. All accounts known to belong to the defendant should be frozen at once. All cheques should be dishonoured for the reasons given above.

2. There are some payments which may be made and which may be debited to the defendant's account. These payments may be loosely described as those which the bank is under some independent obligation to make.

Thus, payments under a letter of credit or a bank guarantee, credit card transaction, and cheques drawn by the defendant which are supported by a cheque guarantee card may all be paid and debited to the defendant's account: see *Z Ltd v A* [1982] 1 All ER 556 at 563, 570 and 576. However, it appears that the sums from any commercial transaction which are paid into the defendant's account will then be covered by the injunction: *Intraco Ltd v Notis Shipping Corporation* [1981] 2 Lloyd's Rep 256.

3. Unless expressly stated in the injunction, certain assets held by the bank are not to be frozen by the bank. Specifically mentioned by the court are: (a) shares or title deeds held by the bank as security; (b) articles in a safe deposit in the name of the defendant; (c) future assets, that is, any assets which come within the control of the bank subsequently to the date on which the bank is served with the order save in so far as any of these assets are specifically referred to in the injunction; (d) money held in a joint account which is in the name of the defendant and any other person or persons.

Unfortunately, these guidelines may be safely relied upon only if the injunction is carefully drawn so as to include specific terms which conform to the first set of guidelines. Since the granting of the injunction, and its terms, fall within the discretion of the granting judge and since the exercise of this discretion must inevitably be influenced by the specific facts before him or her, bankers and other third parties can by no means be assured that injunctions will necessarily be so favourably drawn. In particular, the items of property mentioned in the last guideline must be considered as 'frozen' unless the terms of the injunction specifically relieve the bank from responsibility.

COSTS OF ENFORCEMENT

[12.15] The concern for the interests of third parties is also shown in the practice of requiring the applicant to meet many of the costs of enforcement. In *Sea Rose Ltd v Seatrain in (UK) Ltd* [1981] 1 Lloyd's Rep 556 the injunction was granted only on the basis that the plaintiff, who naturally wished to notify the bank of the existence of the injunction, undertake to pay costs incurred by the banker in searching for relevant accounts of the defendant. In the absence of a centralised computing system, the costs of such a 'trawl' for the accounts may be substantial.

The perceived ability of the applicant to pay such costs may itself be a factor in the decision to grant a Mareva injunction. In *Gilfoyle Shipping Services Ltd v Binosi Pty Ltd* [1984] 2 NZLR 742 the applicant offered to meet the costs of requiring the ship and crew to remain in Timaru. The third party shipowner expressed doubts about the ability of the applicant to meet such costs; this appeared to be one of the factors considered by Barker J in refusing the injunction.

DOCUMENTARY CREDITS

INTRODUCTION

[12.16]   The modern documentary letter of credit has been called 'the crankshaft of modern commerce': see Chorley, *Law of Banking*, 6th ed, Sweet & Maxwell, London, p 225. Although its current form is primarily a product of the twentieth century, its antecedents lie in the earliest days of travel when communication was poor and carrying cash was even riskier than it is today. It is also interesting to note that some of the most recent developments in the letter of credit, the so-called 'standby credit' are closer in form to the old style of letter of credit than to the new. For a more detailed discussion of the history of the modern documentary letter of credit, see E P Ellinger, *Documentary Letters of Credit*, University of Singapore Preso, Singapore, 1970.

TRAVELLERS' LETTERS

[12.17]   A traveller's letter of credit is a letter addressed by a person with international connections to one or more of those overseas associates, requesting that the overseas associate provide the named bearer of the letter, the traveller, with certain financial accommodation and to debit the writer of the letter with the sums advanced. The writer of the letter is called the issuer, the bearer is known as the beneficiary. The addressee of the letter goes under different names depending upon the accommodation which he or she is to provide.

The benefit to the traveller is obvious, but there are other benefits of the arrangement. The issuer of letters is very likely to be the addressee of letters of credit issued by parties to whom letters have been addressed. In a perfect world, the financial accommodation provided by a given addressee could be precisely cancelled by accommodation provided by a reciprocal arrangement. In practice, of course, things do not balance out quite so nicely, but they do balance partially, with the consequence that much of the settlement of debts between issuers and addressees of the letters of credit could be settled by adjustment in their respective books. There is a substantial reduction in the need to move money, which, in the days when travellers' letters were widely used, usually meant precious metal.

Cash credits

[12.18]   The traveller's letter of credit was classified according to the type of accommodation provided by the addressee. The earliest, and in some ways the most common, was a cash credit. By presentation of the letter of credit at the office of the addressee and establishing his or her identity, the beneficiary would be able to draw cash up to the limit which was stated in the letter.

Discount facility

[12.19]   There were a number of refinements on the simple cash credit. When the parties were bankers, it was often desirable that the advancement of cash be accompanied by some form of bill of exchange. In the simplest form, the customer would draw a demand bill payable to him or herself or to the addressee of the letter of credit. The equivalent today would be a letter which guaranteed the addressee that he or she would be reimbursed for cheques drawn by the beneficiary of the letter, a kind of cheque guarantee system. Another form of the letter requested that the addressee discount bills drawn upon the issuer by the beneficiary of the letter.

In both of these cases, in order for the credit to be of the utmost value to the beneficiary, it could be stipulated that the addressee would discount the bills without recourse to the beneficiary.

Letter of introduction for security purposes

[12.20] There was one further refinement which was added as the popularity of the traveller's letter of credit increased. A letter of introduction, called in some cases a 'letter of indication' was drawn separately. This letter was either carried by the beneficiary or was sent directly to the addressee and contained personal information about the beneficiary which was intended to assist in the identification process. The letter of introduction would also carry a specimen signature.

It was clearly important that the letter of credit be carried separately from the letter of introduction, for otherwise a forger would have the best of both worlds. Indeed, the early letters were issued with stern warnings that the letter of credit should be carried separately from the letter of introduction.

Travellers' letters of credit are seldom used today, but they have been replaced by mechanisms that clearly derive from the credit themselves, but are more suited to the larger number of people who travel in modern times. The two most popular forms of modern travel facility are travellers' cheques and credit cards.

MODERN REPLACEMENTS

[12.21] Travellers' cheques are a direct descendant of the traveller's letter of credit. In *Rhodes v London and County Bank* (1880) 1 LDAB 90 the plaintiff had arrangements with the defendant bank whereby he was issued with 'circular notes' and a letter of introduction. The 'circular notes' appear to have been a kind of accounting device whereby the financial institution which made advances to the bearer of the notes and the letter of introduction could easily obtain reimbursement from the issuer.

The modern travellers' cheque may or may not be a bill of exchange, since the form of many travellers' cheques does not satisfy the requirements of s 8(1) of the Bills of Exchange Act 1909: see the discussion at [6.99]. From a functional point of view, the issuer of the travellers' cheque usually charges a fee for issuing, typically 1 per cent, but the issuer also has the use of the traveller's money from the time of issue of the cheques until such time as the issuer is called upon to pay. This concept of a 'prepaid' payment instrument is being revived today in the form of a prepaid 'credit card'. The instrument may be used by organisations to provide expenses for members without the risk of liability for member overspending. It also provides a convenient way of providing honoraria or of making simple gifts.

The letter of credit has also been replaced by the third party credit card. Functionally, this seems very much like the letter of credit, for the cards are issued by banks and other large organisations whose credit is recognised as being reliable. Legally, the third party credit card is distinct from the letter of credit: see [9.85]. Further, instead of being primarily a means of obtaining cash from financial institutions, the cards are primarily a means of obtaining goods and services from merchants who have agreed to honour the cards.

Whereas the third party credit card is somewhat similar to the letter of credit which asks the addressee to provide cash, the cheque guarantee card is very similar to the discount letter of credit which requests the addressee to negotiate the traveller's bills of exchange. The cards are issued to their customers by banks or other organisations. The issuing institution 'guarantees' that the customer's cheque will be met by the bank provided it does not exceed a ceiling amount. Cheque guarantee cards, although very popular in the United Kingdom, are not used in Australia.

MODERN USES

[12.22]   Although the letter of credit has been largely replaced as a financial facility for travellers, it has been adapted in a different form for commercial use, particularly when the transaction is international. In all cases, the motivation for the use of credits is the same. The credit of a major bank or other financial institution is substituted for or added to that of one of the parties to the transaction.

Safe method of payment in international sales

[12.23]   This substitution may be illustrated by a consideration of the major use of letters of credit, that is, facilitating an international sale of goods by the substitution of a reliable paymaster who will stand in the shoes of the buyer. An exporter in country A may know little about the financial standing of the importer in country B, or, even worse, the exporter may know enough to be concerned that payment may be delayed. Nor is concern about the solvency of the trading partner confined to the seller, for the buyer must also be certain that property in the goods is transferred from the seller before payment is made, for otherwise the financial collapse of the seller could leave the buyer without the money and without the goods.

The early solution to this problem was known as a 'documents against payments' or 'documents against acceptance' clause, usually abbreviated in the contract to D/P and D/A respectively. In each case the seller would hand shipping and other contract documents to a local bank which discounts the seller's bill of exchange. The documents are then presented by a correspondent bank to the buyer who receives the documents in exchange for payment (in the case of D/P) or the buyer's acceptance of the seller's bill of exchange (in the case of D/A).

The letter of credit is a better solution which serves the interests of both the buyer and the seller. The credit of the issuing bank is substituted for the credit of the buyer, so that the seller can be certain that payment will be made. On the other hand, the buyer can be certain that payment will not be made until such time as the goods are actually shipped, for the 'documentary' part of the documentary letter of credit means that the seller must present certain documents to the bank before payment will be made: see [12.83] for a discussion of the documents involved in a documentary letter of credit.

[12.24]   The entire operation has been summarised neatly by Denning LJ in *Pavia & Co SPA v Thurmann-Nielsen* [1952] 2 QB 84 at 88:

> The sale of goods across the world is now usually arranged by means of confirmed credits. The buyer requests his banker to open a credit in favour of the seller and in pursuance of that request the banker, or his foreign agent, issues a confirmed credit in favour of the seller. This credit is a promise by the banker to pay money to the seller in return for the shipping documents. Then the seller, when he presents the documents, gets paid the contract price. The conditions of the credit must be strictly fulfilled, otherwise the seller would not be entitled to draw on it.

The use of the word 'confirmed' in the quotation would no longer be considered proper: see [12.46].

It is important to understand that the promise by the bank is to the beneficiary/seller. It is a separate contract which calls for the banker to pay provided only that the seller tenders the documents called for by the terms of the credit. The contract between the banker and the seller is independent of the contract between the buyer and seller, an independence which is so important that it is given a name, the 'autonomy principle': see the discussion at [12.47].

Standby credits

[12.25]   The use of the documentary credit to facilitate international trade has one salient characteristic. Its abuse is controlled by the fact that neither the buyer nor the seller is ever in possession of the documents and the money at the same time. Valuable goods, more precisely, documents of title to the goods, must be tendered in exchange for payment. Not only are the buyer and the seller both protected, but the banker who has issued the credit also has a security interest in the goods by virtue of the documents of title: see [12.110].

In recent years the letter of credit has been adapted to serve a quite different function, one which does not provide the mutual protection of the documentary credit used in trade.

[12.26]   The 'standby credit' originated in the United States where banks were not permitted to give bank guarantees. Particularly in construction work, it may be that delays in the performance of the contract will be very costly to the person for whom the building is being constructed. As a guard against this possibility, it is common to call for 'performance guarantees' from the builder. If the building falls behind schedule or is not completed within the contractual time, the guarantor may be called upon to pay a fixed sum to defray the expenses associated with the late completion.

It will be appreciated that it may be controversial to determine whether or not a large construction project is or is not on schedule. One solution is to provide that experienced builders should act as referees to determine if the project is or is not on schedule. This solution will protect both parties, but is expensive and time-consuming. The other solution is to leave the decision solely in the hands of one of the contracting parties.

Surprisingly, this is the solution that has led to the use of the standby credit. The credit is in the form of an ordinary documentary credit, but the only document called for is a written notice from the beneficiary that the project is not on schedule.

A similar arrangement is the so-called 'first demand guarantee' which is used in Commonwealth countries. The document is in the form of a guarantee that, say, the project will be on schedule, but there is a 'conclusive evidence' clause which states that a written demand from the beneficiary shall be conclusive evidence that the guarantee is due and owing. The first demand guarantee and the standby letter of credit perform exactly the same function and it would seem that both are governed by the same law: see, for example, Denning MR in *Edward Owen Engineering Ltd v Barclays Bank International Ltd* [1978] QB 159; [1978] 1 All ER 976.

The 'standby credit' originated in the United States where banks are forbidden from issuing guarantees. In a triumph of form over substance, it has been held that the standby credit, properly worded, is not a bank guarantee: *Fair Pavilions Inc v First National City Bank* 281 NYS 2d 23 (1967); *Wichita Eagle & Beacon Pub Co v Pacific National Bank* 343 F Supp 323 (N D Cal 1971); *Fidelity Bank v Lutheran Mutual Insurance Co* 465 F 2d 211 (1972); *Barclays Bank DCO v Mercantile National Bank* 481 F 2d 1224.

Commercial documentary credits

[12.27]   Letters of credit are most often referred to as 'documentary credits' in order to emphasise the modern reliance on documents. The obligation to the beneficiary is not absolute, but is conditional upon the presentation of documents in conformity with the terms of the credit. Of course, in the standby credit, it might be very easy for the beneficiary to obtain the required documents, but in the ordinary sale of goods, the documents are an essential feature of the commercial operation of the credit.

A sample transaction

[12.28]   The prototypical use of a documentary letter of credit is as a means of payment in an international sale. The contract of sale will call for the buyer to obtain a letter of credit in favour of the seller. The buyer must approach his or her bank and make the necessary arrangements. When the bank agrees to open the credit, it becomes the 'issuing' bank. The buyer is known as the 'applicant' or the 'account party'. The seller is the 'beneficiary' of the credit.

Although the issuing bank could notify the seller directly, it is more common to do so through the services of a bank located in the same place as the seller. This 'advising bank' will ordinarily be a bank which has business connections with the issuing bank, a so-called 'correspondent bank'. The advising bank does not necessarily assume any responsibility for the credit beyond making timely notification to the seller of the existence and terms of the credit.

The terms of the credit will usually, although not always, contain a statement that it is 'irrevocable', that is, that it represents a binding promise by the issuing bank that the seller will be paid provided only that the seller fulfils his or her obligation to present documents which conform to those listed in the credit. So far then as payment is concerned, the seller may, indeed must, look to the issuing bank rather than to the buyer.

In order to be paid the seller must present the documents stipulated in the credit. The credit may provide that the documents must be presented to the issuing bank, but this is clearly not convenient or sensible from the seller's point of view. There are two solutions. The first is that the documents are forwarded to the issuing bank by a local bank which assumes no liability or responsibility. The second is that there is a 'nominated' bank which is authorised by the issuing bank to make the payment. The seller may then present the documents to the nominated bank for inspection. This inspection must be completed in a reasonable time, not to exceed seven banking days following the receipt of the documents.

Assuming that the documents are satisfactory, the seller is entitled to be paid according to the terms of the credit. This may require 'sight payment', that is, payment immediately, deferred payment or payment by accepting or negotiating the seller's draft (bill of exchange).

Although this arrangement is an improvement for the seller, it may not be entirely satisfactory. The seller may prefer to be able to look to a local bank, one known to the seller and to which he or she may have ready access in the event of any problem. Of course, one way to achieve this would be to require that the buyer make arrangements so that the local bank would be the issuing bank, but this is not a commercially sensible solution since the buyer has no connections with a local bank.

The solution is to have a local bank 'confirm' the credit. The confirming bank adds, in effect, its own promise to that of the issuing bank. In so doing, the confirming bank is relying upon its business connections with the issuing bank and its knowledge of its creditworthiness. The seller/beneficiary obtains a 'local defendant'. The promise made by the confirming bank is in all respects the same as that of the issuing bank.

One of the most important concepts in the law of documentary credits is the 'autonomy principle': the promise made by the issuing and the confirming bank is independent of the underlying contract of sale or other obligation which gives rise to the letter of credit. Although this principle is not absolute, it is very difficult for the buyer to halt payment of the letter of credit on the basis of some underlying contractual dispute with the seller.

Classification by mode of realisation

[12.29] As will be noted from the brief description above, there are numerous ways in which a credit may be realised. It is common commercial terminology to refer to credits in these ways.

• Acceptance credits

[12.30] Thus, in an 'acceptance credit' the obligation of the issuing bank is to accept bills drawn on it, provided such bills are drawn in conformity with the terms of the credit and are presented together with the other required documentation. The purpose of such an arrangement is, of course, to allow the beneficiary to discount the accepted bill in the appropriate markets; the bank is essentially lending its credit to the beneficiary. From a functional point of view, the beneficiary is carrying more of the costs of the finance than in other arrangements.

• Clean credits

[12.31] A 'clean' or 'sight' credit provides for payment against documents. Ordinarily, the documents required will include a sight draft drawn either on the issuing bank or on the account party by the beneficiary. In either case, when a bill is included, it is intended that the payment should be without recourse to the drawer of the instrument since recourse to the drawer would destroy the commercial advantages of an irrevocable credit.

• Discount credits

[12.32] In a 'discount credit', also called a 'negotiation credit', the issuing bank promises to pay either to the holder or to the drawer bills drawn in conformity with the credit and accompanied by the appropriate documents.

• Straight/negotiation credits

[12.33] A further form of classification which is sometimes used is based on the identity of individuals who may rely on the promise made by the issuing bank in the credit. In a 'straight credit' the issuing bank's commitment is to the beneficiary only, although the benefits of that might be extended to other banks by virtue of the issuing bank requesting them to participate in the realisation of the credit.

By contrast, a 'negotiation credit' is an open-ended engagement by the issuing bank. The promise is to all drawers, indorsers and bona fide holders of drafts drawn under the terms of the credit that the drafts will be paid without recourse. An example of the 'negotiation credit' is found in *Banco Nacional Ultramarino v First National Bank of Boston* 289 F 169 (1923) where the letter contained the following words: 'We hereby agree with the drawers, indorsers, and bona fide holders of bills drawn and negotiated in compliance with the terms of this credit that said bills will be duly honored on presentation at our counter in Boston.'

Non-legal classifications

[12.34] There are a number of non-legal classifications which are commonly used when referring to credits. Since there is little uniformity in this usage, it is crucial for banker and lawyer alike to discover precisely what is being discussed when certain terms are used.

• *Revolving credits*

[12.35] A 'revolving credit' is generally for a fixed amount and has an expiry date as in the normal credit, but there is a clause which permits automatic renewal to the upper limit following each transaction on the credit. It is merely a device to obviate the necessity and expense of issuing new and identical credits when it is contemplated by the parties that there will be a series of similar transactions. The 'automatic renewal' usually permits total outstanding drawings under the credit to be at a certain level.

• *Import/export credits*

[12.36] Credits are sometimes referred to as 'import' or 'export' credits depending upon whether their function is to facilitate an import or an export transaction. Similarly, credits may be referred to as 'sterling' or 'dollar' credits depending upon the currency in which they are payable.

• *Deferred payment credits*

[12.37] A fairly recent innovation is the 'deferred payment' credit. It is in the same form as a standard credit which promises payment against documents, but rather than being required to pay immediately, the bank is to pay at some later time.

• *Red clause credits*

[12.38] A 'red clause' credit has as its object to assist a seller who needs periodic finance in order to acquire the goods which are the subject matter of the underlying contract. The credit authorises the intermediary bank to make limited advances to the seller prior to shipment. The credit derives its name from the fact that traditionally the clause authorising pre-shipment payment was printed in red ink.

BASIC PRINCIPLES

[12.39]   If the documentary letter of credit is to fulfil its purpose of providing a reliable method of payment in international transactions, it is obviously important that there should be as few disputes as possible concerning their operation. One method of assuring this is to standardise the law relating to documentary credits.

THE UCP

[12.40]   The Uniform Customs and Practice for Commercial Documentary Credits (UCP) is an attempt to standardise the terms and conditions on which bankers will issue and act on commercial credits. The original version was formulated in 1933 by the International Chamber of Commerce. While widely accepted in many countries, the London bankers decided against adopting the terms of the 1933 version, with the result that the United Kingdom and Commonwealth countries went their own way. Given the dominant position of these countries in world trade at the time, the UCP was generally considered to be unsuccessful in achieving a standardisation.

The situation changed with the revision of the UCP in 1962. Further revisions were made in 1974 and 1983, the final drafts being the result of cooperation of a number of international bodies, including representatives from the Socialist trading countries. The latest revision came into operation on 1 January, 1994. It contains significant amendments intended to deal with changes in international transport and communications. The revision is known as the 1993 revision: see ICC Publication 500.

The UCP is one of the most successful attempts at legal standardisation. At the current time, the terms of UCP are incorporated by reference into virtually every letter of credit. The UCP is not law, but the terms are, by virtue of express inclusion, binding on the parties as contractual terms. Of course, there may still be differences in interpretation of the terms in different legal systems, but an ongoing effort by the International Chamber of Commerce is combined with a general willingness of courts to give effect to foreign decisions to yield a law which comes very close to being a truly international law of letters of credit.

Because of this universality, the articles of the UCP will be given close attention when discussing the law of credits, keeping in mind always that they act merely as contractual terms between the parties.

The formal application of the UCP is by means of inclusion in the credit itself. When so incorporated, the UCP articles are binding on all parties unless otherwise expressly stipulated in the credit: Art 1 UCP.

DEFINITION OF A LETTER OF CREDIT: 1993 REVISION

[12.41]   The definition of a letter of credit was expanded somewhat in the 1983 revision to make it clear that standby credits are within the scope of the UCP. The 1993 revision again elaborated upon the definition to clarify that a bank may issue a credit on its own behalf, that is, without the need for an application by another party, and to include expressly the concept of a 'negotiation' credit: see [12.33]. The current definition is:

> Article 2 For the purposes of these articles, the expressions 'documentary credit(s)' and 'standby letter(s) of credit' used herein (hereinafter referred to as 'credit(s)'), mean any arrangement, however named or described, whereby a bank (the 'issuing bank'), acting at the request and on the instructions of a customer (the 'applicant') or on its own behalf, (i) is to make a payment to or to the order of a third party (the 'beneficiary'), or is to pay or accept bills of exchange (draft(s)) drawn by the beneficiary, or (ii) authorises another bank to effect such payment, or to accept and pay such bills of exchange (draft(s)), or (iii) authorises another bank to negotiate, against stipulated document(s), provided that the terms and conditions of the credit are complied with.

For the purposes of the UCP, branches of a bank in different countries are considered another bank: Art 2 UCP.

The applicant for the credit is also called the 'account party' in much of the literature on credits. In a credit which is used to facilitate an international sale of goods, the account party will be the buyer; in a standby credit, the account party will be the person who is in a position similar to the principal debtor in an ordinary guarantee.

[12.42] Note that the definition contemplates that the issuing party will be a bank. There is, of course, no reason why the basic mechanism of the letter of credit should not be used when the issuing party is a non-bank. If such a credit included the UCP by reference, then there is a fundamental contradiction. However, it is thought that, as a matter of construction, the UCP would be interpreted in a way which would permit its application in the obvious way. An American case has held that a bank may be a confirming bank when the credit has been issued by a mortgage broker: *Barclays Bank (DCO) v Mercantile National Bank* [1973] 2 Lloyd's Rep 541. Although the decision was based on the Uniform Commercial Code, there seems no reason why the same result would not be reached by an application of general principles: see H C Gutteridge and M Megrah, *The Law of Bankers' Commercial Credits*, 7th ed, Europa, London, 1985, p 8.

The issued credit must clearly indicate the mode of realisation, that is, whether the payment is to be a 'sight payment', is to be deferred, or by acceptance or negotiation of a draft: Art 10(a) UCP. The credit should also specify a 'nominated bank' which is authorised to make the payment according to the terms of the credit itself. The credit may be a 'negotiation' credit in which any bank is a nominated bank, that is, any bank is authorised to give value for the drafts and/or documents called for by the credit: Art 10(b) UCP.

Merely being named as a nominated bank does not place the named bank under any obligation to the beneficiary. The nominated bank may refuse to participate in the credit entirely, or it may agree to receive the documents with or without examination for the purpose of forwarding them to the issuing bank. It is only if the nominated bank agrees to operate the credit and that agreement is communicated to the beneficiary that it comes under any liability to make payment by the means specified in the credit: Art 10(c) UCP.

However, by naming the nominated bank the issuing bank authorises the nominated bank to pay according to the terms of the credit and, if the nominated bank does so, the issuing bank undertakes to reimburse it in accordance with the provisions of the UCP: Art 10(d) UCP.

REVOCABLE/IRREVOCABLE

[12.43]   Perhaps the most important classification is that into revocable and irrevocable credits. Roughly speaking, a revocable credit may be cancelled or modified without notice to the beneficiary, although, as will be noted below, the issuing banker may be responsible for certain transactions which have already been completed.

Since one of the commercial reasons for using credits is to be certain of payment arrangements, it will be appreciated that a revocable credit is almost useless to a seller of goods since it may be amended or cancelled by the issuing bank at any time without any prior notice to the beneficiary: Art 8(a); and see *Cape Asbestos Co v Lloyds Bank Ltd* [1921] WN 274. Consequently, it was rather astonishing to find that the basic position in previous versions of the UCP was that given in Art 7(c) of the 1983 Revision: 'In the absence of [a contrary] indication the credit shall be deemed to be revocable.' This anomaly has been corrected in the 1993 Revision: although a credit should clearly indicate whether it is revocable or irrevocable, the 'default' credit is now irrevocable: Art 6(b) and (c) UCP.

A seller of goods who has actually shipped the goods, which must be done before the standard credit may be drawn upon, will be placed in a very embarrassing position if the credit is cancelled without notice before the documents are presented. The result of this is that a revocable credit has very little commercial value and, indeed, it would appear that there are few revocable credits in use.

Of course, if the beneficiary operates the credit prior to any amendment or cancellation then the issuing bank is bound by the transaction and must reimburse the nominated bank which has paid (or incurred a deferred payment obligation) in conformity with the credit: Art 8(b).

[12.44]   The undertaking of a bank which issues an irrevocable credit is quite different. The banker promises the beneficiary that, provided the documents presented to the nominated bank conform to the credit and are presented within the time specified by the credit, payment will be made in the manner stipulated by the credit: Art 9(a). Similarly, a bank which confirms an irrevocable credit undertakes to operate the credit provided that the stipulated documents are presented to the confirming bank or to any other nominated bank and that the terms and conditions of the credit are complied with: Art 9(b). A bank which is requested to add its confirmation but is not prepared to do so must notify the issuing bank as soon as possible: Art 9(c).

With the exception of certain amendments to transferable credits (see [12.117]), an irrevocable credit may not be amended or cancelled without the agreement of each of the major participants: the issuing bank, the confirming bank (if any) and the beneficiary: Art 9(d). No proposed amendment binds the beneficiary until the beneficiary communicates his or her acceptance of the amendment: Art 9(d)(iii). This notice may be given explicitly to the advising bank or implicitly by tendering documents which conform to the proposed amendments: Art 9(c)(iii).

The issuing bank is bound by its proposed amendments from the time of issuing the amendments, but if there is a confirming bank it may choose not to extend its confirmation to the amendments. In the latter case the confirming bank is authorised to advise the beneficiary of the proposed amendment provided that it also advises both the beneficiary and the issuing bank of its decision to withhold confirmation: Art 9(c)(ii).

Amendments must be accepted or rejected in whole, and the UCP expressly provides that a partial acceptance of amendments contained in one and the same advice of amendment is to be given no effect: Art 9(c)(iv).

Of course, if there is an amendment made without the consent of the account party, then the banker would no longer be entitled to be reimbursed after the credit is paid.

WHEN DOES THE CREDIT BECOME IRREVOCABLE?

[12.45]   The definition of irrevocable credit is defective in that it does not state when the credit becomes irrevocable. There are two opposing points of view. One is that the credit becomes irrevocable when it is communicated to the beneficiary and the beneficiary acts upon it: see Rowlatt J in *Urquhart Lindsay & Co Ltd v Eastern Bank Ltd* [1922] 1 KB 318. The other view is that the credit becomes irrevocable from the time that it is communicated to the beneficiary, with no need for action: see Greer J in *Dexters Ltd v Schenker & Co* (1923)14 Ll L Rep 586. The latter view seems preferable from a commercial point of view since it is impossible for the issuing bank to know when the beneficiary has 'acted' or, indeed, to place a very precise meaning on 'acted': Ellinger (E P Ellinger, *Documentary Letters of Credit*, Singapore University Press, Singapore, 1973, p 9) discusses the point in some detail.

CONFIRMED/UNCONFIRMED

[12.46]   In the normal course of events, notice to the beneficiary of a credit opened by the issuing bank is communicated through an intermediate bank located in the place where the beneficiary carries on business. This intermediate bank may be merely an agent of the issuing bank whose sole duty is to notify the beneficiary, or it may be that the intermediary bank is to assume obligations directly to the beneficiary. In the first instance, the intermediary is an 'advising bank', in the second a 'confirming bank'.

Some of the older cases use the expression 'confirmed' in discussing a credit which is irrevocable. That is clearly the case with Lord Denning's speech in *Pa via & Co SPA v Thurmann-Nielsen* [1952] 2 QB 84 at 88 quoted above. In more recent times, however, the meaning of the two expressions have become separate and distinct. Today, a credit is 'confirmed' only if an intermediary bank assumes a direct obligation to the beneficiary: see the discussion in *Panoutsos v Raymond Hadley Corporation of New York* [1917] 2 KB 473. The advantage to the beneficiary is that he or she may look to a local bank for performance of the credit rather than a bank which is very likely to be in the place where the account party, the buyer in the case of a sale of goods, is located. This is particularly important if the issuing bank refuses to pay, for if the beneficiary has a case to argue, it will be very much cheaper to sue a local defendant than one which is located in a foreign country: see, for example, *Edward Owen Engineering Ltd v Barclays Bank International Ltd* [1978] QB 159, where it appeared that the would-be plaintiff could not even obtain a visa to pursue a suit against Libyan buyers.

The UCP provides for confirmation of irrevocable credits only. A confirmation made at the request or authorisation of an issuing bank constitutes a separate undertaking by the confirming bank that it will be responsible to the beneficiary for the operation of the credit. The confirming bank also takes on certain responsibilities for other banks. If the credit calls for acceptance by a drawee bank, the confirming bank promises that it will accept the drafts if the drawee bank stipulated in the credit does not do so, and that it will pay previously accepted drafts if the nominated drawee bank does not do so: Art 9(b)(iii).

THE AUTONOMY PRINCIPLE

[12.47]   In a typical letter of credit arrangement, there are at least three separate contracts. There is the underlying contract, usually of sale, which is the reason for the existence of the letter of credit, there is the contract between the issuing banker and the buyer (or other account party) and there is the contract between the issuing banker and the beneficiary.

These contracts are obviously not independent in the business sense, for the letter of credit would not ordinarily exist without the underlying contract of sale. The question to be addressed in this section is whether or not the contracts are independent in the legal sense. The problem most commonly arises when there is a dispute between the buyer and seller prior to payment. Since withholding of payment is one of the strongest bargaining chips that any buyer has, it is understandable that the buyer should wish to stop the bank from making payment under the letter of credit until such time as the dispute is resolved.

If the contracts between the banker and each of the parties are somehow subservient to the underlying contract, then it seems reasonable that the buyer might be able to stop payment. But if the buyer is to have a free hand to stop payment, then the letter of credit mechanism becomes much less attractive to sellers. Further, if the payment can only be stopped for 'good' reasons, then who is to arbitrate on the particular dispute?

[12.48] Perhaps for these reasons, it has long been recognised that the letter of credit is a separate contract. This is known as the 'autonomy principal' and was judicially firmly established surprisingly late in the development of letter of credit law.

As if to put the matter beyond all doubt, the principle is now enshrined in the UCP:

> Article 3 Credits, by their nature, are separate transactions from the sales or other contract(s) on which they may be based and banks are in no way concerned with or bound by such contract(s), even if any reference whatsoever to such contract(s) is included in the credit. Consequently, the undertaking of a bank to pay, accept and pay Draft(s) or negotiate and/or to fulfil any other obligation under the Credit, is not subject to claims or defences by the Applicant resulting from his relationships with the Issuing Bank or the Beneficiary.

[12.49] The principle is illustrated by *Urquhart Lindsay & Co v Eastern Bank Ltd* [1922] 1 KB 318. The plaintiff company had sold machinery under a contract which called for payment by an irrevocable documentary credit issued by the defendant bank. The contract of sale provided for several shipments of the machinery and also contained a clause which called for a variation in the contract price in certain circumstances, but there was no reference to such matters in the credit itself. After several shipments had been made, the buyers claimed that the price on the next shipment should be reduced under the variation clause. The sellers did not agree. The buyers instructed the defendant banker to refuse to make the payment under the letter of credit for any amount over the sum which the buyers claimed was the correct price.

The bank carried out the instructions of its customer, the buyer, and refused payment when the documents were produced. The court held that the bank was not entitled to do so, that far from the letter of credit being a contract that was subservient to the contract of sale, it was a fully autonomous contract. Indeed, if there was a conflict between the contract of sale and the letter of credit, the court appeared to say that it was the contract of sale which might need to be rewritten.

Explaining the obligations of the parties, Rowlatt J said ([1922] 1 KB 318 at 323):

> ... the defendants undertook to pay the amount of invoices for machinery without qualification, the basis of this form of banking facility being that the buyer is taken for the purpose of all questions between himself and his banker, or between his banker and the seller, to be content to accept the invoices of the seller as correct. It seems to me that, so far from the letter of credit being qualified by the contract of sale, the latter must accommodate itself to the letter of credit.

Furthermore, the court held that, on the breach of the contract to pay under the letter of credit, the bank became liable to pay damages which were to be assessed as on the repudiation of the contract as a whole. The bank had argued that there was a mere failure to make a payment and that, analogous to debt, there could be no assessment of damages beyond the amount of the payment in question. The court rejected the bank's argument, holding that the bank was liable for all damages which flowed from the breach and that the sellers were under no obligation to take an action to obtain payment in some other way; in particular, they were not obliged to take the lesser amount offered by the buyers.

[12.50]   In the absence of fraud on the part of the seller, the issuing banker is not entitled to refuse payment by any reference to the underlying contract of sale and this is true even when the issuing banker is in a position to know that the seller is in breach of the contract with the buyer and that the breach is severe enough to entitle the buyer to reject the documents: see [12.47]. As to the nature of fraud see *United City Merchants (Investments) Ltd and Glass Fibres and Equipment Ltd v Royal Bank of Canada* [1979] 2 Lloyd's Rep 498 and [12.54].

The question of autonomy most often comes before the court when the account party seeks to prevent the bank from paying the beneficiary. Since the *Urquhart Lindsay* case, the bank will not willingly consent to a request from the account party. Indeed, the banker would be well advised to advise the account party to seek such an injunction in all cases where the account party wishes to stop the operation of the credit. By so doing, the bank protects itself from both the beneficiary and its own customer. The injunction may be sought against either the bank or the beneficiary. There are a number of reported cases where the account party has sought an injunction; most have been unsuccessful.

[12.51]   In *Hamzeh Malas & Sons v British Imex Industries* [1958] 2 QB 127; [1957] 2 Lloyd's Rep 549 the buyer/seller contract called for the goods to be delivered in instalments. It was alleged that the first instalment was defective and the buyers sought an injunction which would restrain the sellers from drawing on the credit until the rights of the parties under the contract of sale had been determined. The case is noteworthy for the fact that the English Court of Appeal held that the court had the power to grant such an injunction, but refused to do so on the basis that the credit constituted a separate contract. Jenkins LJ [1957] 2 Lloyd's Rep 549 said (at 550):

> ... the opening of a confirmed letter of credit constitutes a bargain between the banker and the vendor of the goods, which imposes upon the banker an absolute obligation to pay ...

[12.52]   There have also been cases where the account party has sought to gain an injunction which will prevent the bank from paying. In *Discount Records Ltd v Barclays Bank Ltd* [1975] 1 WLR 315 the plaintiffs had ordered goods from a French company. When the first shipments arrived, many of the cartons were simply rubbish. Some of the cartons had shipping marks which appeared to have been changed or tampered with.

Once again, the court affirmed its jurisdiction to grant an injunction which would prevent the operation of the credit, but once again refused to do so. Megarry J noted that the courts should be slow to interfere with bankers' credits except in very grave circumstances since the importance of maintaining commercial confidence in such arrangements is of the utmost importance.

But the court also noted that an injunction was quite improper here for quite another reason. The contract between the bank and the account party was a contract which was separate from the contract of sale. If the banker did the wrong thing under that contract by paying when payment should not be made, then the remedy was in damages for the breach of contract. If, on the other hand, the banker did the correct thing in paying, where was the ground for an injunction? It appears that an injunction will be seriously considered only when to refuse one would result in an irretrievable injustice.

[12.53] The High Court of Australia has also refused to grant injunctions to prevent payment of first demand guarantees where the application was based on an alleged breach of the underlying transaction: see *Wood Hall Ltd v The Pipeline Authority* (1979) 141 CLR 443. The reasons for refusing the injunction were the usual 'commercial efficacy' ones. However, the High Court also made some comments in the case which would have the effect of weakening the autonomy principle. Gibbs J, with whom Barwick CJ and Mason J agreed, expressly found that the underlying contract entitled the beneficiary to claim against the guarantees and refused to speculate on what effect the opposite conclusion might have had: at 490. Stephen J went so far as to say (at 493):

> Had the construction contract itself contained some qualification upon the Authority's power to make a demand under a performance guarantee, the position might well have been different.

This dicta has been applied by Giles J to grant an injunction where the underlying contract contained restriction clauses on the beneficiary's right to call against a first demand bond: *Tenore Pty Ltd v Roleystone Pty Ltd* (Supreme Court, NSW, (Giles J), 14 September 1990, unreported); see also *Pearson Bridge (New South Wales) Pty Ltd v State Rail Authority of New South Wales* (Supreme Court, NSW, (Yeldham J), 28 June 1982, unreported).

Presumably the result of these cases might be different in instruments which are expressed to be subject to the UCP since Art 3 expressly provides that the credit is to be autonomous 'even if any reference whatsoever to such contract(s) is included in the credit'.

The autonomy principle does not prevent a bank from claiming a set-off as against the beneficiary where the beneficiary is indebted to the bank at least where the bank's claim is a liquidated sum which has arisen from the very banking transaction which gave rise to the letter of credit: see *Hongkong and Shanghai Banking Corp v Kloeckner & Co* [1989] 3 All ER 513.

THE FRAUD EXCEPTION

[12.54] The autonomy principle, important as it is, must necessarily yield in certain cases. It has already been noted that the courts have repeatedly asserted that there is a power to grant an injunction to prevent the operation of credits when the circumstances so dictate.

The only circumstance in which injunctions have in fact been granted are those where fraud is involved, and recent cases have even narrowed this exception considerably. Interestingly enough, it is an American case which is always cited as authority for the so-called fraud exception to the autonomy principle.

[12.55] In *Sztejn v J Henry Schroder Banking Corporation* 31 NYS (2d) 631 (1941) the plaintiff contracted to purchase a quantity of bristles from an Indian firm. As partial fulfilment of that contract the plaintiff arranged with the defendant to open an irrevocable letter of credit in favour of the Indian sellers. The complaint alleged that the seller filled some 50 crates with cow-hair and other worthless material with an intent to defraud the plaintiff.

The plaintiff was seeking a declaration that the letter of credit was void and an injunction preventing the defendant banking corporation from paying pursuant to the letter of credit. It is fundamental to the understanding of the case to recognise that it came before the court under a motion for dismissal filed by the defendant and that the procedure called for the court to assume that the facts alleged, in particular the fraud, had been proved by the plaintiff.

The court held that the plaintiff would, under those assumptions, be entitled to injunctive relief. It emphasised that this was under the assumption of fraud, that the bill of exchange which would be presented for payment under the letter of credit was still in the hands of the seller, the bank had been given notice of the fraud and the banker was willing to postpone payment pending an adjudication of the rights and obligations of the other parties.

Since the qualifications mentioned by the court are often overlooked, it is worth reflecting on the very clear words of Shientag J (at 635):

> If it had appeared from the face of the complaint that the bank presenting the draft for payment was a holder in due course, its claim against the bank issuing the letter of credit would not be defeated even though the primary transaction was tainted with fraud.

[12.56] The English court considered the *Sztejn* case in *Discount Records Ltd v Barclays Bank* [1975] 1 Lloyd's Rep 444; discussed above at [12.52]. It is worth noting that the court found insufficient evidence of fraud in the *Discount Records* case to justify an application of the fraud exception. Given the facts of that case, it is difficult to see how extrinsic, that is, non-documentary, fraud could be shown. Also note that the court considered it very relevant that the bill of exchange might be in the hands of a holder in due course.

[12.57] The scope of the fraud rule has received clarification by the House of Lords in *United City Merchants v Royal Bank of Canada* [1983] AC 168;

[1982] All ER 780. The second plaintiff was an English company which sold manufacturing equipment to a Peruvian company. There was an agreement between them to double the invoice price as a means of circumventing Peruvian exchange control regulations, the excess to be deposited in an American bank on behalf of the Peruvian company. A Peruvian bank issued a letter of credit to cover the transaction and the defendant bank confirmed. The rights under the credit were assigned to the first plaintiff.

The credit expired on December 15, 1976 and shipment of the goods was not accomplished until the day after. The court found that there was fraud in that an employee of the loading brokers had improperly dated the bill of lading in order to make it appear that loading was timely. However, the employee was not acting on behalf of the plaintiff beneficiary of the letter of credit.

When the documents were presented to the Royal Bank of Canada, the confirming bank, for payment, it came to the attention of the bankers that the ship had not in fact arrived in port on the day on which the bill of lading was dated. It was clear to the bank that the bill of lading was defective and that there was some fraud which resulted at least in a false date appearing in the documentation. It is a contractual term of a CIF contract that the seller present the buyer with correct shipping documents, so that the seller was in breach of the CIF obligations even though there was no fault on the part of the seller.

The bank refused to pay, claiming the fraud exception. There were further complications due to the conspiracy to avoid the Peruvian exchange control regulations, but those are separate to the issues in the fraud part of the case. The House of Lords held that the bank was obliged to pay. It is worth quoting Lord Diplock at some length:

> If, on their face, the documents presented to the confirming bank by the seller conform with the requirements of the credit as notified to him by the confirming bank, that bank is under a contractual obligation to the seller to honour the credit, notwithstanding that the bank has knowledge that the seller at the time of presentation of the conforming documents is alleged by the buyer to have, and in fact has already, committed a breach of his contract with the buyer for the sale of the goods to which the documents appear on their face to relate, that would have entitled the buyer to treat the contract of sale as rescinded and to reject the goods and refuse to pay the seller the purchase price. The whole commercial purpose for which the system of confirmed irrevocable documentary credits has been developed in international trade is to give to the seller an assured right to be paid before he parts with control of the goods that does not permit of any dispute with the buyer as to the performance of the contract of sale being used as a ground for non-payment or reduction or deferment of payment.

To this general statement of principle as to the contractual obligations of the confirming bank to the seller, there is one established exception: that is, where the seller, for the purpose of drawing on the credit, fraudulently presents to the confirming bank documents that contain, expressly or by implication, material representations of fact that to his or her knowledge are untrue. Although there does not appear among the English authorities any case in which this exception has been applied, it is well established in the American cases of which the leading or 'landmark' case is *Sztejn v J Henry Schroder Banking Corporation* (1941) 31 NYS 2d 631. This judgment of the New York Court of Appeals was referred to with approval by the English Court of Appeal in *Edward Owen Engineering Ltd v Barclays Bank International Ltd* [1978] QB 159.

It seems likely that the 'one established exception' may be somewhat too narrowly stated in the *United City Merchants* case. It is generally thought that there must be fraud on the part of the beneficiary in order to come within the exception, and that fraud may not necessarily be limited to statements in the documents required to be presented under the terms of the credit, although no doubt some consequence of the fraud will appear there.

[12.58] In Australia the concept of fraud may be somewhat wider. In *Hortico (Australia) Pty Ltd v Energy Equipment Co (Australia) Pty Ltd* (1985) 1 NSWLR 545 the Commonwealth Bank issued a first demand performance guarantee in favour of Hortico to secure the supplier's obligation. Hortico made a demand on the bond and the supplier applied for an injunction to prevent payment. In the course of his judgment, Young J considered that the equitable doctrine of 'fraud on a power' might apply. He added that (at 554):

> ... with commercial transactions such as the present, the courts have consist-
> ently taken a 'hands off' approach, and it does not seem to me that anything
> short of actual fraud would warrant this Court in intervening, though it may
> be that in some cases (not this one), the unconscionable conduct may be so
> gross as to lead to exercise of the discretionary power.

[12.59] The rule as to presentation of documents known to be false may also be wider than that proposed by *United City Merchants*. In *Contronic Distributors Pty Ltd v Bank of New South Wales* [1984] 3 NSWLR 110 it was held that the beneficiary of a commercial letter of credit may be restrained from presenting the letter of credit for payment or having payment made against it where the documents which are needed to require payment are to its knowledge false.

Further, it is not just the account party who has the right to seek such an injunction. Both the bank issuing a letter of credit and any person who will suffer the loss in the event of payment against false documents may restrain payment against the letter of credit.

[12.60] A restraining injunction will not be given merely because the documents do not conform to the known facts. In *Inflatable Toy Co Pty Ltd v State Bank of New South Wales* [1994] 34 NSWLR 243 it was noted that commercial people often are 'not fussed' when documents indicate a state of affairs which is contrary to what is actually happening. The injunction will only be granted when the court is convinced that there is a particularly strong prima facie case of fraud.

The problem of fraud or forgery by the beneficiary or by some other person in the transaction is far from solved. The American trend seems to indicate a greater willingness to grant injunctions when there is evidence of fraud. Since the law of documentary credits should be kept uniform throughout the world, we can hope to see some better treatment of the subject in the next revision of the UCP.

THE EFFECT OF THE TRADE PRACTICES ACT

[12.61]   The account party applied for an injunction to prevent the beneficiary from drawing on performance bonds in *Olex Focas Pty Ltd v Skodaexport Co Ltd* [1996] 70 ALJR 983. There were two classes of bonds. The first were referred to by Batt J as performance bonds, the second as 'mobilisation/procurement' guarantees. The mobilisation guarantees were with respect to advances made to the account party.

The account party sought injunctions on the grounds of fraud and, more interestingly, on the grounds that drawing on the bonds would be 'unconscionable' within the meaning of s 51AA of the Trade Practices Act 1974.

Batt J considered that there were no grounds for granting the injunction at common law. He noted that there were only three circumstances in which a documentary credit would be restrained. These are (1) when there is a clear case of fraud of which the bank is aware at (probably) the time of payment; (2) where the documents are forged; and (3) possibly where the underlying contract is illegal. Batt J was of the view that the principles of restraining performance bonds were the same as those relating to letters of credit, noting that the case of forged documents is unlikely to be relevant to the performance bond.

As to the question of 'unconscionability', Batt J considered that there was no reason to restrain the beneficiary with respect to the first class of bond. He noted that calling on performance bonds with a view to exerting commercial pressure on the account party was not, of itself, unconscionable: see *Wood Hall Ltd v Pipeline Authority* (1979) 141 CLR 443 where the High Court upheld a right to demand even though work was nearly finished and the avowed purpose was to exert pressure to force the account party into a more favourable settlement of the dispute. See also *Burleigh Forest Estate Management Pty Ltd v Cigna Insurance Australia Ltd* [1992] 2 Qd R 54.

However, Batt J was of the view that the Trade Practices Act 1974 made 'substantial inroad' into the law of letters of credit and performance bonds. He noted that acting within one's strict legal rights might be 'unconscionable' for the purposes of s 51AA: *Stern v McArthur* (1988) 165 CLR 489.

The factual peculiarity of the 'mobilisation' bonds were that 90 per cent of the advances guaranteed had already been repaid. The guarantees were with respect to these advances only, and the beneficiary's interest could have been protected by a partial demand or by a full demand under only one of the guarantees.

Under these somewhat special circumstances, Batt J was willing, reluctantly it must be said, to grant an injunction pending a hearing by the Court of Appeal. The injunction was only to the extent that the advances had already been repaid, so that the beneficiary was free to call upon the bonds for the amounts that had not been repaid.

The Court of Appeal refused to extend the injunctions to the other performance bonds. The beneficiaries gave an undertaking that they would not call upon the mobilisation guarantees beyond the amount of the advances outstanding. A request by the account party that undertakings be required with respect to the proceeds of any demand was refused. Charles JA noted that in his view, the only circumstances in which an injunction was justified at common law was where the demand was clearly fraudulent, citing *Bolivantar Oil SA v Chase Manhattan Bank* [1984] 1 Lloyd's Rep 251.

It remains to be seen if there are other circumstances in which the courts will find that it is 'unconscionable' to draw against a performance bond. The factual circumstances in *Skodaexport* were unusual in that it was easy to determine that the purpose of the bonds could be fulfilled while still granting a partial injunction. It would be unlikely that a court will find drawing to be 'unconscionable' where the fulfilment of purpose is not so clearly demonstrable.

FORGED DOCUMENTS

[12.62]   It is important to understand that a bank which pays against inaccurate or forged documents is still entitled to reimbursement provided only that the documents appear on their face to be in accordance with the terms of the credit. Put another way, the banks do not warrant that the documents are genuine. The UCP goes further, providing that banks assume no liability for the form, sufficiency, accuracy, genuineness, falsification or legal effect of any document: Art 15.

Even in the absence of the express terms of the UCP, courts had held that a person tendering documents does not warrant their authenticity nor does tendering documents amount to a representation that they are genuine: see, for example, *Guaranty Trust Co of New York v Hannay & Co* [1918] 2 KB 623.

THE PARTIES

[12.63]   Many of the legal problems associated with documentary credits arise because of the multiplicity of parties, their contractual relationships and the interaction of the credit with these other contracts. It might be that these problems should be analysed within a multilateral theory of contracts. We have no such theory in the common law world; we are restricted to analysis by means of our bilateral theory of contract.

THE BUYER AND SELLER

[12.64]   The buyer who is obliged under a contract of sale to arrange for the opening of a credit in favour of a seller must do so a reasonable period of time before the beginning of the period allowed for shipment under the contract of sale. It is clear that the seller is entitled to ship at any time during the contractual period and the credit must be available early enough that shipping arrangements may be made with confidence that the payment by credit will be made: *Pavia & Co SPA v Thurmann-Nielsen* [1952] 2 QB 84. Consequently, in a CIF contract, it is not sufficient for the buyer to open the credit at some time during the contractual shipment period since the seller, who is responsible for making the shipping arrangements, must be given a reasonable period of time in which to make shipping arrangements. What is reasonable will, of course, depend upon the facts of the particular contract.

It might be thought that different considerations would apply in an FOB contract since it is the buyer who is obliged to make the shipping arrangements. However, the English Court of Appeal has held that the same rule applies: *Sinason-Teicher Inter-American Grain Corporation v Oil Cakes and Oilseeds Trading Co Ltd* [1954] 1 WLR 1394.

[12.65] When the buyer-seller contract calls for the opening of a credit, it is with the expectation that the seller will receive payment from the nominated bank. That is indeed the usual course of events, but from a legal point of view we must ask if the opening of the letter itself is sufficient to satisfy the payment obligation of the buyer or if it has some other effect.

The contract between the buyer and the seller may completely specify the method by which the buyer is to discharge the payment obligation, but more often it is remarkably silent on the issue. Of course, the contract may call for the buyer to open a credit in favour of the seller, but the parties seldom contemplate the effect of opening the credit if the course of the transaction does not proceed as contemplated. What happens, for example, if the issuing bank becomes insolvent? Is the buyer entitled to present the documents directly to the seller, even if the credit is still on foot? What happens if the bank wrongly refuses to pay?

Some of these questions may be answered on general principles. It seems that when the contract calls for the opening of a credit, then the seller must evidently attempt to be paid under the credit. Only if that attempt fails would he or she be justified in attempting to present the documents directly to the buyer: *Soproma SpA v Marine & Animal By Products Corporation* [1966] 1 Lloyd's Rep 367.

But there have been arguments raised to the effect that the mere opening of the credit in conformity with the contract of sale is itself complete payment. If the credit fails, then that is the seller's bad luck; having been paid for, the goods must now be delivered.

[12.66] This view received some support from the High Court of Australia in *Saffron v Societe Miniere Cafrika* (1958) 100 CLR 231. The seller had tendered documents which were not in conformity with the credit and payment was refused. Ordinarily, as mentioned above, this would leave the seller in control of the goods, but in the *Saffron* case the buyer achieved control of the goods, then claiming that payment had been made by virtue of the credit being opened. The court said (at 244):

> It would ... be wrong to consider the question without regard to the kind of letter of credit for which the contract provides. A provision for payment by revocable letter of credit could hardly be regarded in any circumstances as negativing payment in the event of revocation. At the other end of the scale a provision for payment by irrevocable and confirmed letter of credit ... might perhaps not unreasonably be regarded as a stipulation for the liability of the confirming bank in place of that of the buyer. Where the stipulation is for an irrevocable but not confirmed credit there would be less reason for regarding the provision of the credit as being all that is required by the buyer in any circumstances.

[12.67] Of course, it is perfectly possible for the seller to contract that the buyer's obligation is extinguished by the mere opening of the credit, but the consequences are so serious for the seller that it does not seem reasonable to infer the result merely from the fact that the seller has requested that the credit be confirmed even when the seller names the confirming bank. The reason for such a term is not to relieve the buyer of all liability, but rather to avoid problems by having a reliable paymaster who is located in the country of the seller. This is the view that was taken by the English Court of Appeal in *W J Alan & Co Ltd v El Nasr Export and Import Co* [1972] QB 189. The court approved the statement of the trial judge (Orr J [1971] 1 Lloyd's Rep 401) who said that it seems:

> wrong that the primary obligation of the buyer to pay the price should be treated as extinguished unless there is some clear indication that both parties so intended and it seems to me that the provision for payment by way of letter of credit which is an arrangement not for the benefit of the seller alone, but of both parties, falls far short of any such indication, and as far as authority goes, I think that on the whole the balance of such authority as there is favours the same view.

[12.68] These questions have been reformulated by Lord Denning in terms of whether the credit is absolute payment, conditional payment, or no payment at all. The consequences of each are as follows (*W J Alan & Co Ltd v El Nasr Export and Import Co* [1972] 2 QB 189 at 209 and 210):

> If the letter of credit is absolute payment of the price, the consequences are these: The seller can only look to the banker for payment. He can in no circumstances look to the buyer. The seller must present the documents to the banker and get payment from him in cash or get him to accept sight or time drafts. If the banker does not take up the documents, the seller will retain them, resell and sue the banker for damages. If the banker takes up the documents in exchange for time drafts, and the banker afterwards becomes insolvent, the seller must prove in the liquidation. He cannot sue the buyer ...
>
> If the letter of credit is conditional payment of the price, the consequences are these: the seller looks in the first instance to the banker for payment; but, if the banker does not meet his obligations when the time comes for him to do so, the seller can have recourse to the buyer. The seller must present the documents to the banker ... It may mean that the buyer (if he has already paid the

bank) will have to pay twice over. So be it. He ought to have made sure that he employed a 'reliable and solvent paymaster' ...

If the letter of credit is no payment at all, but only a means by which payment may be obtained ... the consequences are these: the seller ought to present the documents to the banker. If he does not do so, he will be guilty of laches in enforcing his security and the buyer will be discharged ... But if on the presentation the banker fails or refuses to take up the documents then ... the seller will be entitled to take the documents round to the buyer ... and demand that he takes them up and pay the price ...

As a result of this analysis, I am of the opinion that ... [the letter of credit] operates as conditional payment of the price.

THE BUYER AND ISSUING BANKER

[12.69]   When the account party instructs his or her banker to open a credit, there will usually be an express undertaking in the application that the account party will put the banker in funds to meet the obligations under the credit, but even if there is no express clause there is an implied undertaking to the same effect. In any case, the matter is put beyond doubt by Art 18(c) which holds an instructing party liable for any charges incurred by the instructed party in the course of carrying out the instructions. In the event that the credit stipulates that charges are for the account of some third party, the applicant acts as a guarantor in that if the charges cannot be collected the applicant is liable for them: Art 18(c)(ii).

There is a conflict of views as to the rights of the account party who has placed the banker in funds to meet a credit. On the one hand, it is clear that the banker must use the funds for the purpose of meeting the credit and no other: *Farley v Turner* (1857) 26 LJ Ch 710. On the other hand, there is an old case which has held that the account party has only a right to prove in the bankruptcy or liquidation in the event that the banker fails before the funds have been so applied: *Re Barned's Banking Co; Massey's case* (1870) 39 LJ Ch 635. It may be that the effect of more recent decisions such as *Barclays Bank Ltd v Quistclose Investments Ltd* [1970] AC 567 would have the effect of giving the account party a proprietary right in the funds: see [3.11].

[12.70]   The articles of the UCP which regulate the relationships between the account party and the issuing bank absolve the bank from most responsibility. There is an obligation on the bank to examine the documents with reasonable care to see that they appear on their face to be in accordance with the terms and conditions of the credit but the banker assumes no responsibility for the 'form, sufficiency, accuracy, genuineness, falsification or legal effect' of any of the documents: see Art 15. These limitations on liability are reasonable when it is recalled that the banker is not expected, indeed not entitled, to go behind the documents.

The remaining articles which exempt the bank from liability are rather less understandable, for the banker assumes no liability for matters which are solely within the control of the banker, yet which are disastrous for the account party in the event that the banker performs his or her duty negligently. Thus, Art 16:

> Banks assume no liability or responsibility for the consequences arising out of delay and/or loss in transit of any messages, letters or documents, or for delay, mutilation or other errors arising in the transmission of any telecommunication. Banks assume no liability or responsibility for errors in translation or interpretation of technical terms, and reserve the right to transmit credit terms without translating them.

Article 17 exempts bankers from any liability due to disruptions by any cause beyond their control, including acts of God, riots, civil commotions, insurrections, wars, strikes and lockouts. Further, if the credit has expired during any of these disruptions the bank will not, in the absence of specific instructions, operate the credit upon the resumption of business: Art 17.

Whenever a bank utilises the services of another bank it does so for the account and at the risk of the account party: Art 18(a). Even if the instructing bank has chosen the instructed bank (as is usually the case) the instructing bank assumes no liability or responsibility if there is any failure to carry out their instructions: Art 18(b).

TELETRANSMITTED ADVICE

[12.71] At one time, it was common to advise credits by cable. Much more common today is the telex advice and various forms of 'electronic mail' are beginning to be used. Article 12 of the 1983 Revision addressed the problem, but it was clear that the section contemplated that the 'normal' case would be that the 'real' credit would be advised by mail and that the electronic advice was merely an early indication that the credit would be issued.

Article 11 of the 1993 Revision, while still permitting 'early warning' electronic messages, clearly assumes that the electronic message may be the primary, indeed the only, form of advice. Thus, provided the issuing bank instructs the advising bank by an authenticated teletransmission, the teletransmission is deemed to be the operative credit instrument. No mail confirmation should be sent, and if there is a later mail confirmation it is inoperative. The term 'authenticated teletransmission' is not defined in the UCP, but doubtless would include answerback telex systems, SWIFT messages and other forms of electronic communications which provide some assurance that both the sender and the receiver are who they purport to be.

If the ordinary mail message is to be the operative credit, then the issuing bank may include in the teletransmission words such as 'full details to follow' or, better, state that the later mail message is to be the operative credit. In such a case, the presumption of Art 11(i) that the teletransmission is the operative credit is rebutted: Art 11(ii).

A bank must be careful in giving these 'pre-advice' instructions. A pre-advice of an irrevocable credit must only be given if the bank is prepared to issue the operative credit. Unless explicitly stated in the pre-advice, the issuing bank is irrevocably committed to issue without delay a credit in terms which are not inconsistent with the pre-advice: Art 11(c).

THE ADVISING BANK

[12.72]   The relationship between the issuing bank and the intermediary bank depends to some extent upon what it is that the intermediary is called upon to do. However, in the absence of any express agreement to the contrary, it seems that the relationship is one of principal and agent. Consequently, if the intermediary has complied with the instructions given to it by the issuing bank, then it is entitled to reimbursement of any payments properly made by it.

When the intermediary is a nominated bank which pays or negotiates the drafts of the beneficiary, it will ordinarily be acting as the agent of the issuing banker. Provided that the payment or negotiation is in complete conformity with the conditions of the credit, the intermediary will be entitled not only to reimbursement, but to the indemnity of an agent. Care must be taken here, however, for there can arise situations where it will be held that the intermediary bank is acting outside the terms of the credit: see [12.75]ff.

[12.73]   It is not uncommon for the issuing bank to request the intermediary bank to claim reimbursement from a third bank. The UCP regulates the situation in some detail: Art 19. The intermediary is referred to as the 'claiming bank' and the third party bank which is to provide payment is the 'reimbursing bank'. The issuing bank is under an obligation to provide the reimbursing bank 'in good time' with instructions and authorisation to honour the claim. The issuing bank is not, of course, relieved of liability if the reimbursing bank fails to provide reimbursement, and it is obliged to pay interest to the claiming bank if the reimbursement is delayed: Arts 19(c), (d).

Interestingly, the UCP forbids the issuing bank from demanding that a claiming bank supply a certificate of compliance with the terms and conditions of the credit when claiming from the reimbursing bank: Art 19(c).

[12.74]   The beneficiary will generally have no rights to force the intermediary nominated bank to fulfil any of its obligations unless the intermediary has become a confirming bank. Aside from the common law position of want of privity, the UCP provides in Art 3(b) that the beneficiary can never avail himself or herself of the contractual relationships which exist between banks or between the account party and the issuing bank.

There is, of course a direct contract (the credit itself) between the issuing bank and the beneficiary, but the issuing bank will, in an ordinary international sale of goods, be located in another country. This is one of the main reasons why beneficiaries desire confirmation from a local bank.

[12.75]   If the local bank is only an advising bank, it is necessary for the banker to take some care in dealing with the letter of credit. In *Aotearoa International v Westpac Banking Corporation* [1984] 2 NZLR 34 Aotearoa was the beneficiary of a letter of credit which had been issued by an overseas bank.

The local Westpac bank acted as an advising bank only; the letter was not confirmed. The letter of credit, which incorporated the terms of the UCP, called for the usual shipping documents and for a bill of exchange drawn on the issuing bank by the beneficiary.

The parties had a rather unusual procedure which was customarily followed in these letter of credit transactions. The beneficiary would sign, as drawer, a blank form of a bill of exchange and leave it with the bank to be filled up when the precise figures were available. That procedure was followed on this occasion, but during the filling up of the form, a typing error was made. The form was destroyed and a new form was completed and 'signed' by one of the bank officials per pro the name of the beneficiary.

The completed form was presented, together with the rest of the shipping documents, for payment under the letter of credit, but due to deficiencies in the documentation, payment was refused by the issuing bank. In the meantime, the advising bank had credited the account of the beneficiary, imposing no conditions on the crediting of the account. In the words of the court, the bank 'negotiated' the letter of credit.

The advising bank claimed to be able to recover from the beneficiary, either as a holder of the bill of exchange or by virtue of a general right of recourse which, it was said, an advising bank has against the beneficiary when the letter of credit is 'negotiated' in the manner described here.

Although the bank clearly had the authority to fill in the original form of the bill of exchange, there was no authority to sign a new form even though it was filled up in the same way that the old one should have been. Consequently, the beneficiary was not liable on the bill as their signature had been placed there without their authority.

[12.76]   As to the general right of recourse, the court held that there was no such right. In the course of the judgment, Tompkins J said (at 50):

> It is my conclusion that in the absence of a valid bill or any contractual agreement whereby the plaintiff agreed to indemnify the first defendant, the first defendant has no right of recourse against the plaintiff arising from the first defendant having negotiated the letter of credit when the United Commercial Bank as the issuing bank has failed to pay.

The lesson for advising bankers is very clear. When crediting funds under a credit in which the bank is acting as an advising bank only, it should be made clear that it is a conditional credit and that the letter is not being 'negotiated'. It will not always be sensible to rely upon the bill of exchange, for some letters of credit do not call for a bill and the customer will usually draw the bill 'without recourse' in any event.

THE CONFIRMING BANK

[12.77]   Surprisingly, there seems to be no judicial consideration of the extent of the liability of a bank which confirms the issuing bank's credit. Most authors indicate that the matter will depend upon the precise wording used, but there seems agreement that in the absence of very clear wording to the contrary, there is no guarantee of the issuing bank's obligations: J Paget, *Law of Banking*, 9th ed, Butterworths, London, 1982, p 546 (the matter does not appear to be discussed in later editions); Gutteridge and Megrah, op cit, p 82. So, for example, if the beneficiary chose to tender documents directly to the issuing bank and that bank were to fail before making actual payment, then the beneficiary could not look to the confirming bank since the beneficiary would no longer have control of the documents. On the other hand, it is clear that there is a direct undertaking by the confirming bank to the beneficiary which is similar in terms to the undertaking of the issuing bank: Art 9(b).

Some credits call for time drafts to be drawn by the beneficiary seller on the buyer. It is sometimes argued that the bank's responsibility ends when the buyer/applicant has accepted the draft, an argument which has been generally discredited: Gutteridge and Megrah, op cit, p 23. The 1993 Revision makes the point that credits should not be issued available by drafts on the applicant, but that if the credit does so provide the banks will consider the drafts as additional documents: Arts 9(a)(iv), 9(b)(iv).

A recent case on the responsibility of a confirming bank has discredited a similar argument, namely that the confirming bank's responsibility to the beneficiary does not arise if the buyer refuses to accept the draft.

[12.78]   In *Forestal Mimosa Ltd v Oriental Credit Ltd* [1986] 2 All ER 400 the defendant was a confirming bank of a letter of credit which contained a marginal note incorporating the UCP as part of the terms of the contract. The buyers refused to accept bills drawn upon them and the defendant bank claimed that they were only liable if the buyers in fact accepted the bills. If the terms of the credit were read without reference to the UCP, then this would be a reasonable construction, in spite of the fact that such a construction would nullify the usual commercial effects of a credit, since it would mean that the buyers could unilaterally render the credit ineffective.

At first instance the court held that the defendant bank was justified in not paying. In reaching this conclusion, the court approached the construction of the credit by ignoring the UCP; if the terms interpreted in such a fashion could solve the problem at hand, then there would be no need to resort to the UCP. In other words, the UCP was only to be consulted for the purpose of filling in any gaps which might remain.

The Court of Appeal held that this was the incorrect approach. The terms of the UCP must rank equally with the other express terms of the credit. It might be that if there was a conflict then the express terms of the credit might prevail, but the terms were to be construed so as to prevent such a contradiction if at all possible. The court held that it was possible to read the credit in such a fashion and that in so doing, it was clear that Art 10(b)(iii) of the 1983 Revision placed responsibility on the bank. That Article reads:

> When an issuing bank authorises or requests another bank to confirm its irrevocable credit and the latter has added its confirmation, such confirmation constitutes a definite undertaking of such bank (the confirming bank), in

addition to that of the issuing bank, provided that the stipulated documents are presented and that the terms and conditions of the credit are complied with: (iii) if the credit provides for acceptance—to accept drafts drawn by the beneficiary if the credit stipulates that they are to be drawn on the confirming bank, or to be responsible for their acceptance and payment at maturity if the credit stipulates that they are to be drawn on the applicant for the credit or any other drawee stipulated in the credit.

The defendant bank also argued that there were discrepancies in the documents which were serious enough to cast doubts on their authenticity, but the court held that there was no substance to the argument. As noted above, the interpretation argued by the bank would have had the effect of rendering the credit of little commercial value.

OBLIGATION OF THE INSPECTING BANK

[12.79]   We have already noted the duty of the bank to examine documents with reasonable care. The UCP provides that banks must examine stipulated documents with 'reasonable care' to ascertain whether they appear, on their face, to comply with the requirements of the credit: Art 13(a). The standard is that of international banking practice as reflected in the UCP: Art 13(a).

The question of the extent to which a banker must examine the documents has arisen on several occasions. Perhaps the strongest statement on the matter is by Scrutton LJ in *National Bank of Egypt v Hannevig's Bank* (1919) 3 LDAB 213:

> ... to assume that ... a bank is bound carefully to read through all bills of lading presented to it in ridiculously minute type and full of exceptions, to read through the policies and to exercise a judgment as to whether the legal effect of the bill of lading and the policy is, on the whole, favourable to their clients, is an obligation which I should require to investigate considerably before I accepted it in that unhesitating form.

When the documents are rejected as not being in conformity with the terms of the credit, there is nothing to stop the beneficiary from attempting to rectify the documentary deficiency and presenting the documents again. This might be the case, for example, if the deficiency was merely an oversight in obtaining a certificate of quality. Again, it may be possible to get the issuer of an offending document to reissue the document in a form which complies with the terms of the credit. All such activity requires time, however, and it may be that the resubmission of the documents cannot be made within the time before the credit expires.

[12.80]   It has occasionally been alleged that the bank owes a duty to the beneficiary to discover all defects in the documents at the time of the first presentation, thus giving the beneficiary the optimum chance of correcting the deficiencies in time. The legal form of this argument is that the bank is estopped from raising new reasons for rejection after it has rejected the documents for some other reason. The argument was rejected firmly in *Skandinaviska Aktiebolaget v Barclays Bank Ltd* (1925) 22 Ll L Rep 523 at 525:

It is suggested ... by the plaintiff ... that they have a grievance because the defendant bank did not in the first instance raise the objections that are now raised to the documents, but referred the matter to their customer in Hull and simply sent forward the customer's complaints, which were not in the first instance based upon the documents, but which were based on some untenable contention which he put forward; and it is suggested that by that means the defendants had either by estoppel or waiver, by some rule of law applicable in this country, deprived themselves of the right that they would otherwise have had of resisting the claim. I am clearly of the opinion they have not done so. They were in an intermediate position. They had the usual feelings of banking courtesy towards the foreign bank with whom they had had dealings for a long time, and they desired, and the intention was, to see whether, notwithstanding those objections which were being raised by the customer, the transaction could not be carried through as it ought to have been. I do not think that by doing that and by leaving unstated until the later stage the valid objections— valid in law—to the documents which had been taken by the plaintiff bank, English law can deprive them of any right whatsoever.

If the issuing, confirming or nominated bank decides to reject the documents, then there is an obligation on the bank to notify the bank from which the documents were received or the beneficiary promptly in accordance with Art 14(d). The notice must identify all discrepancies in respect of which the bank has refused the documents, and must also state whether it is holding the documents at the disposal of the presenter or is returning them to the presenter: Art 14(d)(ii). Failure to do so may result in the bank being precluded from rejecting the documents: Art 14(e).

ACCEPTANCE OF DOCUMENTS 'UNDER RESERVE'

[12.81]   There are circumstances where the banker to whom the documents are presented believes that the documents do not strictly comply with the terms of the credit. In such a circumstance, the banker could reject the documents, but if the buyer and seller are known to each other or if one or the other has a particularly good relationship with the banker, it might be that the parties would wish for the deal to go ahead in spite of the discrepancies.

The solution that is often adopted is that the banker will accept the documents 'under reserve', forward them to the issuing bank who will in turn consult with their customer concerning the acceptability of the documents. If the seller is known to the intermediary banker, payment may well be made, again, 'under reserve'. Until recently, the words 'under reserve' had not been sufficiently tested in the courts for their legal meaning to be certain.

[12.82]   The court in *Banque de l'Indochine et de Suez SA v J H Rayner (Mincing Lane) Ltd* [1982] 2 Lloyd's Rep 476 was faced with precisely this problem. It was found by the court that the remitting bank genuinely believed that there were discrepancies in the documents which would have justified nonpayment, the beneficiary genuinely believed that the bank was wrong and that payment should have been made, and both parties hoped that notwithstanding the alleged discrepancies the issuing bank would, with the concurrence of the account party, take up the documents and reimburse the intermediary bank. The intermediary bank made the payment to the benefici-ary 'under reserve'.

At first instance Parker J summed up the two possible interpretations of the phrase, at 479:

> The question which arises appears to me to be 'did the parties, in such circum-stances, by paying and accepting under reserve intend that the bank should be entitled to repayment notwithstanding that it was in law obliged to pay when it did; or was it merely intended that the position of the bank should be pro-tected to the extent that the customer should not thereafter be entitled to resist a demand for repayment on the ground that the payment was unqualified and that he was therefore entitled to retain the payment even if one or more of the irregularities was in law valid.'

Parker J thought that the correct interpretation was the first, but the Court of Appeal reversed the decision: [1983] 1 Lloyd's Rep 228. According to Kerr LJ, 'under reserve' meant (at 234):

> ... that payment was to be made under reserve in the sense that the beneficiary would be bound to repay the money on demand if the issuing bank should reject the documents, whether on its own initiative or on the buyer's instructions.

Of course, if the intermediary bank was under a contractual obligation, then the beneficiary has rights against the bank for a breach of contract. How-ever, a right of suit against the bank is very much less valuable than being able to retain the payment.

The 1993 Revision incorporates these procedures. Article 14(f) provides that the 'remitting bank' may notify the issuing or confirming bank that it has operated the credit 'under reserve' or against an indemnity in respect of cer-tain indemnities. In such a case, the issuing and/or confirming bank remain under their obligations as provided by the UCP, and the reserve or indemnity is a matter solely between the remitting bank and the party which presented the discrepant documents: Art 14(f).

THE DOCUMENTS

[12.83]   One of the most fundamental concepts in the law of documentary credits is that the parties deal only in documents, not in goods or whatever the underlying transaction is about. This principle is enshrined in the UCP:

> Article 4 In credit operations all parties concerned deal with documents, and not with goods, services and/or other performances to which the documents may relate.

THE PRINCIPLE OF STRICT COMPLIANCE

[12.84]   Since the parties are dealing in documents, and since the obliga-tion of the bank to pay only arises 'provided that the stipulated documents are presented and that the terms and conditions of the credit are complied with', there are bound to be questions concerning the meaning of 'stipulated docu-ments' and of when there is 'compliance': see Art 9 UCP.

It is clear that both terms relate only to conditions which are actually embodied in the credit and that no external factors will be considered. So, for example, in one case it was the custom of a bank to send a standard memorandum to all beneficiaries of credits which had been opened by the bank; the court held that the contents of the memorandum were not part of the credit and could not be used to impose conditions on the beneficiary: *Banque de l'Indochine et de Suez SA v J H Rayner (Mincing Lane) Ltd* [1982] 2 Lloyd's Rep 476. Of course, if the credit itself contained a clause which incorporated the memorandum as part of its terms, then the result would be different.

The UCP calls for banks to examine stipulated documents with 'reasonable care' to determine compliance: Art 13. The article elaborates by indicating that the standard is that of international banking practice as reflected in the UCP.

[12.85]   The view of the courts concerning the tender of documents is illustrated by Donaldson J in *Golodetz & Co Inc v Czarnikow-Rionda Co Inc; the Galatia* [1979] 2 Lloyd's Rep 450 at 451:

> A tender of documents which, properly read and understood, calls for further inquiry or are such as to invite litigation is clearly a bad tender. But the operative words are 'properly read and understood'. I fully accept that the clause on this bill of lading makes it unusual, but properly read and understood it calls for no inquiry and it casts no doubt at all upon the fact that the goods were shipped in apparent good order and condition or upon the protection which anyone is entitled to expect when taking up such a document whether as a purchaser or as a lender on the security of the bill.

Perhaps more clearly and succinctly, in *Hansson v Hamel and Horley Ltd* [1922] 2 AC 36 Lord Sumner said (at 46):

> These documents have to be handled by banks; they have to be taken up or rejected promptly and without any opportunity for prolonged inquiry; they have to be such as can be re-tendered to sub-purchasers, and it is essential that they should so conform to the accustomed shipping documents as to be reasonably and readily fit to pass current in commerce.

[12.86]   The kind of difficulties which might arise when the parties depart from the 'dealing in documents' principle are illustrated in *Banque de l'Indochine et de Suez SA v J H Rayner (Mincing Lane) Ltd* [1982] 2 Lloyd's Rep 476. The credit called for the goods to be shipped on a conference line vessel. Note that this is quite different from calling for tender of a document which states that the goods are shipped on a conference line vessel. The defendants claimed that since no document was called for, the statement could be ignored. Both Parker J and the Court of Appeal rejected this argument, instead holding that the statement meant what it clearly did not say, namely that some documentary evidence must be tendered as part of the documentation which would attest to the fact that the carrying ship was a conference line vessel.

The 1993 Revision has a different solution to the problem encountered in the *Rayner* case: if a credit contains any condition without stating the documents to be presented, the condition is to be deemed as not stated and banks are instructed to ignore it: Art 13(c). This seems a less acceptable solution than that arrived at by the Court of Appeal since an oversight could lead to a major condition of the credit to be incorrectly stated. The *Rayner* decision would give effect to the real intent of the parties while the UCP gives effect to the minor oversight.

GENERAL CONTENT AND ORIGINALITY

[12.87]   The introduction of electronic communications technology has blurred the meaning of familiar concepts like 'original document'. If a document is first prepared on a computer then printed out on an adjacent printer, most people would say that the printed copy is the original. If the printer is located in a different place it seems that nothing important has changed, and the document would still be 'original'. What if the electronic 'document' is sent to a distant computer before the document is printed? Why should it make any difference if the document is printed more than once? What about faxed documents?

The UCP approaches these problems in the way that one would expect: let the document speak for itself. Article 20(b) authorises banks to accept, in the absence of any indication in the credit to the contrary, documents which have been produced (or appear to have been reproduced) by reprographic, automated or computerised systems or as carbon copies provided only that the document tendered is marked original and, where necessary, appears to be signed.

Further, a 'signature' may be affixed by handwriting, by facsimile signature, by perforated signature, by stamp, by symbol, or by any other mechanical or electronic method of authentication: Art 20(b). Similarly, if the credit calls for the document to be authenticated, validated, legalised, visaed, certified or any other condition which indicates a similar requirement, the condition will be satisfied by any signature, mark, stamp or label that appears on its face to satisfy the condition: Art 20(d).

DOCUMENTARY DESCRIPTION OF THE GOODS

[12.88]   A credit which is being used to facilitate an international sale of goods will call for a description of the goods in various documents. In virtually all cases, a commercial invoice will be required and there may be other documents which contain descriptions of more or less generality of the goods.

The UCP has relatively little to say about the description of the goods. Article 41(c) provides:

> The description of the goods in the commercial invoice must correspond with the description in the credit. In all other documents, the goods may be described in general terms not inconsistent with the description of the goods in the credit.

[12.89]   In *JH Rayner v Hambro's Bank* [1943] 1 KB 37; [1942] 2 All ER 694 the credit called for 'Coromandel groundnuts in bags'. Although this was the expression used in the commercial invoice, the bill of lading described the shipment as 'machine-shelled groundnut kernels'. The Hambro's bank refused to pay, a decision which was upheld by the English Court of Appeal. The court rejected the argument that the two descriptions meant the same thing, a fact which was, apparently, well known to anyone in the groundnut trade. A banker cannot be expected to have knowledge of the customs and terms of trade.

The decision has been criticised, but it seems likely that when a bill of lading contains terms and descriptions which are not in the credit, then such a document is 'inconsistent with the description of the goods in the credit'. So, if the bill of lading had merely said 'Groundnuts', it is thought that the tender would have been good: see Gutteridge and Megrah, op cit, p 150.

[12.90] Although the documents must necessarily be consistent among themselves, does the full description of the goods need to be found in one document only or is it possible to read the documents as a whole to find if the description meets the requirements of the credit? The matter arose before Devlin J, in *Midland Bank v Seymour* [1955] 2 Lloyd's Rep 147, who said (at 152):

> ... there are only two alternatives that are open to anyone endeavouring to construe the document. One is that each of the documents must contain all the particulars, and the other is that all the documents between them — that is the set of documents — must contain all the particulars. That, of course, is subject to this obvious qualification, that each document (if it has not to contain all the particulars) must contain enough of the particulars to make it a valid document.

The bill of lading did not contain any reference to the quality although such a reference was to be found in the other required documents. Devlin J held that under the above principle of construction the tender was good. Of course, if the credit expressly calls for a particular document to contain the description, then the document must do so.

[12.91] In *Soproma SpA v Marine & Animal By-Products Corporation* [1966] 1 Lloyd's Rep 367 the contract of sale and the letter of credit described the goods as 'Chilean Fish Full Meal, steamdried, minimum 70% protein'. The sellers' invoice referred to 'Chilean Fish Full Meal, 70% protein'. By an error, the shipper's invoice was also included in the documents. It described the goods as 'Chilean Fishmeal minimum 67% protein' and the certificate of quality said 'the analysis or composition of the goods is in accordance with the following analysis: Protein 67 per cent minimum' and a second certificate stated 'Protein 69.7 per cent'.

McNair J held that there was a sufficient general description of the goods in the bill of lading, but that the inconsistencies in the descriptions of the protein contents made the documents an unacceptable tender under the letter of credit. He also noted that the shippers' invoice was probably irrelevant in law although it might have afforded the buyers with a reason for doubting the true protein content of the goods.

[12.92] The range of documentation called for will vary greatly from credit to credit, but there is a core of documents which will be included in virtually every credit which is being used to facilitate an international sale of goods. Where the carriage of the goods is by sea, this core consists of a bill of lading, a commercial invoice and a policy of marine insurance. It is imperative that the banker dealing with international transactions be familiar with the basics of each of these documents.

One of the striking features of the 1993 Revision is its expanded treatment of transport documents. The 1983 Revision contained a single heading 'Transport Documents' that covered the field in six articles. The 1993 Revision identifies nine different types of transport documents and treats each of them in detail.

As with many of the changes in the UCP, this one has been forced by changing technology. The rise of container shipping has allowed the goods to be packed in the container at the consignor's premises. The container is then carried by road and/or rail to a port where it is loaded onto a ship to be carried to a foreign port. At the foreign port the container is offloaded and again carried by road and/or rail to the consignee's place of business where it is unloaded. Since it makes little sense to issue a new document for every stage of carriage, a document known as the 'combined transport' bill of lading or as a 'Multimodal Transport Document' has been used to facilitate the demands of container transport.

Not all of the changes in the 1993 Revision can be attributed to a change in practice. There has also been a clear change in drafting philosophy which attempts to spell out the details for each major form of transport document. This is done at the cost of some repetition.

The bill of lading

[12.93] A bill of lading serves three purposes. First, it is a document of title to the goods; as such, it represents the goods and may be pledged or sold. Second, it is evidence of the contract of carriage between the consignor and the shipper. Third, it is a receipt given by the carrier which acknowledges receipt of the goods. It is negotiable in the sense that the rights of the consignor may be transferred to another party, although these rights are not transferred free of existing equities: see, for example, *Lickbarrow v Mason* (1794) 5 Term Rep 683; *Burdick v Sewell* (1884) 13 QBD 159.

It is its role as a document of title which makes the bill of lading so important to bankers who are engaged in financing international trade, for the use of the bill of lading means that the scheme of trading in documents instead of goods is feasible.

• *Clean/unclean transport documents*

[12.94] The carrier of goods may be responsible for damage to them which occurs during the course of carriage. In order to guard against this liability, carriers will put 'clauses' on transport documents which indicate any existing defects in the appearance or packaging of the goods. This seemingly harmless practice causes great difficulties in international trade, not the least of which is the operation of the UCP.

A 'clean' transport document is one which does not contain a clause which expressly declares a defective condition of either the goods or the packaging: Art 32(a). Documents which are not 'clean' are known as 'unclean' or 'claused'. Banks are directed to refuse a tender of transport documents which are unclean unless the credit expressly stipulates clauses which are acceptable: Art 32(b).

It is not always easy to decide if a superimposed clause has the effect of making the document a claused rather than a clean document. Paget argues that the question is broader than that suggested by the UCP since there may be clauses which do not relate to the condition of the goods or packaging but which nevertheless make the document an unacceptable one. As an example, it is said that documents containing a clause 'Freight paid by cheque' are refused by London bankers on the basis that there is a reasonable doubt that the credit authorises the banker to accept such a document: Paget, op cit, p 672; Gutteridge and Megrah, op cit, p 141.

- *Shipped/received transport documents*

[12.95]   A 'shipped' bill of lading states that the goods have been loaded on board the named ship. Some bills of lading are 'received' bills, that is they state only that the goods have been received for shipment. The received bill is a natural outgrowth of modern port facilities where the goods may be kept for several days pending their turn in the loading process.

Generally speaking, a 'received' bill of lading is not a good tender, either under a CIF contract or a documentary credit which calls for a bill of lading: *Diamond Alkali Export Corporation v Bourgeois* [1921] 3 KB 443. Fortunately, received bills may be transformed into shipped bills by virtue of a notation on the bill itself which verifies that the goods have actually been shipped.

[12.96]   This terminology and practice has been carried over to other transport documents which cover carriage by sea. Such documents must indicate that the goods have been loaded on board or shipped on a named vessel. This may be indicated by preprinted words on the document, but if not then the document must contain a notation which gives the date on which the goods were loaded on board. That date will be deemed to be the date of shipment: see Arts 23, 24 and 25. If the document actually names an 'intended vessel' then there must be a notation on the document which identifies the date on which the goods have been loaded on board and the name of the vessel (even if it is the 'intended vessel').

In modern transport practice even bills of lading may contain an indication that the goods were taken in charge at some place other than the port of loading. If that is the case, then the bill must contain an 'on board' notation which indicates the port of loading (which must, of course, be that stipulated in the credit) and the name of the vessel on which the goods have been loaded: see Arts 23 and 24.

Documents which evidence receipt/dispatch

[12.97]   The bill of lading is the only document which functions traditionally as a document of title. This makes the bill of lading a preferred document in many financing transactions since the document itself may be used to provide security over the goods. This role is, however, independent of its function as a transport document, ie, a document which serves as evidence of the receipt and/or dispatch of the goods and, possibly, as evidence of the contract of carriage.

When there is no intention to deal with goods which are in transit, there is no need for a document of title. So, for example, in carriage by air where the goods are in transit for relatively short periods of time, the standard transport document has always been the air waybill. A waybill is a document which evidences receipt and possibly dispatch of the goods by the carrier. The waybill need not be produced in order to receive the goods at their destination, so it is a popular form of document when the 'documents' are to be transmitted electronically.

The UCP recognises five types of documents that are similar to the waybill. These are the multimodal transport document (although this may include documents of title), the air transport document, a road, rail or inland waterway transport document, the post receipt and the courier/expedited delivery service document. In each case, the UCP specifies in some detail the information which must be shown on the document.

[12.98]   From the commercial point of view, the most important piece of information contained in these documents is the date of dispatch. The reason for this is that the date of dispatch will usually be a condition of the contract of sale, breach of which gives grounds for rejection by the buyer. Because of the different practices associated with each document, the requirements as to the date of dispatch differ.

Unless otherwise indicated by special notation, the date of issuance of a multimodal transport document is taken to be the date of dispatch. An air transport document must contain a specific notation as to the date of dispatch if the credit calls for an actual date of dispatch. Rail, road and inland waterway transport documents are treated like multimodal transport documents in this respect. Post receipts have a stamp or authentication, and the date of this is deemed to be the date of shipment unless the document contains a specific notation to the contrary. Any document issued by a courier service or an expedited delivery service must indicate a date of pick-up or receipt, and that date is taken to be the date of dispatch: see generally Arts 26–29.

Stale bills

[12.99]   A 'stale' bill of lading is one which is tendered so late that it is not possible for the documents to reach the consignee before the arrival of the goods. For many years, bankers would refuse to pay against stale bills of lading, even though they were tendered within the time before the credit expired and even though the terms of the credit were fully met in all other respects. The practice seemed to have little to recommend it and the 1974 version of the UCP addressed the matter directly. The 1993 Revision provides that credits should stipulate both an expiry date for the presentation of documents and, if the credit calls for a transport document, a time after the date of shipment during which presentation must be made to operate the credit: Art 43(a). If the post-shipment time is not specified, the UCP directs that transport documents must be presented no later than 21 days after the date of shipment or the date of the expiry of the credit, whichever is earliest: Art 43(a).

The transhipment problem

[12.100] The operation of documentary credits which are being used to facilitate international trade is influenced by the requirements of the most common form of international sale contracts, namely the CIF contract. The CIF contract is essentially a sale of goods which is effected by a sale of documents. If the documents are in order, then the buyer must pay for the goods even if it is known that the goods have been lost before the presentation of the documents and before property in the goods has passed to the buyer.

The scheme which allows this contract to operate efficiently is the concept of continuous documentary cover. For example, in the situation mentioned above, the buyer's rights are against the policy of marine insurance. It is clear that this documentary coverage must be continuous in the sense that damage to or loss of the goods must, in so far as possible, provide the party at risk with rights of recovery against the carrier or against the insurer.

It is for this reason that CIF contracts require that the bill of lading, the document which gives rights against the carrier, must cover the carriage from the port of origin to the port of destination: *E Clemens Horst Co v Biddell Bros* [1912] AC 18; *Hansson v Hamel and Horley Ltd* [1922] 2 AC 36; *Holland Colombo Trading Society Ltd v Alawdeen Segu Mohammed Khaja* [1954] 2 Lloyd's Rep 45.

The problem is that of transhipment, that is, the unloading of the goods at some intermediate port and the reshipment on a new ship which will then carry the goods to the original destination. The second carrier will issue a bill of lading, but it will be issued to the original carrier. The first carrier will disclaim all responsibility for the ongoing carriage. One solution to this problem is the so-called 'through bill of lading' which is issued by the first carrier but purports to cover the entire voyage. There is little authority on the legal effects of a through bill: for a discussion, see *Hansson v Hamel and Horley Ltd* [1922] 2 AC 36. For these reasons, the general rule is that transhipment is prohibited in a CIF contract. Furthermore, it is very common for a documentary credit to contain a term which prohibits transhipment.

[12.101]   Unfortunately, most bills of lading contain a printed clause which gives the carrier unlimited rights to tranship. It has never been finally decided if the tender of such a bill of lading may be defective under a CIF contract, but as regards credits, the point is now clear both as to the tender of through bills and bills which contain transhipment clauses. Even if the credit prohibits transhipment, banks will accept bills of lading or non-negotiable sea waybills which incorporate clauses stating that the carrier reserves the right to tranship: Arts 23(d)(ii), 24(d)(ii). They will also accept these documents even if the document clearly indicates that transhipment will take place, provided that the relevant cargo is shipped in containers, trailers and/or LASH barges, and provided that the entire ocean carriage is covered by one and the same document: Arts 23(d)(i) and 24(d)(i).

A multimodal transport document which indicates that transhipment will or may take place will be acceptable even though the credit prohibits transhipment provided only that the entire carriage is covered by one and the same document: Art 26(b). The same rule applies to air transport documents, road, rail, and inland waterway transport documents: Arts 27(c), 28(d).

Marine insurance

[12.102]   It will be recalled that the insurance policy is a vital element in the operation of CIF contracts. It is considered so fundamental that a buyer is entitled to receive a valid policy even if it is known that the goods have arrived safely and may repudiate the contract if a valid policy is not among the tendered documents: *Orient Co Ltd v Brekke and Howlid* [1913] 1 KB 531.

A policy is a document which actually embodies the contract between the insurer and the insured. The marine insurance policy is governed by the Marine Insurance Act 1909 and the benefits of the policy may be transferred.

[12.103]   There are two documentation problems related to insurance. The first is that when a policy of insurance is first negotiated, it will usually be not with an insurer directly but with a broker. The broker will issue a 'cover note' which is legally binding so far as the initial insured is concerned, but which does not, of course, contain the terms of the contract of insurance, nor is it transferable. However, because of the delay which may occur between the issue of the cover note and the policy, sellers sometimes have wished to tender the cover note as the insurance documentation. If the credit does not explicitly authorise this, then a cover note issued by a broker is not an acceptable insurance document: Art 34(c). Similarly, unless expressly authorised by the contract, a cover note is not a good tender under a CIF contract: *Manbre Saccharine Co v Corn Products Co* [1919] 1 KB 198. It has been suggested that a certificate which incorporates the terms of the contract might be good tender: *Donald H Scott & Co Ltd v Barclays Bank Ltd* [1923] 2 KB 1.

[12.104]   The second problem concerns the move to so-called 'open cover' policies. A large exporter who makes frequent shipment might arrange with an insurance company for a general cover of all exports. In practice, this means that there is only one policy which places certain ceilings on the amounts to be insured. When the exporter ships goods, the insurer is notified and the goods are covered. It is clearly impossible for the seller to include the policy, yet any certificate issued by the insurer or the insured suffers from the same legal deficiencies as the broker's cover note. The 1993 Revision of the UCP has accepted that commercial practice has changed: unless the credit forbids it, banks will accept an insurance certificate of a declaration under an open cover: Art 34(d). If a credit calls for a certificate of a declaration under an open cover, an insurance policy is good tender in lieu of: Art 34(d).

[12.105]   It is customary in CIF contracts for the insurance to be the CIF price of the goods plus 10 per cent to allow the buyer a profit in the event of the loss of the goods. The UCP incorporates this practice for CIF and C&I, that is 'cost and insurance paid to the named port of destination', contracts by calling for a minimum insurance cover of the CIF or the C&I cost plus 10 per cent: Art 34(f)(ii). This is no problem if the CIF or C&I cost is determinable from the documents. If the price is not so discernible, then the minimum amount is 110 per cent of the amount of the credit or 110 per cent of the gross amount of the invoice, whichever is greater: Art 34(f)(ii). These amounts are, of course, 'defaults' to be applied in the absence of any specific instructions to the contrary in the credit.

[12.106]   It is of the utmost importance that the applicant for the credit specify the risks to be covered by any tendered insurance documents since failing specific instructions banks will accept insurance documents as tendered without any responsibility for risks covered: Art 35(b). This could have disastrous results for the applicant buyer of goods, particularly if the tendered documents are substantially less than called for by the underlying contract. In specifying the risks to be covered, phrases such as 'usual risks' or 'customary risks' must not be used since banks will accept documents as tendered without responsibility for risks not covered: Art 24(a). This is a sensible solution since these phrases, although they may be quite meaningful for the parties in the trade, are meaningless to bankers.

The invoice

[12.107]   The commercial invoice is the only one of the three basic documents which is likely to be able to provide a full description of the goods. It is important therefore that the description contained therein should be in terms identical with those called for in the credit. Unless otherwise stipulated in the credit, an acceptable commercial invoice must appear to be issued by the named beneficiary and made out in the name of the applicant: Art 37(a); there is an exception to this rule for transferable credits: see [12.117].

A problem which sometimes arises is that the invoice is for an amount in excess of the amount of the credit. This may be because the invoice covers more goods than identified in the credit or because the parties always intended that the credit should cover part of the payment only. If the terms of the credit do not address the problem directly, the UCP gives the bank the option of rejecting the documents or operating the credit for the invoice amount, provided of course that the invoice amount is not in excess of the amount permitted by the credit: Art 37(b).

[12.108]   The descriptions of quantity and quality are particularly important, and many disputes have concerned the conformity of descriptions which in other circumstances might seem to be of little importance. Thus, it has been suggested that an invoice which describes 1,000,000 kilograms (1000 metric tons) would not be a good tender under a credit which calls for 1000 tons: see Gutteridge and Megrah, op cit, p 172.

It is surprising common for terms to be included in a contract to allow for the inevitable small variations of price and/or amount of goods. This can cause problems in credits where it has been said that the 'de minimus' rule does not apply: see [12.84]. If words such as 'about', 'approximately', 'circa' or any similar expression is used in connection with the amount of the credit, the quantity of goods or the unit price of goods, then banks will accept a difference not to exceed 10 per cent more or less than that specified in the credit: Art 39(a). Where the credit does not use such words, and provided the credit does not stipulate the contrary, a tolerance of 5 per cent more or less is acceptable in the quantity of goods except where the credit states the quantity in terms of a stated number of packing units or individual items: Art 39(b). In no case, however, may the amount of the drawing exceed the amount of the credit.

Other documents

[12.109]   It is very common for contracts and credits to call for additional documents. The range of possible certificates and documents is so wide and the possibility of verifying their authenticity in any reasonable amount of time causes considerable difficulty. The UCP gives a wide licence to bankers to accept documents which appear to be what is called for; in view of the diversity of such documents, it would seem difficult to place a greater responsibility on banks, given the usual requirements of making a prompt decision without the need to make background investigations.

Credits should state precisely who is to issue a document. Contracts between the parties often call for a document to be issued by a 'first class', 'well known', 'qualified', 'independent', 'official', 'competent' or 'local' person or organisation. This may be acceptable in the contract between the parties where the terms may have an established trade meaning, but they are unacceptable descriptions in credits where the decisions must be made by bankers with no experience in the particular trade. If such terms are used, a bank may accept the document as presented provided that it appears on its face to be in compliance with the other terms and conditions of the credit: Art 20(b).

Similarly, banks will accept documents as presented if the credit is silent as to who should issue the document, the wording of the document or the data content of the document: Art 21. The only requirement in such a case is that the data content of tendered documents must be consistent with other stipulated documents: Art 21.

SECURITY OVER DOCUMENTS/GOODS

[12.110]   When the credit is one which is used to facilitate an international sale of goods, the documents of title to the goods may be used as a security. Even when the bank does not rely entirely upon the goods as security, there is no doubt that they provide a useful adjunct to any other securities that the bank may have taken from the account party.

It is customary that the form used for application will contain a clause which authorises the bank to take possession of and to sell the goods in the event of a non-payment, but even without such a clause, it seems likely that the banker would have an implied pledge of the documents. It has been said that the intermediary bank would have an implied pledge of the documents, although the comments were admittedly obiter: see Scrutton LJ in *Guaranty Trust Co of New York v Hannay* [1918] 2 KB 623.

[12.111]   When the documents include a bill of lading, there is little difficulty, for the bill of lading is a document of title to the goods so that a pledge of the document is equivalent to a pledge of the goods themselves. The goods may be pledged merely by the indorsement and delivery of the bill. Furthermore, the bill of lading does not cease to be a document of title when the carriage itself is completed. It has been held that the contract of carriage is a combined contract of transportation of the goods by sea and a contract of bailment, so that until the goods are released from the bailment the bill of lading remains a good document of title: see Diplock LJ in *Barclays Bank Ltd v Commissioners of Customs and Excise* [1963] 1 Lloyd's Rep 81.

There is somewhat more difficulty when the documents do not include a document of title. This will be the case when the goods are shipped by air, in which case the shipping document is the air waybill, or when there is a combined transport which calls for a multimodal transport document. The waybill generally evidences the receipt of the goods by the carrier and names the consignee. The carrier should deliver the goods only to the named consignee. Consequently, these documents cannot be used to obtain a pledge, but there is no reason why the bank should not have a charge over the goods by means of a letter of hypothecation: see Chapter 10. Further, if the waybill names the bank as consignee, it may be that the bank can obtain a pledge of the goods.

TRUST RECEIPTS

[12.112]   If the applicant for the credit is able to place the banker in funds to meet the credit, then the documents may be delivered immediately. However, very often the applicant/buyer will need to resell and/or reship the goods to a sub-purchaser in order to obtain the funds. If the issuing banker wishes to retain security over the goods, this presents something of a problem. The solution is the 'letter of trust'.

[12.113]   At common law parting with the possession of the goods will usually determine a pledge, but it has always been possible to part with them for a specific purpose without losing all security rights. The specific purpose, in this case, is to allow the account party to sell or ship the goods. The 'letter of trust' embodies an agreement between the account party and the banker whereby the banker agrees to release the goods to the account party for the above limited purpose and the account party in return agrees that the documents, the goods, and the proceeds of the goods when resold will be held in trust for the bank. The validity of the arrangement was upheld by the House of Lords in *North Western Bank v Poynter, Son, & Macdonalds* [1895] AC 56.

The case also illustrates one way in which the arrangement may be very beneficial to the bank. The goods were released to the account party who shipped the goods to a subpurchaser. Before all of the payments were made, the account party became insolvent. The question was whether the bank was entitled to receive the balance of the purchase price or if it must prove along with general creditors. The House of Lords upheld the arrangement with the consequence that the bank was entitled to the balance of the purchase price.

Releasing the documents to the customer is not without its risks, for whereas the pledge is a legal security, the security under the letter of trust is an equitable one. The precise nature of the security is not entirely clear. Davis (A G Davis, *The Law Relating to Commercial Letters of Credit*, 3rd ed, Butterworths, London, 1963) argues that the letter of trust is not a true trust situation but is a combination of bailment, agency and trust. Since the bank's interest is only equitable, a purchaser of the goods who has no notice of the banker's interest will defeat the banker's interest provided the purchase has been for value and in good faith.

The validity of letters of trust has been challenged on a number of occasions. It has been claimed that the arrangement constitutes an unregistered charge on book debts or an unregistered bill of sale. These attempts have all failed, the most comprehensive analysis being that in *Re David Allester Ltd* [1922] 2 Ch 211.

TRANSFERRING CREDITS

[12.114]   Suppose that A wishes to purchase goods for the purpose of resale. A contracts with a supplier to provide the goods and may be required to procure a letter of credit in favour of the supplier. Similarly, A may require that the sub-buyer obtain a letter of credit in which A is the beneficiary. The commercial problem is this: A would like to use the credit in A's favour as a security for, or a substitute for, the letter of credit which A is obliged to open in favour of the supplier.

A simple minded solution would be to ask the sub-buyer to open the letter of credit in favour of the supplier, thereby simplifying the transaction and reducing the costs. However, this is not a sensible commercial decision for two reasons. In the first place, the sub-buyer will be paying a higher price for the goods, so the amounts will not match. Second, where A is buying a large bulk of goods for the purpose of supplying smaller purchasers there will be a number of sub-buyers. Third, and importantly, A, for good commercial reasons, may not wish for the sub-buyers to be aware of the identity of the supplier.

BACK-TO-BACK CREDITS

[12.115]   A more sophisticated solution is known as 'back-to-back' credits. The sub-buyer is asked to open a credit in favour of A, and A opens a credit in favour of the supplier. The important feature is that each of the credits must have identical terms save for the amount and possibly the dates during which it is permissible to operate the credits. A may request the letter of credit from the sub-buyer to be deposited with A's bank as a security for the establishment of the credit in favour of the supplier.

There are several problems with back-to-back credits. If the stipulations as to documents are not identical, then the primary aim of using the first letter as security for the second may fail, for a good tender by the supplier may fail to be a good tender by A to the sub-buyer. Unexpected insolvencies may also upset the operation of inter-connected credits.

[12.116]   When the credits are standby credits, other problems may arise. *Commercial Banking Co of Sydney Ltd v Patrick Intermarine Acceptances Ltd* (1978) 52 ALJR 404 shows the dangers inherent in attempting to use back-to-back credits. In this case, the credits were standby credits which were intended to secure some financing arrangements. PIAL, a large merchant bank, borrowed some A$1.5 million from the State Electricity Commission of Victoria (SECV). The purpose of the borrowing was to make a loan to a finance house, First Leasing. First Leasing was an Australian subsidiary of the First National Bank of Boston. In order to secure the loan from SECV, PIAL made arrangements whereby the Commercial Banking Co of Sydney opened a standby credit in favour of SECV. The credit could be drawn upon by means of a certificate from SECV to the effect that repayment of the loan to PIAL had been demanded but not received.

PIAL also required security from the Boston bank in the form of a standby credit in favour of PIAL which could be operated by a statement from PIAL to the effect that the First Leasing loan repayment had been demanded but not received. There was an undertaking by PIAL that if it was necessary to call on the Boston credit then they would lodge with the CBC their draft and any documents called for by the Boston credit.

The arrangement was perfectly good security for the CBC in the event of the failure of First Leasing, but what happened in fact was that PIAL went into liquidation before the loans became due. SECV called on the credit which had been opened by CBC and were, of course, paid.

The CBC argued that by virtue of that payment they were entitled to an equitable charge on the debt owed to PIAL. This argument was dismissed by Lord Diplock in the Privy Council (at 407):

> Their Lordships find it impossible to imply, from the provision that in a certain event the Commercial Bank should have a proprietary interest in Boston's

liability to PIAL, a provision that, if that liability should never arise, the Commercial Bank should have a proprietary interest in a different liability of a different person to PIAL.

Note that the CBC could have protected themselves very easily by taking an assignment of the First Leasing debt. Even an equitable assignment would have protected them from the liquidation of PIAL. It appears that the failure of PIAL was the one event that the bank never considered.

TRANSFERABLE CREDITS

[12.117]   The solution provided by the UCP is the 'transferable' credit. A, called the 'first beneficiary', requests the sub-buyers to open a transferable credit. A may then request the transferring bank (named in the credit) to make the credit available in whole or in part to one or more other beneficiaries: see Art 48(a).

The UCP is not very friendly to transferable credits. Words which might be thought adequate to indicate transferability are not: 'divisible', 'fractional' 'assignable' and 'transmissible' do not make the credit transferable and the banks are instructed to disregard them. Only the word 'transferable' will render a credit transferable: see Art 48(b). The transferring bank is under no obligation to make any transfer except to the extent and in the manner that it has expressly consented to: Art 48(c).

The UCP permits only a single transfer in the sense that the second beneficiary may not transfer the credit to a third beneficiary: Art 48(g). This does not prohibit the first beneficiary from making fractional transfers in favour of several second beneficiaries, provided of course, that the total sums do not exceed the value of the original credit: Art 48(g).

[12.118]   The strength of a transferable credit is that the terms of operation do not change, thus overcoming one of the major problems of back-to-back credits. The UCP specifically provides that the transferred credit must be on the same terms as the original except for those details which are essential to account for the interests of the first beneficiary. So, it is permissible to reduce or curtail the amount of the credit, any unit price stated therein, the expiry date, the last date for presentation of documents and the period of shipment: Art 48(h). It is also permissible to increase the percentage requirement for insurance cover, and to substitute the name of the first beneficiary for that of the applicant unless the credit specifically requires otherwise: Art 48(h).

In order to meet the commercial requirements of the arrangement, the UCP also allows the first beneficiary to substitute his or her own invoices and/or drafts for those of the second beneficiary provided that the amounts are not in excess of the amount stipulated in the original credit. The first beneficiary may also substitute a new unit price. When this substitution is made, the first beneficiary is entitled to draw under the credit for the difference between his or her invoices and those of the second beneficiary: Art 48(i).

When this 'substitution' option exists, the transferring bank has the right to call for the substituted documents to be exchanged for the invoices and drafts of the second beneficiary. If the first beneficiary fails to provide the substituted documents on the first demand by the transferring bank, the transferring bank may deliver to the issuing bank the documents received from the second beneficiary. This is done without any further responsibility to the first beneficiary: Art 48(j).

One of the major reasons why the UCP prevents multiple transfers is the problem of making amendments to the credit. First, the first beneficiary may not wish for amendments to be passed on to the second beneficiary. The UCP permits the first beneficiary to instruct the transferring bank that he or she retains the right to refuse to allow advisement of amendments. When that it done, the transferring bank must advise the second beneficiary of the instructions regarding amendments: Art 48(d).

The second problem concerning amendments arises when there is more than one second beneficiary. One or more of the second beneficiaries may agree to proposed amendments while one or more may not agree. In that case, the amended credit is operative as regards those who have agreed, while the terms and conditions of the original credit are operative with respect to those second beneficiaries who have not agreed: Art 48(e).

ASSIGNMENT OF CREDITS

[12.119]   The problem of transferability is made much more difficult by the possibility of assigning some or all of the benefits of the credit, a possibility which is governed by the law relating to the assignment of benefits under a contract. A contractual right is a chose in action and normally such rights may be assigned either legally, for example, under the equivalent of s 12 Conveyancing Act 1919 (NSW), or equitably. In either case, the assignee is subject to any equity which may have attached to the assignor: see Chapter 10. Generally speaking, only those contractual benefits which are essentially personal cannot be assigned. It has been said that the substitution of one person for another should be confined to those situations where it can make no difference to the person on whom the obligation lies to which of the two persons he or she is to discharge it: *Tolhurst v Associated Portland Cement Manufacturers (1900) Ltd* [1902] 2 KB 660 (CA); [1903] AC 414 (HL).

The general view appears to be that the benefit of credits can be assigned under our law, but it appears that the precise question has never been litigated. Of course, when the credit is operated by means of a bill of exchange, then the drawer and drawee of the bill must be as specified in the credit. If the bill is a time draft, then payment will ultimately be made to the holder of the bill and it seems that assignment of the proceeds will have no effect, at least so far as the operation of the credit is concerned.

Dangers for the assignee

[12.120] From the standpoint of the assignee, the procedure is fraught with uncertainty and difficulty. Nothing will be paid until such time as the beneficiary complies strictly with the terms of the credit; since the assignee is not usually in a position to know if the conditions have been fulfilled and is not usually in a position to influence that fulfilment, he or she will be uncertain as to the time or even the fact of payment.

Sometimes the assignee will, in order to overcome these difficulties, require that the documents be delivered for inspection and so that the assignee might have the opportunity of correcting any deficiencies in the documentation. In such a circumstance, the assignee may also wish to tender the documents directly. Unfortunately, this may not be possible if the decision of an Austrian commercial court is correct.

The Singer & Friedlander case

[12.121] In *Singer & Friedlander v Creditanstalt-Bankverein* [1981] Com LR 69 the defendants opened a letter of credit in favour of one Aronson to be payable against a commercial invoice and warehouse receipts. The letter was for nearly $10 million and was to pay for a consignment of drugs. The plaintiff bankers were supplying finance to Aronson and as part of the security arrangements the credit was to be assigned to them. This was done in the following terms: I hereby irrevocably and unconditionally assign to you all my rights and benefits under documentary credit.

The documents were given to the plaintiffs, but when they were finally presented, payment was refused on several grounds, including that the purported assignment could give the assignee no right to present the documents to the issuing bank. Fraud was alleged and it was said that Aronson could not himself have presented the documents and claimed payment.

The court held that there had been no transfer of the letter of credit in accordance with the provisions of the UCP. The court went on to argue that to allow the third party presentation of documents would violate the prohibition on transferability:

> It would contradict the nature of the non-transferable letter of credit if in addition to the proceeds the beneficiary could also transfer the right to realise his claim by presentation of documents in conformity with the letter of credit or to impede the paying out of the proceeds by not presenting the documents. If also the right to present (or not to present) the documents were declared transferable the non-transferable letter of credit would come close to the transferable letter of credit so that the two notions could hardly be distinguished.

The matter of assignment remains one on which the law is unsettled. The decision of the Austrian court has not been entirely satisfactory, not the least because it failed to deal adequately with certain communications between the parties which occurred before the attempted presentation of the documents. It might have been hoped that the 1983 Revision of the UCP could have dealt with the matter.

Assignment of proceeds

[12.122]   Of course, even if the whole of the benefit of the credit may not be assigned, it is still possible to assign the proceeds of the credit, a possibility which is expressly recognised by the UCP in Art 49:

> The fact that a credit is not stated to be transferable shall not affect the beneficiary's right to assign any proceeds to which he may be, or may become, entitled under such credit, in accordance with the provisions of the applicable law. This article relates only to the assignment of proceeds and not to the assignment of the right to perform under the Credit itself.

The first sentence of this article dates from the 1974 Revision, but the last is new in the 1993 Revision, presumably a response to the *Singer & Friedlander* case.

INDEX

REFERENCES ARE TO PARAGRAPHS